ELEVENTH EDITION

THE LEGAL AND REGULATORY ENVIRONMENT OF BUSINESS

ELEVENTH EDITION

THE LEGAL AND REGULATORY ENVIRONMENT OF BUSINESS

Robert N. Corley
Distinguished Professor of Legal Studies Emeritus, University of Georgia

O. Lee Reed
Professor of Legal Studies, University of Georgia

Peter J. Shedd
Professor of Legal Studies, University of Georgia

Jere W. Morehead
Associate Professor of Legal Studies, University of Georgia

Boston   Burr Ridge, IL   Dubuque, IA   Madison, WI   New York   San Francisco
St. Louis   Bangkok   Bogotá   Caracas   Lisbon   London   Madrid   Mexico City
Milan   New Delhi   Seoul   Singapore   Sydney   Taipei   Toronto

Irwin/McGraw-Hill

A Division of The **McGraw·Hill** *Companies*

THE LEGAL AND REGULATORY ENVIRONMENT OF BUSINESS
Copyright © 1999 by The McGraw-Hill Companies, Inc. All rights reserved. Previous editions
© 1963, 1968, 1973, 1977, 1981, 1984, 1987, 1990, 1993 and 1996 by McGraw-Hill. Printed in
the United States of America. Except as permitted under the United States Copyright Act of
1976, no part of this publication may be reproduced or distributed in any form or by any
means, or stored in a data base or retrieval system, without the prior written permission of
the publisher.

This book is printed on acid-free paper.

1 2 3 4 5 6 7 8 9 0 VNH/VNH 9 3 2 1 0 9 8

ISBN 0-07-365429-9

Vice president and editorial director: *Michael W. Junior*
Publisher: *Craig D. Beytien*
Sponsoring editor: *Karen M. Mellon*
Developmental editor: *Christine Scheid*
Marketing manager: *Kenyetta Giles*
Project manager: *Carrie Sestak*
Production supervisor: *Michael R. McCormick*
Designer: *Kiera Cunningham*
Compositor: *Carlisle Communications, Ltd.*
Typeface: *10/12 New Aster*
Printer: *Von Hoffmann Press, Inc.*

Library of Congress Cataloging-in-Publication Data
The legal and regulatory environment of business / Robert N. Corley
 . . . [et al.]. — 11th ed.
    p.   cm.
   Includes index.
   ISBN 0-07-365429-9
   1. Industrial laws and legislation—United States.   2. Trade
regulation—United States.   3. Commercial law—United States.
I. Corley, Robert Neil.
KF1600.C6   1999   98-20992
346.7307—dc21

http://www.mhhe.com

ABOUT THE AUTHORS

Robert N. Corley is a Distinguished Professor of Legal Studies Emeritus of the University of Georgia. He received his J.D. and B.S. degrees from the University of Illinois, where he taught for eighteen years. He was admitted to the Illinois Bar in 1956. Professor Corley is past president of the American Business Law Association and a past member of the editorial board of the *American Business Law Journal.* In 1985 he was awarded the Senior Faculty Award of Excellence by the American Business Law Association. Winner of numerous teaching awards at both the undergraduate and graduate levels, he has also taught in several national executive development programs. Since 1964 he has been senior author of *The Legal Environment of Business.* His contributions have shaped the content of the entire legal environment of business field.

O. Lee Reed holds a J.D. degree from the University of Chicago and a B.A. degree from Birmingham-Southern College. Presently, he is Professor of Legal Studies at the University of Georgia. The author of many scholarly articles, he is former editor-in-chief of the *American Business Law Journal.* He also has served as president of the Southeastern Regional Business Law Association. In 1992 he became president of the Academy of Legal Studies in Business. Professor Reed has received teacher-of-the-year awards from both undergraduate and graduate student organizations. He has been co-author of *The Legal and Regulatory Environment of Business* since 1977.

Peter J. Shedd is a Professor of Legal Studies in the Terry College of Business at the University of Georgia where he received both B.B.A. and J.D. degrees. Professor Shedd has extensive experience as a teacher, researcher, and author of business-related texts. He has been an active member of the Academy of Legal Studies in Business and its Southeastern Regional. In 1994, Professor Shedd was elected to the Executive Committee of the National Academy. He will serve as its president during 1998–99. In addition to being a member of the State Bar of Georgia, Professor Shedd is a member of the American Arbitration Association. He is an experienced mediator and arbitrator.

Jere W. Morehead is an Associate Professor of Legal Studies at the University of Georgia where he received his J.D. degree. Prior to joining the Georgia faculty, Professor Morehead served as an Assistant United States Attorney in the Department of Justice, where he specialized in the prosecution of white-collar crime. He currently serves as Editor-in-Chief of the *American Business Law Journal* and is past president of the International Law Section of the Academy of Legal Studies in Business. Professor Morehead is the recipient of several distinguished teaching awards and has served as a visiting faculty member at the University of Michigan. He has authored many scholarly articles on the subjects of jury selection, export controls, and peer review.

PREFACE

It is traditional for college textbooks to begin with a preface. Since the contents of the preface are unlikely topics for testing, most students probably skip the preface and begin their study at Chapter One. Hopefully, most of those teaching the subject matter of the text not only read the Preface but find it useful in many ways. Therefore, this Preface is primarily directed at those teaching the legal and regulatory environment of business courses.

As background about the authors, I note that the four authors include three presidents of The Academy of Legal Studies in Business (formerly the American Business Law Association) and two editors-in-chief of the *American Business Law Journal*. Collectively, they have almost a century of experience in teaching and have won numerous teaching and research awards. The text originated at the University of Illinois at Urbana-Champaign and since 1975 it has been a product of the University of Georgia, in Athens.

Two foundation studies of business schools in the 1950s provided the motivation to develop this text. Those studies suggested that business law courses as taught in the post-World War II era were no longer relevant. As a young assistant professor in the late 1950s, I concluded that the findings of these studies were probably correct and that if I desired a lifetime teaching career, these recommendations ought to be heeded.

Now more than 40 years later, this is my eleventh and possibly last preface. During these eleven editions, my original co-author, Professor Robert L. Black of the University of Illinois, retired from active participation, and three colleagues from the University of Georgia joined the author team. Professor O. Lee Reed joined in 1976, Professor Peter Shedd in 1984, and Professor Jere Morehead in 1990. Each has made valuable contributions, and collectively they are responsible for most of the material in this edition.

The history of prior editions is helpful in understanding the contents of this edition. In 1963, McGraw-Hill published the first edition, then entitled *The Legal Environment of Business*. At that time, law courses in business schools covered such private law topics as contracts, negotiable instruments, business organizations, and property. The emphasis was on business transactions between parties, and the students were taught the "black letter" rules of law that governed these transactions. Such courses have been known as "traditional" business law.

As previously noted, the first edition arose out of findings that the traditional business law course did not adequately educate business students. Issues relating to government regulation of business were considered to be more relevant than these private law subjects because new legal theories had brought expanded rights to employees, consumers, investors, and others. These new rights, which imposed corollary duties on businesses, were usually enforced by governmental agencies. Thus, our new approach emphasized public rather than private law and legal relationships rather than business transactions. *The Legal Environment of Business* title became considered to be a new approach to law in the business curriculum.

As new editions were prepared, additional subjects were added and much of the original coverage was expanded. From the beginning the legal environment approach reflected a belief in the importance of trends in the law and the importance of ethics to legal studies. Subsequent revisions continued to stress trends and ethics. Each revision also attempted to cover areas of current importance to the legal environment and to eliminate topics no longer relevant.

Over the life of this text most accredited schools of business have come to require or offer a Legal Environment of Business course. During this period, the law has become more and more pervasive in every aspect of business. Decisions of the Supreme Court have become as important to the business community as legislation by Congress. Appointments to the Supreme Court receive significant media attention. Thus, the trend toward more and more legal environment courses in business schools closely paralleled the trend in society to use law and litigation as primary tools for social engineering.

In 1992, the American Assembly of Collegiate Schools of Business revised its accreditation standards to include courses covering the legal and regulatory environment of business, emphasizing even more the public law approach. This eleventh edition, like its predecessors, strives to prepare its users for those legal issues they are likely to face as well as the regulatory matters that they will encounter as active business persons.

Changes in the Eleventh Edition

In the preparation of this edition, we continue the trend of shortening the text. This edition is shorter, both in terms of the number of pages and chapters. There are now 15 chapters as compared to 18 chapters in the tenth edition and 20 in the ninth. This reduction was achieved by reorganizing materials and by recognizing that some areas of the law such as antitrust are not as relevant today as before.

The text was reduced in part to enable users to cover the entire text or at least almost all of it in one semester or one quarter. Fifteen chapters in fifteen weeks is a realistic schedule. Chapters of approximately 35 pages constitute a rigorous but realistic weekly workload for students.

The chapter reductions were achieved as follows:

1. Antitrust was reduced from two chapters to one. Much of the space saving was the result of the lack of any realistic enforcement of the laws relating to mergers and acquisitions. Mega-mergers are the order of the day in many fields, including accounting and finance.

2. The torts and product liability chapters were combined. Much of the material that was of primary interest to trial lawyers but of little significance to managers has been eliminated. The approach of this new chapter is on matters of law that are relevant to managers.

3. Securities regulation was combined with the chapter on business organizations. While securities law is of continuing importance, recent trends toward deregulation have made many of the technical aspects less relevant.

In addition to reducing the length of the text, there are the following new features:

1. The authors have used the tobacco industry as a model for discussing legal issues. This industry faces every conceivable legal problem and the causes of these problems are not only understood but are of significant personal importance to students. Not only is tort and product liability of the tobacco industry in the news on a daily basis, so also are attempts by governmental agencies and Congress to regulate that industry. Constitutional issues such as freedom of speech arise, as do antitrust issues such as fixing the price of tobacco leaves. Almost every chapter contains material relating to the tobacco industry.

2. The review questions at the end of each chapter contain one question for each section in the order of the chapter presentation. These are designed to emphasize the most important point in each section as an aid to the students as they prepare for examinations.

Pedagogy

Each chapter contains the following pedagogical elements:

Business Decisions—This element, introduced first in the ninth edition, is continued here. At the beginning of each chapter is a statement of facts that highlights one or more of the substantive aspects of the chapter.

Cases—We have included portions of actual court decisions that illustrate the parties' arguments and the court's resolution of the issues raised. From these cases, we have deleted most of the procedural aspects, citations, and footnotes. While the resulting edited cases are much shorter than in their original form, the heart of the opinions remain. There are 31 new cases in this edition.

Case Questions—Following each case is a series of questions that are designed to help the student understand the key points raised in the case. These questions are a continuation in this eleventh edition.

Concept Summaries—When it is most helpful, a summary of the preceding textual discussion is provided. In this way, complex or lengthy presentations are easily reviewable by the reader.

Key Terms—At the conclusion of the text of each chapter is a list of the words or phrases that are introduced in the chapter. The glossary, at the end of the book, contains definitions for these key terms.

Supplements

Instructor's Resource Manual   *ISBN: 0-07-365430-2*

This manual consists of the teaching outline section, transparency masters, a case brief supplement, and video guide.

The teaching outline section makes up the bulk of this Instructor's Manual, which is organized by text chapter. This section corresponds with the headings in the text, and typically includes suggestions on points of emphasis, answers to the case questions that appear within each chapter of the text, cases for discussion, and additional matters for discussion. Each chapter of this manual also includes a list of references that might be useful secondary sources of information; a suggested answer to the Business Decision that begins each chapter of the text; and suggested answers to all of the end-of-chapter review questions, including the Tobacco Industry Box questions. The Case Brief section of the IM contains a brief of each edited case found in the text. For ease of use, the briefs are numbered by chapter in the order that they appear in the text, and on the bottom right-hand corner of each page, there is a reference to the page in the text where the edited case appears. The tear-out format of this supplement allows instructors to remove any material and incorporate it into their lecture notes.

Test Bank   *ISBN 0-07-365436-1*

By Ernest King of Univ. of Southern Mississippi, instructors can test students' mastery of concepts as the instructors create exams with the use of this Test Bank. Organized by chapter, the Test Bank contains at least 40 multiple-choice questions, 20 true/false questions, and 10 essay questions per chapter, including 1–2 from each Tobacco Industry Box scenario. Many of the questions have been modified to correspond with the text's revision. Answers immediately follow each question.

PowerPoint Presentation Slides   *ISBN 0-07-366044-2*

A brand new supplement to this edition is the PowerPoint Presentation slides. These slides are a replication of those used by Peter Shedd, and contain an outline for classroom lecture.

Computerized Test Bank (Windows Version)   *ISBN 0-07-365432-9*

The computerized Test Bank contains all the multiple-choice, true/false, and essay questions included in the above-described print Test Bank. This powerful system allows tests to be prepared quickly and easily. Instructors can view questions as they are selected for a test; scramble questions; add, delete, and edit questions; select questions by type, objective, and difficulty level; and view and save tests. For Mac copies, please contact your Irwin/McGraw-Hill sales rep.

Irwin/McGraw-Hill Business Law Case Videos   *ISBN 0-07-228386-6*

The adopters of the eleventh edition can obtain Irwin/McGraw-Hill's 20 case videos for classroom use. These contemporary dramatizations of business law issues sometimes focus on issues within a particular chapter, or may span different chapters. A Video Case Guide can be found at the end of the Instructor's Manual, which outlines the facts, questions, issues, and decision for each video segment.

Acknowledgments

Finally, on behalf of the author team, I would like to thank a number of people. First, without the typing skills of Mary Evans, the manuscript would not have been so professionally presented. The team is once again grateful for her work with manuscript drafts.

Second, the team is in the debt of Karen Mellon, our editor, and Carrie Sestak, the project manager. Together, they provided the support needed to make this eleventh edition possible.

Third, the following colleagues provided valuable insight during the review process for which each author is grateful. We thank them all for sharing their expertise with us.

Paul Fiorelli	*Xavier University*
James Hill	*Central Michigan University*
Thomas Hughes	*University of South Carolina*
Michael King	*California State University-Long Beach*
John McGee	*Southwest Texas State University*
Lisa Moran	*Santa Rosa Junior College*
James Owens	*California State University-Chico*
Michael Pustay	*Texas A & M University*

Finally, but certainly not last, I want to thank all of the professors who have used or are using this text. Your feedback has been and continues to be important. Please feel free to share your thoughts with us. You may contact any of my co-authors directly at the Terry College of Business, University of Georgia, Athens, Georgia, 30602 or through the Irwin/McGraw-Hill Publishing Company.

Robert N. Corley

TO THE STUDENT

How to Study The Legal and Regulatory Environment of Business

To gain the most from this textbook, you should learn how to study written material effectively. You can achieve effective study through use of the SQ3R method, a method widely taught by study-skills psychologists for learning textual material.

SQ3R stands for **survey, question, read, recite,** and **review.** As a study method, it has dramatically improved the grade-point averages of most students who have practiced it. It is based upon the concept that active study of written material improves memory and comprehension of information far better than passive reading. Unfortunately, many students have not recognized the difference between active study and mere passive reading.

Students often read a textbook chapter exactly as they would read a novel or a magazine article. They begin with the first sentence of the chapter and read straight through the material, pausing only to underline occasionally. This way of reading may be suitable for a novel, but it is quite inappropriate for a textbook. Psychologists insist that an active study method must begin with a **survey** of the material to be read. If you plan to spend two hours studying a thirty-page chapter, take three to five minutes in the beginning and survey the chapter. First, read the bold-type section headings (each chapter of this book is divided into numbered sections). Second, read a sentence or two from the text of each section. The purpose of this survey is to familiarize you with the topics covered in the chapter. Fight the tendency to stop your surveying process in order to comprehend all of the concepts you are surveying. Comprehension is not the goal of surveying.

Following the survey of all the sections, go back to the beginning of the chapter: Ask yourself a **question** before reading each section. Ask it aloud, if possible, but silently if circumstances demand. The important thing is actually to "talk to yourself." Normally, each section heading can easily be turned into a question. If the section heading reads **Stare Decisis,** ask yourself the question, "What does stare decisis mean?"

Only after asking a question are you finally ready to **read** a chapter section. In reading keep your question in mind. By so doing you will be reading for a purpose: To discover the answer to your question.

Upon finishing each section, stop and **recite** the answer to your question. As an example, at the end of the section on stare decisis say to yourself, "Stare decisis refers to the legal tradition that a judge in a given case will follow the precedent established in similar cases decided by courts in the jurisdiction." According to psychologists, to recite this way greatly aids memory. Recitation also lets you know whether or not you have understood the material just read.

The last step of the SQ3R method is **review.** When devoting two hours to the study of a chapter, take the final fifteen minutes of the time to review the material. Review the questions taken from the headings of each chapter section and recite the answers to them, rereading material if necessary to answer accurately.

While the SQ3R method may be used effectively to study any subject, the **case briefing system** is uniquely designed to aid in the study of court decisions. In studying law, students frequently write up case briefs of each decision they read. Whether you are required to write up every decision is up to your individual instructor. However, the case briefing system provides an excellent framework for comprehending complicated judicial reasoning processes, and you should brief cases whether required to do so or not.

To avoid getting lost in a maze of judicial terminology, you should ask yourself a standard set of questions about each case decision and read to discover the answers to these questions. These standard questions lie at the heart of the case briefing system. They are:

1. Who is the plaintiff and who is the defendant?
2. What are the facts of the case? (Who did what to whom? What is the behavior complained of?)
3. Did the plaintiff or the defendant win in the lower court(s), and which party is appealing? (All decisions in this textbook come from appellate courts.)
4. What was the legal issue or issues appealed?
5. Does the plaintiff or the defendant win on the appeal?
6. What rules of law and reasoning does the appellate court use in deciding the issue?

Here is an illustration of a written case brief. It is a brief of the first case in the book, which is found on page 43. Before looking at the brief you should now read that case. To understand the case you need to know that a "summary judgment" occurs when a court determines that no genuine factual dispute exists and that either the plaintiff or the defendant is entitled to judgment as a matter of law. No evidence is presented before a jury. The court (judge) rules in favor of the plaintiff or the defendant on the basis of what the law is rather than on what facts (who did what to whom, etc.) are believed.

Case Brief

WORLD-WIDE VOLKSWAGEN CORP. v. WOODSON, 100 S.Ct. 559 (1980)
[The notation following the name of the case indicates that the case may be

found in volume 100 of the *Supreme Court Reporter,* starting on page 559. The Supreme Court decided the case in 1980.]

Plaintiff and Defendant

The plaintiff (who brings the lawsuit against the defendant by filing a complaint) is Woodson. The defendants are the German manufacturer of the Audi automobile, Volkswagen of America (the importer), World-Wide Volkswagen (the wholesale distributor), and Seaway (the retail dealership).

Facts

The plaintiff Woodson, a resident of New York, purchased an Audi from a retail dealership in New York. Woodson drove the car to Oklahoma. While in Oklahoma, Woodson was injured in an accident caused by a defect in the car. He sued the dealership and the other defendants in an Oklahoma state court. The dealership and the importer objected to the Oklahoma court's personal jurisdiction (legal power to decide the case concerning the plaintiff and defendants).

Lower Courts

The Oklahoma trial court and appellate courts rejected the arguments that they lacked the jurisdiction to decide the case. The U.S. Supreme Court agreed to hear an appeal on the basis of constitutional due process.

Issue Appealed

Do the courts of Oklahoma have jurisdiction over a nonresident automobile dealer and its wholesale distributor in a products liability case, when the defendants' only connection with Oklahoma is the fact that an automobile sold in New York to a New York resident became involved in an accident in Oklahoma?

Who Wins

The dealer and the wholesale distributor win.

Reasoning

1. A state court may assert personal jurisdiction over a nonresident defendant only as long as there are "minimum contacts" between the defendant and that state. The due process clause requires this standard.

2. This standard protects the defendant from having to defend himself in a distant or inconvenient place. It also ensures that states will not reach out beyond their boundaries and disturb the balance imposed by the federal system of our government.

3. The dealer and wholesaler carried on no activity whatsoever in Oklahoma; thus they may not be sued in that state.

O. Lee Reed

TABLE OF CONTENTS

TABLE OF CASES

INTRODUCTION TO LAW

1

Business Decision

"Calling" All Smokers

As a business consultant, you are retained by a consortium representing to-bacco manufacturing companies. This group seeks your expertise to apply cost-benefit analysis in the defense of legal actions being filed against them by persons injured through the use of tobacco products. As you ponder this task, you begin making a list of questions, including the following:

What types of lawsuits have been and are likely to be filed against these manufacturing companies?

What legal theories provide the bases for these suits?

How likely is it that the plaintiffs will be successful and what is the financial exposure?

How expensive is it to take cases through the entire litigation process?

Which alternatives to litigation are most cost effective?

Most of the business courses you take are designed to prepare you to be a manager and make decisions. The education of future managers is essentially a study of processes and systems. And just as an understanding of the profit motive and our competitive economic system is essential for an educated businessperson, so is knowledge of the law, its processes, our legal system, and the legal environment.

Since business today is conducted within a legal environment, no transaction could be entered into with confidence without a legal system to govern the rights and duties of the parties. Moreover, the interest of society in protecting both commerce and individuals has resulted in many laws regulating the conduct of business. Knowledge of these laws and regulations is also an indispensable ingredient of a business education. As you begin the study of the legal and regulatory environment of business, keep in mind the reason for your study: The law serves as a compass and guide to most business decisions. It provides a general direction for decisions and frequently a specific answer to questions of what a business may or may not do. The law often operates through the fear of sanctions if a decision is contrary to law and legal principles.

This text is designed to highlight for you the legal and regulatory environment in which you will conduct your business activities. However, the law and our legal system are not the only matters that will influence your business decisions. Other matters that deserve your consideration include economic incentives, your personal ethical standards, and your organization's view of its responsibility to society. Throughout the study of the material in this book, you should remember to ask yourself—what is the reason for this legal requirement and how does it interact with these other matters?

This chapter, as an introduction to the entire text, discusses a variety of laws and methods of their interpretation and application. Specifically in this chapter you will be introduced to the following broad topics.

- · What is law?
- · Sources of law
- · Legal sanctions

What is Law?

In this portion of our introduction, you will discover that while the use of the word "law" is commonplace in our daily lives, the meaning of this term is far from exact. Indeed, an appreciation of the broad meaning of "the law" is essential at the outset of your study in this course. The following sections provide background material that will help you gain this appreciation.

1. Definitions of Law

If you hear someone ask the question, "What is *law?*," what comes to your mind? Make a list of the various meanings and application of the word *law;* compare your list with your classmates. Remember, there are no right or wrong answers at this point. The purpose of this exercise and discussion is to broaden your instincts about the law and its influence.

In response to the question in the preceding paragraph, it is common to have someone list something like — "laws are the rules we live by." This is a good general description, but the phrase is overly general. This definition of *law* must be given some context. We often hear players or broadcasters refer to "illegal" plays in sporting events. For example, "that was an illegal block" might be used in either football or basketball. These sporting games must be played with players and coaches following rules ("laws" of the games) to avoid chaos. However, these types of rules ("laws") are not what you will be studying in this text.

To provide the context of "laws" as used in the text, you should consider the following examples of how laws provide guidance to the business community.

Law as Commands

Law is often considered to be a command: You shall do this (that which is right) or you shall not do that (that which is wrong). As a command, law is prescribed by a superior, and the inferior is bound to obey. The criminal law is essentially a body of commands flowing from the people as a whole to people as individuals telling them what they may or may not do.

Many areas of our law do not "command compliance" in the same technical sense as the criminal law. They simply give an aggrieved party a remedy against another one who violates the law in these areas. Civil courts usually do not require compliance but instead impose liability for noncompliance. The sanction of liability provides the motivation for proper conduct.

Law as a Means of Social Control

The law is also a means for controlling people's conduct and for changing society; it deals with social interests. When social interests recognize a right in one person, courts create machinery to assist the person with this right in obtaining redress against the person with the duty or obligation if the duty is not performed or if the obligation is unfulfilled. By this concept, law has four characteristics:

1. It is a scheme of social control.
2. It protects social interests.
3. It accomplishes its purpose by recognizing a capacity in persons to influence the conduct of others.
4. It provides courts and legal procedures to help the person with this capacity.

This definition of law casts judges as social engineers. It operates in decisions regarding environmental protections, employment discrimination issues, and personal rights, such as abortions and prayer in school.

Law as Justice

The foregoing definitions imply that law regulates human conduct and that through courts it resolves controversies. The goal of law is justice, but law and justice are not synonymous. Justice has been defined as that which is founded in fairness, honesty, and righteousness. It is the attempt of honorable persons to do that which is fair. Justice is the purpose and end of government and civil society. Apparently, the achievement of justice depends upon the concept of right and wrong in the society involved. One goal of justice in our society, as stated in the Declaration of Independence, is to secure for all "life, liberty, and the pursuit of happiness."

Like the law, the word "justice" is subject to a variety of applications. For example, social justice recognizes more rights and duties than does legal justice, although the trend of the law is toward equating these concepts. Perfect justice would require that all persons discharge all their obligations and duties so that all other persons may enjoy all their rights and privileges. Our society through law determines which rights and duties will be protected and strives through its judicial system for perfect justice. Of course, the law is incapable of perfect justice because it is in the hands of imperfect people and operates with imperfect procedures. Throughout your studies, keep in mind the policy implications and personal preferences of policy makers that impact the goal that laws (as the means) achieve justice (as the desired end).

2. Classifications of Law

The law often has been described as a "seamless web" in which principles are hopelessly and endlessly intertwined. However, there are ways to classify legal subjects that advance understanding of the law and legal principles.

Common Law and Civil Law

An important method of classifying law is according to the system in which it is created. Rules of law created by the courts through judicial decisions are referred to as the **common law.** Courts "make law" as part of the process of deciding cases and controversies before them. The case law created in this process is based on a doctrine known as **stare decisis.** This doctrine is based on the notion that prior decisions provide guidance that should be followed in subsequent cases involving the same questions of law. Thus, where a rule of law has been announced and followed by courts so that the rule has become settled by judicial decision, a **precedent** is established for future cases. The common law system originated in England. Therefore, because of our nation's close historical association with England, the common law system is of significant importance in the United States. Indeed, many state constitutions specifically adopted the common law of England as the beginning point of those states' legal systems.

The civil law systems found in France and Spain are quite different from the common law system. **Civil law** systems rely primarily on legislative enactments, rather than judicial decisions, for law. Any court in a civil law system must defer to the legislation for the answer to a legal issue. The courts' decisions do not become precedent. Future cases also must be resolved by reference to applicable legislation. Only Louisiana, among the various states, follows a civil law system. This is due to Louisiana's historical ties with France.

Public and Private Law

Another way of classifying the law is to divide it into matters of public law and matters of private law. **Public law** involves those matters that involve the regulation of society as opposed to individuals interacting. Examples of public law include constitutional law, administrative law, and criminal law.

Constitutional law involves the interpretation and application of either the federal or a state constitution. **Administrative law** describes the legal principles that apply to government agencies, bureaus, boards, and commissions. **Criminal law** encompasses all legal aspects of crime. In each of these areas, society, or "the people," are directly involved in the issues. Their interests are represented by a governmental agency, officer, or official whose obligation it is to see that justice is accomplished and the ends of society achieved. Public law provides a major portion of the legal environment of business. For this reason much of the material in subsequent chapters deals

TABLE 1–1   Subdivisions of the Classifications of Legal Subjects

The Law of Contracts	*The Law of Torts*	*The Law of Property*
Sales of goods	Assault and battery	Real property
Commercial paper	Slander and libel	Personal property
Secured transactions	Invasion of privacy	Leases
Bank deposits and collections	Interference with contracts	Bailments
Creditor's rights	Conversion	Wills
Consumer protection	Negligence	Trusts and estates
Debtor protection	Product liability	Mortgages

with constitutional and administrative areas of public law and their application to business.

Private law encompasses those legal problems and relationships that exist between individuals. Private law is traditionally separated into the law of contracts, the law of torts, and the law of property.

Contract law addresses agreements between two parties. **Tort law** addresses wrongs other than a breach of contract, by which one party injures another. **Property law** deals with all aspects of ownership and possession of both tangible things and intangible rights. Our whole economic system is based upon the rights of individuals to acquire and use private property. Table 1–1 provides a further breakdown of these private law topics.

Civil Law and Criminal Law

Another means of classifying the law is to divide it into civil law and criminal law. For administrative purposes, courts usually separate criminal actions from all other lawsuits. *Civil* cases may include suits for breach of contract or tort cases, such as suits for personal injuries. Typically, they involve a request for damages or other appropriate relief that does not involve punishment of the wrongdoer. *Criminal* cases involve a representative of government attempting to prove the wrong committed against society and seeking to have the wrongdoer punished by the court system.

Substantive Law and Procedural Law

Another important classification or distinction in law is between substance and procedure. **Substantive law** defines the legal relationship of people with other people or between them and the state. Thus, the rules of law governing the creation or enforcement of a contractual promise are substantive in nature. **Procedural law** deals with the method and means by which substantive law is made and administered. The time allowed for one party to sue another and the rules of law governing the process of the lawsuit are examples of procedural laws. Thus, substantive rules of law define rights and duties, while procedural rules of law provide the machinery for enforcing those rights and duties.

Judicial procedures involve the conduct of lawsuits and appeals and the enforcement of judgments. The rules for conducting civil trials are different from those for criminal trials. For example, each party may call the other party to the witness stand for cross-examination in a civil trial, but the defendant may not be required to testify in a criminal case. Procedural problems sometimes arise concerning papers filed in lawsuits, the admission of evidence, and various other techniques involved in trying the case. They are the rules of the game. In the next chapter, you will study these procedural aspects of law in greater depth.

Sources of Law

The total body of law by which we are governed comes from four basic sources:

1. Constitutions
2. Legislation
3. The rules, regulations, and decisions of administrative agencies, called administrative law
4. Judicial decisions

The next four sections provide you with details about these sources. Remember that these discussions are introductory. Other chapters provide detailed discussions of some sources, such as the federal constitution in Chapter 5 and the regulatory administrative agencies in Chapter 6. Examples of how legislation and judicial decisions make up our legal and regulatory environment of business are found throughout this book. By way of emphasizing the fundamental importance of the judiciary, section 7 explores the power of judicial review. Section 8 discusses the nature of the judicial process.

3. Constitutions

In our system, the constitution of the governmental unit is its basic and supreme law. The U.S. Constitution is basic to our federal government. By and large, most state constitutions are modeled after the U.S. Constitution. State constitutions provide the same general structure for government, dividing it into executive, legislative, and judicial branches and giving each branch checks and balances on the others. In addition to providing the government structure, constitutions define the powers and functions of the various branches.

There is an important distinction between the federal and state constitutions. The U.S. Constitution was a delegation of authority from the states, which were the basic sovereigns, to the federal government. All powers not contained in our federal constitution are retained by the state. Whereas the U.S. Constitution contains grants of power to the federal government, state constitutions generally contain limitations on the power of the state government.

4. Legislation

Our formal written laws are known as **legislation** because they are created and adopted by elected representatives serving in the legislative branch of government. Legislative bodies exist at all levels of government, including not only the federal Congress but also state general assemblies, city councils, and many other local government bodies that adopt or enact laws. Legislation in its broad sense also includes treaties entered into by the executive branch of government and ratified by the Senate.

Legislation enacted by Congress or a state legislature is usually referred to as a **statute.** Laws passed by local governments are frequently called **ordinances.** Compilations of legislation at all levels of government are called **codes.** For example, we have local traffic codes covering such matters as speed limits, and state laws, such as the Uniform Commercial Code, that cover all aspects of commercial transactions. The statutes of our federal government are compiled in the United States Code.

Uniformity of Legislation

Uniformity in the law may be achieved either by federal legislation or by the enactment of the same law by all states. The latter method has been attempted by a legislative drafting group known as the National Conference of Commissioners on Uniform State Laws. These commissioners endeavor to promote uniformity by drafting model acts. When approved by the National Conference, proposed uniform acts are recommended to the state legislatures for adoption.

More than 100 uniform laws, mostly related to business activities, have been drafted and presented to the various state legislatures. The response of the states in adopting these proposed laws has varied. A few of the uniform laws have been adopted by all the states. Sometimes a state adopts the uniform law in principle but changes some of the provisions to meet local needs. As a result, there are "nonuniform state laws."

The most significant uniform law for business is the **Uniform Commercial Code** (UCC). It was prepared for the stated purpose of collecting in one body the law that "deals with all the phases which may ordinarily arise in the handling of a commercial transaction from start to finish." Thus it covers the law as it relates to the sale of goods, the use of commercial paper to pay for them, the banking system, and the giving of security to ensure that the purchase price will be paid. The Uniform Commercial Code is limited to commercial transactions involving personal property and is not applicable to contracts for the sale of real estate or to contracts for personal services. While the UCC, due to its private law orientation, is not a matter of significant focus in this text, its provisions are discussed in Chapter 8 on contracts.

Interpretation of Legislation

Legislation often is written in general terms. The precise meaning of the law often is unclear. In our legal system, it is up to the judiciary to determine the meaning of general language in a legislative enactment and apply it to the limited facts of a case. The court's purpose in interpreting a statute or an ordinance is to determine the intent of the legislature when the statute was enacted. Such a process is called **statutory construction.**

One technique of statutory interpretation is to examine the **legislative history** of an act to determine the purpose of the legislation or the evil it was designed to correct. Courts try to find the legislative intent by examining the debates of the legislative body, the committee reports, amendments that

TABLE 1–2   Rules of Statutory Construction

Rules Based on the Type of Law
- Taxing laws shall be *strictly* construed.
- Criminal laws shall be *strictly* construed.
- Statutes in derogation of the common law shall be *strictly* construed.
- Remedial statutes shall be *liberally* construed.

Rules Based on Words
- Words generally are given their *plain* or *usual* meaning.
- Technical words are given their *technical* meaning.
- Words are given meaning by the *context* in which they are used.

Other Rules
- If two statutes cover the same topic, they will be construed as *consistent* with each other if possible.
- If two statutes conflict so that they cannot both be in effect, the latter one is presumed to have *repealed* the earlier one.
- Exemptions from statutes are construed *strictly* against the party claiming the exemption.

were rejected, and other matters that transpired prior to the adoption of the statute. Legislative history may supply the legislative intent, but many of the questions of interpretation that confront courts were not foreseen by the legislators. The actual task for a court often is to determine what the legislature *would have* intended had it considered the question.

Resort to legislative history is not the only means of ascertaining the legislative intent. Courts have developed rules of statutory construction that are frequently followed in determining the legislative intent. These rules recognize that the courts do not actually know what the legislature intended. By following an appropriate rule of construction, courts assume that the legislature intended a certain meaning. Table 1–2 summarizes some of the more frequently used rules of statutory construction.

5. Administrative Rules, Regulations, and Decisions

As stated in the preceding sections, legislation often is adopted and signed into law even though it is written in broad, general terms. Legislative bodies, recognizing the need for greater specificity, often authorize the creation of administrative agencies to provide clarity and enforcement of a legal area. Examples of such actions include the establishment of the Environmental Protection Agency (EPA), the Securities and Exchange Commission (SEC), and the Occupational Safety and Health Administration (OSHA).

Each of these agencies and hundreds more regulate business activities through the adoption of rules and regulations. Administrative agencies also can be empowered to investigate businesses to determine if laws have been violated. Many agencies can hold their own hearings resulting in findings of a business's guilt or innocence. Other agencies can prosecute alleged violations of the rules and regulations.

Section 12 of this chapter discusses possible penalties for violations of administrative rules, regulations, and decisions. Chapter 6 provides further details on the creation, operation, and impact of agencies. Suffice it, for now, to say that almost every business activity is regulated to some degree by the administrative process at the federal, state, or local level.

6. Judicial Decisions

In our common law systems, courts create rules of law through interpreting legislation (as in section 4, above) and by deciding cases or controversies that are not resolved by reference to legislation. In either of these settings, when a court decides a case, particularly upon an appeal from a lower court decision, the court writes an **opinion** setting forth, among other things, the reasons for its decision. From these written opinions, rules of law can be deduced, and these make the case law that constitutes common law. The decisions set forth later in the text are cases that have been decided by courts of review. All cases that have been decided are available to interested persons for use in legal research, as are the statutory enactments of legislatures.

Advantages

As stated earlier in this introduction, the precedent-oriented nature of the common law system is founded on the doctrine of stare decisis. Stare decisis arose from the desire of courts as well as society for certainty and predictability in the law. In addition, following precedent was expedient. The common law, through precedent, settled many legal issues and brought stability into many areas of the law, such as contracts. Relying on prior decisions, individuals could then act with reasonable certainty as to the legality of their conduct.

Disadvantages

The benefits of the doctrine of stare decisis and the common law system are counterbalanced by some significant disadvantages. While these burdens are discussed in the remainder of this section, you should keep in mind that we do not consider these disadvantages as destroying the benefits of certainty, predictability, and stability.

Volume, Time & Expense.   First, notwithstanding the fact that common law arose out of a desire for certainty and is designed to create it, common law creates a great deal of uncertainty in the law. The sheer volume of judicial decisions, each possibly creating precedent, makes the "law" beyond the comprehension of lawyers and judges, let alone the rest of us. Large law firms employ lawyers whose sole task is to search the case reports for the law to be used in lawsuits and in advising clients. Access to hundreds of volumes of cases is required. Due to this volume of cases, the common law system does not provide the level of certainty and predictability envisioned by its English creators so many centuries ago.

Instead, it requires hundreds of hours of research time. Since lawyers often charge by the hour, the cost of doing research to "find the applicable law" is becoming increasingly expensive. Although computer search tools are helpful in reducing the time required to locate appropriate cases, the increasing volume of such cases that must be read carefully causes expenses to climb.

Furthermore, conflicting precedents frequently are discovered. Additional time and expense is required to prepare persuasive arguments as to which of the precedents found is the most applicable to resolving the current case.

No Precedent Exists.   Second, in many cases the law cannot be found by searching cases. The law that is used to decide many cases must be made as part of the decision process. Many years ago a legal scholar, in discussing this aspect of case law, observed[1]:

> It is the judges that make the common law. Do you know how they make it? Just as a man makes laws for his dog. When your dog does anything you want to break him of, you wait till he does it, and then beat him for it. This is the way you make laws for your dog: and this is the way the judges make laws for you and me. They won't tell a man beforehand what it is he should not do—they won't so much as allow of his being told: they lie by till he has done something which they say he should not have done, and then they hang him for it. What way, then, has any man of coming at this dog-law? Only by watching their proceedings: by observing in what cases they have hanged a man, in what cases they have sent him to jail, in what cases they have seized his goods, and so forth.

Dicta.   Third, there is an important distinction between precedent and unnecessary opinions of judges. A judicial decision, as authority for future cases, is limited by the facts upon which it is founded and the rules of law upon which the decision actually is based. Frequently courts make comments on matters not necessary to the decision reached. Such expressions, called **dicta,** lack the force of a judicial settlement. Strictly speaking, they are not precedent that courts will be required to follow within the rule of stare decisis. However, dicta may be followed if they are sound and just, and dicta that have been repeated frequently are often given the force of precedent. Moreover, even though a statement by a court is not pure precedent, it does express the court's opinion, and to the extent that the court is knowledgeable about the subject matter, the court's opinion carries some weight.

Rejecting Precedent.   Fourth, one of the major reasons that the case law system leads to uncertainty is that a precedent may be changed or reversed. Since case law is susceptible to change, absolute reliance on it is not possible.

Case law created by the judiciary can be changed by the judiciary. The common law is not set in stone to be left unchanged for decades and centuries. As Justice William O. Douglas observed[2]:

> Inherent in the common law is a dynamic principle which allows it to grow and to tailor itself to meet changing needs within the doctrine of stare decisis,

---

[1]Bentham, *Works* 235, quoted in 1 Steffen and Levi, *Cases and Materials on the Elements of the Law* 207 (3d ed., 1946).

[2]The Eighth Annual Benjamin N. Cardozo Lecture delivered before the Association of the Bar of the City of New York on April 12, 1949. By permission from Justice William O. Douglas.

which, if correctly understood, was not static and did not forever prevent the courts from reversing themselves or from applying principles of common law to new situations as the need arose. If this were not so, we must succumb to a rule that a judge should let others "long dead and unaware of the problems of the age in which he lives, do his thinking of him."

Courts usually hesitate to reject a precedent or to change case law. The assumption is made that a principle or rule of law announced in a former judicial decision, if unfair or contrary to public policy, will be changed by legislation.

Precedent has more force in trial courts than in courts of review, which have the power to make precedent in the first instance. However, stare decisis does not mean that former decisions *always* will be followed, even by trial courts. A former ruling may have been erroneous or the conditions upon which it was based may have changed or may no longer exist. The doctrine does not require courts to multiply their errors by using former mistakes as authority and support for new errors. Thus, just as legislatures change the law by new legislation, courts change the law, from time to time, by reversing or modifying former precedents.

Judges are subject to social forces and changing circumstances just as are legislatures. The personnel of courts changes, and each new generation of judges has a responsibility to reexamine precedents and to adapt them to changing conditions. This responsibility is especially present in cases involving constitutional issues. A doctrine known as *constitutional relativity* stands for the proposition that the meaning of the language found in the Constitution is relative to the time in which it is being interpreted. The doctrine has been used frequently by the Supreme Court to give effect to society's attitudes. Under this concept, great weight is attached to social forces and needs, as the court sees them, in formulating judicial decisions. As the attitudes and problems of society change, precedent changes.

Some comments from justices indicate their attitude toward precedent. For example, Justice Wanamaker in the case of *Adams Express Co. v. Beckwith,* 100 Ohio St. 348 (1919), said:

> A decided case is worth as much as it weighs in reason and righteousness, and no more. It is not enough to say "thus saith the court." It must prove its right to control in any given situation by the degree in which it supports the rights of a party violated and serves the cause of justice as to all parties concerned.

Or as Justice Musmanno stated in the case of *Bosely v. Andrews,* 393 Pa. 161 (1958):

> Stare decisis is the viaduct over which the law travels in transporting the precious cargo of justice. Prudence and a sense of safety dictate that the piers of that viaduct should be examined and tested from time to time to make certain that they are sound, strong and capable of supporting the weight above. . . . A precedent, in law, in order to be binding, should appeal to logic and a genuine sense of justice. What lends dignity to the law founded on precedent is that, if analyzed, the particularly cited case wields authority by the sheer force of its self-integrated honesty, integrity, and rationale. A precedent cannot, and should not, control, if its strength depends alone on the fact that it is old, but may crumble at the slighted probing touch of instinctive reason and natural justice.

The extent to which precedent is followed varies a great deal depending on the subject matter of the litigation. If the dispute involves subject areas of private law, such as torts, contracts, or property, there is much greater deference to precedent than if the subject area is constitutional law. The fact that precedent is to be given great weight in the areas of private law does not mean that courts will continue to follow a rule of private law where the reasoning behind the rule no longer exists. Even here, precedents are reversed as the needs of society change. The belief that the meaning of the Constitution is relative to the times in which it is being interpreted results in less deference to precedent in constitutional law cases. To the extent that courts provide leadership in bringing about social, political, and economic change, they are likely to give less weight to precedent and more weight to other factors.

Conflict of Laws.   A fifth disadvantage of stare decisis arises because our country consists of 50 sovereign states. Each creates its own body of common law. The law as it develops on a case-by-case basis in different states varies from state to state. Moreover, the federal legal system is superimposed on the state systems, thus creating additional bodies of judge-made laws.

When a case or controversy involves more than one state, the difficulty arising from conflicting precedents is compounded. In case law, differences among the states are common and exist in every area of the law.

In cases involving transactions or occurrences with contact with more than one state, the question must always be asked: Which state law applies? To answer this question a body of law has developed primarily through judicial decisions, which is referred to as **conflict of laws.** The decisions that constitute this body of law simply determine which state's substantive law is applicable to any given question when more than one state is involved. This usually arises where all or some of the facts occur in one state and the trial is held in another. For example, the conflict-of-laws rules for tort actions are, in most cases, that the law of the place of injury is applicable. Thus, if a car accident occurred in Missouri but suit was brought in an Illinois state court, the judge would apply the law of Missouri in determining the rights of the parties.

Courts hold several different views about which law to select in resolving issues involving contracts. Some favor the law of the state where the contract was made, others favor the law of the place of performance, and still others have adopted a grouping of contacts theory, which uses the law of the state with the most substantial contact with the contract. This latter theory has also been applied in a few tort cases. In the criminal law, the law of the place of the crime is the applicable substantive law. Table 1–3 illustrates typical conflict-of-laws principles.

In a multistate situation, the first problem confronting the court is to select the appropriate state to turn to for legal precedent on substantive issues. Once this determination has been made, the court's business is then to review the citations of authority advanced by the opposing attorneys to determine which of that state's case decisions to apply in following the doctrine of stare decisis.

TABLE 1–3   Sample Conflict-of-Laws Principles

Substantive Law Issue	*Law to Be Applied*
1. Liability for injury caused by tortious conduct	1. State in which injury was inflicted or State in which injury was received
2. Validity of a contract	2. State in which contract was made or State in which it is to be performed or State with most significant contacts with the contract or State specified in the contract
3. Inheritance of real property	3. State of real property's location
4. Inheritance of tangible personal property	4. State of domicile of deceased
5. Validity of a marriage	5. State of celebration
6. Child custody	6. State of domicile of child
7. Workers' compensation	7. State of employment

Therefore, it must be recognized that there is a body of law used to decide conflicts between the precedents of the various states. This body of law is especially significant in our modern society with its ease of communication and transportation. The trend toward uniform statutes and codes has tended to decrease these conflicts, but many of them still exist. So long as we have a federal system and fifty separate state bodies of substantive law, the area of conflict of laws will continue to be of substantial importance in the application of the doctrine of stare decisis.

Concept Summary: Problems in Common Law

1. Volume of cases creates uncertainty and high costs to the legal system.
2. On many issues, law is not clear or there is no actual precedent.
3. Dicta are not precedent, although they are sometimes taken as such.
4. Precedent is often rejected or overturned.
5. Conflict-of-laws issues exist in many cases.

7. Judicial Review

The most significant of the powers of the judiciary is **judicial review,** which is the power to review laws passed by the legislative body and to declare them to be unconstitutional and thus void. It also allows the courts to review actions taken by the executive branch and to declare them unconstitutional.

Although the Constitution does not expressly provide that the judiciary shall be the overseer of the government, the net effect of this doctrine is to make it so. Chief Justice John Marshall in *Marbury v. Madison*, U.S. (1 Cranch) 137 (1803), announced the doctrine of judicial review using in part the following language and reasoning:

> It is a proposition too plain to be contested, that the constitution controls any legislative act repugnant to it; or that the legislature may not alter the constitution by an ordinary act. . . .
>
> Certainly, all those who have framed written constitutions contemplate them as forming the fundamental and paramount law of the nation, and consequently, the theory of every such government must be, that an act of the legislature, repugnant to the constitution, is void. . . .
>
> It is, emphatically, the province and duty of the judicial department, to say what the law is. Those who apply the rule to particular cases, must of necessity expound and interpret that rule. If two laws conflict with each other, the courts must decide on the operation of each. So, if a law be in opposition to the constitution; if both the law and the constitution apply to a particular case, so that the court must either decide that case, conformable to the law, disregarding the constitution; or conformable to the constitution, disregarding the law; the court must determine which of these conflicting rules governs the case: this is of the very essence of judicial duty. If then, the courts are to regard the constitution, and the constitution is superior to any ordinary act of the legislature, the constitution, and not such ordinary act, must govern the case to which they both apply.

As individual jurists exercise the power of judicial review, they do so with varying attitudes and philosophies. Some judges believe that the power should be used very sparingly, although others are willing to use it more often. Those who believe that the power should not be used except in unusual cases are said to believe in **judicial restraint.** Those who think that the power should be used whenever the needs of society justify its use believe in **judicial activism.** All members of the judiciary believe in judicial restraint and all are activists to some extent. Often a jurist may be an activist in one area of the law and a firm believer in judicial restraint in another. Both judicial restraint and judicial activism describe attitudes or tendencies by matters of degree. Both terms are also used to describe general attitudes toward the exercise of the power of judicial review.

Judicial Restraint

The philosophy of judicial restraint developed naturally from the recognition that, in exercising the power of judicial review, the courts are overseeing coequal branches of government. When the power of judicial review is used to set aside decisions by the other branches of government, the courts are wielding great power. It follows that logic and a commitment to the constitutional system dictate that this almost unlimited power be exercised with great restraint.

Those who believe in judicial restraint think that many constitutional issues are too important to be decided by courts unless absolutely necessary and are to be avoided if there is another legal basis for a decision. They believe the proper use of judicial power demands that courts refrain from determining the constitutionality of an act of Congress unless it is absolutely necessary to a decision of a case. This modest view of the role of the judiciary is based on the belief that litigation is not the appropriate technique for bringing about social, political, and economic change.

The philosophy of judicial restraint is sometimes referred to as *strict constructionism*, or *judicial abstention.* Strict constructionists believe that the Constitution should be interpreted in light of what the Founding Fathers intended. They place great weight on the debates of the Constitutional Convention and the language of the Constitution. Those who promote judicial abstention hold that courts should decide only those matters they must to resolve actual cases and controversies before them. Courts should abstain from deciding issues whenever possible, and doubts about the constitutionality of legislation should be resolved in favor of the statute. Cases should be decided on the facts if possible and on the narrowest possible grounds.

Those who believe in judicial restraint feel that social, political, and economic change in society should result from the political process rather than from court action. Justice John Marshall Harlan in *Reynolds v. Sims*, 84 S.Ct. 1362 (1964), epitomized this philosophy when, in dissenting from a reapportionment decision, he stated in part:

> The vitality of our political system, on which in the last analysis all else depends, is weakened by reliance on the judiciary for political reform. . . . These decisions give support to a current mistaken view of the Constitution and the constitutional function of this Court. This view, in a nutshell, is that every major social ill in the country can find its cure in some constitutional "principle," and that this Court should "take the lead" in promoting reform when other branches of government fail to act. The Constitution is not a panacea for every blot upon the public welfare, nor should this Court, ordained as a judicial body, be thought of as a general haven for reform movements. The Constitution is an instrument of government, fundamental to which is the premise that in a diffusion of governmental authority lies the greatest promise that this nation will realize liberty for all its citizens. This Court, limited in function in accordance with that premise, does not serve its high purpose when it exceeds its authority, even to satisfy justified impatience with the slow working of the political process.

Judges who identify with judicial restraint give great deference to the political process. They believe that the courts, especially the federal courts, ought to defer to the actions of the states and of the coordinate branches of government unless these actions are clearly unconstitutional. They allow the states and the federal legislative and executive branches wide latitude in finding solutions to the nation's problems.

Judicial restraint jurists have a deep commitment to precedent. They overrule cases only when the prior decision is clearly wrong. They try to refrain from writing their personal convictions into the law. They do not view the role of the lawyer and the practice of law as that of social reform. To them, reform is the function of the political process.

Followers of judicial restraint often take a pragmatic approach to litigation. Whenever possible, decisions are based on the facts rather than a principle of law. Reviewing courts exercising judicial restraint tend to accept the trial court decisions unless they are clearly wrong on the facts or the law. If there is any reasonable basis for the lower court decision, it will not be reversed. Such courts often engage in a balancing approach to their decisions.

TABLE 1–4   Typical Judicial Restraint Decisions

1. Male-only draft is not a denial of equal protection of the law.
2. States can regulate nuclear power.
3. States can tax the foreign income of multinational corporations.
4. Prayer in the legislature does not violate the First Amendment.
5. Unanimous verdicts are not required, and juries may consist of fewer than twelve persons.
6. A federal law cannot require state law enforcement officers to conduct background checks on gun purchasers.
7. Class action suits require actual notice to members of the class.
8. Congress cannot create religious freedoms pursuant to Section 5 of the Fourteenth Amendment.
9. Seniority has preference over affirmative action layoffs.
10. State and local employees are subject to the Federal Fair Labor Standards Act.

They weigh competing interests. For example, justices who adhere to judicial restraint often weigh the rights of the person accused of crime with the interests of the victim and of society in determining the extent of the rights of the accused in criminal cases.

Throughout most of our history, judicial restraint has been the dominant philosophy. Today, most of the justices of the U.S. Supreme Court usually follow this philosophy, but all courts to some degree are activist. Table 1–4 illustrates typical judicial restraint decisions. The court allowed these decisions by other branches of government and the political process to stand.

Judicial Activism

Those who believe in the philosophy of judicial activism believe that courts have a major role to play in correcting wrongs in our society. To them, courts must provide leadership in bringing about social, political, and economic change because the political system is often too slow or unable to bring about those changes necessary to improve society. Activists tend to be innovative and less dependent on precedent for their decisions. They are value oriented and policy directed. Activist jurists believe that constitutional issues must be decided within the context of contemporary society and that the meaning of the Constitution is relative to the times in which it is being interpreted. To activists, the courts, and especially the Supreme Court, sit as a continuing constitutional convention to meet the needs of today.

During the 1950s and 1960s, there was an activist majority on the Supreme Court. This activist majority brought about substantial changes in the law, especially in such areas as civil rights, reapportionment, and the criminal law. For example, the activist court of this period ordered desegregation of public schools and gave us the one-man, one-vote concept in the distributing of legislative bodies. Earl Warren, Chief Justice during this period, used to request that lawyers appearing before the Court address themselves to the effect of their clients' positions on society. "Tell me why your position is 'right' and that of your opponent is 'wrong' from the standpoint of society" was a common request to lawyers arguing cases before him.

Activist courts tend to be more result conscious and to place less reliance on precedent. Activists are often referred to as liberals, but that description

TABLE 1–5 Typical Judicial Activist Decisions

1. Busing is a valid technique to achieve school desegregation.
2. Legislative apportionment must be based on population and not area.
3. No prayer is to be permitted in school.
4. The *Miranda* warning shall be given to all criminal suspects prior to interrogation.
5. Statutes outlawing abortion are unconstitutional.
6. Female pensions must be the same as male pensions, even though, on average, females live longer.
7. There shall be equal pay for comparable worth.
8. Residency requirement for public assistance violates equal protection.
9. State laws that require teaching "creation science" as well as evolution are unconstitutional.
10. Certain public employees, such as public defenders, cannot be fired because of political affiliation.

is too narrow to explain their belief in the role of the judiciary as an instrument of change. Activists also believe that justices must examine for themselves the great issues facing society and then decide these issues in light of contemporary standards. Otherwise, they believe we are governed by the dead or by people who are not aware of all of the complexities of today's problems.

Table 1–5 illustrates typical judicial activist decisions. These examples are of decisions in which the judiciary has imposed its will on society.

8. The Nature of the Judicial Process

In deciding cases and in examining the powers discussed in the prior sections, courts are often faced with several alternatives. They may decide the case by use of existing statutes and precedents as they of necessity have a deep commitment to the common law system. Yet they may also refuse to apply existing case law or may declare a statute to be void as unconstitutional. Also, if there is no statute or case law, the court may decide the case and create law in the process. However, case law as a basis for deciding controversies often provides only the point of departure from which the difficult labor of the court begins. The court must examine and compare cases cited as authority to it so it can determine not only which is correct but also whether the principles or rules of law contained therein should be followed or rejected as no longer valid. In reaching and preparing its decision, the court must consider whether the law as announced will provide justice in the particular case and whether it will establish sound precedent for future cases involving similar issues.

The foregoing alternatives raise several questions: Why do courts reach one conclusion rather than another in any given case? What formula, if any, is used in deciding cases and in determining the direction of the law? What forces tend to influence judicial decisions when the public interest is involved?

There is, obviously, no simple answer to these questions. Many people assume that logic is the basic tool of the judicial decision. But Justice Oliver Wendell Holmes stated, "the life of the law has not been logic; it has been experience."[3] Other's argue that courts merely reflect the attitudes of the times and simply follow the more popular course in decisions where the public is involved.

Justice Benjamin Cardozo, in a series of lectures on the judicial process,[4] discussed the sources of information judges utilize in deciding cases. He stated that if the answer were not clearly established by statute or by unquestioned precedent, the problem was twofold: "He [the judge] must first extract from the precedents the underlying principle, the *ratio decidendi;* he must then determine the path or direction along which the principle is to work and develop, if it is not to wither or die." The first part of the problem is separating legal principles from dicta so that the actual precedent is clear. Commenting on the second aspect of the problem, Cardozo said:

> The directive force of a principle may be exerted along the line of logical progression; this I will call the rule of analogy or the method of philosophy; along the line of historical development; this I will call the method of evolution; along the lines of the customs of the community; this I will call the method of tradition; along the lines of justice, morals and social welfare, the *mores* of the day; and this I will call the method of sociology.

In Cardozo's judgment, the rule of analogy was entitled to certain presumptions and should be followed if possible. He believed that the judge who molds the law by the method of philosophy is satisfying humanity's deep-seated desire for certainty. History, in indicating the direction of precedent, often illuminates the path of logic and plays an important part in decisions in areas such as real property. Custom or trade practice has supplied much of the direction of the law in the area of business. All judicial decisions are at least in part directed by the judge's viewpoint on the welfare of society. The end served by law must dictate the administration of justice, and ethical considerations, if ignored, will ultimately overturn a principle of law.

Noting the psychological aspects of judges' decisions, Cardozo observed that it is the subconscious forces that keep judges consistent with one another. In so recognizing that all persons, including judges, have a philosophy that gives coherence and direction to their thought and actions whether they admit it or not, he stated:

> All their lives, forces which they do not recognize and cannot name, have been tugging at them—inherited instincts, traditional beliefs, acquired conviction; and the resultant is an outlook on life, a conception of social needs, . . . which when reasons are nicely balanced, must determine where choice shall fall. In this mental background every problem finds its setting. We may try to see things as objectively as we please. None the less, we can never see them with any eyes except our own. To that test they are all brought—a form of pleading or an act of parliament, the wrongs of paupers or the rights of princes, a village ordinance or a nation's charter.

In the following comments, Cardozo summarized his view of the judicial process.

---

[3]Holmes, *The Common Law* 1 (1938).

[4]Cardozo, *The Nature of the Judicial Process* (1921). Excerpts are used by permission from the Yale University Press.

THE NATURE OF THE JUDICIAL PROCESS

Benjamin N. Cardozo

. . . My analysis of the judicial process comes then to this, and little more: logic, and history, and custom, and utility, and the accepted standards of right conduct are the forces which singly or in combination shape the progress of the law. Which of these forces shall dominate in any case must depend largely upon the comparative importance or value of the social interests that will be thereby promoted or impaired. One of the most fundamental social interests is that law shall be uniform and impartial. There must be nothing in its action that savors of prejudice or favor or even arbitrary whim or fitfulness. Therefore in the main there shall be adherence to precedent. There shall be symmetrical development, consistently with history or custom when history or custom has been the motive force, or the chief one, in giving shape to existing rules, and with logic or philosophy when the motive power has been theirs. But symmetrical development may be bought at too high a price. Uniformity ceases to be a good when it becomes uniformity of oppression. The social interest served by symmetry or certainty must then be balanced against the social interest served by equity and fairness or other elements of social welfare. These may enjoin upon the judge the duty of drawing the line at another angle, of staking the path along new courses, of marking a new point of departure from which others who come after him will set out upon their journey.

If you ask how he is to know when one interest outweighs another, I can only answer that he must get his knowledge just as the legislator gets it, from experience and study and reflection; in brief, from life itself. Here, indeed, is the point of contact between the legislator's work and his. The choice of methods, the appraisement of values, must in the end be guided by like considerations for the one as for the other. Each indeed is legislating within the limits of his competence. No doubt the limits for the judge are narrower. He legislates only between gaps. He fills the open spaces in the law. How far he can go without traveling beyond the walls of the interstices cannot be staked out for him upon a chart. He must learn it for himself as he gains the sense of fitness and proportion that comes with years of habitude in the practice of an art. Even within the gaps, restrictions not easy to define, but felt, however impalpable they may be, by every judge and lawyer, hedge and circumscribe his action. They are established by the traditions of the centuries, by the example of other judges, his predecessors and his colleagues, by the collective judgment of the profession, and by the duty of adherence to the pervading spirit of the law. . . . None the less, within the confines of these open spaces and those of precedent and tradition, choice moves with a freedom which stamps its action as creative. The law which is the resulting product is not found, but made. The process, being legislative, demands the legislator's wisdom. . . .

Legal Sanctions

Several methods are used to encourage or to force compliance with and obedience to the law. These methods, often called **sanctions,** may be used against a person who has failed to comply with the law. The sanctions are in effect a form of punishment for violating the law. Sanctions also have a preventive function. The threat of sanctions usually results in compliance with the requirements of law.

Because punishment is used to secure obedience to the law, the Fourteenth Amendment to the Constitution of the United States provides in part: "No State shall . . . deprive any person of life, liberty or property without due process of law." This provision recognizes that the law is enforced by taking a person's life, freedom, or property. The taking of property from a person may be for the benefit of society generally, as a fine, or for the benefit of another person, as an award of damages. Most laws are enforced through the threat of or actual imposition of financial costs. The right of an individual to take another person's money or property because of the failure of the latter to meet the requirements of the law is known as a **remedy.** As you study the following sections, identify the remedies available to those seeking the money or property of another through the use of legal processes.

9. For Criminal Conduct

A *crime* is a public wrong against society. Criminal cases are brought by the government on behalf of the people. The people are represented by a state's attorney or U.S. attorney or other public official. When a person is convicted of a crime, one of the following punishments may be imposed:

1. Death
2. Imprisonment
3. Fine
4. Removal from office
5. Disqualification from holding any office and from voting

Among the purposes of such punishment are to protect the public and to deter persons from wrongful conduct.

10. For Breach of Contract

The conduct of business is primarily a series of contracts, or legal relationships created between individuals by their own agreement. Business organizations are based on the law of contracts, which makes promises by which the parties create the legal rights and duties enforceable by courts.

When one party to a contract fails to do what he or she agreed to do, a **breach of contract** has occurred. The usual remedy for a breach is a suit for dollar damages. These damages, called **compensatory damages,** are awarded to make the victim of the breach "whole" in the economic sense. Such damages compensate the party for all losses that are the direct and foreseeable result of the breach of contract. The objective is that the party be in as good a position as he or she would have been in had the contract been performed. Damages do not make most parties totally "whole," however, because they do not as a general rule include attorney's fees. Unless the contract or some special law provides to the contrary, parties to the contract litigation pay their own attorneys.

In addition to compensatory damages, breach-of-contract cases may award consequential damages when the breaching party knew or had reason to know that special circumstances existed that would cause the other party to suffer additional losses if the contract were breached.

There are other remedies available for a breach of contract. If a breach by one party is serious enough, the other party may be permitted to rescind or cancel the contract. In some circumstances, the remedy of an injured party may be a decree of **specific performance**—an order by the court commanding the other party actually to perform the bargain as agreed. Much of the litigation today, especially in the federal courts, involves one corporation suing another for breach of contract.

11. For Tortious Conduct

A **tort** is a civil wrong other than a breach of contract committed against persons or their property for which the law gives a right to recover damages. It differs from a crime, which is a wrong against society, although the same act—assault, for example—may be a wrong both against a person and against society.

Tort liability is based on two premises:

1. In a civilized society persons will not intentionally injure others or their property.
2. All persons will exercise reasonable care and caution in their activities.

The first premise has resulted in a group of torts called **intentional torts.** These include such traditional wrongs as assault and battery, false imprisonment, libel, slander, trespass, and conversion of personal property. This group of torts also includes relatively new torts such as interference with contractual relationships and invasion of privacy. The second premise has led to the general field of tort liability known as **negligence.** Negligence is the failure to exercise the degree of care the law requires under the circumstances. Conduct that is negligent under some circumstances may not be negligent in others.

Each of these premises creates liability for wrongful conduct because a party is at fault. Our legal system in effect says, "If you are at *fault* and cause injury to another or his property, you shall compensate the injured party for the loss with money." Such compensation often involves hundreds of thousands or even millions of dollars. Before concluding that some verdicts are too large, ask yourself, "How much money would it take to make the plaintiff whole?" Keep in mind that the objective of a damage award in a tort case is to compensate the plaintiff for a proven loss or injury caused by the intentional or negligent conduct of another. The award is designed to compensate the injured party in full measure for the total harm caused.

In addition to compensatory damages, some tort cases allow plaintiffs to recover **punitive** or **exemplary damages.** These are money damages awarded one party to punish the other's conduct and to deter others from such conduct in the future. These awards often bear little or no relationship to the actual damages sustained. Punitive damages are frequently awarded in intentional tort cases. They can also be awarded when business conduct is oppressive, malicious, or otherwise indicative of the breaching party's intent to harm the other party.

12. For Violating Statutes and Regulations

Statutes at both the federal and state levels of government impose a variety of sanctions for violating the statutes or regulations of administrative agencies adopted to accomplish statutory purposes. These sanctions are often similar to those imposed for criminal conduct, breach of contract, or tortious conduct. Many statutes, for example, impose a fine for a violation and authorized damages to injured parties as well.

The laws designed to protect our competitive economic system from anticompetitive behavior provide a good example of the use of sanctions to control business conduct. The Sherman Antitrust Act of 1890 as amended authorizes four sanctions to enforce its provisions:

1. It is a crime punishable by fine, imprisonment, or both to violate many of the provisions.
2. Courts may use a court order called an **injunction** either to prevent future violations or to correct the impact of past violations. The injunction may prevent anticompetitive behavior or it may even force the breakup of a corporation, as it did for the former American Telephone and Telegraph Company.
3. Persons who suffer injury as a result of noncompliance may sue wrongdoers for *triple* damages.
4. Any property owned in violation of the act that is being transported from one state to another is subject to seizure by and forfeiture to the United States.

The third remedy affords relief to persons injured by another's violation of the antitrust laws. Such victims are given the right to collect three times the damages they have suffered plus court costs and reasonable attorney's fees. Normally, the objective of awarding money damages to individuals in a private lawsuit is to place them in the position they would have enjoyed, as nearly as this can be done with money, had their rights not been invaded. The triple-damage provisions of the antitrust laws, however, employ the remedy of damages to punish a defendant for a wrongful act in addition to compensating the plaintiff for actual injury. Today it is perhaps the most important remedy of all, because it allows one's competitors as well as injured members of the general public to enforce the law if government fails to do so. It also imposes financial burdens on violators far in excess of any fine that could be imposed as a result of a criminal prosecution. This significant liability, moreover, may be far in excess of the damages that can be awarded against any one defendant, because the liability of defendants is similar to liability based on tort law and is said to be joint and several. For example, assume that ten companies in an industry conspire to fix prices and that the total damages caused by the conspiracy equal $100 million. Also, assume that nine of the defendants settle out of court for $25 million. The remaining defendant, if the case is lost, would owe $275 million ($3 \times 100 - 25$).

Other areas of the law discussed later in this text have similar sanctions. Violations of the securities regulations can result in both criminal sanctions and civil damages. They are covered in Chapter 7. Labor law authorizes the awarding of back pay with job reinstatement to workers who are victims of unfair labor practices. It is covered in Chapter 12. The laws on discrimination in employment have similar sanctions. They are covered in Chapter 13. As you study the various aspects of regulation, keep in mind that the administrative sanctions are modeled after the traditional sanctions for violating statutes. However, they often go further and impose attorney's fees as well.

Concept Summary: Legal Sanctions

1. Persons and businesses convicted of criminal conduct may be fined, imprisoned, or both.
2. A party that breaches a contract may be required to pay as compensatory damages to the other party the sum of money required to make the victim whole. In addition, special circumstances may justify consequential damages.
3. A tort victim is entitled to collect as damages the amount of money necessary to compensate the injured party for the total harm caused by the intentional or negligent conduct of the wrongdoer.
4. Punitive damages may be awarded in the case of intentional torts.
5. Statutes and regulations issued by government agencies often authorize sanctions similar to those used in the criminal law, contracts, and torts. They usually go further by using a multiplier for damages and award attorney's fees as well.

A Current Business Example

In the Business Decision at the beginning of this chapter a number of questions are proposed. These questions arise from a remarkable set of events which have developed over the past three years, since the publication of the preceding edition, involving the tobacco industry. These events have had and likely will continue to have a substantial impact on our lives. While this textbook's primary objective is to prepare future business managers to make good decisions in a variety of situations, using the tobacco industry's recent history allows the reader to comprehend that the legal and regulatory environment is pervasive and significant.

For nearly four decades, cigarette manufacturers have faced (and defeated) claims that their products harm users. In the 1960s the surgeon general began requiring that all cigarette packages contain a clearly stated warning. This warning has been increased from "cigarettes *may be* hazardous to health" to "cigarettes *are* hazardous to health." Advertising of cigarettes was banned from television. Throughout these early years, no one successfully litigated and established that cigarette manufacturers were liable for any injury caused by the use of their products. However, in March 1996, history changed. The Liggett Group agreed to settle with five states its potential liability for the health care costs associated with citizens smoking. Liggett agreed to pay $41 million over a 25-year period. In this settlement, the company admitted (for the first time) that its personnel knew that nicotine was addictive and harmful to smokers' health. Further, Liggett began sharing documents about the known addictive aspects of cigarette smoking. Since that settlement, events have moved rapidly to the point that in an effort to settle claims filed by state attorneys general, the major cigarette manufacturing companies have agreed to pay $368.5 billion over 25 years in return for their potential liability being limited through a structured settlement.

This story of cigarette manufacturing companies allows us to illustrate that the various topics covered in this text apply to most business situations. While your business might not be subjected to the same public scrutiny as cigarette manufacturers, the reference to this industry throughout the book hopefully will enlighten you as to the scope and impact of the legal and regulatory environment. Because details are presented throughout this text, the "Tobacco Industry Box" summarizes the scope of the cigarette manufacturing industry example.

Tobacco Industry Box

Impact of Legal and Regulatory Environment of the Cigarette Manufacturing Industry

Chapter	Topic	Example
Chapter 2	Litigation	Thousands of Lawsuits Filed Against Companies
Chapter 3	Alternatives to Litigation	Proposed Settlement
Chapter 4	Ethics	Behavior of Manufacturers
Chapter 5	Constitutional Free Speech	Ban of Joe Camel Advertising
Chapter 6	Administrative Regulation	Food & Drug Administration's Proposed Regulation of Nicotine
Chapter 7	Formation or Reorganization of Companies	Possible Actions Taken by Manufacturers
Chapter 8	Contracts	Various Aspects of Settlement and Confidentiality Agreements
Chapter 9	Torts/Product Liability	Foundation of Wrongful Injury Claims
Chapter 10	Criminal Laws	Potential Perjury Charges Arising from Executives' Testimony before Congress
Chapter 11	Antitrust	Possible Combination of Manufacturing Companies; Potential Price Discrimination; Price Fixing
Chapter 12	Employment & Labor Laws	Wrongful Termination Claims if Market Demands Cause a Reduction in Workforce
Chapter 14	Environmental Laws	Governments' Response to Claims from Second-hand Smoke
Chapter 15	International Transactions	Potential Overseas Market for Cigarettes

Key Terms

Administrative law   4
Breach of contract   20
Civil law   4
Code   7
Common law   4
Compensatory damages   20
Conflict of laws   12
Constitutional law   4
Contract law   5
Criminal law   4
Dicta   10
Exemplary damages   21
Injunction   22
Intentional tort   21
Judicial activism   14
Judicial restraint   14
Judicial review   13
Legislation   6
Legislative history   7

Negligence   21
Opinion   9
Ordinance   7
Precedent   4
Private law   5
Procedural law   5
Property law   5
Public law   4
Punitive damages   21
Remedy   20
Sanctions   19
Specific performance   20
Stare decisis   4
Statute   7
Statutory construction   7
Substantive law   5
Tort   21
Tort law   5
Uniform Commercial Code   7

Review Questions and Problems

What Is Law?

1. *Definitions of Law*
   Describe three ways to define the term *law*. Can you think of other definitions or uses of "law"?

2. *Classifications of Law*
   (a) What are at least four methods of classifying laws?
   (b) Explain what each classification means.

Sources of Law

3. *Constitutions*
   The federal constitution serves a different purpose from the constitutions of the states. Describe this distinction of purposes.

4. *Legislation*
   (a) When legislation is not clearly written, what governmental body ultimately interprets legislation?
   (b) Why is legislative history important in the interpretation process?

5. *Administrative Rules, Regulations, and Decisions*
   Why are administrative agencies important to businesses and its people?

6. *Judicial Decisions*
   (a) What are the advantages and disadvantages of the precedent-oriented legal system under the doctrine of stare decisis? Explain.
   (b) Alex was on a coast-to-coast trip by automobile. While passing through Ohio, Alex had a flat tire. It was fixed by Sam's Turnpike Service Station, and later, while Alex was driving in Indiana, the tire came off and Alex was injured. Alex was hospitalized in Indiana, so he sued Sam in Indiana for the injuries. What rules of substantive law will the Indiana court use to determine if Sam is at fault? Explain.

7. *Judicial Review*
   Describe the two judicial philosophies and the basic principles followed by a judge under each philosophy.

8. *The Nature of the Judicial Process*
   (a) According to Justice Cardozo, what are the five key forces that shape a judge's work.
   (b) What comparison does Justice Cardozo make regarding the judge's job?

Legal Sanctions

9. *For Criminal Conduct*
   Describe the five potential punishments that may be assessed against one found guilty of a crime.

10. *For Breach of Contract*
    What is the basic purpose of compensatory damages?

11. *For Tortious Conduct*
    (a) What is a tort?
    (b) What type of damages, beyond compensatory, is often sought in a tort case?

12. *For Violating Statutes and Regulations*
    Why does Congress allow plaintiffs to seek triple damages against the violator of some statutes?

Terminology Review

For each term in the left-hand column, match the most appropriate description in the right-hand column.

1. Precedent

2. Stare decisis

3. Private v. public law

4. Procedural law

5. Ordinance

6. Dicta

7. Specific performance

8. Injunction

a. A classification of law that focuses on how many people are impacted by the law

b. A court order to stop some action or event

c. A legislative enactment at the local level

d. A judge's decision or opinion that is to be followed in the future

e. A remedy that orders a contracting party to complete what was promised

f. Rules that guide how the law is to be created or enforced

g. The doctrine that means "let the decision stand"

h. An opinion of a judge that goes beyond what is needed to decide the merits of a case

2

COURTS AND LITIGATION

Business Decision

To Defend or to Settle

You are the owner of a small firm that manufactures lawn mowers. While using one of your products, a person suffers severe injury and now is suing, claiming that your product was negligently designed because it did not adequately protect the user. You have no experience with the legal system. You learn that lawyers charge as much as $250 per hour and must be paid whether they win or lose their cases. You are surprised at what must happen before a trial can occur to determine who is at fault. First, your lawyer may move to dismiss the case on jurisdictional grounds. If that fails, both sides will take costly depositions of likely witnesses. You will have to turn over reams of internal documents related to the design of your mower. Each side also will have to pay several hundred dollars per hour for experts as the lawyers prepare the case. These experts will have to be paid again when they testify at trial. As the time for the trial approaches, each side will spend money trying to discern the most sympathetic type of jury. Years after the lawsuit was first filed, the parties will be sitting in the courtroom waiting for jury selection to begin. More money will have been spent defending this case than the plaintiff was seeking when the lawsuit was first filed. Many questions come to mind:

Should you have settled the case at the beginning?

Has your attorney been getting rich at your expense?

Were all of his actions necessary for your defense?

What has happened to the notion of swift and sure justice in the United States?

Is discovery more of a burden than a help?

Can a small businessperson still obtain a fair jury of his or her peers?

To appreciate how law affects business, a manager needs a thorough understanding of the court system and how a case is developed from the filing of a lawsuit to the collection of a judgment against the losing party. Managers frequently are involved in the litigation process as either parties or witnesses in a case.

Chapter 2 first examines the personnel who operate our courts, including a discussion of the role of judges, jurors, and lawyers in a case. It next explores the organizational structure of both the state and federal court systems and the differences between courts of law and courts of equity. The chapter then explains the various parties involved in a case and reviews important concepts such as standing to sue, personal jurisdiction, and class action suits. The next sections then consider the various pretrial matters that often occur in a case such as discovery requests, motions to the court, and penalties for engaging in unprofessional practices or pursuing frivolous claims. Finally, the conduct of the trial itself is scrutinized and various posttrial issues are considered.

By the time you have completed this chapter, you should have an understanding of the court system, an appreciation of how complex litigation has become, and greater sensitivity to how a lawsuit often is an immense drain of time, money, and energy on a business manager.

Personnel

Before we look at the court system, some background and understanding of the individuals who operate our court system is helpful. Judges apply the law to the facts. Jurors find or determine the facts from conflicting evidence, and the facts as found by the jury are given great deference. In the process of representing clients, lawyers present evidence to the jury and argue the law to the court. Collectively, these persons conduct the search for truth.

1. Judges and Justices

The individuals who operate our courts are usually called judges. In some appellate courts, such as the U.S. Supreme Court, members of the court are called justices. In this discussion, we will refer to trial court persons as judges and reviewing court persons as justices.

In all cases, the function of the trial judge is to determine the applicable rules of law to be used to decide the case. Such rules may be procedural or substantive. In cases tried without a jury, the judge is also responsible for finding the facts. In cases tried before a jury, the function of the jury is to decide questions of fact. In all cases, the judge is responsible for deciding questions of law.

Trial judges are the main link between the law and the citizens it serves. The trial judge renders decisions that deal directly with people in conflict. These judges have the primary duty to observe and to apply constitutional limitations and guarantees. They bear the burden of upholding the dignity of the courts and maintaining respect for the law.

Justices do more than simply decide an appeal—they often give reasons for their decisions. These reasoned decisions become precedent and a part of our body of law that may affect society as a whole as well as the litigants.

So in deciding cases, justices must consider not only the result between the parties but also the total effect of the decision of the law. In this sense, their role is similar to that of legislators. When reviewing appeals, justices are essentially concerned with issues of *law;* issues of *fact* normally are resolved at the trial court level.

For these reasons, the personal characteristics required for a justice are somewhat different from those for a trial judge. The manner of performing duties and the methods used also vary between trial and reviewing courts. A trial judge who has observed the witnesses is able to use knowledge gained from participation as an essential ingredient in his or her decisions. A justice must spend most of the time in the library studying the briefs, the record of proceedings, and the law in reaching decisions.

The judiciary, because of the power of judicial review, has perhaps the most extensive power of any branch of government. Lower court judges' decisions may be reviewed by a reviewing court, but they have almost absolute personal immunity from legal actions against them based on their judicial acts.

2. Jurors

It is important to understand the role of the jury as a fact-finding body. Since litigation may involve both questions of law and questions of fact, the deference given to the decisions of a jury is very important. Trial by jury is a cherished right guaranteed by the Bill of Rights. The Sixth and Seventh Amendments to the Constitution guarantee the right of trial by jury in both criminal and civil cases. The **petit jury** is the trial jury that returns a verdict in both situations.

In civil cases the right to trial by a jury is preserved in suits at common law when the amount in controversy exceeds $20. State constitutions have like provisions guaranteeing the right of trial by jury in state courts.

Historically, a jury consisted of twelve persons. Today many states and some federal courts have rules of procedure that provide for smaller juries in both criminal and civil cases. Such provisions are constitutional since the Constitution does not specify the *number* of jurors—only the *types* of cases that may be brought to trial before a jury at common law. Several studies have found no discernible difference between results reached by a 6-person jury and those reached by a 12-person jury. As a result, many cases are tried before six-person juries today.

In most states, a jury's decision must be unanimous because many believe that the truth is more nearly to be found and justice rendered if the jury acts only on one common conscience. However, there is growing evidence that the requirement of unanimity is taking its toll on the administration of justice in the United States. Holdout jurors contribute to mistrials and many cases are routinely deadlocked by margins of 11–1 or 10–2. Several states have eliminated the requirement of unanimity in their courts in civil cases and two states have done so in criminal cases. While the requirement of unanimity persists at the federal level, several legal commentators have argued that unanimous jury verdicts are not constitutionally mandated and should be eliminated to help restore public confidence in our jury system.

Thanks to a series of sensationalized trials, the jury system has been subject to much criticism. Many argue that jurors are not qualified to distinguish fact from fiction, that they vote their prejudices, and that their emotions are too easily swayed by skillful trial lawyers. However, most members of the bench and bar feel the right to be tried by a jury of one's peers in criminal cases is as fair and effective a method of ascertaining the truth and giving an accused his or her "day in court" as has been devised. The jury system protects persons from government oppression and from politically motivated criminal prosecutions.

As Jeremiah Black, the attorney for the defendant in the famous case of *Ex Parte Milligan*, 71 U.S. 2 (1886), observed:

> I do not assert that the jury trial is an infallible mode of ascertaining truth. Like everything human, it has its imperfection. I only say, that it is the best protection for innocence and the surest mode of punishing guilt that has yet been discovered. It has borne the test of longer experience, and borne it better than any other legal institution that ever existed among men.

While jurors generally do not take notes as the trial progresses, Arizona and several other states are permitting jurors to do so. Jurors normally do not give reasons for their decisions, although some special verdicts may require juries to answer a series of questions. Actually, it would be almost impossible for the jury to agree on the reasons for its verdict. A jury may agree as to the result but disagree on some of the facts, and different jurors may have different ideas on the significance of various items of testimony.

Many individuals attempt to avoid jury duty. Some lose money because of time away from a job or profession. Others may feel great stress in having to help make important decisions affecting the lives of many people. Because so many potential jurors seek relief from jury duty, many trials often end up with more jurors who are unemployed or retired than would otherwise be the case. Today, there is a strong trend toward requiring jury duty of all citizens, irrespective of any hardship that such service may entail. Courts often refuse to accept excuses because jury duty is seen as a responsibility of all citizens in a free society.

One of the most difficult issues facing the judicial system is the right to a trial by jury in very complex and complicated cases that frequently take a long time to try. For example, many antitrust cases involve economic issues that baffle economists, and such cases may last for several months or even years. The average juror cannot comprehend the meaning of much of the evidence, let alone remember it when the time to reach a verdict arrives. As a practical matter, many persons cannot serve on a jury for several weeks or months. For these and other reasons, some experts recommend that the right to a trial by jury be abolished in very complex and time-consuming cases. Several of these complex cases can result in huge verdicts, as demonstrated by Table 2–1. When it comes to upward mobility, jury awards seem to have it made. For 1996 alone, all of the top 8 verdicts were for more than $200 million.

3. Lawyers

Our court system is an adversarial one. While private parties to proceedings in a court may represent themselves without a lawyer, as a practical matter, lawyers are required in most cases.

Since knowledge of court procedures and substantive law is required as a bare minimum in most cases, lawyers serve as the representative combat-

TABLE 2–1 Biggest Jury Verdicts of 1996

Verdict	Plaintiff vs. Defendant	State	Subject
$22 billion	Roxas vs. Marcos	Hawaii	Conversion
$1 billion	Dow Corning Corp. vs. Granite Insurance Co.	Michigan	Insurance Coverage
$369 million	DSC Comm. Corp. vs. Next Level Comm. Corp.	Texas	Trade Secrets
$347 million	Broussard vs. Meineke Discount Muffler Shops, Inc.	North Carolina	Fraud, Breach of Contract, and Unfair Trade Practices
$250 million	Red Wolf vs. Burlington Northern RR Co.	Montana	Wrongful death
$229 million	Cities Service Co. vs. Gulf Oil Corp.	Oklahoma	Breach of contract
$218 million	Houchens vs. Rockwell Int'l. Corp.	Kentucky	Environmental pollution
$204 million	Bartlett vs. Mitchell Energy Corp.	Texas	Water pollution

ants in our court system. They present the evidence, the points of law, and the arguments that are weighed by juries and judges in making their decisions.

A lawyer's first duty is to the administration of justice. As an officer of the court, he or she should see that proceedings are conducted in a dignified and orderly manner and that issues are tried on their merits only. The practice of law should not be a game or a battle of wits, but a means to promote justice. The lawyer's duties to each client require the highest degree of fidelity, loyalty, and integrity.

A lawyer serves in three capacities: counselor, advocate, and public servant. As a counselor, a lawyer by the very nature of the profession knows his or her client's most important secrets and affairs. A lawyer is often actively involved in the personal decisions of clients, ranging from their business affairs and family matters such as divorce to their alleged violations of the criminal law. These relationships dictate that a lawyer meet the highest standards of professional and ethical conduct.

The tension between the business community and the legal profession has been growing in recent years. This conflict has been fueled by the increasing number of lawsuits filed by lawyers on behalf of their clients, by resistance from organized lawyer advocacy groups like the American Bar Association to products liability reform, and by the high costs of attorney fees that businesses must absorb into their costs of doing business. Indeed the proposed tobacco settlement, referenced in Chapter 1, has been threatened by the potential for windfall fees of several hundred million dollars for lawyers that negotiated the $368.5 billion agreement.

Explained in the following Tobacco Industry Box, the state of Florida's 1997 settlement against the tobacco industry also has been threatened by attorney fees.

Tobacco Industry Box

It was August 25, 1997, and Florida's governor and attorney general, Lawton Chiles and Bob Butterworth, affixed their signatures to a settlement with the tobacco industry that was going to pay the state $11.3 billion over 25 years. A key provision in the agreement provided that the tobacco industry would pay the trial team's "reasonable" attorneys fees. What "reasonable" meant was for a panel of arbitrators to determine according to the settlement.

The problem for the state, however, is that five members of the state's trial team have broken ranks with their client over the attorneys fees. Those lawyers—part of a "dream team" hired by Governor Chiles to take on the tobacco industry—argue the state has reneged on the contingent fee contract that promised them 25 percent of any recovery. They argue that the only way the state could take on such a foe as the tobacco industry successfully was to hire them. The only way to afford those high-priced lawyers was to offer a contingency-fee deal. If they won anything for the state, the reward would be equivalent to the risk.

The Governor's office claims the trial team accepted the settlement and, therefore, the provision regarding the payment of attorneys fees. The lawyers say they never agreed to any terms of the settlement. Now, the courts will have to resolve this dispute between the client and counsel that could cost the state over $2 billion in attorneys fees. What answers can you provide to these questions?

- Has the "dream team" become a nightmare for its client? Do lawyer-client lawsuits of this nature erode public confidence in the litigation process?
- What would be "reasonable" attorneys fees in this case? Twenty-five percent of $11.3 billion?

It is obvious that if a lawyer is to give competent advice and adequate representation, he or she must know to the fullest extent possible all the facts involved in any legal problem presented by the client. In attempting to ensure that a lawyer may be fully advised of a client's problems and all matters affecting them, the rules of evidence provide that confidential communications to a lawyer are privileged. The law does not permit a lawyer to reveal such facts and testify against a client, even if called to do so at a trial. This is the attorney-client privilege, and it may extend to communications made to the lawyer's employees in certain cases. This is especially important today because law firms frequently use paralegals to gather facts and assist attorneys.

Organization of the Court System

The federal court system and those in most states contain three levels—trial courts, intermediate reviewing courts, and final reviewing courts. Lawsuits are begun at the **trial court** level, and the results are reviewed at one or more of the other two levels.

4. Jurisdiction

For a court to hear and decide a case at any level, it must have **subject matter jurisdiction,** which is the power over the issues involved in the case. Some state trial courts have what is called general jurisdiction, or the power to hear any type of case. Other state courts have only limited jurisdiction, or the power to hear only certain types of cases. Jurisdiction may be limited as to subject matter, amount in controversy, or area in which the parties live. For example, small-claims courts have jurisdiction only if the amount in the controversy does not exceed a certain sum.

Courts, especially those of limited jurisdiction, may be named according to the subject matter with which they deal. Probate courts deal with wills and the estates of deceased persons, juvenile courts with juvenile crime and dependent children, criminal and police courts with violators of state laws and municipal ordinances, and traffic courts with traffic violations.

Even courts of general jurisdiction cannot attempt to resolve every dispute or controversy that may arise. Some issues are simply nonjusticiable. For example, courts would not attempt to referee a football or basketball game. They would not hear a case to decide how English or math should be taught in the public schools. Moreover, courts do not accept cases involving trivial matters. A motorist sued the New Jersey Highway Authority because one of the tokens he purchased was a "slug." The court stated that "the law does not care about trifles; a claim of 35 cents cannot be considered."

5. State Courts

State court systems are created, and their operations are governed from three sources. First, state constitutions provide the general framework for the court system. Second, the state legislature, pursuant to constitutional authority, enacts statutes that add body to the framework. This legislation provides for various courts, establishes their jurisdiction, and regulates the tenure, selection, and duties of judges. Other legislation may establish the general rules of procedure to be used by these courts. Finally, each court sets forth its own rules of procedure within the statutory bounds. These rules are detailed and may specify, for example, the times when various documents must be filed with the court clerk. Thus, a study of the court system for any particular state must refer to its constitution, such legislation as Civil Practice Acts, and the rules of the various courts. Each state has its own terminology and arrangement for its courts. Figure 2.1 diagrams the court system of a typical state.

Trial Courts

Depending upon the particular state, a general trial court can take on any number of names: the *superior court,* the *circuit court,* the *district court,* or the *court of common pleas.* The State of New York adds to the confusion by referring to its trial court as the *supreme court.* In the past, these basic trial courts also were divided into two branches, one known as a *court of law* and the other as a *court of chancery,* or *equity.*

Courts of **law** were developed to deal with legal disputes where one party was seeking money damages from another. Courts of **chancery** or **equity** were given jurisdiction in cases where the remedy at law (money damages) was deemed inadequate. Such cases include suits for an accounting for money, for cancellation of a contract, for dissolution of a partnership or corporation, for

FIGURE 2.1

Typical state court system.

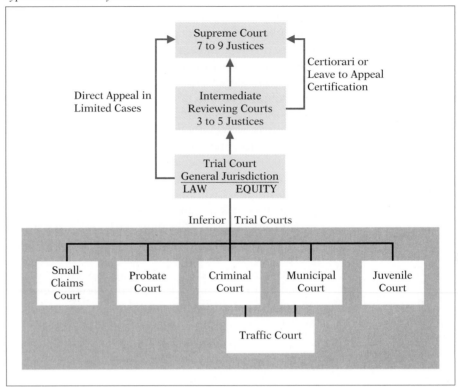

an injunction, to partition or divide real estate among its owners, to quiet title to real estate, and for specific performance of contracts.

Courts of equity use *maxims,* or proverbial sayings, instead of rules of law. Strictly speaking, there are no legal rights in equity, for the decision is based on moral rights and natural justice. A court of equity is a court of conscience in which precedent is secondary to natural justice. Table 2–2 provides some of the typical maxims of equity.

In recent years, many laws have abolished the distinction between law and equity and have combined law and equity into one action known as a *civil action.* The historical distinctions are still important, however, because the right to a jury trial exists in cases at law but usually not in equity. It is necessary to decide whether an action would have been "at law" or "in equity" in order to know if the parties have the right to a trial by jury.

Appellate Courts

The parties to litigation are entitled as a matter of right to a review of their case by a higher court, or an **appeal,** if the requirements of procedural law are followed in seeking the review. In some states there is only one appellate court, which is usually called the supreme court of the state. In more populous states, there often are two levels of reviewing courts—an intermediate level and a court of final resort. In states with two levels of review, the intermediate courts are usually called the **courts of appeal,** and the highest court is again called the **supreme court.** In states with two levels of review-

TABLE 2–2 Typical Maxims of Equity

1. Equity will not allow a right to exist without a remedy.
2. Equity regards as done that which ought to be done.
3. Where there is equal equity, the law must prevail.
4. He who comes into equity must do so with clean hands.
5. He who seeks equity must do equity.
6. Equity aids the vigilant.
7. Equality is equity.

ing courts, most appeals are taken to the lower of the two courts, and the highest court of the state will review only very important cases. Intermediate courts of review typically consist of three to five judges, while seven to nine judges typically make up a state supreme court.

Courts of appeal are essentially concerned with questions of law. Although a party is entitled to one trial and one appeal, he or she may obtain a second review if the higher reviewing court, in the exercise of its discretion, agrees to such a review. The procedure for requesting a second review is to file what is called in some states a *petition for leave to appeal* and in others a petition for a **writ of certiorari.** These procedures are explained more fully in section 6 in this chapter. Deciding such requests is a major function of the highest court in each state. As a practical matter, less than five percent of all such requests are granted.

Small-Claims Courts

One court of limited jurisdiction is especially important to the business community. This court, usually known as **small-claims court,** handles much of the litigation between business and its customers. Small-claims courts are used by businesses to collect accounts and by customers to settle disputes with the business community that are relatively minor from a financial perspective. Such suits are often quite important from the standpoint of principle, however. For example, many persons use small-claims courts to sue for damages caused by defective merchandise or by services poorly performed. Landlord-tenant disputes are another example of controversies decided in these courts.

Small-claims courts have low court costs and simplified procedures. The informality of the proceedings speeds up the flow of cases. The services of a lawyer are not usually required, and some states do not allow lawyers to participate in these proceedings. Such courts usually are subject to a dollar limitation over the suits that may be filed, often ranging from $500 to $5,000.

6. Federal Courts

Article III of the Constitution (see Appendix) provides that judicial power be vested in the Supreme Court and such lower courts as Congress may create. The judicial power of the federal courts has been limited by Congress. Essentially, it extends to matters involving (1) questions of federal law (federal question cases), (2) the United States as a party, (3) controversies among the states, and (4) certain suits between citizens of different states (diversity of citizenship).

Trial Courts

The federal district courts are the trial courts of the federal judicial system. There is at least one such court in every state. These courts have subject matter jurisdiction over all the cases mentioned above. However, items one and four from this list require further discussion as presented in the following paragraphs.

Federal question cases may be based on issues arising out of the U.S. Constitution or out of federal statutes. Any amount of money may be involved in such a case, and it need not be a suit for damages. For example, a suit to enjoin a violation of a constitutional right can be filed in a federal court as a federal question case. These civil actions may involve matters based on federal laws such as those dealing with patents, copyrights, trademarks, taxes, or employment discrimination. The rights guaranteed by the Bill of Rights of the Constitution also may be the basis for a federal question case.

Diversity of citizenship requires that all plaintiffs be citizens of different states from all defendants. If a case involves a party on one side that is a citizen of the same state as a party on the other, there will then be no diversity of citizenship and thus no federal jurisdiction. Courts have held that it is the citizenship of the real party in interest in the case that determines whether diversity of citizenship exists. For example, diversity jurisdiction is based on the citizenship of all members of a partnership.

The fact that business corporations, which are considered persons before the law, are frequently incorporated in one state and have their principal place of business in another state also causes problems in determining when diversity of citizenship exists. For purposes of diversity jurisdiction, a corporation is a citizen of the state of incorporation and also a citizen of the state in which it has its principal place of business. Thus, a Delaware corporation with its principal place of business in Illinois is a citizen of both Delaware and Illinois for purposes of diversity. If any party on the other side of a lawsuit with such a corporation is a citizen of either Illinois or Delaware, there is then no diversity and no federal jurisdiction.

Moreover, questions as to the state in which a corporation has its principal place of business also arise. The total activity of the corporation is examined to determine its principal place of business. This test incorporates both the *place of activities* and the *nerve center* tests. The nerve center test places general emphasis on the locus of the managerial and policy-making functions of the corporations. The place of activities test focuses on production or sales activities. The *total activity* test is not an equation that can provide a simple answer to the question of a corporation's principal place of business. Each case necessarily involves somewhat subjective analysis.

In diversity of citizenship cases, the federal courts have a jurisdictional amount of more than $75,000. If a case involves multiple plaintiffs with separate and distinct claims, *each* claim must satisfy the jurisdictional amount. Thus, in a class action suit, the claim of each plaintiff must meet the $75,000 minimum, unless changed by statute.

Appellate Courts

Under its constitutional authorization, Congress has created 12 U.S. Courts of Appeal plus a special Court of Appeals for the Federal Circuit as intermediate appellate courts in the federal system. This special reviewing court, located in Washington, D.C., hears appeals from special courts such as the U.S. Claims Court and Contract Appeals as well as from administrative decisions such as those made by the Patent and Trademark Office. Other courts, such as the Court of Military Appeals, have been created to handle special subject matter. Figure 2.2 illustrates the federal court system and shows the relationship of state courts and administrative agencies for appellate review.

In addition to these courts of appeal, the federal court system provides for a Supreme Court. Because the litigants are entitled to only one review, or

FIGURE 2.2

The federal court system.

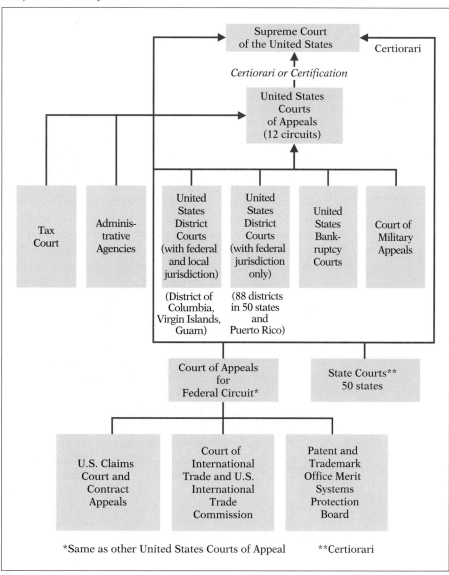

appeal, as a matter of rights, a subsequent review by the U.S. Supreme Court must be obtained through a petition for a writ of certiorari to the Supreme Court.

A petition for a writ of certiorari is a request by the losing party in the Courts of Appeal for permission to file an appeal with the Supreme Court. In such situations, the Supreme Court has discretion as to whether or not it will grant the petition and allow another review. This review is not a matter of right. Writs of certiorari are granted only in cases of substantial federal importance or where there is an obvious conflict between decisions of two or more U.S. Circuit Courts of Appeal in an area of the law that needs clarification.

When the Supreme Court of the United States reviews petitions for a writ of certiorari, the writ is granted if four of the nine justices vote to take the case. The Supreme Court spends a great deal of time and effort in deciding which cases it will hear. It is able to pick and choose those issues with which it will be involved and to control its caseload. In recent years, the Court has been very reluctant to review lower court decisions. In the 1996–97 term of the U.S. Supreme Court, only 80 opinions were issued, the smallest since 1955.

The Supreme Court is far more likely to review and reverse a decision rendered by the Ninth Circuit Court of Appeals—treating it as one commentator noted like a wayward child. In the 1996–97 term, the Supreme Court reviewed 29 rulings from the Ninth Circuit and reversed 28 of them. The District of Columbia Circuit, which has many cases raising significant federal issues, had only one case reviewed during the same term. Many commentators attribute the difference to the judicial activism of the Ninth Circuit, which often is at odds with the philosophy of judicial restraint found in the Supreme Court in recent years. For a more thorough discussion of these two philosophies, please refer to Section 7 of Chapter 1.

The federal district courts and the Courts of Appeal cannot review, retry, or correct judicial errors charged against a state court. Final judgments or decrees rendered by the highest court of a state are reviewed only by the Supreme Court of the United States. State cases reviewed by the U.S. Supreme Court must concern a federal question involving the validity of state action on the grounds that the statute is repugnant to the Constitution, treaties, or laws of the United States. If the case does not involve a federal question, the decision of the highest state court is not subject to review by the Supreme Court of the United States.

Litigation—An Overview

To fully understand the litigation process, you need to be familiar with the terminology used to describe the parties who are adversaries in lawsuits. The next section reviews a variety of relevant terms. Following that, the legal concepts of when a party has the right to file a lawsuit, when a court has power over the parties, and when one person might sue on behalf of a much larger number of other persons, are discussed.

The first of these issues is generally described as *standing to sue*. It is discussed in section 8. If a plaintiff has standing to sue, the court next must determine if it has *personal jurisdiction* over the defendant. This area is discussed in section 9. The third problem area relates to *class action suits,* which involve one or more individuals suing on behalf of all who may have the same grounds for suit. These suits are discussed more fully in section 10.

7. Parties

The party who files a civil action seeking money damages is called the **plaintiff.** The party sued is known as the **defendant.** The term *defendant* also is used to describe the person against whom a criminal charge is filed by the prosecuting state or federal government. When a defendant wants to sue the plaintiff, the defendant files a **counterclaim.** Most jurisdictions use the term **counterplaintiff** and **counterdefendant** to describe the parties to the counterclaim. Thus, the defendant becomes a counterplaintiff and the plaintiff becomes a counterdefendant when a counterclaim is filed.

When the result at the trial court level is appealed, the party appealing is usually referred to as the **appellant,** and the successful party in the trial court is called the **appellee.** Most jurisdictions, in publishing decisions of reviewing courts, list the appellant first and the appellee second, even though the appellant may have been the defendant in the trial court. As a result, the names used in a case are somewhat misleading. When a petition for certiorari is filed to the Supreme Court, the party initiating the petition is the **petitioner** and the other party is known as the **respondent.**

Table 2–3 summarizes the various names given to the parties involved in litigation.

In most state jurisdictions and in federal courts, the law allows all persons to join in one lawsuit as plaintiffs if the causes of action arise out of the same transaction or series of transactions and involve common questions of law or fact. In addition, plaintiffs may join as defendants all persons who are necessary to a complete determination or resolution of the questions involved.

In addition, if a defendant alleges that there cannot be a complete determination of a controversy without the presence of other parties, he or she may bring in new third parties as **third-party defendants.** This procedure usually is followed when there is someone who may have liability to a defendant if the defendant has liability to the plaintiff. For example, assume Never-Fail, Inc., supplies brake shoes to the Ready-to-Go Mechanics Corporation. Ready-to-Go worked on your brakes, and thereafter you were injured when

---

TABLE 2–3 Litigating Parties

Action Filed	*Party Filing the Action*	*Party against Whom the Action Is Filed*
Civil case	Plaintiff	Defendant
Criminal case	State or federal government as represented by a prosecutor	Defendant
Appeal	Appellant	Appellee
Petition for a writ of certiorari	Petitioner	Respondent

your car failed to stop at an intersection. After you filed a lawsuit against Ready-to-Go, it could bring Never-Fail, Inc., into the case as a third-party defendant. In essence, Ready-to-Go is arguing that if it is liable to you, then Never-Fail is liable to Ready-to-Go since the cause of the accident easily could be faulty brake shoes.

8. Standing to Sue

A court's power to resolve a controversy may be limited by the subject matter involved in the case. This power we called subject matter jurisdiction. In addition to showing the court that it has subject matter jurisdiction, a plaintiff must establish that he or she is entitled to have the court decide the dispute, that is, he or she has **standing to sue.**

To establish the required standing, a plaintiff must allege two things. First, the plaintiff must allege that the litigation involves a case or controversy. Courts are not free to litigate matters that have no connection to the law. For example, one business cannot maintain a suit against another business just because the two are competitors. There must be some allegation of a wrong that would create a dispute between plaintiff and defendant.

Second, the plaintiff must allege a personal stake in the resolution of the controversy. This element of standing prevents any individual from asserting the rights of the general public or of a group of which we are not a member. For instance, only a shareholder of one of the two companies involved in a merger could sue to stop the combination of these companies, despite the fact that such a merger may have a substantial adverse impact on competition in general.

In essence, through the standing-to-sue requirements, courts are able to insist that there be an adversarial relationship between plaintiff and defendant. This adversarial relationship helps present the issues to be litigated in sharper focus. To establish standing, plaintiffs must assert their personal legal positions and not those of third parties. Without the requirements of standing, courts would be faced with abstract legal questions of potentially wide public significance, questions generally best left to legislative bodies or administrative agencies.

It is very important to note that standing to sue does not depend upon the merits of the plaintiff's contention that particular conduct is illegal. The presence of standing is determined by the nature and source of the plaintiff's allegations. Standing is determined at the outset of the litigation, not by the outcome. The case that starts on page 41 illustrates the critical nature of standing in winning a lawsuit.

9. Personal Jurisdiction

Jurisdiction refers to the power of a court to hear a case. To have such power, the court must have authority not only over the subject matter of the case but also over the parties to the case. This latter authority is called **personal jurisdiction.** Personal jurisdiction over the plaintiff is obtained when the plaintiff files the suit. Such action indicates voluntary submission to the court's power.

Bennett v. Spear

117 S.Ct. 1154 (1997)

The petitioners are ranch operators and irrigation districts that challenged, under the citizen-suit provision of the Endangered Species Act (ESA), action by the Fish and Wildlife Service and the Secretary of the Interior to maintain minimum water levels on certain reservoirs of the Klamath Irrigation Project. Both the District Court and the Ninth Circuit Court of Appeals rejected the petitioners' complaint for lack of standing because the "recreational, aesthetic, and commercial interests" asserted by the petitioners did not fall within the "zone of interests" protected by the ESA. The lower courts held that only parties alleging an interest in the preservation of endangered species fall within the zone of interests protected by the ESA.

SCALIA, J.: This is a challenge to a biological opinion issued by the Fish and Wildlife Service in accordance with the Endangered Species Act concerning the operation of the Klamath Irrigation Project by the Bureau of Reclamation, and the project's impact on two varieties of endangered fish. The question for decision is whether the petitioners, who have competing economic and other interests in Klamath Project water, have standing to seek judicial review of the biological opinion under the citizen-suit provision of the ESA.

The ESA requires the Secretary of the Interior to promulgate regulations listing those species of animals that are "threatened" or "endangered" under specified criteria, and to designate their "critical habitat." The ESA further requires each federal agency to "insure that any action authorized, funded, or carried out by such agency . . . is not likely to jeopardize the continued existence of any endangered species or threatened species or result in the destruction or adverse modification of habitat of such species which is determined by the Secretary . . . to be critical." If an agency determines that action it proposes to take may adversely affect a listed species, it must engage in formal consultation with the Fish and Wildlife Service, after which the Service must provide the agency with a written statement (the Biological Opinion) explaining how the proposed action will affect the species or its habitat. If the Service concludes that the proposed action will "jeopardize the continued existence of any [listed] species or result in the destruction or adverse modification of [critical habitat,]" the Biological Opinion must outline any "reasonable and prudent alternatives" that the Service believes will avoid that consequence.

The Klamath Project, one of the oldest federal reclamation schemes, is a series of lakes, rivers, dams, and irrigation canals in northern California and southern Oregon. The project was undertaken by the Secretary of the Interior and is administered by the Bureau of Reclamation. In 1992, the Bureau notified the Service that operation of the project might affect the Lost River Sucker and Shortnose Sucker, species of fish that were listed as endangered in 1988. . . .

The Service issued a Biological Opinion which concluded that the "long-term operation of the Klamath Project was likely to jeopardize the continued existence of the Lost River and shortnose suckers." The Biological Opinion identified "reasonable and prudent alternatives" the Service believed would avoid jeopardy, which included the maintenance of minimum water levels on Clear Lake and Gerber reservoirs. The Bureau later notified the Service that it intended to operate the project in compliance with the Biological Opinion. . . .

The petitioners' complaint asserts that the Bureau "has been following essentially the same procedures for storing and releasing water from Clear Lake and Gerber reservoirs throughout the twentieth century," and that "[t]here is no scientifically or commercially available evidence indicating that the populations of endangered suckers in Clear Lake and Gerber reservoirs have declined, are declining, or will decline as a result" of the Bureau's operation of the Klamath Project.

Petitioners' complaint included three claims for relief that are relevant here. The first and second claims allege that the Service's jeopardy determination with respect to Clear Lake and Gerber reservoirs, and the ensuring imposition of minimum water levels, violated the ESA. The third claim is that the imposition of minimum water elevations constituted an implicit determination of critical habitat for the suckers, which violated the ESA, because it failed to take into consideration the designation's economic impact.

The question of standing involves both constitutional limitations on federal-court jurisdiction and prudential limitations on its exercise. To satisfy the "case" or "controversy" requirement of Article III, which is the "irreducible constitutional minimum" of standing, a plaintiff must, generally speaking, demonstrate that he has suffered "injury in fact," that the injury is "fairly traceable" to the actions of the defendant, and that the injury will likely be redressed by a favorable decision.

In addition to the immutable requirements of Article III, the federal judiciary has also adhered to a set of prudential principles that bear on the question of standing. Numbered among these prudential requirements is the doctrine of particular concern in this case: that a plaintiff's grievance must arguably fall within the zone of interests protected or regulated by the statutory provision or constitutional guarantee invoked in the suit.

Congress legislates against the background of our prudential standing doctrine, which applies unless it is expressly negated. The question in the present case is whether the ESA's citizen-suit provision negates the zone-of-interests test (or, perhaps more accurately, expands the zone of interests). We think it does. The first operative portion of the provision says that "any person may commence a civil suit"—an authorization of remarkable breadth when compared with the language Congress ordinarily uses.

It is true that the plaintiffs here are seeking to prevent application of environmental restrictions rather than to implement them. But the "any person" formulation applies to all the causes of action—not only to actions against private violators of environmental restrictions, and not only to actions against the Secretary asserting underenforcement, but also to actions against the Secretary asserting overenforcement. The citizen-suit provision does favor environmentalists in that it covers all private violations of the Act but not all failures of the Secretary to meet his administrative responsibilities; but there is no textual basis for saying that its expansion of standing requirements applies to environmentalists alone. The Court of Appeals therefore erred in concluding that petitioners lacked standing under the zone-of-interests tests to bring their claims under the ESA's citizen-suit provision.

The Government also contends that petitioners' complaint fails to satisfy the standing requirements imposed by the "case" or "controversy" provision of Article III. Given petitioners' allegation that the amount of available water will be reduced and that they will be adversely affected thereby, it is easy to presume specific facts under which petitioners will be injured—for example, the Bureau's distribution of the reduction pro rata among its customers. The complaint alleges the requisite injury in fact. . . .

The judgment of the Court of Appeals is reversed, and the case is remanded for further proceedings consistent with this opinion.

Case Questions

1. What constitutional and prudential limitations impact the question of standing?

2. Why did the Court find the plaintiffs' claims within the "zone of interests" protected by the Endangered Species Act?

3. Does the Court's ruling do damage to the primary purpose behind passage of the Endangered Species Act?

Personal jurisdiction over the defendant usually is obtained by the service of a **summons,** or notice to appear in court, although in some cases it is obtained by the publication of notice and mailing a summons to the last known address. This delivery of notice is referred to as *service of process.* Service of a summons on the defendant usually is valid if it is served upon any member of the household above a specified age and if another copy addressed to the defendant is mailed to the home.

For many years, a summons could not be properly served beyond the borders of the state in which it was issued. However, states now have what are called **long-arm statutes,** which provide for the service of process beyond their boundaries. Such statutes are valid and constitutional if they provide a defendant with due process of law. Under the Fifth Amendment to the Constitution, no person shall "be deprived of life, liberty, or property without due process of law." The Fourteenth Amendment provides that states must also guarantee due process protection. Due process requires that if a defendant is not present within the state where the lawsuit is filed, he or she must have certain minimum contacts with the state so that maintenance of the suit does not offend "traditional notions of fair play and substantial justice."

The typical long-arm statute allows a court to obtain jurisdiction over a defendant even though the process is served beyond its borders if the defendant:

1. Has committed a tort within the state.
2. Owns property within the state that is the subject matter of the lawsuit.
3. Has entered into a contract within the state or transacted the business that is the subject matter of the lawsuit within the state.

Long-arm statutes do not authorize out-of-state service of process in all cases. Personal jurisdiction is obtained under long-arm statutes only when requiring an out-of-state defendant to appear and defense does not violate due process. The case that follows illustrates the extent of constitutional limitations on modern long-arm statutes that allow out-of-state service of process to obtain jurisdiction.

WORLD-WIDE VOLKSWAGEN CORP. V. WOODSON

100 S.Ct. 559 (1980)

Plaintiff-respondent filed a product liability suit in a state court of Oklahoma to recover for personal injuries sustained in an automobile accident. The defendants were the German manufacturer of the Audi automobile, Volkswagen of America (the importer), World-Wide Volkswagen (the wholesale distributor), and Seaway (the retail dealership). The automobile had been purchased from Seaway in the state of New York. All the defendants were served under the Oklahoma long-arm statute. While the manufacturer and the importer filed no challenges to this service, World-Wide and Seaway objected to the Oklahoma court's jurisdiction. These defendants argued that they were New York corporations and that they did no business in Oklahoma. The Oklahoma courts rejected these arguments and found all the defendants liable for the plaintiff's injury. The Supreme Court granted the petitions for certiorari filed by World-Wide and Seaway.

WHITE, J.: . . . The issue before us is whether, consistently with the Due Process Clause of the Fourteenth Amendment, an Oklahoma court may exercise in personam jurisdiction over a nonresident automobile retailer and its wholesale distributor in a products liability action, when the defendants' only connection with Oklahoma is the fact that an automobile sold in New York to New York residents became involved in an accident in Oklahoma. . . .

As has long been settled, and as we reaffirm today, a state court may exercise personal jurisdiction over a nonresident defendant only so long as there exist "minimum contacts" between the defendant and the forum State. The concept of minimum contacts, in turn, can be seen to perform two related, but distinguishable, functions. It protects the defendant against the burdens of litigating in a distant or inconvenient

forum. And it acts to ensure that the States, through their courts, do not reach out beyond the limits imposed on them by their status as coequal sovereigns in a federal system.

The protection against inconvenient litigation is typically described in terms of "reasonableness" or "fairness." We have said that the defendant's contacts with the forum State must be such that maintenance of the suit "does not offend 'traditional notions of fair play and substantial justice.' ". . .

Implicit in this emphasis on reasonableness is the understanding that the burden on the defendant, while always a primary concern, will in an appropriate case be considered in light of other relevant factors, including the forum State's interest in adjudicating the dispute, the plaintiff's interest in obtaining convenient and effective relief, . . . the interstate judicial system's interest in obtaining the most efficient resolution of controversies; and the shared interest of the several States in furthering fundamental substantive social policies. . . .

Thus, the Due Process Clause "does not contemplate that a state may make binding a judgment in personam against an individual or corporate defendant with which the state has no contacts, ties, or relations." Even if the defendant would suffer minimal or no inconvenience from being forced to litigate before the tribunals of another State; even if the forum State has a strong interest in applying its law to the controversy; even if the forum State is the most convenient location for litigation, the Due Process Clause, acting as an instrument of interstate federalism, may sometimes act to divest the State of its power to render a valid judgment.

Applying these principles to the case at hand, we find in the record before us a total absence of those affiliating circumstances that are a necessary predicate to any exercise of state-court jurisdiction. Petitioners carry on no activity whatsoever in Oklahoma. They close no sales and perform no services there. They avail themselves of none of the privileges and benefits of Oklahoma law. They solicit no business there either through salespersons or through advertising reasonably calculated to reach the State. Nor does the record show that they regularly sell cars at wholesale or retail to Oklahoma customers or residents or that they indirectly, through others, serve or seek to serve the Oklahoma market. In short, respondents seek to base jurisdiction on one, isolated occurrence and whatever inferences can be drawn therefrom; the fortuitous circumstance that a single Audi automobile, sold in New York to New York residents, happened to suffer an accident while passing through Oklahoma.

It is argued, however, that because an automobile is mobile by its very design and purpose it was "foreseeable" that the Robinsons' Audi would cause injury in Oklahoma. Yet "foreseeability" alone has never been a sufficient benchmark for personal jurisdiction under the Due Process Clause. . . .

If foreseeability were the criterion, . . . every seller of chattels would in effect appoint the chattel his agent for service of process. His amenability to suit would travel with the chattel. . . . This is not to say, of course, that foreseeability is wholly irrelevant. But the foreseeability that is critical to due process analysis is not the mere likelihood that a product will find its way into the forum State. Rather, it is that the defendant's conduct and connection with the forum State are such that he should reasonably anticipate being haled into court there. . . .

When a corporation "purposefully avails itself of the privilege of conducting activities within the forum State," it has clear notice that it is subject to suit there, and can act to alleviate the risk of burdensome litigation by procuring insurance, passing the expected costs on to customers, or, if the risks are too great, severing its connection with the State. . . . The forum State does not exceed its powers under the Due Process Clause if it asserts personal jurisdiction over a corporation that delivers its products into the stream of commerce with the expectation that they will be purchased by consumers in the forum State.

But there is no such or similar basis for Oklahoma jurisdiction over World-Wide or Seaway in this case. . . . [*Because we find that petitioners have no "contacts, ties, or relations" with the State of Oklahoma, the judgment of the Supreme Court of Oklahoma is reversed*].

Case Questions

1. In determining personal jurisdiction, what factors did the court assess in the relationship among the defendant, the forum, and the litigation?

2. What single factor influenced the Court the most in reaching its decision in this case?

3. Let's assume that parties from different states entered into a contract. What aspects of the relationship would be most important in determining personal jurisdiction over an out-of-state party if a lawsuit was filed claiming breach of contract?

This discussion of jurisdiction relates to civil suits. In criminal suits, the crime must have been committed within the state for the court to have jurisdiction of the case. Jurisdiction over the person of the defendant is obtained by arrest. In the event of arrest in a state other than that in which the crime was committed, the prisoner must be transported back to the state where the crime occurred. This is done by the governor of the state of arrest voluntarily turning the prisoner over to the governor of the requesting state. The process of requesting and transporting the prisoner from one state to another is called **extradition.**

Regardless of the type of case, a defendant may decide not to object to a court's exercise of personal jurisdiction. In other words, a defendant may agree to submit to a court's authority even though personal jurisdiction may not be obtained under the rules discussed in this section. In essence, a defendant may waive or forgo any objection to a court's exercise of personal jurisdiction.

10. Class-Action Suits

A **class-action suit** is one in which one or more plaintiffs file suit on their own behalf and on behalf of all other persons who may have a similar claim. For example, all sellers of real estate through brokers were certified as a class in an antitrust suit against the brokers. All persons suing a drug company, alleging injuries from a product, constituted a class for a tort action. Class-action suits may also be filed on behalf of all shareholders of a named corporation. The number of people constituting a class is frequently quite large. Class-action suits are popular because they often involve matters in which no one member of the class would have a sufficient financial interest to warrant litigation. However, the combined interest of all members of the class not only makes litigation feasible, it quite often makes it very profitable for the lawyer who brings the suit. In addition, such litigation avoids a multiplicity of suits involving the same issue, especially when the issues are complex and the cost of preparation and defense is very substantial.

At the federal level, the Supreme Court has tended to discourage class-action suits. Federal cases require that members of the class be given notice of the lawsuit; actual notice and not merely notice by newspaper publication is usually required. This notice must be given to all members of the class whose names and addresses can be found through reasonable efforts. In addition, those plaintiffs seeking to bring the class action suit must pay all court costs of the action, including the cost of compiling the names and addresses of those in the class. If the trial court denies the plaintiff a right to represent the class, that decision cannot be appealed until there is a final decision in the lawsuit itself. Denial of class-action status making it impractical to continue the litigation does not give grounds for an immediate appeal.

One legal commentator has described the class-action suit as the law's version of a nuclear weapon—it is so destructive no side wants to set it off. A plaintiff's threat to aggregate thousands of individual claims is so powerful that it can destroy a defendant business. However, if the class action fails, the plaintiff wins nothing and loses the investment in the litigation. Simple cost-benefit analysis leads the litigants to settle a class-action suit.

In the past, the federal courts routinely approved class-action settlements provided there was some benefit to the class and a release of all class members' claims. Typically large attorneys' fees were included in the settlements. However, in recent years, the federal courts have begun carefully examining class-action settlements and have developed a much higher standard for approving settlements. A tougher standard is especially important where settlements have been proposed because of the risk that the class representatives and their lawyers could sacrifice the interests of the class in order to financially benefit themselves. Class-action suits in federal courts may be settled on a classwide basis only if the settlement's terms are fair and equitable and only if all the class certification requirements for trial have also been met.

If a class-action suit is in federal court because of diversity of citizenship, the claim of each member of the class must meet the jurisdictional amount of $75,000. This requirement and the aforementioned requirement of notice and settlement have greatly reduced the number of such suits in federal courts. However, the practice of consumers' and plaintiffs' lawyers of combining a single grievance into a lawsuit on behalf of every possible litigant is quite common in state courts. Numerous state class-action statutes allow consumers and others to file suit in state courts on behalf of all citizens of that state. So although the Supreme Court has attempted to reduce class-action cases, it is apparent that public companies are still subject to this type of claim.

Pretrial Procedures

How does a lawsuit begin, and how are issues presented to a court? How does a court decide whether it is the proper place for the lawsuit to be tried? To what extent do the parties in a civil lawsuit learn of the opposing party's legal arguments and factual presentations? How can one party test the validity of the other party's claims prior to trial? And what are the protections against one party harassing another by filing improper or unwarranted lawsuits? These questions arise in the context of pretrial procedures as described in Table 2–4. The following sections provide the answers to these questions.

11. Pleadings

The legal documents that are filed with a court to begin the litigation process are called **pleadings.** Through the contents of the pleadings, the issues to be resolved are brought into sharper focus. Lawsuits begin by a plaintiff filing a pleading, called a **complaint,** with the court clerk. The complaint contains allegations by the plaintiff and a statement or request of the relief sought. The clerk issues the summons, and a court official (usually a sheriff or marshal) delivers the summons and a copy of the complaint to the defendant.

The summons provides the date by which the defendant must respond to the complaint. This response usually takes the form of a written pleading, called an **answer.** The defendant's answer will either admit or deny each allegation of the plaintiff's complaint and may contain affirmative defenses that

TABLE 2–4   Pretrial Proceedings

Plaintiff files complaint.
Complaint and summons served on defendant.
Defendant files motion or answer with possible counterclaim and defenses.
Court rules on motions.
Plaintiff files reply to answer.
Attorneys conduct discovery procedures.
Parties may file motions for summary judgment or judgment on pleadings.
Court conducts pretrial conference.

will defeat the plaintiff's claim. The answer may also contain causes of action the defendant has against the plaintiff. These statements are called *counterclaims*. If the defendant does not respond in any way, the court may enter an order of **default** and grant the plaintiff the relief sought by the complaint.

After receiving an answer that contains one or more counterclaims, the plaintiff files a reply that specifically admits or denies each allegation of the defendant's counterclaims. The factual issues of a lawsuit are thus formed by one party making an allegation and the other party either admitting it or denying it. In this way, pleadings give notice of each party's contentions and serve to set the boundary lines of the litigation.

12. Discovery

Lawsuits are often high drama in the movies and on television. Inevitably in these dramatized courtroom scenes, some element of surprise is the turning point, thereby ensuring a favorable outcome for the popular client or lawyer. In reality, civil litigation seldom concludes with a surprise witness or new piece of evidence. The reason the surprises do not occur is the process of **discovery.**

Purpose
Discovery procedures are designed to take the "sporting aspect" out of litigation and ensure that the results of lawsuits are based on the merits of the controversy and not on the ability, skill, or cunning of counsel. Historically, an attorney who had a weak case on the facts or law could win a lawsuit through a surprise witness at the trial. Today, the law is such that verdicts should not be based on the skill of counsel but on the relative merits of the controversy. Discovery practice is designed to ensure that, prior to trial, each side is fully aware of all the facts involved in the case and of the intentions of the parties. One of its purposes is to aid trial preparation by permitting the parties to learn how a witness will answer questions prior to the actual questioning at the trial. Discovery, in this way, provides a "dress rehearsal" for the trial. Another, perhaps even more important, purpose of discovery is to narrow the issues disputed by the parties. In this way, discovery encourages the settlement of the lawsuit, thereby avoiding the actual trial.

Methods
During the discovery phase of litigation, clients and lawyers need to work very closely together. Several methods of discovery can be utilized, or it might be decided that some methods will not produce new information and thus will be skipped. It is only through the aid of a client that a lawyer can gain the confidence that the discovery is complete and that the case is ready to go to trial.

Typically the least expensive method of discovery is to present a series of written questions to the opposing parties. These questions, called **interrogatories,** must be answered by the party to whom they have been delivered. It is fairly common for plaintiff and defendant to attach a series of interrogatories to their respective pleadings. A common interrogatory is "Please furnish the names and addresses of all persons known to you that witnessed the occurrence which is the subject matter of this lawsuit."

After answers to the interrogatories are received, either party might ask the other to produce specific documents, called **request for production of**

documents, that are important to the lawsuit's outcome. For example, a buyer of merchandise who is suing the seller can request that this defendant produce the original sales contract that contains certain warranties covering the merchandise.

In a personal injury action, the defendant can require the plaintiff to submit to a physical examination by the defendant's expert physician. While the plaintiff may object to the specific doctor, a general objection to the physical examination is not permissible.

The most expensive method of discovery is also the most revealing with regard to preparing for the trial. To conduct discovery to the greatest extent possible, the lawyers will want to take **depositions** of all potential witnesses. In a deposition, the lawyer orally asks questions of the possible witness and an oral response is given. All the spoken words are recorded by a court reporter, and a written transcript is prepared. In this way, a permanent record of the anticipated testimony is created. With depositions, lawyers seldom need to ask a question during a trial to which they do not already know the answer.

Finally, after some or all of these methods of discovery are used, either party may request the other admit that certain issues presented in the pleadings are no longer in dispute. By the **request for an admission,** issues are narrowed, and settlement may become more likely.

Scope

The discovery procedures are intended to be used freely by the parties to litigation without the court's direct supervision. At times a question about the scope of what is discoverable arises, and the party objecting to discovery seeks the judge's opinion. In this setting, a ruling must be given. Generally, judges provide a very broad or liberal interpretation of the degree of discoverable information. The usual rule is that as long as the information sought in discovery will lead to evidence admissible during the trial, the information is discoverable and an objection is overruled.

Although the use of discovery is essential to our system of litigation, it also carries significant costs. In a recent survey of 1,000 judges, abusive discovery was rated highest among the reasons for the high cost of litigation. Discovery imposes several costs on the litigant from whom discovery is sought. These burdens include the time spent searching for and compiling relevant documents; the time, expense, and aggravation of preparing for and attending depositions; the costs of copying and shipping documents; and the attorneys' fees generated in interpreting discovery requests, drafting responses to interrogatories and coordinating responses to production requests, advising the client as to which documents should be disclosed and which ones withheld, and determining whether certain information is privileged. The party seeking discovery also bears costs, including attorneys' fees generated in drafting discovery requests and reviewing the opponent's objections and responses. Both parties incur costs related to the delay discovery imposes on reaching the merits of the case. Finally, discovery imposes burdens on the judicial system; scarce judicial resources must be diverted from other cases to resolve discovery disputes.

The following case illustrates the perils for a business when a judge fails to properly monitor the abuses in the discovery process.

CHUDASAMA V. MAZDA MOTOR CORP.

123 F.3d 1353 (11th Cir. 1997)

Bhupendra Chudasama and his wife, Gunvanti B., purchased a used 1989 Mazda MPV minivan (the "MPV mini-van") from Jays Dodge City, a Columbus, Georgia Dodge dealer. Gunvanti Chudasama was injured when Bhupendra Chudasama lost control of the minivan and it collided with a utility pole. Mrs. Chudasama sustained a broken pelvis and broken facial bones; Mr. Chudasama was uninjured. Mrs. Chudasama's medical bills totaled approximately $13,000, and she lost approximately $5,000 in wages. The accident left the MPV minivan, worth approximately $11,000, beyond repair.

The Chudasamas filed a products liability action against the defendants—Mazda Motor Corp. ("Mazda Japan"), a Japanese company, and Mazda Motor of America, Inc. ("Mazda America"), an American subsidiary of Mazda Japan (collectively "Mazda"). The complaint pointed to two alleged defects in the MPV minivan as the cause of the Chudasamas' accident and resulting injuries: (1) the brakes were likely to cause "the driver's unexpected loss of control . . . in the highway environment of its expected use," and (2) the "doors, side panels and supporting members were inadequately designed and constructed, and fail[ed] to provide a reasonable degree of occupant safety so that they [were] unreasonably likely to crush and deform into the passenger compartment." Their complaint contained four counts: three standard products liability counts—strict liability, breach of implied warranty, and negligent design and manufacture—and one count of fraud. Each count sought compensatory damages to cover Mrs. Chudasama's medical bills and lost wages, and to compensate her for her pain and suffering, Mr. Chudasama for his loss of his wife's "society, companionship and services," and the loss of the vehicle. All but the breach of implied warranty count also sought punitive damages. Following a protracted discovery dispute, the district court entered a default judgment against Mazda for failing to comply with a court order compelling discovery, and the defendant appealed.

TJOFLAT, J.: As has become typical in recent years, both sides initially adopted extreme and unreasonable positions; the plaintiffs asked for almost every tangible piece of information or property possessed by the defendants, and the defendants offered next to nothing and took several steps to delay discovery. In this case, however, the district court never attempted to resolve the parties' disputes and force the parties to meet somewhere in the middle of their respective extreme positions. As a result, what began as a relatively common discovery dispute quickly deteriorated into unbridled legal warfare.

We see no useful purpose in describing the drawn-out discovery battle in detail; a relatively brief summary will suffice. The Chudasamas served Mazda with their first interrogatories and requests for production. Both documents were models of vague and overly broad discovery requests. The production requests, for example, contained 20 "special instructions," 29 definitions, and 121 numbered requests (some containing as many as 11 subparts). Similarly, the interrogatories contained 18 "special instructions," 29 definitions, and 31 numbered interrogatories. "One" interrogatory included five separate questions that applied to each of the 121 numbered requests for production, arguably expanding the number of interrogatories to 635.

The production requests all but asked for every document Mazda ever had in its possession and then some. For example, the Chudasamas sought detailed information about practically all of Mazda's employees worldwide. They requested production of all documents relating to organizational charts, books or manuals of Mazda . . . which will or may assist in identifying and locating those operating divisions, committees, groups, departments, employees, and personnel . . . involved in the conception, market analysis, development, testing, design safety engineering and marketing of the product for all years during which the product has been developed, designed, manufactured and marketed. . . .

In response to the Chudasamas' excessively broad discovery requests, Mazda adopted four different strategies. First, it objected to almost every production request and interrogatory on almost every imaginable ground. While some of its objections were clearly boilerplate and bordered on being frivolous, many were directly on point and raised bona fide questions of law.

Mazda pursued a second strategy for countering the Chudasamas' vague and overbroad discovery requests. It filed a motion to dismiss their fraud count for failure to plead fraud with particularity. Mazda contended that the Chudasamas had failed to point to any specific misrepresentation made by Mazda. . . .

In its motion to dismiss the fraud count, Mazda contended that the Chudasamas failed to allege the "time, place and content of the alleged misrepresentations." The Chudasamas' memorandum in opposition to Mazda's motion argued that the misrepresentations were made in advertisements they had viewed in the past. They needed discovery from Mazda, they said, to find out which particular advertisements they had viewed and relied upon.

Despite the fact that both parties fully briefed Mazda's motion to dismiss, the district court never ruled on it. Although Mazda frequently reminded the district court—over a period of time exceeding a year and a half—that the motion was pending, the only indication in the record that the district court even acknowledged the motion was a statement made at a hearing (over nine months after the motion was filed) suggesting that the motion would be considered after discovery. . . .

Mazda's third strategy was to seek a protective order. Much of the information requested by the Chudasamas involved confidential documents that went to the heart of Mazda's business. They sought marketing studies, internal memoranda, and documentation on the history of the development and design of the MPV minivan and other vehicles. Fearing disclosure of this information to its competitors or to other potential plaintiffs, Mazda sought a "nonsharing" protective order that would keep the information under seal and prohibit the Chudasamas from sharing Mazda's proprietary information with anyone. . . .

Perhaps because it realized that the district court had no intention of ruling on its motion to dismiss the fraud count or its various objections, Mazda adopted a fourth strategy; it withheld a substantial amount of information that it later conceded was properly discoverable.

The district court based its decision to impose sanctions on the Federal Rules of Civil Procedure.

[The Federal Rules] authorize a district court to impose such sanctions "as are just" against a party that violates an order compelling discovery. Included in the list of possible sanctions is an order striking a defendant's answer and entering a default. District courts enjoy substantial discretion in deciding whether and how to impose sanctions under Rule 37. When reviewing an order striking a defendant's pleadings, our review should be particularly scrupulous lest the district court too lightly resort to this extreme sanction, amounting to judgment against the defendant without an opportunity to be heard on the merits.

We recognize that district courts enjoy broad discretion in deciding how best to manage the cases before them. This discretion is not unfettered, however. When a litigant's rights are materially prejudiced by the district court's mismanagement of a case, we must redress the abuse of discretion. The mismanagement of two key parts of this case—Mazda's motion to dismiss the Chudasamas' fraud claim and Mazda's resistance to the Chudasamas' discovery requests—indicates that the district court abused its discretion. . . .

Turning to the facts of the instant case, we note that even the most cursory review of the Chudasamas' shotgun complaint reveals that it contains a fraud count that is novel and of questionable validity. Upon reading the complaint, the district court should have noted that the fraud count dramatically enlarged the scope of the Chudasamas' case. Without the fraud theory, the scope of discovery likely would have been limited to information tending to show that the MPV minivan was a defective product and that Mazda was negligent in designing it. With the fraud theory in the case, on the other hand, the scope of discovery broadened to include Mazda's marketing strategies and safety testing. As a result, the Chudasamas could seek much broader discovery with the fraud count in the complaint than without it.

We conclude that this claim was dubious enough to require the district court to rule on Mazda's motion to dismiss. When the court refused to do so and, instead, allowed the case to proceed through discovery without an analysis of the fraud claim, it abused its discretion. By and large, the Federal Rules of Civil Procedure are designed to minimize the need for judicial intervention into discovery matters. They do not eliminate that need, however.

Having determined that the district court abused its discretion in ordering Mazda to respond to the Chudasamas' requests, we turn to the subsequent sanctions order to determine whether it fell within the district court's broad discretion. The answer is fairly clear: the district court would have been hard pressed to fashion sanctions more severe than those included in its order. Mazda lost nearly everything that was at stake in the litigation and more. In addition to granting costs and attorneys' fees to the Chudasamas, the court struck Mazda's answer and ordered that a default be entered on all claims, reserving damages as the only issue to be tried on the merits. These sanctions were so unduly severe under the circumstances as to constitute a clear abuse of discretion.

For the foregoing reasons, we VACATE both the district court's order compelling discovery and its order granting the appellee's amended motion for sanctions and REMAND this case with the instruction that the Chief Judge of the Middle District of Georgia reassign the case to a different district judge for further proceedings consistent with this opinion.

Case Questions

1. How can a party protect itself from an abusive discovery process?

2. What is the practical consequence of a default judgment being entered against the defendants?

3. Is a ruling of this nature likely to have any impact on the litigation process in this country?

13. Motions

During the pretrial phase of litigation, either plaintiff or defendant or both may attempt to convince the court that there are no questions about the factual setting of the dispute. An argument is presented that there are only questions of law for the judge to resolve. For example, the parties may be in complete agreement that the plaintiff has not been paid by the defendant for the merchandise that was delivered by the plaintiff and received by the defendant. The dispute between these parties is simply whether, under the stated facts, the defendant must pay the plaintiff. This dispute presents only an issue of law, not of fact.

When a question of law is at issue, the parties can seek a pretrial determination of their rights by filing a **motion** with the court. These motions can be made at any point in the litigation process. First, the defendant may, instead of filing an answer, file a pleading that at common law was called a *general demurrer*. Today we call this a *motion to dismiss for failure to state a cause of action*. By this pleading the defendant, in effect, says to the court, "Even if everything the plaintiff says in his complaint is true, he is not entitled to the relief he seeks." For example, the defendant in the case involving the nonpayment for merchandise can argue the plaintiff failed to allege that the defendant ordered the goods. By federal law, merchandise sent unsolicited does not have to be paid for even when it is kept. In essence, the defendant, in the motion to dismiss, argues that the plaintiff failed to plead an essential element of a valid claim.

In addition, a defendant may move to dismiss a suit for reasons that as a matter of law prevent the plaintiff from winning his or her suit. Such matters as a lack of jurisdiction of the court to hear the suit, or expiration of the time limit during which the defendant is subject to suit, may be raised by such a motion. This latter ground is usually referred to as the **statute of limitations.** Each state has prescribed a time limit after which a suit cannot be filed. For example, if the plaintiff fails to sue within the stated period, the defendant is not liable for the nonpayment of the merchandise. (Typically in a situation like the merchandise example, the statute of limitations will be four years from the time the merchandise is received.)

The rules of procedure in the federal court system and in most of the state systems provide for motions for a **judgment on the pleadings** or for **summary judgment.** In the former motion, a party is asking the judge to decide the case based solely on the complaint and the answer. If in the example involving the nonpayment for the merchandise the complaint does contain all the elements needed to state a claim and if the defendant offers no explanation or excuse for nonpayment in the answer, the judge can enter a judgment that the defendant must pay the plaintiff a specified amount. Through this motion, a time-consuming but unnecessary trial can be avoided.

A motion for summary judgment seeks a similar pretrial conclusion to the litigation. However, the party filing this motion is asking the judge to base a decision not only on the pleadings but also on other evidence. Such evidence usually is presented in the form of sworn statements called **affidavits.** The judge also may conduct a hearing and allow the lawyers to argue the merits of the motion for summary judgment. If there is no question of material fact, the judge will decide the legal issues raised by the facts and enter a judgment in favor of one party over the other.

14. Frivolous Cases

Either on a motion by a party or on their own initiative, judges may terminate the litigation process if there is a finding that the lawsuit is frivolous, that is, totally lacking in merit. The difficulty is in the determination of what is frivolous. What initially may appear to be a frivolous complaint may upon the presentation of evidence become a legitimate case.

During the past decade, courts within the federal judiciary and most state court systems have increased the frequency of assessing fines against lawyers who file frivolous cases. For example, Rule 11 of the Federal Rules of Civil Procedure authorizes the imposition of fines for filing frivolous papers. These fines are justified because Rule 11 states:

> The signature of an attorney or party constitutes a certificate by the signer that the signer has read the pleading, motion, or other paper; that to the best of the signer's knowledge, information, and belief formed after reasonable inquiry it is well grounded in fact and is warranted by existing law, and that it is not interposed for any improper purpose, such as to harass or to cause unnecessary delay or needless increase in the cost of litigation.

Most states have a rule similar to Federal Rule 11. The courts have upheld fines against lawyers and clients who sign frivolous documents. These holdings make it essential that businesspeople have thorough discussions with their lawyers about litigation strategies.

The Trial

If efforts to resolve a case through pretrial motions or negotiations have been unsuccessful, the case will proceed to trial as set forth in Table 2–5. A trial normally involves the presentation of evidence to a jury to determine the actual facts in dispute. After the evidence is presented, the judge explains the applicable law to the jury. The jury is asked to deliberate and render a verdict and the trial court must then decide whether to enter a judgment based on the jury's verdict.

15. Jury Selection

As the case is called, the first order of business is to select a jury. Prior to the calling of the case, the court clerk will have summoned prospective jurors. Their names are drawn at random from lists of eligible citizens, and the num-

---

TABLE 2-5 Trial Steps

Voir dire–Parties and their attorneys select jury.
Attorneys present opening statements.
Plaintiff presents evidence through witnesses.
Defendant moves for directed verdict.
Defendant presents evidence through witnesses.
Attorneys present closing arguments.
Court instructs jury on the law.
Jury deliberates and makes decision (verdict).
Judge enters judgment on verdict.
Losing party files posttrial motion.

---

ber of jurors required, between six and twelve, is selected or called into the jury box for the conduct of voir dire examination. **Voir dire** literally means to speak the truth. This examination is a method by which the court and often the attorneys for each party examine each potential juror as to his or her qualifications and ability to be fair and impartial. A party to a lawsuit is entitled to fair and impartial jurors in both civil and criminal cases. Prospective jurors are sworn to give truthful answers to the questions on voir dire.

Either party in the lawsuit may challenge or excuse a prospective juror for a specific reason, or cause. For example, if a prospective juror is related to one of the parties or to a witness or the juror admits bias favoring one side, that person may be excused as a juror because of the specific reason. In addition to the excuses for cause, the plaintiff and defendant are given a certain number of challenges, known as **peremptory challenges,** for which no cause or reason need be given to excuse a prospective juror. The number of peremptory challenges varies from court system to court system and on the type of case being tried. The number also may vary between the parties. For instance, in a criminal case, the defendant may have twelve peremptory challenges, and the government may have only six. The process of voir dire examination continues until all the peremptory challenges are exhausted and a full jury panel is selected.

In the following case, the Supreme Court addresses the issue of whether a party has the unfettered right to use its peremptory challenges to remove individuals from the jury on account of gender.

J.E.B. v. Alabama Ex Rel. T.B.
114 S. Ct. 1419 (1994)

At petitioner's paternity and child support trial, the court assembled a panel of 36 potential jurors, 12 males and 24 females. After the court excused three jurors for cause, only 10 of the remaining 33 jurors were male. The State of Alabama then used 9 of its 10 peremptory challenges to remove male jurors. The petitioner used all but one of his strikes to remove female jurors. As a result, the trial court empaneled an all-female jury. The court rejected petitioner's claim that the Equal Protection Clause of the Fourteenth Amendment prohibits peremptory strikes based solely on gender. The jury subsequently found petitioner to be the father of the child in question and the trial court ordered him to pay child support. After the Alabama Court of Civil Appeals affirmed the decision, the Supreme Court granted certiorari.

BLACKMUN, J.: . . . We have reaffirmed repeatedly our commitment to jury selection procedures that are fair and nondiscriminatory. We have recognized that whether the trial is criminal or civil, potential jurors, as well as litigants, have an equal protection right to jury selection procedures that are free from state-sponsored group stereotypes rooted in, and reflective of, historical prejudice.

Although premised on equal protection principles that apply equally to gender discrimination, all our recent cases . . . involved alleged racial discrimination in the exercise of peremptory challenges. Today we are faced with the question whether the Equal Protection Clause forbids intentional discrimination on the basis of gender, just as it prohibits discrimination on the basis of race. We hold that gender, like race, is an unconstitutional proxy for juror competence and impartiality. . . .

Discrimination on the basis of gender in the exercise of peremptory challenges is a relatively recent phenomenon. Gender-based peremptory strikes were hardly practicable for most of our country's existence, since, until the 19th century women were completely excluded from jury service. So well-entrenched was this exclusion of women that in 1880 this Court, while finding that the exclusion of African-American men from juries violated the Fourteenth Amendment, expressed no doubt that a State may confine the selection of jurors to males.

Many States continued to exclude women from jury service well into the present century, despite the fact that women attained suffrage upon ratification of the Nineteenth Amendment in 1920. States that did permit women to serve on juries often erected other barriers, such as registration requirements and automatic exemptions, designed to deter women from exercising their right to jury service. . . .

This Court consistently has subjected gender-based classifications to heightened scrutiny in recognition of the real danger that government policies that professedly are based on reasonable considerations in fact may be reflective of "archaic and overbroad" generalizations about gender, or based on "outdated misconceptions concerning the role of females in the home rather than in the marketplace and world of ideas. . . ."

Far from proffering an exceptionally persuasive justification for its gender-based peremptory challenges, respondent maintains that its decision to strike virtually all the males from the jury in this case "may reasonably have been based upon the perception, supported by history, that men otherwise totally qualified to serve upon a jury might be more sympathetic and receptive to the arguments of a man alleged in a paternity action to be the father of an out-of-wedlock child, while women equally qualified to serve upon a jury might be more sympathetic and receptive to the arguments of the complaining witness who bore the child."

Even if a measure of truth can be found in some of the gender stereotypes used to justify gender-based peremptory challenges, that fact alone cannot support discrimination on the basis of gender in jury selection. We have made abundantly clear in past cases that gender classifications that rest on impermissible stereotypes violate the Equal Protection Clause, even when some statistical support can be conjured up for the generalization. . . .

Discrimination in jury selection, whether based on race or on gender, causes harm to the litigants, the community, and the individual jurors who are wrongfully excluded from participation in the judicial process. . . . When state actors exercise peremptory challenges in reliance on gender stereotypes, they ratify and reinforce prejudicial views of the relative abilities of men and women. Because these stereotypes have wreaked injustice in so many other spheres of our country's public life, active discrimination by litigants on the basis of gender during jury selection invites cynicism respecting the jury's neutrality and its obligation to adhere to the law. . . .

Our conclusion that litigants may not strike potential jurors solely on the basis of gender does not imply the elimination of all peremptory challenges. . . . Parties still may remove jurors whom they feel might be less acceptable than others on the panel; gender simply may not serve as a proxy for bias. [*The judgment of the Court of Civil Appeals of Alabama is reversed and the case is remanded*].

Case Questions

1. Is a peremptory challenge peremptory if you have to give a nondiscriminatory reason to justify striking a particular juror?

2. What facts made this case an easy one for detecting the existence of discrimination? Will it always be so easy?

3. Is a trial judge normally able to tell whether a lawyer is using peremptory challenges improperly?

The *J.E.B.* case is the most recent decision by the Supreme Court on the controversial subject of discrimination in the jury selection process. The Supreme Court, beginning with the case of *Batson v. Kentucky,* 476 U.S. 79 (1986), declared that the use of peremptory challenges by prosecutors in criminal cases to exclude jurors on the basis of race violated the equal protection clause. In several later cases, the Court expanded its holding in *Batson* to include banning racially discriminatory peremptory challenges by civil litigants and criminal defendants. Given all of the criticism raised about juries today, particularly their ability to decide cases involving celebrity criminal defendants or complex civil issues, we are likely to see further decisions by the Supreme Court clarifying the permissible uses of peremptory challenges in jury selection. Several legal commentators have suggested following the example of England and eliminating the use of peremptory challenges altogether.

16. Other Steps During a Trial

After selecting jurors to hear the case, the attorneys make their opening statements. An opening statement is not evidence; it familiarizes the jury with the essential facts that each side expects to prove. So that the jury may understand the overall picture of the case and the relevancy of each bit of evidence as presented, the lawyers inform the jury of the facts they expect to prove and of the witnesses they expect to call to make such proof.

After the opening statements, the trial continues with the plaintiff introducing evidence to establish the truth of the allegations made in the complaint. Evidence is normally presented in open court by the examination of witnesses and production of documents and other exhibits. After the plaintiff has presented his or her evidence, the defendant may make a motion for a **directed verdict.** The court can only direct a verdict for one party if the evidence, taken in the light most favorable to the other party, establishes as a matter of law that the party making the motion is entitled to a verdict. Just as a plaintiff must *allege* certain facts or have the complaint dismissed by motion to dismiss, he or she must have some *proof* of each essential allegation or lose the case on a motion for a directed verdict.

After the parties have completed the presentation of all the evidence, the lawyers have an opportunity to summarize the evidence. Unlike the opening statements, which involved simply a preview of what was to come, the lawyers in closing argument attempt to convince the jury (or judge if no jury is used) of what the case's outcome should be.

Following the closing arguments, the judge acquaints the jury with the law applicable to the case. These are the **jury instructions.** As the function of the jury is to find the facts and the function of the court is to determine the applicable law, the purpose of jury instructions is to bring the facts and the law together in an orderly manner that will result in a decision. A typical jury instruction might be:

> The plaintiff in his complaint has alleged that he was injured as the proximate cause of the negligence of the defendant. If you find from the evidence that the defendant was guilty of negligence, which proximately caused plaintiff's injuries, then your verdict should be for the plaintiff.

In this instruction, the court is in effect saying that the plaintiff must prove that the defendant was at fault. Thus, the jury is instructed as to the result to be returned if the jurors have found certain facts to be true. At the conclusion of the jury instructions, the judge informs the jurors to begin their deliberations and to return to the courtroom when they have reached a decision.

17. Burden of Proof

The term **burden of proof** has two meanings depending on the context in which it is used. It may describe the burden or responsibility that a person has to come forward with evidence on a particular issue. The party alleging the existence of certain facts usually has the burden of coming forward with evidence to establish those facts.

Burden of proof may also describe the responsibility a person has to be persuasive as to a specific fact. This is known as the *burden of persuasion.* The party with this burden must convince the trier of fact on the issue involved. If a party with the burden of persuasion fails to meet this burden, that party loses the lawsuit. Thus, the burden of persuasion is a legal device used to help determine the rights of the litigating parties.

Criminal Cases

The extent of proof required to satisfy the burden of persuasion varies, depending upon the issue and the type of case. There are three distinct levels of proof recognized by the law. For criminal cases, the burden of proof is described as **beyond a reasonable doubt.** This means that the prosecution in a criminal case has the burden of convincing the trier of fact, usually a jury, that the defendant is guilty of the crime charged and that the jury has no reasonable doubt about the defendant's guilt. This burden of proof does not require evidence beyond any doubt, only beyond a reasonable doubt. A reasonable doubt is one that a reasonable person viewing the evidence might reasonably entertain. This standard is not used in civil cases.

Civil Cases

In civil cases the party with the burden of proof is subject to one of two standards: the **preponderance of evidence** standard or the **clear and convincing proof** standard. The preponderance of evidence standard is used most frequently. It requires that a party convince the jury by a preponderance of evidence that the facts are as he or she contends. Preponderance of evidence is achieved when there is greater weight of evidence in support of the proposition than there is against it. The scales of justice, in other words, tilt more one way than the other. The clear and convincing proof standard is used in situations where the law requires more than a simple preponderance of the evidence but less than proof beyond a reasonable doubt. The scales of justice must tilt heavily one way. Unless the evidence clearly establishes the proposition, the party with the burden of proof fails to sustain it and loses the lawsuit.

18. Deciding the Case

The principal job of the jury is to determine what the facts are and to apply the law, as instructed by the judge, to these facts. The jury's decision is called a **verdict,** and it is announced in the courtroom when the jury's deliberations are completed. An example of a verdict might be "We, the jury, find in favor of the plaintiff and award $1,000,000 to be paid by the defendant" or "We, the jury, find the defendant is not liable to the plaintiff and should pay nothing." The judge must decide whether to accept the verdict. If the judge agrees with the verdict, a **judgment** is entered in favor of the party that won the jury's verdict.

The party who is dissatisfied with the jury's verdict may file a posttrial motion with the judge seeking a **judgment notwithstanding the verdict,** often called JNOV. The judge may enter a judgment opposite to that of the jury's verdict if the judge finds that the verdict is erroneous as a matter of law. The test used by the judge is the same one used to decide a motion for a directed verdict. To grant a motion for a judgment notwithstanding the verdict, the judge must find that reasonable persons viewing the evidence would not reach the verdict the jury returned. Because jurors are presumed to be reasonable, this motion is not frequently granted.

The party who receives the adverse judgment may file a motion for a new trial. This motion may be granted if the judge is convinced that a legal mistake was made during the trial. Because a judge is not usually inclined to acknowledge that mistakes have been made, a motion for a new trial is usually denied. It is from the ruling on this motion that the losing party appeals.

Posttrial Issues

Even after the trial, a number of issues may still exist. First among these is this one: How can a disappointed litigant obtain a review of the trial judge's legal rulings? If the trial court's judgment is final, what can the victorious party do to collect the dollar damages awarded? Finally, can the same subject matter be relitigated? These questions are the subject of the final three sections of this chapter.

19. Appeals

Each state prescribes its own appellate procedure and determines the jurisdiction of its various reviewing courts. Although having knowledge of the procedure used in an appeal is essentially a responsibility for the lawyer, understanding certain aspects of this procedure may assist you in understanding our judicial system. This procedure is described in Table 2–6.

TABLE 2–6   Appellate Review

Party receiving adverse judgment files notice of appeal.
Parties file briefs in reviewing court.
Oral argument made in reviewing court.
Reviewing court announces decision.
Further review may be requested by petition to higher court.
Higher court allows or denies further review.
Final decision (Successful party may require judicial assistance in enforcing the final decision).

Appellate Procedures

Courts of appeal deal with the record of the proceedings in lower court. All the pleadings, testimony, and motions are reduced to a written record, which is filed with the court of review. The court of appeal studies the issues, testimony, and proceedings to determine whether prejudicial errors occurred or whether the lower court reached an erroneous result. In addition to the record, each party files a **brief,** which contains a short description of the nature of the case, the factual situation, the points and authorities on which the party relies, and the argument for reversing or affirming the decision of the lower court, depending on whether the party is an appellant or appellee.

In addition to the brief, the reviewing court is often given the benefit of **oral argument** in deciding the case. The attorneys are given a specified amount of time to explain orally to the court their position in the case. This also gives the court of review an opportunity to question the attorneys about various aspects of the case.

After oral argument, an initial vote of the judges' or justices' impressions is usually taken. The case is assigned to one judge or justice to prepare an opinion. Each judge or justice has a staff of clerks assisting in the preparation of opinions. After the opinion is prepared, it is circulated among the other members of the court. If a majority approve the opinion, it is adopted. Those who disagree may prepare a dissenting opinion. If the review is conducted by an intermediate appellate court, the losing party may petition the highest court in the system for a writ of certiorari.

Deference to Trial Courts

Courts of appeal are essentially concerned with questions of law. However, a reviewing court may be asked to grant a new trial on the ground that the decision in the lower court is contrary to the manifest weight of the evidence found in the record. In the federal courts and in many states, appellate courts are not allowed to disturb factual findings unless they are clearly erroneous. This limitation recognizes the unique opportunity afforded the trial judge in evaluating the credibility of witnesses and weighing the evidence. Determining the weight and credibility of the evidence is the special function of the trial court. An appellate court cannot substitute its interpretation of the evidence for that of the trial court simply because it construes the facts or resolves the ambiguities differently.

20. Enforcement of Judgments and Decrees

After a judgment in a court of law or a decree in a court of equity has become final, either because of the decision on appeal or because the losing party has failed to appeal within the proper time, it may become necessary for the successful party to obtain judicial assistance in enforcing the court decision. The judgment debtor, for example, may not have voluntarily paid the amount of the judgment to the judgment creditor.

The primary enforcement mechanism is for the judgment creditor to request the court's assistance to have the **execution** of the judgment or decree. An execution of a judgment occurs when a court official, such as a sheriff or marshal, seizes some property of the debtor, sells it at public auction, and applies the proceeds to the creditor's claim.

Another form of execution is **garnishment.** This method of enforcement involves having a portion of the debtor's wages paid to the court, which in turn pays the creditor.

21. Res Judicata

Once a decision of the court has become final, it is said to be **res judicata** (the thing has been decided), meaning that a final decision is conclusive on all issues between the parties, whether raised in the litigation or not. Res judicata means either that the case has been finally decided on appeal or that the time for appeal has expired and a cause of action finally determined by a competent court cannot be litigated by the parties in a new proceeding by the same court or in any other court. Res judicata prevents successive suits involving the same factual setting between the same parties and brings disputes to a conclusion. A matter once litigated and legally determined is conclusive between the parties in all subsequent proceedings.

Key Terms

Affidavit   52
Answer   46
Appeal   34
Appellant   39
Appellee   39
Beyond a reasonable doubt   56
Brief   58
Burden of proof   56
Chancery   33
Class-action suit   45
Clear and convincing proof   56
Complaint   46
Counterclaim   39
Counterdefendant   39
Counterplaintiff   39
Court of appeal   34
Default   47
Defendant   39
Deposition   48
Directed verdict   55
Discovery   47
Diversity of citizenship   36
Equity   33
Execution   58
Extradition   44
Federal question case   36
Garnishment   59
Interrogatory   47
Judgment   57
Judgment notwithstanding the verdict   57

Judgment on the pleadings   51
Jury instruction   55
Law   33
Long-arm statutes   42
Motion   51
Oral argument   58
Peremptory challenge   53
Personal jurisdiction   42
Petit jury   29
Petitioner   39
Plaintiff   39
Pleading   46
Preponderance of evidence   56
Request for an admission   48
Request for production of documents   47
Res judicata   59
Respondent   39
Small-claims court   35
Standing to sue   40
Statute of limitations   51
Subject matter jurisdiction   33
Summary judgment   51
Summons   42
Supreme court   34
Third-party defendant   39
Trial court   32
Verdict   56
Voir dire   53
Writ of certiorari   35

Review Questions and Problems

Personnel

1. *Judges and Justices*
   What are the essential responsibilities of a trial judge?

2. *Jurors*
   Why have several states eliminated the requirement of unanimity in jury trials?

3. *Lawyers*
   Name the three critical roles a lawyer serves in society. Why have many lawyers and their business clients had such conflict in recent years?

Organization of the Court System

4. *Jurisdiction*
   Mark, a citizen of Georgia, was crossing a street in Atlanta when he was struck by a car driven by David, a citizen of New York, visiting Atlanta. The car was owned by David's employer, a Delaware corporation that has its principal place of business in Atlanta, Georgia. Mark sues both David and the corporation in federal district court in Atlanta alleging damages in the amount of $500,000. Does the court have subject-matter jurisdiction? Why or why not?

5. *State Courts*
   What are some examples of equitable remedies in litigation?

6. *Federal Courts*
   XYZ makes and markets a product that it believes will help control weight by blocking the human body's digestion of starch. The Food and Drug Administration (FDA) has classified the product as a drug and orders it removed from the market until it can evaluate its use through testing. XYZ disputes the FDA's action and seeks to bring suit in the federal courts. Will the federal courts have jurisdiction to hear the case? Why or why not?

Litigation—An Overview

7. *Parties*
   A building contractor is sued by homeowners alleging that their homes have been poorly constructed resulting in several defects. The contractor seeks to add to the lawsuit a building supplier that it claims provided faulty support beams. Can the contractor add the building supplier as a part to the lawsuit? If so, what is this procedure called and how does it work?

8. *Standing to Sue*
   A group of environmentalists filed a lawsuit challenging commercial fishing in Glacier Bay National Park and sued the Secretary of the Interior and the National Park Service for seeking to prevent more commercial fishing.
   (a) What must the environmentalists show in order to satisfy the requirement of standing to sue in this case?
   (b) At what point should the issue of standing be decided by the court during the course of litigation?

9. *Personal Jurisdiction*
   The New York Gazette is a New York corporation with its principal place of business in New York City. While the *Gazette* sells the majority of its newspapers in the greater New York City area, the *Gazette* also distributes its newspapers throughout the United States and places its printed articles on a website that is read around the world. Shirley, a California resident, brought suit in San Francisco against the *Gazette* over a published article about her and seeks damages for defamation, invasion of privacy, and intentional infliction of emotional distress.
   (a) Is the defendant subject to the jurisdiction of the California courts?
   (b) How should a court analyze a jurisdiction issue of this kind?

10. *Class Action Suits*
    What are the incentives, on both sides of a dispute, in avoiding class action suits?

Pretrial Proceedings

11. *Pleadings*
    Describe the purpose of a complaint and an answer in civil litigation. What is the function of the pleading stage in a lawsuit?

12. *Discovery*
    (a) Why do surprises rarely occur at trial?
    (b) What are some of the key devices a litigant can use in discovery?

13. *Motions*
    Under what circumstances may a court grant a motion for summary judgment?

14. *Frivolous Cases*
    Federal Rule 11 sanctions are available against both lawyers and their clients to curb frivolous litigation. Under what circumstances may sanctions be imposed?

The Trial

15. *Jury Selection*
    At one time, peremptory challenges may be used to strike prospective jurors for any reason. In

light of recent court decisions restricting the use of peremptory challenges, should they be eliminated from litigation?

16. *Other Steps During a Trial*
    What purpose is served by jury instructions? How do they help the jury resolve a case?

17. *Burden of Proof*
    There are three distinct levels of proof required by law depending upon the kind of case involved. Describe them and when they are used.

18. *Deciding the Case*
    When is it appropriate for the judge to enter a judgment notwithstanding the verdict?

Postrial Issues

19. *Appeals*
    Describe the purpose of an appellate brief. An oral argument.

20. *Enforcement of Judgments and Decrees*
    How may a winning party go about enforcing a judgment?

21. *Res Judicata*
    What important purpose does res judicata serve in civil litigation?

Terminology Review

For each term in the left-hand column, match the most appropriate description in the right-hand column.

1. Petit jury

2. Subject-matter jurisdiction

3. Writ of certiorari

4. Personal jurisdiction

5. Standing to sue

6. Class-action suit

7. Depositions

8. Peremptory challenges

9. Directed verdict

10. Preponderance of evidence

a. When the highest court grants review of a lower court's ruling

b. The power of a court over the parties involved in litigation

c. Typically granted to a defendant when the plaintiff fails to present sufficient evidence at trial to justify a jury verdict

d. The fact-finding body during trial

e. The power of a court over the issues involved in the case

f. The burden of proof normally applied in civil cases

g. A type of case in which one or more plaintiffs file a lawsuit on behalf of a much larger group

h. A discovery process that involves the sworn questioning of potential witnesses outside of court.

i. Demonstrating a personal interest in the lawsuit as a plaintiff

j. The power granted each litigant to reject a certain number of prospective jurors

3

ALTERNATIVE DISPUTE RESOLUTION SYSTEMS

Business Decision

Designing A System

Your employer, Let's-Get-It-Done, has a history of multiple employee disputes. These disputes range from claims of illegal discrimination to general complaints of worker dissatisfaction with supervisors. You have been assigned the task of changing the organization's culture. You are considering implementing alternatives to litigation, which has been the typical method of solving disputes.

What are possible alternative dispute resolution systems (ADRs)?

Should employees be required to sign a contract that an ADR method will be used before any lawsuit is filed against the organization?

As the previous chapter points out, and as the Business Decision illustrates, litigation may not always be the best way to settle disputes. In a business relationship, it is neither feasible nor practical to litigate each dispute that arises. Time is money, and one small delay can cause larger and longer delays down the line. In addition, the emotional and financial costs of litigation may be quite high.

Many business relationships can be irreparably damaged through litigation. To help avoid this harm and to help ensure productive, ongoing relationships, a number of alternatives to litigation have developed. These are known as alternative dispute resolution (ADR) systems.

Figure 3.1 illustrates an array of ADR systems. They are arranged along a spectrum of highest cost (in terms of dollars, time, and emotions) to lowest cost. While any given factual situation may cause the items on this spectrum to shift places, this figure presents a generally accepted view of ADR techniques.

It is important to remember two things at the outset of this discussion. First, ADR techniques are used in conjunction with litigation. Thus, it is very common for a matter to be arbitrated or mediated or settled through negotiations during the pretrial process discussed in the preceding chapter.

Figure 3.1

Scale of alterative dispute resolution systems

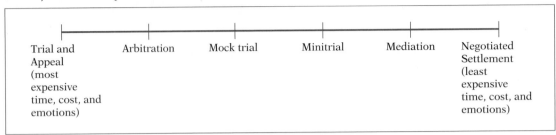

However, disputing parties do not have to begin a lawsuit to use any form of ADR. In this chapter, you will study how ADR systems relate to formal litigation and how they are utilized independently from the litigation process.

The second thing to keep in mind about ADR systems is that their use by disputing parties may be part of a contractual relationship between these parties. For example, it is an effective dispute resolution tool to have the parties' preferred ADR system specified in the contract. However, an ADR technique may be agreed to by disputing parties after the dispute arises even if they did not foresee the possibility of needing to use a dispute resolution system.

In this chapter, you will study ADR systems in the order presented in Figure 3.1. This material is presented under the following major headings:

- Movement to Arbitration
- Arbitration Procedures
- Mock and Minitrials
- Mediation
- Negotiated Settlements

Movement to Arbitration

In an **arbitration,** disputing parties submit their dispute to a neutral third party, called an **arbitrator.** This arbitrator is empowered by the parties to reach a binding decision resolving the controversy. Throughout this century, the legal system has turned more and more to arbitration. Historically, arbitration has been the most popular formal ADR process.

Arbitration may result when parties to a dispute agree to submit their disagreement to an arbitrator, when parties to a business contract include an arbitration clause in their agreement in case a dispute arises, or when legislation requires that this particular type of dispute be arbitrated.

Of particular importance in creating a positive perception and use of arbitration is the Federal Arbitration Act. This law is discussed in more detail in section 2 below. However, first you will be introduced to some general reasons parties often choose to arbitrate disputes. Sections 3 and 4 discuss specific types of arbitration and how they have contributed to the movement toward increased use of this ADR method.

1. Reasons to Arbitrate

The primary reason for the increased use of arbitration is the laudable goal of providing a relatively quick and inexpensive resolution of disputes. Arbitration not only helps the parties avoid the expense of litigation but also provides a means of avoiding the formalities of the courtroom. Formal pleadings, for example, and other procedural steps such as discovery and the rules of evidence are usually not used in an arbitration hearing.

Arbitration also serves to help ease congested court dockets. A primary function of arbitration is to serve as a substitute for and not a prelude to litigation. It is a private proceeding with no public record available to the press and others. Thus, by keeping their dispute private, adversaries may be more likely to preserve their business relationship.

Arbitration also has the advantage of submitting many disputes to experts for solutions. For example, if the issue involves whether a building has been properly constructed, the matter could be submitted to an architect for resolution. If it involves a technical accounting problem, it could be submitted to a certified public accountant. The Securities and Exchange Commission (SEC) has approved an arrangement whereby investors with complaints against securities dealers must submit them for arbitration to arbitrators assigned by the various stock exchanges and the National Association of Securities Dealers. These arbitrators are selected because they possess the special knowledge required to determine if a customer of a brokerage house has a legitimate complaint.

Arbitration is of special importance in labor relations, where it provides the grievance procedures under collective bargaining contracts. Arbitration is a means for industrial self-government, a system of private law for all problems that may arise in the workplace.

Table 3–1 illustrates the growing importance and widespread use of arbitration as an alternative dispute resolution system.

2. The Federal Arbitration Act

Prior to the enactment of the Federal Arbitration Act (FAA), our common-law system preferred litigation over arbitration as a means of resolving disputes. In 1925, congressional enactment of the FAA began to change this presumed way of dispute resolution. However, it was not until after the revision and

---

TABLE 3–1 Examples of Contracts with Arbitration Clauses

Stockbroker and client
Commodities broker and customer
Brokerage firm and employee
Attorney* and client
Union-management collective bargaining agreements
Owner-contractor and contractor-subcontractor
Insurance company and insured
Public carrier and shipper of goods

*Most bar associations require lawyers to arbitrate disputes with clients.

reenactment of the FAA in 1947 that courts began to encourage disputing parties to use arbitration instead of litigation. Clearly, the FAA changed public policy perceptions of arbitration and how states can regulate its use. These two impacts of the FAA are discussed now.

Impact on Policy

The FAA covers any arbitration clause in a contract that involves interstate commerce. Under it, courts are to "rigorously" enforce arbitration agreements. A court assumes arbitration was intended unless it can say with positive assurance that the arbitration clause was not intended to include the particular dispute. The federal policy clearly favors arbitration of commercial disputes. The FAA provides that arbitration agreements "shall be valid, irrevocable, and enforceable, save upon such grounds as exist at law or in equity for the revocation of any contract."

The following case illustrates why the Supreme Court has widely accepted arbitration as an ADR tool.

GILMER V. INTERSTATE/JOHNSON LANE CORP.

111 S.Ct. 1647 (1991)

In 1981, Interstate/Johnson Lane Corp. (Interstate) employed Robert Gilmer as a Financial Services Manager. As a condition of his employment, Gilmer had to register as a securities representative with the New York Stock Exchange (NYSE). As a part of this registration process, Gilmer signed an arbitration agreement covering any dispute, claim, or controversy between him and Interstate.

In 1987, when Gilmer was 62 years old, Interstate terminated his employment. Gilmer filed charges with the Equal Employment Opportunity Commission (EEOC) that Interstate's termination of him violated the Age Discrimination in Employment Act (ADEA). Gilmer also filed an ADEA suit against Interstate. Interstate defended this suit by seeking the trial court's dismissal of Gilmer's complaint on the grounds that this complaint must be arbitrated rather than litigated. The district court denied Interstate's motion, but the Fourth Circuit Court of Appeals reversed, thereby dismissing Gilmer's suit. The Supreme Court granted Gilmer's petition for a writ of certiorari.

WHITE, J.: The question presented in this case is whether a claim under the ADEA can be subjected to compulsory arbitration pursuant to an arbitration agreement in a securities registration application. The Court of Appeals held that it could, and we affirm.

The Federal Arbitration Act (FAA) was originally enacted in 1925 and then reenacted and codified in 1947 as Title 9 of the United States Code. Its purpose was to reverse the longstanding judicial hostility to arbitration agreements that had existed at English common law and had been adopted by American courts, and to place arbitration agreements upon the same footing as other contracts. . . . The FAA also provides for stays of proceedings in federal district courts when an issue in the proceeding is referable to arbitration, § 3, and for orders compelling arbitration when one party has failed, neglected, or refused to comply with an arbitration agreement, § 4. These provisions manifest a liberal federal policy favoring arbitration agreements. . . .

In arguing that arbitration is inconsistent with the ADEA, Gilmer . . . raises a host of challenges to the adequacy of arbitration procedures. . . .

Gilmer first speculates that arbitration panels will be biased. However, we decline to indulge the presumption that the parties and arbitral body conducting a proceeding will be unable or unwilling to retain competent, conscientious and impartial arbitrators. In any event, we note that the NYSE arbitration rules, which are applicable to the dispute in this case, provide protections against biased panels. The rules require, for example, that the parties be informed of the employment histories of the arbitrators, and that they be allowed to make further inquiries into the arbitrators' backgrounds. . . . Moreover, the arbitrators are required to disclose any circumstances which might preclude [them] from rendering an objective and impartial determination. The FAA also protects against bias, by providing that courts may overturn arbitration decisions "[w]here there was evident partiality or corruption in the arbitrators." There has been no showing in this case that those provisions are inadequate to guard against potential bias.

Gilmer also complains that the discovery allowed in arbitration is more limited than in the federal courts, which he contends will make it difficult to prove discrimination. It is unlikely, however, that age discrimination claims require more extensive discovery than other claims that we have found to be arbitrable, such as RICO and antitrust claims. Moreover, there has been no showing in this case that the NYSE discovery provisions, which allow for document production, information requests, depositions, and subpoenas, will prove insufficient to allow ADEA claimants such as Gilmer a fair opportunity to present their claims. Although those procedures might not be as extensive as in the federal courts, by agreeing to arbitrate, a party trades the procedures and opportunity for review of the courtroom for the simplicity, informality, and expedition of arbitration. . . .

A further alleged deficiency of arbitration is that arbitrators often will not issue written opinions, resulting, Gilmer contends, in a lack of public knowledge of employers' discriminatory policies, an inability to obtain effective appellate review, and a stifling of the development of the law. The NYSE rules, however, do require that all arbitration awards be in writing, and that the awards contain the names of the parties, a summary of the issues in controversy, and a description of the award issued. In addition, the award decisions are made available to the public. Furthermore, judicial decisions addressing ADEA claims will continue to be issued because it is unlikely that all or even most ADEA claimants will be subject to arbitration agreements. Finally, Gilmer's concerns apply equally to settlements of ADEA claims, which, as noted above, are clearly allowed.

It is also argued that arbitration procedures cannot adequately further the purpose of the ADEA because they do not provide for broad equitable relief and class actions. As the court below noted, however, arbitrators do not have the power to fashion equitable relief. Indeed, the NYSE rules applicable here do not restrict the types of relief an arbitrator may award. . . . It should be remembered that arbitration agreements will not preclude the EEOC from bringing actions seeking class-wide and equitable relief.

An additional reason advanced by Gilmer for refusing to enforce arbitration agreements relating to ADEA claims is his contention that there often will be unequal bargaining power between employers and employees. Mere inequality in bargaining power, however, is not a sufficient reason to hold that arbitration agreements are never enforceable in the employment context. . . . As discussed above, the FAA's purpose was to place arbitration agreements on the same footing as other contracts. Thus, arbitration agreements are enforceable "save upon such grounds as exist at law or in equity for the revocation of any contract." 9 U.S.C. § 2. Of course, courts should remain attuned to well-supported claims that the agreement to arbitrate resulted from the sort of fraud or overwhelming economic power that would provide grounds for the revocation of any contract. There is no indication in this case, however, that Gilmer, an experienced businessman, was coerced or defrauded into agreeing to the arbitration clause in his registration application. . . .

We conclude that Gilmer has not met his burden of showing that Congress, in enacting the ADEA, intended to preclude arbitration of claims under that Act. Accordingly, the judgment of the Court of Appeals is [*affirmed*].

Case Questions

1. What is the basis of Gilmer's complaint against Interstate/Johnson Lane Corp.?

2. Why does Interstate seek to have Gilmer's complaint dismissed by the trial judge?

3. How do the district court and court of appeals resolve this controversy?

4. Describe Gilmer's five arguments in support of litigating rather than arbitrating this controversy and the reasons why the Supreme Court rejects these arguments.

Impact on State Laws

The federal policy favoring arbitration frequently conflicts with state laws favoring litigation as the means to resolve a dispute. Sometimes a state law specifically provides that designated matters are not to be submitted to arbitration. Are these state laws constitutional when applied to businesses engaged in interstate commerce? The Commerce Clause and the Supremacy

Clause of the United States Constitution are often used to set aside such state laws that deny arbitration of certain disputes.

Sometimes the state law does not directly attack the policy of arbitration but only conflicts with it. Note that in the case which follows the statute involved was not intended as a direct attack on the federal policy favoring arbitration. Instead it simply intended to emphasize to the parties that their contract contained an arbitration clause.

DOCTOR'S ASSOCIATES, INC. V. CASAROTTO

116 S. Ct. 1652 (1996)

Doctor's Associates, Inc. (DAI) is the national franchisor of Subway sandwich shops. In April 1988, DAI entered a franchise agreement with Paul Casarotto, which permitted Casarotto to open a Subway shop in Great Falls, Montana. The franchise agreement stated, on page nine and in ordinary type: "Any controversy or claim arising out of or relating to this contract or the breach thereof shall be settled by Arbitration. . . ." In October 1992, Casarotto sued DAI and its agent, Nick Lombardi, in Montana state court, alleging state-law contract and tort claims relating to the franchise agreement. DAI demanded arbitration of those claims, and successfully moved in the Montana trial court to stay the lawsuit pending arbitration. The Montana Supreme Court reversed since this franchise agreement did not meet the standards of the Montana law, which states: "Notice that a contract is subject to arbitration . . . shall be typed in underlined capital letters on the first page of the contract; and unless such notice is displayed thereon, the contract may not be subject to arbitration." Notice of the arbitration clause in the franchise agreement did not appear on the first page of the contract. Nor was anything relating to the clause typed in underlined capital letters. Because the state's statutory notice requirement had not been met, the Montana Supreme Court declared the parties' dispute not subject to arbitration. The U.S. Supreme Court granted certiorari to address the question whether the Montana statute was preempted by the Federal Arbitration Act.

GINSBURG, J.: . . . The Federal Arbitration Act (FAA or Act) declares written provisions for arbitration "valid, irrevocable, and enforceable, save upon such grounds as exist at law or in equity for the revocation of any contract." 9 U.S.C. § 2. Montana law, however, declares an arbitration clause unenforceable unless "notice that [the] contract is subject to arbitration" is "typed in underlined capital letters on the first page of the contract." Mont. Code Ann. § 27-5-114(4) (1995). The question here presented is whether Montana's law is compatible with the federal Act. We hold that Montana's first-page notice requirement, which governs not "any contract," but specifically and solely contracts "subject to arbitration," conflicts with the FAA and is therefore displaced by the federal measure. . . .

Section 2 of the FAA provides that written arbitration agreements "shall be valid, irrevocable, and enforceable, save upon such grounds as exist at law or in equity for the revocation of any contract." 9 U.S.C. § 2. . . . [T]he text of § 2 declares that state law may be applied "if that law arose to govern issues concerning the validity, revocability, and enforceability of contracts generally." Thus, generally applicable contract defenses, such as fraud, duress or

unconscionability, may be applied to invalidate arbitration agreements without contravening § 2.

Courts may not, however, invalidate arbitration agreements under state laws applicable only to arbitration provisions. By enacting § 2, we have several times said, Congress precluded States from singling out arbitration provisions for suspect status, requiring instead that such provisions be placed upon the same footing as other contracts. Montana's § 27-5-114(4) directly conflicts with § 2 of the FAA because the State's law conditions the enforceability of arbitration agreements on compliance with a special notice requirement not applicable to contracts generally. The FAA thus displaces the Montana statute with respect to arbitration agreements covered by the Act. . . .

Applying § 27-5-114(4) here, in contrast, would not enforce the arbitration clause in the contract between DAI and Casarotto; instead, Montana's first-page notice requirement would invalidate the clause. The "goals and policies" of the FAA, this Court's precedent indicates, are antithetical to threshold limitations placed specifically and solely on arbitration provisions. . . . Section 27-5-114(4) of Montana's law places arbitration agreements in a class apart from "any contract," and singularly limits their validity. The State's prescription is thus inconsonant with, and is therefore preempted by, the federal law.

For the reasons stated, the judgment of the Supreme Court of Montana is reversed, and the case is remanded for further proceedings not inconsistent with this opinion. [*Reversed and remanded*].

Case Questions

1. What does the language of § 2 of the Federal Arbitration Act allow the states to do regarding the revocation of arbitration clauses?

2. What does the language of the Montana statute require the parties to do regarding the appearance of an arbitration clause in a contract?

3. What was the holding of the Montana trial court and Montana Supreme Court concerning the enforceability of the arbitration clause in the Subway franchise agreement?

4. Why does the U.S. Supreme Court conclude that the Montana statute cannot be enforced?

3. Statutorily Mandated Arbitration

Another reason why arbitration has become more widespread during the last few decades is that submission to arbitration may be required by state statute. A growing number of states have adopted statutes that require **mandatory arbitration** for certain types of disputes. Those whose disputes fall within the boundaries of the mandatory arbitration statute must submit the dispute to arbitration prior to being allowed to litigate. Based on studies showing that a dispute requiring three days for resolution before a twelve-person jury takes only two to four hours for resolution by an arbitrator, the mandatory arbitration statute is clearly a viable alternative for controlling court congestion.

The arbitrators in the mandatory arbitration process are retired judges and practicing lawyers, usually experienced trial attorneys. A list of eligible arbitrators is maintained by court officials in charge of the mandatory process. Although the parties may agree on using only one arbitrator, mandatory arbitration cases are usually presented to a panel of three. Arbitrators are paid a per-diem fee. The parties involved in the arbitration are responsible for paying these costs.

Types of Cases

Mandatory arbitration statutes cover only a few types of cases. A typical statute might apply the procedure to claims exclusively for money of a small amount, such as those for less than $15,000, not including interest and costs. Some statutes require arbitration of specific subject matter, like issues arising out of divorces. In addition, arbitration is required only in those cases in which a party has demanded a jury trial, as it can be assumed that a judge hearing a case is basically as efficient as an arbitrator.

Procedures

Mandatory arbitration, while requiring substantially less time than litigation, does not necessarily provide speedy justice. The usual procedure for a claim filed in court that is covered by the mandatory arbitration law is to place the claim in the arbitration track at time of filing. At this time the date and time of hearing is assigned, typically eight months from the date of filing.

Discovery procedures may be used prior to the hearing on arbitration. Since no discovery is permitted after the hearing without permission of the court, an early and thorough degree of preparation is necessary to achieve a full hearing on the merits of the controversy. This preparation also prevents the hearing from being used as an opportunity to discover the adversary's case en route to an eventual trial. Most discovery is by interrogatory rather than by deposition.

The arbitrators have the power to determine the admissibility of evidence and to decide the law and the facts of the case. Rulings on objections to evidence or on other issues that arise during the hearing are made by the arbitrators. States have different rules relating to the admissibility of evidence. In most states the established rules of evidence must be followed by the arbitrators. Several jurisdictions, however, do not require hearings to be conducted according to the established rules of evidence. New Jersey law, for example, provides: "The arbitrator shall admit all relevant evidence and shall not be bound by the rules of evidence." Other states leave to the discretion of the arbitrator the extent to which the rules of evidence apply.

4. Voluntary/Contract-Based Arbitration

While the statutes that mandate arbitration of certain types of disputes clearly have increased the use of this ADR method, the larger growth in the number of arbitration cases comes from disputing parties agreeing to arbitrate, not litigate. Recall that this agreement may be a part of a contract that anticipated possible disputes, or the agreement may be by disputing parties that wish to avoid all the expenses associated with the litigation process.

Voluntary arbitration has become such an important part of our commercial transactions that the next part of this chapter examines this type of ADR device in more detail and compares voluntary arbitration with mandatory arbitration.

Arbitration Procedures

The act of referring a matter to arbitration is called **submission.** Submission to arbitration often occurs when the disputing parties agree to use this form of ADR. Such an agreement by the parties is a submission to **voluntary arbitration.** Generally, an agreement to submit an issue to arbitration is irrevocable, and a party that thinks the process is not going well cannot withdraw from the arbitration and resort to litigation.

After the submission, a hearing is conducted by the arbitrator or arbitrators. Both parties are allowed to present evidence and to argue their own points of view. Then a decision, known as an **award,** is handed down. In most states the arbitrator's award must be in writing. The award is valid as long as it settles the entire controversy and states which party is to pay the other a sum of money.

These topics are discussed in the following sections:

- Submissions
- Arbitrators
- Awards
- Judicial Review

5. Submissions

Submission by contract occurs if the parties enter into an agreement to arbitrate an existing dispute. The arbitration agreement is the submission in this case. In addition, the parties may contractually agree to submit to arbitration all issues that may arise in the future. Submission in these circumstances occurs when a demand to arbitrate is served on the other party. This demand is either a notice that a matter is being referred to the arbitrator agreed upon by the parties or a demand that the matter be referred to arbitration.

Most state statutes authorizing voluntary arbitration require the agreement to arbitrate to be in writing. Since the goal of arbitration is to obtain a quick resolution of disputes, most statutes require submission within a stated time period, usually six months, after the dispute arises.

In the absence of a statute, the rights and duties of the parties to a submission are described and limited by their agreement. Parties that have contracted to arbitrate are not required to arbitrate any matters other than those they previously had agreed to arbitrate. Whether a particular dispute is arbitrable is a question for the court, although the parties may agree to arbitrate additional questions.

The issues submitted to arbitration, as framed in the submission, may be questions of fact, questions of law, or mixed questions of fact and law. They may include the interpretation of the arbitration agreement. Sometimes a dispute arises as to whether the parties have agreed to submit an issue to arbitration. In such a case, one party refuses to arbitrate and the other files suit to compel arbitration. The court hearing the case decides the issue of arbitrability but does not decide the basic issue between the parties. The case that follows explains the role of courts when the issue of arbitrability arises.

AT&T Tech., Inc. v. Communications Workers
106 S.Ct. 1415 (1986)

A collective bargaining agreement covering telephone equipment installation workers provided for arbitration of differences arising over interpretation of the agreement. Article 9 provided that the employer was free to exercise certain management functions, including the hiring, placement, and termination of employees. Such issues were excluded from the arbitration clause, but Article 20 prescribed the order in which employees would be laid off when lack of work necessitated itself.

The employer laid off seventy-nine installers, and the union filed a grievance claiming that there was no lack of work and, therefore, that the layoffs violated Article 20. The employer refused to submit the grievance to arbitration on the ground that under Article 9 the layoffs were not arbitrable. The union then sought to compel arbitration by filing suit in federal district court. That court found that the union's interpretation of Article 20 was at least "arguable" and that it was for the arbitrator, not the court, to decide whether that interpretation had merit; accordingly, it ordered the petitioner to arbitrate. The court of appeals affirmed. The employer's petition for a writ of certiorari was granted.

WHITE, J.: . . . The issue presented in this case is whether a court asked to order arbitration of a grievance filed under a collective-bargaining agreement must first determine that the parties intended to arbitrate the dispute, or whether that determination is properly left to the arbitrator.

The principles necessary to decide this case are not new. They were set out by this Court over 25 years ago in a series of cases known as the *Steelworkers Trilogy*. These precepts have served the industrial relations community well, and have led to continued reliance on arbitration, rather than strikes or lockouts, as the preferred method of resolving disputes arising during the term of a collective-bargaining agreement. We see no reason either to question their continuing validity, or to eviscerate their meaning by creating an exception to their general applicability.

The first principle gleaned from the *Trilogy* is that "arbitration is a matter of contract and a party cannot be required to submit to arbitration any dispute which he has not agreed so to submit." This axiom recognizes the fact that arbitrators derive their authority to resolve disputes only because the parties have agreed in advance to submit such grievances to arbitration.

The second rule, which follows inexorably from the first, is that the question of arbitrability—whether a collective-bargaining agreement creates a duty for the parties to arbitrate the particular grievance—is undeniably an issue for judicial determination. Unless the parties clearly and unmistakably provide otherwise, the question of whether the parties agreed to arbitrate is to be decided by the court, not the arbitrator. . . .

The third principle derived from our prior cases is that, in deciding whether the parties have agreed to submit a particular grievance to arbitration, a court is not to rule on the potential merits of the underlying claims. Whether "arguable" or not, indeed even if it appears to the court to be frivolous, the union's claim that the employer has violated the collective-bargaining agreement is to be decided, not by the court asked to order arbitration, but as the parties have agreed, by the arbitrator. The courts, therefore, have no business weighing the merits of the grievance, considering whether there is equity in a particular claim, or determining whether there is particular language in the written instrument which will support the claim. The agreement is to submit all grievances to arbitration, not merely those which the court will deem meritorious.

Finally, where it has been established that where the contract contains an arbitration clause, there is a presumption of arbitrability in the sense that "[a]n order to arbitrate the particular grievance should not be denied unless it may be said with positive assurance that the arbitration clause is not susceptible of an interpretation that covers the asserted dispute. Doubts should be resolved in favor of coverage." Such a presumption is particularly applicable where the clause is as broad as the one employed in this case, which provides for arbitration of "any differences arising with respect to the interpretation of this contract or the performance of any obligation hereunder. . . ."

This presumption of arbitrability for labor disputes recognizes the greater institutional competence of arbitrators in interpreting collective bargaining agreements, furthers the national labor policy of peaceful resolution of labor and thus best accords with the parties' presumed objectives in pursuing collective bargaining. The willingness of parties to enter into agreements that provide for arbitration of specified disputes would be "drastically reduced," however, if a labor arbitrator had the "power to determine his own jurisdiction. . . ." Were this the applicable rule, an arbitrator would not be constrained to resolve only those disputes that the parties have agreed in advance to settle by arbitration, but instead, would be empowered "to impose obligations outside the contract limited only by his understanding and conscience." This result undercuts the longstanding federal policy of promoting industrial harmony through the use of collective-bargaining agreements, and is antithetical to the function of a collective-bargaining agreement as setting out the rights and duties of the parties.

With these principles in mind, it is evident that the Seventh Circuit erred in ordering the parties to arbitrate the arbitrability question. It is the court's duty to interpret the agreement and to determine whether the parties intended to arbitrate grievances concerning layoffs predicated on a "lack of work" determination by the Company. If the court determines that the agreement so provides, then it is for the arbitrator to determine the relative merits of the parties' substantive interpretations of the agreement. It was for the court, not the arbitrator, to decide in the first instance whether the dispute was to be resolved through arbitration. . . .

The issue in the case is whether, because of express exclusion or other forceful evidence, the dispute over the interpretation of Article 20 of the contract, the layoff provision, is not subject to the arbitration clause. That issue should have been decided by the District Court and reviewed by the Court of Appeals; it should not have been referred to the arbitrator.

The judgment of the Court of Appeals is vacated, and the case is remanded for proceedings in conformity with this opinion. [*It is so ordered*].

Case Questions

1. How do the provisions of Articles 9 and 20 in the collective bargaining agreement create a conflict between the employer and the union?

2. What three principles (or rules) does the Supreme Court discuss concerning the issue of when a dispute is arbitrable?

3. Why does the Supreme Court conclude that the trial court and the circuit court of appeals were in error?

6. Arbitrators

Arbitrators generally are chosen by the disputing parties. A provision in the agreement to arbitrate or in the statute that requires the arbitration describes how the arbitrator is selected. Of concern in the selection process are the expertise of the arbitrator and the number of arbitrators to be chosen.

Expertise

One reason arbitration is frequently preferable to litigation is that the dispute can be submitted to an expert for decision. Appraisers can be used to decide disputes about the value of real estate, medical doctors can be used to decide health care disputes, and academicians can be used to decide issues within their area of expertise.

This use of experts is especially important in labor-management relations. Arbitration is the technique used in collective bargaining contracts to settle grievances of employees against their employers. Arbitration is able to resolve disputes arising out of labor contracts without resorting to judicial intervention. It is quick and efficient and minimizes disruption in the workplace. Labor arbitration has attracted a large number of experts—both lawyers and academicians.

Arbitration provides for decision making by experts with experience in the particular industry and with knowledge of the customs and practices of the particular work site. Parties often choose arbitrators based on their knowledge of the "common law of the shop." They expect the arbitrator to look beyond strictly legal criteria to other factors that bear on the proper resolution of a dispute. These factors may include the effect upon productivity of a particular result, its consequences to the morale of the shop, and whether tensions will be heightened or diminished. The ablest judge cannot be expected to bring the same experience and competence to bear upon the determination of a grievance, because he or she cannot be similarly informed.

Number Chosen

Another issue relates to the number of arbitrators to hear a dispute. It is common to use one arbitrator who is considered objective and impartial. Any person the disputing parties agree upon can be an arbitrator. There are no licensing requirements an arbitrator must satisfy. However, an arbitrator often is chosen from a list of qualified arbitrators provided by the American Arbitration Association. The disputing parties are not limited to the list unless they have agreed to make their selection from this list.

It is also common to have a panel of three arbitrators. In such cases, each party selects an arbitrator and the two so selected choose a third. It is not surprising that when this procedure is used, allegations of bias are often made by the losing party. Courts generally do not allow such allegations to form a basis for overturning a panel's award unless there is evidence of overt corruption or misconduct in the arbitration proceedings. Since such evidence usually is difficult to obtain, allegations of bias normally do not impact the results of arbitration.

7. Awards

Generally the award need not, and does not, set forth findings of fact, conclusions of law, or the reasons for it. However, a disclosure of findings and the reasons must be given if the applicable statute, arbitration agreement, or submission so requires. When the arbitrator does provide the basis for decision in the form of an opinion or letter, that document becomes a part of the award.

Because the parties themselves, by virtue of the submission, frame the issues to be resolved and define the scope of the arbitrator's powers, the parties are generally bound by the resulting award. A court will make every reasonable presumption in favor of the arbitration award and the arbitrator's acts and proceedings. The following case illustrates that the U.S. Supreme Court's ruling will favor a broad scope of the arbitrators' authority. Restrictions on this authority will be allowed only when the disputing parties clearly state such limits.

MASTROBUONO V. SHEARSON LEHMAN HUTTON, INC.
115 S.Ct. 1212 (1995)

STEVENS, J. . . . In 1985 petitioners, Antonio Mastrobuono, then an assistant professor of medieval literature, and his wife Diana Mastrobuono, an artist, opened a securities trading account with respondent Shearson Lehman Hutton, Inc. (Shearson), by executing Shearson's standard-form Client's Agreement. Respondent Nick DiMinico, a vice president of Shearson, managed the Mastrobuonos' account until they closed it in 1987. In 1989, petitioners filed this action in the United States District Court for the Northern District of Illinois, alleging that respondents had mishandled their account and claiming damages on a variety of state and federal law theories.

Paragraph 13 of the parties' agreement contains an arbitration provision and a choice-of-law provision. Relying on the arbitration provision and on §§ 3 and 4 of the Federal Arbitration Act (FAA), 9 U.S.C. §§ 3, 4, respondents filed a motion to stay the court proceedings and to compel arbitration pursuant to the rules of the National Association of Securities Dealers. The District Court granted that motion, and a panel of three arbitrators was convened. After conducting hearings in Illinois, the panel ruled in favor of petitioners.

In the arbitration proceedings, respondents argued that the arbitrators had no authority to award punitive damages. Nevertheless, the panel's award included punitive damages of $400,000, in addition to compensatory damages of $159,327. Respondents paid the compensatory portion of the award but filed a motion in the District Court to vacate the award of punitive damages. The District Court granted the motion, and the Court of Appeals for the Seventh Circuit

affirmed. Both courts relied on the choice-of-law provision in Paragraph 13 of the parties' agreement, which specifies that the contract shall be governed by New York law. Because the New York Court of Appeals has decided that in New York the power to award punitive damages is limited to judicial tribunals and may not be exercised by arbitrators, *Garrity v. Lyle Stuart, Inc.*, 353 N.E.2d 793 (1976), the District Court and the Seventh Circuit held that the panel of arbitrators had no power to award punitive damages in this case.

We granted certiorari because the Courts of Appeals have expressed differing views on whether a contractual choice-of-law provision may preclude an arbitral award of punitive damages that otherwise would be proper. We now reverse.

Earlier this Term, we upheld the enforceability of a predispute arbitration agreement governed by Alabama law, even though an Alabama statute provides that arbitration agreements are unenforceable. *Allied-Bruce Terminix Cos. v. Dobson*, 115 S. Ct. 834 (1995). Writing for the Court, Justice Breyer observed that Congress passed the FAA "to overcome courts' refusals to enforce agreements to arbitrate." After determining that the FAA applied to the parties' arbitration agreement, we readily concluded that the federal statute pre-empted Alabama's statutory prohibition.

Petitioners seek a similar disposition of the case before us today. Here, the Seventh Circuit interpreted the contract to incorporate New York law, including the *Garrity* rule that arbitrators may not award punitive damages. Petitioners ask us to hold that the FAA pre-empts New York's prohibition against arbitral awards of punitive damages because this state law is a vestige of the "ancient" judicial hostility to arbitration.

Respondents answer that the choice-of-law provision in their contract evidences the parties' express agreement that punitive damages should not be awarded in the arbitration of any dispute arising under their contract. . . . Regardless of whether the FAA pre-empts the *Garrity* decision in contracts not expressly incorporating New York law, respondents argue that the parties may themselves agree to be bound by *Garrity,* just as they may agree to forgo arbitration altogether. In other words, if the contract says "no punitive damages," that is the end of the matter, for courts are bound to interpret contracts in accordance with the expressed intentions of the parties—even if the effect of those intentions is to limit arbitration. . . .

[R]espondents thus argue that the parties to a contract may lawfully agree to limit the issues to be arbitrated by waiving any claim for punitive damages. On the other hand, we think our decisions . . . make clear that if contracting parties agree to include claims for punitive damages within the issues to be arbitrated, the FAA ensures that their agreement will be enforced according to its terms even if a rule of state law would otherwise exclude such claims from arbitration. Thus, the case before us comes down to what the contract has to say about the arbitrability of petitioners' claim for punitive damages.

Shearson's standard-form "Client Agreement," which petitioners executed, contains 18 paragraphs. The two relevant provisions of the agreement are found in Paragraph 13. The first sentence of that paragraph provides, in part, that the entire agreement "shall be governed by the laws of the State of New York." The second sentence provides that "any controversy" arising out of the transactions between the parties "shall be settled by arbitration" in accordance with the rules of the National Association of Securities Dealers (NASD), or the Boards of Directors of the New York Stock Exchange and/or the American Stock Exchange. The agreement contains no express reference to claims for punitive damages. To ascertain whether Paragraph 13 expresses an intent to include or exclude such claims, we first address the impact of each of the two relevant provisions, considered separately. We then move on to the more important inquiry: the meaning of the two provisions taken together.

The choice-of-law provision, when viewed in isolation, may reasonably be read as merely a substitute for the conflict-of-laws analysis that otherwise would determine what law to apply to disputes arising out of the contractual relationship. Thus, if a similar contract, without a choice-of-law provision, had been signed in New York and was to be performed in New York, presumably "the laws of the State of New York" would apply, even though the contract did not expressly so state. In such event, there would be nothing in the contract that could possibly constitute evidence of an intent to exclude punitive damages claims. Accordingly, punitive damages would be allowed because, in the absence of contractual intent to the contrary, the FAA would pre-empt the *Garrity* rule.

Even if the reference to "the laws of the State of New York" is more than a substitute for ordinary conflict-of-laws analysis and, as respondents urge, includes the caveat, "detached from otherwise-applicable federal law," the provision might not preclude the award of punitive damages because New York allows its courts, though not its arbitrators, to enter such awards. In other words, the provision might include only New York's substantive rights and obligations, and not the State's allocation of power between alternative tribunals. Respondents' argument is persuasive only if "New York law" means "New York decisional law, including that State's allocation of power between courts and arbitrators, notwithstanding otherwise-applicable federal law." But, as we have demonstrated, the provision need not be read so broadly. It is not, in itself, an unequivocal exclusion of punitive damages claims.

The arbitration provision (the second sentence of Paragraph 13) does not improve respondents' argument. On the contrary, when read separately this clause strongly implies that an arbitral award of punitive damages is appropriate. It explicitly authorizes arbitration in accordance with NASD rules; the panel of arbitrators in fact proceeded under that set of rules. The NASD's Code of Arbitration Procedure indicates that arbitrators may award "damages and other relief." NASD Code of Arbitration Procedure P3741(e) (1993). While not a clear authorization of punitive damages, this provision appears broad enough at least to contemplate such a remedy. Moreover, as the Seventh Circuit noted, a manual provided to NASD arbitrators contains this provision:

> "B. Punitive Damages
> "The issue of punitive damages may arise with great frequency in arbitrations. Parties to arbitration are informed that arbitrators can consider punitive damages as a remedy."

Thus, the text of the arbitration clause itself surely does not support—indeed, it contradicts—the conclusion that the parties agreed to foreclose claims for punitive damages.

Although neither the choice-of-law clause nor the arbitration clause, separately considered, expresses an intent to preclude an award of punitive damages, respondents argue that a fair reading of the entire Paragraph 13 leads to that conclusion. On this theory, even if "New York law" is ambiguous, and even if "arbitration in accordance with NASD rules" indicates that punitive damages are permissible, the juxtaposition of the two clauses suggests that the contract incorporates "New York law relating to arbitration." We disagree. At most, the choice-of-law clause introduces an ambiguity into an arbitration agreement that would otherwise allow punitive damages awards. . . . [W]hen a court interprets such provisions in an agreement covered by the FAA, due regard must be given to the federal policy favoring arbitration, and ambiguities as to the scope of the arbitration clause itself resolved in favor of arbitration.

Moreover, respondents cannot overcome the common-law rule of contract interpretation that a court should construe ambiguous language against the interest of the party that drafted it. Respondents drafted an ambiguous document, and they cannot now claim the benefit of the doubt. The reason for this rule is to protect the party who did not choose the language from an unintended or unfair result. That rationale is well-suited to the facts of this case. As a practical matter, it seems unlikely that petitioners were actually aware of New York's bifurcated approach to punitive damages, or that they had any idea that by signing a standard-form agreement to arbitrate disputes they might be giving up an important substantive right. In the face of such doubt, we are unwilling to impute this intent to petitioners.

Finally the respondents' reading of the two clauses violates another cardinal principle of contract construction: that a document should be read to give effect to all its provisions and to render them consistent with each other. We think the best way to harmonize the choice-of-law provision with the arbitration provision is to read "the laws of the State of New York" to encompass substantive principles that New York courts would apply, but not to include special rules limiting the authority of arbitrators. Thus, the choice-of-law provision covers the rights and duties of the parties, while the arbitration clause covers arbitration; neither sentence intrudes upon the other. In contrast, respondents' reading sets up the two clauses in conflict with one another: one foreclosing punitive damages, the other allowing them. This interpretation is untenable.

We hold that the Court of Appeals misinterpreted the parties' agreement. The arbitral award should have been enforced as within the scope of the contract. The judgment of the Court of Appeals is, therefore, [*reversed*].

Case Questions

1. What is the basis of the Mastrobuonos' lawsuit against Shearson Lehman Hutton, Inc.?

2. Why is this case submitted to arbitration rather than being litigated in the courts?

3. What result of the arbitrators is being contested by Shearson Lehman Hutton?

4. How do the District Court and Court of Appeals rule regarding the arbitrators' authority?

5. How does the U.S. Supreme Court interpret the conflict-of-law principles and the arbitration clause?

An arbitrator's award is final on all issues submitted, and it will be enforced by the courts as if it were a judgment of the court. As will be discussed in detail in the next section, awards are not subject to judicial review on the merits of the decision. Only when fraud or other clearly inappropriate action by the arbitrator can be shown is a court willing to reverse the award granted in a voluntary arbitration proceeding.

After the award is made by the arbitrator, it is usually filed with the clerk of an appropriate court. If no objections are filed within a statutory period, it becomes final and enforceable, like a judgment.

A primary distinction between mandatory and voluntary arbitration is the ability of the dissatisfied party to challenge the award. Following the mandatory arbitration, any party who was present at the arbitration hearing, either in person or by counsel, may file a written notice of rejection of the award and request to proceed to trial. The filing of a single rejection is sufficient to enable all parties to proceed to trial on all issues of the case without filing separate rejections.

8. *Judicial Review*

The arbitration process is less time consuming and less costly than litigation only if the parties are limited in seeking judicial review of the arbitrators' awards. From this perspective, voluntary arbitration is a more effective alternative to litigation than mandatory arbitration. The following subsections discuss the extent of judicial review of awards depending on the type of arbitration.

Review of Voluntary/Contract-based Arbitration Awards

Generally, the award resulting from the voluntary arbitration procedure is judged as final. The arbitrator's findings on questions of both fact and law are conclusive. The judicial review of an arbitrator's award is quite restricted and is more limited than the appellate review of a trial court's decision.

Arbitration clauses are liberally interpreted when the issue contested is the scope of the clause. If the scope of an arbitration clause is debatable or reasonably in doubt, the clause is construed in favor of arbitration.

The fact that the arbitrator made erroneous rulings during the hearing, or reached erroneous findings of fact from the evidence, is no ground for setting aside the award because the parties have agreed that he or she should be the judge of the facts. An erroneous view of the law no matter how egregious is binding because the parties have agreed to accept the arbitrator's view of the law. Error of law renders the award void only when it would require the parties to commit a crime or otherwise to violate a positive mandate of the law. Courts do not interfere with an award by examining the merits of the controversy, the sufficiency of the evidence supporting the award, or the reasoning supporting the decision. Were it otherwise, arbitration would fail in its chief purpose: to preclude the need for litigation. Instead of being a substitute for litigation, arbitration would merely be the beginning of litigation. Broad judicial review on the merits would render arbitration wasteful and superfluous.

Judicial review can correct fraudulent or arbitrary actions by an arbitrator. Further, courts of review are sometimes called upon to set aside an award when the decision is allegedly against public policy. In such cases, the reviewing court must establish that an arbitration award is contrary to the public policy which arises from laws and legal precedents. A reviewing court cannot reject an award simply because that court bases public policy on general considerations of presumed public interests. In essence, the scope of review by courts of an arbitrator's award in a voluntary/contract-based arbitration is extremely limited.

Review of Statutorily Mandated Arbitration

While a party may voluntarily consent to almost any restriction upon or deprivation of a right, a similar restriction or deprivation, if compelled by government, must be in accord with procedural and substantive due process of law. Therefore, a higher level of judicial review of an arbitration award is warranted where the arbitration is statutorily mandated.

Laws providing for mandatory arbitration are subject to numerous constitutional challenges. Many courts have generally held that mandatory arbitration statutes that effectively close the courts to the litigants by compelling them to resort to arbitrators for a final and binding determination are void as against public policy and are unconstitutional in that they:

1. Deprive one of property and liberty of contract without due process of law
2. Violate the litigant's Seventh Amendment right to a jury trial and/or the state's constitutional access to courts' provisions
3. Result in the unconstitutional delegation of legislative or judicial power in violation of state constitutional separation-of-powers provisions

Mandatory arbitration may be constitutional, however, if fair procedures are provided by the legislature and ultimate judicial review is available. Courts throughout the United States have uniformly upheld mandatory arbitration statutory schemes as against the constitutional challenges previously mentioned where a dissatisfied party can reject the arbitrator's award and seek a **de novo judicial review** of that award. De novo review means that the court tries the issues anew or for a second time.

In mandatory proceedings, a record of proceedings is required. Also, findings of fact and conclusions of law are essential if there is to be enough judicial review to satisfy due process. Judicial review of mandatory arbitration requires a de novo review of the interpretation and application of the law by the arbitrators.

The right to reject the award and to proceed to trial is the sole remedy of a party dissatisfied with the award. In a sense, the award is an intermediate step in resolving the dispute if the trial itself is desired. The right to reject the award exists without regard to the basis for the rejection. Many jurisdictions authorize fee and cost sanctions to be imposed on parties who fail to improve their positions at the trial after hearing. It is hoped that the quality of the arbitrators, the integrity of the hearings, and the fairness of the awards will keep the number of rejections to a minimum.

The failure of a party to be present, either in person or by counsel, at an arbitration hearing constitutes a waiver of the right to reject the award and seek de novo judicial review. In essence, a party's lack of participation operates as a consent to the entry by the court of a judgment on the award. Since the procedure of mandatory court-annexed arbitration is an integral part of the judicial process of dispute resolution, its process must be utilized either to finally resolve the dispute or as the obligatory step prior to resolution by trial. To allow any party to ignore the arbitration hearing would permit a mockery of this deliberate attempt to achieve an expeditious and less costly resolution of private controversies.

Review under the Federal Arbitration Act

If the arbitration is conducted pursuant to state statute, that statute must be consulted to determine what, if any, grounds are available to challenge an award in court. In cases that involve interstate commerce issues, the provisions of the Federal Arbitration Act control.

Section 10 of the Federal Arbitration Act provides that an arbitration award may be vacated or set aside on any one of four grounds:

(a) Where the award was procured by corruption, fraud, or other undue means

(b) Where the arbitrators were obviously partial or corrupt

(c) Where the arbitrators were guilty of misconduct in refusing to postpone the hearing, upon sufficient cause shown or in refusing to hear evidence pertinent and material to the controversy or of any other misbehavior by which the rights of any party have been prejudiced

(d) Where the arbitrators exceeded their powers or so imperfectly executed them that a mutual, final, and definite award upon the subject matter submitted was not made

As set forth in subsection (a), the Federal Arbitration Act provides that an award can be vacated if it can be proved that it was procured by "corruption, fraud, or other undue means." Undue means is defined as something akin to fraud and corruption. It goes beyond the merely inappropriate or inadequate nature of the evidence and refers to some aspect of the arbitrator's decision or decision making process obtained in some manner that was unfair and beyond the normal process contemplated by the arbitration act. The courts tend to interpret "undue means" in conjunction with the terms "corruption" and "fraud" which precede it, and thus, "undue means" requires some type of bad faith in the procurement of the award.

When the disputing parties each choose an arbitrator and these arbitrators choose a third to make up a three-person panel, the disputing parties may be inclined to charge that the arbitrator chosen by the parties is partial or corrupt. Under subsection (b), the use of "partial or corrupt" in the FAA is interpreted to mean that an arbitrator lacks the ability to consider evidence and to reach a fair conclusion.

Subsection (c) covers arbitral misconduct. The concept of arbitral "misconduct" does not lend itself to a precise definition. Among the actions that have been found to constitute such misconduct on the part of an arbitrator as would warrant vacating an arbitration award are the following:

1. Participation in communications with a party or a witness without the knowledge or consent of the other party
2. Receipt of evidence as to a material fact without notice to a party
3. Holding hearings or conducting deliberations in the absence of a member of an arbitration panel or rendering an award without consulting a panel member
4. Undertaking an independent investigation into a material matter after the close of hearings and without notice to the parties
5. Accepting gifts or other hospitality from a party during the proceedings

An award may likewise be set aside on the basis of procedural error by an arbitration panel if, for instance, the panel arbitrarily denies a reasonable request for postponement of a hearing or commits an egregious evidentiary error, such as refusing to hear material evidence or precluding a party's efforts to develop a full record.

Finally, subsection (d), involving the question of whether the arbitrators exceeded their power, relates to the arbitrability of the underlying dispute. An arbitrator exceeds his or her powers and authority when he or she attempts to resolve an issue that is not arbitrable because it is outside the scope of the arbitration agreement. Conversely, if the issues presented to the arbitrators are within the scope of the arbitration agreement, subsection (d) does not require the court to "review the merits of every construction of the contract."

Concept Summary: Voluntary Versus Mandatory Arbitration

	Voluntary	*Mandatory Arbitration*
Submission	Based on parties' agreement after dispute arises or on contract clause before dispute arises.	Required by state statute.
Procedures	Since process is not tied to a court, it is quick; informal; often with no discovery; and not bound by rules of evidence.	The procedure is associated with a court's supervision; discovery usually is done, and many states require arbitrators to follow the formal rules of evidence.
Review of award	The award is final with no judicial review, unless a party can prove that the arbitrator engaged in fraudulent, arbitrary, or other inappropriate actions.	The court will conduct a de novo hearing as if the arbitration process had not occurred.

Mock and Minitrials

Your study of the preceding material on arbitration hopefully leaves you with the impression that, while arbitration is more efficient (less time consuming and expensive) than litigation, arbitration often is not a simple process. To avoid even the costs of arbitration, some disputes can be resolved through other ADR techniques that utilize aspects of the litigation process. Two such techniques are discussed now.

9. Mock Trials

Recognizing that a jury's function is to determine the facts, attorneys are using a technique called a **mock trial,** in some very significant cases. The attorneys assemble a group of citizens and present their evidence. The jury then deliberates and makes findings. This dress rehearsal gives attorneys insight into jury reaction to the evidence and points up weaknesses in the case. Sometimes issues are tested without introducing evidence. Lawyers argue the case on the basis of assumed facts to the mock jury for a few hours, and this jury returns a verdict.

The verdicts often cause plaintiffs to take a more realistic view of the damages to which they think they are entitled. This "reality test" helps disputing parties to engage in more meaningful negotiations. Through such negotiations, these parties often settle their dispute without having to go through the formal process of either a trial or an arbitration.

10. Minitrials

A **minitrial** is designed to achieve substantial savings in litigation costs and in the time that senior executives have to spend in resolving disputes.

The minitrial is designed to turn a lawsuit back into a business problem. In a minitrial, lawyers focus on the central issues. They present an abbreviated case not to a judge or jury, but to top executives of the disputing companies. Following these presentations, the executives meet without their lawyers to negotiate and to seek a settlement. After hearing from both sides, these executives are able to appreciate the merits and risks of their case. It is this balanced perspective that leads to speedy, economical settlements.

The results from minitrials are often quick. The process is confidential, and the results are invariably better than the results of litigation. Since executives know their business objectives and operations, they can consider options that their lawyers—and certainly the judges and juries—cannot. A minitrial can preserve business relationships that are usually destroyed in the acrimony of litigation.

An actual minitrial between two companies illustrates the value of the process. Their dispute centered on the interpretation of a contract that was twenty years old. Instead of filing a lawsuit, conducting discovery that would include the production of countless documents, the legal counsels conducted a minitrial. Executives met in a Dallas hotel and heard three hours of presentations by both lawyers. Technical experts for each side also participated. Following this presentation, the executives met alone to discuss the dispute. Before dinner, they reached an agreement to settle their dispute.

The attorneys pinpointed the essentials of the dispute, enabling the executives to focus on the basic business interests involved. The executives had a clear understanding of the strengths and weaknesses of their case, and their expertise was productive in reaching a solution. Since the executives had the power to settle, they were able to reach a firm agreement in one day.

Minitrials are successful. They avoid lengthy trials, reduce legal costs, save management time for productive pursuits, and achieve satisfactory settlements. An American Bar Association survey of minitrials showed an 85 percent success rate. Speed, economy, and flexibility were cited as benefits. Even when the negotiators failed to settle immediately, the minitrial process invariably led to a settlement. Today, corporate policy of many large corporations requires the use of ADRs in all major disputes with other corporations.

Mediation

Mediation is the process by which a third person, called a **mediator,** attempts to assist disputing parties in resolving their differences. A mediator cannot impose a binding solution on the parties. However, as an unbiased and disinterested third party, a mediator is often able to help the parties bring about a compromise of a dispute and thus avoid litigation of it.

Like arbitration, the process of mediation may be utilized by the disputing parties as the result of their agreement to mediate. This agreement may have been made as a part of a contract before a dispute arose. For example, the mediation agreement could be made a part of the culture of the organization in the Business Decision at the beginning of this chapter. On the other hand, parties to a dispute may agree that mediation should be attempted as an alternative to litigating their controversy.

Also like arbitration, the mediation process may be required by the trial judge before a complaint can be litigated formally. There is a growing movement to this court-annexed mediation as one means of controlling the heavy case load faced by courts. Rules related to court-annexed mediation are local in nature; thus there are wide variations as to the type of cases that courts require to be mediated. Generally, cases involving domestic-relations issues (such as divorce and child custody) and cases involving a dollar amount in dispute below a stated threshold level are examples of those that are subject to court-annexed mediation.

Unlike arbitration, there is no need for judicial review of the mediation process. If mediation is successful in helping the parties resolve their dispute, it is the parties' agreement—not one imposed on them. If parties agree to settle a controversy, they do not have any reason to complain. The settlement was their mutual choice. If mediation is not successful in helping the parties find a solution, they may continue to litigate or utilize another ADR technique.

In the next three sections, you will review the following topics related to mediation:

- Advantages and disadvantages
- Procedures
- Combination with ADR systems

11. Advantages/Disadvantages

The basic advantage of mediation over litigation and arbitration is that the disputing parties retain full control over the resolution (or lack thereof) of their controversy. Through retaining this control, the parties can decide how much time and effort to put into the mediation process. The fact that mediation is party driven and does not involve even an informal presentation of evidence makes the process much more efficient than other ADR systems. If parties are making progress toward a settlement, the mediation can be continued and perhaps expanded to involve a possible agreement on other potential disputes. When the mediation is not aiding the parties, any of them can stop the process by simply stating that they will not participate further.

This same aspect of the parties controlling the mediation process may be viewed as a disadvantage rather than as an advantage when compared to other ADR systems. Even in the court-annexed mediations, a party usually satisfies the court's order to mediate by simply showing up. Generally, there is no enforcement mechanism that ensures the parties will mediate in good faith.

An additional disadvantage relates to the selection of the neutral mediator. The parties must be able to agree at least on who will be their mediator. Because there is almost always only one mediator, the parties cannot avoid this basic agreement by selecting a member to a panel of mediators. If the disputing parties cannot "get together" to select a mediator, the mediation process cannot begin.

Finally, the requirements for training as a mediator are not universally defined. Furthermore, licensing requirements are nonexistent at present. Therefore, anyone can serve as a mediator. The disputing party should be aware of the experience (or lack thereof) of the party chosen as their mediator. The Federal Mediation and Conciliation Service, the American Arbitration Association, and other similar organizations are a valuable source of credible mediators.

12. Procedures

Despite the fact that mediations are informal and controlled by the disputing parties, the odds for a successful mediation occurring increase greatly when the mediator follows some basic procedures. First, the mediator usually makes an opening statement. During this statement, mediators should explain the procedures they are asking the parties to agree to. In essence, the mediator explains much of what you are reading in this section. Also, any "rules"—such as the common courtesy of not interrupting the party speaking—are specified.

Second, all the parties are allowed to make a statement about their views of this dispute. These statements are made in the presence of each other and the mediator. A party's attorney may be the spokesperson; however, it often is more enlightening when the parties speak for themselves.

Third, the mediator may decide that the process will be more productive if the parties and their attorneys meet with the mediator outside the presence of the other disputant. This private meeting is called a **caucus.** After each side has caucused with the mediator, the mediator may call the parties back together for continued discussions, or the mediator may begin to act as a shuttle diplomat, moving back and forth between the parties who are in separate rooms. Especially during these caucuses, the mediator must win the trust and confidence of each party to the dispute.

Through the good judgment and experience of the mediator, the differences between the parties hopefully will be resolved and a common agreement can be produced. The final step to a successful mediation is the writing down of the basic agreement and the signing of it by the parties.

13. Combination with ADR Systems

The benefit of flexibility related to mediation allows parties to utilize this process in conjunction with other dispute resolution systems. For example, in the middle of heated litigation, parties can agree to mediate just one issue. The resolution of one issue may help the litigation of the remaining issues proceed in a more efficient manner.

One of the more popular variations has given rise to what some people are calling an additional ADR technique. This variation involves the mediation of a dispute. The parties resolve all the matters of contention that they can and they agree to arbitrate the unresolved matters. This variation has become known as **Med-Arb.** The opportunities to use mediation in beneficial ways are limited only by the creativity of the parties involved.

Some laws encourage the parties to be creative in utilizing ADR systems. For example, the Magnuson-Moss Warranty Act provides that if a business adopts an informal dispute resolution system to handle complaints about its product warranties, then a customer cannot sue the manufacturer or seller for breach of warranty without first going through the informal procedures. This law does not deny consumers the right to sue, nor does it compel a compromise solution. It simply allows a manufacturer to require mediation, for instance, before the complaining consumer can litigate.

Negotiated Settlements

It is universally acknowledged that both parties to litigation are losers. The winning party in a lawsuit is a loser to the extent of the attorney's fees—which are often substantial. The fact that the loser usually also has to pay court costs is an added incentive to settlement without litigation.

There are also personal reasons to settle controversies. The desire to compromise is instinctive for many Americans. Most of us dislike trouble, and many fear going to court. The opinions of others are often a motivating force in encouraging amicable settlements.

Businesses tend to settle disputes with customers for two additional reasons. First, it is simply not good business from a goodwill and public relations standpoint to sue a customer. Second, juries are frequently sympathetic to individuals who have suits against large corporations or defendants who are covered by insurance. Close questions of liability, as well as size of the verdict, are more often than not resolved against business concerns because of their presumed ability to pay. As a result, businesses settle many disputes even though they might possibly prevail in litigation.

The process of negotiating has become a major focus of study. We now know that there are certain elements that should be the focus of parties negotiating a possible settlement. To help illustrate two very different styles of negotiation, consider the factual situation in the following box and the sections that follow.

Factual Situation Giving Rise to a Dispute

Mickey Shears and Naomi Hamilton operate a business that manufactures personal computers. The business name is M&N PC's, Inc. The principal market for M&N computers has been buyers for home use. M&N's reputation is based on assembling a high-quality computer for a relatively low price. M&N's biggest problem has been maintaining a large enough, qualified sales force while keeping the price for its computer below the market average.

William Dalton operates a nationwide chain of discount department stores. This chain is known as Bill's Discount Centers. One year ago, Bill's Discount Centers agreed to buy from M&N a minimum of 250 computers (with specifications stated in the contract) per month for six months. The agreed-upon price of each computer was $1,250.

The relationship between M&N and Bill's worked very well. In the fifth month of this initial contract, Bill's agreed to increase its minimum purchase per

concluded

month to 750 computers, and Bill's committed to this monthly purchase for a twelve-month period to begin after the sixth month of the original contract. The price per computer was to remain at $1,250.

M&N was delighted with the arrangement since it allowed M&N to concentrate on increasing its production capacity while reducing the costs of maintaining a large, active sales force.

Unlike the success of its initial relationship with M&N, Bill's began receiving complaints from its customers about the lack of quality of M&N's computers. These complaints were traced by Bill's customer service representatives to the newer computers that M&N was assembling under its expanded production program. Despite its knowledge of these quality-related problems, Bill's never informed M&N of its findings.

The complaints continued to become more numerous. During the fifth month of the twelve-month period, Bill's purchased only 350 computers from M&N. When M&N sent an invoice for the 750 computers specified as the monthly minimum, Bill's refused to pay for any computers over the 350 actually purchased. In the second week of the sixth month, Bill's sent M&N written notice that it was canceling the remainder of the sales contract due to declining quality of M&N's computers. M&N offered to reduce the price per computer to $1,050, but Bill's refused to withdraw its termination letter.

M&N wants to sue Bill's for $7,062,500. This figure is based on the shortfalls of 400 computers in the fifth month times $1,250/computer plus 750 computers times 7 months times $1,250/computer. Prior to filing suit, M&N wants to explore the chances for a negotiated settlement in the hope of salvaging a constructive relationship with Bill's.

14. Position-based Negotiations

The negotiation method instinctively used by most of us is referred to as **positional bargaining.** The parties involved in a dispute state their respective expectations. In the factual situation you just read, Bill's is saying that it owes nothing to M&N. On the other side, M&N is demanding payment of more than $7 million. The difference between these two positions is so wide that it will be difficult to bring these parties into agreement.

Even if Bill's was willing to buy some computers at a revised price and even if M&N agreed to a reduced quantity or selling price, the issue of quality is not being addressed. Does Bill's gain any market advantage in selling an inferior product, albeit at a lower price, to its customers? Clearly not.

If the positions on quantity and price are the only items open for negotiation, Bill's and M&N's are unlikely to reach a satisfactory compromise. Hence, the chances of a negotiated settlement through positional bargaining are minimal. Is there a better method of negotiation?

15. Interest-based Negotiations

A better approach to negotiating among disputing parties has been described as **principled interest-based negotiations** in the book *Getting to Yes* by Roger Fisher, William Ury, and Bruce Patton.* These authors present seven elements that should become the focus of negotiators. The elements will vary in importance depending on the factual situation in dispute and on

---

*Penguin Books, 2d ed., 1991.

the party's individual perspective. However, concentrating on these elements can help remove some of the barriers created by position-based negotiations. The seven elements of interest-based negotiation are as follows:

- Communication
- Relationship
- Interests
- Options
- Legitimacy
- Alternatives
- Commitment

The remainder of this chapter is not sufficient space to discuss each element in detail. Let's just quickly see how focusing on these elements might help M&N and Bill's in their negotiation efforts.

Communication
First, as expressed in the factual situation above, Bill's has not openly explained to M&N the nature of its dissatisfaction. Customer complaints have not been discussed either in general or with specificity. Such information shared with M&N might help it locate a production operations problem. Furthermore, M&N does not appear to be informing Bill's of any difficulties it faced as it expanded its production capacities.

Relationship
Second, these parties would likely benefit by discussing how each could benefit by continuing their relationship of customer and supplier. Can they solve the current problem and maintain, if not enhance, their future business opportunities together?

Interests
Third, have M&N and Bill's communicated their real interests to each other? Perhaps these interests are not mutually exclusive. For example, Bill's might want to expand its offerings in computing technology to customers. M&N might want to dissolve its sales force and concentrate on production of a variety of computers. These interests, once communicated, may help the parties realize that a continuing relationship is in their mutual best interests.

Options
Fourth, M&N and Bill's should brainstorm possible options for consideration. This exploration process is best done with the parties agreeing that an option mentioned is not necessarily a proposal for compromise. One attractive option might be for Bill's to agree to buy all the computers M&N can produce and for Bill's to market these computers under its own name. Rather than severing their business relationship, M&N could become the exclusive supplier of store-brand computers. The renaming of these products also can help overcome the "quality problems" customers associate with M&N's computers.

Legitimacy
Fifth, legitimacy means to apply standards to the topic negotiated—rather than having the parties state an unsupported proposition. Bill's probably will

not be impressed by M&N stating it will improve the quality of its computers. Instead the parties should focus on how quality can be improved and how customers will approve of the improvements. Production engineers may help address the former issue while specific test marketing plans may assist in legitimizing the latter.

Alternatives

Sixth, if the parties understand their alternative to negotiating a settlement and understand the unattractive nature of that alternative, the desire to negotiate, instead of litigating, is enhanced. M&N, for example, may perceive that bankruptcy is a very likely result if this dispute is not resolved. Bill's, on the other hand, may believe that another supplier is readily available. If these alternatives are, in fact, accurate, Bill's has superior bargaining power to that of M&N.

Commitment

Seventh, any successful negotiation must conclude with the parties making realistic commitments that can be put into practice. Perhaps an initial commitment that assists the overall process of negotiation is to have the parties agree that they will continue to meet and focus on these seven elements. Hopefully, the conclusion of the negotiation will be an agreement between the parties that avoids the expense (dollars, time, and emotions) of litigation. If that commitment is not a settlement, then it might be an agreement to utilize an ADR system.

Recent events surrounding the tobacco industry illustrate the basic theme of this chapter—alternatives to litigation often are viewed as attractive. The following box highlights this point.

Tobacco Industry Box

Throughout the 1990s, the major manufacturers of cigarettes faced a growing number of lawsuits filed by state attorneys general for reimbursement of the states' costs for rendering health-related aid to smokers. In light of the potential costs (in terms of time, money, and increasing negative publicity) of litigating these various suits, the manufacturers negotiated to provide the states $368.5 billion in compensation over a 25-year period. In return, the attorneys general agreed to seek congressional support to deny future plaintiffs the benefit of class-action lawsuits against these manufacturers. While individuals would be allowed to pursue their own personal lawsuits, manufacturers would be freed from the worry of one or more class-action suits. In addition to the billions of dollars mentioned above, manufacturers also agreed to establish a trust fund for future plaintiffs. This fund would be created by the manufacturers contributing up to 25 percent of their profits. Significant provisions also were negotiated concerning reducing smoking by teenagers.

This prospective settlement must be approved by Congress and many commentators question whether this political approval will ever occur. Regardless of the outcome in Congress, the events of 1996–97 illustrate that even in massive lawsuits, parties often find that a negotiated settlement is better than further litigation.

Key Terms

Arbitration   64
Arbitrator   64
Award   70
Caucus   83
De novo judicial review   78
Mandatory arbitration   69
Med-Arb   83
Mediation   81

Mediator   81
Minitrial   80
Mock trial   80
Negotiated settlement   84
Positional bargaining   85
Principled interest-based negotiations   85
Submission   70
Voluntary arbitration   70

Review Questions and Problems

Movement to Arbitration

1. *Reasons to Arbitrate*
   List three reasons why arbitration may be a better way to resolve disputes than litigation.

2. *The Federal Arbitration Act*
   (a) A dispute arose between partners. The partnership agreement provided that if the parties were unable to agree on any matter, it would be submitted to arbitration. One partner filed suit asking a court to appoint a receiver for the business. The other insisted on arbitration. How will the dispute be resolved? Why?
   (b) What impact does the FAA have on state laws that prefer the litigation process to arbitration?

3. *Statutory-Mandated Arbitration*
   (a) What is meant by the phrase *statutory-mandated arbitration?*
   (b) Is arbitration required in all cases? Why or why not?

4. *Voluntary/Contract-Based Arbitration*
   How is voluntary/contract-based arbitration distinguished from statutory-mandated arbitration?

Arbitration Procedures

5. *Submissions*
   (a) What is the purpose of a submission in an arbitration?
   (b) What is the proper role of the courts in determining whether a submission to arbitrate is valid?

6. *Arbitrators*
   While conducting an arbitration hearing, an arbitrator allowed laypersons to testify about the cause of injuries to the claimant. The arbitrator awarded dollar damages to be paid to this claimant. May the losing party have this award set aside on the basis that non-expert testimony was allowed? Why or why not?

7. *Awards*
   Generally, what does an arbitrator have to include in the award to make it valid?

8. *Judicial Review*
   (a) Explain why there are different standards of review of arbitration awards depending on whether the arbitration is voluntary or statutorily mandated.
   (b) Barbara and Coal, Inc., disputed the amount of money due as "minimum royalties" under a mineral lease. They submitted the dispute to arbitration, and the arbitrators awarded Barbara $37,214.67. The court held that there was no substantial evidence in the record to support an award of less than the minimum royalty of $75,000 and directed entry of a judgment for that amount. Was it proper for the court to increase the award? Why or why not?

Mock and Minitrials

9. *Mock Trials*
   What is the benefit to lawyers and parties of conducting a mock trial?

10. *Minitrial*
    Describe how a minitrial may assist business executives in their efforts to settle disputes.

Mediation

11. *Advantages/Disadvantages*
    (a) How is a mediation fundamentally different from an arbitration?
    (b) What are some of the advantages and disadvantages of the mediation process?

12. *Procedures*
    What steps usually are followed to ensure an effective mediation? Explain.
13. *Combination with ADR Systems*
    Describe how mediation can be used in conjunction with arbitration.

Negotiated Settlements

14. *Position-Based Negotiations*
    In business disputes, what two items are most likely to dominate a position-based negotiation?

15. *Interest-Based Negotiations*
    (a) Summarize the seven elements of principled interest-based negotiations.
    (b) How does focusing on these elements assist the negotiation process?

Terminology Review

For each term in the left-hand column, match the most appropriate description in the right-hand column.

1. Mock trial

2. Voluntary arbitration

3. Caucus

4. De novo hearing

5. Submission

6. Interest-based negotiation

7. Mediation

8. Award

9. Minitrial

10. Mandatory arbitration

(a) The process involving a neutral third party who attempts to assist the disputing parties but who has no authority to impose a resolution

(b) The decision of an arbitrator

(c) The meeting between a mediator and only one of the disputing parties

(d) The presentation of evidence to a group of citizens with their suggested verdict following

(e) The process required when a statute provides for disputing parties to arbitrate

(f) To try a case as if for the first time

(g) The presentation of a case to business executives as a means of encouraging settlement

(h) The contractual agreement of parties to submit any dispute to arbitration

(i) A method of bargaining involving emphasis on seven elements

(j) The act of referring a dispute to arbitration

CHAPTER

4

ETHICS AND SELF-REGULATION

Business Decision

The Boss's Overbilling

You are a purchasing agent for American Electronics, Inc. Your company has a government contract to supply the military with certain communications equipment. You become aware that your boss, the purchasing manager, is overbilling the government for various parts purchased and for departmental travel expenses.

   Is it ethical for you to keep silent about your boss's overbilling?

   Will your response be different if you learn (1) that your boss is personally pocketing the extra money from the overbilling, or (2) that the extra money is going to the company? Why?

Historian Barbara Tuchman was asked "What's happened to the world of Washington, Adams, and Jefferson?" She replied that we suffer today from "a loss of moral sense, of knowing the difference between right and wrong, and being governed by it." In recent years the emphasis on business ethics shows concern about regaining this moral sense. The close connection between ethics and law makes a discussion of moral sense especially significant to a book on the legal environment.

   Justice Oliver Wendell Holmes wrote, "The law is the witness and external deposit of our moral life. Its history is the history of the moral development of the race." Ethical (or moral) values underlie much law, including the law of how business operates and is regulated, making it important for business students to know about the nature of ethics, sources of ethics, and problems of achieving an ethical business organization. This chapter introduces the study of business ethics by examining the current concern over business ethics. It explores the relationship of morality and ethics and then of ethics and law. Two principal approaches to ethics are presented: formalism and consequentialism.

Next, the chapter looks at ethical values for business decision making. It examines trends and looks at four sources of ethical values:

- Legal regulation
- Professional codes of ethics
- Codes of ethics from business organizations
- Individual values

Finally, the chapter considers the problems faced in achieving an ethical business organization. When in groups, people often decide and act differently from the way they act as individuals. This fact has special significance for ethics in business corporations. The chapter examines how the profit motive and business bureaucracy put pressure on ethical decision making and how ethical reform must begin with the top leadership of business organizations. The importance of open communication to the ethical life of a business organization is emphasized, and several strategies for implementing corporate ethics are presented.

The Business Decision set forth at the beginning of the chapter focuses on the serious potential conflicts between loyalty to your organization, loyalty to your superior, and business fraud. As we see later in this chapter, how we evaluate this problem may depend on the ethical questions we ask ourselves.

Contemporary Business Ethics

U.S. customs agents caught the president of Ann Taylor, a large chain store, trying to avoid paying duty on $125,000 worth of wristwatches for his personal collection. A substantial civil penalty was proposed. At an Ann Taylor board of directors meeting, one director told the president: "This calls into question your integrity." The president resigned from the company.

More than ever before, business ethics are of concern to the business community and to society. In the 1980s few corporations hired people as ethics officers. Today over 20 percent of big companies have ethics officers whose job is to develop ethics policies, listen to complaints of ethics violations, and investigate ethics abuses. Why have business ethics become so important? Several developments help explain the phenomenon.

1. Ethics and Society

Ours is a pluralistic society, formed from many ethnic backgrounds, races, and religions. As a result, we have few shared ethical values to guide behavior. When a business decision maker does not share common values with society in general, any decision made has a greater likelihood of arousing ethical concern than if there is a common code of behavior and universally accepted values. Pluralism fosters concern over values, and in recent years American society has become more openly pluralistic.

The rising concern over business ethics also responds to a decline in public education and the family structure as sources for ethical teaching. Increasingly sensitive to challenges of bias, school systems have reduced their involvement in promoting shared ethical values and increased their emphasis on the teaching of "value-free" facts. At the same time, the rising divorce rate and numbers of single parents, as well as the tendency of both spouses to work outside the home, has decreased the time families spend together and their power in sharing and shaping ethical values.

Increasing economic interdependence also promotes concerns about business ethics. Not even farm families are self-sustaining. Each of us depends on business and industry for our every necessity—food, clothing, shelter, and energy. The marketplace dominates all aspects of life, and how the marketplace is conducted concerns us. The decisions people in business make have a significant impact on us. When there is a labor-management dispute in the coal industry, one source of electricity is threatened. When manufacturers conspire to raise prices, the cost of our goods goes up. The sale of dangerous pesticides or impure drugs threatens our health. A management decision to close a plant may threaten our jobs.

At the same time, the increasing role of the news media makes us more aware of business decisions than ever before. It has become increasingly difficult for large organizations, including businesses and governments, to hide behavior that is questionable. From the collapse of the savings-and-loan industry to the manipulations of the junk-bond market, the news media heighten public attention and concern. What used to be considered purely private is now considered public. The ethical issues that surround nearly every significant business decision are easier to see than they once were.

2. Ethics and Government

These changes in society have been accompanied by changes in the role of government. When business fails to make ethical decisions, when it fails to live up to society's expectations for ethical behavior, government may step in. As the chapters in this book demonstrate, in the last century, government has been increasingly active in regulating business.

In response, business leaders have become increasingly concerned with business ethics precisely because they want to limit further governmental regulation. They recognize that by encouraging ethical conduct and self-regulation within business organizations, they will prevent outside standards from being imposed on them through public law. As a consequence, both business and industry have, in recent decades, developed codes of ethics. Such efforts by professions and businesses to set standards of behavior are evidence of the increasing tendency toward self-regulation.

Federal law also encourages self-regulation. Federal sentencing guidelines reduce criminal fines for legal violations in companies that have taken specific steps to self-police ethical/legal conduct.

The Nature of Ethics

In 1759 Adam Smith wrote, "However selfish man believes himself to be, there is no doubt that there are some elements in his nature which lead him to concern himself about the fortune of others, in such a way that their happiness is necessary for him, although he obtains nothing from it except the pleasure of seeing it." With this statement the author of *The Wealth of Nations* and the "father of the marketplace" recognized that even self-interest can make people behave unselfishly.

What is it that makes us care about the fortunes of others? The next sections examine the nature of ethics. What is morality? What are ethics? How are morality and ethics similar? How do ethics relate to law? What are the major ethical systems? How do these systems apply to business decision making? When you have finished reading these sections, come back to these questions and see if you can answer them.

3. Ethics and Morality

Since earliest childhood we have been told about "right and wrong," "good and bad." It is right (good) to tell the truth. It is right to help others. It is right to obey your parents. It is wrong (bad) to lie. It is wrong to cheat and steal. It is wrong to hurt others. Through such teaching we develop values about right and wrong. These values that guide our behavior constitute our **morality.** In a larger sense, morality is also society's value system.

In society at large the sharing of moral values promotes social cooperation and is a significant means of social control. Shared moral values lead us to accept and trust others. Shared values allow us to recognize when there is proper behavior in others and where limits to behavior rightfully belong. Shared moral values create social harmony.

The sharing of values in business life is as important as it is in other aspects of our lives. Today many businesses try to foster shared moral values in employees. It is right to strive for quality in products and service. It is wrong to discriminate against or harass a person because of race, gender, or religion. One of the successes of many Japanese companies has been to instill shared moral values in their employees.

Internationally, businesses often face problems when they do business with nations with different moral values. What is wrong in the United States may be right somewhere else and vice versa. Is it right to bribe customs officials so that your company's goods can enter a country? Is it wrong for a woman to appear in public without her face covered? Is it right to eat meat and consume alcohol? Is it wrong to talk business on Sunday? On Saturday? On Friday evening? To succeed in international operations, businesses must be sensitive to differences in moral values.

If morals involve what is right and wrong, **ethics** is a systematic statement of right and wrong together with a philosophical system that both justifies and necessitates rules of conduct. In the Judeo-Christian tradition, for example, private ownership of land and goods is highly valued. It is wrong to take something that does not belong to you—hence the rule "Thou shalt not steal."

Ethics involves a rational method for examining our moral lives, not only for recognizing what is right and wrong but also for understanding why we think something is right or wrong. "The unexamined life is not worth living," said the Greek philosopher Socrates. For him ethical self-examination is necessary for a meaningful human life.

The end result of ethical examination is what philosophers call **the good.** The concept of the good is central to the study of morality. *The good* may be defined as those moral goals and objectives we choose to pursue. It serves to define who we are. Thus, *leading a good life* means more than *having the good life*. It means more than material possessions and luxury. It means pursuing intangibles, being concerned, as Adam Smith put it, about the fortunes of others. That many in contemporary society do not achieve the good is evident. Mortimer Adler has observed: "Go on a hiking trip with a typical American and listen to what he talks about. . . . He'll talk about food, the weather, football, money, sex. He may seem to be having a good time, but he lacks much that is needed for the good life." Too often, we confuse a good time with a good life.

In summary, morality involves what we mean by our values of right and wrong. Ethics is a formal system for deciding what is right and wrong and for justifying moral decisions. In everyday language, the terms *morality* and *ethics* are often used interchangeably. This chapter will also sometimes use the two words to mean the same thing.

4. Ethics and Law

Ethics and law have similar or complementary purposes. Both consist of rules to guide conduct and foster social cooperation. Both deal with what is right and wrong. Society's ethical values may become law through legislation or court decisions, and obedience to law is often viewed as being ethically correct.

However, there are also differences between ethics and law. Unlike ethical systems, the legal system is an institution of the state. The state enforces legal rules through civil and criminal sanctions, like monetary damage awards, fines, and imprisonment. Many ethical values (regarding the treatment of animals, for example) are not enforced by the state, and many laws (regarding traffic violations, for example) do not address ethical concerns.

Another difference between ethics and law concerns motivation. Although values found in ethics may be imposed on an individual (by the family, the company, or the law), the motivation to observe moral rules comes from within. On the other hand, even though the values found in law may also be personal ethical values of an individual, the motivation to observe the law comes from outside the individual in the form of state sanctions. As Justice Oliver Wendell Holmes explains:

> You can see very plainly that a bad man has as much reason as a good one for wishing to avoid an encounter with the public force, and therefore you can see the practical importance of the distinction between morality and law. A man who cares nothing for an ethical rule which is believed and practiced by his neighbors is likely nevertheless to care a good deal to avoid being made to pay money, and will want to keep out of jail if he can.

Ethical systems also involve a broader-based commitment to proper behavior than does the law. Law sets only the minimum standards acceptable to a society. As a former chief executive officer of Procter & Gamble points out: "Ethical behavior is based on more than meeting minimum legal requirements. It invariably involves a higher, moral standard."

Ultimately, the commitment to ethical values is superior to mere observance of the law in ensuring responsible business behavior. Legal rules can never be specific enough to regulate all business actions that may have socially undesirable or even dangerous consequences. And lawmakers often do not have the information to know whether specific conduct threatens employees, consumers, or the public generally. They may also lack the consensus to act quickly, or to act at all, in the face of potentially harmful business actions. However, a commitment to acceptable business ethics will usually ensure responsible business behavior.

Two Systems of Ethics

Two principal systems of ethics dominate thinking about morality in Western civilization. They are formalism and consequentialism. Although these two systems are not mutually exclusive in the outcomes of their moral analyses, they begin from different assumptions. Most people adopt elements of both systems in making ethical choices. *It is very important to appreciate how these systems have influenced your own values and moral beliefs even though until now you have been unaware of it.*

5. Formalism

Formalism (also called **deontology**) is an approach to ethics that affirms an absolute morality. A particular act is in itself right or wrong, always and in every situation. For example, lying is wrong. There are no justifications for it, and its wrongness does not depend on the situation in which the lie is told. Formalism is primarily a duty-based view of ethics. To be ethical, you have a duty, or moral obligation, not to lie. You have a duty to keep promises. You have a duty not to divulge confidences.

For the formalist (one who expresses the ethics of formalism), the ethical focus is on the worth of the individual. Individuals have rights, and these rights should not be infringed, even at the expense of society as a whole, because they have an intrinsic moral value to them. The Bill of Rights illustrates this view of the rights of individuals. When the First Amendment states "Congress shall make no law . . . abridging the freedom of speech," it takes the formalist approach.

For the formalist thinker Immanuel Kant (1724–1804), to be ethical requires that you act with a good intent. To have a good intent, you have to act in ways that are ethically consistent. This emphasis on consistency Kant called the **categorical imperative.** You are compelled to act in the way you believe everyone should act. You should never act in a certain way unless you are willing to have everyone else act in the same way. You cannot make an exception for your own action. You cannot say, "I can lie (cheat) (steal) (cause injury), but others should not do this to me (to my family) (to my friends)." Kant said that to make an exception for your own behavior is immoral and unethical. Note the similarities between Kant's categorical imperative and the Golden Rule: "Do unto others as you would have others do unto you."

Formalist thinking raises many questions for business ethics. Are you treating your employees with respect for their rights as individuals, or are you treating them only as units of production to make a profit? If you are

---

TABLE 4–1 Examples of Ethical Formalism

Statement	*Source*
"We hold these truths to be self-evident."	Declaration of Independence
"Thou shalt not steal."	The Ten Commandments
"A sale made because of deception is wrong. . . . The end doesn't justify the means."	Caterpillar Code of Ethics
"There are fundamental values that cross cultures, and companies must uphold them."	Thomas Donaldson, business ethics scholar
"Openness in communications is deemed fundamental."	Business Roundtable
The moral sense is "the sense of what is inherently right and wrong. . . ."	Barbara Tuchman, historian

---

willing to lie about your ability to meet a production schedule in order to get a new customer, are you willing to have the customer lie to you about his or her ability to pay? If you pass on information that was told to you in confidence, are you willing to have your confidences passed on? Can business function with widespread lying, cheating, and stealing and without respect for the rights of individuals?

In his novel *The Turquoise Lament*, John D. MacDonald puts words into the mouth of his Travis McGee character that illustrate well a formalist approach:

> Integrity is not a conditional word. It doesn't blow in the wind or change in the weather. It is your inner image of yourself, and if you look in there and see a man who won't cheat, then you know he never will. Integrity is not a search for the rewards for integrity.

Table 4–1 presents other statements that reflect a formalist approach to ethics in business and nonbusiness situations.

The Social Contract

The social contract theory of Harvard philosopher John Rawls furnishes an important recent example of how formalism has influenced thinking about business and personal ethics. This theory is based not on duty but on contract (agreement).

Social contract theory concerns itself with how to construct a just society given the many inequalities of wealth, knowledge, and social status. Rawls suggests a simple first step in determining the ethical values on which a just society can be built. We should assume that we do not know our age, gender, race, intelligence, strength, wealth, or social status. This step is vital because it keeps us from being self-interested in the ethical values we consider. For example, not knowing our sex or race, will we agree that it is ethical to discriminate in employment compensation based on sex or race? Not knowing our wealth, will we agree that owning property is a fair prerequisite to being able to vote? Not knowing our age or work status, will we agree that it is just for a company to have mandatory retirement of its officers at age sixty-five? Freeing ourselves of self-knowledge, Rawls argues, improves our ability to evaluate the terms of a fair agreement (contract) under which we enter society or join an organization like a corporation.

Placing himself behind a veil of self-ignorance, Rawls proposes two ethical principles. First, everyone is entitled to certain equal basic rights, including liberty, freedom of association, and personal security. Second, although there may be social and economic inequalities, these inequalities must be based on what a person does, not on who a person is, and everyone must have an equal opportunity for achievement. Since there are natural differences of intelligence and strength and persistent social differences of wealth, class, and status, defining "equal opportunity" is crucial to this second ethical principle. Rawls insists that individuals in a just society have the right to an equal place at the starting line. This is as true within a corporation as it is within a country.

Because of its emphasis on individual rights and self-worth, social contract theory has its origin in formalism. It provides a powerful process for ethical business decision making. Social contract theory is especially valuable in international business. In this arena, in the absence of much law, businesses from various cultures must agree as to the terms under which international business is to take place.

6. Consequentialism

The second principal system of ethics is consequentialism. **Consequentialism** (also called **teleology**) concerns itself with the moral consequences of actions rather than with the morality of the actions themselves. For the consequentialist, lying itself is not unethical. It is the consequences, or end results of lying, that must be evaluated for their ethical implications. It is the loss of trust or harm done by lying that is unethical.

If formalism focuses on individual rights, consequentialism focuses on the common good. The ethics of actions are measured by how they promote the common good. If actions increase the common good, they are ethical. If actions cause overall harm to society, they are unethical.

The dominant form of consequentialism is **utilitarianism.** Utilitarianism judges actions by *usefulness*, by whether they serve to increase the common good. For utilitarians, the end justifies the means. But to judge the utility of a particular action, it is necessary to consider alternative courses of action. Only after you consider all reasonable courses of action can you know whether a particular one has the greatest utility.

In 1992 the International Franchising Association (IFA) adopted a new code of ethics. Officers of the association indicated that an important reason for adopting the new code was to head off government regulation of franchising through self-policing. The code states that when a franchiser is going to make a decision about adding a new franchise outlet into an area where a franchisee already owns an existing outlet, it should weigh "the positive or negative effect of the new outlet on the existing outlet." Another factor to be considered is "the benefit or detriment to the franchise system as a whole in operating the new outlet." The motivation of the IFA in adopting the new ethics code and the quoted language of the code suggest a consequentialist ethical view. Table 4–2 illustrates other examples of consequentialism in business and nonbusiness situations.

Although business ethics reflect elements of both formalism and consequentialism, they focus more heavily on the latter. Business leaders feel a

---

TABLE 4–2 Examples of Ethical Consequentialism

Statement	Source
"There is no doubt that ethics pays off at the bottom line."	CEO, Procter & Gamble
"Loss of confidence in an organization is the single greatest cost of unethical behavior."	CEO, KPMG
"The strongest argument for raising the ethics bar boils down to self-interest."	CEO, KPMG
"Cost-benefit analysis (used by various governmental agencies and in business and finance)."	Economic theory, finance theory, and policy studies
"The greatest happiness of the greatest number is the foundation of morals and legislation."	Jeremy Bentham (1748–1832), English social philosopher

---

need to justify what they do in terms of whether or not it produces dividends for their shareholders. Their primary goal or end is to produce a profit. This orientation reflects consequentialism.

The many statements of business leaders that ethics are "good for business" illustrate this point. These statements imply that certain values are important because their end result is useful in increasing productivity and profit rather than because the values are intrinsically good. The way business managers evaluate alternative courses of action through cost-benefit analysis is also a form of utilitarian consequentialism.

The Protestant Ethic

In part, the current focus on consequentialism in business ethics is due to the decline in business life of what has been described as the **Protestant ethic.** With the Protestant Reformation of the sixteenth century came a new emphasis on the importance of the individual. Instead of relying on the intercession of a church hierarchy to achieve grace, each person, Protestants asserted, had the means to address God personally. Thus religion provided the impetus to hard work and achievement. Human desire and indulgence, said Protestants, should be bent to God's will through self-denial, rational planning, and productivity. The Protestant ethic was rooted in a formalist approach: honesty and keeping promises were intrinsically good.

The Protestant ethic was a boon to capitalism. The quest for economic independence fueled commercial growth, which fueled industrial growth, which created our modern consumer society. English social philosophers promoted self-interest as the means to securing the greatest good for society, and American entrepreneurs asserted that "What's good for business is good for America." Along the way, however, the religious basis of the Protestant ethic was eroded by rising wealth and the encouragement of mass consumption. The part of the ethic that supported hard work, success, and rational planning continued, but without the original absolute moral values. The Protestant ethic became transformed into an organizational ethic that supports the modern bureaucratic managerial system. The sociologist Robert Jackall identifies this system as having "administrative hierarchies, standardized work procedures, regularized timetables, uniform policies,

FIGURE 4.1

Formalism versus consequentialism.

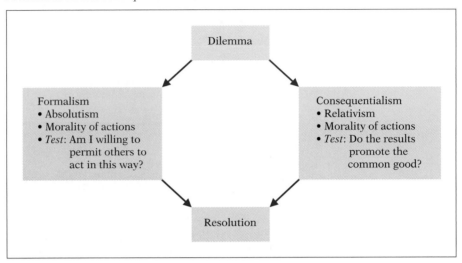

and centralized control." The goal of this system is to produce profit. Business actions are justified by their usefulness in accomplishing the goal. In this century, then, the religious formalism of the Protestant ethic has become a type of utilitarian consequentialism.

7. Comparing the Two Ethical Systems

Formalists and consequentialists can arrive at the same conclusion for an ethical course of action, but they use a different evaluation process (see Figure 4–1). Take as an example a company's decision whether or not to secretly monitor its employees' use of the E-mail system. The company suspects that some employees are using the system for personal business and to spread damaging rumors about the company and its executives. How would formalists and consequentialists approach this decision?

Formalists might say that secret monitoring treats employees only as a means to the end of increasing organizational efficiency and does not respect their self-worth as individuals. The monitoring also does not respect their dignity and their privacy. Formalists might conclude that secret monitoring is unethical. Explaining the problem to the employees and asking for their consent to monitor would be a more ethical action to take.

For a consequentialist, the act of secret monitoring itself is ethically neither right nor wrong. It is the end result that is ethically important. Secret monitoring and the punishment of wrongdoers are useful in improving productivity, which is an appropriate company goal and beneficial to society at large. To that extent secret monitoring is ethically acceptable. But the punishment of wrongdoers will likely reveal to all employees that their E-mail has been secretly monitored. This breach of trust can lower employee morale and lessen employee loyalty to the company. Overall productivity may fall. In examining alternative solutions to the problem, a more beneficial overall solution, and thus a more ethical one, might be to explain the problem to the employees and ask for their consent to monitor all E-mail messages.

This example of the thinking processes of formalists and consequentialists does not exhaust all of the possible approaches that these groups might take to the E-mail problem. It does emphasize the fact that both formalist and consequentialist thinking can lead to the same business decision.

One of the most complex problems of contemporary business ethics concerns the promotion and sale of tobacco products. As you think about the Tobacco Industry Box, bring to bear your new knowledge of formalism and consequentialism.

Tobacco Industry Box

Consider the ethical significance of the following facts:

Tobacco products have been consumed in the United States since at least the early 1600s.

Hundreds of thousands of people are involved in the growing, manufacturing, distributing, and selling of tobacco products.

In the first twenty years of tobacco litigation, juries did not award plaintiffs a single penny against tobacco companies.

Scientists and doctors accept that tobacco consumption is an important contributing factor in cancer and heart disease. Excess consumption of fatty foods and lack of exercise are also contributing factors to these diseases.

Between 300,000 and 400,000 people in the United States die annually due to tobacco consumption.

The average age of beginning tobacco consumption is around sixteen. Almost no one begins tobacco consumption past age twenty-one. Three thousand new teenagers begin tobacco consumption every day.

Tobacco companies spend approximately $5 billion annually in advertising and promoting tobacco sales. The main strategy of tobacco promotion is to associate glamour, excitement, sex, and desirable life images with tobacco consumption.

The law requires that health warnings accompany the advertising and sale of tobacco products.

The nicotine in tobacco is considered addictive. However, millions have stopped tobacco consumption.

Sources of Values for Business Ethics

There are at least four sources of values for business ethics. The sections that follow identify them as:

- Legal regulation
- Professional codes of ethics
- Organizational codes of ethics
- Individual values

8. *Legal Regulation*

Insider trading, bribery, fraudulent practices, and conflicts of interest are often cited as examples of ethical failures. But these practices are illegal as well. That the unethical may be illegal and vice versa is often confusing to students.

The way to understand the ethical-legal relationship is to realize that in our society ethical values frequently become law and that legal regulation can reflect society's ethical values. For example, society's ethical commitment to equal opportunity became law in the Civil Rights Act of 1964, which prohibits employment discrimination based on "race, sex, color, religion, and national origin."

At the same time, the very existence of legal regulation can influence society's view of what is ethical. In 1964, when the Civil Rights Act was passed, few people were concerned about sex discrimination in employment. Opponents of the bill inserted the prohibition against sex discrimination in hopes of preventing its passage. Obviously, these legislators believed that sex discrimination in employment was acceptable and that many others agreed with them. Despite their efforts, however, the Civil Rights Act passed, and over the years, as legal battles involving sex discrimination in employment were fought, Americans' moral sense of the importance of equal employment opportunity regardless of sex caught up with the law. Today a great majority of Americans believe women should not be discriminated against in employment simply because they are women and that such discrimination is wrong. To a significant extent, the law itself contributed to the change in values.

Legal regulation is, then, a significant source of values for business ethics. In fact, many business and professional organizations look to the law when drawing up their codes of ethical conduct. At least five major ethical rules can be drawn from the law. These include:

- Respect for the liberty and rights of others
- The importance of acting in good faith
- The importance of exercising due care
- The importance of honoring confidentiality
- Avoidance of conflicts of interest

The following sections elaborate these concepts. These values derived from legal regulation are appropriate for use in ethical business decision making even when decisions do not involve legal issues.

Liberty and Rights

First, the law requires respect for the liberty and rights of others. We see this requirement in legislation protecting the right of privacy, promoting equal employment opportunity, and guaranteeing freedom of expression and due process of law. In one form or another, these legal rights often appear in ethical codes. Do you think that the concern for individual rights represents formalism or consequentialism?

Good Faith

The law requires that good faith be demonstrated in various economic and other transactions. An example comes from the Uniform Commercial Code, adopted in forty-nine of the fifty states. Article 2 of the UCC on sales law requires that all sales of goods transactions be carried out in *good faith,* which has been interpreted as meaning "honesty in fact" and honesty in intent.

The reverse of good faith is *bad faith,* which can be understood as dishonesty in intent. In cases involving a bad faith withholding of amounts due under insurance policies, some courts and juries have severely punished defendant insurance companies with large punitive damage awards. Acting with an honest intent is the key to understanding good faith. Is looking at the intent of parties to a business contract evidence of formalism or consequentialism?

Due Care

Another ethical value reflecting legal rules requires the exercise of *due care* in our behavior. This value comes from the law of torts, which Justice Oliver Wendell Holmes said "abounds in moral phraseology." Due care derives from society's expectations about how fair and reasonable actions are. Due care promotes the common good. In negligence law, failure to exercise due (or reasonable) care is the principal element that triggers liability against the defendant. Courts have examined due care in negligence cases in terms of a balancing test. The likelihood that the defendant's conduct will cause harmful consequences, taken with the seriousness of the harmful consequences, is balanced against the effort required to avoid the harmful consequences. The balancing test is central to the concept of due care.

Another form of the requirement to exercise due care comes from the Federal Guidelines for Sentencing for Criminal Convictions, which focus specifically on corporate white-collar crime. In determining what punishment a company should receive for the illegal business acts of its employees, the guidelines look at whether the company has "an effective program to prevent and detect violations of the law." An effective program is measured by whether "the organization exercised due diligence in seeking to prevent and detect criminal conduct by its employees and other agents." *Due diligence* is another way of saying "due care."

As with the determination of due care in negligence law, the determination of due diligence in sentencing guidelines requires use of a balancing test. Considering the significance of the balancing test to the exercise of due care (or due diligence), do you think that formalist or consequentialist values are reflected?

Confidentiality

Honoring confidentiality is the fourth major ethical value emerging from the law and legal regulation. The legal requirement of honoring confidentiality appears in agency law generally and in the professional-client relationship in particular. For a CPA to share with unauthorized third parties what has been learned during a client's audit is professional malpractice. Likewise, it is malpractice for an attorney, physician, real estate broker, or any professional agent to tell others what a client (principal) has related in confidence.

In addition to not telling others of a confidence, an agent must in many instances not act on the confidence related by a principal. The insider trading scandals of the 1980s and early 1990s occurred largely because agents improperly traded in the stock market on confidential information provided to them by their principals. The securities laws make it a crime for agents to trade improperly on confidential information.

The legal requirement of honoring confidences contains both formalist and consequentialist ethical values. Can you identify these values?

Conflicts of Interest

Often embodied in business codes of ethics, avoiding conflicts of interest is a final ethical value flowing from the law, especially from agency law. A conflict of interest occurs when one attempts to "serve two masters," and no agent or employee of one principal can secretly work for another whose interest competes with that of the first principal. That is why a real estate agent may not represent both the seller and the buyer in a real estate transaction without permission from both parties.

Conflicts of interest also arise in public service. For instance, it is a conflict of interest for a judge or administrative regulator to make a decision involving a company in which he or she owns stock. Note that in this instance the conflict of interest does not involve "serving two masters." The conflict arises because of the ownership of property that will make it difficult for the judge or regulator to make an unbiased decision. In terms of formalism and consequentialism, how do you evaluate the prohibition against conflicts of interest?

Concept Summary:
Ethical Values from Legal Regulation

- Respect the liberty and rights of others.
- Act in good faith.
- Exercise due care.

- Honor confidentiality.
- Avoid conflicts of interest.

---

9. Professional Codes of Ethics

Another important source of business ethics comes from the historic tradition of the professional codes of ethics. Professions such as law and medicine have long traditions of codes of ethical conduct. Other professions, and more recently business and industry in general, have developed and adopted codes of ethical conduct. Here we use portions of professional codes to demonstrate sources of ethical values that come from the development of group standards for ethical conduct.

We begin with selected excerpts from codes of conduct for two professions: law and accounting. These codes are the American Bar Association Model Rules of Professional Conduct, shown on the following page, and the American Institute of Certified Public Accountants Code of Professional Conduct, which appears on page 106. Take into account that what follows are only short excerpts. These codes in full run many pages.

In spite of their Rules of Professional Conduct, lawyers are sometimes viewed as acting unethically. Is this because unethical people are attracted to the practice of law? Is it because the power conferred by knowing the law corrupts lawyers? Or is it because most nonlawyers do not understand the legal process, so that when they lose legal disputes, they feel it must be because of the other side's "dishonest" lawyers? Is it the emotion invested in legal cases that makes it easy for us to blame others when things do not turn out to our satisfaction? In answering these questions, think about the relationship between law and justice. Does law ensure justice? Are we wrong to hope that it should?

Another important set of group standards is the ethical code of certified public accountants.

From these excerpts, the ethical values expressed in the codes of ethics for lawyers and accountants may seem overly general in nature. But each code has pages of rules that apply to specific situations arising in the lawyer-client and accountant-client relationship. As the state does not enforce these codes, it is not proper to call them law. Yet the professional organizations that have adopted these codes employ specific sanctions to back them up. Lawyers may be disbarred for ethical breaches. Because the state will likely regulate these professions if they do not do so themselves, it is appropriate to term their ethical codes **self-regulation.**

American Bar Association Model Rules of Professional Conduct

As a public citizen, a lawyer should seek improvement of the law, the administration of justice and the quality of service rendered by the legal profession. As a member of a learned profession, a lawyer should cultivate knowledge of the law beyond its use for clients, employ that knowledge in reform of the law and work to strengthen legal education. A lawyer should be mindful of deficiencies in the administration of justice and of the fact that the poor, and sometimes persons who are not poor, cannot afford adequate legal assistance, and should therefore devote professional time and civic influence in their behalf. A lawyer should aid the legal profession in pursuing these objectives and should help the bar regulate itself in the public interest.

Many of a lawyer's professional responsibilities are prescribed in the Rules of Professional Conduct, as well as substantive and procedural law. However, a lawyer is also guided by personal conscience and the approbation of professional peers. A lawyer should strive to attain the highest level of skill, to improve the law and the legal profession and to exemplify the legal profession's ideals of public service. . . .

In the nature of law practice . . . conflicting responsibilities are encountered. Virtually all difficult ethical problems arise from conflict between a lawyer's responsibilities to clients, to the legal system and to the lawyer's own interest in remaining an upright person while earning a satisfactory living. The Rules of Professional Conduct prescribe terms for resolving such conflicts. Within the framework of these Rules many difficult issues of professional discretion can arise. Such issues must be resolved through the exercise of sensitive professional and moral judgment guided by the basic principles underlying the Rules. . . .

The Rules do not, however, exhaust the moral and ethical considerations that should inform a lawyer, for no worthwhile human activity can be completely defined by legal rules. The Rules simply provide a framework for the ethical practice of law.

American Institute of Certified Public Accountants Code of Professional Conduct

These Principles of the Code of Professional Conduct of the American Institute of Certified Public Accountants express the profession's recognition of its responsibilities to the public, to clients, and to colleagues. They guide members in the performance of their professional responsibilities and express the basic tenets of ethical and professional conduct. The Principles call for an unswerving commitment to honorable behavior, even at the sacrifice of personal advantage.

In carrying out their responsibilities as professionals, members should exercise sensitive professional and moral judgments in all their activities.

As professionals, certified public accountants perform an essential role in society. Consistent with that role, members of the American Institute of Certified Public Accountants have responsibilities to all those who use their professional services. Members also have a continuing responsibility to cooperate with each other to improve the art of accounting, maintain the public's confidence, and carry out the profession's special responsibilities for self-governance. The collective efforts of all members are required to maintain and enhance the traditions of the profession.

Members should accept the obligation to act in a way that will serve the public interest, honor the public interest, and demonstrate commitment to professionalism.

A distinguishing mark of a profession is acceptance of its responsibility to the public. The accounting profession's public consists of clients, credit grantors, governments, employers, investors, the business and financial community, and others who rely on the objectivity and integrity of certified public accountants to maintain the orderly functioning of commerce. This reliance imposes a public interest responsibility on certified public accountants. The public interest is defined as the collective well-being of the community of people and institutions the profession serves.

In discharging their professional responsibilities, members may encounter conflicting pressures from among each of those groups. In resolving those conflicts, members should act with integrity, guided by the precept that when members fulfill their responsibility to the public, clients' and employers' interests are best served.

10. Organizational Codes of Ethics

There are few industrywide codes of ethics, so many businesses have adopted ethical codes at the individual organization level. Nearly all large corporations now have their own codes of business ethics, often called codes of conduct. These codes are obviously an important source of business ethics.

The Business Roundtable, a national group of senior business leaders, has identified a general list of topics that organizational codes of business ethics should cover. These include:

- Fundamental honesty and adherence to the law
- Product safety and quality
- Health and safety in the workplace
- Conflicts of interest
- Fairness in selling/marketing practices
- Financial reporting
- Supplier relationships

- Pricing, billing, and contracting
- Trading in securities/using inside information
- Payments to obtain business/Foreign Corrupt Practices Act
- Acquiring and using information about others
- Security
- Political activities
- Protection of the environment
- Intellectual property/proprietary information

Individual companies take different approaches to ethical codes. The Hertz Corporation has a one-page statement of general ethical principles. In part that statement reads: "We will conduct business ethically and honestly in dealing with our customers, suppliers and employees. We will treat our employees in the same fashion as we expect them to treat our customers— with dignity and respect."

Hertz's statement provides only general guidelines to ethical conduct rather than detailed definitions of what kind of ethical behavior the company expects in specific instances. Other companies spell out their expectations for employees' behavior in considerable detail. For instance, the Martin Marietta Corporation Code of Ethics and Standard of Conduct is seventeen pages long and covers a wide variety of company activities and practices.

Many codes of business ethics contain both general statements of shared ethical values and more specific applied examples of these values. General statements of shared values remind employees what their companies stand for and at the same time serve to encourage ethical behavior in situations not covered by specific ethical guides. The applied examples address specific types of business conduct like those listed above by the Business Roundtable.

A majority of organizational codes of business ethics provide sanctions for their violation, up to and including employee termination. As with professional codes of conduct, it is appropriate to call these organizational codes self-regulation. Whether companies pursue ethical self-regulation with enthusiasm and commitment or the codes are mere window dressing to satisfy the government and the general public is an important issue in determining the value of these codes.

11. Individual Values

The ultimate source of ethical values for business decision making comes from the individual. Others can tell you what is right or wrong. They can sanction you for failing to live up to their expectations. But only you can make your behavior ethical. Only you can intend your actions to be honest and fair or to serve the common good.

How to act ethically in every business situation is beyond the scope of this chapter, or that of any book, for that matter. Business life is just too complex. There is no way to create enough rules to cover all possible ethically significant situations, even if they could be identified in advance. However, there are five questions that you can ask yourself that will help you explore your ethical values before making personal or business decisions about what to do.

Have I thought about whether the action I may take is right or wrong? John Smale, former CEO of Procter & Gamble, has said that "there is an ethical dimension to most complex business problems." If this is so, then you should consider whether any decision you propose to make to solve such a problem is ethical or not. The philosopher Hannah Arendt explained that evil often comes from a kind of thoughtlessness. Plato wrote that immoral behavior often flows from ignorance. A major goal of this chapter is to encourage you to think about the ethical implications of what you decide and what you do. It is the first step in leading a good life.

Will I be proud to tell of my action to my family? To my employer? To the news media? An excellent way to uncover whether there are ethical difficulties with a possible decision is to consider how proud you would be to share it with others. Before reaching an important business decision, consider how you would feel about telling your decision to your family, your employer, and the public through the news media. The less proud you are to share your decision with others, the more likely your decision is to be unethical. As Stephen Butler, CEO of KPMG said, "An essential part of an ethics process is identifying issues that would mortify a chief executive if he were to read about them on the front page of the newspaper."

Am I willing for everyone to act as I am thinking of acting? With this question you encompass a major principle of ethical formalism. If you consider suggesting to a coworker that it would be advantageous for him or her to develop a sexual relationship with you, are you willing to have your superior suggest this relationship to you? Or to your friends or a member of your family? Trying to convince yourself that it is acceptable for you to do something but not acceptable for others in your situation to do it is virtually always immoral.

Will my decision cause harm to others or to the environment? Asking this question exposes a significant principle of ethical conse-quentialism: promotion of the common good. Promoting the common good within your business organization is important, but it is even more important to consider whether your decision is good for society.

You can approach this issue of the common good by asking whether your decision will cause harm. If the decision will cause no harm and will advance your business interests, it will also usually advance the good of society by increasing productivity, efficiency, or innovation.

Many business decisions, however, do cause harm to others or to the environment. It is difficult to construct an interstate highway without workers being injured and trees being cut. The point of asking yourself the question about potential harm is so you can weigh the harm against the increase in the common good and so you can evaluate whether an alternative course of action might bring about the same increase in the common good with less harm.

Recall that ethical formalists maintain that harm to some individual rights is never justified by an increase in organizational or common good. But as ethical decision making in business often involves a mixed approach, including both formalism and consequentialism, it is appropriate for you to evaluate potential business decisions by weighing harms against benefits to the common good.

Will my actions violate the law? Both formalists and consequentialists believe that you have an ethical duty to obey the law except in very limited instances. The law provides only minimum standards for behavior, but they are standards that should be observed. Thus, to be ethical, you should always consider whether any business decision you make will require illegal actions.

Sometimes it is not clear whether proposed actions will violate the law. Then you should consult with legal counsel. Many regulatory agencies will also give legal advice about whether actions you are considering are legal or not.

When you are convinced that a law itself is morally wrong, you may be justified in disobeying it. Even then, to be ethical, you must be willing to make public your disobedience and to accept the consequences for it. Both Mohandas Gandhi and Martin Luther King, Jr., deliberately disobeyed laws they thought were morally wrong, and they changed society by doing so. Ultimately they changed both laws and ethics. But they made their disobedience to these laws public, and they willingly accepted punishment for violating them.

Go back now to "The Boss's Overbilling" that opens this chapter, put yourself into that situation, and ask the questions you have just learned. Do the questions help you to explore your ethical values?

Leading an ethical business life may be difficult at times. You will make mistakes. You will be tempted. It is unlikely that you will be perfect. But if you want to be ethical and will work hard toward achieving your goal, you will be rewarded. As with achieving other challenging business objectives, there will be satisfaction in ethical business decision making.

In business as well as in personal life, the key to ethical decision making is wanting to be ethical and having the will to be ethical. If you do not want to be ethical, no code of conduct can make you ethical. Potential harm you may cause to individuals and to society will best be deterred by the threat of legal punishment and the sanctions of professional and corporate codes. You may never get caught, lose your job, or go to jail. But, as Mortimer Adler observed, you will lack "much that is needed for the good life."

Concept Summary:
Self-examination for Self-regulation

- Have I thought about whether the action I may take is right or wrong?
- Will I be proud to tell of my action to my family? To my employer? To the news media?
- Am I willing for everyone to act as I am thinking of acting?

- Will my decision cause harm to others or to the environment?
- Will my actions violate the law?

Achieving an Ethical Business Corporation

The dominant form of organization in modern business is the corporation. Currently, the top 100 manufacturing corporations produce more than two-thirds of the nation's entire manufacturing output. In 1840 the largest manufacturing firm in the United States, the Springfield Armory, employed only 250 workers. Today, many corporations have tens of thousands of employees. Some have hundreds of thousands. In substantial part, the development of the corporate form of business organization made possible this growth in business size.

Ethical problems, however, arise in corporate life that are not present in one's individual experience. In a study published of Harvard MBAs during their first five years following graduation, 29 of 30 reported that business pressures had forced them to violate their own ethical standards. The next sections focus on the ethical problems of an individual in the corporation and suggest several ways of dealing with them.

12. The Obstacles

Some may contend that the corporation by its very nature, with its dependence on a competitive edge and on profit and its limited liability, is so constituted as to make ethical behavior unlikely. That is not true, but there are certain obstacles to ethical corporate behavior that deserve serious consideration.

The Emphasis on Profit

The primary goal of the modern business corporation is to produce profit. Management demands it, the board of directors demands it, and shareholders demand it. Making profit motivates our entire economic system, and it promotes the common good by providing incentive for job creation and the efficient fulfillment of social needs for goods and services.

Unfortunately, with the decline of the Protestant ethic, emphasis on corporate profit alone sometimes conflicts with ethical responsibility. How a profit is made becomes less important than that it is made. Various business scandals illustrate this point.

In many corporations the responsibility for profit making is decentralized. The home office expects a plant in another state to meet certain profit goals, but the home office does not know much about the particular operations of that plant. Meeting profit goals places enormous pressure on the local plant manager. The manager's career advancement depends on the plant's profitability, yet the home office does not appreciate the difficulties under which the plant is operating. In such a situation the overemphasis on profit can easily lead to the manager's taking ethical and legal shortcuts to ensure profit.

The Effect of the Group

The social critic Ambrose Bierce once remarked that the corporation is "an ingenious device for obtaining individual profit without individual responsibility." He was referring to the fact that individuals in large groups such as the corporation feel less responsibility for what happens in the group than they do for what happens in their individual lives. They may also act differently, and to some extent less ethically, in a group.

That individuals will do unethical things as part of a mob which they would never do alone is widely recognized, and the same pattern can be observed in corporate behavior. Within corporations it becomes easy for a researcher not to pass on lately discovered concerns about the possible (yet not certain) side effects of a new skin lotion that upper management is so enthusiastic about. In corporate life it is not difficult to overlook the unethical behavior of a superior when many fellow employees are also overlooking it. And of course, "I did it because everyone else did it" is a common rationalization in groups of all kinds. "Just following orders" is a similar rationalization.

That individuals in groups may feel a diminished sense of responsibility for decisions made and actions taken invites ethical compromise. Coupled with an overemphasis on profit, the group effect increases the difficulty of achieving an ethical business corporation.

Go back once again to "The Boss's Overbilling" at the beginning of the chapter. Does this section help you understand why you are having a difficult time with the problem?

13. The Steps

Despite the obstacles that sometimes stand in the way of ethical corporate behavior, certain steps can be taken to promote business ethics in corporate life.

Involvement of Top Management

To encourage corporate ethics, it is not enough merely to adopt a code of conduct. For the code to change behavior, corporate employees must believe that the values expressed by the code represent the values of the corporation's top management. Top management must act as a role model for values it wishes corporate employees to share.

The sociologist Robert Jackall attributes the importance of a corporation's top management in encouraging business ethics to the bureaucratic system for career advancement. Each employee owes loyalty to his or her immediate corporate superior. As a practical matter, career advancement for the employee is generally tied to career advancement for the superior. In turn, that supervisor has a corporate superior to whom loyalty is owed, and so on up the corporate bureaucratic hierarchy.

Beyond a certain level in corporate bureaucracy, argues Jackall, social indicators about how well an employee "fits in" to the company management are as important as merit performance in securing further career advancement. For this reason, corporate employees tend to be very sensitive to the values of top corporate management and take these values as their own. Due to the interlocking system of loyalties that run between employment levels of the corporate hierarchy, top management's values filter down quite effectively to lower-level employees.

The values adopted by lower-level employees, however, will be top management's *real* values. So if the corporation has a code of conduct that expresses excellent ethical values, but top management shows that it expects profit at any cost, then the values adopted by lower-level employees will likely relate to profit at any cost rather than to values appearing in the code of conduct.

Top management must really believe in the ethical values expressed in codes of conduct for these values to take hold throughout the corporation. But if they do believe them and will communicate this belief through the corporation, there is an excellent chance that these values will be adopted within the corporate group. As Stephen Butler, CEO of KPMG says, "I really believe that corporate ethics are essential for a successful business today, and the CEOs of corporate America are the only ones who can institution-alize them."

Openness in Communication

For ethical corporate values to make their most significant impact on decision making, corporate employees must be willing to talk with each other about ethical issues. "Openness in communication is deemed fundamental," states the Business Roundtable. Openness promotes trust, and without trust even the best-drafted code of ethics will likely fall short of achieving an ethical business corporation.

Beyond helping establish trust, openness in communication is necessary for ethical corporate decision making because of the complexity of information required to evaluate the implications of many business decisions. Without open discussion of these implications among employees and between employees and their superiors, ethical decision making is severely hindered. Information crucial to making an ethical decision may be lacking.

For example, consider the complexity of a firm's decision to sell in other countries a pesticide that is banned for sale in the United States. Evaluating the ethical implications of the sale (assuming there are no legal ones) will demand considerable information. To make a fully informed decision the firm must know:

- What the effects of the pesticide on humans and the environment are
- Why the pesticide was banned in the United States
- Why the pesticide is useful in other countries
- Whether in spite of its ban for use in the United States there may be good reasons to use the pesticide in other countries
- Whether there are alternatives to its use in other countries

The sharing of information about the implications of this pesticide sale will greatly assist the making of an ethical decision about its use. Openness in communication among employees on these implications will be vital in reaching an ethically informed corporate decision about this complex matter.

How is openness in communication on ethical issues promoted within the corporation? There is no single answer. For top management to provide a good role model of concern for speaking out on ethical issues is certainly a right beginning. Another possibility is for employees to meet periodically in small groups to consider either real or hypothetical ethical problems. In general, a shared corporate commitment to the ideal of ethical decision making is important to openness in communication.

Other Strategies

The Business Roundtable looked at the ways more than a hundred major corporations make ethics work. Some of the strategies identified include:

- Management involvement and oversight down the line
- Attention to values and ethics in recruiting and hiring
- Communication programs to inform and motivate employees
- Recognition and reward for exemplary performance, including pay and promotion
- Ombudsmen and hot lines for employee comment and complaint
- Special focus on secrets and vulnerable jobs
- Periodic certification of adherence to standards
- Auditing to ensure compliance
- Enforcement procedures, including discipline and dismissal

14. The Rewards

Of the world's 100 largest economies, 49 of them are countries and 51 are companies. General Motors has greater annual sales than the gross national products of Denmark, Thailand, Turkey, South Africa, or Saudia Arabia. Wal-Mart's economy is larger than that of Poland, Ukraine, Portugal, Israel, or Greece. Because of the size and influence of modern corporations, business ethics take on special significance. Although there are unique problems with promoting ethical corporate decision making, the rewards for making the attempt are important both to business and society.

The Spanish journal *Boletín Círculo* makes four observations about business ethics. A paraphrase of these observations provides a good way to conclude a chapter on ethics and self-regulation:

1. Profits and business ethics are not contradictory. Some of the most profitable businesses have also historically been the most ethical.

2. An ethical organizational life is a basic business asset that should be accepted and encouraged. The reverse is also true. Unethical behavior is a business liability.

3. Ethics are of continuing concern to the business community. They require ongoing reevaluation. Businesses must always be ethically sensitive to changes in society.

4. Business ethics reflect business leadership. Top firms can and should exercise leadership in business ethics.

Business plays a vital role in serving society, and we cannot isolate the impact of important business decisions from their social consequences. For businesses merely to observe the law is not sufficiently responsible. Legal regulation lacks flexibility and is inadequately informed to be the only social guide for business decision making. Ethics belong in business decision making. A business that does not act ethically severs itself from society, from the good, and ultimately from its own source of support.

In reading the next chapters on the regulatory environment, consider how passage of much of the regulation was preceded by breaches of business ethics. If ethical self-regulation does not guide business behavior, legal regulation often follows quickly.

Key Terms

Categorical imperative   96
Consequentialism   98
Deontology   96
Ethics   94
Formalism   96
Morality   94

Protestant ethic   99
Self-regulation   105
Social contract theory   97
Teleology   98
The good   94
Utilitarianism   98

Review Questions and Problems

Contemporary Business Ethics

1. *Ethics and Society*
   Describe the reasons for the rising concern over business ethics.

2. *Ethics and Government*
   How has government action in recent years encouraged increased business attention to ethical matters?

The Nature of Ethics

3. *Ethics and Morality*
   Compare and contrast ethics and morality. What do philosophers call the end result of ethical examination?

4. *Ethics and Law*
   A marketing consultant to your firm comments that being ethical in business means nothing more than obeying the law. Discuss.

Two Systems of Ethics

5. *Formalism*
   As amended in 1988, the Foreign Corrupt Practices Act prohibits bribery as a practice for U.S. companies to use in obtaining business in other countries. In passing the act, Congress expressed the concern that bribery was inherently wrong. Which major system of ethical thought does this concern suggest? Explain.

6. *Consequentialism*
   A recent headline from *The Wall Street Journal* read "U.S. Companies Pay Increasing Attention to Destroying Files." The article discussed how many companies are routinely shredding files in the ordinary course of business to prevent future plaintiffs from obtaining the files and finding incriminating evidence. Is this practice unethical? Evaluate.

7. *Comparing the Two Ethical Systems*
   (a) Is it ethical to advertise tobacco products in association with a desirable, exciting, or sophisticated lifestyle?

   (b) Is it ethical to advertise these products in association with a cartoon character that is appealing to young people?

Sources of Values for Business Ethics

8. *Legal Regulation*
   Explain how in our society, ethical values frequently become law, and how legal regulation can promote change in ethical values. Describe several common ethical values that are found in law.

9. *Professional Codes of Ethics*
   Discuss why lawyers are sometimes viewed as being unethical. Is the average lawyer more or less ethical than the average business manager?

10. *Organizational Codes of Ethics*
    A study of one major company's code of ethics by the Business Roundtable found that the lower the level of employees on the corporate ladder, the greater their hostility and cynicism toward codes of business ethics.
    (a) Why might this be true?
    (b) What can top business management do to change this view?

11. *Individual Values*
    In addition to the five questions listed in the text, can you think of questions to ask yourself to help explore your ethical values before making a business (or personal) decision?

Achieving an Ethical Business Corporation

12. *The Obstacles*
    A *Newsweek* article on business ethics concludes, "Even in today's complex world, knowing what's right is comparatively easy. It's doing what's right that's hard." Explain why this statement may be true in modern corporate decision making.

13. *The Steps*
    Another article from *The Wall Street Journal* carries the headline "Tipsters Telephoning Ethics Hot Lines Can End Up Sabotaging Their Own

Jobs." Discuss why whistle-blowing is unpopular within the corporation. Apply to your discussion what sociologist Robert Jackall said about a sub- ordinate's loyalty to supervisors within the cor- poration. Is whistle-blowing an appropriate sub- ject for corporate ethics codes?

Terminology Review

For each term in the left-hand column, match the most appropriate description in the right-hand column.

1. Morality
2. Ethics
3. The good
4. Formalism

5. Consequentialism

6. Duty

7. Categorical imperative

8. Protestant ethic
9. Social contract theory

a. The total values that we choose to pursue
b. Deontology
c. Teleology
d. A formal statement of values together with a rational method to justify the values
e. To be ethical, actions should be appropriate for universal adoption
f. Helped the early success of Western capital- ism
g. John Rawls advocates using it to construct a just society
h. Concepts of right and wrong
i. Moral obligation

THE CONSTITUTION AND BUSINESS

5

Business Decision

Work, Worship, or Golf

Other retail businesses in the mall in which your sports shoes shop is located have decided to open on Sundays from 12 noon to 6 P.M. You decide to follow suit, but two of your employees refuse to go along, saying it is against their religious beliefs to work on the Sabbath. You terminate their employment. They apply for unemployment compensation, and contend their unemployed status is not their fault. If the state grants them benefits, you will be penalized since your unemployment compensation taxes will go up.

Should you contest their claim?

What would be the result if the employees refuse to work on Sunday because of their desire to play golf on that day?

In this chapter, you will study several basic concepts or clauses that are found in the original Constitution. In particular, sections 1 to 4 cover these basic concepts. In latter parts of this chapter, you will study some of our fundamental freedoms as defined in the amendments to the Constitution. Sections 5 to 7 concentrate on aspects of the First Amendment. The Fourteenth Amendment's provisions are the focus of sections 8 to 9.

Through this material you should gain an appreciation of how the federal government's power to regulate business is created and how this power limits the extent of regulation by state and local governments. You will also gain an understanding that even the federal government's authority to regulate is restricted or limited by what we call constitutional protections.

Basic Concepts

The Constitution contains four concepts or clauses that are of great significance to the regulatory environment of business. They are the separation of powers concept, the supremacy clause, the contract clause, and the commerce clause. Each is discussed in the following sections.

1. Separation of Powers

Our federal system of government is one in which the powers of government are separated horizontally and vertically. The horizontal division separates the power and functions among three equal cobranches of government—the legislative, the executive, and the judicial.

The vertical aspect of **separation of powers** is **federalism** or dual federalism. In a federal system there are two levels of government—a federal level and a state and local level. Each has a separate and distinct role to play. The federal government recognizes that it was created by the states and that states have some sovereignty. The Tenth Amendment reserves some powers to the states and to the people. Congress may not impair the ability of state government to function in the federal system. Likewise, state government may not limit the exercise of powers granted by states to the federal government.

2. Supremacy Clause

In allocating power between federal and state levels of government, the Constitution makes it clear that the Constitution is supreme under all laws and that federal law is supreme over a state law or local ordinance. Under the **supremacy clause** courts may be called upon to decide if a state law is invalid because it conflicts with a federal law. They must construe or interpret the two laws to see if they are in conflict. A conflict exists if the state statute would prevent or interfere with the accomplishment and execution of the full purposes and objectives of Congress.

It is immaterial that a state did not intend to frustrate the federal law if the state law in fact does so. For example, an Arizona statute provided for the suspension of licenses of drivers who could not satisfy judgments arising out of auto accidents, even if the driver was bankrupt. The statute was declared unconstitutional since it was in conflict with the federal law on bankruptcy. The purpose of the Bankruptcy Act is to give debtors new opportunity unhampered by the pressure and discouragement of preexisting debt. The challenged state statute hampers the accomplishment and execution of the full purposes and objectives of the Bankruptcy Act enacted by Congress.

Preemption

Sometimes a federal law is said to preempt an area of law. If a federal law preempts a subject, then any state law that attempts to regulate the same activity is unconstitutional under the supremacy clause. The concept of **preemption** applies not only to federal statutes but also to the rules and regulations of federal administrative agencies. Table 5–1 lists several examples of business-related cases in which the courts have found federal preemption of areas involving business regulations.

The following case illustrates the analysis used to determine whether preemption is intended.

TABLE 5–1 **Examples of State Laws Preempted by Federal Law**

State or Local Law	Preempted by Federal Law
A city conditions renewal of taxicab franchise on settlement of a labor dispute.	National Labor Relations Act
Municipal zoning ordinance governs size, location, and appearance of satellite dish antennas.	Federal Communications Commission Regulation
A state statute permits indirect purchasers to collect damages for overcharges resulting from price-fixing conspiracies.	Sherman Antitrust Act
A state law authorizes a tort claim by workers that a union has breached its duty to ensure a safe workplace.	Labor-Management Relations Act (Landrum-Griffin)
A state law prohibits repeat violators of labor laws from doing business with the state.	National Labor Relations Act
A state nuisance law purports to cover out-of-state sources of water pollution.	Clean Water Act
State criminal prosecution for aggravated battery is filed against corporate officials because of unsafe workplace conditions.	Occupational Safety and Health Act
State statute prohibits use of the direct molding process to duplicate unpatented boat hulls or knowing sale of hulls so duplicated.	Patent Law

BARNETT BANK OF MARION COUNTY, N. A. v. NELSON

116 S.Ct. 1103 (1996)

BREYER, J. The question in this case is whether a federal statute that permits national banks to sell insurance in small towns pre-empts a state statute that forbids them to do so. . . . We conclude that, under ordinary pre-emption principles, the federal statute pre-empts the state statute, thereby prohibiting application of the state statute to prevent a national bank from selling insurance in a small town.

In 1916 Congress enacted a federal statute that says that certain national banks "may" sell insurance in small towns. It provides in relevant part:

"In addition to the powers now vested by law in national [banks] organized under the laws of the United States any such [bank] located and doing business in any place [with a population] . . . [of not more than] five thousand . . . may, under such rules and regulations as may be prescribed by the Comptroller of the Currency, act as the agent for any fire, life, or other insurance company authorized by the authorities of the State . . . to do business [there], . . . by soliciting and selling insurance . . . Provided, however, that no such bank shall . . .

guarantee the payment of any premium . . . And provided further, that the bank shall not guarantee the truth of any statement made by an assured [when applying] . . . for insurance."

In 1974 Florida enacted a statute that prohibits certain banks from selling most kinds of insurance. It says:

"No [Florida licensed] insurance agent . . . who is associated with, . . . owned or controlled by . . . a financial institution shall engage in insurance agency activities . . . ."

The term "financial institution" includes

"any bank . . . [except for a] bank which is not a subsidiary or affiliate of a bank holding company and is located in a city having a population of less than 5,000 . . . ."

Thus, the state statute says, in essence, that banks cannot sell insurance in Florida—except that an unaffiliated small town bank (i.e., a bank that is not affiliated with a bank holding company) may sell insurance in a small town.

In October 1993 petitioner Barnett Bank, an "affiliated" national bank which does business through a branch in a small Florida town, bought a Florida licensed insurance agency. The Florida State Insurance Commissioner, pointing to the state statute, (and noting that the unaffiliated small town bank exception did not apply), ordered Barnett's insurance agency to stop selling the prohibited forms of insurance. Barnett, claiming that the federal statute pre-empted the state statute, then filed this action for declaratory and injunctive relief in federal court.

The District Court held that the federal statute did not pre-empt the state statute . . . . The Eleventh Circuit Court of Appeals, for similar reasons, agreed that the federal statute did not pre-empt the state statute.

We granted certiorari due to uncertainty among lower courts about the pre-emptive effect of this federal statute. We now reverse the Eleventh Circuit.

Did Congress, in enacting the federal statute, intend to exercise its constitutionally delegated authority to set aside the laws of a state? If so, the Supremacy Clause requires courts to follow federal, not state, law.

Sometimes courts, when facing the pre-emption question, find language in the federal statute that reveals an explicit congressional intent to pre-empt state law. More often, explicit pre-emption language does not appear, or does not directly answer the question. In that event, courts must consider whether the federal statute's structure and purpose, or nonspecific statutory language, nonetheless reveal a clear, but implicit, pre-emptive intent. A federal statute, for example, may create a scheme of federal regulation so pervasive as to make reasonable the inference that Congress left no room for the states to supplement it. Alternatively, federal law may be in irreconcilable conflict with state law. Compliance with both statutes, for example, may be a physical impossibility, or the state law may stand as an obstacle to the accomplishment and execution of the full purposes and objectives of Congress.

In this case we must ask whether or not the federal and state statutes are in "irreconcilable conflict." The two statutes do not impose directly conflicting duties on national banks—as they would, for example, if the federal law said, "you must sell insurance," while the state law said, "you may not." Nonetheless, the federal statute authorizes national banks to engage in activities that the state statute expressly forbids. Thus, the state's prohibition of those activities would seem to stand as an obstacle to the accomplishment of one of the federal statute's purposes—unless, of course, that federal purpose is to grant the bank only a very limited permission, that is, permission to sell insurance to the extent that state law also grants permission to do so.

That is what the State of Florida . . . argue(s). They say that the federal statute grants national banks a permission that is limited to circumstances where state law is not to the contrary. In their view, the federal statute removes only federal legal obstacles, not state legal obstacles, to the sale of insurance by national banks. But we do not find this, or the state's related, ordinary pre-emption arguments convincing.

For one thing, the federal statute's language suggests a broad, not a limited, permission. That language says, without relevant qualification, that national banks "may . . . act as the agent" for insurance sales. It specifically refers to "rules and regulations" that will govern such sales, while citing as their source not state law, but the federal Comptroller of the Currency. It also specifically refers to state regulation, while limiting that reference to licensing—not of banks or insurance agents, but of the insurance companies whose policies the bank, as insurance agent, will sell.

For another thing, the federal statute says that its grant of authority to sell insurance is an "addition to the powers now vested by law in national [banks]." In using the word "powers," the statute chooses a legal concept that, in the context of national bank legislation, has a history. That history is one of interpreting grants of both enumerated and incidental "powers" to national banks as grants of authority not normally limited by, but rather ordinarily pre-empting, contrary state law. Thus, this Court, in a case quite similar to this one, held that a federal statute permitting, but not requiring, national banks to receive savings deposits, pre-empts a state statute prohibiting certain state and national banks from using the word "savings" in their advertising. *Franklin Nat. Bank v. New York,* 74 S. Ct. 550 (1954). . . .

The federal statute before us, as in *Franklin Nat. Bank,* explicitly grants a national bank an authorization, permission, or power. And, as in *Franklin Nat. Bank,* it contains no indication that Congress intended to subject that power to local restriction. . . .

We have found nothing elsewhere in the federal statute's background or history that significantly supports the state's arguments. . . .

In light of these considerations, we conclude that the federal statute means to grant small town national banks authority to sell insurance, whether or not a state grants its own state banks or national banks similar approval. Were we to apply ordinary legal principles of pre-emption, the federal law would pre-empt that of the state. . . .

For these reasons, the judgment of the Court of Appeals is [*reversed*].

Case Questions

1. What does the federal law allow banks to do?
2. What does the Florida state law prohibit banks from doing?

3. When considering the possibility of implicit pre-emption, the U.S. Supreme Court mentions two types of analysis. What are these analyses?
4. What is the U.S. Supreme Court's conclusion regarding pre-emption in this case?

3. The Contract Clause

Article I, Section 10, of the Constitution says, "No State shall . . . pass any . . . Law impairing the Obligation of contracts." This is the **contract clause.** It does not apply to the federal government, which does in fact frequently enact laws and adopt regulations that affect existing contracts. For example, the Department of Agriculture from time to time embargoes grain sales to foreign countries, usually as a result of problems in foreign affairs.

The limitation on state action impairing contracts has not been given a literal application. As a result of judicial interpretation, some state laws that affect existing contracts have been approved, especially when the law is passed to deal with a specific emergency situation. On the other hand, this constitutional provision does generally limit alternatives available to state government and prevents the enactment of legislation that changes vested contract rights.

4. The Commerce Clause and Federal Regulation

The power of the federal government to regulate business activity is found in the **commerce clause** of the Constitution. Article I, Section 8, states "Congress shall have Power . . . to regulate Commerce with foreign Nations, and among the several States, and with the Indian Tribes."

This simple-sounding clause has been interpreted as creating at least four important areas involving various aspects of the government regulating business. The following headings within this section illustrate that the commerce clause is viewed as a positive grant of power to the federal government to regulate interstate commerce as well as foreign commerce. This clause also has been interpreted to be a restriction on state and local governments' authority to regulate business, with the issue of taxation being a much litigated area. Because the regulatory issues related to interstate commerce are more numerous and perplexing than those involving foreign commerce, we present the interstate commerce subject matter first.

Interstate Commerce

Throughout our constitutional history the meaning of the phrase in the commerce clause granting the federal government the power to regulate commerce "among the several States" has been extensively litigated. At first this phrase was interpreted to mean interstate commerce as contrasted with intrastate commerce. Later, in a long series of judicial decisions, the power of the federal government was expanded through interpretation to include not only persons *engaged* in interstate commerce but also activities *affecting* interstate commerce.

The power of Congress over commerce is very broad; it extends to all commerce, be it great or small. Labeling an activity a "local" or "intrastate" activity does not resolve the question of whether Congress may regulate it under the commerce clause. The commerce power extends to those intrastate activities that so affect interstate commerce, or the exertion of the power of Congress over it, as to make regulation of them appropriate. Regulation is appropriate if it aids in the effective regulation of interstate commerce. Even activity that is purely intrastate in character may be regulated by Congress, when the activity, combined with like conduct by others similarly situated, substantially affects commerce among the states.

Impact on the State Police Power

The grant of power to Congress over commerce does not contain any provision that expressly excludes states from exercising authority over commerce. Nevertheless, there are definite limitations on the state powers over commerce because of the commerce clause. These limitations reflect the **dominant commerce clause concept.**

The decisions of the Court have established three distinct subject areas of governmental regulation of commerce. Some areas are exclusively federal, some are said to be exclusively local, and still others are such that regulation of them may be dual.

Exclusively Federal. The subject area that is exclusively federal concerns those internal matters where uniformity on a nationwide basis is essential. Any state regulation of such subjects is void whether Congress has entered the field or not.

A classic example of a regulatory area that needs to be limited to the federal government is the opening and closing of airports. Because airlines need access to airports consistent with their routes, havoc could ensue if local authorities were allowed to set the hours that their airports operate. The regulation of the operating hours of airports is best left to the Federal Aviation Administration so that a coordinated effort is present.

Exclusively Local. In theory, those matters that are exclusively within the states' power are intrastate activities that do not have a substantial effect on interstate commerce. As noted in the previous section, it is becoming more and more difficult, if not impossible, to find a subject matter that is truly exclusively local in the sense that it does not affect interstate commerce.

Dual Regulation. Between the two extremes, joint regulation is permissible. This area can be divided into the following three subparts:

- Federal preemption
- Federal regulation but no preemption
- No federal regulation

The first subpart concerns those subjects over which the federal government has preempted the field. By express language or by comprehensive regulation Congress has shown that it intends to exercise exclusive control over the subject matter. When a federal statute has thus preempted the field, *any* state or local law pertaining to the same subject matter is unconstitutional under the commerce clause and the supremacy clause, and the state regulation is void. The net effect of a law that preempts the field makes the subject matter of the law exclusively federal.

The second subpart includes situations in which the federal regulation of a subject matter is not comprehensive enough to preempt the field. Here state regulation is permitted, but when state law is inconsistent or conflicts irreconcilably with the federal statute, it is unconstitutional and void. **Irreconcilable conflicts** exist when it is not possible for a business to comply with both statutes. If compliance with both is not possible, the state law must fall under the supremacy clause and the commerce clause. If compliance with both is reasonably possible, dual compliance is required. This usually has the effect of forcing business to meet the requirements of the law with the greatest burden. For example, if the state minimum wage is $5.35 per hour and the federal is $5.15, employers would be required to pay $5.35 since the conflict can be reconciled.

The commerce clause also invalidates state laws imposing an **undue burden** on interstate commerce. The commerce clause does not prohibit the imposing of burdens on interstate commerce—only the imposition of *undue* burdens. The states have the authority under the police power to regulate matters of legitimate local concern, even though interstate commerce may be affected.

State statutes fall into two categories: those that burden interstate commerce only incidentally and those that affirmatively discriminate against such transactions. For cases in the first category, courts weigh the burdens against the benefits and find undue burdens only if they clearly exceed the local benefits. Cases in the second category are subject to more demanding scrutiny. If a state law either in substance or in practical effect discriminates against interstate commerce, the state must prove not only that the law has a legitimate purpose but also that the purpose cannot be achieved by nondiscriminatory means. If a state law is pure economic protectionism, the courts apply a virtual per se or automatic rule of invalidity.

The third area of possible joint regulation exists where there is no federal law at all. When there is no federal regulation of a subject, state regulation of interstate commerce is permissible, providing, of course, that it does not impose an undue burden on interstate commerce and does not discriminate against interstate commerce in favor of local business.

The commerce clause also has been construed as **prohibiting discrimination** against interstate commerce in favor of intrastate commerce. State and local governments frequently attempt by legislation to aid local business in its competition with interstate business. The commerce clause requires that all regulations be the same for local businesses as for businesses engaged in interstate commerce. A state may not place itself in a position of economic isolation from other states. The following case illustrates the interpretation of the commerce clause as it impacts the discriminatory nature of state regulations.

West Lynn Creamery, Inc. v. Healy

114 S. Ct. 2205 (1994)

The Massachusetts Commissioner of Food and Agriculture found that dairy farmers' costs of production was rais-
ing beyond the level for which they could sell their milk. In response to this finding, Healy (the Commissioner) or-
dered every dealer who handles milk and sells it to retailers to pay a monthly assessment (called a "premium pay-
ment") based on the amount of milk handled. These assessments are distributed to Massachusetts dairy farmers
based on their share of the state's total production of raw milk.

STEVENS, J. . . . Petitioner West Lynn Creamery, Inc., is a milk dealer licensed to do business in Massachusetts. It purchases raw milk, which it processes, packages, and sells to wholesalers, retailers, and other milk dealers. About 97% of the raw milk it purchases is produced by out-of-state farmers. Petitioner LeComte's Dairy, Inc., is also a licensed Massachusetts milk dealer. It purchases all of its milk from West Lynn and distributes it to retail outlets in Massachusetts. . . .

Petitioners West Lynn and LeComte's complied with the pricing order for two months, paying almost $200,000 into the Massachusetts Dairy Equalization Fund. Starting in July 1992, however, petitioners refused to make the premium payments, and respondent commenced license revocation proceedings. Petitioners then filed an action in state court seeking an injunction against enforcement of the order on the ground that it violated the Commerce Clause of the Federal Constitution. The state court denied relief and respondent conditionally revoked their licenses.

The parties agreed to an expedited appellate procedure, and the Supreme Judicial Court of Massachusetts transferred the cases to its own docket. It affirmed, because it concluded that "the pricing order does not discriminate on its face, is evenhanded in its application, and only incidentally burdens interstate commerce." The Court noted that the "pricing order was designed to aid only Massachusetts producers." It conceded that "common sense" indicated that the plan has an "adverse impact on interstate commerce" and that "the fund distribution scheme does burden out-of-State producers." Nevertheless, the Court asserted that "the burden is incidental given the purpose and design of the program." Because it found that the "local benefits" provided to the Commonwealth's dairy industry "outweigh any incidental burden on interstate commerce," it sustained the constitutionality of the pricing order. We granted certiorari and now reverse. . . .

Because of their distorting effects on the geography of production, tariffs have long been recognized as violative of the Commerce Clause. In fact, tariffs against the products of other States are so patently unconstitutional that our cases reveal not a single attempt by any State to enact one. Instead, the cases are filled with state laws that aspire to reap some of the benefits of tariffs by other means. . . .

Massachusetts' pricing order is clearly unconstitutional. Its avowed purpose and its undisputed effect are to enable higher cost Massachusetts dairy farmers to compete with lower cost dairy farmers in other States. The "premium payments" are effectively a tax which makes milk produced out of State more expensive. Although the tax also applies to milk produced in Massachusetts, its effect on Massachusetts producers is entirely (indeed more than) offset by the subsidy provided exclusively to Massachusetts dairy farmers. Like an ordinary tariff, the tax is thus effectively imposed only on out-of-state products. The pricing order thus allows Massachusetts dairy farmers who produce at higher cost to sell at or below the price charged by lower cost out-of-state producers. If there were no federal minimum prices for milk, out-of-state producers might still be able to retain their market share by lowering their prices. Nevertheless, out-of-staters' ability to remain competitive by lowering their prices would not immunize a discriminatory measure. In this case, because the Federal Government sets minimum prices, out-of-state producers may not even have the option of reducing prices in order to retain market share. The Massachusetts pricing order thus will almost certainly cause local goods to constitute a larger share, and goods with an out-of-state source to constitute a smaller share, of the total sales in the market. In fact, this effect was the motive behind the promulgation of the pricing order. This effect renders the program unconstitutional, because it, like a tariff, neutralizes advantages belonging to the place of origin. . . .

Respondent advances four arguments against the conclusion that its pricing order imposes an unconstitutional burden on interstate commerce: (A) Because each component of the program—a local subsidy and a non-discriminatory tax—is valid, the combination of the two is equally valid; (B) The dealers who pay the order premiums (the tax) are not competitors of the farmers who receive disbursements from the Dairy Equalization Fund, so the pricing order is not discriminatory; (C) The pricing order is not protectionist, because the costs of the program are borne only by Massachusetts dealers and consumers, and the benefits are distributed exclusively to Massachusetts farmers; and (D) the order's incidental burden on commerce is justified by the local benefit of saving the dairy industry from collapse. We discuss each of these arguments in turn.

Even granting respondent's assertion that both components of the pricing order would be constitutional standing alone, the pricing order nevertheless must fall. A pure subsidy funded out of general revenue ordinarily imposes no burden on interstate commerce, but merely assists local business. The pricing order in this case, however, is funded principally from taxes on the sale of milk produced in other States. By so funding the subsidy, respondent not only assists local farmers, but burdens interstate commerce. The pricing order thus violates the cardinal principle that a State may not benefit in-state economic interests by burdening out-of-state competitors.

More fundamentally, respondent errs in assuming that the constitutionality of the pricing order follows logically from the constitutionality of its component parts. By conjoining a tax and a subsidy, Massachusetts has created a program more dangerous to interstate commerce than either part alone. . . . [W]hen a nondiscriminatory tax is coupled with a subsidy to one of the groups hurt by the tax, a state's political processes can no longer be relied upon to prevent legislative abuse, because one of the in-state interests which would otherwise lobby against the tax has been mollified by the subsidy. So, in this case, one would ordinarily have expected at least three groups to lobby against the order premium, which, as a tax, raises the price (and hence lowers demand) for milk: dairy farmers, milk dealers, and consumers. But because the tax was coupled with a subsidy, one of the most powerful of these groups, Massachusetts dairy farmers, instead of exerting their influence against the tax, were in fact its primary supporters.

Respondent's argument would require us to analyze separately two parts of an integrated regulation, but we cannot divorce the premium payments from the use to which the payments are put. It is the entire program—not just the contributions to the fund or the distributions from that fund—that simultaneously burdens interstate commerce and discriminates in favor of local producers. The choice of constitutional means—nondiscriminatory tax and local subsidy—cannot guarantee the constitutionality of the program as a whole. . . .

Respondent also argues that since the Massachusetts milk dealers who pay the order premiums are not competitors of the Massachusetts farmers, the pricing order imposes no discriminatory burden on commerce. This argument cannot withstand scrutiny. Is it possible to doubt that if Massachusetts imposed a higher sales tax on milk produced in Maine than milk produced in Massachusetts that the tax would be struck down, in spite of the fact that the sales tax was imposed on consumers, and consumers do not compete with dairy farmers? For over 150 years, our cases have rightly concluded that the imposition of a differential burden on any part of the stream of commerce—from wholesaler to retailer to consumer—is invalid, because a burden placed at any point will result in a disadvantage to the out-of-state producer.

Respondent also argues that "the operation of the Order disproves any claim of protectionism," because "only in-state consumers feel the effect of any retail price increase . . . [and] the dealers themselves . . . have a substantial in-state presence." This argument, if accepted, would undermine almost every discriminatory tax case. State taxes are ordinarily paid by in-state businesses and consumers, yet if they discriminate against out-of-state products, they are unconstitutional. . . .

More fundamentally, respondent ignores the fact that Massachusetts dairy farmers are part of an integrated interstate market. The Massachusetts producers who deliver milk to dealers in that regulated market are participants in the same interstate milk market as the out-of-state producers who sell in the same market and are guaranteed the same minimum blend price by the federal order. The fact that the Massachusetts order imposes assessments only on Massachusetts sales and distributes them only to Massachusetts producers does not exclude either the assessments or the payments from the interstate market. To the extent that those assessments affect the relative volume of Class I milk products sold in the marketing area as compared to other classes of milk products, they necessarily affect the blend price payable even to out-of-state producers who sell only in non-Massachusetts markets. The obvious impact of the order on out-of-state production demonstrates that it is simply wrong to assume that the pricing order burdens only Massachusetts consumers and dealers.

Finally, respondent argues that any incidental burden on interstate commerce "is outweighed by the 'local benefits' of preserving the Massachusetts dairy industry." In a closely related argument, respondent urges that "the purpose of the order, to save an industry from collapse, is not protectionist." If we were to accept these arguments, we would make a virtue of the vice that the rule against discrimination condemns. Preservation of local industry by protecting it from the rigors of interstate competition is the hallmark of the economic protectionism that the Commerce Clause prohibits. . . . Whether a State is attempting to "enhance thriving and substantial business enterprises" or to "subsidize . . . financially troubled" ones is irrelevant to Commerce Clause analysis.

The judgment of the Supreme Judicial Court of Massachusetts is [*reversed*].

Case Questions

1. What two-step program did the Massachusetts Commissioner of Food and Agriculture implement to "save" the state's dairy farmers?

2. How did the Massachusetts court system decide this case?

3. What four arguments were made by the respondent justifying the assessment and distribution program?

4. How did the U.S. Supreme Court respond to each of these arguments?

Concept Summary: Possible Subjects for Government Regulation

Exclusively Federal Subjects

- Any state regulatory law is unconstitutional under the supremacy and commerce clauses.

Exclusively Local Subjects

- The impact on state and local government of laws based on the commerce clause is very limited; very few subjects, if any, are exclusively local.

Possible Dual Regulation Subjects

- Federal law preempts the field. The subject matter is considered exclusively federal.

- Federal law does not preempt the field. A state law is unconstitutional if it:
  1. Is in irreconcilable conflict with federal law
  2. Constitutes an undue burden on interstate commerce
  3. Discriminates against interstate commerce in favor of intrastate commerce

- No federal law. A state law is unconstitutional if it:
  1. Constitutes an undue burden on interstate commerce
  2. Discriminates against interstate commerce in favor of intrastate commerce

---

State Taxation

Taxation is a primary form of regulation. Therefore, taxes imposed by state and local governments are subject to the limitations imposed by the commerce clause. The commerce clause limits property taxes, income taxes, and sales or use taxes levied by state and local governments on interstate commerce. Since taxation distributes the cost of government among those who receive its benefits, interstate commerce is not exempt from state and local taxes. The purpose of the commerce clause is to ensure that a taxpayer engaged in interstate commerce only pays its fair share of state taxes.

To prevent multiple taxation of the same property or income of interstate businesses, taxes are apportioned. **Apportionment** formulas allocate the tax burden of an interstate business among the states entitled to tax it. The commerce clause requires states to use reasonable formulas when more than one state is taxing the same thing.

To justify the tax, there must be sufficient contact, connection, tie, or link between the business and the taxing state. In other words, there must be sufficient local activities to justify the tax in a constitutional sense. This connection is called the **nexus.** A business operating in a state directly benefits from its police and fire protection, the use of its roads, and the like. Indirectly, it will be able to recruit employees more easily if they have easy access to good schools, parks, and civic centers. If the state gives anything for which it can reasonably expect payment, then the tax has a sufficient nexus. In cases involving property taxes, the term *taxable situs* is used in place of nexus, but each is concerned with the adequacy of local activities to support the tax.

The concepts of undue burdens against interstate commerce and discrimination against interstate commerce through taxation are the same as these concepts as applied to other forms of regulation. Taxes that differ from those levied on intrastate commerce cannot be levied on interstate commerce.

Foreign Commerce

The first part of the commerce clause grants the federal government power to regulate foreign commerce. The power to regulate foreign commerce is vested exclusively in the federal government, and it extends to all aspects of foreign trade. In other words, the power to regulate foreign commerce is total. The federal government can prohibit foreign commerce entirely. In recent years, for example, the federal government has imposed trade embargoes on countries such as South Africa, Iraq, Bosnia, and Haiti. It can also allow commerce with restrictions.

That the federal power to regulate foreign commerce is exclusive means state and local governments may not regulate such commerce. State and local governments sometimes attempt directly or indirectly to regulate imports or exports to some degree. Such attempts generally are unconstitutional. However, a state may regulate activities that relate to foreign commerce if such activities are conducted entirely within the state's boundaries. For example, the U.S. Supreme Court has upheld a state tax on the leases of cargo containers used in international trade. This decision was based on the tax being fairly apportioned to the use of the cargo containers within the state. Hence, the Court concluded that the state tax did not violate the foreign commerce clause.*

Regulation and Basic Freedoms

The First Amendment to the Constitution of the United States establishes the following basic freedoms:

- Freedom of religion
- Freedom of speech
- Freedom of the press
- Freedom of assembly
- The right to petition the government for a redress of grievances

---

*Itel Containers Int'l Corp. v. Huddleston, 113 S.Ct. 1095 (1993).

Usually we do not think of these freedoms in a business context; we think of them as the personal rights of individuals in a free society. There are, however, very important aspects of these freedoms relating to economic opportunity and business activity.

As the impact of these basic freedoms on government is studied, four important aspects should be kept in mind. First, basic constitutional rights are not absolutes. Second, the extent of any limitation on a basic constitutional guarantee depends upon the nature of the competing public policy. Cases involving the Bill of Rights almost always require courts to strike a balance either between some goal or policy of society and the constitutional protection involved or between competing constitutional guarantees. For example, such cases may involve conflict between the goal of protecting an individual's or business's reputation and the right of another to speak freely about that reputation. The courts are continually weighing the extent of constitutional protections.

Third, constitutional guarantees exist in order to remove certain issues from the political process and the ballot box. They exist to protect the minority from the majority. Freedom of expression (press and speech) protects the unpopular idea or viewpoint. Freedom of assembly allows groups with ideologies foreign to most of us to meet and express their philosophy. The Bill of Rights protects the "worst" among us even more than it does the "best."

Finally, constitutional rights vary from time to time and may be narrowly interpreted during emergencies such as war or civil strife. Even during peacetime constitutional principles are constantly reapplied and reexamined.

5. Freedom of Religion

The First Amendment states that Congress shall make no law "respecting an establishment of religion" (the **establishment clause**) "or prohibiting the free exercise thereof" (the **free exercise clause**). These clauses guarantee freedom of religion through the separation of church and state.

Most business-related freedom of religion cases involve the free exercise clause. The Supreme Court has held that the denial of unemployment benefits to a worker who refused a position because the job would have required him to work on Sunday violated the free exercise clause of the First Amendment. Thus the law requires that the owner of the business either allow the person to have Sunday off or allow the state to pay unemployment compensation and increase the business's taxes.

Freedom of religion has been used to challenge legislation requiring the closing of business establishments on Sunday. Although the motive for such legislation may be, in part, religious, there are also economic reasons for such legislation. As a result, if a law is based on economic considerations, it may be upheld if its classifications are reasonable and in the public interest. However, many such laws have been held invalid as a violation of the First Amendment.

Other examples of freedom-of-religion cases that concern business are presented in Table 5–2.

TABLE 5–2 Examples of Freedom of Religion Issues Affecting Business

	Case Decisions	
	Yes	*No*
Is it constitutional to apply the Fair Labor Standards Act (minimum-wage law) to a nonprofit religious organization?	X	
Is it constitutional to apply the labor laws relating to union elections to parochial school teachers?		X
Is a state law constitutional that provides Sabbath observers with an absolute and unqualified right not to work on their Sabbath?		X
Is religious belief justification for refusing to participate in the Social Security system?		X
Does the 1964 Civil Rights Act, which obligates employers to make reasonable accommodations of employees' religious beliefs, violate the First Amendment's establishment clause?		X
May a state impose a 6 percent sales tax on religious merchandise sold in the state by religious organizations?	X	
May a state exempt religious periodicals from a sales tax that applies to all other periodicals?		X

6. Freedom of the Press

The publishing business is the only organized private business given explicit constitutional protection. The First Amendment states that "Congress shall make no law . . . abridging the freedom of . . . the press." This guarantee essentially authorizes a private business to provide organized scrutiny of government.

Freedom of the press is not absolute. The press is not free to print anything it wants without liability. Rather, freedom of the press is usually construed to prohibit **prior restraints** on publications. If the press publishes that which is illegal or libelous, it has liability for doing so. This liability may be either criminal or civil for damages.

There are many examples of limitations on freedom of the press. For example, courts have allowed the Federal Communications Commission to censor "filthy" words on television. The power of the commission extends to upholding the public's interest in responsible broadcasting.

A major area of litigation involving freedom of the press involves **defamation.** The tort theory known as **libel** is used to recover damages as a result of printed defamation of character. Libel cases compensate individuals for harm inflicted by defamatory printed falsehoods. Since the threat of a libel suit could have a chilling effect on freedom of the press and on the public's rights to information, the law has a different standard for imposing liability when the printed matter concerns an issue of public interest and concern. If the person involved is a public official or figure, a plaintiff seeking damages for emotional distress caused by offensive publications must prove actual **malice** in order to recover. *Actual malice* includes knowledge that the printed statements were false or circumstances showing a reckless disregard for whether they were true or not. If the plaintiff is not a public figure or public official, there is liability for libelous statements without proof of malice.

7. Freedom of Speech

Freedom of speech, sometimes referred to as freedom of expression, covers both verbal and written communications. In addition, it covers conduct or actions considered **symbolic speech.** Although freedom of speech is not absolute, it is as close to being absolute as any constitutional guarantee. It exists to protect the minority from the majority. It means freedom to express ideas antagonistic to those of the majority. Freedom of speech exists for thoughts many of us hate and for ideas that may be foreign to us. It means freedom to express the unorthodox, and it recognizes that there is no such thing as a false idea.

The issue of freedom of speech arises in many business situations. Cases involving picketing, for example, especially with unions, often are concerned with this issue. The right to picket peacefully for a lawful purpose is well recognized. A state or local law that prohibits all picketing would be unconstitutional since the act of picketing, itself, is a valuable form of communication. However, a state law that limits picketing or other First Amendment freedoms may be constitutional if:

· The regulation is within the constitutional power of government
· It furthers an important or substantial governmental interest
· It is unrelated to suppression of free expression
· The incidental restriction on First Amendment freedoms is no greater than is essential to further the government's interest

Under these principles, laws that prevent pickets from obstructing traffic and those designed to prevent violence would be constitutional. For example, a Texas statute that prohibits "mass picketing," defined as picketing by more than two persons within 50 feet of any entrance or of one another, does not violate the First Amendment. The Supreme Court has held that a city ordinance prohibiting picketing in front of an individual residence was constitutional. The law was enacted to prevent picketing of the homes of doctors who perform abortions. It did not ban all residential picketing and met the four tests previously noted.

Courts may limit the number of pickets to preserve order and promote safety, but they will not deny pickets the right to express opinions in a picket line. For example, a court order preventing a client from picketing her lawyer was held to be a violation of the First Amendment. Freedom of speech even extends to boycotts of a business for a valid public purpose such as the elimination of discrimination.

Freedom of expression does not protect obscene materials. The community's interest in banning such material outweighs any First Amendment interests. The difficult issues in obscenity cases are defining obscenity and determining whether or not items involved are obscene. A movie, book, or magazine is obscene and subject to state regulation if it violates a three-part test:

· If it, taken as a whole, appeals to a prurient interest in sex
· If it portrays, in a clearly offensive way, sexual conduct as specifically defined by the applicable state law
· If it, taken as a whole, does not have serious literary, artistic, political, or scientific value

In deciding whether allegedly obscene work has "literary, artistic, political, or scientific value," a court must determine not whether an ordinary member of any given community would find serious literary, artistic, political, or scientific value in a work, but whether a reasonable person would find such value in the material taken as whole.

In some free-speech cases, an individual whose own speech or conduct may not be prohibited is nevertheless permitted to challenge a statute limiting speech because it also threatens other people not before the court. The person is allowed to challenge the statute because others who may desire to engage in legally protected expression may refrain from doing so. They may fear the risk of prosecution, or they may not want to risk having a law declared to be only partially invalid. This is known as the **overbreadth doctrine.** It means that the legislators have gone too far in seeking to achieve a goal.

For example, an airport authority resolution declared the central terminal area "not open for First Amendment activities." The resolution was unconstitutional under the First Amendment overbreadth doctrine. The resolution reached the "universe of expressive activity" and in effect created a "First-Amendment-Free Zone" at the airport. Nearly every person who entered the airport would violate the resolution, since it bars all First Amendment activities, including talking and reading.

Commercial Speech

Historically, **commercial speech** was not protected by the First Amendment. However, in the 1970s the Supreme Court began to recognize that free commercial speech was essential to the public's right to know. Therefore, today, freedom of speech protects corporations as well as individuals. The public interests served by freedom of expression protect the listener as well as the speaker. Freedom of expression includes freedom of information or the rights of the public to be informed. Since corporations may add to the public's knowledge and information, they also have the right to free speech. Although freedom of speech for corporations may not be coextensive with the right of an individual, it may not be limited without a compelling state interest in doing so. State regulatory commissions often seek to limit the activities of public utilities. Such attempts usually run afoul of the First Amendment. The following case explains why and to what extent commercial speech is protected.

44 LIQUORMART, INC. V. RHODE ISLAND

116 S. Ct. 1495 (1996)

The State of Rhode Island allows advertising of alcoholic beverage prices only in the stores where the alcohol is sold. State law bans such advertising "outside the licensed premises." 44 Liquormart, Inc., a licensed retailer, ran a newspaper ad stating the low prices at which peanuts, potato chips, and Schweppes mixers were being offered, identifying various brands of packaged liquor, and including the word "WOW" in large letters next to the pictures of vodka and rum bottles. As a result of this ad, the Rhode Island Liquor Control Administrator assessed 44 Liquormart a fine of $400. 44 Liquormart paid the fine and sought a declaratory judgment in Federal District Court that the Rhode Island off-premise advertising law was in violation of the First Amendment's free speech protection.

STEVENS, J. . . . The parties disagreed . . . about the impact of the ban on the promotion of temperance in Rhode Island. On that question the District Court heard conflicting expert testimony and reviewed a number of studies.

In his findings of fact, the District Judge first noted that there was a pronounced lack of unanimity among researchers who have studied the impact of advertising on the level of consumption of alcoholic beverages. He referred to a 1985 Federal Trade Commission study that found no evidence that alcohol advertising significantly affects alcohol abuse. Another study indicated that Rhode Island ranks in the upper 30% of States in per capita consumption of alcoholic beverages; alcohol consumption is lower in other States that allow price advertising. After summarizing the testimony of the expert witnesses for both parties, he found "as a fact that Rhode Island's off-premises liquor price advertising ban has no significant impact on levels of alcohol consumption in Rhode Island."

As a matter of law, he concluded that the price advertising ban was unconstitutional because it did not "directly advance" the State's interest in reducing alcohol consumption and was "more extensive than necessary to serve that interest.". . .

The Court of Appeals reversed. It found "inherent merit" in the State's submission that competitive price advertising would lower prices and that lower prices would produce more sales. . . .

Advertising has been a part of our culture throughout our history. Even in colonial days, the public relied on "commercial speech" for vital information about the market. Early newspapers displayed advertisements for goods and services on their front pages, and town criers called out prices in public squares.

In accord with the role that commercial messages have long played, the law has developed to ensure that advertising provides consumers with accurate information about the availability of goods and services. In the early years, the common law, and later, statutes, served the consumers' interest in the receipt of accurate information in the commercial market by prohibiting fraudulent and misleading advertising. It was not until the 1970's, however, that this Court held that the First Amendment protected the dissemination of truthful and nonmisleading commercial messages about lawful products and services.

In *Bigelow v. Virginia*, 95 S. Ct. 2222 (1975), we held that it was error to assume that commercial speech was entitled to no First Amendment protection or that it was without value in the marketplace of ideas. The following Term in *Virginia Bd. of Pharmacy v. Virginia Citizens Consumer Council, Inc.*, 96 S.Ct. 1817 (1976),

we expanded on our holding in *Bigelow* and held that the State's blanket ban on advertising the price of prescription drugs violated the First Amendment. *Virginia Pharmacy Bd.* reflected the conclusion that the same interest that supports regulation of potentially misleading advertising, namely the public's interest in receiving accurate commercial information, also supports an interpretation of the First Amendment that provides constitutional protection for the dissemination of accurate and nonmisleading commercial messages. We explained:

> Advertising, however tasteless and excessive it sometimes may seem, is nonetheless dissemination of information as to who is producing and selling what product, for what reason, and at what price. So long as we preserve a predominantly free enterprise economy, the allocation of our resources in large measure will be made through numerous private economic decisions. It is a matter of public interest that those decisions, in the aggregate, be intelligent and well informed. To this end, the free flow of commercial information is indispensable.

. . . At the same time, our early cases recognized that the State may regulate some types of commercial advertising more freely than other forms of protected speech. Specifically, we explained that the State may require commercial messages to "appear in such a form, or include such additional information, warnings, and disclaimers, as are necessary to prevent its being deceptive," and that it may restrict some forms of aggressive sales practices that have the potential to exert "undue influence" over consumers. . . .

In *Central Hudson Gas & Elec. Corp. v. Public Serv. Comm'n of N.Y.*, 100 S. Ct. 2343 (1980), we took stock of our developing commercial speech jurisprudence. In that case, we considered a regulation "completely" banning all promotional advertising by electric utilities. Our decision acknowledged the special features of commercial speech but identified the serious First Amendment concerns that attend blanket advertising prohibitions that do not protect consumers from commercial harms. . . .

In reaching its conclusion, the majority explained that although the special nature of commercial speech may require less than strict review of its regulation, special concerns arise from "regulations that entirely suppress commercial speech in order to pursue a nonspeech-related policy." In those circumstances, "a ban on speech could screen from public view the underlying governmental policy." As a result, the Court concluded that "special care" should attend the review of such blanket bans, and it pointedly remarked that "in recent years this Court has not approved a blanket ban on commercial speech unless the speech itself was flawed in some way, either because it was deceptive or related to unlawful activity."

As our review of the case law reveals, Rhode Island errs in concluding that all commercial speech regulations are subject to a similar form of constitutional review simply because they target a similar category of expression. The mere fact that messages propose commercial transactions does not in and of itself dictate the constitutional analysis that should apply to decisions to suppress them.

When a State regulates commercial messages to protect consumers from misleading, deceptive, or aggressive sales practices, or requires the disclosure of beneficial consumer information, the purpose of its regulation is consistent with the reasons for according constitutional protection to commercial speech and therefore justifies less than strict review. However, when a State entirely prohibits the dissemination of truthful, nonmisleading commercial messages for reasons unrelated to the preservation of a fair bargaining process, there is far less reason to depart from the rigorous review that the First Amendment generally demands. . . .

In this case, there is no question that Rhode Island's price advertising ban constitutes a blanket prohibition against truthful, nonmisleading speech about a lawful product. There is also no question that the ban serves an end unrelated to consumer protection. Accordingly, we must review the price advertising ban with special care mindful that speech prohibitions of this type rarely survive constitutional review.

The State argues that the price advertising prohibition should nevertheless be upheld because it directly advances the State's substantial interest in promoting temperance, and because it is no more extensive than necessary. Although there is some confusion as to what Rhode Island means by temperance, we assume that the State asserts an interest in reducing alcohol consumption.

In evaluating the ban's effectiveness in advancing the State's interest, we note that a commercial speech regulation "may not be sustained if it provides only ineffective or remote support for the government's purpose." For that reason, the State bears the burden of showing not merely that its regulation will advance its interest, but also that it will do so "to a material degree." The need for the State to make such a showing is particularly great given the drastic nature of its chosen means—the wholesale suppression of truthful, nonmisleading information. Accordingly, we must determine whether the State has shown that the price advertising ban will significantly reduce alcohol consumption. . . .

Although the record suggests that the price advertising ban may have some impact on the purchasing patterns of temperate drinkers of modest means, the State has presented no evidence to suggest that its speech prohibition will significantly reduce market-wide consumption. Indeed, the District Court's considered and uncontradicted finding on this point is directly to the contrary. Moreover, the evidence suggests that the abusive drinker will probably not be deterred by a marginal price increase, and that the true alcoholic may simply reduce his purchases of other necessities.

In addition, as the District Court noted, the State has not identified what price level would lead to a significant reduction in alcohol consumption, nor has it identified the amount that it believes prices would decrease without the ban. Thus, the State's own showing reveals that any connection between the ban and a significant change in alcohol consumption would be purely fortuitous.

As is evident, any conclusion that elimination of the ban would significantly increase alcohol consumption would require us to engage in the sort of speculation or conjecture that is an unacceptable means of demonstrating that a restriction on commercial speech directly advances the State's asserted interest. Such speculation certainly does not suffice when the State takes aim at accurate commercial information for paternalistic ends.

The State also cannot satisfy the requirement that its restriction on speech be no more extensive than necessary. It is perfectly obvious that alternative forms of regulation that would not involve any restriction on speech would be more likely to achieve the State's goal of promoting temperance. As the State's own expert conceded, higher prices can be maintained either by direct regulation or by increased taxation. Per capita purchases could be limited as is the case with prescription drugs. Even educational campaigns focused on the problems of excessive, or even moderate, drinking might prove to be more effective.

As a result, even under the less than strict standard that generally applies in commercial speech cases, the State has failed to establish a "reasonable fit" between its abridgment of speech and its temperance goal. It necessarily follows that the price advertising ban cannot survive the more stringent constitutional review that *Central Hudson* itself concluded was appropriate for the complete suppression of truthful, nonmisleading commercial speech.

Because Rhode Island has failed to carry its heavy burden of justifying its complete ban on price advertising, the judgment of the Court of Appeals is therefore [*reversed*].

Case Questions

1. To what extent did Rhode Island attempt to regulate the commercial speech of alcohol beverage prices?

2. What were the holdings of the District Court and the Court of Appeals?

3. What standard of review does the Supreme Court use in analyzing regulations of commercial speech?

4. Why does the Rhode Island regulation fail to satisfy this standard of review?

In light of your study of the preceding case, the issue of regulating advertising of tobacco products is an interesting consideration. How would you respond to the questions asked in the following Tobacco Industry Box?

Tobacco Industry Box

Suppose that you are a staff member of the Federal Trade Commission and that you are responsible for protecting the public against unfair methods of competition. You have been asked to research how the federal government can restrict a cigarette manufacturing company's advertising campaign. Through use of cartoon characters, this campaign is supposedly directed toward increasing smoking among young persons. Your supervisor wants to know whether the government can ban the use of a particular cartoon character that surveys show appeals to teenagers. Specifically, what answers can you provide to the following questions:

- Is a private company's advertising protected by the Constitution's Free Speech clause?
- What alternatives do you have if a direct governmental ban of advertising is prohibited?

The Fourteenth Amendment

The Fourteenth Amendment to the Constitution states, "No state shall make or enforce any law which shall abridge the privileges or immunities of citizens of the United States; nor shall any state deprive any person of life, liberty or property, without due process of law, nor deny to any person within its jurisdiction the equal protection of the laws." Two of this amendment's provisions are of very special importance to businesspeople—the **due process clause** and the **equal protection clause.**

8. Due Process of Law

- The term "due process of law" as used in the Fourteenth Amendment is probably involved in more litigation than any other constitutional phrase. It cannot be narrowly defined. The term describes fundamental principles of liberty and justice. Simply stated, due process means "fundamental fairness and decency." It means that *government* may not act in a manner that is arbitrary, capricious, or unreasonable. The clause does not prevent private individuals or corporations, including public utilities, from acting in an arbitrary or unreasonable manner. The due process clause applies only to state action and not to the actions of individuals or businesses.

The issues in due process cases are usually divided into questions of **procedural due process** and **substantive due process.** Procedural due process cases often are concerned with whether proper notice has been given and a proper hearing has been conducted. Such cases frequently involve procedures established by statute. However, many cases involve procedures that are not created by statute. For example, the due process clause has been used to challenge the procedure used in the dismissal of a student from a university medical school. Substantive due process issues arise when property or other rights are directly affected by governmental action.

In essence, the due process clause can be invoked anytime procedures of government are questioned in litigation. For example, in recent years, the Supreme Court has used the due process clause as its justification for defining the limits for a jury awarding punitive damages to a plaintiff in a civil lawsuit. The following case illustrates the use of the due process clause.

BMW OF NORTH AMERICA, INC. V. GORE

116 S. Ct. 1589 (1996)

In January 1990, Dr. Ira Gore purchased in Birmingham, Alabama a new BMW automobile for $40,750.88. After nine months, Dr. Gore noticed that the paint was flawed. He was told by the proprietor of "Slick Finish" that his car had been repainted. Upon inquiring at the BMW dealership where he purchased the car, Dr. Gore was told that his car had been repainted prior to its sale. BMW acknowledged that it had a nationwide policy that if the cost of repairing damages done during manufacturing or transportation did not exceed 3% of the retail value, the car was sold as new. If such repairs exceeded the 3% figure, the car was used by the company for a period of time and then sold as a used vehicle. The actual cost of repairs to Dr. Gore's car was $601.37. Since this was well below the 3% stated in BMW's policy, the car was sold as new, and Dr. Gore was not informed of the repairs. Feeling that he had been defrauded, Dr. Gore filed a lawsuit against BMW.

STEVENS, J. . . . Dr. Gore asserted that his repainted car was worth less than a car that had not been refinished. To prove his actual damages of $4,000, he relied on the testimony of a former BMW dealer, who estimated that the value of a repainted BMW was approximately 10 percent less than the value of a new car that had not been damaged and repaired. To support his claim for punitive damages, Dr. Gore introduced evidence that since 1983 BMW had sold 983 refinished cars as new, including 14 in Alabama, without disclosing that the cars had been repainted before sale at a cost of more than $300 per vehicle. Using the actual damage estimate of $4,000 per vehicle, Dr. Gore argued that a punitive award of $4 million would provide an appropriate penalty for selling approximately 1,000 cars for more than they were worth. . . .

The jury returned a verdict finding BMW liable for compensatory damages of $4,000. In addition, the jury assessed $4 million in punitive damages, based on a determination that the nondisclosure policy constituted "gross, oppressive or malicious" fraud.

BMW filed a post-trial motion to set aside the punitive damages award. . . .

The trial judge denied BMW's post-trial motion, holding, inter alia, that the award was not excessive. On appeal, the Alabama Supreme Court also rejected BMW's claim that the award exceeded the constitutionally permissible amount. . . .

The Alabama Supreme Court did, however, rule in BMW's favor on one critical point: The court found that the jury improperly computed the amount of punitive damages by multiplying Dr. Gore's compensatory damages by the number of similar sales in other jurisdictions. Having found the verdict tainted, the court held that "a constitutionally reasonable punitive damages award in this case is $2,000,000," and therefore ordered a remittitur in that amount. . . .

Because we believed that a review of this case would help to illuminate the character of the standard that will identify constitutionally excessive awards of punitive damages, we granted certiorari.

[Here the Court summarizes that states have legitimate interests in protecting citizens from unlawful and deceptive trade practices. However, the Court notes that one state cannot attempt to regulate commercial behavior in all states by awarding excessive punitive damages. The Court then turns to the due process requirements surrounding the award of punitive damages.]

Elementary notions of fairness enshrined in our constitutional jurisprudence dictate that a person receive fair notice not only of the conduct that will subject him to punishment but also of the severity of the penalty that a State may impose. Three guideposts, each of which indicates that BMW did not receive adequate notice of the magnitude of the sanction that Alabama might impose for adhering to the nondisclosure policy adopted in 1983, lead us to the conclusion that the $2 million award against BMW is grossly excessive: the degree of reprehensibility of the nondisclosure; the disparity between the harm or potential harm suffered by Dr. Gore and his punitive damages award; and the difference between this remedy and the civil penalties authorized or imposed in comparable cases. We discuss these considerations in turn.

Degree of Reprehensibility

Perhaps the most important indicium of the reasonableness of a punitive damages award is the degree of reprehensibility of the defendant's conduct. . . .

In this case, none of the aggravating factors associated with particularly reprehensible conduct is present. The harm BMW inflicted on Dr. Gore was purely economic in nature. The presale refinishing of the car had no effect on its performance or safety features, or even its appearance for at least nine months after his purchase. BMW's conduct evinced no indifference to or reckless disregard for the health and safety of others. To be sure, infliction of economic injury, especially when done intentionally through affirmative acts of misconduct, or when the target is financially vulnerable, can warrant a substantial penalty. But this observation does not convert all acts that cause economic harm into torts that are sufficiently reprehensible to justify a significant sanction in addition to compensatory damages.

Dr. Gore contends that BMW's conduct was particularly reprehensible because nondisclosure of the repairs to his car formed part of a nationwide pattern of tortious conduct. Certainly, evidence that a defendant has repeatedly engaged in prohibited conduct while knowing or suspecting that it was unlawful would provide relevant support for an argument that strong medicine is required to cure the defendant's disrespect for the law. Our holdings that a recidivist may be punished more severely than a first offender recognize that repeated misconduct is more reprehensible than an individual instance of malfeasance.

In support of his thesis, Dr. Gore . . . asserts that the state disclosure statutes supplement, rather than supplant, existing remedies for breach of contract and common-law fraud. Thus, according to Dr. Gore, the statutes may not properly be viewed as immunizing from liability the nondisclosure of repairs costing less than the applicable statutory threshold. . . .

We recognize, of course, that only state courts may authoritatively construe state statutes. As far as we are aware, at the time this action was commenced no state court had explicitly addressed whether its State's disclosure statute provides a safe harbor for nondisclosure of presumptively minor repairs or should be construed instead as supplementing common-law duties. A review of the text of the statutes, however, persuades us that in the absence of a state-court determination to the contrary, a corporate executive could reasonably interpret the disclosure requirements as establishing safe harbors. In California, for example, the disclosure statute defines "material" damage to a motor vehicle as damage requiring repairs costing in excess of 3 percent of the suggested retail price or $500, whichever is greater. . . . We simply emphasize that the record contains no evidence that BMW's decision to follow a disclosure policy that coincided with the strictest extant state statute was sufficiently reprehensible to justify a $2 million award of punitive damages. . . .

Finally, the record in this case discloses no deliberate false statements, acts of affirmative misconduct, or concealment of evidence of improper motive, . . . We accept, of course, the jury's finding that BMW suppressed a material fact which Alabama law obligated it to communicate to prospective purchasers of repainted cars in that State. But the omission of a material fact may be less reprehensible than a deliberate false statement, particularly when there is a good-faith basis for believing that no duty to disclose exists.

That conduct is sufficiently reprehensible to give rise to tort liability, and even a modest award of exemplary damages, does not establish the high degree of culpability that warrants a substantial punitive damages award. Because this case exhibits none of the circumstances ordinarily associated with egregiously improper conduct, we are persuaded that BMW's conduct was not sufficiently reprehensible to warrant imposition of a $2 million exemplary damages award.

Ratio

The second and perhaps most commonly cited indicium of an unreasonable or excessive punitive damages award is its ratio to the actual harm inflicted on the plaintiff. The principle that exemplary damages must bear a "reasonable relationship" to compensatory damages has a long pedigree. . . . Our decisions . . . endorsed the proposition that a comparison between the compensatory award and the punitive award is significant. . . .

The $2 million in punitive damages awarded to Dr. Gore by the Alabama Supreme Court is 500 times the amount of his actual harm as determined by the jury. Moreover, there is no suggestion that Dr. Gore or any other BMW purchaser was threatened with any additional potential harm by BMW's nondisclosure policy. . . .

Of course, we have consistently rejected the notion that the constitutional line is marked by a simple mathematical formula, even one that compares actual and potential damages to the punitive award. Indeed, low awards of compensatory damages may properly support a higher ratio than high compensatory awards, if, for example, a particularly egregious act has resulted in only a small amount of economic damages. A higher ratio may also be justified in cases in which the injury is hard to detect or the monetary value of noneconomic harm might have been difficult to determine. . . .

Sanctions for Comparable Misconduct

Comparing the punitive damages award and the civil or criminal penalties that could be imposed for comparable misconduct provides a third indicium of excessiveness. . . . [A] reviewing court engaged in determining whether an award of punitive damages is excessive should accord substantial deference to legislative judgments concerning appropriate sanctions for the conduct at issue. . . . In this case the $2 million economic sanction imposed on BMW is substantially greater than the statutory fines available in Alabama and elsewhere for similar malfeasance.

The maximum civil penalty authorized by the Alabama Legislature for a violation of its Deceptive Trade Practices Act is $2,000; other States authorize more severe sanctions, with the maxima ranging from $5,000 to $10,000. Significantly, some statutes draw a distinction between first offenders and recidivists; thus, in New York the penalty is $50 for a first offense and $250 for subsequent offenses. None of these statutes would provide an out-of-state distributor with fair notice that the first violation—or, indeed

the first 14 violations—of its provisions might subject an offender to a multimillion dollar penalty. Moreover, at the time BMW's policy was first challenged, there does not appear to have been any judicial decision in Alabama or elsewhere indicating that application of that policy might give rise to such severe punishment.

The sanction imposed in this case cannot be justified on the ground that it was necessary to deter future misconduct without considering whether less drastic remedies could be expected to achieve that goal. The fact that a multimillion dollar penalty prompted a change in policy sheds no light on the question whether a lesser deterrent would have adequately protected the interests of Alabama consumers. . . .

The fact that BMW is a large corporation rather than an impecunious individual does not diminish its entitlement to fair notice of the demands that the several States impose on the conduct of its business. Indeed, its status as an active participant in the national economy implicates the federal interest in preventing individual States from imposing undue burdens on interstate commerce. While each State has ample power to protect its own consumers, none may use the punitive damages deterrent as a means of imposing its regulatory policies on the entire Nation.

. . . [W]e are not prepared to draw a bright line marking the limits of a constitutionally acceptable punitive damages award. . . . [H]owever, we are fully convinced that the grossly excessive award imposed in this case transcends the constitutional limit. Whether the appropriate remedy requires a new trial or merely an independent determination by the Alabama Supreme Court of the award necessary to vindicate the economic interests of Alabama consumers is a matter that should be addressed by the state court in the first instance.

The judgment is reversed, and the case is remanded for further proceedings not inconsistent with this opinion. [*Reversed and remanded*].

Case Questions

1. What is the basis of the trial jury's award of $4,000,000 in punitive damages?

2. Why did the Alabama Supreme Court reduce the punitive damages award from $4,000,000 to $2,000,000?

3. What are the three issues that the U.S. Supreme Court examines in evaluating whether a punitive damages award violates the due process clause?

4. Does the U.S. Supreme Court define the constitutional limits of punitive damages awards in terms of dollars?

Incorporation Doctrine

The due process clause has thus played a unique role in constitutional development—one that was probably not anticipated at the time of its ratification. This significant role has been to make most of the provisions of the Bill of Rights applicable to the states. The first phrase of the First Amendment begins: "Congress shall make no law." How then are state and local governments prohibited from making such a law? Jurists have used the due process clause of the Fourteenth Amendment to "incorporate" or "carry over" the Bill of Rights and make these constitutional provisions applicable to the states. Starting in 1925, the Supreme Court began applying various portions of the first eight amendments to the states using the due process clause of the Fourteenth Amendment as the reason for this incorporation and application.

The role of the due process doctrine goes well beyond incorporation. For example, the Fifth Amendment contains a due process clause applicable to the federal government. The Fourteenth Amendment contains a due process clause applicable to state and local governments. Due process essentially means the same thing under both amendments. Through the due process clause, all of the constitutionally guaranteed freedoms we have discussed in this chapter and in Chapter 10 have been incorporated into the Fourteenth Amendment and are applicable to the state government's regulation of our personal and professional lives.

9. Equal Protection

The Fourteenth Amendment's equal protection language is also involved in a great deal of constitutional litigation. No law treats all persons equally; laws draw lines and treat people differently. Therefore, almost any state or local law imaginable can be challenged under the equal protection clause. It is obvious that the equal protection clause does not always deny states the power to treat different persons in different ways. Yet the equal protection clause embodies the ethical idea that law should not treat people differently without a satisfactory reason. In deciding cases using that clause to challenge state and local laws, courts use three distinct approaches. One is the traditional, or **minimum rationality,** approach, and a second is called the **strict scrutiny** approach. Some cases are analyzed as falling in between these approaches. Courts in these cases use the **quasi–strict scrutiny** approach.

As a practical matter, if the traditional (minimum rationality) approach is used, the challenged law and its classifications are usually found *not* to be a violation of equal protection. On the other hand, if the strict scrutiny test is used, the classifications are usually found to be unconstitutional under the equal protection clause.

Minimum Rationality

Under the minimum rationality approach, the classification will survive an equal protection challenge if it has a *rational* connection to a *permissible* state end. A permissible state end is one that is not prohibited by another provision of the Constitution. It qualifies as a legitimate goal of government. The classification must have a reasonable basis (not wholly arbitrary), and the courts will assume any state of facts that can be used to justify the classification. These laws often involve economic issues or social legislation such as welfare laws.

Such laws are presumed to be constitutional because courts recognize that the legislature must draw lines creating distinctions and that such tasks cannot be avoided. Only when no rational basis for the classification exists is it unconstitutional under the equal protection clause. For example, a state law restricting advertising to company-owned trucks was held valid when the rational basis test was applied to it since it is reasonable to assume less advertising on trucks provides for safer roads.

Strict Scrutiny

Under the strict scrutiny test, a classification will be a denial of equal protection unless the classification is necessary to achieve a *compelling* state purpose. It is not enough that a classification be permissible to achieve any state interest; it must be a compelling state objective. To withstand constitutional challenge when this test is used, the law must serve important governmental objectives and the classification must be substantially related to achieving these objectives.

The strict scrutiny test is used if the classification involves either a suspect class or a fundamental constitutional right. A suspect class is one that has such disabilities, has been subjected to such a history of purposeful unequal treatment, or has been placed in such a position of political powerlessness that it commands extraordinary protection from the political process of the majority. For example, classifications directed at race, national origin, and legitimacy of birth are clearly suspect. As a result, the judiciary strictly scrutinizes laws directed at them. Unless the state can prove that its statutory classifications have a compelling state interest as a basis, the classifications will be considered a denial of equal protection. Classifications that are subject to strict judicial scrutiny are presumed to be unconstitutional. The state must convince the court that the classification is fair, reasonable, and necessary to accomplish the objective of legislation that is compelling to a state interest.

The following case is a culmination of the others discussed therein confirming this role of strict scrutiny analysis.

Adarand Constructors, Inc. v. Pena

115 S. Ct. 2097 (1995)

O'CONNOR, J. . . . In 1989, the Central Federal Lands Highway Division (CFLHD), which is part of the United States Department of Transportation (DOT), awarded the prime contract for a highway construction project in Colorado to Mountain Gravel & Construction Company. Mountain Gravel then solicited bids from subcontractors for the guardrail portion of the contract. Adarand, a Colorado-based highway construction company specializing in guardrail work, submitted the low bid. Gonzales Construction Company also submitted a bid.

The prime contract's terms provide that Mountain Gravel would receive additional compensation if it hired subcontractors certified as small businesses controlled by "socially and economically disadvantaged individuals." Gonzales is certified as such a business; Adarand is not. Mountain Gravel awarded the subcontract to Gonzales, despite Adarand's low bid. Federal law requires that a subcontracting clause similar to the one used here must appear in most federal agency contracts, and it also requires the clause to state that "the contractor shall presume that socially and economically disadvantaged individuals include Black Americans, Hispanic Americans, Native Americans, Asian Pacific Americans, and other minorities, or any other individual found to be disadvantaged by the [Small Business] Administration pursuant to section 8(a) of the Small Business Act." Adarand claims that the presumption set forth in that statute discriminates on the basis of race in violation of the Federal Government's Fifth Amendment obligation not to deny anyone equal protection of the laws. . . .

The contract giving rise to the dispute in this case came about as a result of the Surface Transportation and Uniform Relocation Assistance Act of 1987, a DOT appropriations measure. Section 106(c)(1) of STURAA provides that "not less than 10 percent" of the appropriated funds "shall be expended with small business concerns owned and controlled by socially and economically disadvantaged individuals." STURAA adopts the Small Business Act's definition of "socially and economically disadvantaged individual," including the applicable race-based presumptions, and adds that "women shall be presumed to be socially and economically disadvantaged individuals for purposes of this subsection." . . .

After losing the guardrail subcontract to Gonzales, Adarand filed suit against various federal officials in the United States District Court for the District of Colorado, claiming that the race-based presumptions involved in the use of subcontracting compensation clauses violate Adarand's right to equal protection. The District Court granted the Government's motion for summary judgment. The Court of Appeals for the Tenth Circuit affirmed. It understood our decision in *Fullilove v. Klutznick*, 100 S. Ct. 2758 (1980), to have adopted "a lenient standard, resembling intermediate scrutiny, in assessing" the constitutionality of federal race-based action. Applying that "lenient standard," as further developed in *Metro Broadcasting, Inc. v. FCC*, 110 S. Ct. 2997 (1990), the Court of Appeals upheld the use of subcontractor compensation clauses. We granted certiorari. . .

In 1978, the Court confronted the question whether race-based governmental action designed to benefit such groups should also be subject to "the most rigid scrutiny." *Regents of Univ. of California v. Bakke*, 98 S. Ct. 2733, involved an equal protection challenge to a state-run medical school's practice of reserving a number of spaces in its entering class for minority students. The petitioners argued that "strict scrutiny" should apply only to "classifications that disadvantage 'discrete and insular minorities.' " *Bakke* did not produce an opinion for the Court, but Justice Powell's opinion announcing the Court's judgment rejected the argument. In a passage joined by Justice White, Justice Powell wrote that "the guarantee of equal protection cannot mean one thing when applied to one individual and something else when applied to a person of another color." He concluded that "racial and ethnic distinctions of any sort are inherently suspect and thus call for the most exacting judicial examination." . . .

Two years after *Bakke*, the Court faced another challenge to remedial race-based action, this time involving action undertaken by the Federal Government. In *Fullilove v. Klutznick*, the Court upheld Congress' inclusion of a 10% set-aside for minority-owned businesses in the Public Works Employment Act of 1977. As in *Bakke*, there was no opinion for the Court. Chief Justice Burger, in an opinion joined by Justices White and Powell, observed that "any preference based on racial or ethnic criteria must necessarily receive a most searching examination to make sure that it does not conflict with constitutional guarantees." That opinion, however, "did not adopt, either expressly or implicitly, the formulas of analysis articulated in such cases as [*Bakke*]." It employed instead a two-part test which asked, first, "whether the objectives of the legislation are within the power of Congress," and second, "whether the limited use of racial and ethnic criteria, in the context presented, is a constitutionally permissible means for achieving the congressional objectives." It then upheld the program under that test. . . .

In *Wygant v. Jackson Board of Ed.*, 106 S. Ct. 1842 (1986), the Court considered a Fourteenth Amendment challenge to another form of remedial racial classification. The issue in *Wygant* was whether a school board could adopt race-based preferences in determining which teachers to lay off. Justice Powell's plurality opinion observed that "the level of scrutiny does not change merely because the challenged classification operates against a group that historically has not been subject to governmental discrimination," and stated the two-part inquiry as "whether the layoff provision is supported by a compelling state purpose and whether the means chosen to accomplish that purpose are narrowly tailored." In other words, "racial classifications of any sort must be subjected to 'strict scrutiny.' " The plurality then concluded that the school board's interest in "providing minority role models for its minority students, as an attempt to alleviate the effects of societal discrimination," was not a compelling interest that could justify the use of a racial classification. It added that "societal discrimination, without more, is too amorphous a basis for imposing a racially classified remedy," and insisted instead that "a public employer . . . must ensure that, before it embarks on an affirmative-action program, it has convincing evidence that remedial action is warranted. That is, it must have sufficient evidence to justify the conclusion that there has been prior discrimination." . . .

The Court's failure to produce a majority opinion in *Bakke, Fullilove,* and *Wygant* left unresolved the proper analysis for remedial race-based governmental action.

The Court resolved the issue, at least in part, in 1989. *Richmond v. J. A. Croson Co.,* 109 S. Ct. 706 (1989), concerned a city's determination that 30% of its contracting work should go to minority-owned businesses. A majority of the Court in *Croson* held that "the standard of review under the Equal Protection Clause is not dependent on the race of those burdened or benefited by a particular classification," and that the single standard of review for racial classifications should be "strict scrutiny." As to the classification before the Court, the plurality agreed that "a state or local subdivision . . . has the authority to eradicate the effects of private discrimination within its own legislative jurisdiction," but the Court thought that the city had not acted with "a 'strong basis in evidence for its conclusion that remedial action was necessary.' " The Court also thought it "obvious that [the] program is not narrowly tailored to remedy the effects of prior discrimination."

With *Croson,* the Court finally agreed that the Fourteenth Amendment requires strict scrutiny of all race-based action by state and local governments. But *Croson* of course had no occasion to declare what standard of review the Fifth Amendment requires for such action taken by the Federal Government. . . .

A year later, however, the Court took a surprising turn. *Metro Broadcasting, Inc. v. FCC* involved a Fifth Amendment challenge to two race-based policies of the Federal Communications Commission. In *Metro Broadcasting,* the Court repudiated the long-held notion that "it would be unthinkable that the same Constitution would impose a lesser duty on the Federal Government" than it does on a State to afford equal protection of the laws. It did so by holding that "benign" federal racial classifications need only satisfy intermediate scrutiny, even though *Croson* had recently concluded that such classifications enacted by a State must satisfy strict scrutiny. "Benign" federal racial classifications, the Court said,"—even if those measures are not *remedial* in the sense of being designed to compensate victims of past governmental or societal discrimination—are constitutionally permissible to the extent that they serve important governmental objectives within the power of Congress and are substantially related to achievement of those objectives." . . .

By adopting intermediate scrutiny as the standard of review for congressionally mandated "benign" racial classifications, *Metro Broadcasting* departed from prior cases in two significant respects. First, it turned its back on *Croson's* explanation of why strict scrutiny of all governmental racial classifications is essential. . . .

Second, *Metro Broadcasting* squarely rejected one of the three propositions established by the Court's earlier equal protection cases, namely, congruence between the standards applicable to federal and state racial classifications, and in so doing also undermined the other two—skepticism of all racial classifications and consistency of treatment irrespective of the race of the burdened or benefited group. Under *Metro Broadcasting,* certain racial classifications ("benign" ones enacted by the Federal Government) should be treated less skeptically than others; and the race of the benefited group is critical to the determination of which standard of review to apply. *Metro Broadcasting* was thus a significant departure from much of what had come before it.

The three propositions undermined by *Metro Broadcasting* all derive from the basic principle that the Fifth and Fourteenth Amendments to the Constitution protect persons, not groups. It follows from that principle that all governmental action based on race . . . should be subjected to detailed judicial inquiry to ensure that the personal right to equal protection of the laws has not been infringed. These ideas have long been central to this Court's understanding of equal protection, and holding "benign" state and federal racial classifications to different standards does not square with them. . . . Accordingly, we hold today that all racial classifications, imposed by whatever federal, state, or local governmental actor, must be analyzed by a reviewing court under strict scrutiny. In other words, such classifications are constitutional only if they are narrowly tailored measures that further compelling governmental interests. To the extent that *Metro Broadcasting* is inconsistent with that holding, it is overruled. . . .

Because our decision today alters the playing field in some important respects, we think it best to remand the case to the lower courts for further consideration in light of the principles we have announced. The Court of Appeals, following *Metro Broadcasting* and *Fullilove,* analyzed the case in terms of intermediate scrutiny. It upheld the challenged statutes and regulations because it found them to be "narrowly tailored to achieve [their] significant governmental purpose of providing subcontracting opportunities for small disadvantaged business enterprises." The Court of Appeals did not decide the question whether the interests served by the use of subcontractor compensation clauses are properly described as "compelling." It also did not address the question of narrow tailoring in terms of our strict scrutiny cases, by asking, for example, whether there was "any consideration of the use of race-neutral means to increase minority business participation" in government contracting, or whether the program was appropriately limited such that it "will not last longer than the discriminatory effects it is designed to eliminate." . . .

The question whether any of the ways in which the Government uses subcontractor compensation clauses can survive strict scrutiny, and any relevance distinctions such as these may have to that question, should be addressed in the first instance by the lower courts.

Accordingly, the judgment of the Court of Appeals is vacated, and the case is remanded for further proceedings consistent with this opinion. [*Vacated and remanded*].

Case Questions

1. Why was Adarand Constructors, as low bidder on the guardrail subcontract, not awarded the job?
2. What were the holdings of *Bakke, Fullilove,* and *Wygant?* Why did these decisions not resolve the standard of review question?
3. What is the conflict between the opinions in *Croson* and *Metro Broadcasting?*
4. Why is the holding in this case so important? Does this opinion stand for the proposition that affirmative action programs are unconstitutional?
5. Why did the Supreme Court decide not to resolve the issue of which party should be awarded the guardrail subcontract?

Strict judicial scrutiny is applied to a second group of cases, those that involve classifications directed at fundamental rights. If a classification unduly burdens or penalizes the exercise of a constitutional right, it will be stricken unless it is found to be necessary to support a compelling state interest. Among such rights are the right to vote, the right to travel, and the right to appeal. Doubts about such laws result in their being stricken by the courts as a denial of equal protection.

Quasi-Strict Scrutiny

Some cases actually fall between the minimum rationality and strict scrutiny approaches. These cases use what is sometimes called quasi–strict scrutiny tests because the classifications are only partially suspect or the rights involved are not quite fundamental. For example, classifications directed at sex and gender are partially suspect. In cases involving classifications based on sex or gender, the courts have taken this position between the two tests or at least have modified the strict scrutiny approach. Such classifications are unconstitutional unless they are *substantially* related to an *important* government objective. This modified version of strict scrutiny has resulted in holdings that find laws to be valid as well as unconstitutional.

Equal protection cases run the whole spectrum of legislative attempts to solve society's problems. For example, courts have used the equal protection clause to require the integration of public schools. In addition, the meaning and application of the equal protection clause have been central issues in cases involving:

- Apportionment of legislative bodies
- Racial segregation in the sale and rental of real estate
- Laws distinguishing between the rights of legitimates and illegitimates
- The makeup of juries

TABLE 5–3 **Analysis of Equal Protection**

	Minimum Rationality	Quasi–Strict Scrutiny	Strict Scrutiny
Classifications Must Be	Rationally connected to a permissible or legitimate government objective	Substantially related to an important government interest	Necessary to a compelling state interest
	Presumed Valid	*Quasi-Suspect Classes*	*Suspect Classes*
Examples	Height Weight Age Testing School desegregation Veteran's preference Marriage	Sex Gender	Race National origin Legitimacy *Fundamental Rights* To vote To travel To appeal

· Voting requirements
· Welfare residency requirements
· Rights of aliens
· The use of property taxes as the means of financing public schools

The equal protection clause is the means to the end, or goal, of equality of opportunity. As such, it may be utilized by anyone claiming unequal treatment in any case. At the same time the clause will not prevent states from remedying the effect of past discrimination. As you will study in Chapter 13 under the heading of employment discrimination, courts have upheld laws that provide for preferential treatment of minorities if this remedy is narrowly tailored to serve a compelling governmental interest in eradicating past discrimination against the minority group.

Table 5–3 summarizes the legal approaches courts use in analyzing equal protection cases.

Key Terms

Apportionment   126
Commerce clause   121
Commercial speech   131
Contract clause   121
Defamation   129
Dominant commerce clause concept   122
Due process clause   134
Equal Protection Clause   134
Establishment clause   128
Federalism   118
Free exercise clause   128
Irreconcilable conflict   213
Libel   129
Malice   129

Minimum rationality   138
Nexus   127
Overbreadth doctrine   131
Prohibiting discriminaton   123
Preemption   118
Prior restraint   129
Procedural due process   135
Quasi–strict scrutiny   138
Separation of powers   118
Strict scrutiny   138
Substantive due process   135
Supremacy clause   118
Symbolic speech   130
Undue burden   123

Review Questions and Problems

Basic Concepts

1. *Separation of Powers*
   Describe the two concepts that (1) balances power within the federal government and (2) provides distinctions in the role of the federal, state, and local governments.

2. *Supremacy Clause*
   A Florida county adopted an ordinance regulating blood plasma centers in the county. It required that donors take a test for hepatitis and a breath analysis test for alcohol. The Food and Drug Administration (FDA) has promulgated federal regulations establishing minimum standards for the collection of blood plasma. An operator of a blood plasma center filed suit challenging the constitutionality of the ordinances on the ground that they violated the supremacy clause. Decide the case, and give reasons for your decision.

3. *Contract Clause*
   (a) Does the provision of the Constitution apply to the federal government, state government, or both? Explain.
   (b) Does this provision of the Constitution apply to present contractual relationships, future ones, or both? Explain.

4. *Commerce Clause*
   (a) Describe the five factual situations wherein the Commerce Clause might be used to restrict a state or local governmental action. What analysis is used in each situation?
   (b) A Maine statute imposed a tax on trucks. The tax required owners and operators of foreign-based (out-of-state) trucks using Maine highways to purchase either an annual highway use permit or a one-trip permit. Trucks based in-state were exempt. An out-of-state trucker challenged the constitutionality of the statute. Is this Maine statute constitutional? Why or why not?

Regulation and Basic Freedoms

5. *Freedom of Religion*
   Explain the purposes of and distinction between the Establishment Clause and the Free Exercise Clause.

6. *Freedom of Press*
   (a) A promoter of theatrical productions applied to a municipal board (charged with managing a city-leased theater) for a license to stage the play Hair. Relying on outside reports that because of nudity the production would not be in the best interests of the community, the board rejected the application. The promoter sought a court order permitting it to use the auditorium. Why should the court allow the production to proceed?
   (b) What are the distinctions in how the law treats public persons versus private persons with respect to defamation?

7. *Freedom of Speech*
   Silvia, an attorney in Florida, also was a licensed certified public accountant (CPA) and a certified financial planner (CFP). Silvia placed an ad in the yellow pages listing her credentials, including the CPA and CFP designations. The Florida Board of Accountancy reprimanded Silvia for using both the CPA and CFP credential in an ad essentially emphasizing her legal work. Silvia challenged the Board's right to issue this reprimand. What is the legal basis for Silvia's challenge? Explain.

The Fourteenth Amendment

8. *Due Process of Law*
   Explain what is meant by the Incorporation Doctrine and how it was used to expand the impact of the due process clause.

9. *Equal Protection*
   There are three levels of judicial scrutiny under this clause. Describe what these levels are and when they are applicable.

Terminology Review

For each term in the left-hand column, match the most appropriate description in the right-hand column.

1. Defamation

2. Libel

a. The separation of governmental functions between the federal and state governments

b. Used to restrict states' police powers from harming interstate business activity

3. Prior restraint

4. Federalism

5. Malice

6. Overbreadth doctrine

7. Dominant commerce clause

8. Preemption

c. The area of law generally meant to protect a person's or organization's reputation

d. The concept of stopping someone from printing material or delivering a speech

e. The principal whereby the federal government reserves for itself the right to regulate certain activities

f. Proof of intent to cause harm

g. The concept which prohibits governments from enforcing laws that are broader than necessary to accomplish a stated purpose

h. A written form of defamation

THE REGULATORY PROCESS

Business Decision

Sue the Bureaucrats?

You are the chief executive officer of a toy manufacturing firm. Your firm has been inspected by officials of OSHA, the federal Occupational Safety and Health Administration, for alleged violations of workplace safety regulations. The evidence presented to the agency was confusing and conflicting. You feel strongly that the company should not be penalized. Nevertheless your firm has been ordered to pay a substantial fine, and an administrative law judge ordered you to make some very expensive modifications in its manufacturing processes.

Should you continue to seek review of your case before the agency's officials?

Should you appeal by filing a lawsuit to reverse the agency's decision?

If you are successful in court, under what circumstances can you recover your attorney's fees?

For years, it seems, the citizens of this country have complained that "there is too much government." This quoted phrase has as many meanings as there are people saying it. However, in general, the principal reason for this feeling is the vast bureaucracy created by the regulatory process.

Indeed, some commentators have called the administrative agencies a fourth branch of government. Because of the significant impact these agencies can have on businesses and businesspeople, in this chapter, you will study the following:

· Why our governments have come to rely on the regulatory process

· What are the basic functions of administrative agencies

· How these agencies are organized

· When courts will review the actions of agencies

TABLE 6–1   Major Federal Agencies

Name	Functions
Consumer Product Safety Commission (CPSC)	Protects the public against unreasonable risks of injury associated with consumer products
Environmental Protection Agency (EPA)	Administers all laws relating to the environment, including laws on water pollution, air pollution, solid wastes, pesticides, toxic substances, etc.
Federal Aviation Administration (FAA) (part of the Department of Transportation)	Regulates civil aviation to provide safe and efficient use of airspace
Federal Communications Commission (FCC)	Regulates interstate and foreign communications by means of radio, television, wire, cable, and satellite
Federal Reserve Board (FRB)	Regulates the availability and cost of money and credit; the nation's central bank
Federal Trade Commission (FTC)	Protects the public from anticompetitive behavior and unfair and deceptive business practices
Food and Drug Administration (FDA)	Administers laws to prohibit distribution of adulterated, misbranded, or unsafe food and drugs
Equal Employment Opportunity Commission (EEOC)	Seeks to prevent discrimination in employment based on race, color, religion, sex, or national origin and other unlawful employment practices
National Labor Relations Board (NLRB)	Conducts union certification elections and holds hearings on unfair labor practice complaints
Nuclear Regulatory Commission (NRC)	Licenses and regulates the nuclear energy industry
Occupational Safety and Health Administration (OSHA)	Ensures all workers a safe and healthy work environment
Securities and Exchange Commission (SEC)	Enforces the federal securities laws that regulate sale of securities to the investing public

Administrative Agencies

The term **administrative agency** is used to describe all the boards, bureaus, commissions, agencies, and organizations that make up the bureaucracy. The process of regulating business through agencies is described as administrative law. The administrative process occurs at all levels of government.

Table 6–1 lists several of the more important federal agencies and briefly describes their functions. Many of these agencies will be discussed in detail in later chapters. For example, the Securities and Exchange Commission is discussed in Chapter 7, the National Labor Relations Board in Chapter 12, the Equal Employment Opportunity Commission in Chapter 13, and the Environmental Protection Agency in Chapter 14.

As you can see from the Business Decision, the activities of government agencies can have a significant impact on the everyday operations of a business—far more significant, sometimes, than major economic and consumer spending trends or world events. This chapter concerns administrative law—the legal principles relating to regulatory agencies, boards, bureaus, and commissions.

The direct day-to-day legal impact on business of the rules and regulations adopted and enforced by these agencies is probably greater than the impact of the courts or other branches of government. Administrative agencies create and enforce the majority of all laws constituting the legal environment of business. Almost every business activity is regulated to some degree by the administrative process at either the state or federal level.

Although we focus on federal agencies in this chapter, keep in mind that state and local governments also have many agencies. For example, cases involving industrial accidents and injuries to employees are heard by state workers' compensation boards, and most local governments have zoning boards that make recommendations on zoning laws. State governments usually license and regulate intrastate transportation, and state boards usually set rates for local utilities supplying gas and electricity. The principles and problems discussed in this chapter generally apply to the state and local administrative process as well as to the federal. It is clear that almost every aspect of our daily lives is regulated to a substantial degree by the administrative process.

1. Reasons for Agencies

There are many reasons why administrative agencies might be needed. Almost every governmental agency has been created because of a recognized problem in society and from the belief that an agency may be able to help solve the problem. Among the reasons for agencies described in this section are the following:

- To provide specificity
- To provide expertise
- To provide protection
- To provide regulation
- To provide services

Providing Specificity

Legislative branches often cannot legislate in sufficient detail to cover all aspects of many problems. Congress cannot possibly legislate in minute detail, and, as a consequence, it uses more and more general language in stating its regulatory aims and purposes. For example, Congress cannot enact a securities law that covers every possible issue that might arise. Therefore, it delegates to the Securities and Exchange Commission the power to make rules and regulations to fill in the gaps and create the necessary details to make securities laws workable. In many areas an agency has had to develop detailed rules and regulations to carry out a legislative policy.

Nor can courts handle all disputes and controversies that may arise. For example, each year tens of thousands of industrial accidents cause injury or death to workers. If each of these industrial accidents resulted in traditional litigation, the courts simply would not have the time or the personnel to handle the multitude of cases. Therefore, workers' compensation boards decide such claims. Likewise, most cases involving alleged discrimination in employment are turned over to agencies for decision.

Providing Expertise

A reason many agencies are created is to refer a problem or area to experts for solution and management. The Federal Reserve Board (FRB), the Nuclear Regulatory Commission (NRC), and the Food and Drug Administration (FDA) are examples of agencies with expertise beyond that of

Congress or the executive branch. The development of sound policies and proper decisions in many areas requires expertise, and thus we tend to resort to administrative agencies for this expertise. Similarly, administrative agencies often provide needed continuity and consistency in the formulation, application, and enforcement of rules and regulations governing business.

Providing Protection

Many governmental agencies exist to protect the public, especially from the business community. Business has often failed to regulate itself, and the lack of self-regulation has often been contrary to the public interest. For example, the failure of business to voluntarily refrain from polluting many streams and rivers as well as the air led to the creation of the Environmental Protection Agency (EPA). The sale of worthless securities to the investing public was a major reason for the creation of the Securities and Exchange Commission (SEC). The manufacture and sale of dangerous products led to the creation of the Consumer Product Safety Commission (CPSC). Americans tend to turn to a governmental agency for assistance whenever a business or business practice may injure significant numbers of the general public. The prevailing attitude has been that the government's duty is to protect the public from harm.

Providing Regulation

Agencies are often created to replace competition with regulation. When a firm is given monopoly power, it loses its freedom of contract, and a governmental body is given the power to determine the provisions of its contracts. For example, electric utility companies are usually given a monopoly in the geographic area which they serve. A state agency such as a public service commission then has the power to set the rate structure for the utility. Similar agencies have regulated transportation and banking because of the difference of bargaining power between the business and the public. Regulation is often a substitute for competition.

Providing Services

Many agencies were created simply out of necessity. If we are to have a mail service, a post office is necessary. Welfare programs require government personnel to administer them. Social Security programs necessitate that there be a federal agency to determine eligibility and pay benefits. The mere existence of most government programs automatically creates a new agency or expands the functions of an existing one.

2. Functions of Agencies

Administrative agencies tend to possess functions of the other three branches of government, including:

- Rule making
- Adjudicating
- Advising
- Investigating

FIGURE 6.1

The powers of administrative agencies.

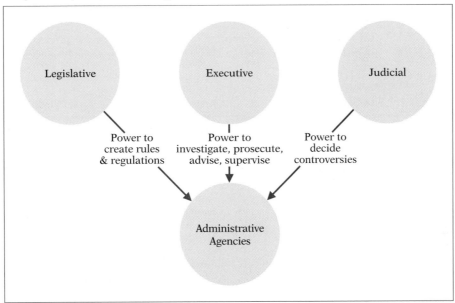

These functions do not concern all administrative agencies to the same degree. Some agencies are primarily adjudicating bodies, such as industrial commissions that rule on workers' compensation claims. Others are primarily supervisory, such as the SEC, which oversees the issue and sale of investment securities. To be sure, most agencies perform all these functions to some degree in carrying out their responsibilities. Figure 6–1 illustrates how these functions have been delegated to these agencies.

Rule Making

Agencies exercise their **quasi-legislative** power by issuing rules and regulations that have the force and effect of law. These rules and regulations may be used to resolve an issue if they are relevant to any issue involved in an adjudicative proceeding. Before rules and regulations are adopted, interested parties are given an opportunity to be heard on the desirability and legality of the proposals.

Guidelines are also issued by agencies to supplement rules. Guidelines are administrative interpretations of the statutes that an agency is responsible for enforcing. Often, guidelines are issued to help businesses determine whether certain practices may or may not be viewed as legal. For example, the Federal Trade Commission and the Justice Department have issued guidelines concerning which mergers are legal and which ones are likely to be challenged as illegal.

Rules and regulations may apply to a business practice irrespective of the industry involved, or they may apply only to an industry. For example, Occupational Safety and Health Administration (OSHA) rules may cover anyone using certain equipment, or a rule may be drafted so that its coverage is limited to an industry such as drug manufacturing.

TABLE 6–2   Fines Imposed by Various Federal and State Administrative Agencies

Company	Violation	Fine	Agency
Paine Webber Group, Inc.	Misleading thousands of investors regarding risky limited partnerships	$302.5 million	SEC
Various Entities	In fiscal 1996, total criminal, civil, and administrative fines	$173 million	EPA
Hercules	Safety infractions in plant	$6 million	OSHA
DeCoster Egg Farm	Unsanitary working and living conditions (included company-owned trailer park)	$3.6 million	OSHA
Air of Miami	Mishandling of hazardous materials and loading of cargo	$1.5 million	FAA

While guidelines can be helpful in understanding an agency's policy, these guidelines do not have the same force of law as rules and regulations do.

Adjudicating

The **quasi-judicial** function involves both fact finding and applying law to the facts. If violations of the law are found, sanctions, such as a fine or other penalty, may be imposed. Fines are often quite substantial (see Table 6–2). In addition, an agency may order that a violator stop (cease) the objectionable activity and refrain (desist) from any further similar violations. This type of agency action is called a **cease and desist order.** Violations of a cease and desist order are punishable by fines, which can be as much as $10,000 per day.

Many cases before agencies are settled by agreement before a final decision, just as most lawsuits are settled. Such a settlement results in the issuance of a **consent order,** which requires that the organization or individual accused admit to the jurisdiction of the agency and waive all rights to seek a judicial review. There is no admission that the business has been guilty of a violation of the law, but there is an agreement not to engage in the business activities that were the subject of the complaint. A consent order saves considerable expense and has the same legal force and effect as a final cease and desist order issued after a full hearing.

Advising

The advisory function of an administrative agency may be accomplished by making reports to the president or to Congress. For example, an agency may propose new legislation to Congress, or it may inform the attorney general of the need for judicial action due to violations of the law. Agencies also report information to the general public that should be known in the public interest, and they publish advisory opinions. For example, a commission may give advice as to whether a firm's proposed course of action might violate any of the laws that commission administers. Advisory opinions are not as binding as formal rulings, but they do give a business an indication of the view an agency would take if the practice in question were challenged formally. The advisory opinion is a unique device generally not available in the judicial system, as courts deal only with actual cases and controversies.

Investigating

One of the major functions of all agencies is to investigate activities and practices that may be illegal. Because of this investigative power, agencies can gather and compile information concerning the organization and business practices of any corporation or industry engaged in commerce to determine whether there has been a violation of any law. In exercising their investigative functions, agencies may use the subpoena power and require reports, examine witnesses under oath, and examine and copy documents, or they may obtain information from other governmental offices. This power of investigation complements the exercise of the agency's other powers, especially the power to adjudicate.

Federal law makes it a crime to make any false or fraudulent statement in any matter within the jurisdiction of a federal agency. A person may be guilty of a violation without proof that he or she had knowledge that the matter was within the jurisdiction of a federal agency. As a result, information furnished to an agency must be truthful.

3. Organization of Agencies

Administrative agencies, boards, or commissions usually consist of five to seven members, one of whom is appointed as chair. Laws creating the regulatory body usually specify that no more than a simple majority of the members (three of the five or four of the seven) may belong to the same political party. Appointments at the federal level require Senate confirmation, and appointees are not permitted to engage in any other business or employment during their terms. They may be removed from office by the president only for inefficiency, neglect of duty, or malfeasance in office.

Regulatory agencies require staffs to carry out their duties. While each agency has its own distinctive organizational structure to meet its responsibilities, most agencies have persons performing certain functions common to all agencies. Because agencies have quasi-legislative and quasi-judicial functions as well as the usual executive ones, the organizational chart of an agency usually embraces the full range of governmental duties. Figure 6–2 shows an organizational chart outlining the general functions and duties of administrative agencies.

In General

The chairperson is designated as such at the time of nomination by the president and is the presiding officer at agency meetings. The chairperson usually belongs to the same political party as the president and, while an equal in voting, is somewhat more important than the other agency members because of visibility and the power to appoint staff. For example, the chairman

FIGURE 6.2

Organizational chart of typical agency, board, or commission.

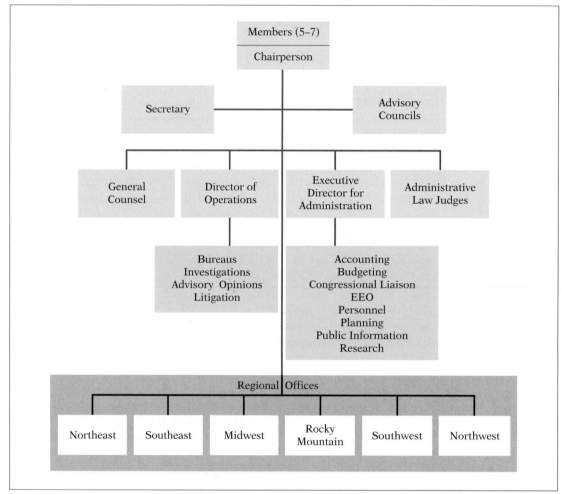

of the Federal Reserve Board is often in the news, while the other board members are relatively unknown.

The secretary is responsible for the minutes of agency meetings and is legal custodian of its records. The secretary usually signs orders and official correspondence and is responsible for publication of all actions in the *Federal Register*. The secretary also coordinates the activities of the agency with others involved in the regulatory process.

The office of **general counsel** is so important in many agencies that the appointment usually requires Senate approval. The general counsel is the chief law officer and legal adviser. He or she represents the agency in court and often makes the decision to file suit or pursue other remedies. The general counsel has significant impact on policy and is often as powerful as a commissioner or board member.

Advisory councils are persons not employed by the agency but interested in its mission. Persons serving on councils are usually selected because of their expertise. For example, the Consumer Product Safety Commission has an advisory council in poison prevention packaging and another on flammable fabrics. These councils provide for interaction between regulators and those being regulated.

The executive director for administration is the chief operating official of an agency and supervises usual administrative functions such as accounting, budgeting, and personnel. Research and planning are usually also supervised by the executive director. Since agencies spend a great deal of time lobbying with Congress, most of them have a legislative liaison, reporting to the executive director for administration.

The duties and suborganization of the director of operations vary greatly from agency to agency. These operating bureaus are assigned specific areas of activity. For example, at the EPA, one group will be concerned with clean air and another with water problems.

Regional offices investigate alleged violations of the law. In addition, they usually have an educational function. Many regional offices have their own administrative law judges and special legal counsel.

Quasi-judicial Staff

Administrative law judges, who are employed by the agency, perform the adjudicative fact-finding functions. Like other types of judges, administrative law judges are protected from liability for damages based on their decisions. This protection is called **immunity.** Because these administrative law judges must exercise independent judgment on the evidence presented, they must be free from pressures possibly asserted by the parties.

These administrative law judges hear cases of alleged law violations and apply the law to the facts. The members of the agency board or commission hear only appeals from the decisions of the administrative law judges. The judges are organizationally separate from the rest of the agency so that the quasi-judicial function will be performed impartially. Administrative law judges use prior decisions or precedent. In addition, they must follow the procedural rules of the agency as well as its policy directives.

Quasi-judicial proceedings usually begin with a complaint filed by the agency. The complaint is often the result of an investigation of information received from a consumer or other person affected by business conduct that may be illegal. The complaint contains allegations of fact concerning the alleged illegal conduct. The business or individual accused of some legality is called the respondent. After the formal complaint is served, the respondent files an answer to the charges and allegations. The case is then assigned to an administrative law judge. At the hearing, counsels for the agency and the respondent produce evidence to prove or disprove the allegations of fact in the complaint and answer. The judge rules on the admissibility of evidence, rules on motions made by counsel, and renders an initial decision that includes a statement of findings and conclusions, along with reasons for them, as to all material issues of fact and law. The ruling also includes an order the judge deems appropriate in view of the evidence in the record. This order becomes final if not challenged within thirty days after it is filed. On the appeal, the agency, board, or commission reviews the record of the initial decision and has all the powers it could have exercised if it had rendered that decision itself.

4. Influencing Agency Decisions

As discussed in section 2, agencies adopt rules and regulations. Due process of law requires that before a rule or regulation may be adopted by an agency, interested parties be given notice of the proposed rules and an opportunity to express their views on them. Agencies give public notice of proposed rules and hold public hearings on them.

At public hearings, interested parties are allowed to present evidence in support of, or in opposition to, a proposed rule or regulation. As a result, the best means of influencing a quasi-legislative decision of an administrative agency is to participate in the adoption process.

Agencies are not politically responsible, in the sense that they are elected by the people. However, it is clear that they react, sometimes dramatically, to the force of public opinion. For example, during the 1990s the Food and Drug Administration became much more visible to the public as this agency addressed labeling and packaging issues related to nutrition and other health concerns.

Letters designed to obtain action or a change in policy to agencies from citizens may be effective. These are probably even more effective if directed to a member of Congress, who in turn asks the agency for an official response or explanation. At various times, an agency may find itself bombarded with official congressional inquiries into its activities. Investigations may result in budget cutbacks. Just the threat of such a proceeding is often sufficient to cause a review of administrative policy.

Furthermore, each branch of government has some control over the administrative process. The executive branch normally appoints the top officials of an agency with the advice and consent of the legislative branch. In addition, the executive branch makes budget recommendations to the legislature and has veto power over its statutes. The legislature can review and control administrative activity by abolishing the agency, enacting specific legislation contrary to rules adopted by the agency, more explicitly defining limitations on the agency's activities, providing additional procedural requirements for the agency's adjudications, or limiting appropriations of funds to the agency.

Judicial Review of Agency Decisions

What alternatives are available to a person, business, or industry unhappy with either rules and regulations that have been adopted or with the quasi-judicial decisions? What are the powers of courts in reviewing decisions of administrative agencies? What chance does a party upset with an agency's decision have in obtaining a reversal of the decision? How much deference is given to an agency's decisions? Answers to these questions must be clearly understood to appreciate the role of administrative agencies in our system. These answers also help in understanding the Business Decision—"Sue the Bureaucrats?"

The following section discusses a requirement that must be satisfied by the parties challenging an agency's rule making or adjudicating function. Then, in sections 6 through 8, you will see that the issues before a court reviewing an agency's decision vary depending on whether a quasi-legislative or quasi-judicial decision is being reviewed.

5. Standing to Sue

Any party seeking the judicial review of any administrative agency's decision must be able to prove *standing to sue*. To establish standing, the challenging party must address two issues.

Reviewability

First, is the action or decision of the agency subject to judicial review? Not all administrative decisions are reviewable. The Federal Administrative Procedure Act provides for judicial review except where "(1) statutes preclude judicial review or (2) agency action is committed to agency discretion by law." Few statutes actually preclude judicial review, and preclusion of judicial review by inference is rare. It is most likely to occur when an agency decides not to undertake action to enforce a statute. For example, prison inmates asked the Food and Drug Administration (FDA) to ban the use of lethal injections to carry out the death penalty. It refused to do so. The Supreme Court held that this decision of the FDA was not subject to judicial review.

Aggrieved Party

Second, is the plaintiff "an aggrieved party"? Generally the plaintiff must have been harmed by an administrative action or decision to have standing. This aspect of standing was discussed in Chapter 2. It is clear that persons who may suffer economic loss due to an agency's action have standing to sue. Recent decisions have expanded the group of persons with standing to sue to include those who have noneconomic interests, such as First Amendment rights.

6. Review of Rule Making

The rule-making function in the administrative process is essentially legislative in character. Administrative agencies are usually created by enactments of the legislature in which the legislative branch is generally said to delegate certain responsibility or quasi-legislative power to the agency. Just as laws enacted by the legislature must be within its power as established by the Constitution or be void, rules and regulations established by an administrative body must be within the confines of its grant of power from the legislature or a court will find them void.

However, once having determined that an act of the legislature is constitutional or a rule of an agency is authorized, the courts will not inquire into its wisdom or effectiveness. An unwise or ineffectual law may be corrected by political action at the polls; an unwise rule or regulation adopted by an agency may be corrected by the legislature that gave the agency power to make the rule in the first place.

There are two basic issues in litigation challenging the validity of a rule made by an administrative agency. First, is the delegation valid? Second, has the agency exceeded its authority?

Is Delegation Valid?

Delegation of quasi-legislative authority to administrative agencies is subject to two constitutional limitations:

· It must be definite.

· It must be limited.

First, delegation of authority must be definite or it will violate due process. Definiteness means that the delegation must be set forth with sufficient clarity so that all concerned, and especially reviewing courts, will be able to determine the extent of the agency's authority. For many reasons, broad language has been held sufficiently definite to meet this test. For example, the term "unfair methods of competition" has been held to be sufficiently definite to meet the requirements of due process.

Second, a delegation of authority must be limited. Delegations must contain standards by which a court can determine whether the limitations have been exceeded. The standards set must meet certain minimum requirements before the agency in question has the power to act in a certain area, and the rules promulgated by the agency must follow these standards and limitations imposed by the law establishing the agency if they are to be upheld. Also, procedural safeguards must exist to control arbitrary administrative action and any administrative abuse of discretionary power.

Just as broad language has been approved as being sufficiently definite for a delegation to be valid under the due process clause, so also have broad standards been approved to meet the limited-power test since the 1930s. Today, it is generally agreed that delegations of authority to make rules may be in very broad language. For example, the delegation of authority to make such rules as the "public interest, convenience and necessity may require" is subject to a valid standard.

The general language used in delegating quasi-legislative authority usually involves grants of substantial discretion to an agency. It must be kept in mind that this delegation of discretion is to the agency and not to the judiciary. Therefore, courts cannot interfere with the discretion given to the agency and cannot substitute their judgment for that of the agency. In essence, there is a policy of deference by the judges to the decision of the administrators. This practice of deference further emphasizes why a businessperson's influence on the rule-making process is greater in the administrative process than through appellate procedures (see section 4, above).

The following case illustrates the actual language used by the Supreme Court to express this philosophy of deference. It demonstrates the expansive discretion given to administrative agencies and how slow courts are to substitute their judgment for that of the administrative process.

NATIONSBANK OF NORTH CAROLINA, N.A. v. VARIABLE ANNUITY LIFE INSURANCE COMPANY

115 S.Ct. 810 (1995)

NationsBank sought permission from the Comptroller of the Currency to sell annuities. When this permission was granted as "incidental to the business of banking," Variable Annuity Life Insurance Co. (VALIC) filed suit challenging the Comptroller's decision. The District Court upheld the Comptroller's ruling, but the Fifth Circuit Court of Appeals reversed. NationsBank petitioned the Supreme Court for review and certiorari was granted.

GINSBURG, J. Petitioner NationsBank of North Carolina, N. A., a national bank based in Charlotte, and its brokerage subsidiary sought permission from the Comptroller of the Currency for the brokerage subsidiary to act as an agent in the sale of annuities. Annuities are contracts under which the purchaser makes one or more premium payments to the issuer in exchange for a series of payments, which continue either for a fixed period or for the life of the purchaser or a designated beneficiary. When a purchaser invests in a "variable" annuity, the purchaser's money is invested in a designated way and payments to the purchaser vary with investment performance. In a classic "fixed" annuity, in contrast, payments do not vary. Under the contracts NationsBank proposed to sell, purchasers could direct their payments to a variable, fixed, or hybrid account, and would be allowed periodically to modify their choice. . . .

The Comptroller granted NationsBank's application. He concluded that national banks have authority to broker annuities within "the business of banking". . . .

Authorizing national banks to "carry on the business of banking," the National Bank Act provides that such banks shall have power—

> To exercise . . . all such incidental powers as shall be necessary to carry on the business of banking; by discounting and negotiating promissory notes, drafts, bills of exchange, and other evidences of debt; by receiving deposits; by buying and selling exchange, coin, and bullion; by loaning money on personal security; and by obtaining, issuing, and circulating notes . . . . The business of dealing in securities and stock by the [bank] shall be limited to purchasing and selling such securities and stock without recourse, solely upon the order, and for the account of, customers, and in no case for its own account, and the [bank] shall not underwrite any issue of securities or stock.

. . . As the administrator charged with supervision of the National Bank Act, the Comptroller bears primary responsibility for surveillance of "the business of banking" . . . We have reiterated:

> It is settled that courts should give great weight to any reasonable construction of a regulatory statute adopted by the agency charged with the enforcement of that statute. The Comptroller of the Currency is charged with the enforcement of banking laws to an extent that warrants the invocation of this principle with respect to his deliberative conclusions as to the meaning of these laws.

Under the formulation now familiar, when we confront an expert administrator's statutory exposition, we inquire first whether the intent of Congress is clear as to the precise question at issue. If so, that is the end of the matter. But if the statute is silent or ambiguous with respect to the specific issue, the question for the court is whether the agency's answer is based on a permissible construction of the statute. If the administrator's reading fills a gap or defines a term in a way that is reasonable in light of the legislature's revealed design, we give the administrator's judgment controlling weight. . . .

[T]he Comptroller determined, in accord with the legislature's intent, that "the business of banking" . . . covers brokerage of financial investment instruments, and is not confined to the examples specifically enumerated. He then reasonably concluded that the authority to sell annuities qualifies as part of, or incidental to, the business of banking. National banks, the Comptroller observed, are authorized to serve as agents for their customers in the purchase and sale of various financial investment instruments and annuities are widely recognized as just such investment products.

By making an initial payment in exchange for a future income stream, the customer is deferring consumption, setting aside money for retirement, future expenses, or a rainy day. For her, an annuity is like putting money in a bank account, a debt instrument, or a mutual fund. Offering bank accounts and acting as agent in the sale of debt instruments and mutual funds are familiar parts of the business of banking.

In sum, modern annuities, though more sophisticated than the standard savings bank deposits of old, answer essentially the same need. By providing customers with the opportunity to invest in one or more annuity options, banks are essentially offering financial investment instruments of the kind congressional authorization permits them to broker. Hence, the Comptroller reasonably typed the permission NationsBank sought as an "incidental power . . . necessary to carry on the business of banking." . . .

We respect as reasonable the Comptroller's conclusion that brokerage of annuities is an "incidental power . . . necessary to carry on the business of banking." . . . Accordingly, the judgment of the Court of Appeals for the Fifth Circuit is [*Reversed*].

Case Questions

1. What did NationsBank want to do that required permission from the Comptroller of the Currency?

2. What was the basis of VALIC's objection to the Comptroller's grant of permission to NationsBank?

3. How did the district court and appellate court rule in this case?

4. What is the reasoning behind the Supreme Court deferring to the Comptroller's ruling?

Authority Exceeded?

Although it is highly unlikely that a court would hold a delegation invalid because of indefiniteness or lack of standards, from time to time courts do find that agencies exceed their authority. Courts will hold that an agency exceeds its authority if an analysis of legislative intent confirms the view that the agency has gone beyond that intent, however noble its purposes may be. The following case is typical of those in which an agency adopted a rule for a good reason but it was found to be beyond the authority of the agency.

MCI Tel. Corp. v. American Tel. & Tel. Co.

114 S.Ct. 2223 (1994)

In 1934, Congress passed the Communications Act authorizing the Federal Communications Commission (FCC) to regulate rates charged for communication services. Section 203 of this Act requires that long-distance telephone companies file their rates with the FCC and then charge only the filed rates. Subsection 203(b)(2) allows the FCC to modify any requirement of these filing procedures.

To facilitate competition during the 1980s in the long-distance telephone industry, the FCC issued a series of regulations that exempted every nondominant long-distance telephone company from filing its rates. (This FCC ruling is referred to as its detariffing policy.) In essence, the FCC's regulations meant that only AT&T (as the dominant long-distance telephone company) had to file its rates. Other long-distance companies, such as MCI, did not have to file the rates they charged.

AT&T challenged the FCC's authority to exempt companies from the § 203 filing requirements. After the FCC issued a Report and Order concluding that its detariffing policy was within its authority under the Communications Act, AT&T sought review by the D.C. Circuit Court of Appeals. That court reversed the FCC's order and concluded that the FCC had exceeded its authority. The FCC and MCI petitioned for certiorari, which was granted.

SCALIA, A.: . . . Section 203 of the Communications Act contains both the filed rate provisions of the Act and the Commission's disputed modification authority. It provides in relevant part:

> (b)(2) The Commission may, in its discretion and for good cause shown, modify any requirement made by or under the authority of this section either in particular instances or by general order applicable to special circumstances or conditions except that the Commission may not require the notice period specified in paragraph (1) to be more than one hundred and twenty days.

. . . The dispute between the parties turns on the meaning of the phrase "modify any requirement" in § 203(b)(2). Petitioners argue that it gives the Commission authority to make even basic and fundamental changes in the scheme created by that section. We disagree. The word "modify" . . . has a connotation of increment or limitation. Virtually every dictionary we are aware of says that "to modify" means to change moderately or in minor fashion.

In support of their position, petitioners cite dictionary definitions contained in or derived from a single source, Webster's Third New International Dictionary 1452 (1976) ("Webster's Third"), which includes among the meanings of "modify," "to make a basic or important change in." Petitioners contend that this establishes sufficient ambiguity to entitle the Commission to deference in its acceptance of the broader meaning, which in turn requires approval of its permissive detariffing policy. In short, they contend that the courts must defer to the agency's choice among available dictionary definitions. . . .

Since an agency's interpretation of a statute is not entitled to deference when it goes beyond the meaning that the statute can bear, the Commission's permissive detariffing policy can be justified only if it makes a less than radical or fundamental change in the Act's tariff-filing requirement. The Commission's attempt to establish that no more than that is involved greatly understates the extent to which its policy deviates from the filing requirement, and greatly undervalues the importance of the filing requirement itself. . . .

Bearing in mind, then, the enormous importance to the statutory scheme of the tariff-filing provision, we turn to whether what has occurred here can be considered a mere "modification." The Commission stresses that its detariffing policy applies only to non-dominant carriers, so that the rates charged to over half of all consumers in the long-distance market are on file with the Commission. It is not clear to us that the proportion of customers affected, rather than the proportion of carriers affected, is the proper measure of the extent of the exemption. . . . But even assuming it is, we think an elimination of the crucial provision of the statute for 40% of a major sector of the industry is much too extensive to be considered a "modification." . . .

Apart from its failure to qualify as a "modification," there is an independent reason why the Commission's detariffing policy cannot come within the § 203(b)(2) authority to modify. That provision requires that when the Commission proceeds "by general order" (as opposed to when it acts "in particular instances") to make a modification, the order can only apply "to special circumstances or conditions." Although that is a somewhat elastic phrase, it is not infinitely so. It is hard to imagine that a condition

shared by 40% of all long-distance customers, and by all long-distance carriers except one, qualifies as "special" within the intent of this limitation. . . .

We do not mean to suggest that the tariff-filing requirement is so inviolate that the Commission's existing modification authority does not reach it at all. Certainly the Commission can modify the form, contents, and location of required filings, and can defer filing or perhaps even waive it altogether in limited circumstances. But what we have here goes well beyond that. It is effectively the introduction of a whole new regime of regulation (or of free-market competition), which may well be a better regime but is not the one that Congress established.

The judgment of the Court of Appeals is [*affirmed*].

Case Questions

1. What does § 203 of the Communications Act require the FCC to do?

2. What was the legal rationale for the FCC's adoption of its detariffing policy?

3. How does the Supreme Court interpret the word "modify"?

4. The Court gives two reasons why it concludes the FCC has exceeded its authority. What is the basis of the second reason?

7. Review of Adjudications: Procedural Aspects

Judicial review of agencies' adjudications by its very nature is quite limited. Legislatures have delegated authority to agencies because of their expertise and knowledge, and courts usually exercise restraint and resolve doubtful issues in favor of an agency. For example, courts reviewing administrative interpretations of law do not always decide questions of law for themselves. It is not unusual for a court to accept an administrative interpretation of law as final if it is warranted in the record and has a rational basis in law. Administrative agencies are frequently called upon to interpret the statute governing an agency, and an agency's construction is persuasive to courts.

Administrative agencies develop their own rules of procedure unless mandated otherwise by an act of the legislature. These procedures are far less formal than judicial procedures, because one of the functions of the administrative process is to decide issues expeditiously. To proceed expeditiously usually means, for example, that administrative agencies are not restricted by the strict rules of evidence used by courts. Such agencies cannot ignore all rules, but they can use some leeway. They cannot, for example, refuse to permit any cross-examination or unduly limit it. Because an agency "is frequently the accuser, the prosecutor, the judge and the jury," it must remain alert to observe accepted standards of fairness. Reviewing courts are, therefore, alert to ensure that the true substance of a fair hearing is not denied to a party to an administrative hearing.

The principle that federal administrative agencies should be free to fashion their own rules of procedure and pursue methods of inquiry permitting them to discharge their duties grows out of the view that administrative agencies and administrators will be familiar with the industries they regulate. Thus, they will be in a better position than courts or legislative bodies to design procedural rules adapted to the peculiarities of the industry and the tasks of the agency involved.

In reviewing the procedures of administrative agencies, courts lack the authority to substitute their judgment or their own procedures for those of the agency. Judicial responsibility is limited to ensuring consistency with statutes and compliance with the demands of the Constitution for a fair hearing. The latter responsibility is based on the due process clause. Due process usually requires a hearing by an agency, but on occasion sanctions may be imposed prior to the hearing.

Two doctrines guide courts in the judicial review of agency adjudications:

- Exhaustion of remedies
- Primary jurisdiction

Exhaustion of Remedies

The doctrine of **exhaustion of remedies** is a court-created rule that limits when courts can review administrative decisions. Courts refuse to review administrative actions until a complaining party has exhausted all of the administrative remedies and procedures available to him or her for redress. Judicial review is available only for final actions by an agency. Preliminary orders such as a decision to file a complaint are not reviewable. Otherwise, the administrative system would be denied important opportunities to make a factual record, to exercise its discretion, or to apply its expertise in its decision making. Also, exhaustion allows an agency to discover and correct its own errors, and thus it helps to dispense with any reason for judicial review. Exhaustion clearly should be required in those cases involving an area of the agency's expertise or specialization; it should require no unusual expense. It should also be required when the administrative remedy is just as likely as the judicial one to provide appropriate relief. The doctrine of exhaustion of remedies avoids the premature interruption of the administrative process. In general, it is probably more efficient for that purpose to go forward without interruption.

However, when there is nothing to be gained from the exhaustion of administrative remedies and when the harm from the continued existence of the administrative ruling is great, the courts have not been reluctant to discard this doctrine. This is especially true when very fundamental constitutional guarantees such as freedom of speech or press are involved or when the administrative remedy is likely to be inadequate. Also, probably no court would insist upon exhaustion when the agency is clearly acting beyond its jurisdiction (because its action is not authorized by statute or the statute authorizing it is unconstitutional) or where it would result in irreparable injury (such as great expense) to the petitioner. Finally, an exception to the doctrine is fraud. If an agency is acting fraudulently, immediate access to the court is appropriate.

The following case illustrates one more limitation to the doctrine of exhaustion of remedies. The Administrative Procedures Act, referred to in this case, is a federal law originally passed in 1946. This law governs the procedures used by federal administrative agencies, including the scope of judicial review of agencies' actions.

DARBY V. CISNEROS

113 S.Ct. 2539 (1993)

R. Gordon Darby is a self-employed real estate developer in South Carolina. He specializes in the development and management of multifamily rental projects. Lonnie Garvin is a mortgage banker who assists developers, like Darby, in obtaining single-family mortgage insurance from the Department of Housing and Urban Development (HUD).

Single-family mortgage insurance is preferable over multifamily mortgage insurance because the latter involves greater oversight and control by HUD over the development project. Garvin arranged the single-family mortgage insurance by avoiding HUD's Rule of Seven. This rule prevented rental properties from receiving single-family mortgage insurance if the developer/borrower already had financial interests in seven or more rental properties in the same project or subdivision.

On behalf of Darby, Garvin used straw purchasers who applied for the single-family mortgage insurance, closed the loan, and then transferred the ownership back to Darby. HUD officials in South Carolina assured Darby that the use of Garvin's plan was legal.

Three of Darby's rental projects were financially unsuccessful. When Darby defaulted, HUD became responsible for the payment of over $6.6 million in mortgage insurance claims. After these defaults, in June 1989, HUD prohibited Darby and Garvin from participating in any program in South Carolina administered by HUD. Two months later, Darby and Garvin were notified that HUD was proposing to debar them from further participation in all HUD procurement contracts and in any nonprocurement transactions with any federal agency.

Darby and Garvin appealed the order of nonparticipation and the proposed debarment. In April 1990, an Administrative Law Judge (ALJ) found that the financing method used by Darby and Garvin was "a sham which improperly circumvented the Rule of Seven." However, the ALJ also concluded that this financing method had been revealed to local HUD officials and that Darby and Garvin lacked any criminal intent. The ALJ held that indefinite debarment would be punitive; however, he did order Darby and Garvin to be debarred for a period of 18 months. This order of the ALJ was labeled an "Initial Decision and Order." No further administrative review of this "Initial Decision and Order" was sought.

Darby and Garvin filed suit in federal district court on May 31, 1990. They asked the federal district judge to declare the ALJ's order invalid as punitive in violation of HUD's own debarment regulations. The secretary of HUD moved to dismiss the suit on the grounds that Darby and Garvin failed to exhaust their administrative remedies within HUD.

The federal district judge granted Darby and Garvin's motion for summary judgment. The Court of Appeal reversed, stating that exhaustion of administrative remedies is required prior to seeking judicial relief. Darby and Garvin's petition for a writ of certiorari was granted.

BLACKMUN, J.: This case presents the question whether federal courts have the authority to require that a plaintiff exhaust available administrative remedies before seeking judicial review under the Administrative Procedures Act (APA), where neither the statute nor agency rules specifically mandate exhaustion as a prerequisite to judicial review. At issue is the relationship between the judicially created doctrine of exhaustion of administrative remedies and the statutory requirements of § 10(c) of the APA. . . .

Section 10(c) of the APA bears the caption "Actions reviewable." It provides in its first two sentences that judicial review is available for "final agency action for which there is no other adequate remedy in a court," and that "preliminary, procedural, or intermediate agency action . . . is subject to review on the review of the final agency action." The last sentence of § 10(c) reads:

Except as otherwise expressly required by statute, agency action otherwise final is final for the purposes of this section whether or not there has been . . . an application . . . for an appeal to superior agency authority.

Petitioners argue that this provision means that a litigant seeking judicial review of a final agency action under the APA need not exhaust available administrative remedies unless such exhaustion is expressly required by statute or agency rule. According to petitioners, since § 10(c) contains an explicit exhaustion provision, federal courts are not free to require further exhaustion as a matter of judicial discretion.

. . . Respondents concede that petitioners' claim is "final" under § 10(c), for neither the National Housing Act nor applicable HUD regulations require that a litigant pursue further administrative appeals prior to seeking judicial review. However, even though nothing in § 10(c) precludes judicial review of petitioners' claim, respondents argue that federal courts remain free under the APA to impose appropriate exhaustion requirements.

We have recognized that the judicial doctrine of exhaustion of administrative remedies is conceptually distinct from the doctrine of finality:

> The finality requirement is concerned with whether the initial decisionmaker has arrived at a definitive position on the issue that inflicts an actual, concrete injury; the exhaustion requirement generally refers to administrative and judicial procedures by which an injured party may seek review of an adverse decision and obtain a remedy if the decision is found to be unlawful or otherwise inappropriate.

Whether courts are free to impose an exhaustion requirement as a matter of judicial discretion depends . . . on whether Congress has provided otherwise. . . . We therefore must consider whether § 10(c), by providing the conditions under which agency action becomes "final for the purposes of" judicial review, limits the authority of courts to impose additional exhaustion requirements as a prerequisite to judicial review.

It perhaps is surprising that it has taken over 45 years since the passage of the APA for this Court definitively to address this question. . . .

The text of the APA leaves little doubt that petitioners are correct. Under § 10(a) of the APA, "[a] person suffering legal wrong because of agency action, or adversely affected or aggrieved by agency action within the meaning of a relevant statute, is entitled to judicial review thereof." Although § 10(a) provides the general right to judicial review of agency actions under the

APA, § 10(c) establishes when such review is available. When an aggrieved party has exhausted all administrative remedies expressly prescribed by statute or agency rule, the agency action is "final for the purposes of this section" and therefore "subject to judicial review" under the first sentence. . . . § 10(c), by its very terms, has limited the availability of the doctrine of exhaustion of administrative remedies to that which the statute or rule clearly mandates.

. . . Congress clearly was concerned with making the exhaustion requirement unambiguous so that aggrieved parties would know precisely what administrative steps were required before judicial review would be available. If courts were able to impose additional exhaustion requirements beyond those provided by Congress or the agency, the last sentence of § 10(c) would make no sense. . . . Section 10(c) explicitly requires exhaustion of all intra-agency appeals mandated either by statute or by agency rule; it would be inconsistent with the plain language of § 10(c) for courts to require litigants to exhaust optional appeals as well. . . .

[W]ith respect to actions brought under the APA, Congress effectively codified the doctrine of exhaustion of administrative remedies in § 10(c). Of course, the exhaustion doctrine continues to apply as a matter of judicial discretion in cases not governed by the APA. But where the APA applies, an appeal to "superior agency authority" is a prerequisite to judicial review only when expressly required by statute or when an agency rule requires appeal before review and the administrative action is made inoperative pending that review. Courts are not free to impose an exhaustion requirement as a rule of judicial administration where the agency action has already become final under § 10(c).

The judgment of the Court of Appeals is reversed, and the case is remanded for further proceedings consistent with this opinion. [*Reversed and remanded*].

Case Questions

1. Why did Darby want to use single-family (rather than multifamily) mortgage insurance?

2. How did Garvin arrange the loan transactions to be able to obtain the single-family mortgage insurance?

3. What was the holding of the Administrative Law Judge?

4. What is the applicability of the doctrine of exhaustion of remedies under § 10(c) of the APA?

Primary Jurisdiction

A doctrine similar to exhaustion of remedies is known as **primary jurisdiction.** *Exhaustion* applies when a claim must go in the first instance to an administrative agency alone. *Primary jurisdiction* applies when a claim is originally filed in the courts. It comes into play whenever enforcement of the claim requires the resolution of issues that, under a regulatory scheme, have been placed within the special competence of an administrative body. In such a case, the judicial process is suspended pending referral of such issues to the administrative body for its views. Primary jurisdiction ensures uniformity and consistency in dealing with matters entrusted to an administrative body. The doctrine is invoked when referral to the agency is preferable because of its specialized knowledge or expertise in dealing with the matter in controversy. Statutes such as those guaranteeing equal employment opportunity that create a private remedy for dollar damages sometimes require resort to an administrative agency as a condition precedent to filing suit. Some of these are federal statutes that require referral to state agencies. In these cases, referral must occur, but the right to sue is not limited by the results of the administrative decision.

8. Review of Factual Determinations

When it reviews the findings of fact made by an administrative body, a court presumes them to be correct. A court of review examines the evidence by analyzing the record of the agency's proceedings. It upholds the agency's findings and conclusions on questions of fact if they are supported by substantial evidence in the record. In other words, the record must contain material evidence from which a reasonable person might reach the same conclusion as did the agency. If substantial evidence in support of the decision is present, the court will not disturb the agency's findings, even though the court itself might have reached a different conclusion on the basis of other conflicting evidence also in the record. For example the determination of credibility of the witnesses who testify in quasi-judicial proceedings is for the agency to determine and not the courts.

The following case provides a further example that courts will not disturb an agency's finding of fact and interpretation of law as long as the court can conclude that there is a reasonable basis for the agency's conclusion.

HOLLY FARMS CORPORATION V. NATIONAL LABOR RELATIONS LABOR BOARD
116 S.Ct. 1396 (1996)

GINSBURG, J. . . . Petitioner Holly Farms Corporation, a wholly owned subsidiary of Tyson Foods, Inc., is a vertically integrated poultry producer headquartered in Wilkesboro, North Carolina. Holly Farms' activities encompass numerous poultry operations, including hatcheries, a feed mill, an equipment maintenance center, and a processing plant.

"Broiler" chickens are birds destined for human food markets. Holly Farms hatches broiler chicks at its own hatcheries, and immediately delivers the chicks to the farms of independent contractors. The contractors then raise the birds into full-grown broiler chickens. Holly Farms pays the contract growers for their services, but retains title to the broilers and supplies the food and medicine necessary to their growth.

When the broilers are seven weeks old, Holly Farms sends its live-haul crews to reclaim the birds and ferry them to the processing plant for slaughter. The live-haul crews—which typically comprise nine chicken catchers, one forklift operator, and one live-haul driver—travel in a flat-bed truck from Holly Farms' processing plant to the farms of the independent growers. At the farms, the chicken catchers enter the coops, manually capture the broilers, and load them into cages. The forklift operator lifts the caged chickens onto the bed of the truck, and the live-haul driver returns the truck, with the loaded cases and the crew, to Holly Farms' processing plant. There, the birds are slaughtered and prepared for shipment to retail stores.

In 1989, the Chauffeurs, Teamsters and Helpers, Local 391 (Union), filed a representation petition with the National Labor Relations Board (Board or NLRB), seeking an election in a proposed unit that included live-haul employees working out of Holly Farms' Wilkesboro processing plant. Over Holly Farms' objection, the Board approved the bargaining unit, ruling that the live-haul workers were "employees" protected by the National Labor Relations Act (NLRA or Act), rather than "agricultural laborers" excluded from the Act's coverage. . . . [T]he Board ordered the corporation to bargain with the Union as the representative of the unit.

The United States Court of Appeals for the Fourth Circuit enforced the Board's order. The court held that the Board's classification of the live-haul workers as "employees," rather than "agricultural laborers," rested "on a reasonable interpretation of the Act." . . .

Other Federal Courts of Appeals . . . have held that live-haul workers employed by vertically integrated poultry producers are engaged in "agriculture." We granted certiorari to resolve the division of authority.

The NLRA's protections extend only to workers who qualify as "employees" under § 2(3) of the Act. The term "employee," NLRA § 2(3) states, "[does] not include any individual employed as an agricultural laborer." No definition of "agricultural laborer" appears in the NLRA. But annually since 1946, Congress has instructed, in riders to Appropriations Acts for the Board: "Agricultural laborer," for NLRA § 2(3) purposes, shall derive its meaning from the definition of "agriculture" supplied by § 3(f) of the Fair Labor Standards Act of 1938 (FLSA). Section § 3(f) of the FLSA provides:

> "Agriculture" includes farming in all its branches and among other things includes the cultivation and tillage of the soil, dairying, the production, cultivation, growing, and harvesting of any agricultural or horticultural commodities . . . , the raising of livestock, bees, fur-bearing animals, or poultry, and any practices (including any forestry or lumbering operations) performed by a farmer or on a farm as an incident to or in conjunction with such farming operations, including preparation for market, delivery to storage or to market or to carriers for transportation to market.

. . . If a statute's meaning is plain, the Board and reviewing courts must give effect to the unambiguously expressed intent of Congress. When the legislative prescription is not free from ambiguity, the administrator must choose between conflicting reasonable interpretations. Courts, in turn, must respect the judgment of the agency empowered to apply the law to varying fact patterns, even if the issue with nearly equal reason [might] be resolved one way rather than another. . . .

Holly Farms argues that under the plain language of the statute, the catching and loading of broilers qualifies as work performed "on a farm as an incident to" the raising of poultry. The corporation emphasizes that § 3(f) of the FLSA enumerates "preparation for market" and "delivery to storage or to market" among activities that count as "agriculture." The live-haul employees' work, Holly Farms concludes, thus falls within the domain of the FLSA exemption and, accordingly, enjoys no NLRA protection.

We find Holly Farms' position to be a plausible, but not an inevitable, construction of § 3(f). Hence, we turn to the Board's position, examining only its reasonableness as an interpretation of the governing legislation.

While agreeing that the chicken catchers and forklift operators work "on a farm," the Board contends that their catch and cage work is not incidental to farming operations. Rather, the work is tied to Holly Farms' slaughtering and processing operations, activities that do not constitute "farming" under the statute. . . .

We find the Board's answer reasonable. Once the broilers have grown on the farm for seven weeks, the growers' contractual obligation to raise the birds ends, and the work of the live-haul crew begins. The record reflects minimal overlap between the work of the live-haul crew and the independent growers' raising activities. The growers do not assist the live-haul crews in catching or loading the chickens; their only responsibilities are to move certain equipment from the chicken coops prior to the crews' arrival, and to be present when the crews are on the farms. Nor do the live-haul employees play any role in the growers' performance of their contractual undertakings.

The record, furthermore, supports the Board's conclusion that the live-haul crews' activities were conjoined with Holly Farms' processing operations, rather than with farming. The chicken catchers, forklift operators, and truckdrivers work as a unit. They all work out of the processing plant in Wilkesboro, located three miles from the hatcheries. Crew members begin and end each shift by punching a timeclock at the processing plant and are functionally integrated with other processing-plant employees. . . .

In sum, we find persuasive the Board's conclusion that the collection of broilers for slaughter was an activity serving Holly Farms' processing operations, and not Holly Farms' own or the independent growers' farming operations. Again, we stress that the reviewing court's function is limited. For the Board to prevail, it need not show that its construction is the best way to read the statute; rather, courts must respect the Board's judgment so long as its reading is a reasonable one. Regardless of how we might have resolved the question as an initial matter, the Board's decision here reflects a reasonable interpretation of the law and, therefore, merits our approbation. The judgment of the Court of Appeals is accordingly [*affirmed*].

Case Questions

1. What is the order of the NLRB from which Holly Farms objects?
2. What are the respective arguments of Holly Farms and the Chauffeurs, Teamsters and Helpers union with regard to the "employees" in this case?
3. What is the holding of the Fourth Circuit Court of Appeals?
4. How does the Supreme Court rule in this case? Why?

As the preceding case exemplifies, it is apparent that on review, courts do not (1) reweigh the evidence, (2) make independent determinations of fact, or (3) substitute their view of the evidence for that of the agency. However, courts do determine if there is substantial evidence to support the action taken. But in their examination of the evidence, all that is required is evidence sufficient to convince a reasonable mind to a fair degree of certainty. Thus, substantial evidence is that which a reasonable mind might accept as adequate to support the conclusion.

For the courts to exercise their function of limited review, an agency must provide a record that sets forth the reasons and basis for its decision. If this record shows that the agency did not examine all relevant data and that it ignored issues before it, a court may set aside the agency's decision because such a decision is arbitrary and capricious. Agencies cannot assume their decisions. They must be based on evidence, and the record must support the decision.

After reading this section and the preceding ones, do you understand why it is important for businesses to take seriously the procedures within the administrative agency? The deference courts give to agencies' decisions makes the Business Decision at the chapter opening an easy one. The chances of winning a reversal are slight at best.

Concept Summary: Judicial Review of Agency Decisions

1. Regardless of whether a party is challenging an agency's rule making or adjudication, that party must have standing to sue.

2. To establish standing to sue, the challenger must show the reviewing court that the agency's decision is subject to review and that the challenger is personally affected by the agency's decision.

3. When the decision challenged involves the agency's rule-making function, the court must determine if the agency's authority was validly delegated.

4. If the delegation of authority is definite and limited, the court will decide if the agency has exceeded its authority. If the answer is no, the agency's rule will be upheld.

5. When the decision challenged involves the agency's adjudicatory function, the law requires the challenger to exhaust the available administrative

concluded

remedies and the court to determine whether an agency should have primary jurisdiction.

6. The factual findings of an agency are presumed to be correct.

7. Courts are not permitted to substitute their personal views for the agency's findings and conclusions if a reasonable person could reach the same result as the agency.

8. An agency's expertise is entitled to great deference and will not be reversed unless it is clearly erroneous.

9. Equal Access to Justice Act

If a business is successful in challenging an administrative agency's decision, that business may be able to collect attorneys' fees. The Equal Access to Justice Act (EAJA) requires the federal government to pay the reasonable attorneys' fees of small businesses, nonprofit groups, and most individuals who can show they were unjustly treated by the federal government. Prior to the enactment of this law, small companies often were reluctant to take on the U.S. government because of litigation costs. The government was at a great advantage because of the number of attorneys and other resources it has. This law enables the "little guy" to fight the bureaucracy. It should be recognized that awards for legal expenses are not available to just anyone. Congress limited eligibility to persons whose net worth does not exceed $1 million and businesses with no more than $5 million net worth and 500 employees. Charitable and religious tax-exempt organizations qualify if they have 500 or fewer employees. The law also grants legal fees only to parties that overcome the government's position in court, administrative proceedings, or a settlement. Even then, the government agency is not required to pay if it can show that its original position was substantially justified.

The word "substantially" means to be justified in substance or in the main, not justified to a high degree. The action must be justified to a degree that could satisfy a reasonable person and must have reasonable basis in both law and fact. For the position of the government to be substantially justified, so that the award of attorneys' fees under the Equal Access to Justice Act is not appropriate, the government's position must be more than merely undeserving of sanctions for frivolity.

Under the EAJA, the amount of fees awarded must "be based upon prevailing market rates for the kind of quality of the services furnished, except that . . . fees shall not be awarded in excess of $75 per hour unless the court determines that an increase in the cost of living or a special factor, such as the limited ability of qualified attorneys for the proceedings involved, justifies a higher fee."

Criticism of Administrative Agencies

The independent regulatory agencies and the administrative process face many problems and are subjected to a great deal of criticism. Many of the common criticisms are summarized in the box that follows. Agencies are often charged with being too vast to be efficient and effective. One of the major criticisms of the fourth branch of government is its high cost.

Criticisms of Administrative Process

Relating to Personnel

1. Government has difficulty in hiring and retaining the best-qualified people. Salaries are often not competitive, and advancement is often slower than in the private sector. Also, some people are overqualified for their positions.

2. The reward system usually does not make a significant distinction between excellent, mediocre, and poor performances. There are few incentives to improve productivity and job performance.

3. It is very difficult, if not impossible, to discharge unsatisfactory employees. Transfers of employees are easier to accomplish than discharges.

4. The *Peter Principle,* which holds that people are promoted to their level of incompetence, is obviously present in many administrative agencies.

5. Personnel in many top positions are selected for political reasons. They often lack the necessary expertise to run an effective organization.

Relating to Procedures

1. Delay in the decision-making process is quite common. There often is no reason to expedite decisions, and a huge backlog of cases is common in agencies such as EEOC.

2. The administrative process is overwhelmed with paperwork and with meetings.

3. Rules and regulations are often written in complex legal language—"legalese"—which laypeople cannot understand.

4. There is often a lack of enforcement procedures to follow up on actions taken to ensure compliance.

5. The administrative process can be dictatorial; there may be too much discretionary power, often unstructured and unchecked, placed in many bureaucratic hands. Formal as well as informal administrative action can amount to an abuse of power.

Relating to Substance

1. There are so many agencies making rules and regulations directed at the business community that the rules and regulations often overlap and are in conflict.

2. Some agencies are accused of "sweetheart regulations," or favoring the industry or industries they regulate over the public interest. This may arise as a result of the "revolving door" relationship. Regulators are often persons who had former high executive positions in the industries they regulate. The reverse is also true: people in high-paying jobs in certain industries often were regulators of those very industries.

3. Many actions for illegal conduct end only with consent orders. A business accused of a violation agrees not to violate the law in the future without admitting any past violation. Such actions have little deterrent effect on others, and little or no punishment is imposed for illegal conduct.

4. The volume of rules adopted by agencies is beyond the ability of the business community to keep up with and comply with.

5. Enforcement of some laws varies over time.

10. The Cost of Regulation

Regulation is a form of taxation. It directly increases the cost of government. But these direct costs of regulation are only a small fraction of the indirect costs. Regulation significantly adds to the cost of doing business, and these costs are passed on to the taxpaying, consuming public. The consumer, for whose protection many regulations are adopted, pays both the direct cost of regulation (in taxes) and the indirect cost (when purchasing products and services).

The existence of a governmental agency usually forces a business subject to the agency's jurisdiction to create a similar bureaucracy within its own organization to deal with the agency. For example, the existence of EEOC has caused most large corporations to designate affirmative action officers. These employees assist their companies in complying with the laws, rules, and regulations enforced by EEOC. Whenever a bureaucracy exists, firms dealing with it must have internal groups with responsibilities that are the mirror image of the agency.

Other costs the public must absorb result from agency regulations that inhibit competition and innovation. Regulation has protected existing companies by creating a barrier to entry into a market. Regulation tends to protect "cozy competition" to the extent that, quite often, the parties that object the most to deregulation are the businesses being regulated.

Perhaps the most disturbing additional cost to the business community is the cost of paperwork. The burden of the paperwork involved in filing applications, returns, reports, and forms is overwhelming and a major cost of doing business.

Historically, there was little or no cost-benefit analysis when new rules and regulations were proposed. Government has tended only to assess the benefits accruing from a cleaner environment, safer products, healthier working conditions, and so on, in deciding to embark upon vast new regulatory programs. The primary focus of policy making by way of such social regulation has not been on balancing the costs of the programs with their potential benefits. The public, and especially consumers, has frequently been forced to pay for many things it did not want or need in the sense that the cost far exceeded the benefits.

The Problem with Assessing Costs

At first glance, the application of cost-benefit analysis to the administrative process would seem to make sense. However, on closer examination, it is obvious that in many cases it is not possible to weigh the costs against the benefits of regulation.

How do you apply cost-benefit analysis to a rule dealing with human life? How much dollar benefit is to be assigned to a life in measuring it against the cost? Assume that a Department of Transportation rule requiring air bags in all new automobiles sold adds a cost of $800 to each car. Assume also that it saves 50,000 lives per year. Is the cost worth the benefit? Your answer may depend on whether you are one of the 50,000. Cost-benefit analysis becomes ethically awkward when there is an attempt to place a dollar value on things not usually bought and sold, such as life, health, or mobility.

Tobacco Industry Box

The proposed settlement, discussed in chapter 3, to end the litigation between the state attorneys general and the major cigarette manufacturers contained an interesting aspect involving the regulatory process—specifically the Food and Drug Administration (FDA). A major issue between these litigants has been the impact of nicotine on smokers. For years, the cigarette manufacturers publicly denied that there were any addictive qualities of nicotine. In fact, these manufacturers had conducted numerous studies about how the manipulation of nicotine in cigarettes influenced the addictive nature of smoking.

> *continued*
>
> In the settlement, it is proposed that the FDA will fully regulate nicotine as an addictive drug by the year 2009. The timing of this grant of authority to the FDA is subject to congressional approval or modification.

Key Terms

Administrative agency   148
Administrative law judge   155
Cease and desist order   152
Consent order   152
Exhaustion of remedies   162

General counsel   154
Immunity   155
Primary jurisdiction   164
Quasi-judicial   152
Quasi-legislative   151

Review Questions and Problems

Administrative Agencies

1. *Reasons for Agencies*
   This chapter discusses five reasons for having administrative agencies. Give an example for each reason.

2. *Functions of Agencies*
   Describe the four possible functions of an administrative agency.

3. *Organization of Agencies*
   (a) Why is the position of General Counsel of an administrative agency so important?
   (b) What is the purpose of the administrative law judges within administrative agencies?

4. *Influencing Agency Decisions*
   Suppose that a company is interested in a newly proposed regulation on clean air by the Environmental Protection Agency. What should this company do to provide its input on this EPA regulation?

Judicial Review of Agency Decisions

5. *Standing to Sue*
   What are the two issues that must be considered by courts to determine whether a person has standing to challenge an agency's decision?

6. *Review of Rule Making*
   Again there are two issues that must be addressed by courts when they review the rule-making (quasi-legislative) functions of agencies. What are these two issues? Explain each.

7. *Review of Adjudications: Procedural Aspects*
   Plaintiffs purchased state lottery tickets and were winners along with seventy-six others. The state had advertised that $1,750,000 would be the prize, but it only distributed $744,471. Plaintiff sued the lottery director, alleging fraud in the conduct of the lottery. The state lottery law provides for administrative hearings upon complaints charging violations of the lottery law or of regulations thereunder. It also allows any party adversely affected by a final order to determination of the administrative agency to seek judicial review. Must the plaintiffs exhaust their administrative remedies? Why or why not?

8. *Review of Factual Determinations*
   What standard of review do courts use to decide whether to uphold the factual determinations made by an administrative agency?

9. *Equal Access to Justice Act*
   A congressman filed an administrative complaint with the Federal Election Commission, alleging various violations of the Federal Election Campaign Act by several different groups that made campaign contributions. Dissatisfied with the progress of the FEC's investigation, he filed suit against the FEC in federal district court, seeking to compel agency action. The court found that the agency action was "arbitrary and capricious." Does this entitle him to an award of attorney's fees under the Equal Access to Justice Act? Why or why not?

Criticism of Administrative Agencies

10. *The Cost of Regulation*
    Why has there been so little use of cost-benefit analysis when judging the merits of agencies' actions?

Terminology Review

For each term in the left-hand column, match the most appropriate description in the right-hand column:

1. CPSC

   a. Protects the public from anticompetitive behavior and unfair and deceptive business practices; a law enforcement agency

2. EPA

   b. Licenses and regulates the nuclear energy industry

3. FCC

   c. Protects the public against unreasonable risks of injury associated with consumer products

4. FTC

   d. Seeks to prevent discrimination in employment based on race, color, religion, sex, or national origin and other unlawful employment practices

5. FDA

   e. Regulates interstate and foreign communications by means of radio, television, wire, cable, and satellite

6. EEOC

   f. Ensures all workers a safe and healthy work environment

7. NLRB

   g. Enforces the federal securities laws that regulate the sale of securities to the investing public

8. NRC

   h. Administers laws to prohibit distribution of adulterated, misbranded, or unsafe food and drugs

9. OSHA

   i. Conducts union certification elections and holds hearings on unfair labor practice complaints

10. SEC

   j. Administers all laws relating to the environment, including laws on water pollution, air pollution, solid wastes, pesticides, toxic substances, etc.

BUSINESS ORGANIZATIONS AND SECURITIES REGULATION

Business Decision

Before You Start

You and two of your college roommates have discussed plans to open a restaurant. You intend to attract college-age students who are health- and fitness-minded to your restaurant. You and your co-owners agree that each will invest equally in terms of time and money. However, in addition to contributions made by each of you, another $700,000 is essential for the restaurant to succeed.

What type of organization is best suited for this business activity?

Who will manage the restaurant during times that you and your co-owners are not present?

What liabilities do you and your co-owners face?

What laws and regulations do you and your co-owners need to be aware of concerning raising the additional funds needed?

The questions asked in the preceding Business Decision describe the three topics covered in this chapter. First, you will be exposed to the variety of issues that arise when deciding which form of organization is best for a given business activity. Second, you will learn about how all businesses rely on people or other organizations, as agents, to achieve the goals established for the business. Third, you will be introduced to some basic matters that must be considered whenever money is solicited from public investors to finance a business activity.

Forms of Business Organizations

Businesspeople conduct their activities and strive to accomplish their goals through a variety of organizational forms. To select which form is best, numerous factors need to be reviewed.

173

In the following sections, you are introduced to some of the basic factors that deserve careful analysis. Then the possible options of organizational forms are presented as alternative choices.

1. Factors to Consider

Significant factors to consider in selecting the best organizational form for a particular business activity include:

- The cost of creating the organization
- The continuity or stability of the organization
- The control of decisions
- The personal liability of the owners
- The taxation of the organization's earnings and its distribution of profits to the owners

In this section, each of these factors is defined so that you can more easily apply their meaning in sections 2 through 8.

Creation
The word "creation" means the legal steps required to form a particular business organization. At times, a businessperson may be concerned with how much it will cost to have each form established. Usually, the cost of creation is not a major factor in considering which form of business organization a person will choose to operate a business. The most significant creation-related issues are how long it will take to create a particular organization and how much paperwork is involved.

Continuity
Another factor to consider when selecting the best organizational form for a business activity is the continuity of the organization. How is the organization's existence tied to its owners? By this question the meaning of the word "continuity" becomes associated with the stability or durability of the organization.

The crucial issue with this continuity factor is the method by which a business organization can be dissolved. A **dissolution** is any change in the ownership of an organization that changes the legal existence of the organization. In essence, the questions become: Is the organization easily dissolved? What impact does a dissolution of the organizational form have on the business activity of that organization?

Managerial Control
The factor of control concerns who is managing the business organization. Often this issue is of vital importance to the owners. The egos of business-people can cause them to insist on equal voices in management. As you study this factor under each organizational form, keep in mind the difficulties that can arise when a few strong-willed business owners disagree with one another. Usually when people are excited about getting started in a business opportunity (like a new restaurant), methods of resolving these potential deadlocks are not viewed as really important. However, consideration of

potential conflict and mechanisms to resolve disputes are essential to consider when selecting a form for a business venture.

Liability

When considering the liability factor, you should ask yourself—to what degree is the owner of a business personally liable for the debts of the business organization? Generally, businesspeople want to limit their personal liability. While there are organizations that appear to accomplish this goal, you will see that such promises might be misleading when actually conducting business transactions. Nevertheless, this liability factor is very important and deserves significant consideration as it relates to each of the organizational forms presented below.

Taxation

This factor often is viewed as the most critical when selecting the form of business organization. At issue is: How is the income earned by the business taxed? How is the money distributed to the business owners taxed? Is it possible that owners may have to pay taxes on money that is attributed to them as income but which they have not actually received? The answers to these questions provide much needed guidance when deciding which form of organization is best suited for a business's operation.

People have stated that the double taxation of corporate income should be avoided by selecting a different form of organization. As you will see, there are specific advantages to creating the organizational forms that are "single taxed." However, advantages also exist when an organization is subject to the supposed "double tax."

2. Selecting the Best Organizational Form

Before we begin with an explanation of the various organizational forms that are available to businesspeople, two terms that relate to the number of owners of a business organization are presented. Some organizations are owned by only a few persons. Such organizations are said to be **closely held.** Family-owned and -operated businesses are common examples of closely held organizations. Other businesses may be owned by hundreds, if not thousands, of persons. These organizations are **publicly held** ones. Examples of publicly held businesses include those whose stock is traded on a public exchange.

You should understand that the decision of selecting an appropriate organizational form usually is limited to those situations involving the few owners of a closely held business. When a business is publicly held by a large number of owners, the form of organization usually is a corporation. The reason for this corporate form being used is that shareholders can transfer their ownership interests without interfering with the organization's management.

Business is conducted under a variety of legal forms. The three basic forms are sole proprietorships, partnerships, and corporations. Hybrid forms take on the attributes of both a partnership and a corporation. These forms include the limited partnership, the S corporation, and the limited liability company or partnership. Each of these organizational forms are discussed in the following six sections.

3. Sole Proprietorships

As the name implies, a **sole proprietorship** is a business owned by only one person. A sole proprietorship is the easiest and least expensive business organization to create. In essence, the proprietor obtains whatever business licenses are necessary and begins operations. The sole proprietor is in total control of his or her business's goals and operations and is personally obligated for the debts of the proprietorship. A sole proprietorship is not taxed as an organization. All the proprietorship's income subject to taxation is attributed to the proprietor.

4. Partnerships

Whenever two or more people wish to own a business together, a partnership is a possible organizational form. In general, a **partnership** is an agreement between two or more persons to share a common interest in a commercial endeavor and to share profits and losses. The word "persons" in the previous sentence should be interpreted broadly enough to allow not only individuals but also business organizations to form a partnership. For example, two or more individuals, an individual and a corporation, a partnership and a corporation, or any combination of these entities may agree to create a business organization called a partnership.

Due to the potentially complex relationships established through a partnership, factors to consider when studying the appropriateness of this organizational form are presented under subheadings that correspond to the items in section 1, above.

Creation

When compared to other forms of business organizations (other than the sole proprietorship), a partnership is easily formed. The cost of forming a partnership is relatively minimal. In addition, the creation of a partnership is made easier since it does not need to get permission from each state in which it does business.

The key to a partnership's existence is satisfying the elements of its definition:

1. Two or more persons,
2. A common interest in business, and
3. Sharing profits and losses.

If the parties conduct their affairs in such a way as to meet these definitional elements, a partnership exists regardless of whether the persons involved call themselves partners or not.

Since the existence of a partnership is based on the partners' agreement, it is possible that this agreement is implied from the conduct or actions of the parties. Partners should never rely on implied agreements. Rather, their agreement should be explicitly stated among the parties and drafted into a formal document. The formal agreement is called the **articles of partnership.**

Since a partnership is created by agreement, the partners select the name of the partnership. This right of selection is subject to two limitations in many states. First, a partnership may not use any word in the name, such as "company," that would imply the existence of a corporation. Second, if the name is other than that of the partners, the partners must give notice as to their actual identity under the state's **assumed-name statute.** Failure to comply with this disclosure requirement may result in the partnership's being denied access to courts, or it may result in criminal actions being brought against those operating under the assumed name.

Continuity

A general partnership is dissolved any time there is a change in the partners. For example, if a partner dies, retires, or otherwise withdraws from the organization, the partnership is dissolved. Likewise, if a person is added as a new partner, there is a technical dissolution of the organization. Therefore, it generally is said that the partnership organization is easily dissolved. Even if the partnership agreement provides that the partnership will continue for a stated number of years, any partner still retains the power to dissolve the organization. Although liability may be imposed on the former partner for wrongful dissolution in violation of the agreement, the partnership nevertheless is dissolved.

A dissolution does not necessarily destroy the business of a partnership. Dissolution is not the same thing as terminating an organization's business activity. Termination involves the winding up or liquidating of a business; dissolution simply means the legal form of organization no longer exists.

To prevent problems that may arise when a partner dies or withdraws from a partnership, the articles of partnership should include a **buy and sell agreement.** This agreement, which needs to be entered into when the business entity is created, provides for the amount and manner of compensation for the interest of the deceased or withdrawing owner.

Buy and sell agreements frequently use formulas to compute the value of the withdrawing partner's interest and provide for the time and method of payment. In the case of death, the liquidity needed is often provided by the cash proceeds from life insurance taken out on the life of the deceased and made payable to the business or to the surviving partners. Upon payment of the amount required by the buy and sell agreement to the estate of the deceased, the interest of the deceased ends, and all the surviving partners can continue the business.

Managerial Control

In a general partnership, unless the agreement provides to the contrary, each partner has an equal voice in the firm's affairs, with an equal right to possess partnership property for business purposes. The partners may agree to divide control in such a way as to make controlling partners and minority partners. To avoid a deadlock among partners, care should be taken to design mechanisms to avoid or at least handle the disputes that will arise when partners share managerial control.

Liability

All partners in a general partnership have unlimited liability for their organization's debts. These partners' personal assets, which are not associated with the partnership, may be claimed by the partnership's creditors. From a creditor's perspective, this personal liability of each partner extends to the organization's entire debt, not just to a pro rata share. These partners are **jointly and severally liable** for the partnership's obligations. For example, assume that a general partnership has three partners and that it owes a creditor $300,000. If it is necessary to collect the debt, this creditor can sue all three partners jointly for the $300,000. As an alternative, the creditor can sue any one partner or any combination of two for the entire $300,000. Among the partners, anyone who has to pay the creditor more than her or his pro rata share of the liability usually can seek contribution from the remaining partners.

Taxation

Like proprietorships, partnerships are not a taxable entity. The fact that this type of organization pays no income tax does not mean that the profits of the partnership are free from income tax. A partnership files an information return that allocates to each partner his or her proportionate share of profits or losses from operations, dividend income, capital gains or losses, and other items that would affect the income tax owed by a partner. Partners then report their share of such items on their individual income tax returns, irrespective of whether they have actually received the items.

This aspect of a partnership is an advantage to the partners if the organization suffers a net loss. The pro rata share of this loss is allocated to each partner, and it can be used to reduce these partners' personal taxable income. However, by this same reasoning, a partnership is a disadvantage if the organization retains any profits made by the organization for the purpose of expansion. Suppose a partnership with three equal partners has $30,000 in net income. If the partnership keeps this money, there still is a constructive distribution of $10,000 to each partner for tax purposes. Assuming that these partners are in a 28 percent personal income tax bracket, they each would have to pay $2,800 in taxes even though they actually received nothing from the partnership.

Concept Summary: Advantages and Disadvantages of Partnerships

The basic law relating to partnerships is found in the Uniform Partnership Act, which has been adopted by every state except Louisiana. According to this statute, the partnership form of organization generally has the following advantages:

1. A partnership is easily formed because it is based on a contract among persons.
2. Costs of formation are not significant.
3. Partnerships are not a tax paying entity.
4. Each partner has an equal voice in management, unless there is a contrary agreement.
5. A partnership may operate in more than one state without obtaining a license to do business.
6. Partnerships generally are subject to less regulation and less governmental supervision than are corporations.

Offsetting these advantages, the following aspects of partnerships have been called disadvantages:

1. For practical reasons, only a limited number of people can be partners.
2. A partnership is dissolved anytime a partner ceases to be a partner, regardless of whether the reason is withdrawal or death.
3. Each partner's liability is unlimited, contrasted with the limited liability of a corporate shareholder.
4. Partners are taxed on their share of the partnership's profits, whether the profits are distributed or not. In other words, partners often are required to pay income tax on money they do not receive.

5. Corporations

The third basic organizational form which might be used to operate a business is the corporation. A **corporation** is an artificial, intangible entity created under the authority of a state's law. A corporation is known as a **domestic corporation** in the state in which it is incorporated. In all other states, this corporation is called a **foreign corporation.** As a creature of state legislative bodies, the corporation is much more complex to create and to operate than other forms of businesses. These legal complexities associated with the corporation are presented below in a structure that parallels the preceding section so that comparisons with partnerships can be easily made.

Creation

A corporation is created by a state issuing a **charter** upon the application of individuals known as **incorporators.** In comparison with partnerships, corporations are more costly to form. Among the costs of incorporation are filing fees, license fees, franchise taxes, attorneys' fees, and the cost of supplies, such as minute books, corporate seals, and stock certificates. In addition to these costs of creation, there also are annual costs in continuing a corporation's operation. These recurring expenses include annual reporting fees and taxes, the cost of annual shareholders' meetings, and ongoing legal-related expenses.

The formal application for corporate charter is called the **articles of incorporation.** These articles must contain the proposed name of the corporation. So that persons dealing with a business will know that it is a corporation, the law requires that the corporate name include one of the following words or end with an abbreviation of them: "corporation," "company," "incorporated," or "limited." In addition, a corporate name must not be the same as, or deceptively similar to, the name of any domestic corporation or that of a foreign corporation authorized to do business in the state to which the application is made. The corporate name is an asset and an aspect of goodwill. As such, it is legally protected.

In addition to the proposed corporate name, the articles of incorporation usually will include the proposed corporation's period of duration, the purpose for which it is formed, the number of authorized shares, and information about the initial corporate officials.

Once drafted, these papers are sent to the appropriate state official (usually the secretary of state), who approves them and issues a corporate charter. Notice of this incorporation usually has to be advertised in the local newspaper in order to inform the public that a new corporation has been created. The initial board of directors then meets, adopts the corporate bylaws, and approves the sale of stock. At this point, the corporation becomes operational.

If a corporation wishes to conduct business in states other than the state of incorporation, that corporation must be licensed in these foreign states. The process of qualification usually requires payment of license fees and franchise taxes above and beyond those paid during the initial incorporation process. If a corporation fails to qualify in states where it is conducting business, the corporation may be denied access to the courts as a means of enforcing its contracts.

Continuity

In contrast to a partnership, a corporation usually is formed to have perpetual existence. The law treats a corporation's existence as distinct from its owners' status as shareholders. Thus, a shareholder's death or sale of her or his stock does not affect the organizational structure of a corporation. This ability to separate management from ownership is an often cited advantage of the corporation.

While the sale of stock by a major shareholder or the shareholder's death has no legal impact on the organization's existence, this event may have a very real adverse impact on that corporation's ability to do business. The shareholder may have been the driving force behind the corporation's success. Without this shareholder, the corporation's business may fail.

Managerial Control

In the corporate form of organization, the issue of control is complicated by three groups. First, the **shareholders** elect the members of the board of directors. These **directors** set the objectives or goals of the corporation, and they appoint the officers. These **officers,** such as the president, vice president, secretary, and treasurer, are charged with managing the daily operations of the corporation in an attempt to achieve the stated organizational objectives or goals. Thus, which one of these three groups really controls the corporation?

To answer this question effectively, you must realize that the issue of who controls a corporation varies depending on the size of the ownership base of the organization. In essence, matters of managerial control require us to examine the publicly held corporation as distinct from the closely held corporation.

Publicly Held Corporations.   In very large corporations, control by management (a combination of the directors and officers) is maintained with a very small percentage of stock ownership through the use of corporate records and funds to solicit **proxies.** Technically, a proxy is an agent appointed by a shareholder for the purpose of voting the shares. Management can, at corporate expense, solicit the right to vote the stock of shareholders unable to attend the meetings at which the directors of the company are elected. An outsider must either own sufficient stock to elect the directors or must solicit proxies at his or her own expense. The management of a large corporation usually can maintain control with only a small minority of actual stock ownership.

Closely Held Corporations.   Unlike the situation with a large, publicly held corporation, one shareholder (or at least a small group of shareholders) may be able to control a closely held corporation. This can result because this individual (or the group) can own an actual majority of the issued shares. This majority can control the election of a board of directors. In fact, the shareholders with the largest amount of stock are often elected to this board of directors. The directors, in turn, elect officers, who again may be the shareholders with the largest interests. In a very real sense, those who own a majority of a closely held corporation can rule with near absolute authority.

What are the rights of those who do not possess control in a closely held corporation—the so-called minority interest? To a large degree, the owners of the minority interest are subject to the whim or caprice of the majority. The majority may pay themselves salaries that use up profits and may never declare a dividend. However, the minority interest is not without some rights, because the directors and officers stand in a fiduciary relation to the corporation and to the minority shareholders if the corporation is closely held. This relation imposes a duty on directors to act for the best interests of the corporation rather than for themselves individually.

If the majority is acting illegally or oppresses the rights of the minority shareholders, a lawsuit known as a **derivative suit** may be brought by a minority shareholder on behalf of the corporation. Such suits may seek to enjoin the unlawful activity or to collect damages for the corporation. For example, contracts made between the corporation and an interested director or officer may be challenged. If sued, the burden is on the director or officer (who may be the majority shareholder) to prove good faith and inherent fairness in such transactions.

The basic difficulty of owning a minority interest in a closely held corporation arises from the fact that there is no ready market for the stock should the shareholder desire to dispose of it. Of course, if there is a valid buy and sell agreement, then there is a market for the stock. Thus, like with partnerships, buy and sell agreements are absolutely essential in closely held corporations.

Liability

The legal ability to separate a corporation's shareholders from its managers means that the owners are liable for the debts of the corporation only to the extent of those shareholders' investment in the cost of the stock. Thus, corporate shareholders are said to have **limited personal liability.**

The generalization that the investors in a corporation have limited liability but those in a partnership have unlimited liability is too broad and needs qualification. To be sure, someone investing in a company listed on the New York Stock Exchange will incur no risk greater than the investment, and the concept of limited liability certainly applies. However, if the company is a small, closely held corporation with limited assets and capital, it will be difficult for it to obtain credit on the strength of its own net worth. As a practical matter, shareholders will usually be required to add their own individual liability as security for borrowing. For example, if the XYZ Company seeks a loan at a local bank, the bank often will require the owners, X, Y, and Z, to personally guarantee repayment of the loan.

This is not to say that shareholders in closely held corporations do not have some degree of limited liability. Shareholders have limited liability for contractlike obligations that are imposed as a matter of law (such as taxes). Liability also is limited when the corporate obligation results from torts committed by company employees while doing company business.

Even in these situations, the mere fact of corporate existence does not mean the shareholders will have liability limited to their investment. When courts find that the corporate organization is being misused, the corporate entity can be disregarded. This has been called **piercing the corporate veil.** When this veil of protection has been pierced, the shareholders are treated like partners who have unlimited liability for their organization's debts.

The **alter-ego theory,** by which the corporate veil can be pierced, may also be used to impose personal liability upon corporate officers, directors, and stockholders. If the corporate entity is disregarded by these officials themselves, so that there is such a unity of ownership and interest that separateness of the corporation has ceased to exist, the alter-ego theory will be followed and the corporate veil will be pierced.

The following case shows that courts have a great deal of authority when the issue is whether or not to pierce the corporate veil and hold shareholders personally liable.

CASTLEBERRY V. BRANSCUM

721 S.W.2d 270 (Tex. 1986)

SPEARS, J.: Joe Castleberry sued Texan Transfer, Inc. and Byron Branscum and Michael Byboth, individually, on a promissory note signed by the corporation for Castleberry's shares in the closely held corporation. The jury found that Branscum and Byboth used Texan Transfer as a sham to perpetrate a fraud. Based on the jury findings, the trial court rendered judgment against Texan Transfer, disregarding its corporate organization (fiction) to hold both Byboth and Branscum individually liable. The court of appeals reversed. . . . We reverse the court of appeals judgment and affirm the trial court, because under the applicable law there was some evidence to support the jury's verdict . . . and disregarding the corporate fiction is a fact question for the jury.

Disregarding the Corporate Fiction

The corporate form normally insulates shareholders, officers, and directors from liability for corporate obligations; but when these individuals abuse the corporate privilege, courts will disregard the corporate fiction and hold them individually liable. We disregard the corporate fiction, even though corporate formalities have been observed and corporate and individual property have been kept separately, when the corporate form has been used as part of a basically unfair device to achieve an inequitable result.

Specifically, we disregard the corporate fiction:

1. when the fiction is used as a means of perpetrating fraud;

2. where a corporation is organized and operated as a mere tool or business conduit of another corporation;

3. where the corporate fiction is resorted to as a means of evading an existing legal obligation;

4. where the corporate fiction is employed to achieve or perpetrate monopoly;

5. where the corporate fiction is used to circumvent a statute; and

6. where the corporate fiction is relied upon as a protection of crime or to justify wrong.

Many Texas cases have blurred the distinction between alter ego and the other bases for disregarding the corporate fiction and treated alter ego as a synonym for the entire doctrine of disregarding the corporate fiction. However . . . alter ego is only one of the bases for disregarding the corporate fiction: "where a corporation is organized and operated as a mere tool or business conduit of another corporation."

Alter ego applies when there is such unity between corporation and individual that the separateness of the corporation has ceased and holding only the corporation liable would result in injustice. It is shown from the total dealings of the corporation and the individual, including the degree to which corporate formalities have been followed and corporate and individual property have been kept separately, the amount of financial interest, ownership and control the individual maintains over the corporation, and whether the corporation has been used for personal purposes. Alter ego's rationale is: "if the shareholders themselves disregard the separation of the corporate enterprise, the law will also disregard it so far as necessary to protect individual and corporate creditors."

The basis used here to disregard the corporate fiction, a sham to perpetrate a fraud, is separate from alter ego. It is sometimes confused with intentional fraud; however, "[n]either fraud nor an intent to defraud need be shown as a prerequisite to disregarding the corporate entity; it is sufficient if recognizing the separate corporate existence would bring about an inequitable result." . . . Thus, we held that note holders could disregard the corporate fiction without showing common-law fraud or deceit when the circumstances amounted to constructive fraud. In *Tigrett v. Pointer*, the Dallas Court of Appeals disregarded the corporate fiction, stating correctly that "[w]hether [the individual] misled them or subjectively intended to defraud them is immaterial . . . [f]or the action was so grossly unfair as to amount to constructive fraud."

To prove there has been a sham to perpetrate a fraud, tort claimants and contract creditors must show only constructive fraud. We distinguished constructive from actual fraud in *Archer v. Griffith:*

> Actual fraud usually involves dishonesty of purpose or intent to deceive, whereas constructive fraud is the breach of some legal or equitable duty which, irrespective of moral guilt, the law declares fraudulent because of its tendency to deceive others, to violate confidence, or to injure public interests.

Because disregarding the corporate fiction is an equitable doctrine, Texas takes a flexible fact-specific approach focusing on equity. . . . Dean Hildebrand, a leading authority on Texas corporation law, stated well the equitable approach: "When this [disregarding the corporate fiction] should be done is a question of fact and common sense. The court must weigh the facts and consequences in each case carefully, and common sense and justice must determine [its] decision." . . . [The court then reviewed the evidence and concluded.]

. . . A jury could find that Byboth and Branscum manipulated a closely held corporation, Texan Transfer, and formed competing businesses to ensure that Castleberry did not get paid. Castleberry had lit-

tle choice but to sell his shares back to the corporation. While this evidence may be no evidence of intentional fraud, constructive fraud, not intentional fraud, is the standard for disregarding the corporate fiction on the basis of a sham to perpetrate a fraud.

In determining if there is an abuse of the corporate privilege, courts must look through the form of complex transactions to the substance. The variety of shams is infinite, but many fit this case's pattern: a closely held corporation owes unwanted obligations; it siphons off corporate revenues, sells off much of the corporate assets, or does other acts to hinder the ongoing business and its ability to pay off its debts; a new business then starts up that is basically a continuation of the old business with many of the same shareholders, officers, and directors. . . . [*We reverse the court of appeals' judgment and affirm the trial court's judgment*].

Case Questions

1. Which of the six justifications for piercing the corporate veil best describes the alter-ego theory?
2. What justification does this court use to pierce the corporate veil of Texan Transfer?
3. What actions of Byboth and Branscum amounted to fraud?

Taxation

Corporations must pay income taxes on their earnings. Table 7–1 sets forth these tax rates as of the end of 1997.

The fact that there is a separate corporate income tax may work as an advantage. For example, if the corporation makes a profit that is to be retained by the corporation to support growth, no income is allocated to the shareholders. These shareholders will not have their personal taxable income increased, as would a partner in a similar situation. In addition, the corporate rate may be lower than the individual rates.

But corporations also have tax disadvantages. Suppose a corporation suffers a loss during a given tax year. The existence of the corporate tax works

TABLE 7–1   Corporate Tax Rates*

Income	Tax Rate
$0–$50,000	15%
$50,000–$75,000	25%
$75,000–$10,000,000	34%
over $10,000,000	35%

*In addition to these rates, there are excess taxes when corporate taxable income exceeds $100,000. These taxes increase again if corporate taxable income exceeds $15,000,000.

as a disadvantage, since this loss cannot be distributed to the shareholders in order to reduce their personal tax liability. Indeed, a net operating loss to a corporation can be used only to offset corporate income earned in other years. And the allocation of such a loss can be carried back only for three years and carried forward for fifteen years. (Note: There are many different rules concerning specialized carryover situations. The Internal Revenue Code should be examined prior to relying on the general rule just stated.)

Perhaps a greater disadvantage of the corporate tax occurs when a profit is made and the corporation wishes to pay a dividend to its shareholders. The money used to pay this dividend will have been taxed at the corporate level. It is then taxed again because the shareholder must take the amount of the dividend into his or her own personal income. The rate of this second tax depends on the personal tax rate of the shareholder receiving the dividend. This situation has been called the **double tax** on corporate income. A similar situation of double taxation occurs when a corporation is dissolved and its assets are distributed to shareholders as capital gains. Yet, as the discussion next indicates, the double tax may not be as big a disadvantage as it appears at first.

Avoiding Double Taxation. Corporations have employed a variety of techniques for avoiding the double taxation of corporate income. First, reasonable salaries paid to corporate officials may be deducted in computing the taxable income of the business. Thus, in a closely held corporation in which all or most shareholders are officers or employees, this technique may avoid double taxation of substantial portions of income. As might be expected, the Internal Revenue Code disallows a deduction for excessive or unreasonable compensation and treats such payments as dividends. Therefore, the determination of the reasonableness of corporate salaries is often a tax problem in that form of organization.

Second, corporations provide expense accounts for many employees, including shareholder employees. These are used to purchase travel, food, and entertainment. When so used, the employee, to some extent, has compensation that is not taxed. In an attempt to close this tax loophole, the law limits deductions for business meals and entertainment to 50 percent of the cost. Meal expenses and entertainment are deductible only if the expenses are directly related to or associated with the active conduct of a trade or business. For a deduction, business must be discussed directly before, during, or directly after the meal. Additionally, meal expenses are not deductible to the extent the meal is lavish or extravagant. Thus, the use of the expense account to avoid taxation of corporate income is subject to numerous technical rules and limitations.

Third, the capital structure of the corporation may include both common stock and interest-bearing loans from shareholders. For example, assume that a company needs $100,000 cash to go into business. If $100,000 of stock is issued, no expense will be deducted. However, assume that $50,000 worth of stock is purchased by the owners and $50,000 is lent to the company by them at 10 percent interest. In this case, $5,000 interest each year is deductible as an expense of the company and thus subject to only one tax as interest income to the owners. Just as in the case of salaries, the Internal Revenue Code has a counteracting rule relating to corporations that are undercapitalized. If the corporation is undercapitalized, interest payments will be treated as dividends and disallowed as deductible expenses.

The fourth technique for avoiding double taxation, at least in part, is simply not to pay dividends and to accumulate the earnings. The Internal Revenue Service seeks to compel corporations to distribute those profits not needed for a business purpose, such as growth. When a corporation retains earnings in excess of $250,000, there is a presumption that these earnings are being accumulated to avoid a second tax on dividends. If the corporations cannot rebut this presumption, an additional tax of 27½ percent is imposed on the first $100,000 unreasonably accumulated in excess of $250,000. For undistributed earnings above this amount, the penalty tax equals 38½ percent of the unreasonable accumulation.

Fifth, a corporation may elect to file under Subchapter S of the Internal Revenue Code. This election eliminates the corporate tax; this subject is discussed further in section 7 of this chapter.

6. Limited Partnerships

A limited partnership basically has all the attributes of a partnership except that one or more of the partners are designated as **limited partners.** This type of partner is not personally responsible for the debts of the business organization. However, these limited partners are not permitted to be involved in the control or operations of the limited partnership. The management is left in the hands of one or more **general partners** who remain personally liable for the organization's debts.

Concept Summary: Advantages and Disadvantages of Corporations

The usual advantages of the corporate form of organization include the following:

1. This form is the best practical means of bringing together a large number of investors.

2. Control may be held by those with a minority of the investment.

3. Ownership may be divided into many unequal shares.

4. Shareholders' liabilities are limited to their investments.

5. The organization can have perpetual existence.

6. In addition to being owners, shareholders may be employees entitled to benefits such as workers' compensation.

Among the frequently cited disadvantages of the corporate organization are the following:

1. The cost of forming and maintaining a corporation, with its formal procedural requirements, is significant.

2. License fees and franchise taxes often are assessed against corporations but not partnerships.

3. A corporation must be qualified in all states where it is conducting local or intrastate business.

4. Generally, corporations are subject to more governmental regulation at all levels than are other forms of business.

5. Corporate income may be subject to double taxation.

The attributes of a general partnership and a corporation that combine to make the limited partnership an attractive alternative form of business organization are discussed under the subheadings that follow.

Creation and Continuity

Like a general partnership, a limited partnership is created by agreement. However, as in the case of a corporation, state law requires that the contents of a certificate must be recorded in the county where the partnership has its principal place of business. An additional copy has to be filed in every community where the partnership conducts business or has an office. If an accurate certificate is not on record and the limited partnership continues its operation, the limited partners become liable as general partners.

The principles guiding dissolutions of partnerships also apply to limited partnerships if there is a change in the general partners. However, a limited partner may assign his or her interest to another without dissolving the limited partnership.

Managerial Control and Liability

In a limited partnership, the general partners are in control. Limited partners have no right to participate in management.

The true nature of the limited partnership being a hybrid is in the area of owners' liability. Traditionally, the general partners in a limited partnership have unlimited liability. However, the limited partners are not personally liable for the partnership's debts. These limited partners' liability typically will not exceed the amount of their investments.

A limited partner who participates in the organization's management becomes liable as a general partner if a third party had knowledge of the limited partner's activities. The following actions by a limited partner do not constitute participation in management in such a way that the advantage of limited liability is lost:

- Acting as an agent or employee of the partnership
- Consulting with or advising a general partner
- Acting as a guarantor of the partnership's obligations
- Inspecting and copying any of the partnership's financial records
- Demanding true and full information about the partnership whenever circumstances render it just and reasonable
- Receiving a share of the profits or other compensation by way of income
- Approving or disapproving an amendment to the partnership's certificate
- Voting on matters of fundamental importance such as dissolution, sale of assets, or change of the partnership's name
- Having contribution returned upon dissolution

7. S Corporations

Beginning in 1958, the federal government permitted shareholders of certain corporations to unanimously elect to have their organization treated like a partnership for income tax purposes. This election is made possible through the language of subchapter S of the Internal Revenue Code. Today, organizations that are subject to this election often are referred to simply as **S corporations.**

The S corporation has all the legal characteristics of the corporation previously discussed in this chapter. The one exception to this similar treatment is that shareholders in the S corporation are responsible for accounting on their individual income tax returns for their respective shares of their organization's profits or losses. In essence, these shareholders can elect to have their business organization treated, for tax purposes, as if it were a partnership. Through this election, the shareholders avoid having a tax assessed on the corporate income itself. Even though the S corporation does not pay any taxes, like a partnership, it must file an information return with the Internal Revenue Service. The following case involves the U.S. Supreme Court deciding whether it is the corporate or shareholder's personal return on which the statute of limitations for challenges is based.

BUFFERD V. COMMISSIONER

113 S.Ct. 927 (1993)

WHITE, J.: On his 1979 income tax return, petitioner, a shareholder in a Subchapter S corporation, claimed as "pass-through" items portions of a deduction and a tax credit reported on the corporation's return. The question presented is whether the 3-year period in which the Internal Revenue Service is permitted to assess petitioner's tax liability runs from the filing date of the individual return or the corporate return. . . .

Subchapter S of the Internal Revenue Code was enacted in 1958 to eliminate tax disadvantages that might dissuade small businesses from adopting the corporate form and to lessen the tax burden on such businesses. The statute accomplishes these goals by means of a pass-through system under which corporate income, losses, deductions, and credits are attributed to individual shareholders in a manner akin to the tax treatment of partnerships. . . .

Petitioner was treasurer and a shareholder of Compo Financial Services, Inc., an S corporation. On February 1, 1980, Compo filed a return for the tax year of December 26, 1978 to November 30, 1979 as required by § 6037(a) of the Code. On that return, Compo reported a loss deduction and an investment tax credit arising from its partnership interest in a venture known as Printers Associates. Petitioner and his wife filed a joint return for 1979 on April 15, 1980. Their return claimed a pro rata share of the deduction and credit reported by Compo pursuant to the pass-through provisions of Subchapter S.

Code § 6501(a) establishes a generally applicable statute of limitations providing that the Internal Revenue Service may assess tax deficiencies within a 3-year period from the date a return is filed. That limitations period may be extended by written agreement. In March 1983, before three years had passed from the time the joint return was filed, petitioner agreed to extend the period in which deficiencies arising from certain claims on the return could be assessed against him. No extension was obtained from Compo with respect to its return for the 1978–1979 tax year.

In 1987, the Commissioner determined that the loss deduction and credit reported by Compo were erroneous and sent a notice of deficiency to petitioner based on the loss deduction and credit that he had claimed on his return. In the Tax Court, petitioner contended that the Commissioner's claim was time barred because the disallowance was based on an error in Compo's return, for which the 3-year assessment period had lapsed. The Tax Court found for the Commissioner. . . . The Court of Appeals for the Second Circuit affirmed, holding that, where a tax deficiency is assessed against the shareholder, the filing date of the shareholder's return is the relevant date for purposes of § 6501(a). Because another Court of Appeals has a contrary view, we granted certiorari.

. . . We have no doubt that the courts below properly concluded, as the Commissioner argued, that it is the filing of the petitioner's return that triggers the running of the statutory period.

The Commissioner can only determine whether the taxpayer understated his tax obligation and should be assessed a deficiency after examining that taxpayer's return. Plainly, then, "the" return referred to in § 6501(a) is the return of the taxpayer against whom a deficiency is assessed. Here, the Commissioner sought to assess taxes which petitioner owed under the Code because his return had erroneously reported a loss and credit to which he was not entitled. The fact that the corporation's return erroneously asserted a loss and credit to be passed through to its shareholders is of no consequence. In this case, the errors on the corporate return did not and could not affect the tax liability of the corporation, and hence the Commissioner could only assess a deficiency against the stockholder-taxpayer whose return claimed the benefit of the errors. . . .

We hold that the limitations period within which the Internal Revenue Service must assess the income tax return of an S corporation shareholder runs from the date on which the shareholder's return is filed. The judgment of the Court of Appeals is [*affirmed*].

Case Questions

1. When was the S corporation's tax return filed?
2. When did Mr. and Mrs. Bufferd file their personal return?
3. When did the IRS assert a challenge claiming that the Bufferds' return contained inaccurate information?
4. What transpired to allow the IRS to claim a challenge beyond the three-year period following the filing of the personal return?
5. Why does the Court conclude that the three-year period of review is based on the shareholder's personal return rather than the S corporation's return?

There are many technical rules of tax law involved in S corporations. However, as a rule of thumb, this method of organization has distinct advantages for a business operating at a loss because the loss is shared and immediately deductible on the returns of the shareholders. It is also advantageous for businesses capable of paying out net profits as earned. In the latter case, the corporate tax is avoided. If net profits must be retained in the business, subchapter S tax treatment is disadvantageous because income tax is paid on earnings not received, and there is a danger of double taxation to the individual because undistributed earnings that have been taxed once are taxed again in the event of the death of a shareholder. Thus, the theoretical advantage of using an S corporation to avoid double taxation of corporate income must be carefully qualified.

8. Limited Liability Companies

The **limited liability company** is a relatively new organizational alternative. In 1977, Wyoming was the first state to pass a law permitting the creation of this type of business organization.

In 1988, the Internal Revenue Service ruled that limited liability companies (LLCs) would be treated as nontaxable entities, much like partnerships, for federal income tax purposes. Following this ruling, states rushed to pass legislation authorizing businesspeople to operate their businesses as LLCs. In essence, its owners have more flexibility than with the S corporation while not having to struggle with the complexities of the limited partnership.

In the true sense of a hybrid, an LLC has characteristics of both a partnership and a corporation. For example, an LLC is created through filings much like those used when creating a corporation. **Articles of organization** are filed with a state official, usually the secretary of state. Instead of "incorporators," the term **organizers** is used. The name of any LLC must acknowledge the special nature of this organizational form by including the phrase "limited liability company," or "limited company," or some abbreviation, such as "LLC" or "LC." An LLC created in a state other than the one in which it is conducting business is called a foreign LLC. Like a foreign corporation, this LLC must apply to the state to be authorized to transact business legally. An LLC also must file annual reports with the states in which it operates.

The owners of LLCs are called **members** rather than shareholders or partners. Membership in LLCs is not limited to individuals. Unlike in the S corporation, a business organization can be an owner in any LLC. The transferability of a member's interest is restricted in the fashion of a partner as opposed to the free transferability of a corporate shareholder. Anytime a member dies or withdraws from the LLC, there is a dissolution of the business organization. However, the business of a dissolved LLC is not necessarily adversely impacted if the remaining members decide to continue business. Either as provided in the articles of organization or by agreement of the remaining members within ninety days of the withdrawing member's disassociation, the business of the LLC may be continued rather than wound up.

The managerial control of an LLC is vested in its members, unless the articles of organization provide for one or more **managers.** Regardless of whether members or managers control the LLC, a majority of these decision makers decide the direction of the organization. In a few situations enumerated in the state law authorizing LLCs, unanimous consent of the members is required for the organization to make a binding decision. Similarly to partners in a partnership, members of LLCs make contributions of capital. They have equal rights to share in the LLC's profits and losses, unless these members have agreed otherwise. When a member is in the minority with respect to decisions being made on behalf of the LLC, that dissenting member has rights very much like a dissenting shareholder in a corporation. These rights include bringing a derivative lawsuit against the controlling members of the LLC. Ultimately, a dissenting member has the right to sell the membership interest to the other members of the LLC.

For liability purposes, members do act as agents of their LLC. However, they are not personally liable to third parties. Thus, these members have attributes of both partners and shareholders with respect to liability.

Finally, state laws and the IRS recognize LLCs as nontaxable entities. While the LLC appears to have many advantages, do not forget that careful analysis is needed in every situation to determine whether this type of tax treatment is in the members' best interests.

A variation of the LLC is known as the **limited liability partnership.** This organization often is used by professionals, such as doctors, lawyers, and accountants.

9. Making the Decision

There usually is no absolutely right answer to the question, Which organizational form is best for a particular business's operation? Hopefully the preceding sections have presented you with some helpful background material to consider when this important decision is made.

The criteria used to select a form or organization needs to be reviewed periodically. This review should be done in consultation with close advisers such as attorneys, accountants, bankers, and insurers. These people weigh the factors and costs involved and then select the most suitable organizational form for the business's needs at that time. Because this selection process balances advantages against disadvantages, the decision often is to choose the least objectionable form of organization.

Agency

Once the organizational form is selected and created, the law on the conduct of business becomes our primary focus. Practically all business transactions involve agents. In the next three sections, general principles of the law of agency are introduced, illustrated, and discussed.

10. Terminology

Basically the application of agency law involves the interaction among three parties. While individuals usually are these parties, agency relationship can involve business organizations. Figure 7–1 illustrates a three-step approach to understanding how the law views the purpose of agency relationship.

First, a **principal** interacts with someone (or some organization) for the purpose of obtaining that second party's assistance. This second party is the **agent.** Second, the agent (on behalf of the principal) interacts with a **third party.** Third, the usual legal purpose of the agent is to create a binding relationship between the principal and third party. Typically, the agent will want Step 3 to involve the understanding that any liability created by Steps 1 and 2 is replaced by the new principal-third party relationship. To accomplish this substitution, the agent must remember to comply with the following duties owed to the principal:

· A duty of loyalty to act for the principal's advantage and not to act to benefit the agent at the principal's expense
· A duty to keep the principal fully informed
· A duty to obey instructions
· A duty to account to the principal for monies handled

In studying the law of agency, keep in mind that the employer/business organization is the principal and the employee is the agent. Whether employee conduct creates liability for the employer is the usual agency issue facing businesses. Such issues may involve either contracts or torts.

FIGURE 7.1

Illustration of the Agency Relationship

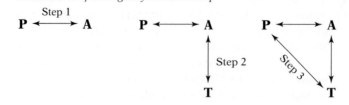

11. Contractual Liability

For an employee to bind the employer to a contract the employee negotiates with a third party, the employer must have authorized the employee's actions. Contractual authority can take the following forms:

Actual authority

- Expressed, written authority
- Expressed, oral authority
- Implied authority
- Apparent authority

Only when one of these types of authority is present will Step 3 in Figure 7–1 occur.

A simple example, taken from the Business Decision, may help illustrate the concept of authority. Suppose, as an owner of the restaurant, you hire Alex to be an evening manager. You discover that the restaurant is running low on coffee. You write a note to your friend, Terry, the manager of the local grocery store, asking Terry to allow Alex to charge $100 worth of coffee to your restaurant's account at the grocery store. You give this note to Alex with instructions to purchase the coffee and deliver the note to Terry. If Terry allows Alex to charge $100 worth of coffee, is your restaurant liable to pay $100 to the grocery store? The answer is yes, because Alex had **actual authority** which was expressed in a writing.

Now suppose a week later, you send Alex to the same grocery store to buy pound cake and yogurt. This time you call Terry on the phone and ask that Alex be allowed to charge the cost of the cake and yogurt. Once again, your restaurant is contractually liable to pay for this purchase since Alex was actually authorized to contract through your expressed oral statement to Terry.

What if, sometime later, you and your co-owner are out of town and Alex is in charge of the restaurant for the evening. Alex, realizing that the tuna salad is in short supply, goes to Terry's grocery store and charges to the restaurant $60 worth of tuna fish. Upon your return, you find a bill from Terry for this purchase. Legally, do you have to pay it? Again, the answer is yes! This time Alex's actions contractually bind the restaurant to Terry since Alex had **implied authority** to do what was necessary for the restaurant's benefit. This implied authority arises from the position Alex holds as evening manager and by the history of the express authority situations.

Finally, suppose that you terminate Alex's employment. In retaliation, Alex goes to Terry's grocery store and charges a variety of groceries that are consistent with the food your restaurant serves. When you get the bill from Terry, is the restaurant liable? Answer—yes. Even though Alex lacks any actual (expressed or implied) authority, your failure to notify Terry of Alex's termination left Alex with **apparent authority.** Due to the history of Alex representing your restaurant, it is reasonable for Terry to assume that this incident is one more in the series of Alex's properly charging items to the restaurant's account. To prevent this unwanted liability from occurring, you should have let Terry know that Alex is no longer employed. This notice would destroy the existence of apparent authority.

It should be noted that in this last scenario, involving the existence of apparent authority, you would have a claim against Alex for the monies you had to pay Terry. Alex's liability to you arises because Alex breached the duty of loyalty owed to the restaurant.

12. Tort Liability

The legal elements of a tort are discussed in Chapter 9. For the purposes of this brief discussion, accept that a tort is a breach of a duty that causes injury. An agent who causes harm to a third party may create legal liability owed by the principal to that third party. The accomplishment of this vicarious liability depends on whether the agent was acting within the scope of employment when the tort occurred. Details of this type of liability are presented in Chapter 9 under the section heading "Respondeat Superior."

The type of business organization in existence determines the extent of responsibility for agents' torts. In essence, partners are liable for all transactions entered into by any partner in the scope of the partnership business and are similarly liable for any partner's torts committed while she or he is acting in the course of the firm's business. Each partner is in effect both an agent of the partnership and a principal, being capable of creating both contract and tort liability for the firm and for copartners and likewise being responsible for acts of copartners. Shareholders of corporations and members of LLCs are protected from tort liability that exceeds the amount of their investment.

Public Investment—Securities Regulation

The regulation of securities began as part of the program to help the United States overcome the great depression of the early 1930s. These securities laws are designed to give potential investors sufficient information so they can make intelligent investment decisions based on factual information rather than on other, less certain criteria.

It is these securities laws that require the roommates in the Business Decision to be very careful if they solicit potential investors. Because specific information must be provided to potential investors, getting into business cannot be done quickly.

13. What is a Security?

Because the objective of securities laws is to protect uninformed people from investing their money without sufficient information, the term **security** has a very broad definition. Indeed, the federal securities laws provide the following definition:

> "Security" means any note, stock, treasury stock, bond, debenture, evidence of indebtedness, certificate of interest or participation in any profit-sharing agreement, collateral-trust certificate, preorganization certificate or subscription, transferable share, investment contract, voting-trust certificate, certificate of deposit for a security, fractional undivided interest in oil, gas, or other mineral

rights, or in general, any interest or instrument commonly known as a "security," or any certificate of interest or participation in, temporary or interim certificate for receipt for, guarantee of, or warrant or right to subscribe to or purchase, any of the foregoing.[1]

As this definition indicates, the word "security" includes much more than corporation stock. Historically, the Supreme Court has held that a security exists when one person invests money and looks to others to manage the money for profit.

14. Securities and Exchange Commission

The **Securities and Exchange Commission (SEC)** is an administrative agency created in 1934 that is responsible for administering the federal securities laws. The SEC consists of five commissioners appointed by the president for five-year terms. In addition to these commissioners, the SEC employs staff personnel such as lawyers, accountants, security analysts, security examiners, and others.

The SEC has both quasi-legislative and quasi-judicial powers. Under its quasi-legislative power, it has adopted rules and regulations relating to financial and other information that must be furnished to the Commission. Other rules prescribe information that must be given to potential investors. The SEC also regulates the various stock exchanges, utility holding companies, investment trusts, and investment advisers. Under its quasi-judicial power, the SEC also is involved in a variety of investigations.

15. Securities Act of 1933: Going Public

The **Securities Act of 1933** is a disclosure law governing the initial sale of securities to the public. This law makes it illegal to use the mails or any other means of interstate communication or transportation to sell securities without disclosing certain financial information to potential investors.

The information given must not be untrue or even misleading. If this information is not accurate, liability may be imposed upon the issuer, the underwriter, the controlling person(s), or the seller of the security.

The act recognizes three sanctions for violations:

- Criminal punishment
- Civil liability, which may be imposed in favor of injured parties in certain cases
- Equitable remedy of an injunction

This law requires that securities subject to its provisions be registered prior to any sale and that a prospectus be furnished to any potential investor prior to any sale being consummated. The **registration statement** includes a detailed disclosure of financial information about the issuer and the controlling individuals involved in the offering of securities for sale to the public.

---

[1]15 U.S.C.A. § 77b(1). This definition is a part of the 1933 Securities Act. It is virtually identical to the definition of security found in the 1934 Securities Exchange Act.

A **prospectus** must be furnished to any interested investor, and it must conform to the statutory requirements. Like the registration statement, the prospectus contains financial information related to the issuer and controlling persons. The prospectus supplies the investor with sufficient facts (including financial information) so that he or she can make an intelligent investment decision. The SEC has adopted rules relating to the detailed requirements of the prospectus. The major requirements are detailed facts about the issuer and financial statements, including balance sheets and statements of operations of the issuer.

Theoretically, any security may be sold under the act, provided the law and the rules and regulations enacted under it are followed. The law does not prohibit the sale of worthless securities. An investor may "foolishly" invest his or her money, and a person may legally sell the sky if the statutory requirements are met. In fact, the prospectus must contain the following in capital letters and boldface type:

> THESE SECURITIES HAVE NOT BEEN APPROVED OR DISAPPROVED BY THE SECURITIES AND EXCHANGE COMMISSION NOR HAS THE COMMISSION PASSED UPON THE ACCURACY OR ADEQUACY OF THIS PROSPECTUS. ANY REPRESENTATION TO THE CONTRARY IS A CRIMINAL OFFENSE.

Under the Federal Securities Act of 1933, both civil and criminal liability may be imposed for violations. Criminal liability results from a willful violation of the act or fraud in *any* offer or sale of securities. Fraud also occurs when any material fact is omitted, causing a statement to be misleading. The penalty is a fine of up to $10,000 or five years in prison or both.

Civil liability arises when responsible parties fail to prepare the required documentation or file or provide documents that contain untrue statements of material facts, omit material facts, or create misleading information. The basic civil remedy sought by a wronged investor is the return of their investment. Typically, a plaintiff needs only to prove that an error exists in the required documentation. A plaintiff does not need to prove reliance under the 1933 Securities Act. This means that good faith (no intent to violate the law) is not a valid defense under the act. However, a very important defense for experts such as accountants is the **due diligence defense.**

To establish this defense, the expert must prove that a reasonable investigation of the financial statements of the issuer and controlling persons was conducted. As the result of this investigation, an expert exercising due diligence must prove that there was no reason to believe any of the information in the registration statement or prospectus was false or misleading.

16. Securities Exchange Act of 1934: Being Public

Whereas the Securities Act of 1933 deals with original offerings of securities, the **Securities Exchange Act of 1934** regulates transfers of securities after the initial sale. The 1934 act, which created the Securities and Exchange Commission, also deals with regulation of securities exchanges, brokers, and dealers in securities.

The Securities Exchange Act makes it illegal to sell a security on a national exchange unless a registration is effective for the security. Registration under the 1934 act differs from registration under the 1933 act. Registration under the 1934 act requires filing prescribed forms with the applicable stock exchange and the SEC.

Provisions relating to stockbrokers and dealers prohibit the use of the mails or any other instrumentality of interstate commerce to sell securities unless the broker or the dealer is registered. The language is sufficiently broad to cover attempted sales as well as actual sales. Brokers and dealers must keep detailed records of their activities and file annual reports with the SEC.

The 1934 act covers numerous situations, but three are of critical importance to every business manager. These are presented under the subheadings of fraud, insider transactions, and nonpublic information.

Fraud

Most of the litigation under the Securities and Exchange Act of 1934 is brought under Section 10(b) of the act and Rule 10b–5 of the SEC which declare that it is unlawful to use the mails or any instrumentality of interstate commerce or any national securities exchange to defraud *any person* in connection with the *purchase or sale* of any security. Defendants in such cases tend to fall into four general categories:

- Insiders
- Broker-dealers
- Corporations whose stock is purchased or sold by plaintiffs
- Those, such as accountants, who aid and abet or conspire with a party who falls into one of the first three categories

Liability under Rule 10b–5 may be imposed on an accountant even though he or she performs only an unaudited write-up. An accountant is liable for errors in financial statements contained in a prospectus or other filed report even though unaudited if there are errors he or she knew or should have known. Even when performing an unaudited write-up, an accountant must undertake at least a minimal investigation into the figures supplied to him or her and cannot disregard suspicious circumstances.

A plaintiff in a suit under Rule 10b–5 must prove damages. The damages of a defrauded purchaser are actual out-of-pocket losses or the excess of what was paid over the value of what was received. A buyer's damages are measured at the time of purchase.

Computation of a defrauded seller's damages is more difficult. A defrauding purchaser usually benefits from an increase in the value of the securities, while the plaintiff seller loses this increase. Courts do not allow defrauding buyers to keep these increases in value. Therefore, the measure of the seller's damages is the difference between the fair value of all that the seller received and the fair value of what he or she would have received had there been no fraud, except where the defendant received more than the seller's loss. In this latter case, the seller is entitled to the defendant's profit. As a result, defendants lose all profits flowing from the fraudulent conduct.

Plaintiffs under Rule 10b–5 are also entitled to consequential damages. These include lost dividends, brokerage fees, and taxes. In addition, courts may order payment of interest on the funds. Punitive damages are not permitted as they are in cases of common law fraud based on state laws. This distinction results from the language of the 1934 act, which limits recoveries to actual damages.

Insider Transactions

The second important provision of the 1934 act is Section 16, which concerns insider transactions. An **insider** is any person who:

- Owns more than 10 percent of any security
- Is a director or an officer of the issuer of the security

The SEC defines an officer for insider trading purposes as the executive officers, accounting officers, chief financial officers, and controllers. The SEC also examines the individual investor's function within the company rather than the title of the position held.

Section 16 and SEC regulations require that insiders file, at the time of the registration or within ten days after becoming an insider, a statement of the amount of such issues of which they are the owners. The regulations also require filing within ten days after the close of each calendar month thereafter if there has been any change in such ownership during that month. This filing must indicate the change in an insider's ownership interest.

The reason for prohibiting insiders from trading for profit is to prevent the use of information that is available to an insider but not to the general public. Because the SEC cannot determine for certain when nonpublic information is improperly used, Section 16 creates a presumption that any profit made within a six-month time period is illegal. These profits are referred to as **short-swing profits.** Thus, if a director, officer, or principal owner realizes profits on the purchase and sale of a security within a six-month period, the profits legally belong to the company or to the investor who purchased it from or sold it to an insider, resulting in the insider's profit and the investor's loss. The order of the purchase and sale is immaterial. The profit is calculated on the lowest price in and highest price out during any six-month period. Unlike the required proof of intent to deceive under Section 10(b), the short-swing profits rule of Section 16 does not depend on any misuse of information. In other words, short-swing profits by insiders, regardless of the insiders' state of mind, are absolutely prohibited.

While the SEC enforces the requirements of Section 16 that insiders file certain documents, the SEC does not enforce the provision that prohibits insiders from engaging in short-swing profits. This provision of Section 16 is enforced by civil actions filed by the issuer of the security or by a person who owns a security of the issuer.

Nonpublic Information

The SEC's concern for trading based on nonpublic information goes beyond the Section 16 ban on short-swing profits. Indeed, a person who is not technically an insider but who trades securities without disclosing nonpublic information may violate Section 10(b) and Rule 10b–5. The SEC takes the position that the profit obtained as the result of a trader's silence concerning information that is not freely available to everyone is a manipulation or deception prohibited by Section 10(b) and Rule 10b–5. In essence, the users of nonpublic information are treated like insiders if they can be classified as tippees.

A **tippee** is a person who learns of nonpublic information from an insider. In essence, a tippee is viewed as a temporary insider. A tippee is liable for the use of nonpublic information because an insider should not be allowed to do indirectly what he or she cannot do directly. In other words, a tippee is liable for trading or passing on information that is nonpublic.

The SEC's campaign against the use of nonpublic information has an interesting history which is beyond the scope of this text. However, the following recent case illustrates a major victory for the SEC-proposed **misappropriation theory.** Note also, this case presents the specific language of Section 10(b) and Rule 10b–5.

UNITED STATES V. O'HAGAN
117 S. Ct. 2199 (1997)

GINSBURG, J.: . . . Respondent James Herman O'Hagan was a partner in the law firm of Dorsey & Whitney in Minneapolis, Minnesota. In July 1988, Grand Metropolitan PLC (Grand Met), a company based in London, England, retained Dorsey & Whitney as local counsel to represent Grand Met regarding a potential tender offer for the common stock of the Pillsbury Company, headquartered in Minneapolis. Both Grand Met and Dorsey & Whitney took precautions to protect the confidentiality of Grand Met's tender offer plans. O'Hagan did no work on the Grand Met representation. Dorsey & Whitney withdrew from representing Grand Met on September 9, 1988. Less than a month later, on October 4, 1988, Grand Met publicly announced its tender offer for Pillsbury stock.

On August 18, 1988, while Dorsey & Whitney was still representing Grand Met, O'Hagan began purchasing call options for Pillsbury stock. Each option gave him the right to purchase 100 shares of Pillsbury stock by a specified date in September 1988. Later in August and in September, O'Hagan made additional purchases of Pillsbury call options. By the end of September, he owned 2,500 unexpired Pillsbury options. . . . O'Hagan also purchased, in September 1988, some 5,000 shares of Pillsbury common stock, at a price just under $39 per share. When Grand Met announced its tender offer in October, the price of Pillsbury stock rose to nearly $60 per share. O'Hagan then sold his Pillsbury call options and common stock, making a profit of more than $4.3 million.

The Securities and Exchange Commission (SEC or Commission) initiated an investigation into O'Hagan's transactions, culminating in a 57-count indictment. The indictment alleged that O'Hagan defrauded his law firm and its client, Grand Met, by using for his own trading purposes material, nonpublic information regarding Grand Met's planned tender offer. . . .

A divided panel of the Court of Appeals for the Eighth Circuit reversed all of O'Hagan's convictions. Liability under § 10(b) and Rule 10b–5, the Eighth Circuit held, may not be grounded on the "misappropriation theory" of securities fraud on which the prosecution relied. . .

Decisions of the Courts of Appeals are in conflict on the propriety of the misappropriation theory under § 10(b) and Rule. . . . We granted certiorari and now reverse the Eighth Circuit's judgment. . . .

In pertinent part, § 10(b) of the Exchange Act provides:

> It shall be unlawful for any person, directly or indirectly, by the use of any means or instrumentality of interstate commerce or of the mails, or of any facility of any national securities exchange— . . .
>
> (b) To use or employ, in connection with the purchase or sale of any security registered on a national securities exchange or any security not so registered, any manipulative or deceptive device or contrivance in contravention of such rules and regulations as the [Securities and Exchange] Commission may prescribe as necessary or appropriate in the public interest or for the protection of investors.

The statute thus proscribes (1) using any deceptive device (2) in connection with the purchase or sale of securities, in contravention of rules prescribed by the Commission. The provision, as written, does not confine its coverage to deception of a purchaser or seller of securities; rather, the statute reaches any deceptive device used in connection with the purchase or sale of any security.

Pursuant to its § 10(b) rulemaking authority, the Commission has adopted Rule 10b–5, which, as relevant here, provides:

> It shall be unlawful for any person, directly or indirectly, by the use of any means or instrumentality of interstate commerce, or of the mails or of any facility of any national securities exchange,
>
> (a) To employ any device, scheme, or artifice to defraud, [or] . . .
>
> (c) To engage in any act, practice, or course of business which operates or would operate as a fraud or deceit

upon any person, in connection with the purchase or sale of any security.

. . . Under the "traditional" or "classical theory" of insider trading liability, § 10(b) and Rule 10b–5 are violated when a corporate insider trades in the securities of his corporation on the basis of material, nonpublic information. . . .

The "misappropriation theory" holds that a person commits fraud "in connection with" a securities transaction, and thereby violates § 10(b) and Rule 10b–5, when he misappropriates confidential information for securities trading purposes, in breach of a duty owed to the source of the information. Under this theory, a fiduciary's undisclosed, self-serving use of a principal's information to purchase or sell securities, in breach of a duty of loyalty and confidentiality, defrauds the principal of the exclusive use of that information. In lieu of premising liability on a fiduciary relationship between company insider and purchaser or seller of the company's stock, the misappropriation theory premises liability on a fiduciary-turned-trader's deception of those who entrusted him with access to confidential information.

The two theories are complementary, each addressing efforts to capitalize on nonpublic information through the purchase or sale of securities. The classical theory targets a corporate insider's breach of duty to shareholders with whom the insider transacts; the misappropriation theory outlaws trading on the basis of nonpublic information by a corporate "outsider" in breach of a duty owed not to a trading party, but to the source of the information. The misappropriation theory is thus designed to protect the integrity of the securities markets against abuses by outsiders to a corporation who have access to confidential information that will affect the corporation's security price when revealed, but who owe no fiduciary or other duty to that corporation's shareholders.

In this case, the indictment alleged that O'Hagan, in breach of a duty of trust and confidence he owed to his law firm, Dorsey & Whitney, and to its client, Grand Met, traded on the basis of nonpublic information regarding Grand Met's planned tender offer for Pillsbury common stock. This conduct, the Government charged, constituted a fraudulent device in connection with the purchase and sale of securities.

We agree with the Government that misappropriation, as just defined, satisfies § 10(b)'s requirement that chargeable conduct involve a "deceptive device or contrivance" used "in connection with" the purchase or sale of securities. We observe, first, that misappropriators, as the Government describes them, deal in deception. A fiduciary who "[pretends] loyalty to the principal while secretly converting the principal's information for personal gain," "dupes" or defrauds the principal. . . .

Deception through nondisclosure is central to the theory of liability for which the Government seeks recognition. As counsel for the Government stated in explanation of the theory at oral argument: "To satisfy the common law rule that a trustee may not use the property that [has] been entrusted [to] him, there would have to be consent. To satisfy the requirement of the Securities Act that there be no deception, there would only have to be disclosure." . . .

[F]ull disclosure forecloses liability under the misappropriation theory: Because the deception essential to the misappropriation theory involves feigning fidelity to the source of information, if the fiduciary discloses to the source that he plans to trade on the nonpublic information, there is no "deceptive device" and thus no § 10(b) violation—although the fiduciary-turned-trader may remain liable under state law for breach of a duty of loyalty.

We turn next to the § 10(b) requirement that the misappropriator's deceptive use of information be "in connection with the purchase or sale of [a] security." This element is satisfied because the fiduciary's fraud is consummated, not when the fiduciary gains the confidential information, but when, without disclosure to his principal, he uses the information to purchase or sell securities. The securities transaction and the breach of duty thus coincide. This is so even though the person or entity defrauded is not the other party to the trade, but is, instead, the source of the nonpublic information. A misappropriator who trades on the basis of material, nonpublic information, in short, gains his advantageous market position through deception; he deceives the source of the information and simultaneously harms members of the investing public.

The misappropriation theory targets information of a sort that misappropriators ordinarily capitalize upon to gain no-risk profits through the purchase or sale of securities. . . .

The misappropriation theory comports with § 10(b)'s language, which requires deception "in connection with the purchase or sale of any security," not deception of an identifiable purchaser or seller. The theory is also well-tuned to an animating purpose of the Exchange Act: to insure honest securities markets and thereby promote investor confidence. Although informational disparity is inevitable in the securities markets, investors likely would hesitate to venture their capital in a market where trading based on misappropriated nonpublic information is unchecked by law. An investor's informational disadvantage vis-a-vis a misappropriator with material, nonpublic information stems from contrivance, not luck; it is a disadvantage that cannot be overcome with research or skill.

In sum, considering the inhibiting impact on market participation of trading on misappropriated information, and the congressional purposes underlying § 10(b), it makes scant sense to hold a lawyer like O'Hagan a § 10(b) violator if he works for a law firm representing the target of a tender offer, but not if he works for a law firm representing the bidder. The text of the statute requires no such result. The misappropriation at issue here was properly made the subject of a § 10(b) charge because it meets the statutory requirement that there be "deceptive" conduct "in connection with" securities transactions. . . .

. . . [T]he misappropriation theory, as we have examined and explained it in this opinion, is both consistent with the statute and with our precedent. Vital to our decision that criminal liability may be sustained under the misappropriation theory, we emphasize, are two sturdy safeguards Congress has provided regarding scienter. To establish a criminal violation of Rule 10b–5, the Government must prove that a person "willfully" violated the provision. Furthermore, a defendant may not be imprisoned for violating Rule 10b–5 if he proves that he had no knowledge of the rule. . . .

The Eighth Circuit erred in holding that the misappropriation theory is inconsistent with § 10(b). The Court of Appeals may address on remand O'Hagan's other challenges to his convictions under § 10(b) and Rule 10b–5. . . . [*Reversed and remanded*].

Case Questions

1. What was O'Hagan accused of doing that was illegal?

2. What is the theory that the SEC argues is the basis of O'Hagan's wrongdoing?

3. How did the trial court and the appellate court rule in this case?

4. What reasons did the Supreme Court give for finding that the misappropriation theory is appropriate?

5. According to the Supreme Court, when and against whom did the misappropriation occur?

The SEC continues to focus its enforcement efforts on the misuse of nonpublic information at all levels of transactions. The SEC's efforts are aided by the fact that the civil penalty for gaining illegal profits with nonpublic information is three times the profits gained. In addition, companies that fail to prevent these violations by employees may be civilly liable for triple damages.

The following concept summary not only highlights the various provisions discussed in this section, it also emphasizes the significant criminal sanctions under the 1934 act.

Concept Summary: Liability Under the Securities Exchange Act of 1934

Fraud (Section 10(b))

Purpose: Creates liability for use of mail or any instrumentality of interstate commerce to defraud any person in connection with the purchase or sale of any security

Plaintiff's case: (1) Proof of defendant's intent to deceive through use of false information or nondisclosure of truthful information; (2) plaintiff's reliance on fraudulent documents; and (3) damages

Defendant's defenses: For (1), no actual fraud was involved; for (2), only aided or abetted fraud; for (3), information was not material

Civil fines: (1) $500,000 per organization; $100,000 per individual and ban from service as director or officer; (2) three times profits for illegal trading on nonpublic information

Insider Information (Section 16 (b))

Purpose: (1) Creates strict liability for any insider making a profit on issuer's securities during any six-month period

concluded

   Plaintiff's case: Proof of the short-swing nature of the profitable transaction
   Defendant's defenses: Proof of no short-swing transaction; good faith (lack of intent) is no defense.
   Civil fines: $500,000 per organization; $100,000 per individual and ban from service as director or officer

Criminal Liability

For false or misleading documents filed: $100,000 fine or five years in prison or both per individual; $500,000 fine per organization
   For trading on nonpublic information: $1 million fine or ten years in prison or both per individual; $10 million fine per organization

Key Terms

Actual authority   191
Agent   190
Alter-ego theory   181
Apparent authority   191
Articles of incorporation   179
Articles of organization   188
Articles of partnership   176
Assumed-name statute   177
Buy and sell agreement   177
Charter   179
Closely held   175
Corporation   179
Derivative suit   181
Director   180
Dissolution   174
Domestic corporation   179
Double tax   184
Due diligence defense   194
Foreign corporation   179
General partner   185
Implied authority   191
Incorporator   179
Insider   196
Jointly and severally liable   177
Limited liability company   188

Limited liability partnership   189
Limited partner   185
Limited personal liability   181
Manager   189
Member   189
Misappropriation theory   197
Officer   180
Organizer   188
Partnership   176
Piercing the corporate veil   181
Principal   190
Prospectus   194
Proxy   180
Publicly held   175
Registration statement   193
S corporation   187
Securities Act of 1933   193
Securities and Exchange Commission (SEC)   193
Securities Exchange Act of 1934   194
Security   192
Shareholder   180
Short-swing profits   196
Sole proprietorship   176
Third party   190
Tippee   196

Review Questions and Problems

Forms of Business Organizations

1. *Factors to Consider*
   List and explain five critical factors to consider when selecting which organizational form is best for a particular business activity.

2. *Selecting the Best Organizational Form*
   (a) What are the three traditional business organizations and the four hybrid forms?
   (b) Explain the distinction between the term "closely held" and "publicly held."

3. *Sole Proprietorships*

   What are the limitations of the sole proprietorship?

4. *Partnerships*

   Terry is the senior partner in an accounting firm. One of Terry's partners performs an audit. The audited firm sues Terry, as the senior partner, for alleged errors in the audit. If Terry is found liable, can Terry sue to collect a pro rata share of this liability from the other partners? Why or why not?

5. *Corporations*

   (a) Who controls the closely held corporation? Explain.

   (b) Describe five techniques that a corporation might use to avoid the double taxation of corporate profits.

6. *Limited Partnerships*

   Laura and Gary have formed a limited partnership, with Gary agreeing to be the general partner. This partnership has purchased supplies from Sam. Sam has received a promissory note signed on behalf of the partnership as payment. If the partnership is unable to pay this note, can Sam hold Gary personally liable? Explain.

7. *S Corporations*

   (a) Although it is technically a corporation, the S corporation has the attributes of which business organization when considering the taxation factor?

   (b) What is the implication of this treatment if the S corporation has a profitable year but does not distribute dividends to its shareholders?

8. *Limited Liability Companies*

   What is the advantage of this organizational form compared to the S corporation?

9. *Making the Decision*

   You and a friend are considering forming a business organization to manufacture and sell widgets. You suspect that the company will show a loss during the first two years of operation. You also know that another manufacturer of widgets has suffered three product liability lawsuits totaling $300,000 within the past year. What form of business organization should be selected under these circumstances? Explain.

Agency

10. *Terminology*

    (a) What are the names given to the three parties typically involved in an agency relationship?

    (b) Describe the general purpose of the agency relationship.

11. *Contractual Liability*

    For several years, Albert acted as a collection agent for Paulette. Recently, Paulette revoked Albert's authority to collect payments from customers. However, neither Paulette nor Albert told any customers of Albert's termination. Yesterday, Theresa, one of Paulette's customers, paid Albert the money owed to Paulette. Albert never gave this money to Paulette. Is Theresa liable to pay Paulette? Why or why not?

12. *Tort Liability*

    Tammy was shopping in Save-a-Lot Grocery Store when Stewart, an employee, brushed Tammy's ankle with a grocery cart. A short time later, while still shopping, Tammy told Stewart that he should say "Excuse me," and then people would get out of his way. Stewart then punched Tammy in the face, knocking her to the floor. If Tammy sues Save-a-Lot, what legal issue must be addressed to determine whether Save-a-Lot is liable?

Public Investment—Securities Regulation

13. *What is a Security?*

    W.J. Howey Company and Howey-in-the-Hills Service, Inc., are Florida corporations under common control and management. Howey Company offers to sell to the public its orange grove, tree by tree. Howey-in-the-Hills Service, Inc., offers these buyers a contract wherein the appropriate care, harvesting, and marketing of the oranges would be provided. Most of the buyers who sign the service contracts are nonresidents of Florida who have very little knowledge or skill needed to care for and harvest the oranges. These buyers are attracted by the expectation of profits. Is a sale of orange trees by the Howey Company and a sale of services by Howey-in-the-Hills Service, Inc., a sale of a security? Why or why not?

14. *Securities and Exchange Commission*

    (a) Give an example of this agency's quasi-legislative authority.

    (b) Give an example of this agency's quasi-judicial authority.

15. *Securities Act of 1933: Going Public*

    (a) Describe the two documents and their purposes required under the 1933 act.

    (b) What is the typical remedy sought by an investor who alleges that one or both of these documents failed to comply with the 1933 act?

16. *Securities Exchange Act of 1934: Being Public*
    (a) What is the basic purpose of § 10(b) and Rule 10b–5?
    (b) If a corporate director of XYZ, Inc. buys 250 shares of XYZ, Inc. on September 1, what is the earliest date that this director can legally sell this stock, assuming no other buy-or-sell transactions?

Terminology Review

For each term in the left-hand column, match the most appropriate description in the right-hand column.

1. Partnership

2. Sole proprietorship
3. Limited partnership

4. Corporation

5. Limited liability company

6. Buy and sell agreement

7. S corporation

8. Accumulated earnings tax

9. Registration statement

10. Prospectus

11. Insider

12. Agent

13. Apparent authority

14. Principal

15. Actual authority

a. A business owned by one person who is personally liable for all losses

b. An artificial being created by a state

c. Imposed when a corporation fails to justify not paying dividends from earnings

d. Created when shareholders elect to be treated as partners for tax purposes

e. Created by an agreement between two or more persons who agree to share profits and losses

f. Provides for compensation to a deceased or withdrawing owner of a business in return for that owner's interest

g. A relatively new organizational form that combines aspects of partnerships and corporations to provide its members with limited liability

h. Exists when some partners are treated like shareholders for liability purposes

i. The document that contains financial and other information. It must be filed with the SEC prior to any sale of a security.

j. A person who owns more than 10 percent of a security of an issuer or who is a director or an officer of an issuer

k. A document or pamphlet that includes the essential information contained in the registration statement; it is filed with the SEC and made available to potential investors

l. An individual or business organization that hires employees to "get the job done"

m. The grant of permission that flows from a principal to an agent, it may be either expressed or implied

n. The impression a third party has when not notified that an agent has been terminated

o. The individual or business organization that represents a principal

CONTRACT LAW AND PRIVATE ENTERPRISE

Business Decision

The Big Mistake

As a new sales representative for Misco Equipment Corporation, you take a customer out to dinner. Before dinner is over, you have shaken hands on a deal to sell the customer nearly a half-million dollars worth of industrial equipment. In writing up the formal contract the next morning, you discover that you misfigured the equipment's price. Your error could cost Misco $60,000. You telephone your customer and explain the situation.

Is the "deal" you made an enforceable contract?

Does the mistake you made permit you to get out of an enforceable contract?

What do you think will happen in this situation?

Real-life contract problems usually involve business-related and people-related considerations as well as legal rules. The Business Decision illustrates this fact. There are legal considerations about:

1. At what point the "deal" became a contract.
2. Whether the verbal "deal" must be in writing to be enforceable.
3. Whether your misfiguring the price excuses your company from having to sell the equipment at that price.

There are also nonlegal business considerations to this situation. If your company tries to get out of the deal, it risks losing the customer's future business. Probably, the company will settle this situation through negotiation rather than litigation. Still, as rapidly growing contract litigation between businesses shows, it is good to know the rules of contract law.

Millions of new contracts—legally enforceable promises—are formed daily in the United States. Businesspeople and consumers alike make

FIGURE 8.1

Elements of a contract.

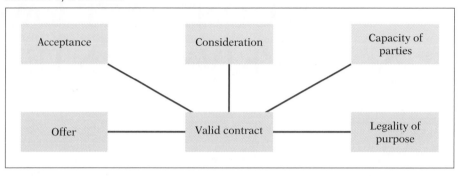

contractual agreements. Over the years, no other area of the law has been as important as the law of contracts in supporting the private enterprise system.

The making of contracts is basic to the understanding of the legal and regulatory environment of business. Labor unions and companies make collective bargaining agreements that are contracts (Chapter 12). Antitrust laws prohibit contracts that restrain trade (Chapter 11). In administrative law the government and businesses make consent order agreements that are a type of contract (Chapter 6). In securities law (Chapter 7) the government regulates the contractual process. Even the Constitution prohibits the states from "impairing the obligation of Contracts" (Article 1, section 10) (Chapter 5).

There are five basic elements of a contract, as shown in Figure 8.1:

· Offer
· Acceptance
· Consideration
· Capacity of parties to contract
· A legal purpose

A substantial part of this chapter focuses on these elements and how they come together to form contracts. Before an agreement can become a legally binding contract, someone must make a specific promise to another and also a specific demand of that person. This is the offer. The other person must accept the terms of the offer in the proper way. Both parties must give consideration to the other. Consideration is the promise to give, or the actual giving, of a requested benefit or the incurring of a legal detriment (i.e., doing something one does not have to). Both parties must be of legal age and sound mind, and the purpose of the agreement cannot be illegal or against public policy. However, before discussing further the formation of contracts, we shall develop the role of contract law in the private enterprise system and consider various classifications of contracts.

Sections of this chapter also discuss other contract law topics, such as the significance of written contracts, the interpretation of contracts, and the performance of contracts. The concluding sections outline trends in contract law and discuss contractual ethics.

A special area of contract law covers the sale of goods. **Goods** are tangible, movable personal property, a category that covers everything from airplanes to flea collars. They do not, however, include services and real estate. Contracts for the sale of goods are covered by the Uniform Commercial Code (UCC), a special body of law adopted in every state except Louisiana, which has related legislation. This chapter recognizes many instances in which the law treats sales of goods differently from other types of contracts. Tell yourself right now that you will be sure to note when contracts involve sales of goods and are covered under the UCC.

Basic Concepts

1. Contract Law in Private Enterprise

When was the last time you entered a contract? Was it last month when you signed an apartment or dorm lease? If so, you must be very hungry. This is because one enters a contract when buying a meal or a snack from a vending machine. Actually, most people contract daily for a great variety of goods and services that they purchase or lease. The rules of contract law underlie the private enterprise system at every turn.

A contract is a legally enforceable promise. It need not usually be a formal, written document, and those who make a contract do not have to use the word "contract" or recognize that they have made a legally enforceable promise. Still, the rules of contract law apply. If the expectations of the parties to a contract are not met, these rules affect legal negotiations or a lawsuit. For instance, contract law says that a restaurant "promises" that its food is fit to eat. Should the restaurant serve a meal that gives the buyer food poisoning, it would now be liable for the injury caused by breaking its promise.

Contract law enables people to make private agreements legally enforceable. Enforceability of agreements is desirable because it gives people the certainty they need to rely on promises contained in agreements. For instance, a shirt manufacturer in Los Angeles must know that it can rely on the promise of a store in Boston to pay for a thousand specially manufactured shirts. The manufacturer is more likely to agree to sew the shirts if it can enforce payment from the buyer, if necessary, under the law of contracts.

In an important sense, then, the law of contracts is vital for our private enterprise economy. It helps make buyers and sellers willing to do business together. Contract law is not as needed in the economy of the People's Republic of China, where the state controls many buying and selling relationships. It is also less needed in countries such as Japan, where centuries of tradition regulate business arrangements. But in the United States the law of contracts promotes certainty that agreements will be kept and permits reliance on promises. It encourages the flow of commerce.

Contract law also provides enormous flexibility and precision in business dealings. It provides flexibility in that you can agree (or require agreement) to literally anything that is not illegal or against public policy. It gives precision in that with careful thinking you can make another agree to exactly the requirements that accomplish even a very complex business purpose. See the Tobacco Industry Box for an example of the precise use of contractual language to accomplish a business purpose.

Tobacco Industry Box

The Confidentiality Agreement

Many companies require employees to sign contractual confidentiality agreements. In these agreements employees promise not to disclose certain things they learn during their employment. Confidentiality agreements are very useful in keeping employees or ex-employees from telling a company's research discoveries, marketing plans, customer lists, and other sensitive information.

Confidentiality agreements are especially important in the tobacco industry. Most medical opinion holds that tobacco is an addictive product that can cause heart and lung disease. What do tobacco industry executives think about these issues? Publicly, the tobacco industry downplays that tobacco is addictive and minimizes tobacco health risks. Discussion within the industry, however, may show concern about the effects of tobacco. Precisely worded confidentiality agreements prohibit tobacco industry employees from revealing documents or discussions at work concerning the risks of tobacco consumption, or even how cigarettes and other tobacco products are made. The tobacco industry can enforce these agreements through court injunctions or damage clauses. Over the years, confidentiality agreements have been very useful in keeping industry information out of the hands of those who wish to sue or regulate the industry.

In 1994 a paralegal who worked for a law firm representing a major tobacco company copied and then released many internal company documents that indicated concern within the tobacco industry over the risks of tobacco consumption. The *New York Times,* the *Washington Post,* and other publications carried stories on the contents of these documents. Not long afterwards, the tobacco industry began negotiating for a comprehensive settlement to the legal claims arising from tobacco consumption and to the government's regulation of the tobacco industry.

2. Sources of Contract Law

Most of the contract law outlined in this chapter is common law (see Chapter 1). The courts have developed principles controlling contract formation, performance, breach, and remedies in countless cases that come to us today in the form of precedents. This judge-made law affects many types of contracts, including real property, service, employment, and general business contracts.

Another source of contract law is legislation. Various states have enacted parts of the common law, sometimes modifying it. The UCC's coverage of the sale of goods is an example of how the legislation may modify the common law of contracts. The making of contracts in specific industries, such as the insurance industry, is also often controlled by legislation.

3. Classification of Contracts

We use a number of terms to help classify different types of contracts. Learning these terms will greatly help you understand contract law.

Executory and Executed Contracts

For instance, an **executory contract** (or term of a contract) is one the contracting parties have not yet performed. An **executed contract** (or term) is one the parties have performed.

Express and Implied-in-Fact Contracts

Many contracts arise from discussions in which parties actually discuss the promised terms of their agreement. These are called **express contracts.** A negotiated purchase of land for construction of a manufacturing plant is an example of an express contract. These are also **implied-in-fact contracts,** which arise from the conduct of the parties rather than from words. For instance, asking a person such as an accountant for professional advice *implies* a promise to pay the going rate for this advice even though you do not make an *express* promise to pay for it.

Quasi-Contract

When one party is unjustly enriched at the expense of another, the law may imply a duty on the first party to pay the second even though there is no contract between the two parties. The doctrine that requires this result is **quasi-contract.** It is a contract *implied in law.*

If a debtor overpays a creditor $5,000, the debtor can force the creditor to return that amount by suing under quasi-contract. It would be an unjust enrichment to allow the creditor to keep the $5,000. Likewise, when John has paid taxes on land, thinking that he owns it, and Mary comes along with a superior title (ownership) to the land and has John evicted, quasi-contract requires that Mary reimburse John for the taxes paid.

Note that quasi-contract is not an answer to every situation in which no contract exists. Over the years, courts have come to apply quasi-contract in a fairly limited number of cases based on unjust enrichment.

Unilateral and Bilateral Contracts

One classification of contracts concerns those that are unilateral and those that are bilateral. A **unilateral contract** involves a present act given in return for a promise of future performance. A promise to pay $50 for a ride to Florida during spring break illustrates the unilateral contract. Another example is catching a bank robber in return for the promise of a reward. In **bilateral contracts,** each party makes a promise to perform for the other: Greshman promises to deliver a deed to the land on October 31; Gomez promises to pay Greshman $50,000 for the land on that date. When it is unclear whether the parties to an agreement intend a unilateral or a bilateral contract, courts usually presume that the contract is bilateral.

Void Contracts

Void contracts are really not contracts at all. They are agreements that lack any one of the essential contractual elements. Often this element is legality of purpose. For example, in states where gambling is illegal, a bet on a football game is void. This usually means that a court will not enforce the betting agreement. The opposite of a void contract is a **valid contract,** which contains all the proper elements of a contract.

Voidable Contracts

A **voidable contract** binds one of the parties to an agreement but gives the other party the option of withdrawing from it. Contracts based on fraud or misrepresentation are two important examples of voidable contracts. **Fraud** involves an intentional misstatement of a material (important) fact that induces one to rely justifiably to his or her injury. Intentionally calling a zircon a diamond and persuading someone to purchase it on that basis is a fraud. Sometimes failures to disclose a material fact can also be a fraud, as when a landowner sells a buyer land knowing that the buyer wishes to build a home on it and does not disclose that the land is underwater during the rainy season. The defrauded party can withdraw from the contract. **Misrepresentation** is simply a misstatement without intent to mislead. However, a contract entered into through misrepresentation is still voidable by the innocent party.

Other examples of voidable contracts are those induced by duress or undue influence. **Duress** means force or threat of force. The force may be physical or, in some instances, economic. **Undue influence** occurs when one is taken advantage of unfairly through a contract by a party who misuses a position of relationship or legal confidence. Contracts voidable because of undue influence often arise when persons weakened by age or illness are persuaded to enter into a disadvantageous contract by a family member or other person.

Concept Summary: Void and Voidable Contracts

A Contract is Void If It Is:

Illegal or against public policy (see § 10)
Lacking in some other essential element

A Contract Is Voidable in Cases of:

Fraud (intent to mislead)
Misrepresentation (unintentional)

Duress (force or threat of force)
Undue influence (misuse of position or legal confidence)
Mutual mistake of fact (see § 7)
Lack of capacity to contract (see § 9)

---

4. Breach of Contract

A party that does not live up to the obligation of contractual performance is said to breach the contract. There are several remedies or solutions available for a breach of contract. These include the following, as discussed in Figure 8.2.

· Negotiated settlement
· Arbitration
· Various damage awards
· Specific performance
· Rescission

Note that the various remedies are usually mutually exclusive. For instance, you could not get both specific performance and rescission for the

FIGURE 8.2

Remedies for breach of contract.

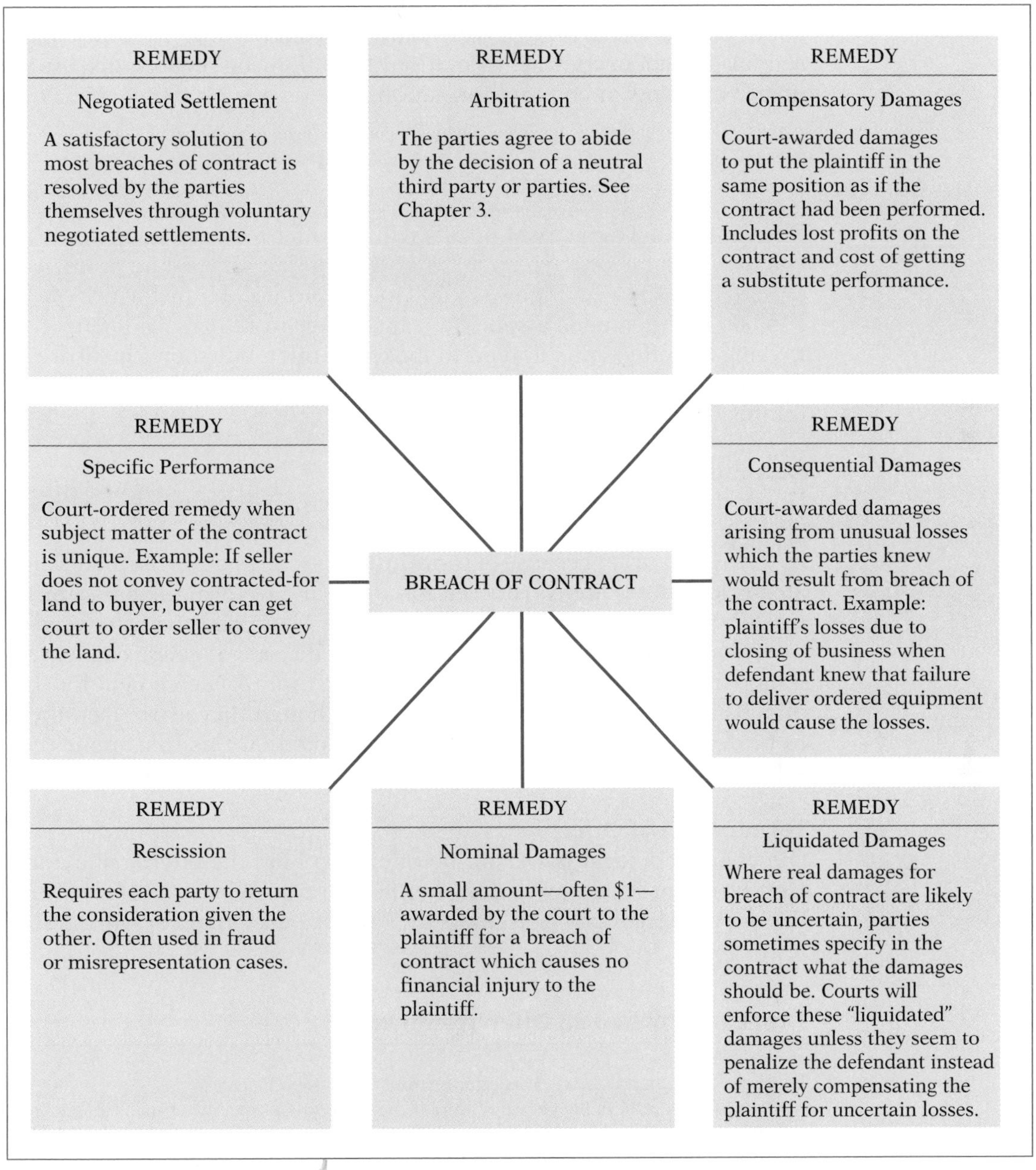

REMEDY	REMEDY	REMEDY
Negotiated Settlement	**Arbitration**	**Compensatory Damages**
A satisfactory solution to most breaches of contract is resolved by the parties themselves through voluntary negotiated settlements.	The parties agree to abide by the decision of a neutral third party or parties. See Chapter 3.	Court-awarded damages to put the plaintiff in the same position as if the contract had been performed. Includes lost profits on the contract and cost of getting a substitute performance.

REMEDY		REMEDY
Specific Performance		**Consequential Damages**
Court-ordered remedy when subject matter of the contract is unique. Example: If seller does not convey contracted-for land to buyer, buyer can get court to order seller to convey the land.	**BREACH OF CONTRACT**	Court-awarded damages arising from unusual losses which the parties knew would result from breach of the contract. Example: plaintiff's losses due to closing of business when defendant knew that failure to deliver ordered equipment would cause the losses.

REMEDY	REMEDY	REMEDY
Rescission	**Nominal Damages**	**Liquidated Damages**
Requires each party to return the consideration given the other. Often used in fraud or misrepresentation cases.	A small amount—often $1—awarded by the court to the plaintiff for a breach of contract which causes no financial injury to the plaintiff.	Where real damages for breach of contract are likely to be uncertain, parties sometimes specify in the contract what the damages should be. Courts will enforce these "liquidated" damages unless they seem to penalize the defendant instead of merely compensating the plaintiff for uncertain losses.

to lessen consequences of

same breach of contract. On the other hand, you might get both compensatory and consequential damages for the same breach of contract.

The victim of a contract breach must **mitigate** damages when possible. To mitigate damages requires the victim to take reasonable steps to reduce them. For example, when a tenant breaches a house lease by moving away before the lease expires, the landlord must mitigate damages by renting the house to another willing and suitable tenant if such a person is available.

Contract Formation

How a contract is formed is one of the most important issues to understand about contract law. Many agreements are void because they lack some essential element of contract formation. The following sections discuss the required elements of contract formation.

5. Offer to Contract

The contractual agreement begins with an offer made to an *offeree* (the person to whom the offer is made). An **offer** contains a specific promise and a specific demand. "I will pay $15,000 for the electrical transformer" promises $15,000 and demands a specific transformer in return. An *offeror* (person making the offer) must intend to make the offer, but courts measure intent objectively, that is, by how others reasonably see it rather than by what the offeror thinks he or she means.

Definiteness of Terms
Under the common law of contracts, contractual terms must be definite and specific. An offer to purchase a house at a "reasonable price" cannot be the basis for a contract because of **indefiniteness.** Most advertisements and catalog price quotes are considered too indefinite to form the basis for a contract unless they are specific about the quality of goods being offered.

However, under the UCC, contracts for the sale of goods can leave open nonquantity terms to be decided at a future time. An agreement for the sale of 500 cameras will bind the parties even though they leave open the price to be decided on delivery in six months. Note that this rule applies only to sales of goods. It does not apply to sales of real estate or services.

Termination of Offer
Offers create a legal power in the offeree to bind the offeror in a contract. However, that legal power does not last forever. When an offer *terminates,* the offeree's legal power to bind the offeror ends. Table 8–1 illustrates the

TABLE 8–1   When an Offer Terminates

By provision in the offer: "This offer terminates at noon Friday."
By lapse of a reasonable period of time if the offer fails to specify a time: What is "reasonable" depends on the circumstances.
By rejection of the offer: "Thank you, but I do not want the widgets you are offering." A **counteroffer** is also a rejection: "Your offer of $10,000 for the land is too low. I will sell it to you for $12,500."
By revocation of the offer: "I regret to inform you that I am withdrawing my offer."
By destruction of the subject matter: The widgets are destroyed by fire before the offer of their sale has been accepted.
By the offeror's death or insanity: Offeror dies before the offer has been accepted.
By the contractual performance becoming illegal: Congress declares that sales of certain computers to Iraq are illegal. This terminates an offer to sell the computers to an Iraqi trading company.

various instances when an offer terminates. The case that follows illustrates two instances of when an offer terminates: the counteroffer and the lapse of a reasonable period of time.

HEALTH AND WELFARE PLAN FOR EMPLOYEES OF REM, INC. v. RIDLER

1997 U.S. App. LEXIS 23878 (8th Cir.)

James Ridler, an employee of REM, Inc., was seriously injured in a motorcycle accident. His employer's medical insurance plan (Plan) paid over $400,000 for his medical care and wage loss benefits. When Ridler sued those responsible for the accident, the Plan claimed Ridler must reimburse the Plan, according to their contract, out of any amount received from those responsible for the accident. The district court ruled the Plan was entitled to full reimbursement, and Ridler appealed. He argued that his attorney James Lord had accepted an offer from the Plan's representative Lavina Reis to compromise the reimbursement claim for $137,000. The Plan asserted that Lord had not accepted the offer, but had proposed a counteroffer that the Plan simply reduce its obligation to Ridler by $137,000, a transaction called a "set-off." The Plan further argued that as it had not agreed to the counteroffer, the original offer had terminated.

PER CURIAM: . . . Lord told Reis, in essence, that the offer was not acceptable and then suggested that the Plan forgo reimbursement for a set-off. This was an attempt to materially alter the terms of the offer, and constitutes a counter-offer. The *Restatement of Contracts* states:

(1) A counter-offer is an offer made by an offeree to his offeror relating to the same matter as the original offer and proposing a substituted bargain differing from that proposed by the original offer.

(2) An offeree's power of acceptance is terminated by his making of a counter-offer, unless the offeror has manifested a contrary intention or unless the counter-offer manifests a contrary intention of the offeree.

Under Minnesota law, an acceptance that seeks to vary, add to or qualify the terms of an offer is not positive and unequivocal, and constitutes a counter-offer and a rejection of the original offer. The district court did not err by finding that Lord's uncontroverted statements presented a counter-offer and a rejection, and terminated his power to accept the original offer.

Moreover, Ridler's attempt to accept the offer on June 13th was not within a reasonable time. The Plan's offer did not contain a specified deadline for acceptance. Therefore, it lapsed after a "reasonable time." According to both the *Second Restatement* and *Corbin on Contracts,* what constitutes reasonable time is a fact question which depends on all the circumstances existing when the offer and attempted acceptance are made. The Plan's reimbursement interest was increased by $130,000 between the time the offer was made and Ridler's attempted acceptance. Despite the fact that only a short period of time had lapsed, the circumstances surrounding the offer had radically changed. The district court did not err by concluding that even if Ridler had not rejected the offer, the acceptance was not made within a reasonable time. [*Affirmed*].

Case Questions

1. Why was Ridler obligated to reimburse the Plan?

2. Why did Ridler argue that he did not have to reimburse the Plan over $400,000, the amount it had paid because of his injuries?

3. Why did the court conclude that the offer made to Ridler had terminated?

6. Acceptance of Offer

Acceptance of an offer is necessary to a binding contract. An offer to enter into a bilateral contract is accepted by the offeree's making the required promise. When Toni offers Aaron certain widgets for $2,500 to be delivered by November 30 on ninety-day credit terms, and Aaron accepts, Aaron is promising to pay $2,500 on ninety-day credit terms.

Unilateral contracts are accepted by performing a requested act, not by making a promise. A company's offer of a $2,500 reward for information leading to the conviction of anyone vandalizing company property is not accepted by promising to provide the information. Only the act of providing information accepts such an offer.

Deposited Acceptance Rule

When does the acceptance become legally binding on the offeror? Unless the offeror specifies a particular time, the acceptance usually binds the parties when the offeree dispatches it. Since the offeree frequently mails the acceptance, the acceptance becomes binding when it is "deposited" with the postal service—hence the **deposited acceptance rule,** also called the **mailbox rule.**

The importance of the deposited acceptance rule is that the offeror cannot revoke the offer once the offeree has accepted it. An added significance is that an offeror's revocation is not effective until the offeree actually receives it. Thus, a deposited acceptance creates a binding contract even though a revocation is also in the mail.

Mirror Image Rule

For an acceptance to create a binding contract, standard contract law requires that the acceptance must "mirror" the offer, that is, must match it exactly. This is the **mirror image rule.** If the acceptance changes the terms of the offer or adds new terms, it is not really an acceptance. It is a *counteroffer.*

The UCC has changed the mirror image rule, especially with regard to merchants contracting for the sale of goods. An acceptance between merchants creates a binding contract even though it proposes new or different terms. The new or different terms become part of the contract unless one of the following takes place:

1. The offer expressly limits acceptance to the original terms.
2. The proposed terms materially (importantly) alter the contract.
3. The offeror rejects the proposed terms.

Silence Not Acceptance

In general, an offeree's failure to reject an offer does not imply acceptance. Another way to say this is that silence is not acceptance. The offeree has no usual duty to reply to the offer even if the offer states that the offeror will treat silence as acceptance.

There are major exceptions to this rule. For instance, parties may have a contract that specifies that future shipments of goods be made automatically unless the offeree expressly rejects them. Many book- and record-club contracts operate in this manner.

A related doctrine looks at the parties' prior *course of dealing*—the way they have done business in the past. Silence may well imply acceptance if the parties previously dealt with each other by having the buyer take shipments from the seller unless the buyer notified the seller in advance not to ship.

Finally, the UCC says that a contract may arise from the *conduct* of a buyer and seller of goods. Emphasis is placed on how the parties act rather than on a formal offer and acceptance of terms.

7. *Voluntary Consent*

To be enforceable, a contract must be voluntarily made. The previously discussed doctrines of fraud, misrepresentation, duress, and undue influence show that a contract is voidable when both parties do not reach it through a voluntary, knowing consent.

Mutual Mistake

What happens when each party misunderstands something very basic and material about a contract? Such a situation goes right to the heart of whether there has been a "voluntary" consent to a contract. When there is a **mutual mistake** as to a material fact inducing a contract, rescission is appropriate. The test of materiality is whether the parties would have contracted had they been aware of the mistake. If they would not have contracted, the mistaken fact is material.

There is a difference between a mutual, or bilateral, mistake and a unilateral mistake. A **unilateral mistake** arises when only one of the parties to a contract is wrong about a material fact. Suppose that Royal Carpet Co. bids $8.70 per yard for certain carpet material instead of $7.80 per yard as it had intended. If the seller accepts Royal Carpet's bid, a contract results even though there was a unilateral mistake.

Now you should understand that in the Business Decision "The Big Mistake" your company will have to perform the contract even though you made a mistake. It was a unilateral mistake.

Mutual Assent

A doctrine similar to mutual mistake is that of **mutual assent.** Mutual assent requires that the "minds" of contracting parties must "meet" before a contract exists. Two parties may sign a piece of paper called a "contract," but if each believes the contract involves something different, there is no mutual assent, no meeting of the minds. There is no real contract.

The next case furnishes a good example of how lack of mutual assent leads to a court's finding that no contract exists. With no meeting of the minds, the parties have not voluntarily consented to anything.

HILL-SHAFER PARTNERSHIP V. CHILSON FAMILY TRUST

799 P.2d 810 (Arizona 1990)

The Chilson Family Trust (seller) owns approximately twenty acres of land on Butler Avenue near Flagstaff, Arizona. Butler Avenue divides about 17.3 acres of the land into two parcels called "Butler North" and "Butler South." A third parcel, called the "Triangle," is a 2.4-acre piece of land north of Butler North.

Hill-Shafer Partnership (buyer) offered to buy from the seller fifteen acres of land north of Butler Avenue, which include Butler North and the Triangle. The offer proposed that the $620,500 price of the land be reduced if a survey showed that the land contained less than fifteen acres. The seller rejected the offer and counteroffered at the same price, insisting that the land be identified by legal description alone, with no possible price reduction. The buyer accepted the offer.

Through error the seller's offer legally described Butler North and Butler South rather than Butler North and the Triangle. When the seller discovered the error, it proposed to change the contract to contain a legal description of Butler North and the Triangle instead of the larger piece of land called Butler North and Butler South. The buyer refused and sued the seller for specific performance of the original contract. The trial court ruled in favor of the seller. On appeal, the Court of Appeal ruled for the buyer. The case is now before the Arizona Supreme Court.

MOELLER, J.: . . . In the case before us . . . we are convinced, as was the trial judge, that reasonable minds could only conclude that there was not mutual assent by the parties. All parties agree that initially all negotiations were directed towards Butler North and the Triangle. Both the appraisal and the letter of intent described and set a price only for the property north of Butler. Buyer's essential contention is that once seller made a counter-offer, the entire posture of the deal changed. Buyer argues that, although it offered to buy only the property north of Butler, once the seller insisted the property be identified by legal description alone, buyer's intent shifted (although uncommunicated to seller) and it thereafter intended to purchase whatever was contained in the legal description, regardless of what it was or where it was.

A careful examination of the deposition testimony demonstrates that no testimony or reasonable inference rebuts seller's testimony that seller only intended to convey the property north of Butler. Absent any such testimony or inference, buyer relies solely on the fact that seller insisted that legal description govern. Our review of the evidence leads us to hold that, under these particular facts, the only reasonable conclusion to be drawn from the evidence is that seller insisted on use of a legal description to avoid a price adjustment based on the actual acreage of the property north of Butler. There is no evidence that the parties ever discussed any property south of Butler. The first and only time Butler South crept into the deal was in the legal description contained in seller's counter-offer. Buyer's agents testified that, although they knew they were purchasing property in the Butler area, they had no specific knowledge of how many acres were involved. Buyer was not even sure seller owned the parcel south of Butler. Seller, on the other hand, was interested only in selling Butler North and the Triangle. . . .

It is well-established that before a binding contract is formed, the parties must mutually consent to all material terms. A distinct intent common to both parties must exist without doubt or difference, and until all understand alike there can be no assent. If one party thinks he is buying one thing and the other party thinks he is selling another thing, no meeting of the minds occurs, and no contract is formed.

The most famous statement of this point of law arose in the case of Raffles v. Wichelhaus [an English case of 1864]. In Raffles, the parties agreed on a sale of goods which was to be delivered from Bombay by the ship "Peerless." In fact, two ships named "Peerless" were sailing from Bombay at different times, and each party had a different ship in mind. The arrival time of the merchandise was of the essence to the contract. Because the understanding of the parties was different as to a material time, no binding contract was formed. . . .

In this case the seller believed the description covered only the property north of Butler. It did not. To an untrained person, the language of a legal description is susceptible of different interpretations. In fact, the parties in this case testified they could not understand the technical terminology of the legal description. Shafer, the buyer, testified the description looked "like Greek" to him. Chilson, the seller, testified that: "I just had to assume that it was correct of what we intended to do, and found out later it wasn't, however." The price of $620,500 was determined after an appraisal of the Triangle and Butler North. Buyer submitted a letter of intent only on the property north of Butler. The property south of Butler was never discussed. Seller believed the description contained in the offer described the property that had been listed and discussed. Had buyer accepted the offer on that basis and with the same intent, a binding contract (subject to reformation) might well have been formed for the sale of the land north of Butler. However, buyer's intent varied from seller's. Buyer's understanding was that it would acquire whatever was included in the legal description, regardless of size or location. We disagree with the court of appeal's conclusion that the preciseness of a legal description, as a matter of law, prevented a rescission based on a misunderstanding.

The evidence supports the trial court's conclusion that, as a matter of law, there was not mutual assent. Therefore, the trial court's grant of summary judgment in favor of the seller is affirmed. The court of appeal's decision is vacated. [*Reversed*].

Case Questions

1. Why do you think the buyer wants the seller specifically to perform the contract? What is the business reason?

2. Why does Justice Moeller discuss *Raffles v. Wichelhaus,* an English case over one hundred years old?

3. Do you think the decision of the Supreme Court of Arizona is a fair one?

In the opinion Justice Moeller mentions the remedy of **reformation.** As applied here, it means that if the seller and buyer had definitely agreed on Butler North and the Triangle but through a drafting mistake the contract legally described Butler North and Butler South, the court would "reform" the contract language to describe Butler North and the Triangle.

8. Consideration

Courts will not enforce contractual promises unless they are supported by **consideration.** Before Robert can enforce a promise made by Peter, Robert must have given consideration, that is, assumed a legal obligation or surrendered a legal right. In a bilateral contract, each party promises something to the other. The binding promises are the consideration. In a unilateral contract, the consideration of one party is a promise; the consideration of the other party is performance of an act. When it is not clear whether there is consideration to support a promise, a court will often examine a transaction as a whole.

Must Be Bargained For

An important part of consideration is that it must be *bargained for.* Sometimes the parties to an agreement specify an insignificant consideration in return for a great one, for example, a promise of $1 in return for a promise to convey 40 acres of land. In such situations a court must decide whether the party promising to convey the land really bargained for the $1 or merely promised to make a gift. Promises to make gifts are not binding, because no bargained-for consideration supports the promise.

Similarly, *prior consideration* is no consideration. For instance, after many years of working at Acme Co., Bigman retires as vice president for financial planning. The company's board of directors votes him a new car every year "for services rendered." One year later the board rescinds this vote. If Bigman sues for breach of contract, he will lose. He gave no consideration to support the board's promise. The past years of service were not "bargained for" by the company's board when it took its vote. The board merely promised to give an unenforceable gift to Bigman.

Agreement Not to Sue

When reasonable grounds for a lawsuit exist, an agreement not to sue is consideration to support a promise. If First Bank agrees not to sue Maria, who has failed to repay a student loan, in return for the promise of Maria's parents to repay the loan, First Bank has given consideration. It has promised to surrender its legal right to sue Maria.

Likewise, suppose that a consulting firm bills a client $5,000 for fifty hours of work at $100 per hour. The client disputes the bill and contends that the consulting firm worked only twenty-five hours and should get only $2,500. If the two parties compromise the bill at $3,500 for thirty-five hours, this agreement binds them both. Each has surrendered the right to have a court determine exactly what amount is owed. Such an agreement and the payment of the $3,500 is an **accord and satisfaction.**

Preexisting Obligation

A party to an agreement does not give consideration by promising to do something that he or she is already obligated to do. For example, suppose a warehouse owner contracts to have certain repairs done for $20,000. In the middle of construction, the building contractor demands an additional $5,000 to complete the work. The owner agrees, but when the work is finished, he gives the contractor only $20,000. If the contractor sues, he will lose. The owner's promise to pay an extra $5,000 is not supported by consideration. The contractor is under a *preexisting obligation* to do the work for which the owner promises an additional $5,000.

If the contractor promised to do something he was not already obligated to do, there would be consideration to support the promise of the additional $5,000. Promising to modify the repair plans illustrates such new consideration.

Consideration Not Necessary

The preexisting obligation rule discussed above does not apply to a sale-of-goods contract. The UCC states that parties to a sale-of-goods contract may make binding modifications to it without both parties giving new consideration. If a buyer of widgets agrees to pay a seller an additional $5,000 over and above the amount already promised, the buyer is bound, although the seller gives only the consideration (widgets) that she is already obligated to give.

Under the UCC, the rules of consideration also do not apply to a **firm offer.** A firm offer exists when a merchant offering goods promises in writing that the offer will not be revoked for a period not to exceed three months. This promise binds the merchant, although the offeree buyer gives no consideration to support it. With offers not involving sales of goods by a merchant, a promise not to revoke an offer must be supported by the offeree's consideration to be binding. Such an arrangement is called an **option.**

An important exception to the rule requiring consideration to support a promise is the doctrine of **promissory estoppel.** This doctrine arises when a promisee justifiably relies on a promisor's promise to his or her economic injury. The promisor must know that the promisee is likely to rely on the promise. As the next case illustrates, promissory estoppel is increasingly used when the facts of a business relationship do not amount to an express or implied contract.

ESQUIRE RADIO & ELECTRONICS v. MONTGOMERY WARD
804 F.2d 787 (2nd Cir. 1986)

Esquire Radio & Electronics (Esquire) helped develop and import consumer electronics products for Montgomery Ward & Co. (Ward). Ward issued import orders to foreign manufacturers for products and spare parts. The orders were shipped to Esquire, which inventoried both products and spare parts for Ward's buyback. Although this arrangement continued for many years, the buyback terms were never expressly set forth. In 1984, Ward terminated its relationship with Esquire and refused to buy Esquire's existing spare-parts inventory. Esquire sued and won in the trial court. Ward appealed.

PIERCE, J.: . . . Notwithstanding the absence of a written agreement, courts applying New York law recognize other enforceable obligations, including oral contracts, implied contracts, and promissory estoppel. In our view, the doctrine of promissory estoppel applies to the facts of this case.

The doctrine of promissory estoppel, as set forth in § 90 of the Restatement of Contracts and as adopted in New York, has three principal requirements: "a clear and unambiguous promise; a reasonable and foreseeable reliance by the party to whom the promise is made; and an injury sustained by the party asserting the estoppel by reason of his reliance."

Here, all three elements are present. As noted above, there was evidence that, on several critical occasions, Ward clearly and unambiguously promised to repurchase accumulated spare parts inventories. The evidence showed that in the 1960s, Fisher, a Ward manager, assured Esquire that Ward would purchase the spare parts and that in the meantime Esquire should consider such inventories as being held on Ward's account. Similarly, at a meeting of executives and managers from both companies in the early 1970s, Esquire specifically expressed its concerns regarding the costs and risks of mounting inventories, and Ward, this time through Senior Vice President Dean Lewis, explicitly advised Esquire not to "concern yourself about the size of the inventory. We will buy the parts." In fact, in 1975, Ward's Parts Specialist, Harris Asher, unilaterally approached Esquire's Sales Vice President, Maffei, to induce Esquire to increase spare parts inventories regarding certain cassette recorders. When Maffei responded that he was concerned about the potential costs of such accumulations, Asher replied, "I don't know what you are concerned about. We are going to buy them from you anyway. We are going to use them." Certainly these specific, clear and unambiguous statements at the very least "suffice[d] to create a factual question" as to whether Ward had promised to repurchase accumulated spare parts during the tenure of the buy-back arrangement. Thus the question of whether there was such a promise was properly submitted to the jury.

We draw the same conclusion as to whether Esquire reasonably and foreseeably relied on Ward's repurchase promises. At the meeting during the early 1970s, Ward's Senior Vice President, Lewis, not only promised that Ward would purchase Esquire's inventories; he also urged Esquire to continue accumulating inventories as it had been doing throughout the period of the buy-back arrangement. While it is true that at that meeting Ward declined to adopt Esquire's proposal that accumulated inventories be stored in Ward's newly opened National Parts Center in Berkeley, Illinois, we think it significant that Ward's stated reason for declining was not that it wished Esquire to bear the risks that spare parts might not be needed, but that the Berkeley facility could not accommodate the size of the accumulated inventory.

Further, in 1975, Asher, Ward's Parts Specialist, not only promised that Ward would buy Esquire's inventories but specifically sought to induce Esquire to accumulate more inventories in reliance on that promise: "You ought to carry more and not be so tight on the quantities." Certainly, based on this evidence the jury rationally could conclude that, over the years, Ward induced Esquire to accumulate spare parts by making several specific promises to repurchase such parts, and that Esquire reasonably and foreseeably relied on such promises.

Finally, we think it is clear that Esquire sustained injury by reason of its reliance on Ward's promises. Esquire continued to accumulate extensive spare parts inventories after repeated assurances by Ward that it would repurchase the inventory, which by the time of termination, exceeded $1.2 million paid by Esquire to Ward for the parts plus shipment costs, including the 5 percent fee charged by the Ward trading company. The bulk of spare parts inventory valuation evidence came from Esquire documents prepared in the ordinary course of business, and admitted in accordance with applicable rules of evidence. Based on this evidence, the jury awarded Esquire what it paid for the spare parts ($1,241,340.95), excluding any benefit of the bargain profit that Esquire would have realized had Ward not repudiated.

Having affirmed the judgment as to spare parts shipments lacking written purchase agreements on the theory of promissory estoppel, we need not reach the question of whether the judgment might equally be affirmed on the basis of implied or oral contract. [*Affirmed*].

Case Questions

1. What are the requirements of promissory estoppel in New York?

2. What did Montgomery Ward do to make the court believe that it had met each of the three promissory estoppel requirements?

3. Do you believe that there was an implied-in-fact contract in this situation?

9. Capacity of Parties to Contract

Capacity refers to a person's ability to be bound by a contract. Courts have traditionally held three classes of persons to lack capacity to be bound by contractual promises:

- Minors (also called "infants")
- Intoxicated persons
- Mentally incompetent persons

Minors

In most states, a *minor* is anyone under age eighteen. Minors usually cannot be legally bound to contractual promises unless those promises involve *necessaries of life* such as food, clothing, shelter, medical care, and—in some states—education. Even for necessaries, minors often cannot be sued for the contract price, only for a "reasonable" value. In a number of states, courts will hold a minor who has misrepresented his or her age to contractual promises.

A contract into which a minor has entered is voidable at the election of the minor. The minor can *disaffirm* the contract and legally recover any consideration that has been given an adult, even if the minor cannot return the adult's consideration. On the other hand, the adult is bound by the contract unless the minor elects to disaffirm it.

The minor may disaffirm a contract anytime before reaching the age of majority (usually eighteen) and for a reasonable time after reaching majority. If the minor fails to disaffirm within a reasonable time after reaching majority, the minor is said to *ratify* the contract. Upon ratification, the minor loses the right to disaffirm.

Intoxicated and Mentally Incompetent Persons

Except when a court has judged an adult to be mentally incompetent, she or he does not lose capacity to contract simply because of intoxication or mental impairment. In most cases involving adult capacity to contract, courts measure capacity by whether the adult was capable of understanding the nature and purpose of the contract. Obviously, the more complex a contractual transaction gets, the more likely a court is to decide that an intoxicated or mentally impaired person lacks capacity to contract and has the right to disaffirm the contract.

10. Illegal Contracts

A basic requirement of a valid contract is *legality of purpose*. A "contract" to murder someone is hardly enforceable in a court of law. Contracts that require commission of a crime or tort or violate accepted standards of behavior (*public policy*) are void. Courts will generally take no action on a void contract, and they will leave the parties to a contract where they have put themselves. Table 8–2 gives common examples of illegal contracts.

There are several exceptions to the general rule that courts will take no action on an illegal contract. A contract may have both legal and illegal provisions to it. In such a case, courts will often enforce the legal provisions and refuse to enforce the illegal ones. For instance, a contract providing services or leasing goods sometimes contains a provision excusing the service provider or lessor from liability for negligently caused injury. Courts usually will not enforce this provision but will enforce the rest of the contract.

The following case shows how even a very large company when contracting with the federal government can have its contracts ruled illegal by the court. In this instance, AT&T seeks reimbursement for cost overruns on an important defense project when Congress has prohibited the kind of contract that AT&T has entered into.

TABLE 8–2 Examples of Illegal Contracts

Gambling agreements (except where permitted)

Contracts for usurious interest (greater interest than allowed by law)

Professional contracts made by unlicensed persons in which a regulatory statute requires licensing

Contracts that unreasonably restrain trade (see Chapter 11)

Many contracts that attempt to limit negligence liability of a seller of goods or services to the public (called **exculpatory contracts**)

Unconscionable contracts involving a sale of goods under the UCC (usually applied when a difference in bargaining power or education leads a merchant to take unreasonable advantage of a consumer)

Other contracts prohibited by statute or against public policy

AMERICAN TELEPHONE AND TELEGRAPH CO. V. UNITED STATES
124 F.3d 1471 (Fed. Cir. 1997)

AT&T agreed to develop an antisubmarine warfare system for the Navy for a fixed price of $34.5 million. When the system ended up costing AT&T a claimed $101 million, AT&T sued and asked the court to reform the contract or award it a sum for unjust enrichment. AT&T claimed that § 8118 of the Department of Defense Appropriations Act prohibited fixed-price contracts in excess of $10 million unless certain procedures were followed. Since the procedures were not followed, the Navy had no authority to make the contract, and the contract was void as illegal. The trial court declared the contract illegal, but granted AT&T unjust enrichment.

PLAGER, J.: . . . In analyzing the problem, it is important to keep clearly in mind what is meant when a contract is termed "illegal," a term used with abandon in the parties' briefs. That term encompasses a broad range of possible defects in contractual arrangements, from contracts that are inherently unenforceable (a contract to murder someone), to contracts in which one party is incompetent to contract (due to age or mental infirmity), to contracts in which a necessary term is omitted (such as price or date of performance), to contracts which are in some respect in violation of a positive rule of law (such as the case here).

The Government argues that the cases that have held contracts to be void or invalid upon the basis of a statutory or regulatory violation have involved provisions that explicitly limited the very authority of the parties to enter into the contract, or expressly prohibited the contract altogether. The Government notes that none of the "illegality" cases cited by AT&T deal with funding deficiencies. In the Government's view, a restriction on the availability of funding is not tantamount to a lack of authority to contract. Therefore, concludes the Government, § 8118 does not render the contract void from its inception.

AT&T responds that the question is not whether § 8118 restricted the Navy's ability to fund fixed price-

type development contracts, but whether the restrictions on the use of funds contained in § 8118 were "mandatory." If so, argues AT&T, a contract entered into in violation of § 8118 is illegal and void.

The Court of Federal Claims concluded that § 8118's requirement for a written determination upholding the pricing integrity of a fixed-price development contract operates as a constraint on the contracting process intended for the protection of both Government and contractor. We agree with the Court of Federal Claims on this point, and affirm its conclusion. The congressional purpose is abundantly clear: "None of the funds provided . . . may be obligated for [certain] fixed price-type contracts." The attempt by the Navy to obligate or expend funds for a contract not properly authorized by Congress is ineffective to either commit or make use of federal dollars. The Government's attempt to contract fails. No valid contract was or could be entered into in face of the express congressional prohibition.

The remaining question is what follows from the conclusion that the "contract" between the parties was an invalid attempt to enter into a contract. AT&T agrees that the contract was void, but seeks reformation of the contract into a cost-based type contract. The trial court correctly differentiated between an otherwise valid contract that contains a prohibited term or clause and one that is void from the inception. The court noted that the former may be amenable to reformation, but that a court has no power to remake that which was never established in the first instance.

The trial court, however, did not end the case there. The court concluded that the consequence of its determinations was to leave the parties with an implied-in-fact contract, with compensation to be awarded on an unjust enrichment basis. We cannot agree. The concept of implied-in-fact contract is not for the purpose of salvaging an otherwise invalid contract. An implied-in-fact contract arises when, in the absence of an express contract, the parties' behavior leaves no doubt that what was intended was a contractual relationship permitted by law. In the case here, the contractual relationship was not permitted by law, and the implied-in-fact contract is not appropriate.

Since AT&T never had a contract with the Government, and it is not entitled in an action in the Court of Federal Claims to relief based on a theory of unjust enrichment, AT&T has not stated a claim upon which relief can be granted. The Government is enti-

tled to judgment in its favor. The decision of the trial court to the contrary, in which it would consider the award of relief to AT&T in this case, is reversed.

This is not to say that AT&T is without any remedy. It would appear that the Government is in possession of goods, the RDA equipment, originally manufactured and owned by AT&T. There is nothing to suggest that AT&T intended to make a gift of that equipment to the Government, and much to suggest the contrary. Whether AT&T may recover the goods, or bring an appropriate action for the value of its wrongful retention and use by the Government, is not before us. [*Affirmed–in part. Reversed–in part*].

Case Questions

1. Why does § 8118 prohibit fixed-price development contracts over $10 million unless certain procedures are followed?

2. What is the effect of illegality on the contract AT&T made with the Navy?

3. What does the court suggest AT&T can do now that the court has declared the contract illegal?

Often, courts will allow an innocent party to recover payment made to a party who knows (or should know) that a contract is illegal. For example, courts will allow recovery of a payment for professional services made by an innocent person to a person who is unlicensed to provide such services.

In some cases courts may allow a person to recover compensation under quasi-contract for services performed on an illegal contract. Recovery may be allowed when an otherwise qualified professional lets his or her license expire and provides services to a client before renewing the license.

Contracts That Restrain Trade

Contracts that restrain trade often are illegal and void. They include contracts to monopolize, to fix prices between competitors, and to divide up markets. Chapter 11 on antitrust law discusses these contracts and their illegality.

Other contracts that restrain trade are important to the efficient operation of business. **Covenants not to compete** are important in protecting employers from having the employees they train leave them and compete against them. They also protect the buyer of a business from having the seller set up a competing business.

However, some covenants not to compete are illegal. Courts will declare such agreements illegal unless they have a valid business purpose, such as to protect the goodwill a business buyer purchases from the seller of the business. Covenants not to compete must also be "reasonable as to time and space." If they restrain competition for too long or in an area too large, the courts will declare them unreasonable and void them as being illegal. Four or five years is generally as long a time as the courts are willing to find reasonable, and even then the length of time must be justified. As to space, the courts will void covenants not to compete any time the area restrained exceeds the area in which the restraining business operates.

11. Written Contracts

Some people have the impression that contracts have to be in writing to be enforceable. In most instances, this is not so. However, it is true that certain contracts must be in writing (or at least evidenced by writing) to be enforceable.

The law requiring that certain contracts be in writing is the **statute of frauds.** Designed to prevent frauds arising from oral contracts, the original English statute is more than 300 years old. Today, every state has its own statute of frauds. Business-related provisions require the following contracts to be in writing:

- Contracts involving an interest in land
- Collateral contracts to pay the debt of another person
- Contracts that cannot be performed within one year
- Sale-of-goods contracts for $500 or more

In some states, the statute of frauds requires that the actual contract between the parties must be in writing. However, most states merely require that the contract be *evidenced* by writing and be signed by the party to be held. This requirement means that the party being sued must have signed a note, memorandum, or another written form short of a formal contract that describes with reasonable certainty the terms of the oral agreement. In sales of goods between merchants, the writing need not always be signed by the party sued. Under certain circumstances, it may be signed by the suing party.

Sale of an Interest in Land

Sales of interests in land are common contracts covered by the statute of frauds. Although "sales of interests in land" covers a contract to sell land, it includes much more. Interests in land include contracts for mortgages, mining rights, easements (rights to use another's land, such as the right to cross it with electric power wires), and leases of longer than one year. However, a contract to insure land or to erect a building is not an interest in land.

The doctrine of **part performance** creates an exception to the requirement that sales of interests in land must be in writing. When a buyer of land has made valuable improvements in it, or when the buyer is in possession of it and has paid part of the purchase price, even an oral contract to sell is enforceable.

In the next case, the plaintiffs argued that part performance enabled them to enforce an oral rental contract of a farm.

WEHRENBERG V. BOOTHE

1997 U.S. App. LEXIS 1066 (10th Cir.)

Loren and Norina Wehrenberg lost their farm through a bank foreclosure. Wayne and Mary Lee Boothe bought the farm from the bank. The Wehrenbergs continued to live on the farm through an agreement with the Boothes. This lawsuit arose when the Boothes refused to sell the property to the Wehrenbergs. The plaintiffs Wehrenberg sued, claiming an oral contract to buy the land after they had lived on it for five years and arguing that part performance defeated the statute of frauds defense raised by the defendants Boothe.

PORFILIO, J.: . . . Plaintiffs do not challenge the district court's determination that the alleged oral contract is governed by Oklahoma's statute of frauds. They contend only that their partial performance of the contract took it out of the statute. To avoid the statute of frauds under Oklahoma law, the party alleging the oral agreement has the burden of establishing clearly the terms of the agreement as well as the acts constituting partial performance. There are four kinds of partial performance sufficient to remove an oral contract for the sale of land from the statute: (1) notorious and exclusive possession of the property under the contract with the seller's knowledge, accompanied by part payment of the consideration; (2) the making of substantial permanent improvements to the land with the knowledge of the seller and under the contract; (3) alteration of the parties' positions pursuant to the contract making restoration to their former positions impossible or impractical; or (4) conduct by the parties that would cause enforcement of the statute in one party's favor to inflict unjust and unconscionable injury on the other party. Whether a party has met its burden of establishing the terms of the alleged contract and sufficient partial performance is a question of fact or mixed question of law and fact.

Even assuming, contrary to the district court's conclusion, that plaintiffs have adequately established the terms of the agreement, we agree with the district court that they have not met their burden of showing partial performance. They contend that they made valuable improvements to the property when they "put up several permanent fences, remediated a salt water well site, rocked in the barn foundation, and reterraced one farm." There is no evidence in the record on appeal that they remediated a well or rocked in the barn foundation. More importantly, they cite no evidence indicating that these improvements were done with the Boothes' knowledge or that they were pursuant to the contract.

Plaintiffs also contend they partially performed the contract when they "invested $17,500 in another farm purchased by the Boothes." Again, there is no evidence that this investment was under the alleged contract or done with the Boothes' knowledge. Additionally, to the extent plaintiffs claim this investment was partial consideration and that they had possession of the property sufficient to satisfy the first test for partial performance, we note that they were evicted from the property under state court orders in 1990. This is obviously inconsistent with the requirement of exclusive possession of the property under the alleged contract.

Finally, plaintiffs contend that they cannot be restored to their former position as owners of the property because the Boothes have sold it and that they would suffer unconscionable injury if the statute is enforced. Plaintiffs do not explain how or point to evidence showing they altered their position as a result of the contract. They admit that there was no contract until after the Boothes had purchased the property at the sheriff's sale; thus, their position as nonowners of the property is not altered by enforcement of the statute. [*Affirmed*].

Case Questions

1. What are the four types of part performance that the court says will defeat a statute of frauds defense relating to an oral contract to sell land?

2. What was the part performance the plaintiffs claimed they had made in this case?

3. Why does the court conclude that the plaintiffs have not made a part performance?

4. If you plan to buy or sell real estate, what should you do to avoid the statute of frauds?

Collateral Promise to Pay Another's Debt

A *collateral promise* is a secondary one. It is not Janet's promise to pay Joan's debt, which is an original or primary promise. A collateral contract arises only from Janet's promise to pay Joan's debt if Joan does not. Under the statute of frauds, only collateral contracts must be in writing.

Cannot Be Performed within One Year

The statute of frauds applies to a contract the parties cannot perform within one year after its making. Courts usually interpret the one-year requirement to mean that the contract must specify a period of performance longer than one year. Thus, an oral contract for services that last twenty months is not enforceable. But an oral contract for services to be completed "by" a date twenty months away is enforceable. The difference is that the latter contract can be performed within one year, even if it actually takes longer than that to perform it.

As interpreted by the courts, the statute of frauds applies only to executory contracts that the parties cannot perform within a year. Once one of the parties has completed his or her performance for the other, that party can enforce an oral multiyear contract.

Sale of Goods of $500 or More

Under the UCC, the statute of frauds covers sales of goods of $500 or more. Modifications to such contracts are also included. Table 8–3 lists exceptions to the writing requirement for sale-of-goods contracts.

Others

In addition to the basic contracts covered by the statute of frauds, other contracts must be in writing in various states. Most states require insurance policies to be written. Several states require written estimates in contracts for automobile repair.

The Parol Evidence Rule

Like the statute of frauds, the **parol evidence rule** influences the form of contracts. This rule states that parties to a complete and final written contract cannot introduce oral evidence in court that changes the intended meaning of the written terms.

The parol evidence rule applies only to evidence of oral agreements made at the time of or prior to the written contract. It does not apply to oral modifications coming after the parties have made the written contract (although the statute of frauds may apply).

Suppose that Chris Consumer wants to testify in court that a merchant of an Ultima washing machine gave him an oral six-month warranty on the machine, even though the $450 written contract specified "no warranties." If the warranty was made after Chris signed the contract, he may testify about its existence. Otherwise, the parol evidence rule prevents him from testifying about an oral agreement that changes the terms of the written contract.

TABLE 8–3   Exceptions to Statute-of-Frauds Requirement That Sale-of-Goods Contracts Be in Writing

Contract for goods specially manufactured for the buyer on which the seller had begun performance

Contract for goods for which payment has been made and accepted or that have been received and accepted

Contract for goods in which the party being sued admits in court or pleadings that the contract has been made

Contract for goods between merchants in which the merchant sued has received a written notice from the other merchant confirming the contract and in which merchant sued does not object to the confirmation within ten days

An exception to the parol evidence rule allows evidence of oral agreement that merely explains the meaning of written terms without changing the terms. Also, oral evidence that changes the meaning of written terms can be given if necessary to prevent fraud.

Other Contract Issues

Once you know how a contract is formed, there are other important contract issues to understand. These issues include interpretation of contracts, assignment of contracts, performance of contracts, and discharge of contracts. The next sections discuss these issues.

12. Interpretation of Contracts

If each party is satisfied with the other's performance under a contract, there is no problem with interpreting the contract's terms. But when disagreement about contractual performance exists, interpretation of the terms often becomes necessary. Courts have devised several rules to assist in interpreting contracts.

Common words are given their usual meaning. "A rose is a rose is a rose," said the poet, and a court will interpret this common word to refer to a flower. However, if the word has a particular *trade usage,* courts will give it that meaning. In a contract in the wine trade, the term "rose" would not refer to a flower at all but to a type of wine.

Some words have special legal meanings. A party to a contract had best appreciate that courts give legal terms their legal meaning. The buyer of radios may think that a contractual phrase calling for "delivery to the buyer on November 20" means that the seller will take the radios to the buyer's place of business, but it does not.

Delivery is a legal term referring to the transfer of possession from the seller to the buyer. It does not make the seller responsible for "shipping" the radios to the buyer. Furthermore, the UCC says that when the contract states no place for delivery, the place of delivery is the seller's place of business. The buyer will have to take delivery of the radios at the seller's place of business on November 20. Because some terms have both common and legal meanings, a person should have an attorney examine contracts drawn up by others.

Many businesses today use printed form contracts. Sometimes the parties to one of these printed contracts type or handwrite additional terms. What happens when the typed or handwritten terms contradict the printed terms? What if the printed terms of a contract state "no warranties," but the parties have written in a ninety-day warranty? In such a case, courts interpret handwritten terms to control typed terms and typed terms to control printed ones (see Figure 8.3). The written warranty will be enforced since the writing is the best evidence of the parties' true intention.

Another rule is that when only one of the parties drafts (draws up) a contract, courts will interpret ambiguous or vague terms against the party that drafts them. Courts often apply this rule to insurance contracts.

FIGURE 8.3

Interpretation of contract terms: Handwriting is the best evidence of intention.

13. Assignment of Contracts

Electronics, Inc., sells 250 radios on credit at $20 apiece to Radio Land Retail. Electronics then sells its rights under the contract to Manufacturers' Credit Co. When payment is due, can Manufacturers' Credit legally collect the $5,000 owed to Electronics by Radio Land? This transaction is controlled by the law of **assignment,** which is a transfer (generally a sale) of rights under a contract. Figure 8.4 shows the transaction and introduces important terms.

There is an important exception to the rule that assignees are subject to assignors' defenses. Under the UCC, an assignee, called a *holder in due course* who takes an assignment of rights through a *negotiable instrument* or *document,* will not be subject to the personal contract defenses of an assignor. To be negotiable, an instrument or document must be signed by the obligor (the party bound by legal obligation) and must contain certain language.

When an assignor assigns rights, he or she makes an implied warranty that the rights are valid. If the assignee is unable to enforce the rights against

FIGURE 8.4

Assignment.

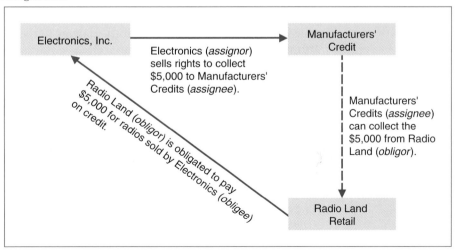

the obligor because of illegality, incapacity, or breach of contract, the assignee can sue the assignor. But the assignor does not guarantee that the obligor is able to pay the claim.

Notice of Assignment

When an assignment is made, an assignee should notify the obligor immediately. Otherwise, the obligor may perform for the obligee-assignor. If Radio Land pays Electronics before being notified by Manufacturers' Credit of the assignment, Radio Land cannot be held liable to Manufacturers' Credit.

A dishonest or careless assignor may assign the same contract rights to two different assignees. Notification of the obligor is especially important in this situation. In most states, the law says that the first assignee to notify the obligor has priority no matter which assignee receives the first assignment of rights.

Contracts That Cannot Be Assigned

Although most contracts can be assigned, certain ones cannot. An assignment that increases the burden of performance to the obligor cannot be assigned. For instance, a right to have goods shipped to the buyer's place of business cannot be assigned by an Atlanta buyer to a Miami buyer if a New York seller has to ship the goods to Miami instead of Atlanta. Similarly, a *requirements contract* to supply a retail buyer with all the radios needed cannot be assigned because it depends upon the buyer's personal situation.

Most states regulate the assignment of wages. They limit the amount of wages a wage earner can assign to protect wage earners and their families.

A party to a contract cannot assign (delegate) performance of duties under a contract when performance depends on the character, skill, or training of that party. Otherwise, duties under a contract can be assigned as well as rights.

14. Contracts Benefiting a Third Party

The performance of a contract may benefit third persons who are not parties to the contract. Such persons are called **third-party beneficiaries.** In general, persons who are not parties to a contract have no rights to sue to enforce the contract or to get damages for breach of contract. However, a third party beneficiary can sue if the parties to the contract *intended* to benefit that person.

For instance, if Ajax Co. owes First National Bank $50,000, and if Ajax performs $50,000 of work for Nadir, Inc., Ajax may contract to have Nadir pay First National $50,000. In this instance, First National is a *creditor beneficiary* of the contract between Ajax and Nadir.

When the performance under a contract is meant as a gift to a third party, that person is a *donee beneficiary*. Donee beneficiaries can sue the party who owes them a performance under a breached contract, but they cannot sue the party who contracted to make them a gift. The beneficiary of a life insurance policy is usually a donee beneficiary.

An *incidental beneficiary* is a third party who unintentionally benefits from a contract. The incidental beneficiary has no rights under a contract. If merchant A contracts to have security service patrol her property—a contract that will likely also protect the other merchants on the block—and if one evening when the service fails to show up merchant B on the block is burglarized, B cannot sue the security service for breach of contract. B is only an incidental beneficiary of the contract between A and the service.

15. Performance of Contracts

At the time parties reach agreement under a contract, the **duty of performance** becomes binding. Each party must perform the consideration promised to the other. Failure to perform breaches the contract.

Conditions

Parties often put conditions into a contract that affect its performance. If something must take place in the future before a party has a duty to perform, it is called a **condition precedent.** For example, a building developer may contract to buy certain land "when the city of Euphoria annexes it." The annexation is a condition precedent to the developer's duty to purchase the land.

A **condition subsequent** excuses contractual performance if some future event takes place. A marine insurance policy that terminates shipping loss coverage "if war is declared" contains a condition subsequent.

Under **concurrent conditions** each party's contractual performance is triggered by the other party's tending (offering) performance. In a contract for the purchase of land, the performing obligations of the seller and buyer are concurrent conditions. The significance of a concurrent condition is that a party must offer to perform before legally holding the other party for nonperformance. The land buyer must offer to pay for the land before suing the seller for failing to perform.

The conditions discussed above may be express or implied. **Express conditions** are set forth in the contract. **Implied conditions** do not appear in the contract but are implied by law.

Levels of Performance

A party to a contract may not always perfectly perform duties under it. The more complex a contract is, the more difficult it is for a party to complete every aspect of performance. Courts generally recognize three levels of specific performance.

1. COMPLETE PERFORMANCE recognizes that a contracting party has fulfilled every duty required by the contract. Payment of money, for example, is a contractual duty of performance that a party can perform completely. A party that performs completely is entitled to a complete performance by the other party and may sue to enforce this right.

2. SUBSTANTIAL PERFORMANCE represents a less-than-complete performance. A contracting party has honestly attempted to perform but has fallen short. Because of the complexity of building contractors' work, they often are able to reach substantial performance but not complete performance. One who substantially performs is entitled to the price promised by the other less that party's damages.

3. MATERIAL BREACH is a level of performance below what is reasonably acceptable. A party that has materially breached a contract cannot sue the other party for performance and is liable for damages arising from the breach.

TABLE 8–4   Events That Discharge a Party to a Contract

Occurrence of a condition subsequent
Nonoccurrence of a condition precedent
Material breach by the other party
Legal surrender of the right to enforce performance (**waiver**)
Mutual agreement to rescind
Expiration of the statute of limitations for enforceability
The substitution by agreement of one party for another on a contract (**novation**)
Impossibility of performance
Commercial impracticality

---

16. Discharge of Contracts

A party to a contract is **discharged** when the party is released from all further obligation of performance. Of course, complete performance discharges a party to a contract. Table 8–4 lists other events that create discharge.

Impossibility of Performance

One event that discharges a party's obligation of performance deserves special attention. A party is discharged because of **impossibility of performance.**

If the subject matter of the contract is destroyed, the contract becomes impossible to perform. When a contract exists for the sale of a building, and the building burns, the seller is discharged from performance. Likewise, when there is a contract for personal services, and the party promising the services becomes ill or dies, the party receives discharge from performances.

The party that promises performance that becomes illegal is also discharged because of impossibility of performance. Mere increased difficulty or reduced profitability, however, does not constitute impossibility of performance.

Commercial Impracticability

Under the UCC a party to a sale-of-goods contract receives discharge from performance because of **commercial impracticability.** The *impracticability* standard is not as difficult to meet as the *impossibility* standard. What constitutes impracticability of performance depends upon the circumstances of the situation. For instance, a manufacturer may be discharged from an obligation to make goods for a buyer when the manufacturer's major source of raw materials is unexpectedly interrupted. But if the raw materials are reasonably available from another supplier, the manufacturer may not receive discharge because of impracticability.

17. Trends in Contract Law

This chapter has given you an appreciation of the influence of contract law on private commercial transactions. To this end, the discussion has centered on the rules of contract law. Legal enforceability of contractual agreements provides an important framework for promoting certainty and efficiency in commercial dealings.

In general, trends in contract law do not affect the basic rules discussed in this chapter. Other chapters in the book develop many of the trends that affect contract law today. They deal with specific types of contracts or the use of contracts in particular situations. Still, several trends not mentioned elsewhere deserve attention here.

Contractual Relationships between Businesses

As commercial transactions have grown increasingly complex, courts and legislatures have created more and more exceptions to traditional, fairly inflexible requirements of contract formation. These exceptions reflect an attempt to accommodate law to the actual reality of business dealings. For instance, UCC provisions on modification of contracts without consideration, open-ended contract terms, and contract formation by course of dealing are exceptions to traditional rules.

Similarly, courts have demonstrated greater willingness in recent years to grant damages based on one party's reasonable reliance on another's promises instead of merely on the party's expectations under a formal contract. This development reflects attempts to conform law to actual behavior in a complicated business world.

Increasingly, businesses are taking contracts to court. A study by University of Wisconsin law professor Mark Galanter shows a several hundred percent rise in contract disputes filed in federal courts since 1960. Today, contract disputes represent the largest single category of cases filed in federal courts. Professor Galanter attributes this growth in contract litigation to businesses suing each other over contractual performance.

Finally, many contracting parties do not seek legal enforcement of breached agreements. Often, parties use arbitration, mediation, and negotiation when business problems arise under contracts. They avoid the time-consuming, expensive, and uncertain litigation process.

Contractual Relationships between Businesses and Employees

A recent statistic asserts that more than half of the country's biggest corporations now have employment contracts for top management. This figure represents a 50 percent increase since 1982. Contract negotiation is becoming increasingly important for many executives.

Most lower-level workers still do not have express contracts with their employers. Employers may terminate the employment of these workers at will. However, courts in growing numbers have been willing to take statements made by employers in personnel manuals and other documents and use them as a basis for implying contract rights for employees.

Contractual Relationships between Businesses and Consumers

A major trend in contract law has been the passage of many statutes affecting contracts between businesses and consumers. Government has stepped in at both the federal and state levels to protect consumers as they make contracts with businesses.

One development affecting business and consumer contracts has been enactment of "plain English" statutes in several states. These states require that standard business and consumer form contracts be written in a clearly understandable way. Drafters of such contracts must avoid legal expressions not ordinarily comprehended by consumers. More than thirty states have related statutes directed specifically at insurance contracts. A number of federal laws affecting readability also apply to specific types of contracts.

18. Contractual Ethics

In general, ethical concerns are increasingly reflected in how courts decide contractual disputes. Although the traditional rules of contract law are still very important, they cannot always be used to predict what courts will do when one party acts in *bad faith* or violates the *expectations* that another party brings to a business arrangement.

Involved in all lawsuits are not only legal issues but also the ethical values that society holds regarding appropriate business practices. Business-persons sometimes argue that jurors do not understand business dealings, and this is likely true. At the same time, however, juries may also be operating from a different set of ethical expectations than a segment of the business community. When this happens, large verdicts against business defendants may surprise the business community.

Eventually, ethical values may provide the basis for legal rules. In contract law the growing use of promissory estoppel and implied contract doctrine shows the willingness of courts to make binding business arrangements that in the past would have been unenforceable without an express contract. It is easy to understand these changes in terms of the good-faith expectations of the parties to business arrangements and in light of society's evolving ethical standards.

Key Terms

Review Questions and Problems

Basic Concepts

1. *Contract Law in Private Enterprise*
   Discuss the importance of contract law to the private market system. How does contract law provide flexibility and precision in business dealings?

2. *Sources of Contract Law*
   (a) What are the sources of contract law?
   (b) What is the UCC?

3. *Classification of Contracts*
   Dalton discovers that an antique car dealer has misrepresented an old car that Dalton bought for $75,000. The dealer represented that the car had been owned by Al Capone, which was untrue. What does it mean to say that the contract for the sale of the car is voidable? Explain.

4. *Breach of Contract*
   Gustavson contracts with Sanders to buy 51 percent of the stock of Gilmet Corporation. When Sanders breaches the contract, Gustavson sues for specific performance. Is specific performance an appropriate remedy under these circumstances? Explain.

Contract Formation

5. *Offer to Contract*
   Condor Equipment Company offers to sell Snappy Jack Biscuits, Inc., a dough-cutting machine. The offer states: "This offer expires Friday noon." On Thursday morning, the sales manager for Condor calls the president of Snappy Jack and explains that the machine has been sold to another purchaser. Discuss whether Condor has legally revoked its offer to Snappy Jack.

6. *Acceptance of Offer*
   Fielding Bros. offers to ship six furnaces to Central City Heating and Cooling Co. for $4,500 cash. Central City accepts on the condition that Fielding give 120 days' credit. Has a contract resulted? Explain.

7. *Voluntary Consent*
   Explain the legal difference between unilateral and bilateral mistake.

8. *Consideration*
   Jefferson and Goldberg enter a contract for the sale of five acres of land at $10,000 per acre. Later, Goldberg, the buyer, asks if Jefferson will agree to modify the contract to $9,000 per acre. (a) Jefferson agrees. Is Jefferson's promise binding on him? (b) Would your answer be different if five used cars were being sold instead of five acres of land?

9. *Capacity of Parties to Contract*
   Describe the circumstances under which an adult lacks the capacity to contract.

10. *Illegal Contracts*
    Hunt signs an equipment lease contract with Edwards Rental. The contract contains a clause stating: "Lessor disclaims all liability arising from injuries caused by use of this equipment." Because the equipment has been improperly serviced by Edwards Rental, Hunt is injured while using it. If Hunt sues, will the disclaimer clause likely be enforced? Explain.

11. *Written Contracts*
    Elegante Haberdashery telephones an order to Nordic Mills for 500 men's shirts at $15 each. Each shirt will carry the Elegante label and have the Elegante trademark over the pocket. After the shirts are manufactured, Elegante refuses to accept delivery of them and raises the statute of frauds as a defense. Discuss whether this defense applies to these facts.

Other Contractual Issues

12. *Interpretation of Contracts*
    Gus contracts to buy a used car from Cars Galore, Inc. The printed contract specifies "no warranties." But Gus and the sales manager of Cars handwrite into the contract a ninety-day guarantee on the transmission. If the transmission fails after sixty days, is there a warranty protecting Gus? Explain.

13. *Assignment of Contracts*
    Franchetti Rifle Distributors assigns a $20,000 claim against Top Gun, Inc., to the Zenith

Collection Agency. When Zenith sues Top Gun, Top Gun asserts that it rejected a shipment of rifles from Franchetti, out of which the claim arose, because they had defective trigger guards. Explain whether Top Gun can properly assert its defense against plaintiff Zenith.

14. *Contracts Benefiting a Third Party*
    What is the distinction between a creditor beneficiary and an incidental beneficiary? Explain.

15. *Performance of Contracts*
    Ace Contracting constructs an office building for Realty Enterprises. Realty's tenants quickly find a number of minor problems with the plumbing and insulation of the new building. When Realty contacts Ace about bringing its work up to standard, Ace promises to correct the problems, but never does. (a) Can Realty rescind the contract? (b) What are Realty's legal remedies?

16. *Discharge of Contracts*
    A tripling of prices by an illegal cartel of uranium producers caused Westinghouse Electric Corp. to default on uranium delivery contracts to a number of utility companies. The companies sued and Westinghouse settled. If the case had gone to trial, what defense might Westinghouse have raised to excuse its nonperformance under the contracts?

17. *Trends in Contract Law*
    Explain why businesses are increasingly suing one another for breach of contract.

18. *Contractual Ethics*
    When do traditional rules of contract law not adequately predict what a court will decide in a contractual dispute? Discuss.

Terminology Review

For each term in the left-hand column, match the most appropriate description in the right-hand column.

1. Accord and satisfaction
2. Assignment
3. Bilateral contract
4. Condition precedent
5. Executory contract
6. Firm offer
7. Material breach
8. Parol evidence rule
9. Quasi-contract
10. Rescission
11. Voidable contract

a. A recovery based on unjust enrichment
b. A merchant's written promise to hold open an offer
c. A contract that binds one party but allows the other party to withdraw legally
d. A future uncertain event that must occur before performance is due
e. A level of contractual performance below what is reasonably acceptable
f. Settlement and payment of a disputed debt by mutual agreement
g. The doctrine that prohibits use of oral evidence to alter or vary the terms of certain written contracts
h. A contract the consideration for which is a binding promise given by each party
i. A remedy that requires that each party return what it got from the other
j. A transfer of contractual rights
k. A contract the parties have not yet performed

TORTS IN THE BUSINESS ENVIRONMENT

Business Decision

Attacked!

You own University Heights Apartments, a business that rents primarily to students. One evening, your tenant Sharon is attacked by an intruder who forces the lock on the sliding glass door of her ground-floor apartment. Sharon's screams attract the attention of Darryl, your resident manager, who comes to Sharon's aid. Together, he and Sharon drive the intruder off, but not before they both are badly cut by the intruder.

Is the intruder liable for what he has done?

Do you have legal responsibilities to Sharon and Darryl?

What should you consider doing at your apartments?

In the Business Decision above the intruder has committed an intentional tort and is, of course, liable for damages. Unfortunately, few such criminals have substantial financial resources, so they are seldom sued. As owner of the apartments, you have a duty to use reasonable care to protect tenants. If the jury does not consider the sliding glass door lock a reasonable protection from intruders, you may be liable to the tenant for negligence. In addition, you may be strictly liable to your injured employee under workers' compensation law. You should consult with an attorney about reasonable steps to take at the apartments to protect your tenants and employees.

The word **tort** means "wrong." Legally, a tort is a civil wrong other than a breach of contract. Most torts involve injuries to persons or property. These injuries may be crimes as well as torts, but the doctrine of tort itself is civil rather than criminal. The usual remedy for a tort is dollar damages. Behavior that constitutes a tort is called *tortious* behavior. One who commits a tort is a *tortfeasor*.

This chapter divides torts into three main categories: intentional torts, negligence torts, and strict liability torts. Intentional torts involve deliberate actions that cause injury. Negligence torts involve injury following a failure to use reasonable care. Strict liability torts impose legal responsibility for injury even though a liable party neither intentionally nor negligently causes the injury.

Important to torts are the concepts of duty and causation. One is not liable for another's injury unless he or she has a *duty* toward the person injured. And, of course, there is usually no liability for injury unless one has *caused* the injury. We explain these concepts under the discussion of negligence, where they are most relevant.

This chapter also covers the topic of damages. The topic concerns the business community because huge damage awards, frequently against businesses, have become common in recent years. Finally, the chapter explores some alternatives to the current tort system, including workers' compensation.

Intentional Torts

An important element in the following torts is *intent,* as we are dealing with intentional torts. **Intent** is usually defined as the desire to bring about certain results. But in some circumstances the meaning is even broader, including not only desired results but also results that are "substantially likely" to result from an action. Recently, employers who knowingly exposed employees to toxic substances without warning them of the dangers have been sued for committing the intentional tort of battery. The employers did not desire their employees' injuries, but these injuries were "substantially likely" to result from the failure to warn.

The following sections explain the basic types of intentional torts. Table 9–1 lists these torts.

1. Assault and Battery

An **assault** is the placing of another in immediate apprehension for his or her physical safety. "Apprehension" has a broader meaning than "fear." It includes the expectation that one is about to be physically injured. The person who intentionally creates such apprehension in another is guilty of the tort of assault. Many times a battery follows an assault. A **battery** is an illegal

---

TABLE 9–1   Types of Intentional Torts

Assault and battery
Intentional infliction of mental distress
Invasion of privacy
False imprisonment and malicious prosecution
Trespass
Conversion
Defamation
Common law business torts
Statutory competitive torts
Constitutional torts

touching of another. As used here, "illegal" means that the touching is done without justification and without the consent of the person touched. The touching need not cause injury.

A store manager who threatens an unpleasant customer with a wrench, for example, is guilty of assault. Actually hitting the customer with the wrench would constitute battery.

2. Intentional Infliction of Mental Distress

Intentional **infliction of mental distress** is a battery to the emotions. It arises from outrageous, intentional conduct that carries a strong probability of causing mental distress to the person at whom it is directed. Usually, one who sues on the basis of an intentional infliction of mental distress must prove that the defendant's outrageous behavior caused not only mental distress but also physical symptoms, such as headaches or sleeplessness.

The most common cases of intentional infliction of mental distress (also called "emotional distress") have concerned employees who have been discriminated against or fired. Many such cases, however, do not involve the type of outrageous conduct necessary for the mental distress tort. In the following case, the court decides whether or not an employer's conduct is outrageous. Pay special attention to the precedent cases the court discusses in its opinion.

VAN STAN V. FANCY COLOURS & COMPANY
125 F.3d 563 (7th Cir. 1997)

WOOD, JR., J.: . . . After Fancy Colours & Company ("Fancy Colours") terminated his employment, Michael D. Van Stan ("Van Stan") sued Fancy Colours contending that it fired him in violation of the Americans with Disabilities Act ("ADA") and that Fancy Colours' conduct in firing him amounted to intentional infliction of emotional distress. A jury awarded Van Stan damages of $150,000 for intentional infliction of emotional distress but determined that Fancy Colours had not violated the ADA. We reverse the entry of judgment against Fancy Colours on the intentional infliction of emotional distress claim.

Under Illinois law, which the parties both agree applies, a plaintiff may recover damages for intentional infliction of emotional distress only if he establishes that (1) the defendant's conduct was extreme and outrageous, (2) the defendant intended to inflict severe emotional distress or knew that there was at least a high probability that his conduct would inflict severe emotional distress, and (3) the defendant's conduct did cause severe emotional distress. Conduct is extreme and outrageous only if "the conduct has been so outrageous in character and so extreme in degree, as

to go beyond all possible bounds of decency. . . ." "Mere insults, indignities, threats, annoyances, petty oppressions, or other trivialities" do not amount to extreme and outrageous conduct, nor does conduct "characterized by malice or a degree of aggravation which would entitle the plaintiff to punitive damages for another tort." Moreover, we judge whether conduct is extreme and outrageous on an objective standard based on all the facts and circumstances of a particular case. Thus, to serve as a basis for recovery, the defendant's conduct must be such that the "recitation of facts to an average member of the community would arouse his resentment against the actor, and lead him to exclaim 'Outrageous!' "

In the employment context, Illinois courts have recognized that personality conflicts and questioning of job performance are "unavoidable aspects of employment" and that "frequently, they produce concern and distress." The courts have reasoned, however, that if such incidents were actionable, nearly all employees would have a cause of action for intentional infliction of emotional distress. Thus, Illinois courts have limited recovery to cases in which the employer's conduct has been truly egregious. See, e.g., *Pavilon v. Kaferly* . . . (the employer, knowing that the plaintiff was susceptible to emotional distress, offered her money for sexual favors, fired her after she refused, and after he fired her, threatened to kill her, to rape her, and to file a legal action challenging her rights to custody of her child and attempted to disrupt her new employment relationship); *Milton v. Illinois Bell Tel. Co.* . . . (the employer engaged in an extensive course of disciplinary and harassing conduct to coerce the plaintiff to falsify work reports).

In contrast, Illinois courts have denied recovery for distress resulting from recognizably reprehensible conduct which has been linked to an employer's legitimate interest. In *Harris v. First Fed. Sav. & Loan Ass'n of Chicago* an Illinois appellate court held that a plaintiff who alleged that her employer criticized, demoted, and discharged her after she reported allegedly criminal activity to her supervisor did not state a claim because she did not allege that her employer engaged in this course of conduct to coerce her into engaging in illegal activity. While the court characterized the employer's conduct as "reprehensible," the court held that it did not rise to the level of extreme and outrageous conduct because the employer merely acted out of displeasure with the plaintiff's exercise of judgment regarding another employee's conduct.

Recognizing this high threshold, this Court and other federal courts applying Illinois law have denied recovery to plaintiffs who alleged that their employers subjected them to a continuous series of intentionally discriminatory acts. For example, in *Harriston* we held that the plaintiff failed to allege conduct that rose to the level of extreme and outrageous conduct even though she contended that among other things her employer refused to allow her to supervise white subordinates, reprimanded her for no reason, refused to allow her to participate in a management incentive fund, forced her out of her management position, promised her a promotion she never received, took away from her major accounts and gave her less lucrative accounts in return, excluded her from office

activities, monitored her telephone calls with an eavesdropping device and ignored concerns of her health and safety after her personal property was damaged on company property. See also *Briggs v. North Shore Sanitary Dist.* (Allegations that the plaintiff's employer and fellow employees hung a pickaninny doll in her office, subjected her to racial slurs, excluded her from office social activities, placed her on probation, and refused to train her properly did not rise to the level of extreme and outrageous conduct, but allegations that co-workers exposed her to toxic fumes for more than eight hours did).

In this case, Van Stan maintains that viewing the evidence in the light most favorable to him, a reasonable jury could have found that Walters [Van Stan's supervisor,] and other Fancy Colours supervisors knew that Van Stan suffered from a bipolar disorder, that Fancy Colours fired Van Stan because his disorder required him to work less hours, that Walters telephoned Van Stan at home while he was on vacation to inform him that he had been terminated and that after Van Stan requested an explanation, Walters falsely told Van Stan that he was being fired for low productivity. While we do not mean to condone such conduct, we do not believe that this course of conduct was akin to the type of egregious conduct present in *Pavilon* and *Milton,* nor do we believe that it exceeded all possible bounds of decency. Thus, as a matter of law Fancy Colours' conduct did not rise to the level of extreme and outrageous conduct, and Fancy Colours is entitled to a judgment in its favor. [*Reversed*].

Case Questions

1. What was the conduct that plaintiff Van Stan claimed was "extreme and outrageous"?

2. What does the court say about what would happen if more "personality conflicts and questioning of job performance" amounted to intentional infliction of mental and emotional distress?

3. Why is the Illinois case in federal court?

In the business world, other examples of infliction of mental distress come about from the efforts of creditors to extract payment from their debtors. Frequent, abusive, threatening phone calls by creditors might provide the basis for a claim of intentional infliction of mental distress. As torts go, this one is of fairly recent origin. It is a judge-made tort, which furnishes a good example of how the courts are becoming increasingly sensitive to the range of injuries for which compensation is appropriate. In some states, courts have gone so far as to establish liability for carelessly inflicted mental distress, such as the distress of a mother who sees her child negligently run down by a delivery truck.

3. Invasion of Privacy

The tort of **invasion of privacy** is one that is still in the early stages of legal development. As the statutes and court cases recognize it, the tort at present comprises three principal invasions of personal interest. An invasion of any one of these areas of interest is sufficient to trigger liability.

Most commonly, liability will be imposed on a defendant who appropriates the plaintiff's name or likeness for his or her own use. Many advertisers and marketers have been required to pay damages to individuals when pictures of them have been used without authorization to promote products, or when their names and identities have been used without permission for promotional purposes. Before using anyone's picture or name, an advertiser must obtain a proper release from that person to avoid possible liability. Appropriating another's name and identity in order to secure credit is an additional example of this invasion-of-privacy tort.

A second invasion of privacy is the defendant's intrusion upon the plaintiff's physical solitude. Illegal searches or invasions of home or possessions, illegal wiretapping, and persistent and unwanted telephoning can provide the basis for this invasion-of-privacy tort. In one case, a woman even recovered damages against a photographer who entered her sickroom and snapped a picture of her. Employers who enter their employees' homes without permission have also been sued successfully for invasions of privacy. If the invasion of privacy continues, it may be enjoined by the court. Jacqueline Kennedy Onassis sought and obtained an injunction that forbade a certain photographer from getting too close to her and her children. Under this tort, the invasion of physical solitude must be highly objectionable to a reasonable person.

The third invasion of personal interest that gives rise to the invasion-of-privacy tort is the defendant's public disclosure of highly objectionable, private information about the plaintiff. A showing of such facts can be the basis for a cause of action, even if the information is true. Thus, publishing in a newspaper that the plaintiff does not pay his or her debts has been ruled to create liability for the defendant creditor. Communicating the same facts to a credit-reporting agency or the plaintiff's employer usually does not impose liability, however. In these cases, there has been no disclosure to the public in general. Also, the news media are protected under the First Amendment when they publish information about public officials and other public figures.

4. False Imprisonment and Malicious Prosecution

Claims of **false imprisonment** stem most frequently in business from instances of shoplifting. This tort is the intentional unjustified confinement of a nonconsenting person. Although most states have statutes that permit merchants or their employees to detain customers suspected of shoplifting, this detention must be a reasonable one. The unnecessary use of force, lack of reasonable suspicion of shoplifting, or an unreasonable length of confinement can cause the merchant to lose the statutory privilege. The improperly detained customer is then able to sue for false imprisonment. Allegations of battery are also usually made if the customer has been touched.

The tort of **malicious prosecution** is often called *false arrest*. Malicious prosecution arises from causing someone to be arrested criminally without proper grounds. It occurs, for instance, when the arrest is accomplished simply to harass someone. In Albany, New York, a jury awarded a man $200,000 for malicious prosecution. His zipper had broken, leaving his fly open, and a store security guard had him arrested for indecent exposure even after he explained that he had not noticed the problem.

5. Trespass

To enter another's land without consent or to remain there after being asked to leave constitutes the tort of **trespass.** A variation on the trespass tort arises when something (such as particles of pollution) is placed on another's land without consent. Although the usual civil action for trespass asks for an injunction to restrain the trespasser, the action may also ask for damages.

Union pickets walking on company property (in most instances), customers refusing to leave a store after being asked to do so, and unauthorized persons entering restricted areas are all examples of trespass. Note that trespass is often a crime as well as a tort. Intentional wrongdoing is frequently criminal.

6. Conversion

Conversion is the wrongful and unlawful exercise of dominion (power) and control over the personal property of another. Conversion deprives the proper owner of lawful rights in the property. The deprivation may be either temporary or permanent, but it must constitute a serious invasion of the owner's rights. Abraham Lincoln once convinced an Illinois court that a defendant's action in riding the plaintiff's horse for 15 miles was not sufficiently serious to be a conversion since the defendant had returned the horse in good condition. The plaintiff had left the horse with the defendant to be stabled and fed.

Conversion arises often in business situations. Stealing property or purchasing stolen property (even innocently) is a conversion. Failing to return properly acquired property at the designated time, delivering property to the wrong party, and destruction and alteration of property are all conversions if the deprivation of ownership rights is serious or long-lasting. Even if she or he intends to return it, one who converts is absolutely liable for any damage done to property. A warehouse operator who improperly transfers stored goods from a designated to a nondesignated warehouse is absolutely liable when a tornado destroys the goods or when a thief steals them.

7. Defamation

Defamation is the publication of untrue statements about another that hold up that individual's character or reputation to contempt and ridicule. "Publication" means that the untruth must be made known to third parties. If defamation is oral, it is called **slander.** Written defamation, or defamation published over radio or television, is termed **libel.**

False accusations of dishonesty or inability to pay debts frequently bring on defamation suits in business relationships. Sometimes, such accusations arise during the course of a takeover attempt by one company of another through an offering to buy stock. In a recent instance, the chairman of one company called the chairman of a rival business "lying, deceitful, and treacherous" and charged that he "violated the standards by which decent men do business." If untrue, these remarks provide a good example of defamation of character. Punitive or punishment damages, as well as actual damages, may be assessed in defamation cases.

Individuals are not the only ones who can sue for defamation. A corporation can also sue for defamation if untrue remarks discredit the way the corporation conducts its business. Untruthfully implying that a company's entire management is dishonest or incompetent defames the corporation.

Because of the First Amendment, special rules regarding defamation apply to the news media. These media are not liable for the defamatory untruths they print about public officials and public figures unless plaintiffs can prove that the untruths were published with "malice" (evil intent, that is, the deliberate intent to injure) or with "reckless disregard for the truth." Public figures are those who have consciously brought themselves to public attention.

Plaintiffs' verdicts in defamation cases are often overturned by appellate courts. Because of the constitutional protection given to speech and the media, appellate judges reexamine trial evidence very closely to determine whether the necessary elements of defamation had been proven.

There are two basic defenses to a claim of defamation. One defense is that the statements made were true. *Truth* is an absolute defense. The second defense is that the statements arose from *privileged communications*. For example, statements made by legislators, judges, attorneys, and those involved in lawsuits are privileged under many circumstances.

Nearly one-third of all defamation suits are currently brought by employees against present and former employers. Often these suits arise when employers give job references on former employees who have been discharged for dishonesty. As a result, many employers will now not give job references or will do no more than verify that former employees did work for them.

8. Fraud

Business managers must be alert to the intentional tort of **fraud.** A fraud is an intentional misrepresentation of a material fact that is justifiably relied upon by someone to his or her injury. An intentional misrepresentation means a lie. The lie must be of a material fact—an important one. The victim of the fraud must justifiably rely on the misrepresentation and must suffer some injury, usually a loss of money or property.

Business frauds often involve the intentional misrepresentation of property or financial status. Lying about business assets or liabilities in order to get credit or a loan is a fraud. Likewise, intentionally misrepresenting that land is free from hazardous wastes when in fact you know that certain toxic chemicals are buried on the land constitutes fraud.

The previous chapter on contracts discussed fraud as voiding a contract. But fraud is also an intentional tort, and one who is a victim of fraud can sue for damages, including punitive or punishment damages. Fraud is both a common law intentional tort and a type of tort covered in many statutes that prohibit lying to a bank or in various documents that businesses must supply to the government. Note that frauds are sometimes also crimes. Chapter 10 discusses criminal frauds.

9. Common Law Business Torts

The label *business torts* embraces several different kinds of torts that involve intentional interference with business relations.

Injurious Falsehood

Injurious falsehood, sometimes called *trade disparagement,* is a common business tort. It consists of the publication of untrue statements that disparage the plaintiff's ownership of property or its quality. General disparagement of the plaintiff's business may also provide basis for liability. As a cause of action, injurious falsehood is similar to defamation of character. It differs, however, in that it usually applies to the plaintiff's property or business rather than character or reputation. The requirements of proof are also somewhat different. Defamatory remarks are presumed false unless the defendant can prove their truth. But in disparagement cases the plaintiff must establish the falsity of the defendant's statements. The plaintiff must also show actual damages arising from the untrue statements.

As an example of injurious falsehood, consider the cases filed by a major home products company. The complaints alleged that the defendants had distributed handouts that associated the company's familiar emblem of moon and stars with satanism—the worship of the devil. At the heart of this tort is the interference with the company's future sales.

Intentional Interference with Contractual Relations

A second type of business tort is **intentional interference with contractual relations.** Inducing employees to breach contracts with their employers can bring liability to third parties. Recently, a brokerage firm in New Orleans sued a competitor and obtained a judgment for several hundred thousand dollars because the competitor had induced a number of the firm's employees to break their employment contracts. In another suit, a jury awarded Pennzoil over $10 billion against Texaco for persuading Getty Oil to breach an agreement of merger with Pennzoil. After Texaco filed for bankruptcy, Pennzoil accepted a settlement of around $3 billion.

Obtaining Trade Secrets

Another variety of business tort arises from wrongfully obtaining a rival's trade secrets. The Fifth Circuit Court of Appeals has defined a **trade secret** as "any formula, pattern, device, or compilation of information which is used in one's business, and which gives him an opportunity to obtain an advantage over competitors who do not know or use it." Information that is general knowledge cannot be a trade secret.

Many times employees who leave their employment to go into competition with their employers are accused of misappropriating trade secrets. An employee may draw upon the general knowledge, skills, and experience he or she has gained in working for a former employer, but it is a tort for the employee to use specific customer lists, documents, or other trade secrets gained through previous employment. In addition to obtaining provable damages, someone whose trade secrets have been misappropriated will usually ask the court to enjoin the defendant from using trade secrets in competition with the plaintiff.

For a trade secret to remain a trade secret, a business must take active steps to keep the information confidential. A major soft-drink manufacturer once withdrew from a consumer market of 400 million people in India rather than reveal the secret of its cola-based mixture, as demanded by the Indian government.

10. Statutory Competitive Torts

Another common law business tort involves **unfair competition.** It includes "palming off" a competitor's goods as one's own, and misappropriating trademarks. In addition to being a common law tort, unfair competition also includes several statutory torts. A statutory tort, of course, is one created by statute. For instance, violation of the antitrust laws is a tort under the Clayton Act (see Chapter 11). The following discussions examine statutory torts of unfair competition involving trademarks, false advertising, patents, and copyrights.

Trademark Infringement

The law of trademarks covers trademarks, service marks, certification marks, and collective marks. A **trademark** is any mark, word, picture, or design that attaches to goods to indicate their source. If the mark is associated with a service, it is a *service mark*. A *certification mark* is used by someone other than its owner to certify the quality, point of origin, or other characteristic of goods or services. Use of a *collective mark* represents membership in a certain organization or association. McDonald's golden arches, the words and design of Coca-Cola, the Good Housekeeping Seal of Approval, the prancing horse of Ferrari, and the "union label" are all marks of one kind or another. In the discussion that follows, all marks are termed "trademarks."

The common law protects the use of trademarks, but since the **Lanham Act** of 1946, the principal protection has come from federal law. Trademark law recognizes that property rights extend beyond ownership of actual goods to the intangible aspects of goodwill that trademarks represent. In forbidding misappropriation of trademarks, the law prevents misappropriation of a company's goodwill and reputation. It protects both the company that owns the mark and the buyer of goods or services who relies upon it.

To acquire the protection of the Lanham Act, a company must register the trademark with the Patent and Trademark Office. A trademark in current use on goods and services in interstate commerce may be registered. Or a company can file an *intent-to-use* statement on a trademark and reserve rights in that mark for up to three years. To be registerable, a mark must be *uniquely distinctive* and *nondescriptive*. A mark that merely describes a use or characteristic of the product cannot generally be registered. A quick-order restaurant, for example, could not register the trademark "Fast Food."

Unauthorized use of a registered trademark constitutes the competitive tort of **infringement.** Infringement exists not only when the exact trademark is copied but also when the mark used resembles the protected trademark enough to confuse the public. The Lanham Act provides that any person who infringes on another's registered trademark in selling or advertising goods or services is liable for damages and subject to injunction. In instances of willful infringement, a court may award triple damages. Wendy's International, Inc., forced dozens of retailers to remove thousands of "Where's the beef?" T-shirts from their shelves. The shirts' manufacturer lacked the fast-food chain's permission to use the trademarked slogan.

A growing problem in recent years has been the deliberate counterfeiting of products. Levi's jeans, Rolex watches, and other well-known brand products have been copied and sold. The U.S. International Trade Commission estimates that the volume of counterfeiting has tripled in recent years.

Now Congress has made deliberate counterfeiting a felony, punishable by jail terms and substantial fines. It is also a federal crime to traffic knowingly in goods containing a counterfeit mark.

To maintain a trademark, the owner must prevent its misuse and unauthorized use. If the public comes to think that a registered trademark represents a general class of goods, rather than a single brand, registration and the right to sue for trademark infringement may be lost. For instance, employees of a popular cola beverage have been instructed always to ask for it at a restaurant by its famous trademarked name. If the restaurant brings a competitor's cola beverage instead of the one ordered, the employees are instructed to object strenuously to the substitution for the trademarked brand. It is all part of the attempt to preserve the uniqueness of the trademark. Table 9–2 gives examples of trademarks that have lost their uniqueness due to general use.

False Advertising

A tort related to but different from trademark infringement is the competitive tort of **false advertising.** The Lanham Act establishes an action for civil damages for any false description or representation of one's goods or services that may damage a competitor. This action need not involve trademark infringement.

Many different kinds of false advertising are actionable under the Lanham Act. For an advertiser to represent its product as "California redwood" when the wood is actually red oak might invite a tort action by anyone legitimately associated with the redwood industry. To portray a picture

---

TABLE 9–2   Trademarks Lost Due to General Use

Aspirin
Cellophane
Thermos
Monopoly (the game)
Escalator

of a competitor's product as one's own, as in an advertisement, is actionably false if the two products are not identical.

Under the Lanham Act company X could sue company Y only when company Y misrepresented its own products. However, in 1988 Congress amended the Lanham Act with the Trademark Law Revision Act. The new law now permits company X to sue company Y when company Y misrepresents company X's product (or service). Prior to 1988 misrepresentations of this latter kind were actionable only under the common law tort of injurious falsehood.

Patent Infringement

In the last century, a government official urged that the Patent Office be closed because there was nothing left to invent. Today, however, inventors file approximately 100,000 new patent applications every year. When granted, **patents** give their holders a seventeen-year legal monopoly over the use and licensing of new processes, products, machines, and other combinations of matter. Design patents can be obtained for shorter time periods. Underlying the grant of patents is the belief that the law should encourage invention by granting inventors exclusive rights to the profits of their efforts for a limited duration.

To be patentable, inventions must be *nonobvious, novel,* and *useful.* They also must be tangible applications of an idea. Discovery of a new fact about the universe—e.g., that individual molecules can be used in computer memory—does not in itself allow the discoverer to patent all future uses of that fact. Only when that fact is specifically applied through design of a new machine or process may it be patented.

Federal patent law permits the holder of a patent to bring a statutory tort action against anyone who infringes on the patent. The principal issues in most patent cases are:

- Whether the patent is valid
- Whether the defendant has infringed the patent

The plaintiff in patent cases usually seeks remedies of injunction and damages. Triple damages are available against defendants found guilty of "willful and wanton" infringement.

Interestingly, having a patent properly registered with the Patent Office does not conclusively establish its validity. It only creates a presumption of validity. In a large percentage of cases involving patents, courts find the patents to be either invalid or otherwise unenforceable. However, that percentage is smaller than before 1982, when the Court of Appeals for the Federal Circuit was created. That court now handles all patent infringement appeals.

New technologies lead to new issues of patent law. Of special current concern is the patentability of computer programs. In *Diamond v. Diehr and Lutton,* the Supreme Court held that a process for curing rubber did not become unpatentable simply because it incorporated a computer program. On the other hand, computer applications of mathematical formulas are not patentable. Another issue of present significance to patent law involves the extent to which new "genetically engineered" life forms can be patented. The Supreme Court has ruled that under some circumstances patent law does apply to protect the inventors of such life forms.

Copyright Infringement

Copyright law protects authors rather than inventors. An author creates works of a literary, dramatic, musical, graphic, choreographic, audio, or visual nature. Ranging from printed material to photographs to records and motion pictures, these works receive automatic federal protection under the Copyright Act of 1976 from the moment the author creates them. The copyright allows the holder to control the reproduction, display, distribution, and performance of a protected work. The copyright runs for the author's lifetime, plus fifty additional years.

Although copyright protection is automatic, a tort action for copyright infringement cannot be begun unless the author has properly filed copies of the protected work with the Copyright Office. And one who infringes on a copyright cannot be held liable for actual or statutory damages unless a copyright symbol or notice accompanies the protected work. When the author has observed the proper formalities, however, she or he may recover actual or statutory damages, attorney's fees, and any profits the infringer has made. Illegally reproduced copies may also be seized, and willful copyright violations are criminal offenses.

The law permits a *fair use* of copyrighted work for teaching, research, and reporting purposes. No royalty payments need be made to the author or composer. Whether or not use of copyrighted material is a "fair" one is a decision that courts must make on a case-by-case basis.

An important challenge to copyright law concerns protecting computer programming. Congress has granted copyright protection to the designs of integrated circuits. These circuits are designed into silicon chips used in computers and other electronic equipment. The new law gives ten years of copyright protection to any chips designed since July 1, 1983. The actual arrangement of an original program's letters and symbols is also copyrightable. But it is usually easy to program in a different way (perhaps use a different programming language) yet achieve almost exactly the same "look and feel" of the original program. Congress and the courts are presently considering how to protect computer programming through both copyright and patent law.

Negligence

The second major area of tort liability involves unreasonable behavior that causes injury. This area of tort is called **negligence.** In the United States more lawsuits allege negligence than any other single cause of action.

Negligence takes place when one who has a duty to act reasonably acts carelessly and causes injury to another. Actually, five separate elements make up negligence, and the following sections discuss these elements. Table 9–3 also summarizes them. In business, negligence can occur when employees cause injury to customers or others, when those invited to a business are injured because the business fails to protect them, when products are not carefully manufactured, when services, such as accounting services, are not carefully provided, and in many other situations. In the Business Decision that begins this chapter, the apartment owner may be negligently

TABLE 9–3   Elements of Negligence

Existence of a duty of care owed by the defendant to the plaintiff
Unreasonable behavior by the defendant that breaches the duty
Causation in fact
Proximate causation
An actual injury

liable to the tenant attacked by the intruder for failing to protect her reasonably.

11. Duty of Care

A critical element of the negligence tort is **duty.** Without a duty to another person, one does not owe that person reasonable care. Accidental injuries occur daily for which people other than the victim have no responsibility, legally or otherwise.

Duty usually arises out of a person's conduct or activity. A person doing something has a duty to use reasonable care and skill around others to avoid injuring them. Whether one is driving a car or manufacturing a product, she or he has a duty not to injure others by unreasonable conduct.

Usually, a person has no duty to avoid injuring others through *nonconduct*. There is no general duty requiring a sunbather at the beach to warn a would-be surfer that a great white shark is lurking offshore, even if the sunbather has seen the fin. There is moral responsibility but no legal duty present.

When there is a special relationship between persons, the situation changes. A person in a special relationship to another may have a duty to avoid unreasonable nonconduct. A business renting surfboards at the beach would probably be liable for renting a board to a customer who was attacked by a shark if it knew the shark was nearby and failed to warn the customer. The special business relationship between the two parties creates a duty to take action and makes the business liable for its unreasonable nonconduct.

In recent years, negligence cases against businesses for nonconduct have grown dramatically. Most of these cases have involved failure to protect customers from crimes. The National Crime Prevention Institute estimates that such cases have increased tenfold since the mid-1970s.

One famous case involved the Tailhook scandal. A group of male naval aviators was sexually groping female guests as they walked down the hallway at a Hilton hotel. (Remember that an unconsented-to touching is an intentional tort.) One of the females who was sexually touched sued the Hilton hotel for negligence in knowing of the aviators' behavior and failing to protect her. A jury awarded her a total of $6.7 million against Hilton.

In the case that follows, the New Jersey Supreme Court determines that an apartment owner is not liable for failing to protect tenants who are off apartment property. Note, however, that the Supreme Court had to reverse both the trial court and the court of appeals.

Kuzmicz v. Ivy Hill Park Apts., Inc.
147 N.J. 510 (N.J. Sup.Ct. 1997)

POLLOCK, J.: . . . Plaintiff Ireneusz Kuzmicz was a tenant of defendant Ivy Hill Park Apartments, Inc. (Ivy Hill), which owns an apartment complex in Newark. On the night of December 8, 1989, Kuzmicz was assaulted on a vacant lot owned by defendant Newark Board of Education (the Board). The lot is located between the complex and a grocery store owned by defendant Great Atlantic & Pacific Tea Company, Inc. (the A & P). The issue is whether under the circumstances of this case Ivy Hill owed Kuzmicz a duty to protect him by mending a bordering fence or warning him of the risk of assault on the Board's property.

The jury awarded Kuzmicz $175,000, apportioning liability: Kuzmicz twenty percent; the Board thirty percent; and Ivy Hill fifty percent. The Appellate Division affirmed. We granted Ivy Hill's petition for certification and now reverse.

Against this background, we consider whether Ivy Hill owed Kuzmicz a duty to protect him from the risk of assault on another's property. Our analysis begins with the fact that Kuzmicz was injured on land that Ivy Hill did not own or control. The question is whether Ivy Hill owed Kuzmicz a duty to protect him by warning him of the risk of off-premises criminal assaults or by making more exhaustive efforts to seal the fence. Ultimately, the determination of the existence of a duty is a question of fairness and public policy. Fairness, not foreseeability alone, is the test. Relevant to the determination of the fairness of the imposition of a duty on a landowner is the nature of the risk, the relationship of the parties, the opportunity to exercise care, and the effect on the public of the imposition of the duty.

Consistent with that analysis, we have found a landlord liable to a tenant for damages resulting from a burglary when the landlord failed to replace a broken dead-bolt lock on the tenant's apartment. The apartment house was in an area where break-ins were common, and the landlord had assured the tenant that it would repair the lock. Furthermore, a regulation of the Department of Community Affairs required the landlord to furnish a working lock. In that context, we held, "[a] residential tenant can recover damages from his landlord upon proper proof that the latter unreasonably enhanced the risk of loss due to theft by failing to supply adequate locks to safeguard the tenant's premises after suitable notice of the defect."

We likewise have imposed liability on a landlord who provides inadequate security for common areas of rental premises for the failure to prevent a criminal assault on a tenant. [T]he apartment was in a high crime area. Burglars and other unauthorized persons previously had broken into the building. Contrary to an administrative regulation, the landlord had not installed a lock on the front entrance. On those facts, we held that "by failing to do anything to arrest or even reduce the risk of criminal harm to his tenants, the landlord effectively and unreasonably enhanced that risk." [T]he criminal act resulting in the imposition of liability on the landlord occurred in the apartment house.

Similarly, we have held that the owner of a supermarket may be liable to a customer who is mugged at night in the market's parking lot. In *Butler v. Acme Markets*, unknown to the customer, seven muggings had occurred in the lot during the preceding year, five in the evenings during the four months preceding the attack in question. To combat the muggings, the market had hired off-duty policemen. At the time of the attack, however, the only guard was inside the market; no one was on duty in the parking lot. In this setting, we held that the market had a duty to protect the customer from foreseeable criminal activity.

[L]andlords and business owners should be liable for foreseeable injuries that occur on their premises. The underlying rationale is that they are in the best position to control the risk of harm. Ownership or control of the premises, for example, enables a party to prevent the harm. That rationale simply does not apply in the present case. Simply stated, existing precedent does not support the imposition of liability on Ivy Hill for Kuzmicz's injuries that occurred on the Board's property.

This case reveals the tragic fact that life in inner cities can be dangerous. Contrary to the dissent's contention, however, Ivy Hill's awareness of criminal activity on the Board's property does not suffice to impose liability on Ivy Hill for that activity. In effect, the dissent would transfer to an innocent property owner the duty to prevent criminal conduct that is more properly the responsibility of others.

Imposing on a landlord a duty to pay a tenant for injuries sustained in a criminal attack on another's property obviously helps to compensate the tenant. The imposition of the duty, however, transfers from one property owner to another the duty to compensate for injuries sustained on the property of the first owner. That duty carries costs, which provide a disincentive to own rental property in urban areas.

If Kuzmicz could recover from Ivy Hill because he was mugged on the Board's property while returning from the A & P, presumably he could recover also for injuries resulting from muggings on the Board's property while returning from work, the movies, the library, a restaurant, or a bar. The other eight thousand tenants, likewise would be entitled to recover against Ivy Hill if they were injured as they crossed the Board's property. If the risk of mugging was foreseeable on other properties in the area, how could the dissent deny recovery if tenants were mugged on those properties? In each instance, according to the dissent's theory, Ivy Hill would have breached a duty of care to the tenant by failing to warn of the risk of criminal activity or by failing to erect an impenetrable barrier between the other properties and the apartment house. To impose a duty on a landlord for the safety of tenants while on property over which the landlord has no control and from which it derives no benefit would be unprecedented. Precedent in this State and elsewhere supports the conclusion that under the circumstances of this case, the landlord does not owe a duty to the tenant for a criminal assault on the Board's property.

We empathize with the desire to compensate the victim of a criminal attack. That desire, however, should not predetermine the existence of the duty of a property owner for off-premises injuries. On these facts, it would be unfair to hold Ivy Hill liable to Kuzmicz for the failure to warn him of the possibility of an assault on the Board's path or for the failure to take greater measures to mend the fence. In so concluding, we do not foreclose the recognition of a landlord's duty to a tenant for off-premises injuries under different facts.

The judgment of the Appellate Division is reversed, and the matter is remanded to the Law Division for the entry of a judgment in favor of Ivy Hill. [*Reversed*].

Case Questions

1. Why does the trial court make the plaintiff Kuzmicz absorb 20 percent of the liability? (Hint. See section 15 on defenses to negligence.)

2. If the attack on Kuzmicz had occurred on apartment property, would the apartment owner have been liable?

3. Note that the Board of Education, which owned the vacant lot where the attack occurred, is held liable in this case.

12. Unreasonable Behavior—Breach of Duty

At the core of negligence is the unreasonable behavior that breaches the duty of care that the defendant owes to the plaintiff. The problem is how do we separate reasonable behavior that causes accidental injury from unreasonable behavior that causes injury? Usually a jury determines this issue, but negligence is a mixed question of law and fact. Despite the trend for judges to let juries decide what the standard of reasonable care is, judges also continue to be involved in the definition of negligence. A well-known definition by Judge Learned Hand states that negligence is determined by "the likelihood that the defendant's conduct will injure others, taken with the seriousness of the injury if it happens, and balanced against the interest which he must sacrifice to avoid the risk."

A special type of aggravated negligence is **willful and wanton negligence.** Although this does not reveal intent, it does show an extreme lack of due care. Negligent injuries inflicted by drunk drivers show willful and wanton negligence. The significance of this type of negligence is that the injured plaintiff can recover punitive damages as well as actual damages.

13. Causation in Fact

Before a person is liable to another for negligent injury, the person's failure to use reasonable care must actually have "caused" the injury. This observation is not so obvious as it first appears. A motorist stops by the roadside to change a tire. Another motorist drives past carelessly and sideswipes the first as he changes the tire. What caused the accident? Was it the inattention of the second motorist or the fact that the first motorist had a flat tire? Did the argument the second motorist had with her boss before getting in the car cause the accident, or was it the decision of the first motorist to visit one more client that afternoon? In a real sense, all these things caused the accident. Chains of causation stretch out infinitely.

Still, in a negligence suit the plaintiff must prove that the defendant actually caused the injury. The courts term this **cause in fact.** In light of the many possible ways to attribute accident causation, how do courts determine if a plaintiff's lack of care, in fact, caused a certain injury? They do so very practically. Courts leave questions of cause in fact almost entirely to juries as long as the evidence reveals that a defendant's alleged carelessness could have been a substantial, material factor in bringing about an injury. Juries then make judgments about whether a defendant's behavior in fact caused the harm.

A particular problem of causation arises where the carelessness of two or more tortfeasors contributes to cause the plaintiff's injury, as when two persons are wrestling over control of the car which strikes the plaintiff. Tort law handles such cases by making each tortfeasor *jointly and severally* liable for the entire judgment. The plaintiff can recover only the amount of the judgment, but she or he may recover it wholly from either of the tortfeasors or get a portion of the judgment from each.

14. Proximate Causation

It is not enough that a plaintiff suing for negligence prove that the defendant caused an injury in fact. The plaintiff also must establish proximate causation. **Proximate cause** is, perhaps, more accurately termed *legal cause*. It represents the proposition that those engaged in activity are legally liable only for the *foreseeable* risk that they cause.

Defining proximate causation in terms of foreseeable risk creates further problems about the meaning of the word "foreseeable." In its application, foreseeability has come to mean that the plaintiff must have been one whom the defendant could reasonably expect to be injured by a negligent act. For example, it is reasonable to expect, thus foreseeable, that a collapsing hotel walkway should injure those on or under it. But many courts would rule as unforeseeable that someone a block away, startled upon hearing the loud crash of the walkway, should trip and stumble into the path of an oncoming car. The court would likely dismiss that person's complaint against the hotel as failing to show proximate causation.

Another application of proximate cause doctrine requires the injury to be caused *directly* by the defendant's negligence. Causes of injury that intervene between the defendant's negligence and the plaintiff's injury can destroy the necessary proximate causation. Some courts, for instance, would hold that it is not foreseeable that an owner's negligence in leaving keys in a parked car should result in an intoxicated thief who steals the car crashing and injuring another motorist. These courts would dismiss for lack of proximate cause a case brought by the motorist against the car's owner.

15. Defenses to Negligence

There are two principal defenses to an allegation of negligence: contributory negligence and assumption of risk. Both these defenses are *affirmative defenses,* which means that the defendant must specifically raise these defenses to take advantage of them. When properly raised and proved, these defenses limit or bar the plaintiff's recovery against the defendant. The defenses are valid even though the defendant has actually been negligent.

Contributory Negligence

As originally applied, the **contributory negligence** defense absolutely barred the plaintiff from recovery if the plaintiff's own fault contributed to the injury "in any degree, however slight." The trend today, however, in the great majority of states is to offset the harsh rule of contributory negligence with the doctrine of **comparative responsibility** (also called *comparative negligence* and *comparative fault*). Under comparative principles, the plaintiff's contributory negligence does not bar recovery. It merely compares the plaintiff's fault with the defendant's and reduces the damage award proportionally. Under comparative responsibility, injury damages of $100,000 would be reduced by the jury to $80,000 if the jury determined that the plaintiff's own fault contributed 20 percent to the injury.

Adoption of the comparative negligence principle seems to lead to more frequent and larger awards for plaintiffs. This was the conclusion of a study by the Illinois Insurance Information Service for the year following that state's adoption of comparative negligence.

Assumption of Risk

If contributory negligence involves failure to use proper care for one's own safety, the **assumption-of-the-risk** defense arises from the plaintiff's knowing and willing undertaking of an activity made dangerous by the negligence of another. When professional hockey first came to this country, many spectators injured by flying hockey pucks sued and recovered for negligence. But as time went on and spectators came to realize that attending a hockey game meant that one might occasionally be exposed to flying hockey pucks, courts began to allow the defendant owners of hockey teams to assert that injured spectators had assumed the risk of injury from a speeding puck.

Assumption of the risk may be implied from the circumstances, or it can arise from an express agreement. Many businesses attempt to relieve themselves of potential liability by having employees or customers agree contractually not to sue for negligence, that is, to assume the risk. Some of these contractual agreements are legally enforceable, but many will be struck down by the courts as being against public policy, especially where a business possesses a vastly more powerful bargaining position than does its employee or customer.

It is important to a successful assumption-of-the-risk defense that the assumption was voluntary. Entering a hockey arena while knowing the risk of flying pucks is a voluntary assumption of the risk. Courts have often ruled, however, that people who imperil themselves while attempting to rescue their own or others' property from a risk created by the defendant have not assumed the risk voluntarily. A plaintiff who is injured while attempting to save his possessions from a fire negligently caused by the defendant is not subject to the assumption-of-the-risk defense.

Concept Summary: Plaintiff v. Defendant in Negligence

Plaintiff Must Prove:

Duty of care owed by defendant to plaintiff
Unreasonable behavior by defendant is a breach of the duty
Defendant's breach in fact caused injury
Injury was foreseeable given defendant's actions (proximate causation)
Injury actually occurred

Defendant May Prove:

Plaintiff's behavior contributed to injury (contributory negligence)
Plaintiff assumed risk

Strict Liability in Tort

Strict liability is a catchall phrase for the legal responsibility for injury-causing behavior that is neither intentional nor negligent. There are various types of strict liability torts, some of which are more "strict" than others. What ties them together is that they all impose legal liability, regardless of the intent or fault of the defendant. The next sections discuss these torts and tort doctrines.

16. Strict Products Liability

A major type of strict tort liability is **strict products liability,** for the commercial sale of defective products. In most states any retail, wholesale, or manufacturing seller who sells an unreasonably dangerous defective product that causes injury to a user of the product is strictly liable. For example, if a forklift you are using at work malfunctions because of defective brakes and you run off the edge of the loading dock and are injured, you can sue the retailer, wholesaler, and manufacturer of the product for strict liability. The fact that the retailer and wholesaler may have been perfectly careful in selling the product does not matter. They are strictly liable.

Strict products liability applies only to "commercial" sellers, those who normally sell products like the one causing injury, or who place them in the stream of commerce. Included as commercial sellers are the retailer, wholesaler, and manufacturer of a product, but also included are suppliers of defective parts and companies that assemble a defective product. Not included as a commercial seller is your next door neighbor who sells you her defective lawnmower. The neighbor may be negligent, for instance, if she knew of the defect that caused you injury and forgot to warn you about it, but she cannot be held strictly liable.

An important concept in strict products liability is that of "defect." Strict liability only applies to the sale of unreasonably dangerous *defective* products. There are two kinds of defects. **Production defects** arise when products are not manufactured to a manufacturer's own standards. Defective brakes on a new car are a good example of a production defect. **Design defects** occur when a product is manufactured according to the manufacturer's standards, but the product injures a user due to its unsafe design. Almost any product that injures a user can be claimed to have a "defective" design. At trial the issue becomes whether or not a jury will agree that the design is defective. Lack of adequate warnings for dangerous products should also be considered a design defect. Dangerous equipment, chemical products, and drugs should always contain proper warnings about use.

In practice, strict products liability is useful in protecting those who suffer personal injury or property damage. It does not protect businesses that have economic losses due to defective products. For instance, a warehouse that loses profits because its defective forklift will not run cannot recover those lost profits under strict products liability. The warehouse would have to sue for breach of contract. However, if the forklift defect causes injury to a worker, the worker can successfully sue the forklift manufacturer for strict products liability.

Under strict products liability, contributory negligence is not a defense but assumption of the risk is. As the Tobacco Industry Box explains, the assumption of the risk defense has protected tobacco manufacturers from health injury liability for many years. Misuse is another defense that defendants commonly raise in product liability cases. Removing safety guards from equipment is a common basis for the misuse defense. Defendants have also argued that if a product meets some federally required standard, it cannot be considered defective. Most courts, however, have ruled that federal standards only set a minimum requirement for safe design and that meeting federal standards does not automatically keep a manufacturer from being sued for strict products liability.

The rapid growth of products and service litigation during the past two decades has brought forth many calls for "tort reform." A number of states have changed their laws to modify the tort doctrines discussed in this section and chapter. At the federal level, tort reform has been strongly advocated although it has not passed as of this writing. Some of the tort reforms proposed or passed by the states include:

- Permitting only negligence actions against retailers and wholesalers unless the product manufacturer is insolvent.
- Eliminating strict liability recovery for defective product design.
- Barring products liability claims against sellers if products have been altered or modified by a user.
- Providing for the presumption of reasonableness defense in product design cases in which the product meets the **state-of-the-art,** that is, the prevailing industry standards, at the time of product manufacture.
- Creating a **statute of repose** that would specify a period (such as twenty-five years) following product sale after which plaintiffs would lose their rights to bring suits for product-related injuries.
- Reducing or eliminating punitive damage awards in most product liability cases.

Tobacco Industry Box

Tobacco-Related Products Liability

Individual plaintiffs have filed hundreds of tobacco-related products liability lawsuits since the 1960s. Prior to 1997, the tobacco company defendants had won all of these cases except one that is still on appeal. In almost every instance, juries have decided that cigarette smokers and other tobacco consumers *assumed the risk* of their habits. The surgeon general's warning that appears in tobacco advertising and the generally known dangers of tobacco consumption put individual consumers on notice of health risks, including heart disease and cancer.

Recently, however, lawsuits brought by non-smoking employees exposed to second-hand smoke have begun to appear. Six-thousand flight attendants filed a class action suit in Florida claiming injury from second-hand smoke. Other employees especially exposed to such smoke include those in the hospitality industry. Non-smokers exposed to second-hand smoke usually cannot be said to have assumed the risk of smoking dangers. The American Medical Association estimates that 40,000 people may die annually from second-hand smoke.

In still another area of tobacco-related products liability, the attorneys general of over 20 states have filed suit against the tobacco companies. They seek to recover reimbursement for Medicaid payments made by the states to cover tobacco-caused medical expense. In Florida, the court awarded the state $11 billion in a Medicaid case. There have been settlements with other states.

Threatened by litigation, the tobacco companies in 1997 agreed with the attorneys general of many states to an overall settlement of tobacco liability. The companies agreed to pay out $368 billion over a 25-year period to compensate for losses related to tobacco consumption. They also agreed to limits on advertising and that smoking is addictive and causes cancer. In return the agreement prohibited future class actions and punitive damage awards against tobacco companies. However, under the agreement Congress must approve these terms, which may not happen. In addition, some of the terms, such as limits on advertising, may be unconstitutional.

---

17. Respondeat Superior

Any time an employee is liable for tortious acts in the *scope of employment*, the employer is also liable. This is because of the tort doctrine of **respondeat superior** ("let the master reply").

The reason for respondeat superior is that the employee is advancing the interests of the employer when the tortious act occurs. If the employee were not doing the work, the employer would have to do it. Therefore, the employer is just as liable as the employee when the employee acts tortiously in carrying out the work. In a sense, the employer has set the employee in motion and is responsible for the employee's acts.

Most respondeat superior cases involve employee negligence. Note, however, that the employer is strictly liable once the employee's fault is established. And it does not matter that the employer warned the employee against the tortious behavior. Because Mary's employer told her to be careful while delivering pizzas does not prevent it from being liable when Mary runs a red light and has an accident.

Some respondeat superior cases involve an employee's intentional tort. If a store's service representative strikes a customer during an argument over the return of merchandise, the store will be liable under respondeat superior. But if the argument concerns football instead of the return of merchandise, the store will not be liable. The difference is that the argument over football is not within the scope of employment.

Usually, the only defense the employer has to the strict liability of respondeat superior is that the employee was outside the scope of employment. Sometimes this defense is made using the language **frolic and detour.** An employee who is on a frolic or detour is no longer acting for the employer. If Mary has delivered her employer's pizzas and is driving to see a friend when an accident occurs, the employer is not liable.

An employer who must pay for an employee's tort under respondeat superior may legally sue the employee for reimbursement. In practice, this seldom happens because the employer carries insurance. Occasionally, an insurer who has paid a respondeat superior claim will sue the employee who caused the claim.

18. Ultrahazardous Activity

In most states, the courts impose strict liability in tort for types of activities they call *ultrahazardous.* Transporting and using explosives and poisons fall under this category, as does keeping dangerous wild animals. Injuries caused from artificial storage of large quantities of liquid also can bring strict liability on the one who stores. In one unfortunate instance, a two-million-gallon vat of molasses burst and drowned a number of passersby in a nearby street. Regardless of whose fault or intent it was, the vat owner is strictly liable in this situation because of ultrahazardous activity.

19. Other Strict Liability Torts

The majority of states impose strict liability upon tavern owners for injuries to third parties caused by their intoxicated patrons. The acts imposing this liability are called **dram shop acts.** Because of the public attention given in recent years to intoxicated drivers, there has been a tremendous increase in dram shop act cases.

Common carriers, transportation companies licensed to serve the public, are also strictly liable for damage to goods being transported by them. Common carriers, however, can limit their liability in certain instances through contractual agreement, and they are not liable for (1) acts of God, such as natural catastrophes; (2) action of an alien enemy; (3) order of public authority, such as authorities of one state barring potentially diseased fruit shipments from another state from entering their state; (4) the inherent nature of the goods, such as perishable vegetables; and (5) misconduct of the shipper, such as improper packaging.

TABLE 9–4   Recent Damage Awards or Settlements in Tort Cases

Defendant	Event Causing Injury	Award or Settlement in Millions of Dollars
Ernst & Young	Accounting malpractice	$400
Dow Corning & Bristol-Myers Squibb	Product (breast implants)	4,750
Exxon	Negligence (oil spill)	100
General Motors	Product (pickup trucks)	105
Honeywell	Patent infringement	1,200
Kinetic Concepts, Inc.	Patent infringement	84
New York City	Negligence (police chase)	100
Nintendo Co.	Patent infringement	208
Pfizer Inc.	Product (heart valves)	215
Procter & Gamble	Defamation	15
Teledyne Continental Motors	Negligence (plane crash)	107
3M	Trade secret misappropriation	116

Damages

One legal scholar concludes that "the crucial controversy in personal injury torts today" is in the area of damages. This is because the average personal injury award has been increasing at nearly double the rate of inflation. For dramatic examples of the size of awards or settlements in some recent cases, examine Table 9–4. The size of damage awards is largely determined by juries, but judges also play a role in damages, especially in damage instructions to the jury and in deciding whether to approve substantial damage awards.

20. Compensatory Damages

Most damages awarded in tort cases compensate the plaintiff for injuries suffered. The purpose of damages is to make the plaintiff whole again, at least financially. There are three major types of loss that potentially follow tort injury and are called **compensatory damages.** They are:

- Past and future medical expenses
- Past and future economic loss (including property damage and loss of earning power)
- Past and future pain and suffering

Compensatory damages may also be awarded for loss of limb, loss of consortium (the marriage relationship), and mental distress.

Calculation of damage awards creates significant problems. Juries frequently use state-adopted life expectancy tables and present-value discount tables to help them determine the amount of damages to award. But uncertainty about the life expectancy of injured plaintiffs and the impact of inflation often makes these tables misleading. Also, awarding damages for pain and suffering is an art rather than a science. These awards measure jury sympathy as much as they calculate compensation for any financial loss. The recent dramatic increases in the size of damage awards helps underline the problems in their calculation. One result is that many individuals and businesses are underinsured for major tort liability.

21. Punitive Damages

Compensatory damages are not the only kind of damages. There are also **punitive damages.** By awarding punitive damages, courts or juries punish defendants for committing intentional torts and for negligent behavior considered "gross" or "willful and wanton." The key to the award of punitive damages is the defendant's motive. Usually the motive must be "malicious," "fraudulent," or "evil." Increasingly, punitive damages are also awarded for dangerously negligent conduct that shows a conscious disregard for the interests of others. These damages punish those who commit aggravated torts and act to deter future wrongdoing. Because they make an example out of the defendant, punitive damages are sometimes called *exemplary damages*.

Presently, there is much controversy about how appropriate it is to award punitive damages against corporations for their economic activities. Especially when companies fail to warn of known danger created by their activities, or when cost-benefit decisions are made at the risk of substantial human injury, courts are upholding substantial punitive damage awards against companies. Yet consider that these damages are a windfall to the injured plaintiff who has already received compensatory damages. And instead of punishing guilty management for wrongdoing, punitive damages may end up punishing innocent shareholders by reducing their dividends.

Many court decisions also overlook a very important consideration about punitive damages. Most companies carry liability insurance policies that reimburse them for "all sums which the insured might become legally obligated to pay." This includes reimbursement for punitive damages. Instead of punishing guilty companies, punitive damages may punish other companies, which have to pay increased insurance premiums, and may punish consumers, who ultimately pay higher prices. As a matter of public policy, several states prohibit insurance from covering punitive damages, but the great majority of states permit such coverage. This fact severely undermines arguments for awarding punitive damages against companies for their economic activities.

Consider also that an award of punitive damages greatly resembles a criminal fine. Yet the defendant who is subject to these criminal-type damages lacks the right to be indicted by a grand jury and cannot assert the right against self-incrimination. In addition, the defendant is subject to a lower standard of proof than in a criminal case. However, defendants in tort suits have challenged awards of punitive damages on a constitutional basis.

Finally, note that the United States is the only country in the world where punitive damages are regularly awarded.

Alternatives to the Tort System

Of common law origin, the tort system has developed slowly over several centuries. Today, the tort system has come under much criticism because of aspects of its development. The **contingency fee,** which permits a plaintiff to sue without first having to pay an attorney, encourages litigation. Others see litigation as promoted by the fact that even if a plaintiff loses a tort action, the plaintiff does not have to reimburse the defendant's often substantial legal expenses. Apprehension about the easy availability of punitive damages and general concern over the role of the civil jury in handing down large damage awards are also directed at the tort system.

Perhaps the most important problem of the tort system, however, is that it is rarely a cost-effective way of compensating those who are injured by others. For example, the Rand Corporation estimates that only 40 to 60 percent of the insurance dollars paid out due to tort litigation go to injured plaintiffs. Litigation expenses, including legal fees, consume the rest.

There are many alternatives to tort litigation. Arbitration (discussed in Chapter 3) is an important one. No-fault insurance, like that found in many states' automobile liability plans, is another. Workers' compensation acts are a third alternative. Because of their importance to the business community, the next section focuses on this alternative. As you read about workers' compensation, consider if it would be possible to apply some variation of workers' compensation to tort situations that do not involve the employer-employee relationship.

22. Workers' Compensation Acts

Around the turn of the century, the tort system was largely replaced in the workplace by a series of workers' compensation acts. These statutes were enacted at both the state and federal level, and they imposed a type of strict liability on employers for accidental workplace injuries suffered by their employees. The clear purpose of these statutes was to remove financial losses of injury from workers and redistribute them onto employers and ultimately onto society.

History

Workers' compensation laws are state statutes designed to protect employees and their families from the risks of accidental injury, death, or disease resulting from their employment. They were passed because the common law did not give adequate protection to employees from the hazards of their work. At common law, anyone was liable in tort for damages resulting from injuries caused to another as a proximate result of negligence. If an employer acted unreasonably and his or her carelessness was the proximate cause of physical injury suffered by an employee, the latter could sue and recover damages from the employer. However, the common law also provided the employer with the means of escaping this tort liability in most cases through three defenses:

· Assumption of the risk
· Contributory negligence
· The fellow-servant rule

For example, assume that employer E knowingly instructed workers to operate dangerous machinery not equipped with any safety devices, even though it realized injury to them was likely. W, a worker, had his arm mangled when it was caught in the gears of one of these machines. Even though E was negligent in permitting this hazardous condition to persist, if W were aware of the dangers that existed, he would be unable to recover damages because he knowingly *assumed the risk* of his injury. In addition, if the injury were caused by *contributory negligence* of the employee as well as the negligence of the employer, the action was defeated. And if the injury occurred because of the negligence of another employee, the negligent employee, rather than the employer, was liable because of the *fellow-servant rule*.

The English Parliament passed a workers' compensation statute in 1897. Today all states have such legislation, modeled to a greater or lesser degree on the English act. These laws vary a great deal from state to state as to the industries subject to them, the employees they cover, the nature of the injuries or diseases that are compensable, the rates of compensation, and the means of administration. In spite of wide variances in the laws of the states in this area, certain general observations can be made about them.

The System

State workers' compensation statutes provide a system to pay workers or their families if the worker is accidentally killed or injured or incurs an occupational disease while employed. To be compensable, the death, illness, or injury must arise out of and in the course of the employment. Under these acts, the negligence or fault of the employer in causing an on-the-job injury is not an issue. Instead, these laws recognize the fact of life that a certain number of injuries, deaths, and diseases are bound to occur in a modern industrial society as a result of the attempts of businesses and their employees to provide the goods and services demanded by the consuming public.

This view leads to the conclusion that it is fairer for the consuming public to bear the cost of such mishaps rather than to impose it on injured workers. Workers' compensation laws create strict liability for employers of accidentally injured workers. Liability exists regardless of lack of negligence or fault, provided the necessary association between the injuries and the business of the employer is present. The three defenses the employer had at common law are eliminated. The employers, treating the costs of these injuries as part of the costs of production, pass them on to the consumers who created the demand for the product or service being furnished.

Workers' compensation acts give covered employees the right to certain cash payments for their loss of income due to accidental, on-the-job injuries. In the event of a married employee's death, benefits are provided for the surviving spouse and minor children. The amount of such awards usually is subject to a stated maximum and is calculated by using a percentage of the wages of the employee. If the employee suffers permanent, partial disability, most states provide compensation both for injuries that are scheduled in the statute and those that are nonscheduled. As an example of the former, a worker who loses a hand might be awarded 100 weeks of compensation at $95 per week. Besides scheduling specific compensation for certain specific injuries, most acts also provide compensation for nonscheduled ones based upon the earning power the employee lost due to his or her injury. In addition to the above payments, all statutes provide for medical benefits.

In some states, employers have a choice of covering their workers' compensation risk with insurance or of being self-insured (that is, paying all claims directly) if they can demonstrate their capability to do so. Approximately 20 percent of compensation benefits are paid by self-insurers. In other states, employers pay into a state fund used to compensate workers entitled to benefits. In these states, the amounts of the payments are based on the size of the payroll and the experience of the employer in having claims filed against the system by its employees.

Workers' compensation laws are usually administered exclusively by an administrative agency called the industrial commission or board, which has quasi-judicial powers. Of course, the ruling of such boards is subject to review by the courts of the jurisdiction in the same manner as the actions of other administrative agencies.

Tests for Determining Compensation

The tests for determining whether an employer must pay workers' compensation to an employee are simply:

1. Was the injury accidental?
2. Did the injury arise out of and in the course of employment?

Because workers' compensation laws benefit workers, courts interpret them liberally to favor workers.

In recent years, cases have tended to expand employers' liability. For instance, courts have held that heart attacks (as well as other common ailments in which the employee has had either a preexisting disease or a physical condition likely to lead to the disease) are compensable as "accidental injuries." One ruling approved an award to a purchasing agent who became mentally ill because she was exposed to unusual work, stresses, and strains. Her "nerve-racking" job involved a business whose sales grew over sixfold in ten years. Factors contributing to her "accidental injury" included harsh criticism by her supervisor, long hours of work, and inability to take vacations due to the requirements of her position.

Likewise, the courts have been liberal in upholding awards that have been challenged on the grounds that the injury did not arise "out of and in the course of employment." Courts routinely support compensation awards for almost any accidental injury that employees suffer while traveling for their employers. A Minnesota Supreme Court decision upheld a lower court award of compensation to a bus driver. On a layover during a trip, the driver had been shot accidentally in a tavern parking lot following a night on the town.

Exclusive Remedy Rule

Recently, some courts have been liberal in their interpretations of the **exclusive remedy rule.** This rule, which is written into all compensation statutes, states that an employee's sole remedy against an employer for workplace injury or illness shall be workers' compensation. In the past few years, courts in several important jurisdictions have created exceptions to this rule. Note that these exceptions recognize in part that workers' compensation laws do not adequately compensate badly injured workers.

Since workers' compensation laws apply only to accidentally injured workers, the exclusive remedy rule does not protect employers who intentionally injure workers. But the issue arises as to how "intentional" such an injury has to be. What if an employer knowingly exposes employees to a chemical that may cause illness in some employees over a long term?

The Future of State Workers' Compensation

Currently, many problems confront the state workers' compensation system. Fifty separate nonuniform acts make up the system. Many acts exclude from coverage groups such as farmworkers, government employees, and employees of small businesses. Many state legislatures have enacted changes in their compensation laws. However, states that have broadened coverage and increased benefits have greatly boosted the cost of doing business within their borders. This discourages new businesses from locating within these states and encourages those already there to move out.

In the last decade, workers' compensation payments have tripled. Many workers exaggerate their injuries to get compensation. At the same time, compensation payments to seriously injured workers are often inadequate, and this has led to attempts to get around the exclusive remedy rule.

As our national economy moves from a manufacturing to a service emphasis, the nature of injuries suffered under workers' compensation programs begins to change. In particular, the number of mental stress claims rises. The National Council on Compensation Insurance states that these claims have increased fivefold in the past few years. Problems of proving (or disproving) mental stress claims bring new concerns for the workers' compensation system.

A major problem concerns slowly developing occupational diseases. Many toxic chemicals cause cancer and other diseases only after workers have been exposed to them over many years. Often it is difficult or impossible for workers or their survivors to recover workers' compensation for such diseases.

One solution to the problems confronting the workers' compensation system would be federal reform. Those advocating such reform have put forth several plans, but Congress has shown little inclination so far to adopt a uniform federal act. However, as the next section reveals, there are already federal compensation acts covering certain segments of the work force.

Key Terms

Review Questions and Problems

Intentional Torts

1. *Assault and Battery*
   Under what theory can an employee sue her employer for merely touching her? Explain.

2. *Intentional Infliction of Mental Distress*
   In business the intentional infliction of mental distress tort has most often involved what type of situation?

3. *Invasion of Privacy*
   Explain the three principal invasions of personal interest that make up invasion of privacy.

4. *False Imprisonment and Malicious Prosecution*
   Explain the difference between false imprisonment and malicious prosecution. In what business situation does false imprisonment most frequently arise?

5. *Trespass*
   In recent months, homeowners downwind from International Cement Company have had clouds of cement dust settle on their property. Trees, shrubbery, and flowers have all been killed. The paint on houses has also been affected. Explain what tort cause of action these homeowners might pursue against International.

6. *Conversion*
   Bartley signs a storage contract with Universal Warehouses. The contract specifies that Bartley's household goods will be stored at Universal's midtown storage facility while he is out of the country on business. Later, without contacting Bartley, Universal transfers his goods to a suburban warehouse. Two days after the move, a freak flood wipes out the suburban warehouse and Bartley's goods. Is Universal liable to Bartley? Explain.

7. *Defamation*
   Acme Airlines attempts to get control of Free Fall Airways by making a public offer to buy its stock from shareholders. Free Fall's president, Joan, advises the shareholders in a letter that

Acme's president, Richard, is "little better than a crook" and "can't even control his own company." Analyze the potential liability of Free Fall's president for these remarks.

8. *Fraud*
   Fraud can be used to void a contract and as a basis for intentional tort. What is the advantage to a plaintiff of suing for the tort of fraud as opposed to using fraud merely as a contractual defense?

9. *Common Law Business Torts*
   You are concerned because several of your employees have recently broken their employment contracts and left town. Investigation reveals that Sly and Company, your competitor in a nearby city, has paid bonuses to your former employees to persuade them to break their contracts. Discuss what legal steps you can take against Sly.

10. *Statutory Competitive Torts*
    (a) The Stillwater Record Corporation discovers that a number of retail stores are selling counterfeit copies of its popular line of environmental records and tapes. Discuss Stillwater's legal rights against the retailers and the counterfeiter.
    (b) Total Truck Renter, Inc., ran advertising that showed both its trucks and the trucks of its biggest competitor. Tricks of photography were used to make Total's trucks appear larger than the competitor's. Actually, the trucks were all of similar size. Is what Total done legally acceptable? Explain.

Negligence

11. *Duty of Care*
    (a) Do you have a duty of care to warn a stranger on the street of the potential danger of broken glass ahead?
    (b) Do you have a duty to warn an employee of similar danger at a place of employment? Explain.

12. *Unreasonable Behavior—Breach of Duty*
    In litigation who usually determines if the defendant's behavior is unreasonable?

13. *Causation in Fact*
    (a) What does it mean to say that "chains of causation stretch out endlessly"?
    (b) What is the standard used by the judge in instructing the jury about causation?

14. *Proximate Causation*
    Explain the difference between proximate causation and causation in fact.

15. *Defenses to Negligence*
    A jury finds Lee, the defendant, liable in a tort case. It determines that José, the plaintiff, has suffered $200,000 in damages. The jury also finds that José's own fault contributed 25 percent to his injuries. Under a comparative negligence instruction, what amount of damages will the jury aware the plaintiff?

Strict Liability in Tort

16. *Strict Products Liability*
    While driving under the influence of alcohol, Joe runs off the road and wrecks his car. As the car turns over, the protruding door latch hits the ground and the door flies open. Joe, who is not wearing his seat belt, is thrown from the car and badly hurt. Joe sues the car manufacturer, asserting that the door latch was defectively designed. Discuss the legal issues raised by these facts.

17. *Respondeat Superior*
    Carlos delivers pizza for Mama Mia's Pizza Parlor. One of his employer's rules is that delivery employees are never to violate posted speed limits. While traveling 50 miles per hour in a 30-mile-per-hour speed zone, Carlos negligently crashes into a city bus. Is Mama Mia's liable for the injuries caused by Carlos? Discuss.

18. *Ultrahazardous Activity*
    Through no one's fault, a sludge dam of the Phillips Phosphate Company breaks. Millions of gallons of sludge run off into a nearby river that empties into Pico Bay. The fishing industry in the bay area is ruined. Is Phillips Phosphate liable to the fishing industry? Explain.

19. *Other Strict Liability Torts*
    Explain when common carriers are not strictly liable for damage to transported goods.

Damages

20. *Compensatory Damages*
    Explain the three types of loss that give rise to compensatory damages.

21. *Punitive Damages*
    During a business lunch, Bob eats salad dressing that contains almond extract. He is very allergic to nuts and suffers a severe allergic reaction. There are complications and Bob becomes almost totally paralyzed. Because Bob had instructed the restaurant waiter and the chef that he might die if he ate any nuts, he sues the restaurant for negligence. Discuss the types of damages Bob may recover.

Alternatives to the Tort System

22. *Workers' Compensation Acts*
    If Corgel fails to wear a hard hat as required by Hammersmith, his employer, and is injured by a falling hammer, can he recover workers' compensation from Hammersmith? Your answer should explain the basis for recovering workers' compensation.

Terminology Review

For each term in the left-hand column, match the most appropriate description in the right-hand column.

1. Assumption of risk

2. Comparative negligence

3. Copyright

4. Defamation

a. The liability of an employer for an employee's torts

b. Damages that punish a defendant for wrongdoing

c. Knowingly encountering a dangerous condition caused by another

d. The legal cause of an injury, which is determined by the "foreseeability" test

5. Duty

6. Proximate causation

7. Punitive damages

8. Respondeat superior

9. Trademark

10. Trespass

e. Reduction of plaintiff's damages by the amount by which plaintiff's own carelessness caused the injury

f. The legal right of an author to control reproduction or performance of a literary, musical, or graphic work

g. Publication of harmful, untrue statements about another

h. The legal responsibility of a person, which arises out of conduct, to act (or not act) in a certain way toward others

i. The tort of entering another's land without consent

j. A mark, word, picture, or design that attaches to goods to indicate their source

THE CRIMINAL LAW AND BUSINESS

Business Decision

Cooking the Books

Your business is in need of additional working capital. You contact your bank and a loan of $500,000 is tentatively approved pending a review of your financial statements. The bank loan officer, who is a close personal friend, tells you to make sure that the financial statements "look good" before mailing them to the bank.

- Should you juggle the figures to make sure the loan is approved?
- Is the bank loan officer a potential grand jury target?
- Do you face additional charges by using the mail to return the financial statement?

In the past several years the United States has faced a crime wave of staggering proportions. Violent crime obviously has contributed to the problem, but white-collar criminals have been responsible for this predicament as well. According to recently released statistics, corporate America is losing an estimated $100 billion annually at the hands of its own workers.

What types of offenses are we talking about when we mention white-collar crime? Embezzlement, making electronic advances to fictitious employees, overcharging customers and pocketing the difference, accepting kickbacks from suppliers in exchange for orders, bid rigging, check forgery, selling trade secrets, falsifying inventories to cover theft, and paying false invoices—all are costing every person in this country hundreds, if not thousands, of dollars. Between 2 percent and 5 percent of each sales dollar is a premium that companies must charge customers to make up for losses due to white-collar crime.

The arrests made in white-collar crime probably represent only the tip of the iceberg. Many of these crimes go unreported by businesses out of a fear of embarrassment. Prosecutors sometimes shy away from filing charges in white-collar cases because juries have more sympathy for nonviolent offenders. One prosecutor told *The New York Times* that "I can wave a pair of bloody underwear in front of a jury and have their undivided attention. But I can wave $100 million in phony loan statements in front of the same jury and just watch their eyes glaze over."

"Cooking the books" illustrates a federal crime. A false financial statement may initially help to get a loan approved; however, as lending institutions suffer losses from bad loans, borrowers who submit false statements to obtain those loans may face prison sentences and stiff fines. Moreover, using the mail to commit a crime may result in additional penalties.

Why is white-collar crime so high today? Some of the perpetrators are motivated by greed and corruption. Others are angry with their employer and use crime as a means of striking back at the company. One reason sometimes advanced for the increase in white-collar crime is that historically the risk of being caught and sent to prison was slight. Bribery of local officials, for example, was frequently considered a legitimate cost of doing business, especially overseas.

Business conduct that historically was unethical or tortious may today be a crime. Legal advice on business decisions that may be of questionable legality is always required, unless of course the business and its employees are committed to avoiding any conduct that is of questionable legality. Table 10–1 illustrates a variety of criminal prosecutions against businesspeople.

This chapter looks first at terms and procedures in criminal law that relate to business. It then considers constitutional issues, specific crimes, and recent sentencing guidelines as well as problems in the criminal justice system. All of these issues are highly relevant for managers seeking to avoid criminal charges against themselves and their businesses.

TABLE 10–1   **Examples of Criminal Charges against Businesspeople**

- A very wealthy Wall Street proxy solicitor who solicits votes for management at corporate annual meetings overcharged clients and padded expense accounts sent to corporate clients. Rather than sue to collect the overcharge, the clients had the proxy solicitor charged with grand larceny and income tax evasion. He pleaded guilty.
- A person attempted to cash a forged check. The business to which the check was presented refused to cash it. The check was destroyed by the forger, who was nevertheless convicted of forgery.
- An advertising agency paid $132,000 to an individual who used part of the money to bribe the tourism minister of a foreign country to hire the agency to win an advertising contract. The agency entered a guilty plea to violating the Foreign Corrupt Practices Act (See Chapter 15).
- A politician was given a campaign contribution by a securities firm that was defrauding the public. The politician was convicted of money laundering under the Money Laundering Control Act (1986) because he knew the money was tainted. This law extends criminal liability to those who knowingly do business with criminals.
- A plaintiff's lawyer in a personal injury case was indicted for fraud when it was discovered that in making the client's case, medical bills had been faked, witnesses bribed, and a pickax used to enlarge the hole in the street where the plaintiff had fallen.
- A holder of tire-sealant franchises was convicted of conspiracy to violate the federal disclosure requirements established by the Federal Trade Commission in selling franchises.

TABLE 10–2   Criminal Offenses

Typical Felonies (Imprisonment for More than One Year and/or Fine)	*Typical Misdemeanors (Jail for Less than One Year and/or Fine)*
Arson	Assault
Bribery	Battery
Burglary	Gambling
Embezzlement	Larceny (petty)
False statements	Littering
Forgery	Prostitution
Larceny (grand)	Public disturbance
Mail fraud	Simple assault
Price fixing	Traffic offenses
Racketeering	Trespass

Terms and Procedures

Several terms and concepts, such as "conspiracy," "knowingly," "willfully," and "nolo contendere," are unique to the criminal law. These concepts are reviewed in the following sections.

1. Terminology

Crimes are classified as **felonies** or **misdemeanors.** This classification is based on the punishment imposed in the event of a conviction. Felonies are punishable by fine or imprisonment in a penitentiary for a period of one year or more, whereas misdemeanors are punishable by a fine or a jail sentence of less than one year. Table 10–2 lists typical offenses under each classification.

In addition, felony cases are commenced by grand jury *indictment,* whereas misdemeanors are usually commenced by the government filing a charge called an *information.* Grand juries are different from petit juries. A grand jury determines if there is sufficient evidence to warrant a trial. A petit jury determines the guilt or innocence of the accused. The role of the grand jury is discussed further below.

Most federal laws declaring conduct to be criminal use the words "knowingly" or "willfully." In this context, **knowingly** means that the criminal act was done voluntarily and intentionally and was not a mistake or accident. While knowledge cannot be established by demonstrating that the accused was negligent, careless, or foolish, knowledge can be inferred if the accused deliberately blinded himself or herself to the existence of a fact. In the context of criminal law, **willfully** means that the act was committed voluntarily and purposely, with the specific intent to do something the law forbids. The intent was either to disobey or to disregard the law.

In criminal cases, the defendant has three possible pleas to enter to an indictment charging a violation: *guilty, not guilty,* or **nolo contendere.** This last plea, Latin for "no contest," allows sentencing just as if the defendant had pleaded or been found guilty. It has the advantage to a defendant of avoiding the cost of trial and effect of a guilty plea or finding in a subsequent civil suit. Criminal convictions may create prima facie cases for civil damage suits, but this effect can be avoided by the nolo contendere plea.

2. The Grand Jury

The Fifth Amendment to the U.S. Constitution provides that before anyone can be tried for serious crime, there must be an indictment by a grand jury. This protection is designed to prevent political trials and unjustified prosecutions by placing a group of citizens between prosecutors and persons accused of major crimes.

A grand jury normally consists of 23 citizens who live within the jurisdiction of the court that would try one accused of a crime. At least 16 persons must be present for the grand jury to hear evidence and vote on cases. For an indictment to be returned, a majority of the grand jury must find that a crime has been committed and that the evidence is sufficient to warrant the accused's standing trial. This determination is **probable cause.**

The grand jury does not attempt to determine if the accused is guilty, only that probable cause exists to believe the accused committed the crime. Since probable cause is the standard for grand jury action, it is not difficult to obtain an indictment. Even an indicted person, however, is entitled to the **presumption of innocence**—to be presumed innocent until found guilty by a petit jury.

Grand juries also serve as an investigative body. Law enforcement officials such as agents for the Federal Bureau of Investigation, U.S. Customs Service, U.S. Postal Service, and Secret Service often act as arms of federal grand juries investigating possible criminal activities. Persons who are the targets or subjects of investigations may be called before grand juries and may be questioned under oath about possible illegal conduct. In such cases the persons subpoenaed to testify before the grand jury are entitled to invoke their Fifth Amendment privilege against compulsory self-incrimination and refuse to answer questions. While they are entitled to have the benefit of legal advice, defense counsel is not allowed to accompany a witness before a grand jury. However, counsel may be outside the grand jury room and thus available for consultation whenever a witness desires it.

Grand jurors may also subpoena business records. These records are then made available to law enforcement personnel for study. Witnesses may be called and questioned about documents and records delivered in response to a subpoena. Some of the issues that may arise from such subpoenas are discussed in the case that follows. In this case, the Supreme Court determined the standards for upholding grand jury subpoenas.

UNITED STATES V. R. ENTERPRISES, INC.
111 S.Ct. 722 (1991)

A federal grand jury sitting in Virginia has been investigating allegations of interstate transportation of obscene materials. The grand jury issued a series of subpoenas to three companies—Model Magazine Distributors, Inc. (Model), R. Enterprises, Inc., and MFR Court Street Books, Inc. (MFR). Model is a New York distributor of sexually oriented paperback books, magazines, and videotapes. R. Enterprises, which distributes adult materials, and MFR . . .are also based in New York. All three companies are wholly owned by Martin Rothstein. The grand jury subpoenas sought a variety of corporate books and records and, in Model's case, copies of 193 videotapes that Model had shipped to retailers in Virginia. All three companies moved to quash the subpoenas, arguing that the subpoenas called for production of materials irrelevant to the grand jury's investigation. . . .

The District Court denied the motions to quash. . . . [T]he court explained in denying MFR's motion to quash that it was "inclined to agree" with "the majority of the jurisdictions," which do not require the Government to make a "threshold showing" before a grand jury subpoena will be enforced. . . . [T]he companies refused to comply with the subpoenas. The District Court found each in contempt and fined them $500 per day, but stayed imposition of the fine pending appeal.

. . . [T]he Court of Appeals quashed the business records subpoenas issued to R. Enterprises and MFR. In doing so . . . it required the Government to clear the three hurdles . . . in the trial context—relevancy, admissibility, and specificity—in order to enforce the grand jury subpoenas. The court concluded that the challenged subpoenas did not satisfy [these] standards, finding no evidence in the record that either company had ever shipped materials into, or otherwise conducted business in Virginia. . . It . . . noted that "any evidence concerning Mr. Rothstein's alleged business activities outside of Virginia, or his ownership of companies which distribute allegedly obscene materials outside of Virginia, would most likely be inadmissible on relevancy grounds at any trial that might occur," and that the subpoenas therefore failed "to meet the requirements that any documents subpoenaed . . . must be admissible as evidence at trial. . . ."

O'CONNOR, J: This case requires the Court to decide what standards apply when a party seeks to avoid compliance with a subpoena *duces tecum* issued in connection with a grand jury investigation.

We granted certiorari to determine whether the Court of Appeals applied the proper standard in evaluating the grand jury subpoenas issued to respondents. We now reverse.

The grand jury occupies a unique role in our criminal justice system. It is an investigatory body charged with the responsibility of determining whether or not a crime has been committed. Unlike this Court, whose jurisdiction is predicated on a specific case or controversy, the grand jury "can investigate merely on suspicion that the law is being violated, or even just because it wants assurance that it is not." The function of the grand jury is to inquire into all information that might possibly bear on its investigation until it has identified an offense or has satisfied itself that none has occurred. As a necessary consequence of its investigatory function, the grand jury paints with a broad brush. . . .

A grand jury subpoena is thus much different from a subpoena issued in the context of a prospective criminal trial, where a specific offense has been identified and a particular defendant charged. . . . In short, the Government cannot be required to justify the issuance of a grand jury subpoena by presenting evidence sufficient to establish probable cause because the very purpose of requesting the information is to ascertain whether probable cause exists.

This Court has emphasized on numerous occasions that many of the rules and restrictions that apply at a trial do not apply in grand jury proceedings. The teaching of the Court's decisions is clear: A grand jury "may compel the production of evidence or the testimony of witnesses as it considers appropriate, and its operation generally is unrestrained by the technical procedural and evidentiary rules governing the conduct of criminal trials. . . ."

This guiding principle renders suspect the Court of Appeals' holding that the standards . . . as to subpoenas issued in anticipation of trial apply equally in the grand jury context. . . . Requiring the Government to explain in too much detail the particular reasons underlying a subpoena threatens to compromise "the indispensable secrecy of grand jury proceedings." Broad disclosure also affords the targets of investigation far more information about the grand jury's internal workings than the Federal Rules of Criminal Procedure appear to contemplate.

The investigatory powers of the grand jury are nevertheless not unlimited. Grand juries are not licensed to engage in arbitrary fishing expeditions, nor may they select targets of investigation out of malice or an intent to harass. In this case, the focus of our inquiry is the limit imposed on a grand jury by Federal Rule of Criminal Procedure 17(c), which governs the issuance of subpoenas *duces tecum* in federal criminal proceedings. The Rule provides that "the court on motion made promptly may quash or modify the subpoena if compliance would be unreasonable or oppressive." . . .

Our task is to fashion an appropriate standard of reasonableness, one that gives due weight to the difficult position of subpoena recipients but does not impair the strong governmental interests in affording grand juries wide latitude, avoiding minitrials on peripheral matters, and preserving a necessary level of secrecy. We begin by reiterating that the law presumes, absent a strong showing to the contrary, that a grand jury acts within the legitimate scope of its authority. . . . Consequently, a grand jury subpoena issued through normal channels is presumed to be reasonable, and the burden of showing unreasonableness must be on the recipient who seeks to avoid compliance. Indeed, this result is indicated by the language of Rule 17(c), which permits a subpoena to be quashed only "on motion" and "if *compliance* would be unreasonable." . . . To the extent that the Court of Appeals placed an initial burden on the Government, it committed error. Drawing on the principles articulated above, we conclude that where, as here, a subpoena is challenged on relevancy grounds, the motion to quash must be denied unless the district court determines that there is no reasonable possibility that the category of materials the Government seeks will produce information relevant to the general subject of the grand jury's investigation. . . .

Applying these principles in this case demonstrates that the District Court correctly denied respondents' motions to quash. It is undisputed that all three companies—Model, R. Enterprises, and MFR—are owned by the same person, that all do business in the same area, and that one of the three, Model, has shipped sexually explicit materials into the Eastern District of Virginia. The District Court could have concluded from these facts that there was a reasonable possibility that the business records of R. Enterprises and MFR would produce information relevant to the grand jury's investigation into the interstate transportation of obscene materials. Respondents' blanket denial of any connection to Virginia did not suffice to render the District Court's conclusion invalid. A grand jury need not accept on faith the self-serving assertions of those who may have committed criminal acts. Rather, it is entitled to determine for itself whether a crime has been committed. . . .[*Reversed*].

Case Questions

1. What presumption does the law afford the acts of a grand jury?

2. Is it fair, given the grand jury's secretive nature, to place the burden of showing unreasonableness on the recipient of the subpoena?

3. Can you envision a factual scenario in which the Court would quash the grand jury subpoena?

Proper functioning of the grand jury system depends upon the secrecy of the proceedings. This secrecy protects the innocent accused from disclosure of the accusations made against him or her before the grand jury. In judicial proceedings, however, transcripts of grand jury proceedings may be obtained if necessary to avoid possible injustice. For example, a defendant may use a grand jury transcript at a trial to impeach a witness, to refresh the witness's recollection, or to test his or her credibility. The disclosure of a grand jury transcript is appropriate only in those cases where the need for it outweighs the public interest in secrecy, and the burden of demonstrating this balance rests upon a private party seeking disclosure.

Grand jury service, especially at the federal level, is often time consuming. Because many investigations take a long time, grand jurors frequently serve for a year to eighteen months. The jury does not meet every day, but meeting at least one day per week or three days in one week per month is common. State grand juries serve shorter terms, but even in these cases service involves a substantial sacrifice by those called to serve.

3. Conspiracies

It is a separate criminal offense for anyone to conspire or agree with someone else to do something that, if carried out, would be a criminal offense. A **conspiracy** is an agreement or a "kind of partnership" for criminal purposes in which each member becomes the agent or partner of every other member. A formal agreement is not required, and all members of the conspiracy need not plan all of the details of the scheme.

The essence of a conspiracy offense is the making of the agreement itself followed by the commission of any overt act. An **overt act** is any transaction or event knowingly committed by a conspirator in an effort to accomplish some object of the conspiracy. Standing alone, the act may be entirely innocent; the context of the conspiracy makes it criminal. For example, driving a car to a bank to pick up a bank robber would constitute an overt act by the driver.

To convict a person of a conspiracy, it is not necessary for the government to prove the conspirators actually succeeded in accomplishing their intended crime. The evidence must show beyond a reasonable doubt that:

- Two or more persons, in some way or manner, came to a mutual understanding to try to accomplish a common and unlawful plan.
- The defendant willfully became a member of such conspiracy.
- During the existence of the conspiracy, one of the conspirators knowingly committed at least one of the overt acts described in the indictment.
- Such overt act was knowingly committed in an effort to carry out or accomplish some object of the conspiracy.

A person may be convicted of conspiracy even if he or she did not know all the details of the unlawful scheme. If a defendant has an understanding of the unlawful nature of a plan and knowingly and willfully joins in that plan on one occasion, that is sufficient evidence for conviction.

The law on conspiracies is often used to "drag in" defendants who did not actually participate in the commission of an offense. A person may become a coconspirator through participation in routine business meetings if the meetings are followed by illegal conduct. If illegal plans or conduct are in the planning process, it is imperative that persons not wishing to participate in the conspiracy disassociate themselves from the process immediately upon discovery of the illegal scheme.

The following "Tobacco Industry Box" illustrates the scope and complexity of investigating conspiracy cases.

Tobacco Industry Box

The U.S. Department of Justice has made it clear that tobacco industry executives and their lawyers face criminal prosecution over whether industry officials lied to government agencies about manipulating nicotine levels in their products. The investigation also centers around allegations that the tobacco industry hatched a conspiracy over 40 years ago to deceive the public about the hazards of smoking.

As a part of the investigation, federal prosecutors have granted immunity from prosecution to several key witnesses. The government has sought assistance from company researchers, scientists, product development employees, and manufacturing officers with knowledge about cigarette development.

The investigation also is examining allegations that the tobacco industry's lawyers were the architects of a scheme to postpone for years public dissemination of research that cigarettes kill. The tobacco industry has hired some of America's top law firms and has legal bills of approximately $600 million a year. At stake is not only whether the FDA should have the power to regulate nicotine in tobacco as a drug, but the possibility of criminal sanctions against tobacco firms and their corporate officers and lawyers.

4. Aiding and Abetting

The charge of **aiding and abetting** another in the commission of a crime is similar to the charge of conspiracy in that guilt may be established without proof that the defendant personally committed every act constituting the alleged offense. The law recognizes that anything a person can do may also be accomplished through direction of another person as his or her agent.

If a person acts under the direction of the defendant or joins the defendant in performing acts with the intent to commit a crime, then the law holds that person responsible for aiding and abetting the crime. Moreover, the law holds the defendant responsible for the acts and conduct of such other persons just as though he or she had committed the acts or engaged in such conduct if the defendant deliberately associated himself or herself in some way with those persons.

Indictments often charge persons both with a conspiracy to commit a crime and with aiding and abetting others to do so. Theses allegations are used to indict persons only minimally involved with the actual substantive crime. To avoid going to trial, many will agree to testify against those more directly involved in return for lesser punishment or even immunity from prosecution. Such charges are frequently dropped, but the value to the government of the conspiracy theory and the charge of aiding and abetting should not be underestimated by corporate officials, who may be potentially liable for criminal acts committed without their direct involvement.

At the state level, a charge similar to the federal charge of aiding and abetting is that a person is an **accessory** to a crime. A person may be an accessory before the crime is committed or after it is committed, in which case the person is accused of being an accessory after the fact. A person who assists a perpetrator of a crime in eluding the police would be such an accessory. *Accessories before the crime* assist in preparation for the crime, and they may be punished the same as the person who committed the crime. *Accessories after the fact* are usually subject to specific penalties for their actions as provided for in the laws declaring assistance of criminals to be unlawful.

Constitutional Issues

Before covering the elements of some of the more important business-related crimes, an understanding of the constitutional protections afforded persons accused of crimes is essential. These protections are in the Bill of Rights. These first ten amendments to the Constitution were adopted to overcome the concern that the Constitution granted power to a central government at the expense of the individual citizen. These rights protect not only persons accused of crimes but also businesses from excessive regulation. As you study the Fourth, Fifth, and Sixth Amendments to the Constitution, notice their impact on the regulatory process.

5. The Fourth Amendment: Illegal Search and Seizure

The Fourth Amendment protects individuals and corporations from **unreasonable searches and seizures.** It primarily protects persons from unwarranted intrusions on their privacy by requiring the police to obtain a court order called a **search warrant.** As a general rule, the search warrant must be obtained by the police prior to a search of a person, any premises, or other property such as the trunk of an automobile. Before a court will issue a search warrant, the police must offer evidence that a crime has been committed and there is cause to believe that the intended search will assist in its investigation.

Fourth Amendment issues usually arise in criminal cases involving search warrants. Typical issues are:

- The validity of searches incident to an arrest
- The validity of search warrants (the presence of probable cause to issue the warrant)
- The validity of consents to searches
- The extent to which property such as automobiles may be searched without a warrant

In recent years, the Fourth Amendment protection has been narrowed by Supreme Court decisions. To protect police officers, courts have held that officers making an arrest do not need a search warrant to search that person and the immediate area around him or her for weapons. Officers are given far more latitude in searching an automobile than in searching a person, a home, or a building. The right to search for evidence also extends to the premises of persons not suspected of criminal conduct. Such premises may include offices of newspapers and attorneys. In addition, during an automobile search a person who does not own the vehicle may not object to its search even if he or she has property in the vehicle.

Moreover, electronic surveillance has been held not to violate the Fourth Amendment if used pursuant to a court-authorized order. Warrantless searches of garbage bags left at curbside of a suspect's home and of property of a foreign citizen seized abroad have both been held to be constitutional, as have aerial observation of a fenced-in backyard of a house. The case of the foreign citizen established the legal principle that the Fourth Amendment does not apply to actions of the federal government involving foreign citizens that take place outside the United States.

Fourth Amendment protection also extends to certain civil matters. For example, building inspectors do not have the right to inspect for building code violations without a warrant if the owner of the premises objects. The Securities and Exchange Commission (SEC) cannot use confidential reports obtained in the course of its routine operations to establish a violation of federal law. Nor can agents from the Occupational Safety and Health Administration (OSHA) conduct unannounced searches of workplaces to inspect for safety hazards and violations of OSHA regulations. The Supreme Court held that the warrantless inspection provisions of the Occupational Safety and Health Act were unconstitutional under the Fourth Amendment. If an owner of a business objects to an inspection, inspectors must go to court and obtain a search warrant. To obtain this warrant, inspectors must show that the standards for conducting an inspection are satisfied; they do not need to show probable cause.

The Supreme Court has upheld a state law that authorized warrantless searches of junkyards. A divided court (5 to 4) said that warrantless searches of junkyards are constitutional because operators of commercial premises in closely regulated industries have a reduced expectation of privacy. The Supreme Court has upheld alcohol and drug testing of railroad employees against a Fourth Amendment challenge. In pervasively regulated industries the privacy interests of the business are weakened and government interests in regulating particular businesses are heightened; thus a warrantless inspection of commercial premises may well be reasonable within the meaning of the Fourth Amendment.

6. The Fifth Amendment: Self-Incrimination

The Fifth Amendment is best known for its protection against compulsory self-incrimination. When a person giving testimony pleads "the Fifth," he or she is exercising the right to this protection. The privilege against self-incrimination protects an accused from being compelled to testify against himself or herself. The Fifth Amendment does not protect the accused from being compelled by the state to produce real or physical evidence. Fingerprints can be taken, as can voice samples and bodily fluids. In order to be testimonial and protected, an accused's communication must itself, explicitly or implicitly, relate to a factual assertion or disclose information.

Issues concerning the Fifth Amendment protection as it relates to a business may arise when a businessperson is called to testify about a business matter or is served with a subpoena requiring the production of records. A businessperson may not be called upon to testify against himself or herself in any governmental hearing such as a congressional proceeding. But the protection against compulsory self-incrimination does not protect a businessperson from having to produce, in court, records prepared in the ordinary course of business. Since the production of records does not compel oral testimony, the Fifth Amendment does not prevent the use of written evidence, including documents in the hands either of the accused or of someone else such as an accountant. Of course, corporate officials, union officials, and partners cannot be required to give oral testimony if such testimony may tend to incriminate them. However, these individuals must produce subpoenaed documents. Therefore, business records can be obtained even if they are incriminating.

Obviously a corporation or other collective entity cannot be called upon to testify; only individuals can do so. Therefore, the protection against compulsory self-incrimination does not apply to corporations or to labor unions or partnerships. These collective entities have no Fifth Amendment right to refuse to submit their books and records in response to a subpoena. The only business protected by the Fifth Amendment privilege against compulsory self-incrimination is a sole proprietorship.

When business records are subpoenaed in a tax investigation, it is often contended that the act of producing the records is itself incriminating. The argument is made that compliance with the subpoena concedes the existence of the papers demanded and their control by the person served. It also would indicate the taxpayer's belief that the papers are those described in the subpoena. The court has indicated that each case depends on its own set of facts, and the act of answering a subpoena may or may not be privileged, depending on those facts. As the following case illustrates, the most important fact is the form of business organization whose records are being sought. If the business is a corporation, then the individual required to supply the records cannot use the Fifth Amendment to avoid producing them.

IN RE GRAND JURY WITNESSES

92 F.3d 710 (8th Cir. 1996)

A federal grand jury in South Dakota was investigating possible criminal violations of the Clean Water Act at a corporation's waste water treatment facility. Two former employees had pleaded guilty to a conspiracy to violate the Clean Water Act, and the grand jury investigation included whether senior corporate officers could be criminally liable as "responsible corporate officer[s]." The corporation has responded to grand jury document subpoenas, acting through its designated document custodians.

Two high-ranking corporate officers, who are not currently targets of the investigation, moved to quash document subpoenas demanding they produce "all documents in your possession" relating to operation of the corporation's waste water treatment plant and to the resulting pollution problems. Rejecting their Fifth Amendment challenge to the subpoenas, the district court denied the motion to quash, ordered the Witnesses to produce "all corporate records in their possession," and held them in contempt for refusing to comply. The Witnesses appealed.

LOKEN, J.: The Fifth Amendment provides that no person "shall be compelled in any criminal case to be a witness against himself." This protection does not apply to the contents of any document that a person has voluntarily prepared. However, when a grand jury subpoenas a person's private papers, the act of producing responsive documents has communicative aspects of its own, wholly aside from the contents of the papers, such as whether a document exists, is genuine, and is in the subpoenaed person's possession. Therefore, depending on the circumstances, the act of producing personal papers may be testimonial self-incrimination protected by the Fifth Amendment. However, the Fifth Amendment does not protect corporations and other "collective entities" from compelled self-incrimination. Because corporate document custodians hold corporate records in a representative rather than a personal capacity, those records cannot be the subject of the [custodian's] personal privilege against self-incrimination.

The Witnesses argue that the district court erred in applying the collective entity doctrine in this case because they were subpoenaed personally, not as corporate document custodians, and because the act of production may compel them to disclose their personal possession of incriminating corporate documents. In other words, the Witnesses claim that they may not be compelled to produce collective entity documents in their possession if that act of production might incriminate them. This issue was decided in the government's favor in *Braswell v. United States*, 108 S.Ct. 2284 (1988). The Witnesses' attempt to distinguish *Braswell* is unpersuasive, at least at this stage of the grand jury proceedings.

In *Braswell*, the government subpoenaed the president and sole shareholder of two corporations to produce all corporate books and records. He moved to quash, arguing that the act of production would incriminate him and the collective entity doctrine should not apply to entities that are his alter ego. The Supreme Court rejected that argument. After thoroughly reviewing its collective entity and act-of-production cases, the Court squarely held, "A custodian may not resist a subpoena for corporate records on Fifth Amendment grounds." Responding to the contention that this rule will subject corporate custodians to personal act-of-production incrimination, the Court explained:

> Although a corporate custodian is not entitled to resist a subpoena on the ground that his act of production will be personally incriminating, we do think certain consequences flow from the fact that the custodian's act of production is one in his representative rather than personal capacity. Because the custodian acts as a representative, the act is deemed one of the corporation and not the individual.

The Witnesses seek to distinguish *Braswell* by arguing that the subpoenas in this case are directed to them personally and call for corporate documents in their personal possession. As numerous cases make clear, this is a distinction without a difference. Fifth Amendment protection does not turn on whether the subpoena is directed to the collective entity, to a person as that entity's document custodian, or to the person individually. The issue is whether the subpoena requires the person to produce corporate records held in a representative capacity. Here, the district court clarified any ambiguity in that regard by ordering the Witnesses to produce "corporate records in their possession." It is irrelevant that the Witnesses are not the corporation's designated document custodians. For Fifth Amendment purposes, any corporate agent with possession, custody, or control of corporate records produces those records in a representative capacity.

As the above-quoted passage from *Braswell* makes clear, our decision that the district court's order to produce must be affirmed does not mean that the Witnesses are doomed to suffer the consequences of act-of-production incrimination. Their private papers remain protected by the Fifth Amendment, and issues of whether a particular document is a private paper or a corporate record may be submitted to the district court in camera.

The order of the district court is [*affirmed*].

Case Questions

1. Why is an individual treated differently from a corporation for the purpose of producing records pursuant to the Fifth Amendment?

2. Would it make any difference in this case if the target of the investigation were the president of the corporation?

3. Why is it necessary, from a practical standpoint, for the Court to require the production of these documents?

The Fifth Amendment also prevents a person from being twice prosecuted for the same offense by the same governmental entity. The **double jeopardy** clause prevents the government from improperly harassing persons by repeatedly charging them for the same infraction.

In the following case businesspersons attempted to use the double jeopardy clause to prevent criminal prosecution following the imposition of civil penalties for violating various federal laws.

HUDSON V. UNITED STATES

118 S.Ct. 488 (1997)

The Government administratively imposed monetary penalties and occupational debarment on petitioners for violation of federal banking statutes, and later criminally indicted them for essentially the same conduct.

Petitioner John Hudson was the chairman and controlling shareholder of the First National Bank of Tipton (Tipton) and the First National Bank of Hammon (Hammon). Petitioner Jack Rackley was president of Tipton and a member of the board of directors of Hammon, and petitioner Larry Baresel was a member of the board of directors of both Tipton and Hammon.

The Comptroller of the Currency (OCC) concluded that petitioners had used their bank positions to arrange a series of loans to third parties, in violation of various federal banking statutes and regulations. OCC issued a "Notice of Assessment of Civil Money Penalty." The notice alleged that the illegal loans resulted in losses to Tipton and Hammon of almost $900,000 and contributed to the failure of those banks. OCC assessed penalties of $100,000 against Hudson and $50,000 each against both Rackley and Baresel. OCC also issued a "Notice of Intention to Prohibit Further Participation" against each petitioner.

Petitioners resolved the OCC proceedings against them by each entering into a "Stipulation and Consent Order." These consent orders provided that Hudson, Baresel, and Rackley would pay assessments of $16,500, $15,000, and $12,500 respectively. In addition, each petitioner agreed not to "participate in any manner" in the affairs of any banking institution without the written authorization of the OCC and all other relevant regulatory agencies.

Petitioners subsequently were indicted in the Western District of Oklahoma in a 22-count indictment on charges of conspiracy, misapplication of bank funds, and making false bank entries. The violations charged in the indictment rested on the same lending transactions that formed the basis for the prior administrative actions brought by OCC. Petitioners moved to dismiss the indictment on double jeopardy grounds.

REHNQUIST, J.: We hold that the Double Jeopardy Clause of the Fifth Amendment is not a bar to the later criminal prosecution because the administrative proceedings were civil, not criminal. . . .

The Double Jeopardy Clause provides that no "person [shall] be subject for the same offense to be twice put in jeopardy of life or limb." We have long recognized that the Double Jeopardy Clause does not prohibit the imposition of punishment. The Clause protects only against the imposition of multiple criminal punishments for the same offense.

Whether a particular punishment is criminal or civil is, at least initially, a matter of statutory construction. A court must first ask whether the legislature, in establishing the penalizing mechanism, indicated either expressly or impliedly a preference for one label or the other. Even in those cases where the legislature has indicated an intention to establish a civil penalty, we have inquired further whether the statutory scheme was so punitive either in purpose or effect as to "transform what was clearly intended as a civil remedy into a criminal penalty."

In making this latter determination, several factors provide useful guideposts, including: (1) whether the sanction involves an affirmative disability or restraint; (2) whether it has historically been regarded as a punishment; (3) whether it comes into play only on a finding of scienter; (4) whether its operation will promote the traditional aims of punishment—retribution and deterrence; (5) whether the behavior to which it applies is already a crime; (6) whether an alternative purpose to which it may rationally be connected is assignable for it; and (7) whether it appears excessive in relation to the alternative purpose assigned. It is important to note, however, that these factors must be considered in relation to the statute on its face, and only the clearest proof will suffice to override legislative intent and transform what has been denominated a civil remedy into a criminal penalty.

Applying traditional double jeopardy principles to the facts of this case, it is clear that the criminal prosecution of these petitioners would not violate the Double Jeopardy Clause. It is evident that Congress intended the OCC money penalties and debarment sanctions to be civil in nature. As for the money penalties, which authorize the imposition of monetary penalties, expressly provide that such penalties are civil. While the provision authorizing debarment contains no language explicitly denominating the sanction as civil, we think it significant that the authority to issue debarment orders is conferred upon the appropriate federal banking agencies. That such authority was conferred upon administrative agencies is prima facie evidence that Congress intended to provide for a civil sanction.

We find that there is little evidence, much less the clearest proof that we require, suggesting that either OCC money penalties or debarment sanctions are so punitive in form and effect as to render them criminal despite Congress' intent to the contrary.

We recognize that the imposition of both money penalties and debarment sanctions will deter others from emulating petitioners' conduct, a traditional goal of criminal punishment. But the mere presence of this purpose is insufficient to render a sanction criminal, as deterrence may serve civil as well as criminal goals.

In sum, there simply is very little showing, to say nothing of the "clearest proof," that OCC money penalties and debarment sanctions are criminal. The Double Jeopardy Clause is therefore no obstacle to their trial on the pending indictments, and it may proceed.

The judgment of the Court of Appeals for the Tenth Circuit is accordingly [*affirmed*].

Case Questions

1. What protections against governmental overreaching are provided by the Double Jeopardy Clause?

2. Under which circumstances could a civil penalty be so punitive as to implicate the Double Jeopardy Clause?

3. Why were the money penalties and debarment sanctions insufficient to render the sanctions criminal in nature?

7. The Sixth Amendment: Trial by Jury

The Sixth Amendment, like the Fifth, provides multiple protection in criminal cases. Essentially, its protections give you the right to:

- A speedy and public trial
- Trial by jury
- Be informed of the charge against you

- Confront your accuser
- Subpoena witnesses in your favor
- Have the assistance of an attorney

The American concept of a jury trial contemplates a jury drawn from a fair cross section of the community. The jury guards against the exercise of arbitrary power by using the commonsense judgment of the community as a hedge against the overzealous or mistaken prosecutor. The jury's perspective on facts is used in preference to the professional or, perhaps, biased response of a judge.

Community participation in administering criminal law is not only consistent with our democratic heritage, it is also critical to public confidence in the fairness of the criminal justice system. Therefore, a state may not restrict jury service only to special groups or exclude identifiable segments playing major roles in the community. For example, a Missouri law that excluded females who requested an automatic exemption from jury duty was unconstitutional as violating the "cross-section" concept. Likewise, minorities may not be systematically excluded from jury duty, either in the eligibility to serve process or in the actual selection process during a trial. As discussed in Chapter 2, peremptory challenges used during voir dire examination cannot be used to deny a defendant a jury of one's peers.

The right to a jury trial does not extend to state juvenile court delinquency proceedings because they are not criminal prosecutions. However, juveniles do have the right to counsel, to confront the witnesses against them, and to cross-examine them.

The right to an attorney exists in any cases where incarceration is a possible punishment. It exists at every stage of the proceeding, commencing with an investigation that centers on a person as the accused. Thus, it can be seen that there are many technical aspects to the Sixth Amendment, and numerous cases still arise concerning it. For example, a criminal defendant's right to counsel of his or her choice may be limited in certain situations by the attorney's prior representation of a corporation. By representing the corporation, an attorney may obtain potentially privileged information from employees who later become adverse witnesses against the corporation or individual officers in criminal prosecutions. These potential conflicts of interest also become very complicated when employees provide incriminating information to corporate counsel on the mistaken belief that he or she represents their interests as well as those of the corporation. Often, however, these interests can be adverse and in direct conflict.

To further complicate the issue of representation, a new 1994 U.S. Department of Justice rule now allows government lawyers to contact workers who are not "high level" in a company without going through the company's legal department. Prosecutors may interview middle managers or line workers about company practices and try to persuade them to blow the whistle on upper management in criminal investigations. Normally, ethical rules would bar an attorney from directly contacting a person who is already represented by counsel. The Justice Department has rejected that rule in the context of corporate counsel primarily on the ground that it would frustrate the development of successful criminal investigations against corporations and corporate officials.

Concept Summary: Constitutional Protections

1. The Bill of Rights contains several provisions that protect persons accused of crimes and protect business from certain regulatory activities.

2. The Fourth Amendment protection against illegal searches and seizures has been narrowed substantially in recent years.

3. The Fifth Amendment protection against compulsory self-incrimination does not protect an accused from being the source of real or physical evidence and does not prevent the use of business records in criminal cases. The protection is limited to testimony that incriminates.

4. The Fifth Amendment protection against double jeopardy is not a bar to subsequent criminal prosecution following the imposition of civil penalties.

5. The Sixth Amendment guarantees that peremptory challenges cannot deny an accused a jury of one's peers and that defendants have a right to counsel.

Specific Crimes

The following sections consider a number of federal crimes that today are relevant to the conduct of business. They are frequently committed even by small businesses. Many of these crimes result in civil suits against a business for dollar damages as well as criminal prosecutions.

8. Endangering Workers

Most of the crimes committed by business are white-collar crimes because they do not involve violence. Businesses are sometimes, however, found guilty of violent crime. A major recent trend in the criminal law is for states to charge corporate officials with crimes such as assault and battery, reckless **endangerment of workers,** and a form of accidental homicide when a worker is injured or killed on the job. These accidents, injuries, and deaths usually occur in manufacturing companies that use extremely dangerous processes. Corporate officials in companies that use mercury, cyanide, or other dangerous chemicals and that do not have adequate safety precautions may face criminal charges when workers are injured or killed as a result of their employment.

When criminal charges are brought in these cases, the defense usually contends that the state criminal laws have been preempted by the federal Occupational Safety and Health Act. While some courts have accepted this argument, most, including such major industrial states as New York, Illinois, and Michigan, have not. On two occasions the Supreme Court has been asked to review the matter and hold that state laws are preempted. It has refused to do so. As a result, in most states company officials can be criminally prosecuted for endangering the health and safety of their employees.

Some states, such as California, have passed specific statutes that require employers to warn employees of life-threatening hazards in the workplace. Failure to do so is a crime. It is likely that additional states will adopt similar legislation in the near future.

9. False Statement to a Bank

Borrowers from banks are routinely required to furnish their financial statements. These statements are intended to supply information to the bank to be used in making its decision on the loan request. Financial statements are relied upon by banks even though many of them are not certified as correct by a certified public accountant. To protect banks and attempt to ensure the accuracy of financial information, the U.S. Code makes it a federal crime for anyone willfully to make a false statement to a federally insured bank or savings and loan association. The proof must show beyond a reasonable doubt that the false statement or report was made with the intent to influence the action of the insured bank or savings and loan association upon an application, advance, commitment, loan or any change or extension thereof. An *insured bank* is one whose deposits are insured by the Federal Deposit Insurance Corporation. An insured savings and loan association is one whose deposits are insured by the Federal Savings and Loan Insurance Corporation.

A statement or report is *false* when made if it relates to a material fact and is untrue and is then known to be untrue by the person making it. A fact is *material* if it is important to the decision to be made by the officers or employees of the institution involved and has the capacity of influencing them in making that decision. It is not necessary, however, to prove that the institution involved was, in fact, influenced or misled. The gist of the offense is an attempt to influence such an institution by willfully making the false statement or report concerning the matter. The maximum penalty for a violation is two years' imprisonment and a $5,000 fine.

10. Fraud

The U.S. Code contains several provisions making it criminal to carry out a scheme to defraud. Two of these provisions cover fraud using the mails and interstate wire communication facilities. Another provision makes it a crime for anyone to transport someone or induce someone to travel in interstate commerce for the purpose of executing a scheme to defraud that person of money or property having a value of $5,000 or more. In addition, a federal law prevents fraud by use of counterfeit access devices, including bank cards, plates, codes, account numbers, or other means of account access to initiate a transfer of funds. The counterfeit or unauthorized access device used must result in at least $1,000 being fraudulently obtained within a one-year period. An *unauthorized access device* is any access device that is lost, stolen, expired, revoked, canceled, or obtained with intent to defraud.

Mail fraud and wire fraud cases require proof beyond a reasonable doubt that the person accused of fraud:

- Had the intent to defraud someone
- Knowingly and willfully devised a scheme to defraud or to obtain money or property by means of false pretenses, representations, or promises
- Used the U.S. Postal Service by mailing some matter or thing for the purpose of executing the scheme to defraud in the case of mail fraud or transmitted by wire in interstate commerce some sound for the purpose of executing the scheme to defraud in the case of wire fraud

A *scheme* is any plan or course of action intended to deceive others. A statement or representation is *false* or *fraudulent* if it relates to a material fact and is known to be untrue or is made with reckless indifference as to its truth or falsity. A statement or representation may also be *false* or *fraudulent* if it constitutes a half truth or effectively conceals a material fact with intent to defraud. A *material fact* is a fact that would be important to a reasonable person in deciding whether to engage or not to engage in a particular transaction.

Intent to defraud means to act knowingly and with the specific intent to deceive someone, ordinarily for the purpose of causing some financial loss to another or bringing about some financial gain to oneself. In many fraud cases the defendant asserts a good-faith defense to the allegations of the indictment. **Good faith** is a complete defense since good faith on the part of a defendant is inconsistent with intent to defraud or willfulness, purposes essential to the charges. The burden of proof is not on the defendant to prove good faith, since he or she has no burden to prove anything. The government must establish beyond a reasonable doubt that the defendant acted with specific intent to defraud.

One who expresses an opinion honestly held or a belief honestly entertained is not chargeable with fraudulent intent even though the opinion is erroneous or the belief is mistaken. Evidence that establishes only that a person made a mistake in judgment or an error in management or was careless does not establish fraudulent intent. On the other hand, an honest belief on the part of the defendant that a particular business venture was sound and would ultimately succeed would not, in and of itself, constitute *good faith* in carrying out that venture if the defendant knowingly made false or fraudulent representations to others with the specific intent to deceive them.

It is not necessary that the material mailed or transmitted by wire was itself false or fraudulent or that the alleged scheme actually succeeded in defrauding anyone. Each separate use of the mails or of the interstate wire facilities that further a scheme to defraud constitutes a separate offense.

To illustrate the importance of these laws, consider the case of a real estate development company operating in Florida. It defrauded thousands of home purchasers by grossly inflating the prices of its homes to unsuspecting out-of-state buyers who were unfamiliar with actual market values. False appraisals were used. The company was fined $500,000 and agreed to make restitution of at least $80 million. The net result was bankruptcy for the company.

11. False Statement to a Federal Agency

The U.S. Code makes it a federal crime for anyone willfully and knowingly to make a false or fraudulent statement to a department or agency of the United States. The false statement must be related to a material matter, and the defendant must have acted willfully and with knowledge of the falsity. It is not necessary to show that the government agency was in fact deceived or misled. The issue of materiality is one of law for the courts. The maximum penalty is five years' imprisonment and a $10,000 fine.

A person may be guilty of a violation without proof that he or she had knowledge that the matter was within the jurisdiction of a federal agency. A businessperson may violate this law by making a false statement to another firm or person with knowledge that the information will be submitted to a government agency. Businesses must take care to avoid puffery or exaggerations in the context of any matter that may come within the jurisdiction of a federal agency.

Due to the sweeping nature of this statute, seven federal appellate courts of appeal had recognized an **exculpatory no** exception for simple denials made in response to government questioning as part of a criminal investigation. This narrow exception protected an individual from prosecution for making a false statement when the person's statement simply denies criminal wrongdoing. The exculpatory no was permitted when a person, in response to governmental questioning, had to choose between three undesirable options: self-incrimination by telling the truth; remaining silent and raising greater suspicions; or denying guilt by making a false statement to the governmental official. Courts permitting this exception believed it balanced the need for protecting the basic functions of government agencies conducting investigations against the Fifth Amendment protection against self-incrimination.

In early 1998, the Supreme Court rejected the exculpatory no exception in the case of *Brogan v. United States*, 118 U.S. 805 (1998). The Court found the exception was not supported by the plain language of the statute and held that the Fifth Amendment does not confer a privilege to lie.

12. Bankruptcy Crimes

Bankruptcy proceedings are conducted in federal courts. To protect the interests of all parties to the proceedings, the U.S. Code makes certain conduct by the debtor and certain conduct by creditors and others a federal crime. These are **bankruptcy crimes.** First, it is a crime for the bankrupt debtor to falsify the information filed in the bankruptcy proceedings. Similarly, it is a crime for anyone to present a false claim in any bankruptcy proceeding.

Any person, including the debtor, in possession of property belonging to the estate of a debtor in bankruptcy, is guilty of a felony if he or she conceals the property from the person charged with control of the property in the bankruptcy proceeding. The law requires that the act of concealment be fraudulent. An act is done fraudulently if done with intent to deceive or cheat any creditor, trustee, or bankruptcy judge. In this context, *conceal* means to secrete, falsify, mutilate, fraudulently transfer, withhold information or knowledge required by law to be made known, or take any action preventing discovery. Since the offense of **concealment** is a continuing one, the acts of concealment may have begun before as well as be committed after the bankruptcy proceeding began.

It is no defense that the concealment may have proved unsuccessful. Even though the property in question is recovered for the debtor's estate, the defendant may still be guilty of concealment. Similarly, it is no defense that there was no demand by any officer of the court or creditor for the property alleged to have been concealed.

13. Racketeer Influenced and Corrupt Organizations Act (RICO)

The most controversial of the federal criminal laws relating to business is the Racketeer Influenced and Corrupt Organizations Act, commonly known as **RICO.** As the name implies, the intent of the law was to impose liability on organized crime. RICO imposes criminal and civil liability upon those businesspersons who engage in certain *prohibited activities* and who engage in interstate commerce. Specifically, liability extends to any person who:

- Uses or invests income from prohibited activities to acquire an interest in or to operate an enterprise
- Acquires or maintains an interest in or control of an enterprise
- Conducts or participates in the conduct of an enterprise while being employed by or associated with it

Each prohibited activity is defined to include, as one necessary element, proof either of a *pattern of racketeering activity* or of *collection of unlawful debt*. **Racketeering** is defined in RICO to mean "any act or threat involving" specified state law crimes, any "act" indictable under various specified federal statutes, and certain federal "offenses." As to the term *pattern*, the statute says only that it "requires at least two acts of racketeering activity" within a ten-year period. It is not otherwise defined. The case that follows defined pattern of activity and led to an expansion of RICO cases.

H.J. INC. v. NORTHWESTERN BELL TELEPHONE COMPANY

109 S.Ct. 2893 (1989)

Petitioners, H.J. Inc., filed a class action RICO suit for an injunction and triple damages on behalf of customers of the defendant—respondent Northwestern Bell Telephone Company (NBT). It alleged that NBT had bribed the members of the Minnesota Public Utilities Commission (MPUC) to approve rates in excess of a fair and reasonable amount. It had done so by paying for parties, meals, tickets to sporting events, and airline tickets for commissioners.

The lower courts dismissed the complaint because all of the acts alleged had been committed to further a single scheme to influence MPUC commissioners to the detriment of NBT's customers and the law requires a pattern of racketeering activity. They concluded that a pattern of activity requires multiple illegal schemes. Other courts of appeal had reached the opposite conclusion on the meaning of the word "pattern."

As a result, the Supreme Court granted certiorari. The government participated as a friend of the court (amicus curiae), referred to in the opinion as "amici."

BRENNAN, J.: . . . Congress has done nothing . . . to illuminate RICO's key requirement of a pattern of racketeering; and as the plethora of different views expressed by the Courts of Appeals . . . demonstrates, developing a meaningful concept of "pattern" within the existing statutory framework has proved to be no easy task.

It is, nevertheless, a task we must undertake in order to decide this case. Our guides in the endeavor must be the text of the statute and its legislative history. We find no support in those sources for the proposition . . . that predicate acts of racketeering may form a pattern only when they are part of separate illegal schemes. Nor can we agree with those courts that have suggested that a pattern is established merely by proving two predicate acts or with

amici in this case who argue that the word "pattern" refers only to predicates that are indicative of a perpetrator involved in organized crime or its functional equivalent. In our view, Congress had a more natural and commonsense approach to RICO's pattern element in mind, intending a more stringent requirement than proof simply of two predicates, but also envisioning a concept of sufficient breadth that it might encompass multiple predicates within a single scheme that were related and that amounted to, or threatened the likelihood of, continued criminal activity.

We begin . . . with RICO's text [which] indicates that Congress envisioned circumstances in which no more than two predicates would be necessary to establish a pattern of racketeering—otherwise it would have drawn a narrower boundary to RICO liability, requiring proof of a greater number of predicates. But, at the same time, the statement that a pattern requires at least two predicates implies that while two acts are necessary, they may not be sufficient.

The legislative history shows that Congress indeed had a fairly flexible concept of a pattern in mind. A pattern is not formed by "sporadic activity," and a person cannot "be subjected to the sanctions simply for committing two widely separated and isolated criminal offenses." Instead, "[t]he term 'pattern' itself requires the showing of a relationship" between the predicates, and of "'the threat of continuing activity.'" It is this factor of *continuity plus relationship* which combines to produce a pattern. RICO's legislative history reveals Congress' intent that to prove a pattern of racketeering activity a plaintiff or prosecutor must show that the racketeering predicates are related, *and* that they amount to or pose a threat of continued criminal activity. . . .

RICO's predicate acts or offenses, and the *relationship* these predicates must bear one to another, are distinct requirements. A party alleging a RICO violation may demonstrate continuity over a closed period by proving a series of related predicates extending over a substantial period of time. Predicate acts extending over a few weeks or months and threatening no further criminal conduct do not satisfy this requirement: Congress was concerned in RICO with long-term criminal conduct. Often a RICO action will be brought before continuity can be established in this way. In such cases, liability depends on whether the *threat* of continuity is demonstrated. . . .

Various *amici* urge that RICO's pattern element should be interpreted . . . so that a defendant's racketeering activities form a pattern only if they are characteristic either of organized crime in the traditional sense, or of an organized-crime-type perpetrator, that is, of an association dedicated to the repeated commission of criminal offenses. . . .

Congress' decision not explicitly to limit RICO's broad terms strongly implies that Congress had in mind no such narrow and fixed idea of what constitutes a pattern as that suggested by *amici* here. . . .

The occasion for Congress' action was the perceived need to combat organized crime. But Congress for cogent reasons chose to enact a more general statute, one which, although it had organized crime as its focus, was not limited in application to organized crime. Congress picked out as key to RICO's application broad concepts that might fairly indicate an organized crime connection, but that it fully realized do not either individually or together provide anything approaching a perfect fit with "organized crime." . . .

RICO, with its very generous definition of "racketeering activity," acknowledges the breakdown of the traditional conception of organized crime, and responds to a new situation in which persons engaged in long-term criminal activity often operate *wholly* within legitimate enterprises. Congress drafted RICO broadly enough to encompass a wide range of criminal activity, taking many different forms and likely to attract a broad array of perpetrators operating in many different ways. We thus decline the invitation to invent a rule that RICO's pattern of racketeering concept requires an allegation and proof of an organized crime nexus. . . .

Petitioner's complaint alleges that at different times over the course of at least a 6-year period the noncommissioned respondents gave five members of the MPUC numerous bribes, in several different forms, with the objective—in which they were allegedly successful—of causing these Commissioners to approve unfair and unreasonable rates for Northwestern Bell. RICO defines bribery as a "racketeering activity," so petitioners have alleged multiple predicate acts.

Under the analysis we have set forth above, and consistent with the allegations in their complaint, petitioners may be able to prove that the multiple predicates alleged constitute "a pattern of racketeering activity," in that they satisfy the requirements of relationship and continuity. The acts of bribery alleged are said to be related by a common purpose, to influence Commissioners in carrying out their duties in order to win approval of unfairly and unreasonably high rates for Northwestern Bell. Furthermore, petitioners claim that the racketeering predicates occurred with some frequency over at least a 6-year period, which may be sufficient to satisfy the continuity requirement. Alternatively, a threat of continuity of racketeering activity might be established at trial by showing that the alleged bribes were a regular way of conducting Northwestern Bell's ongoing business, or a regular way of conducting or participating in the conduct of the alleged and ongoing RICO enterprise, the MPUC. [The judgment is *reversed and remanded*].

Case Questions

1. What is the purpose behind RICO?
2. What is required to show a pattern of racketeering under RICO?
3. Must racketeering activities be a part of organized crime?

TABLE 10–3   Examples of 1997 RICO Cases

Parties	Alleged Illegal Activity	State
Brannon v. Boatmen's Bancshares, Inc.	Bank fraud	Oklahoma
Cannon vs. Nationwide Acceptance Corp.	Loan fraud	Illinois
Ehrich vs. B.A.T. Industries	Scheme to cause cigarette addiction	New Jersey
Emery v. American General Finance, Inc.	Mail fraud	Illinois
Farmers & Merchants National Bank vs. San Clemente Financial Group Securities	Securities fraud	New Jersey
Kaiser vs. Stewart	Insurance fraud	Pennsylvania
McCampbell vs. KPMG Peat Marwick	Accounting fraud	Texas
Schwartz vs. Upper Deck Co.	Gambling fraud	California

The law has been used against a variety of defendants, as Table 10–3 illustrates. Rather than encouraging suits by private persons against organized crime, RICO has encouraged suits against accounting firms, brokerage houses, banks, and other businesses. A recent survey found that more than 75 percent of all RICO suits involve securities frauds and other types of business fraud. Less than 10 percent involve criminal activity generally associated with organized crime. When one considers that RICO cases constitute almost 10 percent of the case load in federal courts, the importance of this statute is apparent. Yet the law has not had its intended impact and needs clarification by Congress, as Justice Brennan suggested in the preceding case.

RICO provides for drastic remedies. Conviction for a violation of RICO carries severe criminal penalties and forfeiture of illegal proceeds, and a person found in a private civil action to have violated RICO is liable for treble, or triple damages, costs, and attorneys' fees. Upon filing a RICO indictment, the government may seek a temporary restraining order to preserve all forfeitable assets until the trial is completed and judgment entered. Such orders can have a wide-ranging impact on third parties who do business with the defendants, including clients, vendors, banks, investors, creditors, dependents, and others.

14. Criminalization of Health Care

The United States spends more than $900 billion annually providing health care, and up to 10 percent of every dollar constitutes fraud and waste. The Department of Justice has assigned 50 FBI agents to specialized investigative units concentrating on health care prosecutions and is actively searching for physicians and businesspersons to prosecute for health care fraud related to false claims under government-sponsored programs such as Medicare, Medicaid, and CHAMPUS. Violators are prosecuted for submitting false claims to the government (see section 11) and/or using the mail to submit the erroneous claims (see section 10). Some of these practices may implicate RICO (section 13) and expose the defendants to even greater criminal liability.

A few recent examples illustrate just how these prosecutions are developed. An oncologist was convicted for filing false claims for administering chemotherapy to patients while he was out of the country. The doctor's defense of claiming that another doctor had been present and "covering" for him failed to convince the jury. A urologist was recently convicted of "upcoding" office visits and billing them as consultations to get more reimbursement from the government. A cardiac pacemaker salesman was convicted of offering to doctors "kickbacks" that consisted of football tickets, educational materials, and even female escorts in exchange for purchasing his firm's equipment.

Financial ties between doctors and laboratories, pharmacies, and suppliers are under scrutiny by the Justice Department. Referral agreements between home health care groups and doctors also are under examination to make sure that no unreported benefit accrues to anyone in these situations. Hospitals and nursing homes are all subject to prosecution for double-billing practices or for charging for equipment that was not used for the benefit of the patient.

15. Sentencing Guidelines

Historically, the fate of a person convicted of a crime depended heavily on the judge doing the sentencing. Some judges were lenient, and others were tough. The sentencing of convicted criminals was sometimes described as "judicial roulette." To make the criminal justice system more just and help ensure that similar crimes receive similar sentences, in the late 1980s a federal sentencing commission developed **sentencing guidelines** for federal crimes.

The published guidelines followed a great deal of study and debate. They use a mathematical approach and assign a number to each type of crime and to all attending circumstances. Some numbers are pluses and some are minuses. Multipliers are used for aggravating circumstances, and tables provide a range of sentences. For example, a first-offense armed robbery offender who stole $20,000 would be given a sentence of 46 to 57 months.

The law authorizes judges to depart from the guidelines when they encounter factors not considered by the commission. If a judge intends to impose a sentence in excess of the guidelines, the defendant must be informed in advance of this fact and of the reasons for the departure. In most cases, judges determine the sentence by relying on a probation officer's report. If the report recommends a penalty tougher than the guidelines, the defendant may review the report in advance, argue against the tougher sentence, and challenge the grounds.

The Federal Sentencing Guidelines have been subject to considerable debate and controversy. Many federal judges have been irked at the loss of control in the sentencing phase of the case, and others have criticized the complexity of the guidelines, which are sometimes hard even for the judges to follow.

The U.S. Sentencing Commission, which administers the guidelines, recently reported to Congress that great disparities still persist in sentencing for some federal offenses. Federal prosecutors often pursue money laundering charges in a broad array of cases because the guidelines impose such harsh sentences. For example, a businessperson who fraudulently obtains

$20,000 of insurance payments and conducts routine financial transactions with the proceeds may be incarcerated for 8–14 months if charged with mail fraud. However, the same defendant would face a jail sentence of 33–41 months if charged under the money laundering statute.

Under the guidelines, either party may appeal based upon a claim that the trial judge did not follow the guidelines properly. The following case illustrates that point and how drastically the sentence may change depending upon the amount of fraud involved.

United States v. Palmer

31 F.3d 259 (5th Cir. 1994)

DAVIS, J.: The United States appeals Gary Palmer's sentence following his plea of guilty to one count of conspiracy to commit bank fraud. Because the district court erred in concluding that the bank suffered no loss, we vacate the sentence and remand.

Gary Palmer was the president of Liberty National Bank of Dallas, Texas, and the principal shareholder of Liberty Bancshares, Inc., the holding company that owned Liberty National Bank. Palmer was also the sole shareholder of the Texas Acceptance Corporation ("TAC"), the affiliate of Liberty National Bank. . . .

In 1993, Palmer pled guilty to one count of bank fraud. The presentence report stated that Palmer's action had caused a loss of $1,900,000. Therefore, the report recommended a nine-level increase in Palmer's offense level [pursuant to the Federal Sentencing Guidelines] for causing a loss of more than $1,000,000 but less than $2,000,000. Palmer objected to the increase and contended that the bank suffered no loss because the three entities—Liberty National Bank, Liberty Bancshares, Inc. and TAC—were a single organization with aligned interests that shared the $1.9 million.

The Government countered that the Bank and Liberty Bancshares were separate entities and that a reduction of Liberty Bancshares' indebtedness did not confer any benefit on the Bank. According to the Government, the principal benefit was to the holding company and the conspirators who owned the holding company. . . .

The district court rejected the presentence report's calculations of the offense level and refused to assess any points for financial loss. Instead, the court determined that the offense level was six and sentenced Palmer to five years of probation. The Government filed a timely notice of appeal. . . .

This court reviews a district court's application of the sentencing guidelines *de novo* and the district court's findings of fact for clear error. . . . The district court concluded that the insured bank sustained no loss because it considered Liberty National Bank, Liberty Bancshares, and TAC as one entity. This led the district court to further conclude that the Bank suffered no loss even though the holding company used some of the Bank's funds to extinguish indebtedness of the holding company and for other purposes which did not improve the financial health of the bank. . . .

We agree with the Government that the district court started from a faulty premise. A benefit to a holding company is not necessarily a benefit to the subsidiary. A holding company can manipulate property and credit of a controlled corporation to benefit itself while damaging the subsidiary. . . .

A large part of the Bank's $1.9 million profit was used to pay off the holding company's loans. Liberty National Bank had no liability for the holding company's loans and thus paying off Liberty Bancshares' indebtedness did not provide a benefit to the Bank.

In sum, the Bank did not benefit from the use of these funds by Liberty Bancshares and others to reduce their indebtedness. Rather, the holding company and its shareholders, such as Palmer, enjoyed the benefit of these payments. . . .

The district court therefore clearly erred in determining that the Bank suffered no loss. . . . We therefore vacate Palmer's sentence and remand this case to the district court to determine the amount of Liberty National Bank's loss consistent with this opinion and for resentencing in light of that loss. [*Vacated and remanded*].

Case Questions

1. Why do the federal sentencing guidelines exist?

2. Why is the nine-level increase in Palmer's offense level so critical to determining his overall sentence?

3. Upon what basis did the Court of Appeals find a loss to Liberty National Bank?

Because corporations cannot be jailed, the sentencing commission has developed special guidelines for sentencing organizations convicted of federal crimes. The emphasis is on monetary penalties. It must be kept in mind, however, that in most criminal cases involving organizations, corporate officers can also be charged. As a result, the guidelines are designed so that the sanctions imposed upon organizations and their agents, taken together, will provide just punishment, adequate deterrence, and incentives for organizations to maintain internal mechanisms for preventing, detecting, and reporting criminal conduct. Punishment and deterrence are goals of the guidelines.

The guidelines for sentencing organizations are based on four general principles:

1. A court must, whenever practicable, order the organization to remedy any harm caused by the offense. The resources expended to remedy the harm should be viewed not as punishment but rather as a means of making victims whole for the harm caused. This principle is designed to eliminate the need for a tort suit and still allow the court to follow the traditional tort theory of damages.

2. If the organization operated primarily for a criminal purpose or primarily by criminal means, the fine should be high enough to divest the organization of all its assets. If this recommendation is followed, the net result is that the organization is eliminated and the fine becomes a "death penalty."

3. The fine range is based on the seriousness of the offense and the culpability of the organization. The seriousness of the offense generally will be determined by examining the financial gains to the defendant or the financial loss to the victim. These amounts will be applied by use of a guideline offense-level fine table. Culpability generally will be determined by the steps taken by the organization prior to the offense to prevent and detect criminal conduct, the level and extent of involvement in or tolerance of the offense by certain personnel, and the organization's actions after an offense has been committed.

4. Probation will be included in the sentence if needed to ensure that another sanction will be fully implemented or to ensure that steps will be taken within the organization to reduce the likelihood of future criminal conduct.

To illustrate how these guidelines would work, assume that a large corporation committed fraud in selling its product to the federal government. Perhaps the test results on the product were falsely reported. If a high official in the company and some middle managers knew that the test results were falsified and the company had a previous conviction of fraud within ten years, the fine would be $20 to $40 million. However, if the company received good points for cooperation with investigators and had an aggressive internal audit program to detect and prevent fraud, the fine would be only $4 to $8 million. In either case, the court would also order *restitution*. The court may also put the business on probation, preventing it from selling stock and paying dividends, or the court may otherwise be involved in major corporate decisions. This probation provision serves to get the attention of senior management and to keep it. Management in a company on probation must prevent violations of federal laws by its employees.

If these new guidelines are followed, some very tough sentences will be imposed on corporations convicted of federal crimes. Criminal conduct will not only not pay; it may also totally destroy a business.

Key Terms

Accessory   270
Aiding and abetting   270
Bankruptcy crime   280
Concealment   280
Conspiracy   268
Double jeopardy   274
Endangerment of workers   277
Exculpatory no   280
Felony   265
Good faith   279
Intent to defraud   279
Knowingly   265

Misdemeanor   265
Nolo contendere   265
Overt act   268
Presumption of innocence   266
Probable cause   266
Racketeering   281
RICO   280
Search warrant   271
Sentencing guidelines   284
Unreasonable search and seizure   270
Willfully   265

Review Questions and Problems

Terms and Procedures

1. *Terminology*
   What is the difference between felonies and misdemeanors?

2. *The Grand Jury*
   (a) Why is a grand jury subpoena different from a trial subpoena?
   (b) What role does the grand jury play in our criminal justice system?

3. *Conspiracies*
   (a) How does the law of conspiracy permit charging defendants who did not actually participate in the commission of an offense?
   (b) What must a businessperson do to avoid being charged with a conspiracy?

4. *Aiding and Abetting*
   Bill is a partner in a CPA firm. Susan, also a partner with this firm, prepares a federal income tax return knowing that it contains false information. Bill reviews the return and questions its accuracy. Susan concedes that the return is false but informs Bill that the client wants the return prepared in this manner. Bill does not prevent Susan from obtaining the taxpayer's signature on the return or later filing it with the IRS. Has Bill aided and abetted in the commission of a crime? Explain.

Constitutional Issues

5. *The Fourth Amendment: Illegal Search and Seizure*
   With respect to OSHA, under what circumstances could a business successfully raise a Fourth Amendment claim against the government?

6. *The Fifth Amendment: Self-Incrimination*
   Sam is the owner of a sole proprietorship. A grand jury, during the course of an investigation of possible bribery in the awarding of several municipal contracts, serves three subpoenas on Sam seeking his business records. Are Sam's records privileged under the Fifth Amendment? Why or why not?

7. *The Sixth Amendment: Trial by Jury*
   What are the essential protections provided by the Sixth Amendment in criminal cases?

Specific Crimes

8. *Endangering Workers*
   Beth was killed when a trench collapsed. An investigation revealed that the trench was 27 feet deep and is without adequate shoring in violation of safety standards. Bob, the president of the firm, is charged with negligent homicide. Is a finding of guilt possible? Why or why not?

9. *False Statement to a Bank*
   In order to convict a person of making a false statement to a bank, what elements of the crime must be shown?

10. *Fraud*
    Why is "good faith" a defense to a charge of mail or wire fraud?

11. *False Statement to a Federal Agency*
    Explain the exculpatory no defense. Why has it been rejected by the Supreme Court?

12. *Bankruptcy Crimes*
    Absolutely critical to a bankruptcy crime is the issue of concealment. Describe that concept. Should it be illegal?

13. *Racketeer Influenced and Corrupt Organizations Act (RICO)*
    RICO has become a major factor in criminal and civil cases involving business conduct. One impact of RICO criminal charges is that many defendants agree to plead guilty to other criminal charges in order to have the RICO charges dismissed. Why do RICO charges produce this result?

14. *Criminalization of Health Care*
    Describe the various federal laws that are used to prosecute corrupt health care providers.

15. *Sentencing Guidelines*
    The U.S. Sentencing Guidelines apply a mathematical formula to sentencing. How do the guidelines operate?

Terminology Review

For each term in the left-hand column, match the most appropriate description in the right-hand column.

1. Grand Jury

2. Conspiracy

3. Search Warrant

4. Self-Incrimination

5. Double-Jeopardy

6. Trial by Jury

7. False Statements

8. Exculpatory No

9. RICO

10. Sentencing Guidelines

a. expansive federal law aimed at controlling abusive business practices

b. sets criminal penalties in federal cases

c. federal body charged with investigating and enforcing the law

d. simple denials in response to questioning in criminal investigation

e. protected by the fifth amendment

f. prevents trial of a person for the same infraction twice

g. criminal if made to a bank or governmental agency

h. may by issued based upon probable cause

i. an agreement with a criminal purpose

j. guaranteed by the sixth amendment in criminal cases

11

ANTITRUST LAWS— REGULATING COMPETITION

Business Decision

What to Do?

You have successfully completed the requirements to become a licensed real estate broker and you have decided to open a real estate firm in your home town. Upon application to join the local Multiple Listing Service (MLS), you learn that you are required to sign an agreement that your firm will charge a seven percent commission rate on all residential sales transactions. The reason given for this standard charge is that it will encourage all MLS agents to find buyers for all the houses for sale. The agreement calls for the commission to be divided as follows:

- Listing Agent/Firm 45%
- Selling Agent/Firm 45%
- Multiple Listing Service 10%

What concerns do you have about this agreement?

Should you sign this agreement?

This chapter discusses laws commonly referred to as antitrust laws. The term "antitrust" is somewhat misleading. Trusts are a legal arrangement used for centuries for such socially desirable purposes as promoting education or caring for spendthrift or incompetent children and for financial and tax planning. A **trust** is a fiduciary relationship concerning property in which one person, known as the **trustee,** holds legal title to property for the benefit of another, known as the **beneficiary.** The trustee has the duty to manage and preserve the property for the use and enjoyment of the beneficiary.

In the last part of the nineteenth century, the trust device was used extensively to gain monopolistic control of several industries. The trust device allowed all or at least a majority of the stock of several companies to be transferred to a trustee. The trustee then was in a position to control the operations and policy making of all the companies. The trust not only controlled production, but also dominated and divided the market and established price levels. The effect of these concentrations was to destroy the free market—"to restrain trade."

The Sherman Act

The first statute that attempted to regulate competition was the **Sherman Act** enacted in 1890. Since the purpose of the Sherman Act was to "bust" the trusts, laws against them became known as the antitrust laws. Today the term is used to describe all laws that intend to promote and regulate competition and make our competitive economic system work.

1. Historical Development

The goal of the Sherman Act is competition. Competition tends to keep private markets working in ways that are socially desirable. It encourages an efficient allocation of resources and stimulates efficiency and product innovation. A competitive system that allows easy entry to and withdrawal from the marketplace is consistent with individual freedom and economic opportunity. In 1958, Justice Hugo Black in *Northern Pacific Ry. Co. v. United States* (356 U.S. 1), reflected on the purpose of the Sherman Act when he stated in part:

> The Sherman Act was designed to be a comprehensive charter of economic liberty aimed at preserving free and unfettered competition as the rule of trade. It rests on the premise that the unrestrained interaction of competitive forces will yield the best allocation of our economic resources, the lowest prices, the highest quality and the greatest material progress, while at the same time providing an environment conducive to the preservation of our democratic, political and social institutions.

The Sherman Act still provides the basic framework for the regulation of competition. It seeks to preserve competition by prohibiting two types of anticompetitive business behavior:

- Contracts, combinations, and conspiracies in restraint of trade or commerce (see section 2)
- Monopolies and attempts to monopolize (see section 3)

In 1914 Congress, recognizing that the Sherman Act needed to be more specific, enacted the **Clayton Act** as an amendment to the Sherman Act and later twice amended the Clayton Act (1936, 1950) to clarify its provisions. The Clayton Act declares that certain enumerated practices in interstate commerce are illegal. These are practices that might adversely affect competition but that were not clear violations under the Sherman Act.

In 1914, Congress also passed the **Federal Trade Commission Act.** This act created the Federal Trade Commission (FTC), an independent administrative agency charged with keeping competition free and fair. The FTC enforces the Clayton Act. In addition, it enforces Section 5 of the FTC Act, which prohibits unfair methods of competition and unfair or deceptive acts or practices.

The antitrust laws are enforced by the federal and state governments and by private parties. The federal government's basic enforcement procedures are utilized through the Department of Justice and the FTC. The Department of Justice alone has the power to bring criminal proceedings, but it shares its civil enforcement powers with the FTC. Antitrust enforcement by state government takes the form of a state attorney general bringing civil suits for damages under the Sherman Act as well as suits for an injunction. In addition to these governmental enforcers, private parties may bring civil suits seeking monetary damages or an injunction as a means of enforcing the antitrust laws.

2. Restraint of Trade

Section 1 of the Sherman Act prohibits contracts, combinations, and conspiracies in **restraint of trade** or commerce. *Contracts* in restraint of trade usually result from verbal or written agreements; *combinations* usually result from conduct; *conspiracies* are usually established by agreement and followed up by some act carrying out the plan of the conspiracy. An express agreement is not required to create a contract in restraint of trade. Such contracts may be implied. For example, discussion of price with one's competitors together with conscious parallel pricing establishes a violation.

Joint activities by two or more persons may constitute a violation of Section 1. The most common contract in restraint of trade is an agreement among competitors to charge the same price for their products **(price fixing).** Such agreements among producers to set prices in advance rather than allow prices to be set by the operations of a free market are obviously anticompetitive and in restraint of trade. Agreements relating to territories of operation also violate Section 1 of the Sherman Act. So does an attempt to extend the economic power of a patent or copyright to unrelated products or services.

The acceptance of an invitation to participate in a plan that is in restraint of interstate commerce is sufficient to establish an unlawful conspiracy. Circumstantial evidence may be used to prove a conspiracy. For example, the simultaneous price increases by three major cigarette producers at a time of declining sales were admissible evidence to prove a conspiracy without direct proof of communication among them.

Sherman Act cases must satisfy an interstate commerce element. The facts must show that an allegedly illegal activity was either in interstate commerce or had a substantial effect on interstate commerce. The facts need not prove a change in the volume of interstate commerce but only that the activity had a substantial and adverse or not insubstantial effect on interstate commerce. In a recent case involving the medical profession, it was held that the Sherman Act is applicable to staff privileges at a hospital. The impact on interstate commerce is readily apparent.

3. Monopoly

Section 2 of the Sherman Act is directed at **monopoly** and the attempts to monopolize any part of interstate or foreign commerce. The law establishes the means to break up existing monopolies and to prevent others from developing. It is directed at single firms and does not purport to cover shared monopolies or oligopolies.

Under Section 2 of the Sherman Act, it is a violation for a firm to monopolize, attempt to monopolize, or conspire to monopolize any part of interstate or foreign commerce. A firm has violated Section 2 if it followed a course of conduct through which it obtained the power to control price or exclude competition. The mere possession of monopoly power is not a violation. There must be proof that the power resulted from a deliberate course of conduct or proof of intent to maintain the power by conduct. Proof of deliberateness is just as essential as proof of the power to control price to exclude competition. Section 2 cases require a definition of the relevant market and a study of the degree of concentration within the market. In defining the relevant market, the courts examine both product market and geographic market. A relevant market is the smallest one wide enough so that products from outside the geographic area or from other producers in the same area cannot compete with those included in the defined relevant market. In other words, if prices are raised or supply is curtailed within a given area while demand remains constant, will products from other areas or other products from within the area enter the market in enough quantity to force a lower price or increased supply?

Some monopoly cases involve products for which there are few or no substitutes. Other cases involve products for which there are numerous substitutes. For example, aluminum may be considered a product that is generally homogeneous. If a firm has 90 percent of the virgin aluminum market, a violation would be established. However, if a firm had 90 percent of the Danish coffee cake market, the decision is less clear, because numerous products compete with Danish coffee cakes as a breakfast product. The relevant product is often difficult to define because of differences in products, substitute products, product diversification, and even product clusters.

Different forms of economic analysis are used in monopoly cases. In monopoly cases, courts examine the conduct of the firm. How did it achieve its market share? Was it by internal growth or acquisition? Does the firm's current conduct tend to injure competition? Note that in the box that follows the illegal conduct was the failure to cooperate with a competitor. This conduct was designed to eliminate the competitor, and it resulted in liability for triple damages.

Example of Monopoly

The case of *Aspen Skiing Co. v. Aspen Highlands Skiing Corp.** provides an example of the kind of factual situation and legal analysis that leads to a finding of a § 2 violation. In the early years of snow skiing in Aspen, three facilities were operated by three distinct companies. The two parties involved in this case were among these competitors. In addition to offering a daily ski-lift ticket for their own mountain, each competitor sold a multiday, interchangeable, all-Aspen ticket.

_____
*105 S.Ct. 2847 (1985).

Aspen Skiing acquired the third facility and opened a fourth. Eventually, this company sold a multiday ticket that allowed its patrons access to only its facilities. As a result of this action, Aspen Highlands lost a significant share of its business. Ultimately, Aspen Highlands sued Aspen Skiing, alleging that the refusal to sell an all-Aspen ticket was an illegal attempt to monopolize the Aspen skiing market.

Aspen Skiing argued that it was not in violation of § 2 of the Sherman Act because nothing in this law required it to do business with a competitor.

concluded

Even though the trial judge agreed with this legal conclusion, the judge instructed the jury that it could find Aspen Skiing in violation of the Sherman Act unless that company persuaded the jury that its conduct was justified by any normal business purpose.

Apparently the jury was not convinced by Aspen Skiing's presentation. The jury rendered a verdict finding Aspen Skiing in violation of § 2 and awarding Aspen Highlands actual damages of $2.5 million. This award was tripled to $7.5 million, and costs and attorneys' fees were added to this amount.

Aspen Skiing was unable to convince either the court of appeals or the United States Supreme Court to reverse this jury verdict. The Supreme Court was particularly influenced by the market studies that showed skiers wanted to have access to the Highlands facilities but refused to ski there due to the lack of an all-area ticket. The Court concluded that the jury was justified in finding that inappropriate motivations to monopolize were behind Aspen Skiing's decision to stop selling the all-area ticket.

4. The Rule of Reason

The Sherman Act was deliberately vague in expectation that the courts would draw the line between legal and illegal conduct with respect to restraint of trade and monopoly. Section 1 of the Sherman Act provides that "every contract, combination . . . , or conspiracy in restraint of trade . . . is declared illegal." However, the United States Supreme Court has held that Congress did not really mean it when it used the word "every." The **rule of reason** was announced in *Standard Oil Co. v. United States* (221 U.S. 1 [1911]). The Supreme Court in that case held that contracts or conspiracies in restraint of trade were illegal only if they constituted *undue* or *unreasonable* restraints of trade and that only *unreasonable* attempts to monopolize were covered by the Sherman Act. As a result, acts that the statute prohibits may be removed from the coverage of the law by a finding that they are *reasonable.*

The *test of reasonableness* asks whether challenged contracts or acts are unreasonably restrictive of competitive conditions. If an agreement promotes competition, it may be legal. If it suppresses or destroys competition, it is unreasonable and illegal.

For purposes of the rule of reason, Sherman Act violations may be divided into two categories. Some agreements or practices are so plainly anticompetitive and so lacking in any redeeming values that they are conclusively presumed to be illegal without further examination under the rule of reason. These agreements have such a pernicious effect on competition that elaborate inquiry as to the precise harm they may cause or a business excuse for them are unnecessary. They are said to be *illegal per se.* It is not necessary to examine them to see if they are reasonable. They are conclusively presumed to be unreasonable. The other category consists of agreements and practices that are illegal only if they impose an unreasonable restraint upon competitors.

The concept of **per se illegality** simplifies proof in cases in which it is applied. When an activity is illegal per se, courts are not required to conduct a complicated and prolonged examination of the economic consequences of the activity to determine whether it is unreasonable. If it is illegal per se, proof of the activity is proof of a violation and proof that it is in restraint of trade. It is unreasonable as a matter of law.

The most common example of an agreement that is illegal per se is one that fixes prices. Agreements among competitors to divide up territories, or to limit the supply of a commodity are also outlawed without proof of any unreasonable effects.

Sometimes one competitor complains to a manufacturer about the conduct of another competitor, especially when that conduct consists of lowering prices to the extent that the complaining competitor cannot compete. Is it legal for a manufacturer to impose restraints on one competitor at the request of the other? Is such conduct illegal per se or is it subject to the rule of reason? Is there a difference between restraints that are directed at price and those that are not? The case that follows discusses these issues.

BUSINESS ELECTRONICS CORPORATION V. SHARP ELECTRONICS CORPORATION
108 S.Ct. 1515 (1988)

SCALIA, J.: . . . In 1968, petitioner (Business Electronics Corporation) became the exclusive retailer in the Houston, Texas area of electronic calculators manufactured by respondent Sharp Electronics Corporation. In 1972, respondent appointed Gilbert Hartwell as a second retailer in the Houston area. During the relevant period, electronic calculators were primarily sold to business customers for prices up to $1000. . . . Petitioner's retail prices were often below respondent's suggested retail prices and generally below Hartwell's retail prices, even though Hartwell too sometimes priced below respondent's suggested retail prices. Hartwell complained to respondent on a number of occasions about petitioner's prices. In June 1973, Hartwell gave respondent the ultimatum that Hartwell would terminate his dealership unless respondent ended its relationship with petitioner within 30 days. Respondent terminated petitioner's dealership in July 1973.

Petitioner brought suit . . . alleging that respondent and Hartwell had conspired to terminate petitioner and that such conspiracy was illegal per se under § 1 of the Sherman Act. . . . [The District Court found in favor of the petitioner but the Fifth Circuit Court of Appeals reversed.] It held that, to render illegal per se a vertical agreement between a manufacturer and a dealer to terminate a second dealer, the first dealer "must expressly or impliedly agree to set its prices at some level, though not a specific one. The distributor cannot retain complete freedom to set whatever price it chooses."

Section 1 of the Sherman Act provides that "every contract, combination in the form of trust or otherwise, or conspiracy, in restraint of trade or commerce among the several States, or with foreign nations, is declared to be illegal." Since the earliest decisions of this Court interpreting this provision, we have recognized that it was intended to prohibit only unreasonable restraints of trade. Ordinarily, whether particular concerted action violates § 1 of the Sherman Act is determined through case-by-case application of the so-called rule of reason—that is, "the factfinder weighs all of the circumstances of a case in deciding whether a restrictive practice should be prohibited as imposing an unreasonable restraint on competition." Certain categories of agreements, however, have been held to be per se illegal, dispensing with the need for case-by-case evaluation. We have said that per se rules are appropriate only for "conduct that is manifestly anticompetitive," that is, conduct " 'that would always or almost always tend to restrict competition and decrease output.' " . . .

Although vertical agreements on resale prices have been illegal per se since 1911, we have recognized that the scope of per se illegality should be narrow in the context of vertical restraints. . . .

We refused to extend per se illegality to vertical nonprice restraints, specifically to a manufacturer's termination of one dealer pursuant to an exclusive territory agreement with another. We noted that especially in the vertical restraint context "departure from the rule-of-reason standard must be based on demonstrable economic effect rather than . . . upon formalistic line drawing." We concluded that vertical nonprice restraints had not been shown . . . to justify per se illegality. Rather, we found, they had real potential to stimulate interbrand competition, "the primary concern of antitrust law."

Moreover, we observed that a rule of *per se* illegality for vertical nonprice restraints was not needed or effective to protect *intra* brand competition. First, so long as interbrand competition existed, that would provide a "significant check" on any attempt to exploit intrabrand market power. In fact, in order to meet that interbrand competition, a manufacturer's dominant incentive is to lower resale prices. Second, the *per se* illegality of vertical restraints would create a perverse incentive for manufacturers to integrate vertically into distribution, an outcome hardly conducive to fostering the creation and maintenance of small businesses. . . .

There has been no showing here that an agreement between a manufacturer and a dealer to terminate a "price cutter," without a further agreement on the price or price levels to be charged by the remaining dealer, almost always tends to restrict competition and reduce output. . . .

Any agreement between a manufacturer and a dealer to terminate another dealer who happens to have charged lower prices can be alleged to have been directed against the terminated dealer's "price cutting." In the vast majority of cases, it will be extremely difficult for the manufacturer to convince a jury that its motivation was to ensure adequate services, since price cutting and some measure of service cutting usually go hand in hand. Accordingly, a manufacturer that agrees to give one dealer an exclusive territory and terminates another dealer pursuant to that agreement, or even a manufacturer that agrees with one dealer to terminate another for failure to provide contractually-obligated services, exposes itself to the highly plausible claim that its real motivation was to terminate a price cutter. Moreover, even vertical restraints that do not result in dealer termination, such as the initial granting of an exclusive territory or the requirement that certain services be provided, can be attacked as designed to allow existing dealers to charge higher prices. . . .

We cannot avoid this difficulty by invalidating as illegal *per se* only those agreements imposing vertical restraints that contain the word "price" or that affect the "prices" charged by dealers. . . . As the above discussion indicates, all vertical restraints . . . have the potential to allow dealers to increase "prices" and can be characterized as intended to achieve just that. In fact, vertical nonprice restraints only accomplish the benefits identified . . . because they reduce intrabrand price competition to the point where the dealer's profit margin permits provision of the desired services. . . . The manufacturer often will want to endure that its distributors earn sufficient profit to pay for programs such as hiring and training additional salesmen or demonstrating the technical features of the product. . . .

In resting our decision upon the foregoing economic analysis, we do not ignore common-law precedent concerning what constituted "restraint of trade" at the time the Sherman Act was adopted. But neither do we give that pre-1890 precedent the dispositive effect some would. The term "restraint of trade" in the statute, like the term at common law, refers not to a particular list of agreements, but to a particular economic consequence, which may be produced by quite different sorts of agreements in varying times and circumstances. . . .

The Sherman Act adopted the term "restraint of trade" along with its dynamic potential. It invokes the common law itself, and not merely the static content that the common law had assigned to the term in 1890. If it were otherwise, not only would the line of *per se* illegality have to be drawn today precisely where it was in 1890, but also case-by-case evaluation of legality (conducted where *per se* rules do not apply) would have to be governed by 19th-century notions of reasonableness. It would make no sense to create out of the single term "restraint of trade" a chronologically schizoid statue, in which a "rule of reason" evolves with new circumstances and new wisdom, but a line of *per se* illegality remains forever fixed where it was.

Of course the common law, both in general and as embodied in the Sherman Act, does not lightly assume that the economic realities underlying earlier decisions have changed, or that earlier judicial perceptions of those realities were in error. It is relevant, therefore, whether the common law of restraint of trade ever prohibited as illegal *per se* an agreement of the sort made here, and whether our decisions under § 1 of the Sherman Act have ever expressed or necessarily implied such a prohibition. . . .

[The court reviewed previous decisions concerning the analysis used under § 1 of the Sherman Act and concluded as follows:] In sum, economic analysis supports the view, and no precedent opposes it, that a vertical restraint is not illegal *per se* unless it includes some agreements on price or price levels. Accordingly, the judgment of the Fifth Circuit is [*affirmed*].

Case Questions

1. What was the business relationship between the petitioner and the respondent?

2. Why did the respondent end its business relationship with the petitioner?

3. What were the holdings of the district court and the Court of Appeal?

4. Why does the Supreme Court conclude that the rule of reason, rather than per se illegality, analysis is preferable in this case?

5. Sanctions

Penalties for violating the law.

The Sherman Act as amended by the Clayton Act recognizes four separate legal sanctions:

1. Violations may be subject to criminal fines and imprisonment.
2. Violations may be enjoined by the courts.
3. Injured parties may collect **triple damages.**
4. Any property owned in violation of Section 1 of the Sherman Act that is being transported from one state to another is subject to a seizure by and forfeiture to the United States.

The first sanction is criminal punishment. Crimes under the Sherman Act are felonies. An individual found guilty may be fined up to $350,000 and imprisoned up to three years. A corporation found guilty may be fined up to $10 million for each offense.

The second sanction of the Sherman Act empowers courts to grant injunctions, at the request of the government or a private party, that will prevent and restrain violations or continued violations of its provisions. An injunction may prevent anticompetitive behavior, or it may even force a breakup of a corporation.

The injunction is frequently used when the success of a criminal prosecution is doubtful. It takes less proof to enjoin an activity *(preponderance of the evidence)* than it does to convict of a crime *(beyond a reasonable doubt).* There have been cases involving this remedy even after an acquittal in a criminal case. In effect, the court ordered the defendant not to do something it had been found innocent of doing.

The third sanction affords relief to persons, including governments, injured by another's violations of the Sherman Act. Section 4 of the Clayton Act authorizes such victims in a civil action to collect three times the damages they have suffered plus court costs and reasonable attorneys' fees. Normally, the objective of awarding money damages to individuals in a private lawsuit is to place them in the position they would have enjoyed, as nearly as this can be done with money, had their rights not been invaded. The triple-damage provisions of the antitrust laws, however, employ the remedy of damages to punish a defendant for a wrongful act in addition to compensating the plaintiff for actual injury. Today it is perhaps the most important sanction for an antitrust violation, because it allows one's competitors as well as injured members of the general public to enforce the law. Legislation also allows both federal and state governments to file a suit for triple damages.

Successful triple-damage suits may impose financial burdens on violators far in excess of any fine that could be imposed as a result of a criminal prosecution. This significant liability may be far in excess of the damages caused by any one defendant, because the liability of defendants is based on tort law and is said to be *joint and several.* For example, assume that ten companies in an industry conspire to fix prices and that the total damages caused by the conspiracy equal $100 million. Also, assume that nine of the defendants settle out of court for $25 million. The remaining defendant, if the case is lost, would owe $275 million ($3 \times 100 - 25$). The Supreme Court has held that there is no right of contribution by the losing party against those that settled prior to the final judgment.

There is a significant relationship between the criminal antitrust prosecution and the civil suit for triple damages. If the defendant in a criminal antitrust suit is convicted or pleads guilty, the plaintiff in the related triple damages suit is greatly aided. This result arises from the criminal case's prima facie evidence that an antitrust violation occurred. The cost of the investigation and preparation needed to prove the existence of an antitrust violation is usually substantial. Being allowed to use the defendant's criminal conviction or guilty plea as proof of the wrong allows the civil plaintiff to concentrate on proving damages, which are then tripled by the court. This automatic proof deriving from the criminal case can be avoided if the defendant enters a plea of *nolo contendere* (no contest) in the criminal case. Since this plea technically is interpreted as avoiding a conviction, the civil plaintiff is left with the burden of proving the antitrust violation.

Concept Summary: Antitrust Sanctions

1. Four sanctions are recognized by the antitrust laws:
   a. Federal criminal penalties
   b. Injunctions ordered by the courts
   c. Triple damages payable to an injured party
   d. Seizure and forfeiture of property owned in restraint of trade if such property is transported between states
2. The federal criminal penalties are, for an individual, up to a $350,000 fine plus up to 3 years in prison, and, for a corporation, up to $10 million in fines.

3. An injunction may prevent anticompetitive behavior.
4. Under the triple-damage sanctions, a defendant cannot seek contribution from other wrongdoers.
5. Liability for triple damages does not extend to an indirect purchaser but may extend to victims whose damages are fixed.
6. To avoid the impact of a guilty plea or a conviction on a pending civil antitrust suit, the criminally accused defendant often pleads nolo contendere (no contest).

---

6. Exemptions

Certain businesses may be exempt from the Sherman Act because of a statute or as the result of a judicial decision. Among activities and businesses for which there are statutory exemptions are insurance companies, farmers' cooperatives, shipping, milk marketing, and investment companies. Activities required by state law are exempt. In addition, normal activities of labor unions are exempt.

These exemptions are narrowly construed and do not mean that every activity of a firm is necessarily exempted simply because most activities are exempted. For example, it has been held that an agreement between an insurance company and a pharmaceutical organization that regulates the price of prescription drugs given to policyholders of the insurance company was not exempt—it was not the business of insurance that was involved in the transaction. It is the business of insurance that is exempt and not the business of insurance companies. Likewise, a labor union would forfeit its exemption when it agreed with one set of employers to impose a certain wage scale on other employer bargaining units. It is only the usual and legitimate union activity that is exempt.

In a 1943 case known as *Parker v. Brown,* the Supreme Court created a **state action exemption** to the Sherman Act. This state action exemption, usually referred to as the **Parker v. Brown doctrine,** was based on the reasoning that the Sherman Act does not apply to state government. When a state acts in its sovereign capacity, it is immune from federal antitrust scrutiny. For example, an unsuccessful candidate for admittance to the Arizona Bar alleged a conspiracy by the Bar examiners in violation of the Sherman Act. He contended that the grading scale was dictated by the number of new attorneys desired rather than by the level of competition and answers on the exam. The courts held that this activity was exempt from the Sherman Act. The grading of bar examinations is, in reality, conduct of the Arizona Supreme Court and thus exempt. Action by the courts is just as immune as actions by the legislature.

Another exemption from the Sherman Act extends to concerted efforts to lobby government officials, regardless of the anticompetitive purposes of the lobbying effort. The doctrine, known as the **Noerr-Pennington doctrine** is based on the First Amendment. For example, Budget Rent-A-Car filed suit against Hertz and National Rent-A-Car because the defendants lobbied officials at three state-owned airports to limit the number of car-rental operations. This lobbying was ruled exempt from the Sherman Act under the First Amendment right to petition government for a redress of grievances and recognition of the value of the free flow of information.

Price Fixing

Agreements relating to the price to be charged for a product or service are in violation of the Sherman Act. Price fixing is clearly in restraint of trade: A competitive system requires that prices be set by the operation of free markets. Since price is the essence of competition, price fixing is illegal per se in all its manifestations: horizontal, vertical, and indirect.

7. Horizontal Price Fixing

Horizontal price fixing is an agreement between competitors to fix prices. The term "price fixing" means more than setting a price. For example, if partners set the price of their goods or service, they have engaged in a form of price fixing but not the type envisioned by the Sherman Act. The price fixing covered by the Sherman Act is that which threatens free competition.

It is no defense to a charge of price fixing that the prices fixed are fair or reasonable. It also is no defense that price fixing is engaged in by small competitors to allow them to compete with larger competitors. The per se rule makes price fixing illegal whether the parties to it have control of the market or not and whether or not they are trying to raise or lower the market price.

It is just as illegal to fix a low price as it is to fix a high price. Maximum-price agreements are just as illegal as minimum-price agreements.

Historically, the Sherman Act was thought to apply only to the sale of goods. Price fixing in the service sector was commonly engaged in by professional persons such as architects, lawyers, and physicians. It was also engaged in by service workers, such as automobile and TV repairpersons, barbers, and refuse collectors. The argument was that persons performing services were not engaged in trade or commerce and thus they were not covered by the Sherman Act. It was also contended by the professionals that there was a "learned profession" exception to the Sherman Act.

In the mid-1970s, the Supreme Court rejected these arguments, and in the following case it held that the Sherman Act covered services, including those performed by the learned professions such as attorneys-at-law. Today, it is just as illegal to fix the price of services as it is to fix the price of goods.

GOLDFARB ET UX. V. VIRGINIA STATE BAR ET AL.

95 S.Ct. 2004 (1975)

BURGER, J.: We granted certiorari to decide whether a minimum fee schedule for lawyers published by the Fairfax County Bar Association and enforced by the Virginia State Bar violates § 1 of the Sherman Act, 15 U.S.C. § 1. . . .

In 1971 petitioners, husband and wife, contracted to buy a home in Fairfax County, Virginia. The financing agency required them to secure title insurance; this required a title examination, and only a member of the Virginia State Bar could legally perform that service. Petitioners therefore contacted a lawyer who quoted them the precise fee suggested in a minimum fee schedule published by respondent Fairfax County Bar Association; the lawyer told them it was his policy to keep his charges in line with the minimum fee schedule which provided for a fee of 1% of the value of the property involved. Petitioners then tried to find a lawyer who would examine the title for less than the fee fixed by the schedule. They sent letters to 36 other Fairfax County lawyers requesting their fees. Nineteen replied and none indicated that he would charge less than the rate fixed by the schedule; several stated that they knew of no attorney who would do so.

The fee schedule the lawyers referred to is a list of recommended minimum prices for common legal services. Respondent Fairfax County Bar Association published the fee schedule although, as a purely voluntary association of attorneys, the County Bar Association has no formal power to enforce it. Enforcement has been provided by respondent

Virginia State Bar which is the administrative agency through which the Virginia Supreme Court regulates the practice of law in that State; membership in the State Bar is required in order to practice in Virginia. Although the State Bar has never taken formal disciplinary action to compel adherence to any fee schedule, it has published reports condoning fee schedules and has issued two ethical opinions indicating fee schedules cannot be ignored. The most recent opinion states that "evidence that an attorney *habitually* charges less than the suggested minimum fee schedule adopted by his local bar association raises a presumption that such lawyer is guilty of misconduct. . . ."

Because petitioners could not find a lawyer willing to charge a fee lower than the schedule dictated, they had their title examined by the lawyer they had first contacted. They then brought this class action against the State Bar and the County Bar alleging that the operation of the minimum fee schedule, as applied to fees for legal services relating to residential real estate transactions, constitutes price fixing in violation of § 1 of the Sherman Act. Petitioners sought both injunctive relief and damages.

[The Court then reviewed the decisions of the lower courts which had resulted in a denial of relief to petitioners.]

We . . . are thus confronted for the first time with the question of whether the Sherman Act applies to services performed by attorneys in examining titles in connection with financing the purchase of real estate.

. . . The County Bar argues that because the fee schedule is merely advisory, the schedule and its enforcement mechanism do not constitute price fixing. Its purpose, the argument continues, is only to provide legitimate information to aid member lawyers in complying with Virginia professional regulations. Moreover the County Bar contends that in practice the schedule has not had the effect of producing fixed fees. The facts found by the trier belie these contentions. . . . The fee schedule was enforced through the prospect of professional discipline from the State Bar, and the desire of attorneys to comply with announced professional norms, the motivation to conform was reinforced by the assurance that other lawyers would not compete by underbidding. This is not merely a case of an agreement that may be inferred from an exchange of price information, for here a naked agreement was clearly shown, and the effect on prices is plain.

Moreover, in terms of restraining competition and harming consumers like petitioners, the price-fixing activities found here are unusually damaging. A title examination is indispensable in the process of financing a real estate purchase, and since only an attorney licensed to practice in Virginia may legally examine a title, consumers could not turn to alternative sources for the necessary service. All attorneys, of course, were practicing under the constraint of the fee schedule. . . . These factors coalesced to create a pricing system that consumers could not realistically escape. On this record respondent's activities constitute a classic illustration of price fixing.

The County Bar argues that Congress never intended to include the learned professions within the terms "trade or commerce" in § 1 of the Sherman Act, and therefore the sale of professional services is exempt from the Act. No explicit exemption or legislative history is provided to support this contention, rather the existence of state regulation seems to be its primary basis. Also, the County Bar maintains that competition is inconsistent with the practice of a profession because enhancing profit is not the goal of professional activities; the goal is to provide services necessary to the community. That, indeed, is the classic basis traditionally advanced to distinguish professions from trades, businesses, and other occupations, but it loses some of its force when used to support the fee control activities involved here.

In arguing that learned professions are not "trade or commerce" the County Bar seeks a total exclusion from antitrust regulation. Whether state regulation is active or dormant, real or theoretical, lawyers would be able to adopt anticompetitive practices with impunity. We cannot find support for the proposition that Congress intended any such sweeping exclusion. The nature of an occupation, standing alone, does not provide sanctuary from the Sherman Act, nor is the public service aspect of professional practice controlling in determining whether § 1 includes professions. Congress intended to strike as broadly as it could in § 1 of the Sherman Act, and to read into it so wide an exemption as that urged on us would be at odds with that purpose.

The language of § 1 of the Sherman Act, of course, contains no exception. . . . Indeed, our cases have specifically included the sale of services within § 1. Whatever else it may be, the examination of a land title is a service; the exchange of such a service for money is "commerce" in the most common usage of that word. It is no disparagement of the practice of law as a profession to acknowledge that it has this business aspect, and is subject to § 1 of the Sherman Act. . . . In the modern world it cannot be denied that the activities of lawyers play an important part in commercial intercourse, and that anticompetitive activities by lawyers may exert a restraint on commerce.

In *Parker v. Brown* 317 U.S. 341 (1943), the Court held that an anticompetitive marketing program "which derived its authority and efficacy from the legislative command of the state" was not a violation of the Sherman Act because the Act was intended to regulate private practices and not to prohibit a State from imposing a restraint as an act of government. Respondent State Bar and respondent County Bar both seek to avail themselves of this so-called state action exemption. . . .

The threshold inquiry in determining if an anticompetitive activity is state action of the type the Sherman Act was not meant to proscribe is whether the activity is required by the State acting as sovereign. Here we need not inquire further into the state action question because it cannot fairly be said that the State of Virginia through its Supreme Court Rules required the anticompetitive activities of either respondent. Respondents have pointed to no Virginia statute requiring their activities. . . . [*Reversed and remanded*].

Case Questions

1. How did the Goldfarbs prove that the attorneys in Fairfax County had agreed on a minimum-fee schedule?

2. In which party's favor had the lower courts ruled?

3. What reasons are given by the Court for holding that the Sherman Act applies to providers of services?

4. How does the Court justify its conclusion that the legal profession is engaged in "trade or commerce"?

TABLE 11–1   Examples of Horizontal Price-Fixing Cases

Business	Type of Case	Sherman Act Violation	Case Result
Archer Daniels Midland Company and others	Criminal and civil	Fixed prices on citric acid	$70 million fine and $35 million civil settlement
Mrs. Baird's Bakery	Criminal and civil	Fixed prices on baked goods	$10 million fine and $18 million settlement
President of Pepsi-Cola Bottling Co.	Criminal	Agreed with Coca-Cola bottler to stop discounts to retailers	4 months in jail, $45,000 fine, 3 years' probation, community service
Southland Corp. and Borden Inc.	Criminal and civil	Rigged bids for dairy products sold to Florida school-milk programs	$8 million combined fine and $2.5 million in civil claims
American Institute of Architects	Civil, injunction	Discouraged competitive bidding, discount fees, and free services	Consent decree that practices would cease plus $50,000 in costs
Fireman's Fund Home Insurance Co., Liberty Mutual Insurance, and Traveler's Corp.	Civil, class action, triple damages	Boycotted Minnesota law requiring workers' compensation rates to be established by competition	$34 million settlement
Kanzaki Specialty Papers Inc. and Mitsubishi Corp.	Criminal	Fixed prices on thermal fax paper	$6.3 million settlement
Delta, United, USAir, American, TWA, and Northwest Airlines	Civil	Use of computerized clearinghouse to fix airfares	$458 million settlement involving the issuance of coupons for future air travel

Some professional groups have attempted to avoid restrictions on price fixing through the use of ethical standards. While such ethical standards are not illegal per se, they are nevertheless anticompetitive and a violation of the Sherman Act. Others have attempted to determine the price of services indirectly by using formulas and relative-value scales. For example, some medical organizations have determined that a given medical procedure would be allocated a relative value on a scale of 1 to 10. Open-heart surgery might be labeled a 9 and an appendectomy a 3. All members of the profession would then use these values in determining professional fees. Such attempts have been uniformly held to be illegal.

Table 11–1 presents examples of recent horizontal price-fixing cases. The companies and industries involved demonstrate the pervasiveness of Sherman Act violations.

8. Vertical Price Fixing

Attempts by manufacturers to control the ultimate retail price for their products is known as **vertical price fixing** or **resale price maintenance.** Such efforts result in part from the desire to maintain a high-quality product image, the assumption being that a relatively high price suggests a relatively high quality. These efforts are also based on a desire to maintain adequate channels of distribution. If one retailer is selling a product at prices significantly below those of other retailers, there is a strong likelihood that the other retailers will not continue to carry the product.

Although most resale price-maintenance schemes run afoul of the Sherman Act, it is possible for a manufacturer to control the resale price of its products. The primary method of legally controlling the retail price is for a manufacturer simply to announce its prices and refuse to deal with those who fail to comply. Under what is commonly referred to as the **Colgate doctrine,** the Supreme Court recognizes that such independent action by a manufacturer is not a per se violation of the Sherman Act. Resale price maintenance is legal only if there is no coercion or pressure other than the announced policy and its implementation. If the manufacturer sits down with the distributor or retailer and gets an agreement that the parties will comply, then there is a violation of Section 1 of the Sherman Act.

Whether or not vertical price fixing should be illegal per se has been a matter of debate among economists and politicians. There is a possibility that a vertical restraint imposed by a single manufacturer or wholesaler may stimulate interbrand competition as it reduces intrabrand competition. This debate produced the following case, in which the Supreme Court announces that the rule of reason is the correct analysis when determining the legality of vertical price fixing situations. The review of previous antitrust cases and analyses make up an important part of this case.

STATE OIL COMPANY V. KHAN

1997 U.S. Lexis 6705 (1997)

O'CONNOR, J.: . . . Respondents, Barkat U. Khan and his corporation, entered into an agreement with petitioner, State Oil Company, to lease and operate a gas station and convenience store owned by State Oil. The agreement provided that respondents would obtain the station's gasoline supply from State Oil at a price equal to a suggested retail price set by State Oil, less a margin of 3.25 cents per gallon. Under the agreement, respondents could charge any amount for gasoline sold to the station's customers, but if the price charged was higher than State Oil's suggested retail price, the excess was to be rebated to State Oil. Respondents could sell gasoline for less than State Oil's suggested retail price, but any such decrease would reduce their 3.25 cents-per-gallon margin.

About a year after respondents began operating the gas station, they fell behind in lease payments. State Oil then gave notice of its intent to terminate the agreement and commenced a state court proceeding to evict respondents. . . .

Respondents sued State Oil . . . alleging . . . that State Oil had engaged in price fixing in violation of § 1

of the Sherman Act by preventing respondents from raising or lowering retail gas prices.

The District Court found that the allegations in the complaint did not state a per se violation of the Sherman Act because they did not establish the sort of "manifestly anticompetitive implications or pernicious effect on competition" that would justify per se prohibition of State Oil's conduct. The District Court held that respondents had not shown that a difference in gasoline pricing would have increased the station's sales; nor had they shown that State Oil had market power or that its pricing provisions affected competition in a relevant market. Accordingly, the District Court entered summary judgment for State Oil on respondents' Sherman Act claim.

The Court of Appeals . . . reversed. The court first noted that the agreement between respondents and State Oil did indeed fix maximum gasoline prices by making it "worthless" for respondents to exceed the suggested retail prices. After reviewing legal and economic aspects of price fixing, the court concluded that State Oil's pricing scheme was a per se antitrust violation under *Albrecht v. Herald Co.* . . .

We granted certiorari to consider two questions, whether State Oil's conduct constitutes a per se violation of the Sherman Act and whether respondents are entitled to recover damages based on that conduct.

Although the Sherman Act, by its terms, prohibits every agreement "in restraint of trade," this Court has long recognized that Congress intended to outlaw only unreasonable restraints. As a consequence, most antitrust claims are analyzed under a "rule of reason," according to which the finder of fact must decide whether the questioned practice imposes an unreasonable restraint on competition, taking into account a variety of factors, including specific information about the relevant business, its condition before and after the restraint was imposed, and the restraint's history, nature, and effect.

Some types of restraints, however, have such predictable and pernicious anticompetitive effect, and such limited potential for procompetitive benefit, that they are deemed unlawful per se. Per se treatment is appropriate once experience with a particular kind of restraint enables the Court to predict with confidence that the rule of reason will condemn it. Thus, we have expressed reluctance to adopt per se rules with regard to restraints imposed in the context of business relationships where the economic impact of certain practices is not immediately obvious.

A review of this Court's decisions leading up to and beyond *Albrecht* is relevant to our assessment of the continuing validity of the per se rule established in *Albrecht*. Beginning with *Dr. Miles Medical Co. v. John D. Park & Sons Co.*, the Court recognized the illegality of agreements under which manufacturers or suppliers set the minimum resale prices to be charged by their distributors. By 1940, the Court broadly declared all business combinations "formed for the purpose and with the effect of raising, depressing, fixing, pegging, or stabilizing the price of a commodity in interstate or foreign commerce" illegal per se. *United States v. Socony-Vacuum Oil Co.* Accordingly, the Court condemned an agreement between two affiliated liquor distillers to limit the maximum price charged by retailers in *Kiefer-Stewart Co. v. Joseph E. Seagram & Sons, Inc.*, noting that agreements to fix maximum prices, "no less than those to fix minimum prices, cripple the freedom of traders and thereby restrain their ability to sell in accordance with their own judgment."

In subsequent cases, the Court's attention turned to arrangements through which suppliers imposed restrictions on dealers with respect to matters other than resale price. In *White Motor Co. v. United States*, the Court considered the validity of a manufacturer's assignment of exclusive territories to its distributors and dealers. The Court determined that too little was known about the competitive impact of such vertical limitations to warrant treating them as per se unlawful. Four years later, in *United States v. Arnold, Schwinn & Co.*, the Court reconsidered the status of exclusive dealer territories and held that, upon the transfer of title to goods to a distributor, a supplier's imposition of territorial restrictions on the distributor was "so obviously destructive of competition" as to constitute a per se violation of the Sherman Act. In Schwinn, the Court acknowledged that some vertical restrictions, such as the conferral of territorial rights or franchises, could have procompetitive benefits by allowing smaller enterprises to compete, and that such restrictions might avert vertical integration in the distribution process. The Court drew the line, however, at permitting manufacturers to control product marketing once dominion over the goods had passed to dealers.

Albrecht, decided the following Term, involved a newspaper publisher who had granted exclusive territories to independent carriers subject to their adherence to a maximum price on resale of the newspapers to the public. Influenced by its decisions in *Socony-Vacuum*, *Kiefer-Stewart*, and *Schwinn*, the Court concluded that it was per se unlawful for the publisher to fix the maximum resale price of its newspapers. The Court acknowledged that "maximum and minimum price fixing may have different consequences in many situations," but nonetheless condemned maximum price fixing for substituting the perhaps erroneous judgment of a seller for the forces of the competitive market. . . .

Nine years later, in *Continental T. V., Inc. v. GTE Sylvania Inc.*, the Court overruled *Schwinn*, thereby rejecting application of a per se rule in the context of vertical nonprice restrictions. The Court acknowledged the principle of stare decisis, but explained that the need for clarification in the law justified reconsideration of *Schwinn*:

> Since its announcement, Schwinn has been the subject of continuing controversy and confusion, both in the scholarly journals and in the federal courts. The great weight of scholarly opinion has been critical of the decision, and a number of the federal courts confronted with analogous vertical restrictions have sought to limit its reach. In our view, the experience of the past 10 years should be brought to bear on this subject of considerable commercial importance.

. . . In *GTE Sylvania*, the Court declined to comment on *Albrecht's* per se treatment of vertical maximum price restrictions, noting that the issue "involved significantly different questions of analysis and policy." Subsequent decisions of the Court, however, have hinted that the analytical underpinnings of *Albrecht* were substantially weakened by *GTE Sylvania*. We noted . . . that vertical restraints are generally more defensible than horizontal restraints. . . . [D]ecisions such as *GTE Sylvania* recognize the possibility that a vertical restraint imposed by a single manufacturer or wholesaler may stimulate interbrand competition even as it reduces intrabrand competition. . . .

Albrecht reflected the Court's fear that maximum price fixing could be used to disguise arrangements to fix minimum prices, which remain illegal per se. Although we have acknowledged the possibility that maximum pricing might mask minimum pricing, we believe that such conduct—as with the other concerns articulated in Albrecht—can be appropriately recognized and punished under the rule of reason. . . .

In overruling *Albrecht,* we of course do not hold that all vertical maximum price fixing is per se lawful. Instead, vertical maximum price fixing, like the majority of commercial arrangements subject to the antitrust laws, should be evaluated under the rule of rea-

son. In our view, rule-of-reason analysis will effectively identify those situations in which vertical maximum price fixing amounts to anticompetitive conduct.

There remains the question whether respondents are entitled to recover damages based on State Oil's conduct. . . . Under the circumstances, the matter should be reviewed by the Court of Appeals in the first instance. We therefore vacate the judgment of the Court of Appeals and remand the case for further proceedings consistent with this opinion. [*Vacate and remand*].

Case Questions

1. How did State Oil Company impose a maximum pricing policy on its retail station?

2. Why does the Court find the rule of reason analysis sufficient to regulate anticompetitive aspects of vertical maximum price fixing?

3. What impact does this decision have on the analysis used to judge the legality of vertical minimum price fixing? On horizontal price fixing?

9. Indirect Price Fixing

The ingenuity of businesspersons produces numerous attempts to fix prices by indirect means. Such attempts to control prices take a variety of forms and appear in diverse circumstances. Some arise out of a desire to protect a channel of distribution or a marketing system. Others result from attempts to keep marginal competitors in business to avoid becoming a monopoly.

In one case, indirect price fixing took the form of an exchange of price information. Economic theory was used to support the assumption that prices would be more unstable and lower if the information had not been exchanged. This case established that conduct directed at price stabilization is per se anticompetitive. The warning to business and industry is clear: Cooperation and cozy relationships between competitors may be illegal.

Concept Summary: Price Fixing

1. Price fixing in the sale of goods or services is illegal per se.

2. It is just as illegal to fix a low price as it is a high price.

3. Ethical standards cannot be used to fix prices.

4. Attempts by manufacturers to control the ultimate sale of their product (vertical price fixing) is as illegal as horizontal price fixing.

5. The Colgate doctrine is an exception in vertical price-fixing cases. It allows a manufacturer to select its customers and to refuse to deal with those who fail to follow its suggested prices.

6. The mere exchange of price information among competitors may constitute a Sherman Act violation.

Other Acts in Restraint of Trade

10. Territorial Agreements

Territorial agreements restrain trade by allocating geographical areas among competitors. They may be either horizontal or vertical. A **horizontal territorial agreement** would be entered into by competing businesses for the purpose of giving each an exclusive territory. For example, if all Oldsmobile dealers in state X agreed to allocate to each an exclusive territory, a horizontal arrangement would exist. It would be illegal per se under the Sherman Act. This is true even if the arrangement is made with a third party. For example, an agreement among competing cable television operators to divide the market in Houston, Texas, was a per se violation even though the agreement required city council approval.

A **vertical territorial agreement** is one between a manufacturer and a dealer or distributor. It assigns the dealer or distributor an exclusive territory, and the manufacturer agrees not to sell to other dealers or distributors in that territory in exchange for an agreement by the dealer that it will not operate outside the area assigned. Such agreements are usually part of a franchise or license agreement. These vertical arrangements are not per se violations; they are subject to the rule of reason.

A vertical territorial restriction that is illegal may result in the awarding of triple damages. If a plaintiff can establish that the interbrand market structure is such that intrabrand competition is a critical source of competitive pressure on price, a plaintiff may recover triple damages. The plaintiff is required to show the nature and effect of the territorial restriction and how it adversely affects market competition.

11. Concerted Activities

Many antitrust cases involve agreements or conduct by competitors that have anticompetitive effects. Competitors sometimes attempt to share some activities or join together in the performance of a function. These are known as **concerted activities.**

Concerted activities are often beneficial to society even though they reduce competition. For example, joint research efforts to find a cure for cancer or to find substitutes for gasoline would seem to provide significant benefits to society. A sharing of technology may be beneficial also. Joint efforts in other areas may reduce costs and improve efficiency, with direct benefit to the public.

Congress has recognized the need to encourage cooperation among competitors. For example, in 1984, the National Cooperative Research Act was enacted. In 1990, Congress created an exception to the Sherman Act so that television industry officials could discuss the development of joint guidelines to limit the depiction of violence on television.

Again in 1993, Congress made it easier for U.S. companies to engage in joint production ventures. The National Cooperative Production Amendments Act does not protect joint production ventures from all possibilities of antitrust violations. Rather, this law provides protection through the following basic provisions:

· Joint production ventures will be subject to the rule of reason analysis rather than the per se illegality standard.

- A joint production venture must notify the Justice Department and the FTC of its plans to engage in joint activities.
- In a private civil antitrust action brought against the joint production venture, the plaintiff can be awarded only actual damages plus costs. The joint production venture will not be subject to triple damages.

Despite these exceptions to the Sherman Act that permit specific joint activities, you should always remain aware that concerted activities among competitors can lead to the severe sanctions discussed in section 5 above.

The Clayton Act

12. Introduction

By 1914, it was obvious that the Sherman Act of 1890 had not accomplished its intended purposes. Practices that reduced competition were commonplace. In order to improve the antitrust laws, Congress in 1914 enacted the Clayton Act and the Federal Trade Commission Act. The Clayton Act is more specific than the Sherman Act in declaring certain enumerated practices in commerce illegal. These were practices that might adversely affect competition but were not themselves contracts, combinations, or conspiracies in restraint of trade; such practices did not go far enough to constitute actual monopolization or attempts to monopolize. Further, the enumerated practices did not have to actually injure competition to be wrongful; they were outlawed if their effect substantially lessened competition or tended to create a monopoly. Thus, the burden of proving a violation was eased. The Clayton Act made it possible to attack in their incipiency many practices which, if continued, eventually could destroy competition or create a monopoly. The idea was to remedy these matters before full harm was done.

Violations of the original Clayton Act were not crimes, and the act contained no sanction for forfeiture of property. However, it did provide that the Justice Department might obtain injunctions to prevent violations. Those persons injured by a violation could obtain injunctive relief in their own behalf and, in addition, were given the right to collect three times the damages they suffered plus court costs and reasonable attorney's fees.

13. Price Discrimination

Section 2 of the Clayton Act as originally adopted in 1914 made it unlawful for a seller to discriminate in the price that is charged to different purchasers of commodities when the effect may be to lessen competition substantially or to tend to create a monopoly in any line of commerce. Discrimination in price on account of differences in the grade, quality, or quantity of the commodity sold, or that makes only due allowance for differences in the cost of selling or transportation was not illegal.

In the 1920s and early 1930s, various techniques such as large-volume purchases with quantity discounts were used by big retailers, especially chain stores, to obtain more favorable prices than those available to smaller competitors. In addition to obtaining quantity discounts, some large businesses created subsidiary corporations that received brokerage allowances as wholesalers. Another method used by big buyers to obtain price advantages was to demand and obtain larger promotional allowances than were given to smaller buyers. The prevalence of these practices led to the enactment in 1936 of the **Robinson-Patman amendment** to Section 2 of the Clayton Act. This statute attempted to eliminate the advantage that a large buyer could secure over a small buyer solely because of the larger buyer's quantity-purchasing ability.

The Robinson-Patman amendment attempts to ensure equality of price to all customers of a seller of commodities for resale. The law protects a single competitor who is victimized by price discrimination. It is a violation both to knowingly give and to receive the benefits of such discrimination. Therefore, the law applies to both sellers and buyers. It is just as illegal to receive the benefit of price discrimination as it is to give a lower price to one of two buyers.

The Robinson-Patman amendment extends only to transactions in interstate commerce; it does not extend to transactions that affect only intrastate commerce. In addition, the law is applicable only to the sale of goods; it does not cover contracts that involve the sale of services or the sale of advertising such as television time.

The Robinson-Patman amendment gives the Federal Trade Commission (FTC) jurisdiction and authority to regulate quantity discounts. It also prohibits certain hidden or indirect discriminations by sellers in favor of certain buyers. Section 2(c) prohibits an unearned brokerage commission related to a sale of goods. For example, it is unlawful to pay or to receive a commission or discount on sales or purchases except for actual services rendered. Section 2(d) outlaws granting promotional allowances or payments on goods bought for resale unless such allowances are available to all competing customers. For example, a manufacturer who gives a retailer a right to purchase three items for the price of two as part of a special promotion must give the same right to all competitors in the market. Section 2(e) prohibits giving promotional facilities or services on goods bought for resale unless they are made available to all competing customers.

The Robinson-Patman amendment makes it a crime for a seller to sell either at lower prices in one geographic area than elsewhere in the United States to eliminate competition or a competitor, or at unreasonably low prices to drive out a competitor. This statute declared **predatory pricing** to be illegal.

Predatory pricing is pricing below marginal cost by a company willing and able to sustain losses for a prolonged period to drive out competition. (It is assumed that the price will later be increased when the competition or competitor is destroyed.) Predatory pricing also involves charging higher prices on some products to subsidize below-cost sales of other products or cutting prices below cost on a product in just one area to wipe out a small local competitor.

The following case illustrates the complexity of the Robinson-Patman amendment.

Texaco Inc. v. Hasbrouck

110 S.Ct 2535 (1990)

Texaco sold gasoline directly to twelve independent Texaco retailers at retail tank wagon (RTW) prices. It also sold gasoline to two wholesale distributors (Gull and Dompier), who in turn supplied stations competing with the

Texaco stations. The sales price to Gull and Dompier was 3¢ and 6¢ per gallon less than the RTW price. As a result, the sales at Texaco stations dropped dramatically.

The Texaco retailers filed suit against Texaco alleging a violation of Section 2(a) of the Robinson-Patman amendment. Texaco contended that the price differential was a legitimate functional discount. The lower courts awarded plaintiffs $449,900 actual damages, and Texaco was granted a writ of certiorari.

STEVENS, J.: . . . . It is appropriate to begin our consideration of the legal status of functional discounts by examining the language of the Act. Section 2(a) provides in part:

> It shall be unlawful for any person engaged in commerce, in the course of such commerce, either directly or indirectly, to discriminate in price between different purchasers of commodities of like grade and quality, where either or any of the purchases involved in such discrimination are in commerce, where such commodities are sold for use, consumption, or resale within the United States or any Territory thereof or the District of Columbia or any insular possession or other place under the jurisdiction of the United States, and where the effect of such discrimination may be substantially to lessen competition or tend to create a monopoly in any line of commerce, or to injure, destroy, or prevent competition with any person who either grants or knowingly receives the benefit of such discrimination, or with customers, of either of them. . . .

The Act contains no express reference to functional discounts. It does contain two affirmative defenses that provide protection for two categories of discounts—those that are justified by savings in the seller's cost of manufacture, delivery or sale, and those that represent a good faith response to the equally low prices of a competitor. As the case comes to us, neither of those defenses is available to Texaco.

In order to establish a violation of the Act, respondents had the burden of proving four facts: (1) that Texaco's sales to Gull and Dompier were made in interstate commerce; (2) that the gasoline sold to them was of the same grade and quality as that sold to respondents; (3) that Texaco discriminated in price as between Gull and Dompier on the one hand and respondents on the other; and (4) that the discrimination had a prohibited effect on competition. . . .

Texaco argues that although it charged different prices, it did not "discriminate in price" within the meaning of the Act, and that, at least to the extent that Gull and Dompier acted as wholesalers, the price differentials did not injure competition.

Texaco's first argument would create a blanket exemption for all functional discounts. Indeed, carried to its logical conclusion, it would exempt all price differentials except those given to competing purchasers.

Since we have already decided that a price discrimination within the meaning of Section 2(a) "is merely a price difference," we must reject Texaco's first argument.

In *FTC v. Morton Salt Co.*, 334 U.S. 37 46–47 (1948), we held that an injury to competition may be inferred from evidence that some purchasers had to pay their supplier "substantially more for their goods than their competitors had to pay." Texaco . . . argues that this presumption should not apply to differences between prices charged to wholesalers and those charged to retailers. Moreover, they argue that it would be inconsistent with fundamental antitrust policies to construe the Act as requiring a seller to control his customers' resale prices. The seller should not be held liable for the independent pricing decisions of his customers. . . .

A supplier need not satisfy the rigorous requirements of the cost justification defense in order to prove that a particular functional discount is reasonable and accordingly did not cause any substantial lessening of competition between a wholesaler's customers and the supplier's direct customers. The record in this case, however, adequately supports the finding that Texaco violated the Act.

The hypothetical predicate for the . . . entire discussion of functional discounts is a price differential "that merely accords due recognition and reimbursement for actual marketing functions." Such a discount is not illegal. In this case, however, . . . there was no substantial evidence indicating that the discounts to Gull and Dompier constituted a reasonable reimbursement for the value to Texaco of their actual marketing functions. Indeed, Dompier was separately compensated for its hauling function, and neither Gull nor Dompier maintained any significant storage facilities. . . .

The longstanding principle that functional discounts provide no safe harbor from the Act is . . . evident from the practice of the Federal Trade Commission, which has, while permitting legitimate functional discounts, proceeded against those discounts which appeared to be subterfuges to avoid the Act's restrictions. . . .

The evidence indicates . . . that Texaco affirmatively encouraged Dompier to expand its retail business and that Texaco was fully informed about the persistent and marketwide consequences of its own pricing policies. Indeed, its own executives recognized that the dramatic impact on the market was almost entirely attributable to the magnitude of the distributor discount and the hauling allowance. . . . The special facts of this case . . . make it peculiarly difficult for Texaco to claim that it is being held liable for the independent pricing decisions of Gull or Dompier.

. . . The competitive injury component of a Robinson-Patman Act violation is not limited to the injury to competition between the favored and the disfavored purchaser; it also encompasses the injury to competition between their customers. This conclusion is compelled by the statutory language, which specifically encompasses not only the adverse effect of price discrimination on persons who either grant or knowingly receive the benefit of such discrimination, but also on "customers of either of them." Such indirect competitive effects surely may not be presumed automatically in every functional discount setting, and, indeed, one would expect that most functional discounts will be legitimate discounts which do not cause harm to competition. At the least, a functional discount that constitutes a reasonable reimbursement

for the purchasers' actual marketing functions will not violate the Act. When a functional discount is legitimate, the inference of injury to competition . . . will simply not arise. Yet it is also true that not every functional discount is entitled to a judgment of legitimacy, and that it will sometimes be possible to produce evidence showing that a particular functional discount caused a price discrimination of the sort the Act prohibits. When such anticompetitive effects are proved—as we believe they were in this case—they are covered by the Act. . . . [*Affirmed*].

Case Questions

1. What four factual elements must be proven by the plaintiff-respondents to establish a Section 2 Robinson-Patman violation?

2. What were the holdings of the lower courts?

3. What is Texaco's argument for charging different prices to its customers?

4. Why does the Court reject Texaco's argument?

The Robinson-Patman amendment recognizes certain exceptions or defenses:

- Sellers may select their own customers in good-faith transactions and not in restraint of trade.
- Price changes may be made in response to changing conditions, such as actual or imminent deterioration of perishable goods, obsolescence of seasonal goods, distress sales under court process, or sales in good faith in discontinuance of business in the goods concerned (changing conditions defense).
- Price differentials based on differences in the cost of manufacture, sale, or delivery of commodities are permitted (**cost justification defense**).
- A seller in good faith may meet the equally low price of a competitor (**good-faith meeting-of-competition defense**).

Concept Summary: Robinson-Patman Amendment

1. It is a violation to sell the same goods to competing buyers for resale at different prices.

2. The law also is violated by a buyer that knowingly receives a lower price.

3. The law does not apply to transactions wholly in intrastate commerce or to transactions that do not involve goods.

4. Price discrimination may result from quantity discounts, unearned brokerage allowances, or promotional allowances.

5. Functional discounts must be based on legitimate marketing functions actually performed.

6. It is a crime for a seller to sell at low prices in an attempt to drive out a competitor.

(concluded)

7. Plaintiffs must prove actual injury to collect triple damages for Robinson-Patman violations.

8. The good-faith meeting-of-competition defense is available to both the seller and the buyer.

14. Special Arrangements

Section 3 of the Clayton Act limits the use of certain types of contractual arrangements involving goods when the impact of these contracts may substantially lessen competition or tends to create a monopoly. These special arrangements include sales contracts that tie one product with another, contracts that contain reciprocal arrangements in which each party is a buyer and a seller, and provisions foreclosing buying or selling with others.

A **tying contract** is one in which a product is sold or leased only on the condition that the buyer or lessee purchase a different product or service from the seller or lessor. A common form of tying arrangement is known as **full-line forcing.** In full-line forcing, the buyer or lessee is compelled to take a complete product line from the seller. Under these arrangements, the buyer cannot purchase only one product of the line. A typical illegal agreement is one in which a clothing manufacturer requires a retailer to carry the manufacturer's full line of articles in order to sell a popular line of shirts.

As this edition is being prepared, the most publicized example of a tying contract, and indeed the most important antitrust case brought by the government in the 1990's, involves Microsoft Corporation. In 1994, Microsoft entered into a consent agreement with the Justice Department. In that agreement, Microsoft promised that it would not tie its internet browser software with its operating system, Windows 3.1. When it released the upgraded Windows 95, Microsoft included its internet browser, Explorer, as part of the new operating system. In 1997, the Justice Department asked a federal district judge in Washington, D.C. to fine Microsoft $1,000,000 a day for every day that it continued to tie Explorer with the purchase of Windows 95. The Justice Department claims that Microsoft is violating the consent agreement. Towards the end of 1997, the district judge refused to impose the fine. He did, however, order Microsoft to stop automatically including the Explorer software with every sale of Windows 95. Developments in this case, including further hearings and appeals, likely will provide interesting discussion of how the antitrust law impacts the marketing of new products—such as Windows 98.

A **reciprocal dealing** arrangement exists when two parties face each other as both buyer and seller. One party offers to buy the other's goods but only if the second party buys other goods from the first party. For example, suppose that Company "A" is a manufacturer of microprocessor chips for personal computers. Further assume that Company "B" manufactures personal computers. A reciprocal dealing occurs if "B" agrees to buy processor chips only if "A" agrees to buy a specified number of "B's" computers for use in "A's" offices.

An **exclusive dealing** contract contains a provision that one party or the other (buyer or seller) will deal only with the other party. For example, a seller of tomatoes agrees to sell only to Campbell Soup. A buyer of coal may agree to purchase only from a certain coal company. Such agreements tend to foreclose a portion of the market from competitors.

15. Illegal Mergers and Acquisitions

The Clayton Act makes certain mergers and acquisitions illegal. **Mergers** are usually classified as horizontal, market extension, vertical, or conglomerate. A **horizontal merger** usually combines two businesses in the same field or industry. The acquired and acquiring companies have competed with each other, and the merger reduces the number of competitors and leads to greater concentration in the industry. A **market extension merger** describes an acquisition in which the acquiring company extends its markets. This market extension may be either in new products **(product extension)** or in new areas **(geographic extension).** For example, if a brewery that did not operate in New England acquired a New England brewery, it would have accomplished a geographic market extension merger.

A **vertical merger** brings together one company that is the customer of the other in one of the lines of commerce in which the other is a supplier. Such a combination ordinarily removes or has the potential to remove the merged customer from the market as far as other suppliers are concerned. It also may remove a source of supply if the acquiring company is a customer of the acquired one. A **conglomerate merger** is one in which the businesses involved neither compete nor are related as customer and supplier in any given line of commerce. Some analysts consider product extension and geographic extension mergers to be conglomerate ones with many characteristics of horizontal ones. In any event, there is a great deal of similarity in the legal principles applied to market extension and to conglomerate mergers.

As originally enacted in 1914, the Clayton Act prohibited only horizontal mergers through the acquisition of stock of one competing company by another. A merger between competitors could be accomplished and was permitted through one acquiring the assets of the other. In 1950, Congress passed the **Celler-Kefauver amendment,** which substantially broadened the coverage of Section 7. First, this amendment plugged the stock-versus-assets loophole. After 1950, the acquisition of assets was also covered by Section 7. Second, the Celler-Kefauver amendment prohibited all acquisitions in which the effect lessened competition substantially in any line of commerce in any section of the country. Thus, the amendment added vertical and conglomerate mergers to the coverage of Section 7. In 1980, Congress expanded coverage by including not only businesses engaged in interstate commerce but also businesses engaged in activities that affect commerce. It also substituted the word "person" for "corporation" so as to include partnerships and sole proprietorships.

In recent years there have been numerous mergers that arguably could have been challenged as a violation of Section 7 of the Clayton Act. Table 11–2 illustrates such mergers during 1995 and 1996. One reason that such mergers are not challenged is international competition. The antitrust

TABLE 11–2   Recent Mergers

Acquiring Company	Acquired Company	$ Value
Time-Warner	Turner Broadcasting	$ 9 billion
Boeing	McDonnell Douglas	$14 billion
Procter & Gamble	Tambrands	$ 2 billion
Travelers Group	Salomon Brothers	$ 9 billion

division of the Justice Department and the Federal Trade Commission take international competitors into account in reviewing the impact of a merger on competition.

Unfair Competition

16. The Role of the FTC

The Federal Trade Commission enforces the Clayton Act. The FTC also enforces Section 5 of the Federal Trade Commission Act, which made "unfair methods of competition" in commerce unlawful. The **Wheeler-Lea amendment** of 1938 added that "unfair or deceptive acts or practices in commerce" are also unlawful under Section 5.

The FTC has broad, sweeping powers and a mandate to determine what methods, acts, or practices in commerce constitute unfair competition. The original Section 5 of the Federal Trade Commission Act outlawed unfair methods of competition in commerce and directed the FTC to prevent the use of such, but it offered no definition of the specific practices that were unfair. The term "unfair methods of competition" was designed by Congress as a flexible concept, the exact meaning of which could evolve on a case-by-case basis. It can apply to a variety of unrelated activities. It is generally up to the FTC to determine what business conduct is "unfair." Great deference is given to the FTC's opinion as to what constitutes a violation and to the remedies it proposes to correct anticompetitive behavior.

The purpose of Section 5 was to establish that anticompetitive acts or practices that fall short of transgressing the Sherman or Clayton Act may be "unfair methods of competition." If a business practice is such that it is doubtful that the evidence is sufficient to prove a Sherman or Clayton Act violation, the FTC may nevertheless proceed and find that the business practice is unfair.

Key Terms

Beneficiary   289
Celler-Kefauver Amendment   311
Clayton Act   290
Colgate doctrine   302
Concerted activities   305

Conglomerate merger   311
Cost justification defense   309
Exclusive dealing   311
Federal Trade Commission Act   290
Full-line forcing   310

Review Questions and Problems

The Sherman Act

1. *Historical Development*
   The Sherman Act, as amended by the Clayton Act, seeks to preserve competition by declaring two types of anticompetitive behavior to be illegal. Describe these two behaviors.

2. *Restraint of Trade*
   All of the orthodontists in your community at their annual holiday party agreed to charge the parents of each child patient a non-refundable fee of $200 prior to beginning any treatment. They also agreed that the charge for an orthodontia procedure would not be less than $2,000. Are these agreements a violation of the Sherman Act? Explain.

3. *Monopoly*
   The Justice Department filed a civil suit claiming Grinnell Corporation had a monopoly in the operation of central station hazard-detecting devices. These security devices are used to prevent burglary and to detect fires. They involve electronic notification of the police and fire departments at a central location. Grinnell, through three separate subsidiaries, controlled 87 percent of that business. It argues that it faces competition from other modes of protection from burglary, and therefore it does not have monopoly power. What argument does the Justice Department have to make to prove its claim that Grinnell is operating an illegal monopoly?

4. *The Rule of Reason*
   (a) Why is it important for courts to use the rule of reason analysis when considering ac-

tions allegedly in violation of the Sherman Act?
   (b) What is the significance of the per se analysis under the rule of reason?

5. *Sanctions*
   (a) Name the four sanctions used to enforce the Sherman Act.
   (b) What is the relationship between the criminal sanction and suits for triple damages?
   (c) What is the impact of the nolo contendere plea?

6. *Exemptions*
   The operators of adult book stores got together and each agreed to contribute $1,000 to a fund for use in lobbying the city council to repeal an ordinance which made the sale of sexually explicit publications a crime. If the operators are charged with violating the antitrust laws, what will be the likely defense? Explain.

Price Fixing

7. *Horizontal Price Fixing*
   The members of a real estate brokers' multiple listing service voted to raise their commission rate from 6 to 7 percent. The bylaws of the association provided for expulsion of any member charging less than the agreed upon commission. If broker Hillary continues to charge 6 percent, can she be expelled legally? Why or why not?

8. *Vertical Price Fixing*
   (a) Describe the situations when a supplier can legally fix the minimum price that a customer must charge to its buyers.

(b) What analysis do courts use when judging the legality of a vertical price-fixing plan? Why is this legal analysis the appropriate one to use?

9. *Indirect Price Fixing*

Assume that all manufacturers of computer chips entered into an agreement whereby each agreed to exchange information as to the most recent price charged or quoted to a consumer. Is this agreement a violation of the Sherman Act? Why or why not?

Other Acts of Restraint of Trade

10. *Territorial Agreements*
    (a) Are franchise agreements which allocate an exclusive territory to the franchisee always illegal? Explain.
    (b) Give an example of a product where intra-brand competition is as important as inter-brand competition.

11. *Concerted Activities*

In response to public pressure, all of the manu-facturers of chewing tobacco agree not to adver-tise on radio or television. The resultant savings is used to reduce the price of the product to con-sumers. Furthermore, the use of chewing to-bacco by teenagers is reduced dramatically. Is the agreement legal? Explain.

The Clayton Act

12. *Introduction*
    (a) Name the sanctions that can be imposed against a violator of the Clayton Act.
    (b) What is the significance of the word "incipi-ency" in Clayton Act enforcement?

13. *Price Discrimination*

You are the sales representative for a manufac-turer of insulation. A customer that accounts for approximately one-third of your sales suddenly asks for a discount because of the volume of its purchases. You are politely told that a refusal will cause the customer to take its business to another manufacturer. Your income is solely from commissions on sales, which are calcu-lated on gross profit margins.

    (a) If you agree to a discount, have you broken any law?

(b) If you have violated a law, what are the po-tential consequences?

(c) If you give the same discount to all cus-tomers, would your actions be illegal? Explain.

14. *Special Arrangements*
    (a) An ice-cream franchiser requires its fran-chisees to purchase all ice cream, cones and syrups from the franchiser. Does this con-tract violate the antitrust laws? Why or why not?
    (b) Would your answer be the same if the con-tract also required the franchisees to pur-chase all of its paper products and cleaning supplies, such as napkins, from the fran-chiser? Explain.

15. *Illegal Mergers and Acquisitions*

The government challenged the acquisition by Procter & Gamble (P&G) of Clorox. Clorox was the leading manufacturer of liquid bleach at the time of the acquisition, accounting for 48 per-cent of the national sales. It was the only firm selling nationally, and the top two firms ac-counted for 65 percent of national sales. P&G is a large, diversified manufacturer of household products, with its primary activity being in the area of soaps, detergents, and cleaners. P&G ac-counted for 54 percent of all packaged detergent sales, and the top three firms accounted for 50 percent of the market. P&G is among the na-tion's leading advertiser. What is the basis for the government's challenge to this acquisition? Explain.

Unfair Competition

16. *The Role of the FTC*
    (a) The FTC has responsibility for preventing unfair methods of competition and unfair and deceptive business practices. Describe three examples of business activities that could be declared unlawful by the FTC pur-suant to these powers.
    (b) Does the FTC have to prove that these exam-ples involve violations of the Sherman or Clayton Acts to be successful in establishing an unfair method of competition or an un-fair or deceptive business practice? Explain.

Terminology Review

For each term in the left-hand column, match the most appropriate description in the right-hand column.

1. Rule of reason

2. Per se illegality

3. Triple damages

4. State action exemption

5. Noerr-Pennington doctrine

6. Horizontal price fixing

7. Resale price maintenance

8. Robinson-Patman

9. Tying contract

10. Horizontal merger

11. Vertical merger

12. Conglomerate merger

13. Celler-Kefauver

a. A merger that combines two businesses that formerly competed with each other in a particular line of commerce

b. When a commodity is sold or leased for use only on condition that the buyer or lessee purchase certain additional products or services from the seller or lessor

c. A rule that states that contracts or conspiracies are illegal only if they constitute an undue or unreasonable restraint of trade or if they unreasonably attempt to monopolize

d. An exemption from the antitrust laws that covers concerted efforts to lobby governmental bodies

e. The analysis used when an activity is inherently anticompetitive

f. An agreement among competitors to charge the same price for goods or services

g. A powerful sanction imposed against those that violate antitrust laws in order to make an example of the wrongdoer while providing a financial incentive to the wronged party to act as an enforcer

h. A type of vertical price fixing that may be legal under the Colgate doctrine

i. An exception to the antitrust laws that protects activities mandated by state law

j. The 1950 amendment to the Clayton Act that broadens the scope of Section 7, thereby making more mergers illegal

k. The 1936 amendment to the Clayton Act that broadens the scope of Section 2, thereby making illegal price discrimination more common

l. A merger in which the businesses that are combined neither compete nor are related as customer and supplier in any given line of commerce

m. A merger that brings together a customer and supplier

EMPLOYMENT AND LABOR LAWS

Business Decision

Cancel the Turkeys

For years, your small electronics company has given all its employees one week's pay and a turkey each Christmas. But now a recession is eroding profitability and the company is operating at a significant loss, so you consider canceling the Christmas presents for this year. The employees have just voted for union representation, and the extra pay and turkeys are not mentioned in the collective-bargaining agreement.

Is a Christmas gift still purely a management decision?

Are you in trouble if you cancel the turkeys?

What is the union's role in the decision?

Throughout the twentieth century, the United States government has passed laws, issued executive orders, and promulgated regulations designed to influence the employment relationship. There are literally hundreds of examples of how laws have impacted the employer and employee. This chapter and the next one focus on two of the most important policy initiatives of the federal government in the employment setting—(1) the union-management relationship and (2) employment discrimination.

To focus on these two topics as our primary concentration does not mean that the other laws and regulations are unimportant. A listing of some of the major laws and the purpose of each appears in Table 12–1. As current and future business managers, a working knowledge of all these laws is vital to your success. However, after a brief discussion of some "hot" employment topics, the focus on labor laws in this chapter and employment discrimination in the next chapter seems appropriate. These subjects are critical to all managers, and they illustrate how legal policies are developed over a period of time as societal needs are perceived.

TABLE 12–1 **Summary of Major Federal Employment Laws**

Law	Purpose
Fair Labor Standards Act	• Provides restrictions on child labor • Provides hourly minimum wage and maximum number of hours before overtime is owed
Social Security Act	• Provides unemployment compensation • Provides disability benefits
Employment Retirement Income Security Act	• Provides requirements for private pension plans
Occupational Safety and Health Act	• Provides standards for safe and healthy working environment
Electronic Communications Privacy Act	• Provides standards to protect privacy
Railway Labor Act, Norris LaGuardia Act, Wagner Act, Taft-Hartley Act, and Landrum-Griffin Act	• Provide national policy for governing the union-management relationship
Civil Rights Acts, Equal Employment Opportunity Act, Pregnancy Discrimination Act, Americans with Disabilities Act, Age Discrimination in Employment Act	• Provide national policy governing employment discrimination

Current Trends and Issues

Before we address labor laws, two other employment topics merit a close examination. The employment-at-will doctrine and worker privacy are important to understand. The following two sections discuss these legal issues and the third section raises some questions concerning how the business manager should handle an employee's complaint prior to taking any action relating to the employee.

1. Limitations on Employment at Will

Historically, unless employees contracted for a definite period of employment (such as for one year), employers were able to discharge them without cause at any time. This is called the **employment-at-will** doctrine.

During the 1930s, employers began to lose this absolute right to discharge employees whenever they desired. The Labor-Management Relations Act prohibited employers from firing employees for union activities. Now, many federal laws limit employers in their right to terminate employees, even at-will employees (see Table 12–2). Some states have also prohibited employers by statute from discharging employees for certain reasons, such as for refusing to take lie detector examinations.

Courts, too, have begun limiting the at-will doctrine. Under contract theory, several courts have stated that at-will employment contracts (which are not written and are little more than an agreement to pay for work performed) contain an implied promise of good faith and fair dealing by the em-

TABLE 12–2 **Federal Statutes Limiting Employment-at-Will Doctrine**

Statute	Limitation on Employee Discharge
Labor-Management Relations Act	Prohibits discharge for union activity or for filing charges under the act
Fair Labor Standards Act	Forbids discharge for exercising rights guaranteed by minimum-wage and overtime provisions of the act
Occupational Safety and Health Act	Prohibits discharge for exercising rights under the act
Civil Rights Act	Makes illegal discharge based on race, sex, color, religion, or national origin
Age Discrimination in Employment Act	Forbids age-based discharge of employees over age forty
Employee Retirement Income Security Act	Prohibits discharge to prevent employees from getting vested pension rights
Clean Air Act	Prevents discharge of employees who cooperate in proceedings against an employer for violation of the act
Clean Water Act	Prevents discharge of employees who cooperate in proceedings against an employer for violation of the act
Consumer Credit Protection Act	Prohibits discharge of employees due to garnishment of wages for any one indebtedness
Judiciary and Judicial Procedure Act	Forbids discharge of employees for service on federal grand or petit juries

ployer. This promise, implied by law, can be broken in certain cases by unjustified dismissal of employees.

Other courts have ruled that the employer's publication of a personnel handbook can change the nature of at-will employment. They have held the employer liable for breach of contract for discharging an employee in violation of statements made in the handbook about discharge procedures.

Many contract and tort exceptions to employment at will have involved one of three types of employer behavior:

- Discharge of employee for performance of an important public obligation, such as jury duty
- Discharge of employee for reporting employer's alleged violations of law (whistle-blowing)
- Discharge of employee for exercising statutory rights

Most of the cases that limit at-will employment state that the employer has violated *public policy*. What does it mean to say that an employer has violated public policy? Is it a court's way of saying that most people no longer support the employer's right to do what it did?

Limitations on discrimination and employment at will evidence a growing concern for the rights of employees in their jobs and may suggest a trend that could lead to some type of broad, legally guaranteed job security. In recent years, unions have also increasingly focused on job-security issues in their bargaining with employers.

2. Workers' Privacy

Individual privacy is such an important part of individual freedom that both legal and ethical questions regarding privacy are bound to multiply in the computer age. While debate continues concerning the need for further federal privacy legislation, many states have passed their own privacy-related statutes. Several states guarantee workers access to their job personnel files and restrict disclosure of personal information to third parties.

Concerns for individual privacy also contributed to passage of the Electronic Communications Privacy Act of 1986 and the 1988 Employee Polygraph Protection Act. Under this latter federal law, private employers generally are forbidden from using lie detector tests while screening job applicants. Current employees may not be tested randomly but may be tested as a result of a specific incident or activity that causes economic injury or loss to an employer's business. The act permits private security companies to test job applicants and allows companies that manufacture or sell controlled substances to test both job applicants and current employees. The Labor Department may seek fines of up to $10,000 against employers who violate the act. Employees are also authorized to sue employers for violating the act.

Another important privacy concern involves drug testing. At present there is no uniform law regarding the drug testing of employees. Many private companies conduct such testing. However, some states have placed some limits on a private company's right to test for drugs.

Public employees are protected from some drug testing by the Fourth Amendment's prohibition against *unreasonable* searches. However, exactly when drug tests are unreasonable is subject to much debate in the courts. In general, public employees may be tested when there is a proper suspicion that employees are using illegal drugs that impair working ability or violate employment rules. Courts have also upheld drug testing as part of required annual medical exams.

The following case combines aspects of the at-will doctrine and workers' expectations of privacy. The case illustrates, at least in the view of this one district court judge, that the expectation of privacy regarding e-mail communication is very limited.

MICHAEL A. SMYTH v. THE PILLSBURY COMPANY
914 F.Supp. 97 (E.D. Pa. 1996)

WEINER, J. In this diversity action, plaintiff, an at-will employee, claims he was wrongfully discharged from his position as a regional operations manager by the defendant. Presently before the court is the motion of the defendant to dismiss pursuant to Rule 12(b)(6) of the Federal Rules of Civil Procedure. For the reasons which follow, the motion is granted.

A claim may be dismissed under Fed.R.Civ.P. 12(b)(6) only if the plaintiff can prove no set of facts in support of the claim that would entitle him to relief. The reviewing court must consider only those facts alleged in the Complaint and accept all of the allegations as true. Applying this standard, we find that plaintiff has failed to state a claim upon which relief can be granted.

Defendant maintained an electronic mail communication system ("e-mail") in order to promote internal corporate communications between its employees. Defendant repeatedly assured its employees, including plaintiff, that all e-mail communications would remain confidential and privileged. Defendant further assured its employees, including plaintiff, that e-mail communications could not be intercepted and used by defendant against its employees as grounds for termination or reprimand.

In October 1994, plaintiff received certain e-mail communications from his supervisor over defendant's e-mail system on his computer at home. In reliance on defendant's assurances regarding defendant's e-mail system, plaintiff responded and exchanged e-mails with his supervisor. At some later date, contrary to the assurances of confidentiality made by defendant, defendant, acting through its agents, servants and employees, intercepted plaintiff's private e-mail messages made in October 1994. On January 17, 1995, defendant notified plaintiff that it was terminating his employment effective February 1, 1995, for transmitting what it deemed to be inappropriate and unprofessional comments over defendant's e-mail system in October, 1994.

As a general rule, Pennsylvania law does not provide a common law cause of action for the wrongful discharge of an at-will employee such as plaintiff. Pennsylvania is an employment-at-will jurisdiction and an employer may discharge an employee with or without cause, at pleasure, unless restrained by some contract.

However, in the most limited of circumstances, exceptions have been recognized where discharge of an at-will employee threatens or violates a clear mandate of public policy. A clear mandate of public policy must be of a type that strikes at the heart of a citizen's social rights, duties and responsibilities. This recognized public policy exception is an especially narrow one. To date, the Pennsylvania Superior Court has only recognized three such exceptions.

First, an employee may not be fired for serving on jury duty. . . . Second, an employer may not deny employment to a person with a prior conviction. . . . And finally, an employee may not be fired for reporting violations of federal regulations to the Nuclear Regulatory Commission. . . .

As evidenced above, a public policy exception must be clearly defined. The sources of public policy can be found in "legislation, administrative rules, regulation, or decision; and judicial decisions . . . Absent legislation, the judiciary must define the cause of action in case by case determinations." . . .

Plaintiff claims that his termination was in violation of public policy which precludes an employer from terminating an employee in violation of the employee's right to privacy as embodied in Pennsylvania common law. . . .

[T]he Restatement (Second) of Torts defines the tort as follows:

> One who intentionally intrudes, physically or otherwise, upon the solitude or seclusion of another or his private affairs or concerns, is subject to liability to the other for invasion of his privacy, if the intrusion would be highly offensive to a reasonable person.

Restatement (Second) of Torts § 652B. Liability only attaches when the intrusion is substantial and would be highly offensive to the ordinary reasonable person. . . .

Applying the Restatement definition of the tort of intrusion upon seclusion to the facts and circumstances of the case sub judice, we find that plaintiff has failed to state a claim upon which relief can be granted. In the first instance, . . . we do not find a reasonable expectation of privacy in e-mail communications voluntarily made by an employee to his supervisor over the company e-mail system notwithstanding any assurances that such communications would not be intercepted by management. Once plaintiff communicated the alleged unprofessional comments to a second person (his supervisor) over an e-mail system which was apparently utilized by the entire company, any reasonable expectation of privacy was lost. Significantly, the defendant did not require plaintiff . . . to disclose any personal information about himself. Rather, plaintiff voluntarily communicated the alleged unprofessional comments over the company e-mail system. We find no privacy interests in such communications.

In the second instance, even if we found that an employee had a reasonable expectation of privacy in the contents of his e-mail communications over the company e-mail system, we do not find that a reasonable person would consider the defendant's interception of these communications to be a substantial and highly offensive invasion of his privacy. Again, we note that by intercepting such communications, the company is not requiring the employee to disclose any personal information about himself or invading the employee's person or personal effects. Moreover, the company's interest in preventing inappropriate and unprofessional comments or even illegal activity over its e-mail system outweighs any privacy interest the employee may have in those comments.

In sum, we find that the defendant's actions did not tortiously invade the plaintiff's privacy and, therefore, did not violate public policy. As a result, the motion to dismiss is granted.

Case Questions

1. To what form of communication did Michael Smyth claim he had a right of privacy?

2. How does the court define the phrase *public policy* as it relates to an exception to discharging at-will employees?

3. What is this court's view of an employee's expected right of privacy to E-mail communications?

4. Why does the court reach this conclusion?

3. Employee Lawsuits

Despite the presence of many examples of the employer violating an employment law, most employers strive to obey the law. They still risk lawsuits, however, including many brought by unsatisfactory employees who have been disciplined, denied promotion, or discharged. How can employers protect themselves from unjustified employee lawsuits?

One important protection against unjustified employee lawsuits is an established system of adequate documentation. Sometimes called the **paper fortress,** this documentation consists of job descriptions, personnel manuals, and employee personnel files.

Before handing anyone an employment application, the employer should insist that the potential candidate carefully study a job description. A well-written job description will help potential applicants eliminate themselves from job situations for which they lack interest or qualification, thus preventing employers from having to dismiss them later and risking lawsuits.

Once a new employee is hired, the employer should give the employee a personnel manual. This manual should include information about employee benefits and should also outline work rules and job requirements. The employer should go over the manual with the employee and answer any questions. Clear identification of employer expectations and policies helps provide a defense against employee lawsuits if subsequent discipline or discharge of the employee becomes necessary. The employer should ask that the employee sign a form indicating receipt of the manual and an understanding of the employer's explanation of its contents.

The employer should enter this form, with all other documentation relevant to an employee's work history, into the employee's personnel file. Regular written evaluations of employee performance should also be entered into the personnel file. A chronological record of unsatisfactory work performance is a very useful defense against unjustified lawsuits following discipline, denial of promotion, or discharge.

Another piece of documentation that helps justify employer decisions is the written warning. Anytime an employee breaks a work rule or performs unsatisfactorily, the employer should issue the employee a written warning and place a duplicate in the personnel file. The warning should explain specifically what work rule the employee violated. In addition, employers should either have an employee sign that he or she has received a written warning or else note in the personnel file that the employee has received a copy of it. The employer should also give the employee the opportunity to place a letter of explanation in the personnel file.

Laws discussed in this chapter and the next one should not prevent employers from discharging unsatisfactory employees. In an actual termination conversation, however, the employer should provide the employee with specific reasons for discharge, taken from the personnel file. Detailed documentation is vital in successfully responding to unjustified employee lawsuits. Even better is to prevent them in the first place through the development, enforcement, and review of company policies that promote legal compliance.

Labor-Management Relationship

The goal of labor law is successful **collective bargaining,** the process by which labor and management negotiate and reach agreements on matters of importance to both. Such matters include wages to be paid workers, hours to be worked, and other terms and conditions of employment. Collective bargaining can be successful only if the bargaining power of the parties is equal. Most laws regulating labor-management relations seek to equalize this bargaining power. As a result, some laws add to the bargaining position of labor and others add to that of management.

The major federal laws that govern labor-management relations are highlighted in Table 12–3. As you read, keep in mind that this chapter is a

TABLE 12–3 **Federal Laws Governing Labor-Management Relations**

Year	Statute	Major Provisions
1914	Clayton Act	1. Exempted union activity from the antitrust laws
1926	Railway Labor Act	1. Governs collective bargaining for railroads and airlines
		2. Created the National Mediation Board to conduct union elections and mediate differences between employers and unions
1932	Norris-LaGuardia Act	1. Outlawed yellow-dog contracts
		2. Prohibited federal courts from enjoining lawful union activities, including picketing and strikes
1935	Wagner Act (National Labor Relations Act)	1. Created the National Labor Relations Board (NLRB)
		2. Authorized the NLRB to conduct union certification elections
		3. Outlawed certain conduct by management as unfair to labor (five unfair labor practices)
		4. Authorized the NLRB to hold hearings on unfair labor practices and correct wrongs resulting from them
1947	Taft-Hartley Act (Labor-Management Relations Act)	1. Outlawed certain conduct by unions as six unfair labor practices
		2. Provided for an eighty-day cooling-off period in strikes that imperil national health or safety
		3. Allowed states to enact right-to-work laws
		4. Created the Federal Mediation and Conciliation Service to assist in settlement of labor disputes
1959	Landrum-Griffin Act (Labor-Management Reporting and Disclosure Act, LMRDA)	1. Created a Bill of Rights for union members
		2. Requires reports to the secretary of labor
		3. Added to the list of unfair labor practices

historical review of when, why, and how the federal government has created laws regulating the labor-management relationship.

4. Laws before 1935

During the time prior to 1935, Congress viewed the labor-management relationship as being unbalanced. In a series of laws which are thought of as being prolabor Congress attempted to correct the perceived inequities. It did so by passing the following:

- The Clayton Act
- The Railway Labor Act
- The Norris-LaGuardia Act

The Clayton Act

The first federal statute of any importance to the labor movement is the **Clayton Act** of 1914, which was passed principally to strengthen the antitrust laws. Between 1890 (when the Sherman Antitrust Act was passed) and 1914, labor unions were weak in their ability to represent employees. At least one reason for the relative strength enjoyed by management was the fact that it could and did argue that employees acting together were restraining trade illegally under the Sherman Act.

The Clayton Act stated that antitrust laws regulating anticompetitive contracts did not apply to labor unions or their members in lawfully carrying out their legitimate activities. This exemption covered only *legitimate* union practices. While the Clayton Act exempted employees from the claim that they were restraining trade through unionization, this law did not expressly grant employees the protected right to join a union. Therefore, the Clayton Act did not balance the bargaining power between labor and management. The latter group remained the stronger one.

The Railway Labor Act

Among the first industries to unionize were the railroads. In 1926, Congress enacted the **Railway Labor Act** to encourage collective bargaining in the railroad industry. The goal was to resolve labor disputes that might otherwise disrupt transportation and result in violence. The act was later extended to airlines; today it applies to both air and rail transportation. It established the three-member **National Mediation Board,** which must designate the bargaining representative for any given bargaining unit of employees in the railway or air transport industries. The board generally does this by holding representation elections.

When the parties to a dispute over proposed contract terms in the transportation industry cannot reach an agreement concerning rates of pay or working conditions, the National Mediation Board must attempt mediation of their differences. If mediation does not resolve their differences, the board encourages voluntary arbitration. If the parties refuse arbitration and the dispute is likely to disrupt interstate commerce substantially, the board informs the president, who then appoints a special emergency board. This emergency board lacks judicial power, but it encourages the parties to reach an agreement by investigating the dispute and publishing its findings of fact and recommendations for settlement. During the investigation, which lasts thirty days, and for an additional thirty days after the report is issued, business is conducted without interruption. The parties, however, have no duty to comply with the special board's proposals. Thus, if no new collective bargaining agreement is reached after the sixty-day period, lockouts by management and strikes by workers become legal.

The Railway Labor Act has played a vitally important role in balancing the labor-management relationship in the transportation industries. However, due to this act's limited application, the management of businesses outside the transportation industry generally continued to have superior bargaining power following 1926.

The Norris-LaGuardia Act

Because of management's superior bargaining power, prior to 1932 management often made it a condition of employment that employees agree not to join a labor union. Such agreements became known as **yellow-dog contracts** on the basis that any employee who would forsake the right to join fellow employees in unionization was a cowardly scoundrel (yellow dog). Passed in 1932, the **Norris-LaGuardia Act** made yellow-dog contracts illegal. In essence, management no longer could explicitly deny an employee the right to unionize.

Seeking injunctions to stop concerted activities had remained an important tool of management in fighting the growth of labor unions. The Norris-LaGuardia Act listed specific acts of persons and organizations participating in labor disputes that were not subject to federal court injunctions. These included:

· Striking or quitting work
· Belonging to a labor organization
· Paying strike or unemployment benefits to participants in a labor dispute
· Publicizing the existence of a labor dispute or the facts related to it (including picketing)
· Peaceably assembling to promote interests in a labor dispute
· Agreeing with others or advising or causing them to do any of the above acts without fraud or violence

Although the Norris-LaGuardia Act greatly restricts the use of injunctions in labor disputes, it does not prohibit them altogether. An injunction may be issued to enjoin illegal strikes, such as ones by public employees. In addition, one seeking an injunction in a labor dispute must meet the test of a stringent, clean-hands rule. No restraining order will be granted to any person who fails to comply with any obligation imposed by law or who fails to make every reasonable effort to settle the dispute.

The Norris-LaGuardia Act restricts the use of federal court injunctions in labor disputes; it does not limit the jurisdiction of state courts in issuing them. The Supreme Court has upheld the jurisdiction of a state court to enjoin a union's work stoppage and picketing in violation of a no-strike clause in its collective bargaining agreement. Due to these limitations and economic conditions that existed in the labor market in 1932, the Norris-LaGuardia Act did not substantially strengthen the organized labor movement.

The Wagner Act

The labor movement received its greatest stimulus for growth with the enactment in 1935 of the National Labor Relations Act, known as the **Wagner Act.** Perhaps most significantly, Congress explicitly affirmed labor's right to organize and to bargain collectively. Recognizing that a major cause of industrial strife was the inequality of bargaining power between employees and employers, Section 7 of the act states:

> Employees shall have the right to self-organization, to form, join, or assist labor organizations, to bargain collectively through representatives of their own choosing, and to engage in concerted activities for the purpose of collective bargaining or other mutual aid or protection.

In addition to this Section 7 right to unionize, the Wagner Act contained several other key provisions. Among these are the following actions approved by Congress:

· Creating the National Labor Relations Board (NLRB) to administer the act

· Providing for employees the right to select a union with exclusive power to act as their collective bargaining agent

· Outlawing certain conduct by employers that generally has the effect of either preventing the organization of employees or emasculating their unions where they do exist; these forbidden acts are called *unfair labor practices*

· Authorizing the NLRB to conduct hearings on unfair labor practice allegations and, if unfair practices are found to exist, to take corrective action including issuing cease and desist orders and awarding dollar damages to unions and employees

5. The National Labor Relations Board

Established by the Wagner Act, the **National Labor Relations Board** operates as an independent agency of the U.S. government. This section discusses the organizational structure of the NLRB, its jurisdiction, and its quasi-judicial function. The following section examines the NLRB's authority to certify unions as the collective bargaining representative of employees. After this introduction to the NLRB, the remainder of the chapter will illustrate the significant role this agency plays in balancing the labor-management relationship.

NLRB Organization

The NLRB consists of five members, appointed by the president with the advice and consent of the Senate, who serve staggered terms of five years each. In addition, there is a general counsel of the board who supervises board investigations and serves as prosecutor in cases before the board. The general counsel supervises operations of the NLRB so that the board itself may perform its quasi-judicial function of deciding unfair labor practice cases free of bias. Administrative law judges are responsible for the initial conduct of hearings in unfair labor practice cases.

The general counsel also is responsible for the conduct of representation elections. In addition, the general counsel is responsible for seeking court orders requiring compliance with the board's orders and represents the board in miscellaneous litigation. The board determines policy questions, such as what types of employers and groups of employees are covered by the labor law. Recall the *Holly Farms* case in Chapter 6 and how courts are bound to defer to the rulings of the NLRB as long as the board members reach a reasonable result. That case helps illustrate the extensive authority and power of the NLRB.

Jurisdiction

Congress gave the NLRB jurisdiction over any business "affecting commerce." Certain employers and employees are, however, specifically exempt from NLRB jurisdiction. These include:

- Employees of federal and state governments
- Employees of political subdivisions of the states
- Persons subject to the Railway Labor Act
- Independent contractors
- Individuals employed as agricultural laborers or domestic servants in a home
- Individuals employed by their spouse or a parent

The NLRB has never been able to exercise fully the powers given it because of budget and time constraints. It has limited its own jurisdiction to businesses of a certain size (Table 12–4 lists these businesses). As a result of

---

TABLE 12–4   NLRB Assumes Jurisdiction over the Following

Nonretail operations with an annual outflow or inflow across state lines of at least $50,000

Retail enterprises with a gross volume of $500,000 or more a year

Enterprises operating office buildings if the gross revenues are at least $100,000 per year

Transportation enterprises furnishing interstate services

Local transit systems with an annual gross volume of at least $250,000

Newspapers that subscribe to interstate news services, publish nationally syndicated features, or advertise nationally sold products and have a minimum annual gross volume of $250,000

Communication enterprises that operate radio or television stations or telephone or telegraph services with a gross volume of $100,000 or more per year

Local public utilities with an annual gross volume of $250,000 per year or an outflow or inflow of goods or services across state lines of $50,000 or more per year

Hotel and motel enterprises that serve transient guests and gross at least $500,000 in revenues per year

All enterprises whose operations have a substantial impact on national defense

Nonprofit hospitals

Private universities and colleges

this policy, federal laws do not cover many small employers, which are subject to applicable state law on labor relations and common law principles. Of course the board may decide to take jurisdiction over any business that affects interstate commerce.

Quasi-judicial Authority

In sections 7, 12, and 13 of this chapter, you will study the various unfair labor practices. Congress has granted the NLRB the authority to conduct the quasi-judicial hearings that are required to investigate and to enforce sanctions if these unfair labor practices occur. This authority is extensive in that the NLRB has discretion to order whatever action is necessary to correct the unlawful practice.

6. Certification of Unions

An employer may voluntarily recognize that its workers desire to have a certain labor union represent them. The employer is free to agree to bargain with the union as the collective bargaining representative of the employees. In actuality, such voluntary recognition occurs in relatively few situations. More common is the NLRB's certification of a union as the bargaining agent for a group of employees. This certification process is the result of an election or occurs through authorization cards. Each of these certification processes is discussed in the next two subsections.

Unionization Elections

Elections are by secret ballot and are supervised by the NLRB. The board decides what unit of employees is appropriate for purposes of collective bargaining and therefore which employees are entitled to vote in the election. It may select the total employer unit, craft unit, plant unit, or any subdivision of the plant.

Obviously, how the board exercises its discretion in this regard may be crucial to the outcome of a given election. If all 100 workers at one plant operated by an employer desire to organize but 400 out of 500 at another of the employer's plants do not, designation of the total employees as the one appropriate bargaining unit would ensure that both plants would remain nonunion.

The NLRB conducts elections upon receipt of a petition signed by at least 30 percent of the employees. In addition, an employer may file a petition for selection of an initial representative. An employer may also file a petition for an election to invalidate certification of an incumbent union. It must show that it doubts, in good faith, the continued support of the union by a majority of the employees. Petitions are used to obtain votes to certify a union or to rescind a union's authority. After any valid election has been conducted by the NLRB, another is not permitted for one year, regardless of whether the union wins or loses the certification vote. Also, an election is not allowed within the term of a collective bargaining agreement or three years after it has been signed, whichever period is shorter.

In the following case, the Supreme Court discusses the union's status as the bargaining agent for the employees.

Auciello Iron Works, Inc. v. National Labor Relations Board

116 S.Ct. 1754 (1996)

SOUTER, J. . . . Petitioner Auciello Iron Works of Hudson, Massachusetts, had 23 production and maintenance employees during the period in question. After a union election in 1977, the NLRB certified Shopmen's Local No. 501, [affiliated with] International Association of Bridge, Structural, and Ornamental Iron Workers, AFL-CIO, as the collective-bargaining representative of Auciello's employees. Over the following years, the company and the Union were able to negotiate a series of collective-bargaining agreements, one of which expired on September 25, 1988. Negotiations for a new one were unsuccessful throughout September and October 1988, however, when Auciello and the Union had not made a new contract by October 14, 1988, the employees went on strike. Negotiations continued, nonetheless, and, on November 17, 1988, Auciello presented the Union with a complete contract proposal. On November 18, 1988, the picketing stopped, and nine days later, on a Sunday evening, the Union telegraphed its acceptance of the outstanding offer. The very next day, however, Auciello told the Union that it doubted that a majority of the bargaining unit's employees supported the Union, and for that reason disavowed the collective-bargaining agreement and denied it had any duty to continue negotiating. Auciello traced its doubt to knowledge acquired before the Union accepted the contract offer, including the facts that 9 employees had crossed the picket line, that 13 employees had given it signed forms indicating their resignation from the Union, and that 16 had expressed dissatisfaction with the Union.

In January 1989, the Board's General Counsel issued an administrative complaint charging Auciello with violation of §§ 8(a)(1) and (5) of the NLRA. An administrative law judge found that a contract existed between the parties and that Auciello's withdrawal from it violated the Act. The Board affirmed the administrative law judge's decision; it treated Auciello's claim of good-faith doubt as irrelevant and ordered Auciello to reduce the collective-bargaining agreement to a formal written instrument. . . . [T]he Court of Appeals thereafter enforced the order as resting on a "policy choice [both] . . . reasonable and . . . quite persuasive." We granted certiorari and now affirm.

The object of the National Labor Relations Act is industrial peace and stability, fostered by collective-bargaining agreements providing for the orderly resolution of labor disputes between workers and employees. To such ends, the Board has adopted various presumptions about the existence of majority support for a union within a bargaining unit, the precondition for service as its exclusive representative. The first two are conclusive presumptions. A union "usually is entitled to a conclusive presumption of majority status for one year following" Board certification as such a representative. A union is likewise entitled under Board precedent to a conclusive presumption of majority status during the term of any collective-bargaining agreement, up to three years. . . .

There is a third presumption, though not a conclusive one. At the end of the certification year or upon expiration of the collective-bargaining agreement, the presumption of majority status becomes a rebuttable one. Then, an employer may overcome the presumption (when, for example, defending against an unfair labor practice charge) by showing that, at the time of [its] refusal to bargain, either (1) the union did not in fact enjoy majority support, or (2) the employer had a good-faith doubt, founded on a sufficient objective basis, of the union's majority support. Auciello asks this Court to hold that it may raise the latter defense even after a collective-bargaining contract period has apparently begun to run upon a union's acceptance of an employer's outstanding offer.

The same need . . . that first prompted the Board to adopt the rule presuming the union's majority status during the term of a collective-bargaining agreement also led the Board to rule out an exception for the benefit of an employer with doubts arising from facts antedating the contract. The Board said that such an exception would allow an employer to control the timing of its assertion of good-faith doubt and thus to "sit on that doubt and . . . raise it after the offer is accepted." The Board thought that the risks associated with giving employers such "unilateral control [over] a vital part of the collective-bargaining process," would undermine the stability of the collective-bargaining relationship, and thus outweigh any benefit that might in theory follow from vindicating a doubt that ultimately proved to be sound.

The Board's judgment in the matter is entitled to prevail. . . .

It might be tempting to think that Auciello's doubt was expressed so soon after the apparent contract formation that little would be lost by vindicating that doubt and wiping the contractual slate clean, if in fact the company can make a convincing case for the doubt it claims. . . . But if doubts about the union's majority status would justify repudiating a contract one day after its ostensible formation, why should the same doubt not serve as well a year into the contract's term? Auciello implicitly agrees on the need to provide some cutoff, but argues that the limit should be expressed as a "reasonable time" to repudiate the contract. That is, it seeks case-by-case determinations of the appropriate time for asserting a good-faith doubt in place of the Board's bright-line rule cutting off the opportunity at the moment of apparent contract formation. Auciello's desire is natural, but its argument fails to point up anything unreasonable in the Board's position.

The Board's approach generally allows companies an adequate chance to act on their preacceptance doubts before contract formation, just as Auciello could have acted effectively under the Board's rule in this case. Auciello knew that the picket line had been crossed and that a number of its employees had expressed dissatisfaction with the Union at least nine days before the contract's acceptance, and all of the resignation forms Auciello received were dated at least five days before the acceptance date. During the week preceding the apparent formation of the contract, Auciello had at least three alternatives to doing nothing. It could have withdrawn the outstanding offer and then, like its employees, petitioned for a representation election. . . . Following withdrawal, it could also have refused to bargain further on the basis of its good-faith doubt, leaving it to the Union to

charge an unfair labor practice, against which it could defend on the basis of the doubt. And, of course, it could have withdrawn its offer to allow it time to investigate while it continued to fulfil its duty to bargain in good faith with the Union. The company thus had generous opportunities to avoid the presumption before the moment of acceptance. . . .

We hold that the Board reasonably found an employer's precontractual, good-faith doubt inadequate to support an exception to the conclusive presumption arising at the moment a collective-bargaining contract offer has been accepted. We accordingly affirm the judgment of the Court of Appeals. . . . [*Affirmed*].

Case Questions

1. What was the basis for Auciello Iron Works to question the Union's right to represent Auciello's employees?

2. When did Auciello refuse to recognize the Union as the certified bargaining agent of Auciello's employees?

3. What are the presumptions about the Union's status as bargaining agent that the Supreme Court refers to in deciding this case?

4. Why does the Supreme Court agree with the NLRB that an unfair labor practice has occurred in this case?

Unionization through Cards

A union seeking to represent employees may solicit cards from them indicating their willingness for the union to represent them. An employer may then recognize the union as the bargaining agent for its employees if the cards are signed by a majority of the employees. An employer, however, is not required to recognize the union based on a majority card showing and always has the option to insist on an election. However, once an employer recognizes the union—no matter how informally—the employer is bound by the recognition and loses the right to seek an election.

Cards also may be used as a substitute for an election if certain conditions are met. The NLRB may issue a bargaining order based on such cards if the cards are unequivocal and clearly indicate that the employee signing the card is authorizing the union to represent him or her. The general counsel of the NLRB is not required to prove that the employees read or understood the cards. If a card states on its face that it authorizes collective bargaining, it will be counted for that purpose unless there is clear proof that the employee was told that it would not be used for that purpose.

7. Unfair Labor Practices by Management

Remember that Congress desired to strengthen the bargaining power of labor unions when it passed the Wagner Act in 1935. A principal means of accom-

TABLE 12–5   Unfair Labor Practices by Management

1. Interference with efforts of employees to form, join, or assist labor organizations or to engage in concerted activities for mutual aid or protection
2. Domination of a labor organization or contribution of financial or other support to it
3. Discrimination in hiring or tenure of employees for reason of union affiliation
4. Discrimination against employees for filing charges or giving testimony under the act
5. Refusal to bargain collectively in good faith with a duly designated representative of the employees

plishing this goal was through the creation of five unfair labor practices by management. These practices, as summarized in Table 12–5, are now illegal.

Conduct may be, and often is, a violation of more than one of the listed unfair labor practices. Indeed, most violations constitute interference with the right to engage in concerted activity (the first category). For example, retaliation against a union leader for filing charges would constitute a violation of both the first and fourth categories.

This section of the chapter attempts to introduce you to these unfair labor practices under the following headings:

- Interfering
- Dominating a Labor Organization
- Discriminating Based on Union Affiliation
- Discriminating as a Result of NLRB Proceedings
- Refusing to Bargain in Good Faith

Interfering

The first unfair labor practice has two distinct parts. First, it is unfair for an employer to interfere with the efforts of employees to form, join, or assist labor organizations. The second part covers interfering with "concerted activities for mutual aid or protection." This violation does not have to involve a union; the act protects any group of employees acting for their mutual aid and protection.

With Unionization.   The first part of this unfair labor practice by management is a catchall intended to guarantee the right of employees to organize and join unions. It clearly prohibits "scare" tactics such as threats by employers to fire those involved in organizing employees or threats to cut back on employee benefits if employees succeed in unionizing. In addition, less obvious activities are outlawed, such as requiring job applicants to state on a questionnaire whether they would cross a picket line in a strike. An employer cannot engage in any conduct calculated to erode employee support for the union.

Interference with unionization may take the form of a carrot as well as a stick. The conferring of benefits by an employer may be an unfair labor practice. In one case, the employer reminded its employees two weeks before a representation election that the company had just instituted a "floating holiday" that employees could take on their birthdays. The union lost the election, but it was set aside by the NLRB. It was an unfair labor practice for the employer to engage in conduct immediately favorable to employees. The conduct interfered with the freedom of choice for or against unionization.

The Business Decision—"Cancel the Turkeys"—should be reconsidered in light of what you have just read. Is it possible that your decision to deny your employees this traditional holiday benefit could be interpreted as an unfair labor practice? How would you prove that you are not retaliating against your employees for their approval of the labor union?

The following case demonstrates the seriousness which the NLRB and the Supreme Court apply to the "employees" right to engage in union activity.

NATIONAL LABOR RELATIONS BOARD V. TOWN & COUNTRY ELECTRIC, INC.
116 S. Ct. 450 (1995)

BREYER, J. Can a worker be a company's "employee," within the terms of the National Labor Relations Act, if, at the same time, a union pays that worker to help the union organize the company? We agree with the National Labor Relations Board that the answer is "yes."

The relevant background is the following: Town & Country Electric, Inc., a nonunion electrical contractor, wanted to hire several licensed Minnesota electricians for construction work in Minnesota. Town & Country (through an employment agency) advertised for job applicants, but, it refused to interview 10 of 11 union applicants (including two professional union staff) who responded to the advertisement. Its employment agency hired the one union applicant whom Town & Country interviewed, but he was dismissed after only a few days on the job.

The members of the Union (the International Brotherhood of Electrical Workers, Locals 292 and 343) filed a complaint with the National Labor Relations Board claiming that Town & Country and the employment agency had refused to interview (or retain) them because of their union membership. An administrative law judge ruled in favor of the Union members, and the Board affirmed that ruling.

In the course of its decision, the Board determined that all 11 job applicants (including the two Union officials and the one member briefly hired) were "employees" as the Act defines that word. The Board recognized that under well-established law, it made no difference that the 10 members who were simply applicants were never hired. Neither, in the Board's view, did it matter (with respect to the meaning of the word "employee") that the Union members intended to try to organize the company if they secured the advertised jobs, nor that the Union would pay them while they set

about their organizing. The Board then rejected the company's fact-based explanations for its refusals to interview or to retain these 11 "employees" and held that the company had committed "unfair labor practices" by discriminating on the basis of union membership.

The United States Court of Appeals for the Eighth Circuit reversed the Board. It held that the Board had incorrectly interpreted the statutory word "employee." In the court's view, that key word does not cover (and therefore the Act does not protect from antiunion discrimination) those who work for a company while a union simultaneously pays them to organize that company. . . .

Because other Circuits have interpreted the word "employee" differently, we granted certiorari. . . .

This case grows out of a controversy about rights that the Act grants to "employees," namely, rights "to self-organization, to form, join, or assist labor organizations, to bargain collectively . . . and to engage in other concerted activities for the purpose of collective bargaining or other mutual aid or protection." We granted certiorari to decide only that part of the controversy that focuses upon the meaning of the word "employee," a key term in the statute, since these rights belong only to those workers who qualify as "employees" as that term is defined in the Act.

The relevant statutory language is the following:

The term "employee" shall include any employee, and shall not be limited to the employees of a particular employer, unless this subchapter explicitly states otherwise, and shall include any individual whose work has ceased as a consequence of, or in connection with, any current labor dispute or because of any unfair labor practice, and who has not obtained any other regular and substantially equivalent employment, but shall not include any individual employed as an agricultural laborer, or in the domestic service of any family or person at his home, or any individual employed by his parent or spouse, or any individual having the status of an independent contractor, or any individual employed as a supervisor, or any individual employed by an employer subject to the Railway Labor Act, as amended from time to time, or by any other person who is not an employer as herein defined.

We must specifically decide whether the Board may lawfully interpret this language to include company workers who are also paid union organizers.

We put the question in terms of the Board's lawful authority because this Court's decisions recognize that the Board often possesses a degree of legal leeway when it interprets its governing statute, particularly where Congress likely intended an understanding of labor relations to guide the Act's application. We add, however, that the Board needs very little legal leeway here to convince us of the correctness of its decision.

Several strong general arguments favor the Board's position. For one thing, the Board's decision is consistent with the broad language of the Act itself—language that is broad enough to include those company workers whom a union also pays for organizing. . . .

For another thing, the Board's broad, literal interpretation of the word "employee" is consistent with several of the Act's purposes, such as protecting "the right of employees to organize for mutual aid without employer interference," and "encouraging and protecting the collective-bargaining process." . . .

Finally, at least one other provision of the 1947 Labor Management Relations Act seems specifically to contemplate the possibility that a company's employee might also work for a union. This provision forbids an employer (say, the company) from making payments to a person employed by a union, but simultaneously exempts from that ban wages paid by the company to "any . . . employee of a labor organization, who is also an employee" of the company. If Town & Country is right, there would not seem to be many (or any) human beings to which this last phrase could apply. . . .

We hold only that the Board's construction of the word "employee" is lawful; that term does not exclude paid union organizers.

For these reasons the judgment of the Court of Appeals is vacated, and the case is remanded for further proceedings consistent with this opinion. [*Vacated and remanded*].

Case Questions

1. Of the 11 applicants involved in this case, how many were hired by Town & Country?

2. Why did the NLRB and the courts assume that all eleven applicants were covered by the phrase *company employee?*

3. What are three arguments that favor the NLRB's ruling that these "employees" are protected by the labor laws?

With Concerted Activities. The term **concerted activity** is given a liberal interpretation in order to create a climate that encourages unionization, collective bargaining, and all that may flow therefrom. For example, some employees refused to work after a heated grievance meeting. They followed their supervisors onto the workroom floor and continued to argue loudly until they were ordered a second time to resume work. The employer issued letters of reprimand alleging insubordination. This was an unfair labor practice. The employees were engaged in a protected activity. The protection of employee conduct at grievance meetings is extended to a brief cooling-off period following an employer's termination of such a meeting. Protection of employees' participation in the meetings themselves would be seriously threatened if the employer could at any point call an immediate halt to the operation of the law simply by declaring the meeting ended.

The concerted-activity concept is quite extensive. In one case, an employer was investigating theft by employees. One employee asked that a union representative be present during her interview. She was refused. The Supreme Court held that the employee had a right to representation when there was a perceived threat to her employment security. The presence of a representative assures other employees in the bargaining unit that they, too, can obtain aid and protection if they wish when there appears to be a threat to their job security. Refusing the assistance at the interview was an unfair labor practice. In addition, the right to engage in concerted activity has been expanded to cover the actions of a sole employee under certain circumstances. If an employee has a grievance that may affect other workers, that employee has rights protected by the concerted-activity language of this unfair labor practice, even though no other worker participates in the activity.

Dominating a Labor Organization

The second unfair labor practice prohibits the domination of a labor organization by employers or their contribution of financial or other support to any union. Under the Wagner Act, any organization of employees must be completely independent of their employers. In the case of a controversy between competing unions, employers must remain strictly neutral. It is an unfair labor practice for the employer to support a union by giving it a meeting place, providing refreshments for union meetings, permitting the union to use the employer's telephone, secretary, or copying machine, or allowing the union to keep cafeteria or vending-machine profits.

Discriminating Based on Union Affiliation

Under the third unfair labor practice, an employer may neither discharge nor refuse to hire an employee to either encourage or discourage membership in any labor organization. Nor may the employer discriminate regarding any term or condition of employment for such purposes. The law does not oblige an employer to favor union members in hiring employees. It also does not restrict him or her in the normal exercise of any employer's right to select or discharge employees. However, the employer may not abuse that right by discriminatory action based on union membership or activities that encourage or discourage membership in a labor organization. For example, the Supreme Court has held that an employer who reports the possible existence of illegal aliens to the Immigration and Naturalization Service engages in an unfair labor practice when that report is closely associated with the employees' approval of a labor union as their bargaining agent.

Again, the issue in the Business Decision relates as much to this unfair labor practice as it does to the first one on interference. Very often acts by an employer may involve several of the statutorily prohibited practices. In essence, you would need thorough documentation that your decision to cancel the turkeys was not motivated by your intent to interfere with or discriminate against union affiliation.

A company may not go partially out of business because some of its employees have organized, nor may it temporarily close that portion of its business that has unionized. If a company closes one plant because a union is voted in, such action discourages union activity at other plants. Partial closings to "chill" unionism are unfair labor practices.

Discriminating as a Result of NLRB Proceedings

Under the fourth unfair labor practice, employees are protected from being discharged or from other reprisals by their employers because they have sought to enforce their rights under the Wagner Act by filing charges or giving testimony in NLRB proceedings. This protection prevents the NLRB's channels of information from being dried up by employer intimidation of complainants and witnesses. An employer cannot refuse to hire a prospective employee because charges have been filed by him or her.

The main defense of any employer accused of reprisal is that he or she discharged or discriminated against the employee for some reason other than filing charges or giving testimony. Most often such cases boil down to trying to prove what motivated the company in pursuing its course of action. If the company can convince the NLRB that the employee was discharged because of misconduct, low production, personnel cutbacks necessitated by economic conditions, or other legitimate considerations, the company will be exonerated. Otherwise, it will be found guilty of this unfair labor practice.

Refusing to Bargain in Good Faith

The fifth unfair labor practice occurs when management refuses to bargain with the collective bargaining representative of its employees. The Wagner Act did not define the phrase "to bargain collectively." Judicial decisions have added the concept of *good faith* to bargaining. To comply with the requirement that they bargain collectively in good faith, employers must approach the bargaining table with fair and open minds and a sincere intent to find a basis of agreement. Refusing to meet at reasonable times with representatives of the other party, refusing to reduce agreements to writing, and designating persons with no authority to negotiate as representatives at meetings are examples of this unfair labor practice.

The employer's duty to bargain collectively includes a duty to provide relevant information needed by a union for the proper performance of its duties as the employees' bargaining representative. For example, data about job-related safety and health must be furnished so that the union can safeguard its members' health and safety.

A more fundamental issue inherent in the requirement that parties bargain collectively is: "About what?" Must the employer bargain with the union about all subjects and all management decisions in which the union or the employees are interested? Are there subjects and issues upon which management is allowed to act alone?

In answering these questions, the law divides issues into two categories—**compulsory bargaining issues** and **voluntary bargaining issues.** Compulsory, or mandatory, bargaining issues are those concerned with wages, hours, and other terms and conditions of employment. Although the parties may voluntarily consider other issues, the refusal by either to bargain in good faith on such other permissive matters is not an unfair labor practice.

Classifying an issue as *compulsory* or *voluntary* is done on a case-by-case basis. For example, questions relating to fringe benefits are compulsory bargaining issues because they are "wages." The NLRB and the courts are called on to decide whether management and labor must bargain with each other on a multitude of issues, as the case that follows illustrates.

Ford Motor Company v. NLRB

99 S.Ct. 1842 (1979)

The petitioner, Ford Motor Company, provided its employees with in-plant cafeteria and vending-machine services. The services were managed by an independent caterer, ARA, but the petitioner had the right to review and approve the quality, quantity, and prices of the food served. When petitioner notified respondent union, which represents the employees, that the cafeteria and vending-machine prices were to be increased, the union requested bargaining over the prices and services. Petitioner refused to bargain, and the union then filed an unfair labor practice charge with the National Labor Relations Board, alleging a refusal to bargain contrary to Section 8(a)(5) of the National Labor Relations Act (NLRA). Taking the view that in-plant food prices and services are "other terms and conditions of employment," the NLRB sustained the charge and ordered petitioner to bargain. The Court of Appeals enforced the order, and the Supreme Court granted certiorari.

WHITE, J.: . . . Because the "classification of bargaining subjects as 'terms or conditions of employment' is a matter concerning which the Board has special expertise," its judgment as to what is a mandatory bargaining subject is entitled to considerable deference. . . .

Construing and applying the duty to bargain and the language of § 8(d), "other terms and conditions of employment," are tasks lying at the heart of the Board's function. With all due respect to the courts of appeals that have held otherwise, we conclude that the Board's consistent view that in-plant food prices and services are mandatory bargaining subjects is not an unreasonable or unprincipled construction of the statute and that it should be accepted and enforced.

It is not suggested by petitioner that an employee should work a full 8-hour shift without stopping to eat. It reasonably follows that the availability of food during working hours and the conditions under which it is to be consumed are matters of deep concern to workers, and one need not strain to consider them to be among those "conditions" of employment that should be subject to the mutual duty to bargain. By the same token, where the employer has chosen, apparently in his own interest, to make available a system of in-plant feeding facilities for his employees, the prices at which food is offered and other aspects of this service may reasonably be considered among those subjects about which management and union must bargain. The terms and conditions under which food is available on the job are plainly germane to the "working environment." Furthermore, the company is not in the business of selling food to its employees, and the establishment of in-plant food prices is not among those "managerial decisions, which lie at the core of entrepreneurial control." The Board is in no sense attempting to permit the Union to usurp managerial decision-making; nor is it seeking to regulate an area from which Congress intended to exclude it. . . .

As illustrated by the facts of this case, substantial disputes can arise over the pricing of in-plant supplied food and beverages. National labor policy contemplates that areas of common dispute between employers and employees be funneled into collective bargaining. The assumption is that this is preferable to allowing recurring disputes to fester outside the negotiation process until strikes or other forms of economic warfare occur. . . .

Ford nevertheless argues against classifying food prices and services as mandatory bargaining subjects because they do not "vitally affect" the terms and conditions of employment . . . and because they are trivial matters over which neither party should be required to bargain.

There is no merit to either of these arguments. . . . As for the argument that in-plant food prices and service are too trivial to qualify as mandatory subjects, the Board has a contrary view, and we have no basis for rejecting it. It is also clear that the bargaining-unit employees in this case considered the matter far from trivial since they pressed an unsuccessful boycott to secure a voice in setting food prices. They evidently felt, and common sense also tells us, that even minor increases in the cost of meals can amount to a substantial sum of money over time. . . .

Ford also argues that the Board's position will result in unnecessary disruption because any small change in price or service will trigger the obligation to bargain. The problem it is said, will be particularly acute in situations where several unions are involved, possibly requiring endless rounds of negotiations over issues as minor as the price of a cup of coffee or a soft drink. . . .

The Board apparently assumes that, as a practical matter, requests to bargain will not be lightly made. Moreover, problems created by constantly shifting food prices can be anticipated and provided for in the collective bargaining agreement. Furthermore, if it is true that disputes over food prices are likely to be frequent and intense, it follows that more, not less, collective bargaining is the remedy. This is the assumption of national labor policy, and it is soundly supported by both reason and experience.

Finally, Ford asserts that to require it to engage in bargaining over in-plant food service prices would be futile because those prices are set by a third-party supplier, ARA. It is true that ARA sets vending machine and cafeteria prices, but under Ford's contract with ARA, Ford retains the right to review and control food services and prices. In any event, an employer can always affect prices by initiating or altering a subsidy to the third-party supplier such as that provided by Ford in this case, and will typically have the right to change suppliers at some point in the future. To this extent the employer holds future, if not present, leverage over in-plant food services and prices.

We affirm, therefore, the Court of Appeals' judgment upholding the Board's determination in this case that in-plant food services and prices are "terms and conditions of employment" subject to the mandatory bargaining under § 8(a)(5) and 8(d) of the National Labor Relations Act. [*Affirmed*].

Case Questions

1. What is the basis of the union arguing that the price of in-plant food is a compulsory bargaining issue?

2. What are the four arguments asserted by Ford to justify its refusal to bargain?

3. How does the Supreme Court respond to these arguments asserted by Ford?

A party to labor negotiations may present a demand relating to a non-mandatory bargaining issue as long as this issue does not have to be resolved before the parties can resolve mandatory bargaining issues. Tying a voluntary bargaining issue to a compulsory bargaining issue results in a failure to bargain in good faith and is in effect an unfair labor practice.

Courts tend to defer to the special expertise of the NLRB in classifying collective bargaining subjects, especially in the area of "terms or conditions of employment." The courts have affirmed board rulings holding that issues such as union dues checkoff, health and accident insurance, safety rules, merit pay increases, incentive pay plans, Christmas and other bonuses, stock purchase plans, pensions, paid vacations and holidays, the privilege of hunting on a reserved portion of a paper company's forest preserve, proposals for effective arbitration and grievance procedures, and no-strike and no-lockout clauses are compulsory bargaining issues. Once again, the issues in the Business Decision—"Cancel the Turkeys"—are governed by this unfair labor practice as well as others.

Remember that neither the employer nor the union is required to make concessions to the other concerning a mandatory subject of bargaining. The law only demands that each negotiate such matters in good faith with the other before making a decision and taking unilateral action. If the parties fail to reach an agreement after discussing these problems, each may take steps that are against the wishes and best interests of the other party. For example, the employer may refuse to grant a wage increase requested by the union, and the union is free to strike.

The Taft-Hartley Act

The Wagner Act opened the door for the rapid growth of the union movement. From 1935 to the end of World War II, the strength and influence of unions grew substantially. Where, prior to the Wagner Act, employers had the greater advantage in bargaining power, by 1946 many persons felt the pendulum had shifted and that unions, with their ability to call nationwide, crippling strikes, had the better bargaining position. To balance the scale, the Labor-Management Relations Act (the **Taft-Hartley Act**) was enacted in 1947 to amend the Wagner Act.

The purposes of the Taft-Hartley Act were to ensure the free flow of commerce by eliminating union practices that burden commerce and to provide procedures for avoiding disputes that jeopardize the public health, safety, or interest. It recognized that both parties to collective bargaining need protection from wrongful interference by the other and that employees sometimes need protection from the union itself. Finally, it sought to protect the public interest in major labor disputes. Congress authorized the creation of the Federal Mediation and Conciliation Service to help achieve the goals of the Taft-Hartley Act. Members of this Service are available to assist the parties in settling labor disputes.

In its attempt to balance the bargaining power between labor unions and management, the Taft-Hartley Act contains the following major provisions:

· Provides for an *eighty-day cooling-off period* in strikes that imperil the nation's health or safety
· Reinforces the employer's freedom of speech in labor-management relations
· Outlaws the *closed-shop* concept but permits *union shops* in the absence of a state *right-to-work* law
· Permits suits by union members for breach of contract against unions
· Creates six unfair labor practices by unions

8. Eighty-Day Cooling-off Period

Somewhat like the thirty-day period provided under the Railway Labor Act, the Taft-Hartley Act provides for an *eighty-day cooling-off period* following certain procedures. This provision was intended to avoid some of the nationwide strikes by steelworkers, mineworkers, autoworkers, and longshoremen that had nearly paralyzed the economy. When a threatened or actual strike or lockout affecting an entire industry or substantial part thereof will, if permitted to occur or to continue, imperil the national health or safety, the eighty-day period may be enforced. The procedure starts with the president recognizing the emergency and appointing a board of inquiry to obtain facts about the threatened or actual strike or lockout. The board studies the situation and reports back to the president. If the board finds that the national health or safety is indeed affected by the strike, then the president, through the attorney general, goes to the federal court for an injunction ordering the union to suspend the strike (or the company to suspend the lockout) for eighty days.

During the eighty-day period, the Federal Mediation and Conciliation Service works with the labor-management parties to try to achieve an agreement. If during this time the reconciliation effort fails, the presidential board holds new hearings and receives the company's final offer. The union members are then allowed to vote on this final proposal by the company. If they vote for the new proposal, the dispute is over and work continues as usual. If they vote against the proposal, the workers may again be called out on strike. At this point, the strike may continue indefinitely until the disagreement causing it is resolved by collective bargaining or unless there is additional legislation by Congress to solve the problem.

Experience has shown that many disputes are settled during the eighty-day period. The injunction provided for in the Taft-Hartley Act may not be used for all strikes and lockouts. This injunction is limited to *national emergency* strikes and lockouts, those that involve national defense or key industries or have a substantial effect on the economy.

9. Free Speech

Employers had complained that the Wagner Act violated their right of free speech. Statements of management alone had been used as the basis of finding an employer guilty of unfair labor practices. To meet this objection, Congress, in Taft-Hartley, added the following provision:

> 8(c) The expressing of any views, argument, or opinion, or the dissemination thereof, whether in written, printed, graphic, or visual form, shall not constitute or be evidence of an unfair labor practice under any of the provisions of this Act, if such expression contains no threat of reprisal or force or promise of benefit.

This provision gives employers limited free speech, at best. It is difficult to make statements that cannot be construed as a threat or a promise. For example, if an employer predicts dire economic events as a result of unionization, such may be an illegal threat if the employer has it within his or her power to make the prediction come true. Whether particular language is coercive or not often depends on the analysis of the total background of facts and circumstances in which it was uttered. To be forbidden, the statements of an employer need not be proved to have been coercive in fact but only to have had a reasonable tendency to intimidate employees under the circumstances.

An employer's threats to withdraw existing benefits if employees unionize is not speech protected by Section 8(c). However, mere predictions and prophecies are protected. For example, in one case an employer's speeches and handbills during the union's organizational campaign stated its intention to fight the union in every legal way possible and to "deal hard" with the union at arm's length if it were voted in. The employer also warned that employees could be permanently replaced if the union called an economic strike. This language was held to fall within the protection of Section 8(c). The right of free speech guaranteed by the Taft-Hartley Act applies to labor unions as well as employers. However, there is a rule prohibiting either side from making election speeches on company time to massed assemblies of employees within 24 hours before an election.

10. Union Shop—Memberships and Fees

A result of the Wagner Act's strong support of unionization was the unintended bargaining power given to unions with respect to an employer's hiring practices. In many bargaining situations the union became so strong that it successfully insisted on management hiring only union members. In essence, to apply for a prospective job, a person would have to join the union. These situations became known as **closed shops.**

One of the major changes brought about by the Taft-Hartley Act was outlawing of the closed shop. This act still permitted the **union shop.** In a union shop contract, the employer agrees that after an employee has been hired that employee must join the union as a condition of continued employment. Under the Taft-Hartley Act, such a requirement may not be imposed until the thirtieth day after employment begins.

One of the sections of the Taft-Hartley Act most distasteful to unions is 14(b), which outlaws the union shop in states that have adopted a right-to-work law. **Right-to-work laws** prohibit agreements requiring membership in a labor organization as a condition of continued employment of a person who was not in the union when hired. Approximately twenty states have right-to-work laws today. Workers in these states who do not belong to a union may not be required to pay representation fees to the union that represents the employees. However, such workers are subject to the terms of the collective bargaining agreement, and the union must handle their grievances, if any, with management.

11. Suits against Unions

Section 301 of the Taft-Hartley Act provides that suits for breach of a contract between an employer and a labor organization can be filed in the federal district courts without regard to the amount in question. A labor organization is responsible for the acts of its agents and may sue or be sued. Any money judgment against it is enforceable only against its assets and not against any individual member. Moreover, individuals cannot be sued for actions such as violating no-strike provisions of a collective bargaining contract.

In addition, members may sue their union and recover the money damages they suffer because of an illegal strike. If a union activity is both an unfair labor practice and a breach of a collective bargaining agreement, the NLRB's authority is not exclusive and does not destroy the jurisdiction of courts under Section 301 of the Taft-Hartley Act.

Many suits against unions are by members alleging a breach of the duty of fair representation. Since workers cannot bargain individually when represented by a union, the union has an implied duty of fair representation to act reasonably, with honesty of purpose, and in good faith. The union is required to represent all the employees in the bargaining unit, including those who are nonunion, impartially and without hostile discrimination.

The duty of fair representation applies not only to the *negotiation* of a collective bargaining agreement but also to the *administration* of the agreement. Unions must fairly represent employers in disputes with the employer regarding the *interpretation* and *application* of the terms of an existing contract.

An employee may file suit against the union and its representatives for damages resulting from breach of their duty of fair representation in processing his or her grievance against the employer. A union may not process a grievance in an arbitrary, indifferent, or careless manner.

Finally, a union member may sue a local union for failing to enforce the international union's constitution and bylaws. Thus, Section 301 of the Taft-Hartley Act authorizes an employer to sue a union for breach of contract as well as employees to sue to enforce either the union-management collective bargaining agreement or a union-contract with a member.

12. Unfair Labor Practices by Unions

Perhaps more than with any other provision of the Taft-Hartley Act, Congress attempted to balance the bargaining power in the labor-management relationship by enacting six unfair labor practices by unions. These were intended to balance the unfair labor practices by management contained in the Wagner Act and discussed in section 7, above. Table 12–6 lists the unfair labor practices by unions as passed in 1947.

TABLE 12–6 Unfair Labor Practices by Unions as Enacted in the Taft-Hartley Act

1. Restraining or coercing an employee to join a union or an employer in selecting representatives to bargain with the union
2. Causing or attempting to cause the employer to discriminate against an employee who is not a union member, unless there is a legal union-shop agreement in effect
3. Refusing to bargain with the employer if it is the NLRB-designated representative of the employees
4. Striking, picketing, or engaging in secondary boycotts for illegal purposes
5. Charging new members excessive or discriminatory initiation fees when there is a union-shop agreement
6. Causing an employer to pay for work not performed (featherbedding)

Three of these illegal practices can be presented in a summary fashion due to the preceding discussions in this chapter or because they have very little impact today. The third unfair labor practice by unions is complementary to the fifth unfair labor practice by management. In essence, Congress requires unions to bargain in good faith as is required of management. The fifth unfair labor practice by unions simply means that unions cannot take advantage of the union-shop agreement by charging unreasonable dues or fees when members and nonmembers are obligated to pay them. Today, the sixth unfair labor practice, involving *featherbedding*, or payment for work not actually performed, is of less importance than when it was enacted in 1947.

The remaining unfair labor practices by unions are presented under the following headings:

- Restraining or Coercing an Employee into Joining a Union
- Causing an Employer to Discriminate against a Nonunion Member
- Striking or Picketing for Illegal Purposes or Engaging in Secondary Boycotts

Restraining or Coercing an Employee into Joining a Union

This unfair labor practice includes misconduct by unions directed toward employees. The law makes it illegal for a union to restrain or coerce employees in the exercise of their rights to bargain collectively, just as it is an unfair labor practice by employers to interfere with the same rights. Employees also are guaranteed the right to *refrain* from union activities unless they are required to join the union by a legal union shop agreement.

Causing an Employer to Discriminate against a Nonunion Member

If a legal union shop agreement is in effect, a labor organization may insist that the employer observe its terms. But even when a legal union shop contract is in effect, the law prohibits a union from attempting to cause an employer to discriminate against an employee who has been denied membership or had his or her membership terminated for some reason other than failure to pay the dues and initiation fees uniformly required of all members. And even if an employee is a member, the union may not cause the employer to discriminate against him or her for not following union rules. This prohibition was designed to prevent the use of the union shop as a means of intimidating employees who were at odds with union officials over their policies.

Striking or Picketing for Illegal Purposes or Engaging in Secondary Boycotts

Jurisdictional strikes are unfair labor practices. A **jurisdictional strike** is used to force an employer to assign work to employees in one craft union rather than another. Since the dispute is between the two unions and not with the employer, the law requires that such disputes be submitted to the NLRB by the unions.

It is also an unfair labor practice for a union to threaten or to coerce by picketing, for example, an employer to recognize or bargain with one union if another one has been certified as the representative of its employees.

It is an unfair labor practice for a union to threaten, coerce, or restrain a third person not party to a labor dispute for the purpose of causing that third person to exert pressure on the company involved in the labor dispute. This law requires that strikes and picketing be directed at the employer with which the union actually has a labor dispute. This dispute protects neutral parties from serious economic injury or even ruin.

An example of illegal secondary activity occurs when a union induces the employees of an employer to strike or engage in a concerted refusal to use, handle, or work on any goods or to perform any service to force the employer to stop doing business with some third person. For example, assume that a supplier (like a bakery) has a work force that is nonunionized. A customer (i.e., a grocery store) has employees who belong to a union. This union would like to be the bargaining representative for the supplier's employees. It would be an illegal secondary boycott for this union to have its members either strike or picket the grocery store in the hope that the grocery store would discontinue its buying from this bakery. The union must deal directly with the bakery.

13. Amendments

Congressional hearings in the 1950s uncovered widespread corruption, violence, and lack of democratic procedures in some labor unions. As a result, Congress passed the **Landrum-Griffin Act,** or Labor-Management Reporting and Disclosure Act (LMRDA), in 1959. Its provisions constitute a "bill of rights" for union members and provide for union reform. Also in this act, Congress included some amendments to the unfair labor practices by management and unions.

In essence, in its continuing attempt to balance the bargaining power in the labor-management relationship, Congress added one unfair labor practice by management and two by unions.

Agreeing to Engage in a Secondary Boycott

You should recall from your reading in the preceding section that unions cannot engage in secondary boycotts. Technically, nothing in that unfair labor practice, as enacted in the Taft-Hartley Act, prohibited a union and an employer from agreeing to engage in a secondary boycott. The original restriction applied only to the unilateral acts of the union. The Landrum-Griffin Act clarified the concern over secondary boycotts by prohibiting a union-management agreement which would adversely impact a neutral third party.

It is also an unfair labor practice for both the employer involved and the union to enter into a **hot-cargo contract.** A hot-cargo contract is one in which an employer voluntarily agrees with a union that the employees should not be required by their employer to handle or work on goods or materials going to or coming from an employer designated by the union as "unfair." Such goods are said to be hot cargo. These clauses were common in trucking and construction labor contracts. The law thus forbids an employer and a labor organization to make an agreement under which the employer agrees to stop doing business with any other employer.

Picketing When Not Certified

In certain cases it is illegal for unions to force an employer to recognize or bargain with the union if it is not currently certified as the duly authorized collective bargaining representative. The purpose is to reinforce the effectiveness of the election procedures employed by the NLRB by outlawing certain tactics used by unions backed by only a minority of the employees of a particular employer. Thus, picketing to force an employer to recognize an uncertified union is an unfair labor practice in the following cases:

1. When the employer has lawfully recognized another union as the collective bargaining representative of its employees
2. When a valid representation election has been conducted by the NLRB within the past twelve months
3. When picketing has been conducted for an unreasonable time, in excess of thirty days, without a petition for a representation election being filed with the NLRB

Including these amendments to the Landrum-Griffin Act, the law on unfair labor practices is summarized in the following box.

Concept Summary: Unfair Labor Practices

By Management

1. Interfering with unionization and concerted activities by employees
2. Dominating a union or contributing to it, financially or otherwise
3. Discriminating in hiring or tenure of employees on the basis of union affiliation
4. Discriminating against employees who seek to enforce their Wagner Act rights
5. Refusing to bargain collectively in good faith
6. Agreeing with a labor organization to engage in a secondary boycott

By Unions

1. Restraining or coercing an employee to join a union
2. Causing an employer to discriminate against a nonunion member
3. Refusing to bargain collectively in good faith
4. Striking, picketing, or engaging in secondary boycotts for illegal purposes
5. Charging excessive or discriminatory fees
6. Causing an employer to pay for work not performed
7. Picketing to force an employer to recognize or bargain with an uncertified union
8. Agreeing with an employer to engage in a secondary boycott

Tobacco Industry Box

At the end of 1997 in Washington state, a federal district judge certified 60 private health and welfare trusts as representatives of 500,000 union members in a class-action lawsuit against tobacco companies. This suit seeks reimbursement for costs incurred in treating smoking-related illnesses. This suit in Washington is the first class-action involving union members and the tobaco industry. As of the end of 1997, class-action lawsuits against tobacco companies included those by private health-care plans representing approximately 30 million people.

The proposed national settlement for $368.5 billion, discussed in chapter 1 and elsewhere, is asking Congress to ban these types of class-action suits.

Key Terms

Clayton Act   324
Closed shop   339
Collective bargaining   323
Compulsory bargaining issue   335
Concerted activity   333
Employment at will   318
Hot-cargo contract   343
Jurisdictional strike   342
Landrum-Griffin Act   342
National Labor Relations Board (NLRB)   326

National Mediation Board   324
Norris-LaGuardia Act   325
Paper fortress   322
Railway Labor Act   324
Right-to-work law   339
Taft-Hartley Act   337
Union shop   339
Voluntary bargaining issue   335
Wagner Act   326
Yellow-dog contract   325

Review Questions and Problems

Current Trends and Issues

1. *Limitations on Employment at Will*
   Terry was hired as an assistant manager by the Assurance Manufacturing Company. There was no specified time period related to Terry's employment. During Terry's first day at work, the Personnel Director of Assurance gave Terry a copy of the Employees' Handbook. In this handbook, Assurance stated that no employee would be terminated without a justifiable explanation. Five months after beginning work at Assurance, Terry was notified that after an additional two weeks there would be no further job for Terry at Assurance. When Terry asked why this termination was occurring, the Personnel Director told Terry "that under state law no reason for termination has to be given. In essence, you are an employee only for as long as Assurance desires, Terry." What is the best argument Terry can make that the employment at-will doctrine is not applicable in this situation? Explain.

2. *Workers' Privacy*
   Discuss three examples of how an employer may invade an employee's privacy at the workplace.

3. *Employee Lawsuits*
   (a) What is meant by the phrase "paper fortress?"
   (b) How does maintaining a paper fortress aid the employer when the employee claims unfair treatment?

Labor-Management Relationship

4. *Laws before 1935*
   (a) What is the specific purpose of (1) the Clayton Act, (2) the Railway Labor Act, and (3) the Norris-LaGuardia Act?
   (b) Why did these laws not increase laborers' bargaining power to the degree that is considered equal to management's bargaining power?

The Wagner Act

5. *National Labor Relations Board*
   Describe the nature and limitations of the NLRB's jurisdiction.

6. *Certification of Unions*
   The NLRB conducted a certification election, and the union won by a vote of 22-20. Management refused to bargain with this union. The reason for this refusal to recognize the union as the employees' bargaining agent was that the union had used "recognition slips" as a means of indicating the employees' support for the union. Several employees testified that they signed these slips to avoid the payment of the initiation fee. Further, at least a few employees indicated that they thought they had to vote for the union since they had signed a recognition slip. Should the NLRB set aside this election of the union? Explain.

7. *Unfair Labor Practices by Management*
   (a) List the five unfair labor practices created by the Wagner Act.
   (b) Describe a situation for each of these unfair labor practices.

Taft-Hartley Act

8. *Eighty-Day Cooling-Off Period*
   (a) Under what circumstances is the President authorized to order parties in a labor dispute back to work for 80 days?
   (b) Describe the procedures that must be followed to invoke this cooling-off period.

9. *Free Speech*
   The Personnel Director of your company has been asked to talk with the employees about the benefits and detriments of voting for or against the union in an upcoming certification election. What should this Director keep in mind about the Free Speech Clause in the Taft-Hartley Act? Explain.

10. *Union Shop - Membership and Fees*
    Pat lives in a state that has enacted a right-to-work law. The company which employs her has recognized the United Clerical Workers (UCW) as the bargaining representative of its workers. The union has sought to collect union dues or their equivalent from Pat. Is she required to pay them? Why or why not?

11. *Suits Against Unions*
    Ed is discharged for allegedly stealing property from his employer. He asks his union to have him reinstated because his discharge violates the collective bargaining agreement in force. However, the union does not investigate the incident until it is too late to file a request for arbitration under the collective bargaining agreement. Assuming that Ed is innocent of the charges, does he have any rights against the union? Explain.

12. *Unfair Labor Practices by Unions*
    (a) List the six unfair labor practices created by the Taft-Hartley Act.
    (b) Describe a situation for each of these unfair labor practices.

13. *Amendments*
    (a) What were two basic purposes for Congress passing the Landrum-Griffin Act?
    (b) What are the two additional unfair labor practices added by this law?

Statutory Identification

Identify the federal statute that accomplished each of the following:

a. Exempted union activity from the antitrust laws

b. Created the National Labor Relations Board (NLRB)

c. Allowed states to enact right-to-work laws

d. Outlawed certain conduct by management as unfair to labor (unfair labor practices)

e. Governed collective bargaining for railroads and airlines

f. Prohibited federal courts from enjoining lawful union activities, including picketing and strikes

g. Established bill of rights for union members

h. Provided for an eighty-day cooling-off period in strikes that imperil national health or safety

i. Outlawed yellow-dog contracts

j. Created the Federal Mediation and Conciliation Service

DISCRIMINATION IN EMPLOYMENT

Business Decision

"Just Good Fun"

When Maria Suarez got her new job, she was happy. As an oil rigger, she would make enough money to support herself and her two children. But after a week of working with a primarily male crew, her happiness was gone. Her co-workers were the reason. At first the men made unwelcome comments about her body. Then sexual graffiti mentioning her name appeared. When she came to work one morning a nude female picture was pinned to one of the rigs. Her name had been scrawled across the bottom. Maria complained to the crew foreman, who referred her to the site manager. "Let's ignore it for a while," he told Maria. "It's just good fun. The men are testing you. You've got to fit in."

What are Maria's legal rights in this situation?

What would you do if you were the site manager?

Do you think Maria should just try to "fit in"?

In recent years avoiding discrimination lawsuits has become the primary legal issue in employment. Even the President of the United States has been sued for employment discrimination. This chapter discusses what constitutes employment discrimination and how to avoid discrimination lawsuits.

"Just Good Fun" illustrates an important antidiscrimination employment issue. Today, women need not put up with a sexually offensive work environment in order to keep a job. The Civil Rights Act of 1964 makes an employer liable for failing to take prompt steps to correct such an environment once the employer knows that it exists. If you are the site manager, you should immediately notify all employees what constitutes offensive conduct and tell them they must stop it or face penalties. If specific employees are known to be responsible, they should be warned. Depending on the circumstances, some companies have transferred or even discharged offenders.

Laws prohibiting discrimination exist at both the federal and state levels. In the opening sections of the chapter we focus on antidiscrimination laws at the federal level. The Civil Rights Act of 1964 (including its 1991 amendments) is the principal such law. It prohibits certain discrimination based on race, sex, color, religion, and national origin. Other antidiscrimination laws covered are the Equal Pay Act, the Civil Rights Act of 1866 (called Section 1981), the Age Discrimination in Employment Act, and the Americans with Disabilities Act. The chapter concludes with a section on how to avoid or minimize unjustified employment discrimination lawsuits and a section on trends in employment discrimination litigation.

The Civil Rights Act of 1964

"That all men are created equal" was one of the "self-evident" truths recognized by the Founding Fathers in the Declaration of Independence. However, equality among all our citizens clearly has been an ideal rather than a fact. The Constitution itself recognizes slavery by saying that slaves should count as "three fifths of all other Persons" for determining population in House of Representatives elections. And of course, that all *men* are created equal says nothing about women, who did not even get a constitutionally guaranteed right to vote until 1920.

Nowhere have effects of inequality and discrimination been felt more acutely than in the area of job opportunity. Historically, common law permitted employers to hire and fire virtually at will, unless restrained by contract or statute. Under this system, white males came to dominate the job market in their ability to gain employment and their salaries and wages.

Although the Civil Rights Act of 1866 contains a provision that plaintiffs now widely use in employment discrimination cases, such use is recent. Passage of labor law in the 1920s and 1930s marks the first significant federal limitation on the relatively unrestricted right of employers to hire and fire. Then, in connection with the war effort, President Franklin D. Roosevelt issued executive orders in 1941 and 1943 requiring a clause prohibiting racial discrimination in all federal contracts with private contractors. Subsequent executive orders in the 1950s established committees to investigate complaints of racial discrimination against such contractors. Affirmative action requirements on federal contracts followed from executive orders of the 1960s.

The most important statute eliminating discriminatory employment practices, however, is the federal Civil Rights Act of 1964, as amended by the Equal Employment Opportunity Act of 1972 and the Civil Rights Act of 1991.

1. General Provisions

The provisions of Title VII of the Civil Rights Act of 1964 apply to employers with 15 or more employees. They also cover labor unions and certain others (see Table 13–1). The major purpose of these laws is to eliminate job discrimination based on race, color, religion, sex, or national origin. Discrimination for any of these reasons is a violation of the law, except that employers, employment agencies, and labor unions can discriminate on the basis of religion,

TABLE 13–1   Employers and Others Covered by Title VII

Private employers with fifteen or more employees
Labor unions with fifteen or more members
Employment agencies
State and local governments
Public and private educational institutions
Federal government (in most instances)

sex, or national origin where these are **bona fide occupational qualifications (BFOQs)** reasonably necessary to normal business operations. Title VII also permits discrimination if it results unintentionally from a seniority or merit system.

The types of employer action in which discrimination is prohibited include:

· Discharge
· Refusal to hire
· Compensation
· Terms, conditions, or privileges of employment

Employment *agencies* are prohibited from either *failing to refer* or from *actually referring* an individual for employment on the basis of race, color, religion, sex, or national origin. This prohibition differs from the law binding *employers*, where it is unlawful only to fail or refuse to hire on discriminatory grounds—the affirmative act of hiring for a discriminatory reason is apparently not illegal. For example, assume that a contractor with a government contract seeks a qualified African American engineer and requests an employment agency to refer one. The agency complies with the request. Unless a white applicant was discriminated against, the employer likely did not break the law; but the employment agency, by referring on the basis of color, unquestionably *did* violate Title VII.

Employers, unions, and employment agencies are prohibited from discriminating against an employee, applicant, or union member because he or she has made a charge, testified, or participated in an investigation or hearing under the act or otherwise opposed any unlawful practice.

Note that regarding general hiring, referrals, advertising, and admissions to training or apprenticeship programs, Title VII allows discrimination only on the basis of religion, sex, or national origin and only where these considerations are bona fide occupational qualifications. For example, it is legal for a Baptist church to refuse to engage a Lutheran minister. EEOC guidelines on sex discrimination consider sex to be a bona fide occupational qualification, for example, where it is necessary for authenticity or genuineness in hiring an actor or actress. The omission of *race* and *color* from this exception must mean that Congress does not feel these two factors are ever bona fide occupational qualifications.

Additional exemptions exist with respect to laws creating preferential treatment for veterans and hiring based on professionally developed ability tests that are not designed or intended to be used to discriminate. Such tests must bear a relationship to the job for which they are administered, however.

2. Enforcement Procedures

The Civil Rights Act of 1964 created the Equal Employment Opportunity Commission (EEOC). This agency has the primary responsibility of enforcing the provisions of the act. The EEOC is composed of five members, not more than three of whom may be members of the same political party. They are appointed by the president, with the advice and consent of the Senate, and serve a five-year term. In the course of its investigations, the EEOC has broad authority to hold hearings, obtain evidence, and subpoena and examine witnesses under oath.

Under the Equal Employment Opportunity Act of 1972, the EEOC can file a civil suit in federal district court and represent a person charging a violation of the act. However, it must first exhaust efforts to settle the claim. Remedies that may be obtained in such an action include reinstatement with back pay for the victim of an illegal discrimination and injunctions against future violations of the act by the defendant. Since discrimination complaints can take years to litigate and may involve large employee classes, the size of awards and settlements is sometimes many millions of dollars (see Table 13–2). However, the median award in employment discrimination cases is much less and plaintiffs only win about half the cases.

In 1991 Congress amended the Civil Rights Act to allow the recovery of compensatory and punitive damages of up to $300,000 per person. These damages are in addition to other remedies such as job reinstatement and back pay. Compensatory damages include damages for the pain and suffering of discrimination. Punitive damages are appropriate whenever discrimination occurs with "malice or with reckless or callous indifference to the

TABLE 13–2   Recent Awards or Settlements in Discrimination Cases

Defendant	Plaintiff(s)	Award or Settlement
First Union	Older Employees	$ 58.5 million
Johnson & Johnson	Female	11.7 million
Lucky Stores, Inc.	Females	107.0 million
Miller Brewing Co.	Male	24.5 million
Northwest Airlines	Females	52.5 million
Publix Super Markets	Females	81.5 million
Shoney's Inc.	African Americans	132.5 million
Texaco, Inc.	African Americans	176.0 million

Percentage Win Rate and Median Award in Employment Discrimination Cases by Category—1995

Category	Percentage Win Rate	Award
Age	54%	$219,000
Race	47%	147,799
Disability	54%	110,345
Sex	48%	106,728
Pregnancy	65%	87,500
Sexual Harassment	53%	38,500

Source: Jury Verdict Research, Inc.

federally protected rights of others." Very important, the 1991 amendments allow compensatory and punitive damages *only* when employers are guilty of *intentional* discrimination.

In enacting Title VII of the Civil Rights Act of 1964, Congress made it clear that it did not intend to preempt states' fair employment laws. Where state agencies begin discrimination proceedings, the EEOC must wait sixty days before it starts action. Furthermore, if a state law provides relief to a discrimination charge, the EEOC must notify the appropriate state officials and wait sixty days before continuing action.

An employee must file charges of illegal discrimination within 180 days after the unlawful practice occurred. If the EEOC does not act within a certain time period, the employee may personally file a civil action in federal district court against the employer.

To win a Title VII civil action, a plaintiff must initially show that actions taken by the employer were likely based on an illegally discriminatory basis, such as race. Generally, the plaintiff must prove either disparate (unequal) treatment or disparate impact. In proving **disparate treatment,** the plaintiff must convince the court that the employer *intentionally* discriminated against the plaintiff. If discrimination is a motivating factor, an employer's practice is illegal even though other factors (such as customer preference) also contributed.

In a **disparate impact** case the plaintiff must prove that the employer's policies had a discriminatory effect on a group protected by Title VII. The employer can defeat the plaintiff's claim by proving the **business necessity defense.** This defense requires that the employer prove that the policies used are job related and based on business necessity. However, the plaintiff can still establish a violation by showing that other policies would serve the legitimate interests of business necessity without having undesirable discriminatory effects.

In the following case the Supreme Court explains disparate treatment and disparate impact. It then extends disparate impact theory to apply to subjective as well as to objective employer evaluations of employees.

WATSON V. FORT WORTH BANK & TRUST

108 S.Ct. 2777 (1988)

Petitioner Clara Watson worked for the respondent Fort Worth Bank & Trust. After she was denied four different promotions by her supervisors, all of whom were white, she filed a discrimination charge with the EEOC. Exhausting her administrative remedies, she filed suit in federal district court. Both the district court and the Court of Appeals ruled that Ms. Watson must prove intentional discrimination. These courts ruled that subjective promotion policies could not be tested under disparate impact theory. Ms. Watson petitioned the Supreme Court for a writ of certiorari. Certiorari was granted.

O'CONNOR, J.: . . . Several of our decisions have dealt with the evidentiary standards that apply when an individual alleges that an employer has treated that particular person less favorably than others because of the plaintiff's race, color, religion, sex, or national origin. In such "disparate treatment" cases, which involve "the most easily understood type of discrimination," the plaintiff is required to prove that the defendant had a discriminatory intent or motive. In order to facilitate the orderly consideration of relevant evidence, we have devised a series of shifting evidentiary burdens that are "intended progressively to sharpen the inquiry into the elusive factual question of intentional discrimination." Under the scheme, a prima facie case is ordinarily established by proof that the employer, after having rejected the plaintiff's application for a job or promotion, continued to seek applicants with qualifications similar to the plaintiff's. The burden of proving a prima facie case is "not onerous," and the employer in turn may rebut it simply by producing some evidence that it had legitimate, nondiscriminatory reasons for the decision. If the defendant carries this burden of production, the plaintiff must prove by a preponderance of all the evidence in the case that the legitimate reasons offered by the defendant were a pretext for discrimination. . . .

In *Griggs v. Duke Power Co.*, this Court held that a plaintiff need not necessarily prove intentional discrimination in order to establish that an employer has violated . . . [Title VII]: In certain cases, facially neutral employment practices that have significant adverse effects on protected groups have been held to violate the Act without proof that the employer adopted those practices with a discriminatory intent. The factual issues and the character of the evidence are inevitably somewhat different when the plaintiff is exempted from the need to prove intentional discrimination. The evidence in these "disparate impact" cases usually focuses on statistical disparities, rather than specific incidents, and on competing explanations for those disparities. . . .

This Court has repeatedly reaffirmed the principle that some facially neutral employment practices may violate Title VII even in the absence of a demonstrated discriminatory intent. We have not limited this principle to cases in which the challenged practice served to perpetuate the effects of pre-Act intentional discrimination. Each of our subsequent decisions, however, involved standardized employment tests or criteria. . . . In contrast, we have consistently used conventional disparate-treatment theory, in which proof of intent to discriminate is required, to review hiring and promotion decisions that were based on the exercise of personal judgment or the application of inherently subjective criteria. . . .

The parties present us with stark and uninviting alternatives. Petitioner contends that subjective selection methods are at least as likely to have discriminatory effects as are the kind of objective tests at issue in *Griggs* and our other disparate impact cases. Furthermore, she argues, if disparate impact analysis is confined to objective tests, employers will be able to substitute subjective criteria having substantially identical effects, and *Griggs* will become a dead letter. Respondent and the United States (appearing as amicus curiae) argue that conventional disparate treatment analysis is adequate to accompany Congress' purpose in enacting Title VII. They also argue that subjective selection practices would be so impossibly difficult to defend under disparate impact analysis that employers would be forced to adopt numerical quotas in order to avoid liability. . . .

We are persuaded that disparate impact analysis is in principle no less applicable to subjective employment criteria than to objective or standardized tests. In either case, a facially neutral practice, adopted without discriminatory intent, may have effects that are indistinguishable from intentionally discriminatory practices. It is true, to be sure, that an employer's policy of leaving promotion decisions to the unchecked discretion of lower level supervisors should itself raise no inference of discriminatory conduct. Especially in relatively small businesses like respondent's, it may be customary and quite reasonable simply to delegate employment decisions to those employees who are most familiar with the jobs to be filled and with the candidates for those jobs. It does not follow, however, that the particular supervisors to whom this discretion is delegated always act without discriminatory intent. Furthermore, even if one assumed that any such discrimination can be adequately policed through disparate treatment analysis, the problem of subconscious stereotypes and prejudices would remain. In this case, for example, petitioner was apparently told at one point that the teller position was a big responsibility with "a lot of money . . . for blacks to have to count." Such remarks may not prove discriminatory intent, but they do suggest a lingering form of the problem that Title VII was enacted to combat. If an employer's undisciplined system of subjective decisionmaking has precisely the same effects as a system pervaded by impermissible intentional discrimination, it is difficult to see why Title VII's proscription against discriminatory actions should not apply. In both circumstances, the employer's practices may be said to "adversely affect [an individual's] status as an employee, because of such individual's race, color, religion, sex, or national origin." We conclude, accordingly, that subjective or discretionary employment practices may be analyzed under the disparate impact approach in appropriate cases.

Having decided that disparate impact analysis may in principle be applied to subjective as well as to objective practices, we turn to the evidentiary standards that should apply in such cases. It is here that the concerns raised by respondent have their greatest force. Respondent contends that a plaintiff may establish a prima facie case of disparate impact through the use of bare statistics, and that the defendant can rebut this statistical showing only by justifying the challenged practice in terms of "business necessity" or "job relatedness."

We do not believe that disparate impact theory need have any chilling effect on legitimate business practices. We recognize, however, that today's extension of that theory into the context of subjective selection practices could increase the risk that employers will be given incentives to adopt quotas or to engage in preferential treatment. Because Congress has so clearly and emphatically expressed its intent that Title VII not lead to this result, we think it imperative to explain in some detail why the evidentiary standards that apply in these cases should serve as adequate safeguards against the danger that Congress recognized. Our previous decisions offer guidance, but today's extension of disparate impact analysis calls for a fresh and somewhat closer examination of the constraints that operate to keep that analysis within its proper bounds.

First, we note that the plaintiff's burden in establishing a prima facie case goes beyond the need to show that there are statistical disparities in the employer's work force. The plaintiff must begin by identifying the specific employment practice that is challenged. Although this has been relatively easy to do in some challenges to standardized tests, it may sometimes be more difficult when subjective selection criteria are at issue. . . .

Once the employment practice at issue has been identified, causation must be proved; that is, the plaintiff must offer statistical evidence of a kind and degree sufficient to show that the practice in question has caused the exclusion of applicants for jobs or promotions because of their membership in a protected group. Our formulations, which have never been framed in terms of any rigid mathematical formula, have consistently stressed that statistical disparities must be sufficiently substantial that they raise such an inference of causation. . . .

Nor are courts or defendants obliged to assume that plaintiff's statistical evidence is reliable. "If the employer discerns fallacies or deficiencies in the data offered by the plaintiff, he is free to adduce countervailing evidence of his own." . . .

A second constraint on the application of disparate impact theory lies in the nature of the "business necessity" or "job relatedness" defense. Although we have said that an employer has "the burden of showing that any given requirement must have a manifest relationship to the employment in question," such a formulation should not be interpreted as implying that the ultimate burden of proof can be shifted to the defendant. On the contrary, the ultimate burden of proving that discrimination against a protected group has been caused by a specific employment practice remains with the plaintiff at all times. Thus, when a plaintiff has made out a prima facie case of disparate impact, and when the defendant has met its burden of producing evidence that its employment practices are based on legitimate business reasons, the plaintiff must "show that other tests or selection devices, without a similarly undesirable racial effect, would also serve the employer's legitimate interest in efficient and trustworthy workmanship." . . .

In the context of subjective or discretionary employment decisions, the employer will often find it easier than in the case of standardized tests to produce evidence of a "manifest relationship to the employment in question." It is self-evident that many jobs, for example those involving managerial responsibilities, require personal qualities that have never been considered amenable to standardized testing. In evaluating claims that discretionary employment practices are insufficiently related to legitimate business purposes, it must be borne in mind that "[c]ourts are generally less competent than employers to restructure business practices, and unless mandated to do so by Congress they should not attempt it." . . . In sum, the high standards of proof in disparate impact cases are sufficient in our view to avoid giving employers incentives to modify any normal and legitimate practices by introducing quotas or preferential treatment. . . . The judgment of the Court of Appeals is vacated, and the case is remanded for further proceedings consistent with this opinion. [*It is so ordered*].

Case Questions

1. What are *subjective* promotion policies?
2. Does the Court apply disparate impact analysis or disparate treatment analysis to subjective promotion policies?
3. After the *Watson* case, what does a plaintiff have to prove to establish disparate impact discrimination?

Before the 1991 Civil Rights Act amendments, employees or the EEOC sometimes claimed that proving racial or gender statistical imbalances in a work force established illegal discrimination. They claimed that such imbalances showed illegal discrimination, much like disparate impact discrimination, even in the absence of proof of an employer's discriminatory

---

TABLE 13–3   **Examples of Disparate Impact on Race**

Denying employment to unwed mothers when minorities have a higher rate of illegitimate births than whites

Refusing to hire people because of poor credit rating when minorities are disproportionately affected

Refusing to hire people with arrest records when minorities have higher arrest rates than whites

Giving hiring priority to relatives of present employees when minorities are underrepresented in the work force

Using discriminatory personnel tests that have no substantial relation to job qualification

---

intent. However, the 1991 amendments state that the showing of a statistically imbalanced work force is not enough *in itself* to establish a violation of Title VII.

3. Discrimination on the Basis of Race or Color

The integration of African Americans into the mainstream of American society is the primary objective of the Civil Rights Act of 1964. Title VII, which deals with employment practices, is the key legal regulation for achieving this goal. Without equal employment opportunities, African Americans can hardly enjoy other guaranteed rights, such as access to public accommodations.

Title VII prohibits discriminatory employment practices based on race or color that involve *recruiting, hiring,* and *promotion* of employees. Of course, intentional discrimination in these matters is illegal, but, as previously stated, policies with disparate impact are also forbidden. Such discrimination arises from an employer's policies or practices that apply equally to everyone but that discriminate in greater proportion against minorities and have no relation to job qualification. Table 13–3 gives examples of disparate impact on race. Often at issue in disparate impact cases is whether a discriminatory policy or practice relates to job qualification. Courts require proof, not mere assertion, of job relatedness before upholding an employer's discriminatory personnel test or other practice.

The law also prohibits discrimination in *employment conditions* and *benefits.* EEOC decisions have found such practices as the following to be violations:

- Permitting racial insults in the work situation
- Maintaining all-white or all-black crews for no demonstrable reasons
- Providing better housing for whites than blacks
- Granting higher average Christmas bonuses to whites than blacks for reasons that were not persuasive to the Commission

It is important to appreciate that Title VII prohibits employment discrimination against members of all races. In one recent case, a federal court jury awarded a white senior air traffic official $500,000 in damages against the Federal Aviation Administration. The official charged the FAA had demoted him and replaced him with an African American following complaints that blacks were underrepresented in senior management levels. Note that this case did not involve affirmative action (see Section 10).

4. Discrimination on the Basis of National Origin

Title VII's prohibition against national origin discrimination protects various ethnic groups in the workplace. In a recent case, the court ruled that Title VII had been violated when a bakery employee of Iranian descent was called "Ayatollah" in the workplace by the assistant manager and other employees. After he complained, he was fired.

Discrimination concerning the speaking of a native language frequently causes national-origin lawsuits under Title VII. For instance, courts have ruled illegal an employer's rule against speaking Spanish during work hours when the employer could not show a business need to understand all conversations between Hispanic employees. On the other hand, some courts have held that if jobs require contact with the public, a requirement that employees speak some English *may* be a bona fide occupational qualification.

Direct foreign investment in the United States has doubled and redoubled in recent years. This increasing investment has presented some unusual issues of employment discrimination law. For instance, many commercial treaties with foreign countries give foreign companies operating in the United States the right to hire executive-level employees "of their choice." Does this mean that foreign companies in the United States can discriminate as to their managerial employees on a basis forbidden under Title VII? In 1982, the Supreme Court partially resolved this issue by ruling that the civil rights laws applied to a Japanese company that did business through a subsidiary incorporated in this country.

5. Discrimination on the Basis of Religion

As was noted, religious corporations, associations, or societies can discriminate in all their employment practices on the basis of religion, but not on the basis of race, color, sex, or national origin. Other employers cannot discriminate on the basis of religion in employment practices, and they must make **reasonable accommodation** to the religious needs of their employees if it does not result in undue hardship to them.

In one case the Supreme Court let stand a lower court ruling that employees cannot be required to pay union dues if they have religious objections to unions. The case determined that a union violated Title VII by forcing a company to fire a Seventh Day Adventist who did not comply with a collective-bargaining agreement term that all employees must pay union dues. The union argued unsuccessfully that it had made reasonable accommodation to the worker's religious beliefs by offering to give any dues paid by him to charity. However, in another case the Supreme Court ruled that a company rightfully fired an employee who refused to work on Saturdays due to religious belief. The Court said that the company did not have to burden other employees by making them work Saturdays.

A growing source of religious discrimination lawsuits concerns employees who for religious reasons refuse to perform some task required by the employer. For example, in one case a vegetarian bus driver refused to distribute hamburger coupons on his bus, asserting religious beliefs. When his employer fired him, he sued. The parties settled the case for $50,000. Note that even if an employer wins such a lawsuit, it can cost the employer $100,000 or

TABLE 13–4   Examples of Illegal Sex Discrimination

Type of Business	Violation
Radio station	Refusing to hire a female newscaster because "news coming from a woman sounds like gossip"
Bank	Allowing males but not females to smoke at their desks
Utility company	Allowing women to retire at age 50 but requiring men to wait until age 55
International business	Failing to promote women to overseas positions because foreign clients were reluctant to do business with women
Hospital	Firing a pregnant X-ray technician for health reasons instead of giving her a leave of absence
Manufacturing firm	Failing to stop repeated, offensive sexual flirtations by some of its employees

more to defend itself. Since 1990, Title VII complaints filed annually with the EEOC based on religious discrimination have almost doubled.

6. Discrimination on the Basis of Sex

Historically, states have enacted many laws designed supposedly to protect women. For example, many states by statute have prohibited the employment of women in certain occupations such as those that require lifting heavy objects. Others have barred women from working during the night or more than a given number of hours per week or day. A federal district court held that a California state law that required rest periods for women only was in violation of Title VII. Some statutes prohibit employing women for a specified time after childbirth. Under EEOC guidelines, such statutes are not a defense to a charge of illegal sex discrimination and do not provide an employer with a bona fide occupational qualification in hiring standards. Other EEOC guidelines forbid employers:

- To classify jobs as male or female
- To advertise in help-wanted columns that are designated male or female, unless sex is a bona fide job qualification

Similarly, employers may not have separate male and female seniority lists.

Table 13–4 gives examples of prohibited acts of sex discrimination under Title VII.

Whether sex is a bona fide occupational qualification (and discrimination is thus legal) has been raised in several cases. The courts have tended to consider this exception narrowly. In the following instances involving hiring policy, *no* bona fide occupational qualification was found to exist:

- A rule requiring airline stewardesses, but not stewards, to be single
- A policy of hiring only females as flight cabin attendants
- A rule against hiring females with preschool-age children, but not against hiring males with such children
- A telephone company policy against hiring females as switchers because of the alleged heavy lifting involved on the job

In the telephone company case, the court held that for a bona fide occupational qualification to exist, there must be "reasonable cause to believe, that is, a factual basis for believing, that all or substantially all women would be unable to perform safely and efficiently the duties of the job involved." The Supreme Court has indicated that for such a qualification to exist, sex must be provably relevant to job performance.

Sexual Harassment

A common type of illegal sex discrimination in the workplace is **sexual harassment.** The typical sexual harassment case involves a plaintiff who has been promised benefits or threatened with loss if she or he does not give sexual favors to an employment supervisor. Such a case is also called a "quid pro quo" (this for that) case. Under Title VII and agency law, an employer is liable for this sex discrimination.

Another type of sexual harassment is the **hostile work environment,** one in which co-workers make offensive sexual comments or propositions, engage in suggestive touching, show nude pictures, or draw sexual graffiti. In 1986 the Supreme Court in *Meritor Savings Bank v. Vinson* ruled that Title VII prohibits "an offensive or hostile working environment," even when no economic loss occurs. By so ruling, the Court acknowledged that the work environment itself is a condition of employment covered by Title VII. Now you should understand why it is so important for the employer in "Just Good Fun" to act promptly to correct the hostile environment.

In 1993 the Supreme Court again addressed the hostile work environment issue. Specifically, the Court was asked to determine whether, before a person could sue under Title VII, a hostile work environment had "to seriously affect [his or her] psychological well-being" or "cause injury."

In *Harris v. Forklift Systems, Inc.,* the Court ruled that illegal sexual harassment goes beyond that which causes "injury." It includes any harassment reasonably perceived as "hostile and abusive."

In 1998 the Supreme Court confronted the issue of whether Title VII covered harassment of an employee by other employees of the same sex.

ONCALE V. SUNDOWNER OFFSHORE SERVICES, INC.

118 S. Ct. 998 (1998)

SCALIA, J.: In late October 1991, Joseph Oncale was working for respondent Sundowner Offshore Services on a Chevron U.S.A., Inc., oil platform in the Gulf of Mexico. He was employed as a roustabout on an eight-man crew which included respondents John Lyons, Danny Pippen, and Brandon Johnson. Lyons, the crane operator, and Pippen, the driller, had supervisory authority. On several occasions, Oncale was forcibly subjected to sex-related, humiliating actions against him by Lyons, Pippen and Johnson in the presence of the rest of the crew. Pippen and Lyons also physically assaulted Oncale in a sexual manner, and Lyons threatened him with rape.

Oncale's complaints to supervisory personnel produced no remedial action; in fact, the company's Safety Compliance Clerk, Valent Hohen, told Oncale that Lyons and Pippen "picked [on] him all the time too," and called him a name suggesting homosexuality. Oncale eventually quit—asking that his pink slip reflect that he "voluntarily left due to sexual harassment and verbal abuse." When asked at his deposition why he left Sundowner, Oncale stated "I felt that if I didn't leave my job, that I would be raped or forced to have sex."

Title VII of the Civil Rights Act of 1964 provides, in relevant part, that "it shall be an unlawful employment practice for an employer . . . to discriminate against any individual with respect to his compensation, terms, conditions, or privileges of employment, because of such individual's race, color, religion, sex, or national origin." We have held that this not only covers "terms" and "conditions" in the narrow contractual sense, but "evinces a congressional intent to strike at the entire spectrum of disparate treatment of men and women in employment."

Title VII's prohibition of discrimination "because of . . . sex" protects men as well as women, and in the related context of racial discrimination in the workplace we have rejected any conclusive presumption that an employer will not discriminate against members of his own race. If our precedents leave any doubt on the question, we hold today that nothing in Title VII necessarily bars a claim of discrimination "because of . . . sex" merely because the plaintiff and the defendant (or the person charged with acting on behalf of the defendant) are of the same sex.

Courts have had little trouble with that principle in cases where an employee claims to have been passed over for a job or promotion. But when the issue arises in the context of a "hostile environment" sexual harassment claim, the state and federal courts have taken a bewildering variety of stances. Some, like the Fifth Circuit in this case, have held that same-sex sexual harassment claims are never cognizable under Title VII. Other decisions say that such claims are actionable only if the plaintiff can prove that the harasser is homosexual (and thus presumably motivated by sexual desire). Still others suggest that workplace harassment that is sexual in content is always actionable, regardless of the harasser's sex, sexual orientation, or motivation.

Courts and juries have found the inference of discrimination easy to draw in most male–female sexual harassment situations, because the challenged conduct typically involves explicit or implicit proposals of sexual activity; it is reasonable to assume those proposals would not have been made to someone of the same sex. The same chain of inference would be available to a plaintiff alleging same-sex harassment, if there were credible evidence that the harasser was homosexual. But harassing conduct need not be motivated by sexual desire to support an inference of discrimination on the basis of sex. A trier of fact might reasonably find such discrimination, for example, if a female victim is harassed in such sex-specific and derogatory terms by another woman as to make it clear that the harasser is motivated by general hostility to the presence of women in the workplace. A same-sex harassment plaintiff may also, of course, offer direct comparative evidence about how the alleged harasser treated members of both sexes in a mixed-sex workplace. Whatever evidentiary route the plaintiff chooses to follow, he or she must always prove that the conduct at issue was not merely tinged with offensive sexual connotations, but actually constituted "discrimination . . . because of . . . sex."

And there is another requirement that prevents Title VII from expanding into a general civility code: As we emphasized in *Meritor* and *Harris*, the statute does not reach genuine but innocuous differences in the ways men and women routinely interact with members of the same sex and of the opposite sex. The prohibition of harassment on the basis of sex requires neither asexuality nor androgyny in the workplace; it forbids only behavior so objectively offensive as to alter the "conditions" of the victim's employment. "Conduct that is not severe or pervasive enough to create an objectively hostile or abusive work environment—an environment that a reasonable person would find hostile or abusive—is beyond Title VII's purview." We have always regarded that requirement as crucial, and as sufficient to ensure that courts and juries do not mistake ordinary socializing in the workplace—such as male-on-male horseplay or intersexual flirtation—for discriminatory "conditions of employment."

We have emphasized, moreover, that the objective severity of harassment should be judged from the perspective of a reasonable person in the plaintiff's position, considering "all the circumstances." In same-sex (as in all) harassment cases, that inquiry requires careful consideration of the social context in which particular behavior occurs and is experienced by its target. A professional football player's working environment is not severely or pervasively abusive, for example, if the coach smacks him on the buttocks as he heads onto the field—even if the same behavior would reasonably be experienced as abusive by the coach's secretary (male or female) back at the office. The real social impact of workplace behavior often depends on a constellation of surrounding circumstances, expectations, and relationships which are not fully captured by a simple recitation of the words used or the physical acts performed. Common sense, and an appropriate sensitivity to social context, will enable courts and juries to distinguish between simple teasing or roughhousing among members of the same sex, and conduct which a reasonable person in the plaintiff's position would find severely hostile or abusive.

Because we conclude that sex discrimination consisting of same-sex sexual harassment is actionable under Title VII, the judgment of the Court of Appeals for the Fifth Circuit is reversed, and the case is remanded for further proceedings consistent with this opinion. [*Reversed and remanded*].

Case Questions

1. Before the decision in this case, what had the lower courts decided about whether same-sex harassment could violate Title VII?

2. Did the Court determine that the harassment of Oncale violated Title VII? Explain.

3. Does flirting violate Title VII? Explain.

Pregnancy Discrimination Act

The Pregnancy Discrimination Act amended the Civil Rights Act in 1978. Under it, employers can no longer discriminate against women workers who become pregnant or give birth. Thus, employers with health or disability plans must cover pregnancy, childbirth, and related medical conditions in the same manner as other conditions are covered. The law covers unmarried as well as married pregnant women. It also states that an employer cannot force a pregnant woman to stop working until her baby is born, provided she is still capable of performing her duties properly. And the employer cannot specify how long a leave of absence must be taken after childbirth. Coverage for abortion is not required by the statute unless an employee carries to term and her life is endangered or she develops medical complications because of an abortion. If a woman undergoes an abortion, though, all other benefits provided for employees, such as sick leave, must be provided to her.

Note that sex discrimination applies to discrimination against men as well as women. For example, under the Pregnancy Discrimination Act the Supreme Court ruled unlawful an employer's health insurance plan that covered the pregnancies of female employees but did not cover the pregnancies of male employees' wives.

Equal Pay Act

Other federal legislation that pertains to sex discrimination in employment includes the Equal Pay Act of 1963. Presently administered by the EEOC, the act prohibits an employer from discriminating on the basis of sex in the payment of wages for equal work performed. For jobs to be equal, they must require "equal skill, effort, and responsibility" and must be performed "under similar working conditions." Discrimination is allowed if it arises from a seniority system, a merit system, a piecework production system, or any factor other than sex.

The focus of Equal Pay Act cases is whether the male and female jobs being compared involve "equal" work. Courts have recognized that *equal* does not mean *identical;* it means *substantially* equal. Thus, courts have ruled "equal" the work of male barbers and female beauticians and of male tailors and female seamstresses. Differences in male and female job descriptions will not totally protect employers against charges of equal-pay infractions. The courts have held that "substantially equal" work done on different machines would require the employer to compensate male and female employees equally.

In 1983, the Supreme Court ruled that discriminatory male and female pay differences can also be illegal under Title VII. In *County of Washington v. Gunther,* the Court decided that plaintiffs can use evidence of such pay differences to help prove intentional sex discrimination, even when the work performed is not substantially equal. Relying on the *Gunther* case, at least one lower court has held that women must be paid equally with men who perform comparable work. A federal district court ruled that the state of Washington discriminated against secretaries (mostly women) by paying them less than maintenance and other personnel (mostly men). However, the **comparable worth** theory is highly controversial, and other courts have not agreed with the theory.

Sexual Orientation Discrimination

The courts have not interpreted Title VII to prohibit discrimination against employees based on their sexual orientation, or whether they are gay, lesbian, bisexual, or heterosexual. Instead, the courts have defined the word "sex" in Table VII to refer only to gender, to whether someone is female or male. Eleven states, however, and numerous cities do forbid discrimination based on sexual orientation. It seems likely that Congress will soon amend antidiscrimination law to protect employees from discrimination based on sexual orientation.

Employment Practices That May Be Challenged

In studying the Civil Rights Act, it is useful to consider several specific employment practices that employees or job applicants may challenge as discriminatory. These practices include:

- Setting testing and educational requirements
- Having height and weight requirements for physical labor
- Maintaining appearance requirements
- Practicing affirmative action
- Using seniority systems

The following sections take a close look at these practices.

7. Testing and Educational Requirements

Employers have used a number of tools to help them find the right person for the right job in hiring and promoting employees. Among these are interviews, references, minimum educational requirements (such as a high school diploma), and personnel tests. Obviously, interviewers can be biased, even if they try not to be. One study indicated that interviewers tended to select tall men for sales positions because interviewers *subconsciously* related height to potential sales success. References may not be so reliable, either. A previous employer's letter may reflect personal biases against an applicant that were not related to job performance.

At the other extreme, an employer may give a poor employee a top recommendation because of sympathy or fear of a lawsuit in case the letter is somehow obtained by the employee. Advocates of personnel tests in the selection process feel they are very valuable in weeding out the wrong persons for a job and picking the right ones. They believe reliance on test results eliminates biases that interviewers or former employers who give references may have.

Tests, however, can have a *disparate impact* on job applicants, discriminating on the basis of race, sex, color, religion, or national origin. Setting educational standards such as requiring a high school diploma for employment can also have a disparate impact. To avoid discrimination challenges, employers must make sure that all testing and educational requirements are job related and necessary for the business.

In the past, some employers have "race normed" employment tests. *Race norming* is the practice of setting two different cutoff test scores for employment based on race or one of the other Title VII categories. For example, on a race-normed test, the minimum score for employment of white job applicants might be set at 75 out of 100. For minority applicants, the minimum score might be set at 65. *The Civil Rights Act amendments of 1991 specifically prohibit the race norming of employment tests.*

8. Height and Weight Requirements

Minimum or maximum height or weight job requirements apply equally to all job applicants, but if they have the effect of screening out applicants on the basis of race, national origin, or sex, the employer must demonstrate that such requirements are validly related to the ability to perform the work in question. For example, maximum size standards would be permissible, even if they favored women over men, if the available work space were too small to permit large persons to perform the duties of the job properly. Most size requirements have dictated minimum heights or weights, often based on a stereotyped assumption that a certain amount of strength that smaller persons might not have probably was necessary for the work. In one case, a 5-foot, 5-inch, 130-pound Hispanic won a suit against a police department on the basis that the department's 5-foot, 8-inch minimum height requirement discriminated against Hispanics, who often are shorter than that standard. He was later hired when he passed the department's physical agility examination, which included dragging a 150-pound body 75 feet and scaling a 6-foot wall.

9. Appearance Requirements

Employers often have set grooming standards for their employees. Those regulating hair length of males or prohibiting beards or mustaches have been among the most common. Undoubtedly, motivation for these rules stems from the feeling of the employer that the image it projects to the public through its employees will be adversely affected if their appearance is not "proper." It is unclear whether appearance requirements are legal or illegal, since there have been rulings both ways. Refusing to hire applicants because of a company policy prohibiting "handlebar" and "Fu Manchu" mustaches and bushy hairstyles was found illegal. Although the policies appeared neutral on their surface, it was held that they had a disparate impact against blacks.

In another case, a black employee argued that he was wrongfully fired for breaking a company rule prohibiting beards. Dermatologists testified that the plaintiff had a condition called "razor bumps" (which occurs when the tightly curled facial hairs of black men become ingrown from shaving) and that the only known cure was for him not to shave. Although the federal appeals court found that the plaintiff was prejudiced by the employer's regulation, it held in favor of the company, ruling that its *slight racial impact* was justified by the *business necessity* it served. However, a conflicting opinion in still another case upheld an employee's right to wear a beard because of razor bumps.

10. Affirmative Action Programs and Reverse Discrimination

Since the 1940s, a series of presidential executive orders have promoted nondiscrimination and **affirmative action** by employers who contract with the federal government. The authority for these orders rests with the president's executive power to control the granting of federal contracts. As a condition to obtaining such contracts, employers must agree contractually to take affirmative action to avoid unlawful discrimination in recruitment, employment, promotion, training, rate of compensation, and layoff of workers.

The affirmative action requirement means that federally contracting employers must actively recruit members of minority groups being underused in the work force. That is, employers must hire members of these groups when there are fewer minority workers in a given job category than one could reasonably expect, considering their availability. In many instances, employers must develop written affirmative action plans and set goals and timetables for bringing minority (or female) work forces up to their percentages in the available labor pool.

The Labor Department administers executive orders through its Office of Federal Contract Compliance Programs (OFCCP). The OFCCP can terminate federal contracts with employers who do not comply with its guidelines and can make them ineligible for any future federal business. For instance, it required Uniroyal, Inc., to give its female employees an estimated $18 million in back pay to compensate for past employment discrimination. The alternative was elimination of $36 million of existing federal contracts and ineligibility for future federal business.

In the early 1980s, the Labor Department eased OFCCP regulations on 75 percent of the firms that do business with the federal government. Firms with fewer than 250 employees and federal contracts of under $1 million no longer must prepare written affirmative action plans for hiring women and minorities. The OFCCP has also begun to limit its use of back pay awards to specific individuals who can show an actual loss due to violation of OFCCP guidelines.

Not all affirmative action programs are imposed on employers by the government. Many employers have adopted programs voluntarily or through collective bargaining agreements with unions. These affirmative action programs have sometimes subjected employers to charges of **reverse discrimination** when minorities or women with lower qualifications or less seniority than white males are given preference in employment or training. Even though such programs are intended to remedy the effects of present or past discrimination or other barriers to equal employment opportunity, white males have argued that the law does not permit employers to discriminate against *them* on the basis of race or sex any more than it allows discrimination against minorities or women.

In *United Steelworkers of America v. Weber,* the Supreme Court ruled legal under Title VII a voluntary affirmative action plan between an employer and a union. The plan required that at least 50 percent of certain new work trainees be black. The Court noted that the plan did not require that white employees be fired or excluded altogether from advancement. It was only a temporary measure to eliminate actual racial imbalance in the work force.

The *Weber* case provoked much controversy. Some scholars questioned whether the Supreme Court might reverse *Weber* or limit its application. In further upholding affirmative action against charges of reverse discrimination, the next case seems to answer those questions.

JOHNSON V. SANTA CLARA COUNTY TRANSPORTATION AGENCY

107 S.Ct. 1442 (1987)

The district court ruled that the agency had violated Title VII. When the Court of Appeals reversed, the Supreme Court granted certiorari.

BRENNAN, J.: . . . In December 1978, the Santa Clara County Transit District Board of Supervisors adopted an Affirmative Action Plan (Plan) for the County Transportation Agency. The Plan implemented a County Affirmative Action Plan, which had been adopted, declared the County, because "mere prohibition of discriminatory practices is not enough to remedy the effects of past practices and to permit attainment of an equitable representation of minorities, women and handicapped persons." Relevant to this case, the Agency Plan provides that, in making promotions to positions within a traditionally segregated job classification in which women have been significantly underrepresented, the Agency is authorized to consider as one factor the sex of a qualified applicant.

In reviewing the composition of its work force, the Agency noted in its Plan that women were represented in numbers far less than their proportion of the county labor force in both the Agency as a whole and in five of seven job categories. Specifically, while women constituted 36.4% of the area labor market, they composed only 22.4% of Agency employees. Furthermore, women working at the Agency were concentrated largely in EEOC job categories traditionally held by women: women made up 76% of Office and Clerical Workers, but only 7.1% of Agency Officials and Administrators, 8.6% of Professionals, 9.7% of Technicians, and 22% of Service and Maintenance workers. As for the job classifications relevant to this case, none of the 238 Skilled Craft Worker positions was held by a woman. The Plan noted that this underrepresentation of women in part reflected the fact that women had not traditionally been employed in these positions, and they had not been strongly motivated to seek training or employment in them "because of the limited opportunities that have existed in the past for them to work in such classifications."

The assessment of the legality of the Agency Plan must be guided by our decision in [*United Steelworkers of America v. Weber*]. In that case, the Court addressed the question whether the employer violated Title VII by adopting a voluntary affirmative action plan designed to "eliminate manifest racial imbalances in traditionally segregated job categories." . . .

We upheld the employer's decision to select less senior black applicants over the white respondent, for we found that taking race into account was consistent with Title VII's objective of "break[ing] down old patterns of racial segregation and hierarchy." As we stated:

> It would be ironic indeed if a law triggered by a Nation's concern over centuries of racial injustice and intended to improve the lot of those who had "been excluded from the American dream for so long" constituted the first legislative prohibition of all voluntary, private, race-conscious efforts to abolish traditional patterns of racial segregation and hierarchy. . . .

We noted that the plan did not "unnecessarily trammel the interests of the white employees," since it did not require the "discharge of white workers and their replacement with new black hirees." Nor did the plan create "an absolute bar to the advancement of white employees," since half of those trained in the new program were to be white. Finally we observed that the plan was a temporary measure, not designed to maintain racial balance, but to "eliminate a manifest racial imbalance." As Justice BLACKMUN's concurrence made clear, *Weber* held that an employer seeking to justify the adoption of a plan need not point to its own prior discriminatory practices, nor even to evidence of an "arguable violation" on its part. Rather, it need only point to a "conspicuous . . . imbalance in traditionally segregated job categories." Our decision was grounded in the recognition that voluntary employer action can play a crucial role in furthering Title VII's purpose of eliminating the effects of discrimination in the workplace, and that Title VII should not be read to thwart such efforts. . . .

In reviewing the employment decision at issue in this case, we must first examine whether that decision was made pursuant to a plan prompted by concerns similar to those of the employer in *Weber*. Next, we must determine whether the effect of the plan on males and non-minorities is comparable to the effect of the plan in that case. . . .

In evaluating the compliance of an affirmative action plan with Title VII's prohibition on discrimination, we must be mindful of "this Court's and Congress' consistent emphasis on the 'value of voluntary efforts to further the objectives of the law.' " The Agency in the case before us has undertaken such a voluntary effort, and has done so in full recognition of both the difficulties and the potential for intrusion on males and non-minorities. The Agency has identified a conspicuous imbalance in job categories traditionally segregated by race and sex. It has made clear from the outset, however, that employment decisions may not be justified solely by reference to this imbalance, but must rest on a multitude of practical, realistic factors. It has therefore committed itself to annual adjustment of goals so as to provide a reasonable guide for actual hiring and promotion decisions. The Agency earmarks no positions for anyone; sex is but one of several factors that may be taken into account in evaluating qualified applicants for a position. As both the Plan's language and its manner of operation attest, the Agency has no intention of establishing a work force whose permanent composition is dictated by rigid numerical standards.

We therefore hold that the Agency appropriately took into account as one factor the sex of Diane Joyce in determining that she should be promoted to the road dispatcher position. The decision to do so was made pursuant to an affirmative action plan that represents a moderate, flexible, case-by-case approach to effecting a gradual improvement in the representation of minorities and women in the Agency's work force. Such a plan is fully consistent with Title VII, for it embodies the contribution that voluntary employer action can make in eliminating the vestiges of discrimination in the workplace. Accordingly, the judgment of the Court of Appeals is [*affirmed*].

Case Questions

1. How does the Court justify affirmative action plans?

2. Does an employer have to admit prior discriminatory practices before adopting a voluntary affirmative action plan? Explain.

3. Why does the Court make a point of saying "the Agency has no intention of establishing a work force whose permanent composition is dictated by rigid numerical standards"?

Note the difference between taking affirmative action and setting a "quota." Affirmative action is taken to help correct historic work force imbalances and usually has target goals that are pursued for a limited time. On the other hand, quotas set rigid standards for various groups, such as that 50 percent of the work force must be female. The 1991 Civil Rights Act amendments prohibit the setting of quotas in employment.

The EEOC has issued guidelines intended to protect employers who set up affirmative action plans. These guidelines indicate that Title VII is not violated if an employer determines that there is a reasonable basis for concluding that such a plan is appropriate and the employer takes *reasonable* affirmative action. For example, if an employer discovers that it has a job category where one might expect to find more women and minorities employed than are actually in its work force, the employer has a reasonable basis for affirmative action.

In 1995 the Supreme Court decided *Adarand Constructors, Inc. v. Pena*. The Court emphasized in this important case that government-imposed affirmative action plans are subject to *strict judicial scrutiny* under equal protection guaranteed by the Fifth and Fourteenth Amendments. To be constitutional, such plans must now be supported by a *compelling interest*. The

Adarand decision will make it constitutionally difficult to justify some government-imposed affirmative action plans. Much litigation has followed that tests the constitutionality of various plans.

In 1996, California voters approved the controversial Proposition 209. In relevant part it says that "the state shall not discriminate against, or grant preferential treatment to, any individual or group on the basis of race, sex, color, ethnicity, or national origin in the operation of public employment, public education, or public contracting." The Supreme Court refused to hear an appeal from a lower court decision that upheld Proposition 209 against constitutional challenge and the assertion it violated federal civil rights law. Although Proposition 209 *does not* affect private employer affirmative action plans required by federal law, it does illustrate the current opposition that many Americans have to affirmative action. Polls show that almost three-fourths of the general population disapproves of affirmative action. Nearly 50 percent of African Americans also oppose it.

11. Seniority Systems

Seniority systems give priority to those employees who have worked longer for a particular employer or in a particular line of employment of the employer. Employers may institute seniority systems on their own, but in a union shop they are usually the result of collective bargaining. Their terms are spelled out in the agreement between the company and the union. Seniority systems often determine the calculation of vacation, pension, and other fringe benefits. They also control many employment decisions such as the order in which employees may choose shifts or qualify for promotions or transfers to different jobs. They also are used to select the persons to be laid off when an employer is reducing its labor force. As a result of seniority, the last hired are usually the first fired. Decisions based on seniority have been challenged in recent years as violating the laws relating to equal employment opportunity. Challenges often arose when recently hired members of minority groups were laid off during periods of economic downturn. Firms with successful affirmative action programs often lost most of their minority employees.

Section 703(h) of the Civil Rights Act of 1964 provides that, in spite of other provisions in the act, it is not an unlawful employment practice for an employer to apply different employment standards under a bona fide (good-faith) seniority system if the differences are not the result of an *intention* to discriminate. In *Memphis Fire Dept. v. Stotts* the Supreme Court ruled that discrimination resulting from application of a seniority system was lawful even when it affected minorities hired or promoted by affirmative action.

Other Statutes and Discrimination in Employment

Although the Civil Rights Act of 1964 is the most widely used antidiscrimination statute, there are other important antidiscrimination laws. They include the Civil Rights Act of 1866, the Age Discrimination in Employment Act, the Americans with Disabilities Act, and various state and local laws. The following sections examine these laws.

12. Civil Rights Act of 1866

An important federal law that complements Title VII of the 1964 Civil Rights Act is the Civil Rights Act of 1866. One provision of that act, known as **Section 1981,** provides that "all persons . . . shall have the same right to make and enforce contracts . . . as enjoyed by white citizens." Since union memberships and employment relationships involve contracts, Section 1981 bans racial discrimination in these areas.

The courts have interpreted Section 1981 as giving a private plaintiff most of the same protections against racial discrimination that the 1964 Civil Rights Act provides. In addition, there are at least two advantages to the plaintiff who files a suit based on Section 1981. First, there are no procedural requirements for bringing such a suit, while there are a number of fairly complex requirements plaintiffs must follow before bringing a private suit under Title VII. For instance, before a plaintiff can file a lawsuit against an employer, the plaintiff must file charges of discrimination with the EEOC and have that agency fail to bring an action against the employer. By using Section 1981, a plaintiff can immediately sue an employer in federal court without first going through the EEOC.

A second advantage to Section 1981 is that under it the courts can award unlimited compensatory and punitive damages. There are no capped limits as there are under Title VII. As a practical matter, parties alleging racial discrimination usually sue under both Section 1981 and Title VII.

Note that Section 1981 does not cover discrimination based on sex, religion, national origin, age, or handicap. As interpreted by the courts, this section applies only to *racial* discrimination. However, what is race? The Supreme Court has held that being of Arabic or Jewish ancestry constitutes "race" as protected by Section 1981. The Court stated that when the law was passed in the nineteenth century, the concept of race was much broader than it is today. Race then included the descendants of a particular "family, tribe, people, or nation." Has the Court opened the door for a white job applicant to sue a black employer for discrimination under Section 1981?

In *Patterson v. McLean,* the Supreme Court interpreted Section 1981 to apply only to the actual hiring or firing of employees based on race. Under this interpretation, Section 1981 did not offer protection against discrimination such as a hostile working environment. But the Civil Rights Act amendments of 1991 redefined Section 1981 to include protection against discrimination in "enjoyment of all benefits, privileges, terms and conditions of the contractual relationship." Thus Section 1981 now also protects against hostile environment discrimination.

13. Discrimination on the Basis of Age

Neither the Civil Rights Act nor the Equal Employment Opportunity Act forbids discrimination based on age. However, the Age Discrimination in Employment Act (ADEA) does. It prohibits employment discrimination against employees ages 40 and older, and it prohibits the mandatory retirement of these employees. Only bona fide executives and high policymakers of private companies can be forced into early retirement. The ADEA also invalidates retirement plans and labor contracts that violate the act.

Remedies for a violation of the ADEA include reinstatement of an improperly fired employee, front pay for future earnings loss if no reinstatement, back pay, and injunctions, as well as attorney's fees. In the case that follows, the Supreme Court confronts the interesting case of how an employee's wrongdoing should affect the remedies in her age-discrimination lawsuit against her employer. Note the purposes the Court says the ADEA serves.

McKennon v. Nashville Banner Publishing Co.

513 U.S. 352 (1995)

Alleging that her discharge by the Nashville Banner Publishing Co. violated the ADEA, Christine McKennon sued her employer. After she admitted in her deposition that she had copied some of her employer's confidential documents in anticipation of being discharged, the trial court granted judgment for the Banner. The court held that McKennon's misconduct was grounds for her termination and that the ADEA gave her no remedy. The Supreme Court granted certiorari.

KENNEDY, J. . . . The ADEA, enacted in 1967 as part of an ongoing congressional effort to eradicate discrimination in the workplace, reflects a societal condemnation of invidious bias in employment decisions. The ADEA is but part of a wider statutory scheme to protect employees in the workplace nationwide. The substantive antidiscrimination provisions of the ADEA are modeled upon the prohibitions of Title VII. Its remedial provisions incorporate by reference the provisions of the Fair Labor Standards Act of 1938. When confronted with a violation of the ADEA, a district court is authorized to afford relief by means of reinstatement, backpay, injunctive relief, declaratory judgment, and attorney's fees. In the case of a willful violation of the Act, the ADEA authorizes an award of liquidated damages equal to the backpay award. The Act also gives federal courts the discretion to "grant such legal or equitable relief as may be appropriate to effectuate the purpose of [the Act]."

The ADEA and Title VII share common substantive features and also a common purpose: "the elimination of discrimination in the workplace." Congress designed the remedial measures in these statutes to serve as a "spur or catalyst" to cause employers "to self-examine and to self-evaluate their employment practices and to endeavor to eliminate, so far as possible, the last vestiges" of discrimination. Deterrence is one object of these statutes. Compensation for injuries caused by the prohibited discrimination is another. The ADEA, in keeping with these purposes, contains a vital element found in both Title VII and the Fair Labor Standards Act: it grants an injured employee a right of action to obtain the authorized relief. The private litigant who seeks redress for his or her injuries vindicates both the deterrence and the compensation objectives of the ADEA. It would not accord with this scheme if after-acquired evidence of wrongdoing that would have resulted in termination operates, in every instance, to bar all relief for an earlier violation of the Act.

The objectives of the ADEA are furthered when even a single employee establishes that an employer has discriminated against him or her. The disclosure through litigation of incidents or practices which violate national policies respecting nondiscrimination in the work force is itself important, for the occurrence of violations may disclose patterns of noncompliance resulting from a misappreciation of the Act's operation or entrenched resistance to its commands, either of which can be of industry-wide significance. The efficacy of its enforcement mechanisms becomes one measure of the success of the Act.

McKennon's misconduct was not discovered until after she had been fired. The employer could not have been motivated by knowledge it did not have and it cannot now claim that the employee was fired for the nondiscriminatory reason. Our inquiry is not at an end, however, for even though the employer has violated the Act, we must consider how the after-acquired evidence of the employee's wrongdoing bears on the specific remedy to be ordered. . . . The proper boundaries of remedial relief in the general class of cases where, after termination, it is discovered that the employee has engaged in wrongdoing must be addressed by the judicial system in the ordinary course of further decisions, for the factual permutations and the equitable considerations they raise will vary from case to case. We do conclude that here, and as a general rule in cases of this type, neither reinstatement nor front pay is an appropriate remedy. It would be both inequitable and pointless to order the reinstatement of someone the employer would have terminated, and will terminate, in any event and upon lawful grounds.

The proper measure of backpay presents a more difficult problem. Resolution of this question must give proper recognition to the fact that an ADEA violation has occurred which must be deterred and compensated without undue infringement upon the employer's rights and prerogatives. The object of compensation is to restore the employee to the position he or she would have been in absent the discrimination, but that principle is difficult to apply with precision where there is after-acquired evidence of wrongdoing that would have led to termination on legitimate grounds had the employer known about it. Once an employer learns about employee wrongdoing that would lead to a legitimate discharge, we cannot require the employer to ignore the information, even if it is acquired during the course of discovery in a suit against the employer and even if the information might have gone undiscovered absent the suit. The beginning point in the trial court's formulation of a rem-

edy should be calculation of backpay from the date of the unlawful discharge to the date the new information was discovered. In determining the appropriate order for relief, the court can consider taking into further account extraordinary equitable circumstances that affect the legitimate interests of either party. An absolute rule barring any recovery of backpay, however, would undermine the ADEA's objective of forcing employers to consider and examine their motivations, and of penalizing them for employment decisions that spring from age discrimination.

The judgment is reversed, and the case is remanded to the Court of Appeals for the Sixth Circuit for further proceedings consistent with this opinion. [*Reversed and remanded*].

Case Questions

1. What did the plaintiff McKennon do wrong?
2. Why is McKennon denied reinstatement?
3. Why does the Court say McKennon should not be denied all remedies under the ADEA because of her wrongdoing?
4. How did her wrongdoing affect the back pay she could receive under the ADEA?

In one case under the act, Standard Oil Company of California agreed to pay $2 million in back wages to 160 employees who had been laid off and were over forty. Thus, if persons over forty are just as qualified as younger workers to handle their jobs, they usually must be kept. To cut costs, some companies have discriminated against older, higher-ranking, and higher-paid employees by replacing them with younger, lower-salaried persons who are equally competent to handle the job. This cost cutting is also illegal. One decision awarded three former department store executives $2.3 million for such discrimination. In another case, a firm transferred a sixty-year-old man to a job that required him to stand for long periods. When he died, his widow, arguing that the transfer had been an attempt to induce him to retire, obtained a judgment against the firm for $750,000 in damages for illegal age discrimination.

An important area of age discrimination litigation exists when age is a bona fide occupational qualification. It is recognized that as people grow older, their physical strength, agility, reflexes, hearing, and vision tend to diminish in quality. However, this generally provides no legal reason for discriminating against older persons as a class. Although courts will uphold job-related physical requirements if they apply on a case-by-case basis, they frequently find as illegal those policies that prohibit the hiring of persons beyond a maximum age or that establish a maximum age beyond which employees are forced to retire for physical reasons. Thus, one court ruled that a mandatory retirement age of 65 was illegally discriminatory as applied to the job of district fire chief. To the contrary, another court ruled that the airlines could impose a maximum age for hiring a new pilot in light of a Federal Aviation Administration–mandated retirement age for pilots.

Courts have disagreed on whether remedies for violation of the act include, in addition to reinstatement and wages lost, damages for the psychological trauma of being fired or forced to resign illegally. One federal district court awarded $200,000 to a victim of age discrimination who was an inventor and scientist, for the psychological and physical effects suffered from being forced into early retirement at age 60. Also awarded were out-of-pocket costs of $60,000 and attorneys' fees of $65,000. Note that *willful* violations of the act entitle discrimination victims to *double damages.*

Since the 1978 amendments to the act, age discrimination claims have grown rapidly. In recent years, they have more than doubled in number.

14. Discrimination on the Basis of Disabilities

According to a Harris poll, two-thirds of all disabled Americans between the ages of 16 and 64 are not working, even though most of them want to work. To help those with disabilities get work, Congress in 1990 passed the Americans with Disabilities Act (ADA). Major provisions of this act prohibit employment discrimination against the disabled.

To prevent disability discrimination in general, the ADA prohibits employers from requiring a preemployment medical examination or asking questions about a job applicant's medical history. Only after a job offer has been given can the employer condition employment on an employee's passing a job-related medical exam or on the employee's responses to job-related medical questions.

Under the ADA **disability** is defined as "any physical or mental impairment that substantially limits one or more of an individual's major life activities." "Physical and mental impairment" includes physical disorders or conditions, disease, disfigurement, amputation affecting a vital body system, psychological disorders, mental retardation, mental illness, and learning disabilities. "Major life activities" include the ability to perform manual tasks, walk, see, hear, speak, learn, breathe, care for oneself, or work.

Not included by the ADA as protected disabilities are homosexuality, sexual behavior disorders, compulsive gambling, kleptomania, and disorders resulting from *current* drug or alcohol use. The emphasis on current drug or alcohol use means that employees who have successfully recovered or are successfully recovering from drug or alcohol disabilities are protected from employment discrimination.

What about people with acquired immunodeficiency syndrome (AIDS)? Does having it make an employee disabled under the ADA? The answer to this question is yes. Although those who test positive for the AIDS virus may not initially have any obvious physical or mental disability, they are disabled in the sense that others' fear of them can interfere with their ability to work, which is a major life activity.

The ADA prohibits employers of fifteen or more employees (also unions with fifteen or more members and employment agencies) from discriminating against the qualified disabled with respect to hiring, advancement, termination, compensation, training, or other terms, conditions, or privileges of employment. **Qualified disabled** are defined as those with a disability who, with or without reasonable accommodation, can perform the essential functions of a particular job position.

The ADA does not require employers to hire the unqualified disabled, but they must make reasonable accommodation so disabled employees can succeed in the workplace. Reasonable accommodation is the process of adjusting a job or work environment to fit the needs of disabled employees. It may include:

- Making the work facilities accessible and usable to disabled employees
- Restructuring jobs or modifying work schedules
- Purchasing or modifying necessary equipment for use by the disabled
- Providing appropriate training materials or assistance modified to fit the needs of disabled employees

Note that an employer need make only reasonable accommodation for disabled employees. The employer can plead *undue hardship,* defined as "an action requiring significant difficulty or expense," as a reason for not accommodating the needs of disabled employees. The ADA specifies that in evaluating undue hardship, the cost of the accommodation, the resources of the employer, the size of the employer, and the nature of the employer's business be considered.

Remedies under the ADA are basically the same remedies available under the Civil Rights Act, including hiring, reinstatement, back pay, injunctive relief, and compensatory and punitive damages. As with the Civil Rights Act, compensatory and punitive damages are not available for policies that merely have disparate impact. They are available for intentional discrimination and for other employer actions such as failing to make reasonable accommodation for known job applicant or employee disabilities.

In some ways, the ADA merely follows the rights available under the Civil Rights Act and applies them to protect the disabled. But the ADA is much more detailed than the Civil Rights Act. What a disability is, what constitutes discrimination, and what constitutes reasonable accommodation are all specifically defined. It will be interesting to see if the high degree of definition in the ADA reduces litigation challenging the meaning of its provisions. Also worthy of seeing will be whether the ADA is flexible enough to deal with discrimination not specifically mentioned in the act.

In addition to a title (or section) prohibiting employment discrimination against the disabled, the ADA has several other titles. The most important one forbids discrimination against the disabled in public accommodations, including restaurants, bars, hotels, theaters, retail stores, service establishments, parks, museums, libraries, schools, and transportation facilities.

The ADA replaces the Rehabilitation Act of 1973 as the primary federal law protecting the disabled. However, the Rehabilitation Act, which applies only to employers doing business with the government under a federal contract for $2,500 or more, still requires that such employers have a qualified affirmative action program for hiring and promoting the disabled.

Concept Summary: Illegal Employment Practices

Unless bona fide occupational qualifications or business necessity can be proved, federal law prohibits recruiting, hiring, promoting, and other employment practices that involve disparate treatment or produce a disparate impact on the basis of:

Race or color
National origin
Religion

Sex
Test scores and educational requirements
Height and weight
Appearance
Age
Disabilities

15. Discrimination in Getting and Keeping Health Insurance

Beginning July 1, 1997, a new act prohibits group health plans and health insurance issuers from discriminating against employees based on certain factors. The Health Insurance Portability and Accountability Act (HIPAA) forbids group plans and issuers from excluding an employee from insurance coverage or requiring different premiums based on the employee's health status, medical condition or history, genetic information, or disability.

The act primarily prevents discrimination against individual employees in small businesses. Before the act, individual employees with an illness like cancer or a genetic condition like sickle cell anemia were sometimes denied coverage in a new health plan. The small size of the plan deterred insurers from covering individual employees whose medical condition might produce large claims. The act denies insurers the right to discriminate on this basis. It also guarantees that insured employees who leave their old employer and join a new employer are not denied health insurance. As of this writing, the exact meanings of many HIPAA provisions are still unclear.

Note, however, that the act only applies to prevent discrimination in group health insurance plans. It does not apply to individuals who purchase individual health insurance. Congress is considering legislation to extend HIPAA's antidiscrimination provisions to individual insurance. Behind HIPAA and proposals for new legislation is the concern that new forms of genetic testing will allow insurers and employers to identify and discriminate against individuals who may in the future develop certain medical conditions.

16. Other Federal Legislation

Other federal legislation dealing with employment discrimination includes the National Labor Relations Act of 1936. The National Labor Relations Board has ruled that appeals to racial prejudice in a collective bargaining representation election constitute an unfair labor practice. The NLRB has also revoked the certification of unions that practice discriminatory admission or representation policies. Additionally, employers have an obligation to bargain with certified unions over matters of employment discrimination. Such matters are considered "terms and conditions of employment" and are thus mandatory bargaining issues. Note that the reverse discrimination issue in the *Weber* case (p. 362) arose because of an affirmative action plan in a collective bargaining contract.

Finally, various other federal agencies may prohibit discriminatory employment practices under their authorizing statutes. The Federal Communications Commission, for example, has prohibited employment discrimination by its licensees (radio and TV stations) and has required the submission of affirmative action plans as a condition of license renewal.

17. State Antidiscrimination Laws

Federal laws concerning equal employment opportunity specifically permit state laws imposing additional duties and liabilities. In recent years, fair employment practices legislation has been introduced and passed by many state legislatures. When the federal Equal Employment Opportunity Act became effective, forty states had such laws, but their provisions varied considerably. A typical state act makes it an unfair employment practice for any employer to refuse to hire or otherwise discriminate against any individual because of his or her race, color, religion, national origin, or ancestry. If employment agencies or labor organizations discriminate against an individual in any way because of one of these reasons, they are also guilty of an unfair employment practice. State acts usually set up an administrative body, generally known as the Fair Employment Practices Commission, which has the power to make rules and regulations and hear and decide charges of violations filed by complainants.

State antidiscrimination laws sometimes protect categories of persons not protected by federal law. For example, some protect persons from employment discrimination based on weight. Others protect persons from discrimination based on sexual preference.

As indicated in Chapter 9 on torts, discrimination plaintiffs can also sue employers under various state common law causes of action, like negligence, assault, battery, intentional infliction of mental distress, and defamation. Under common law, plaintiffs can usually receive unlimited compensatory and punitive damages, and greater numbers of plaintiffs seem to be suing under common law. In Las Vegas a jury awarded over $5 million against the Hilton Hotel and in favor of a plaintiff who had been sexually groped at an aviators' Tailhook convention. The jury determined that the hotel had been negligent in failing to provide adequate security.

18. Trends in Employment Discrimination and Litigation

Several current trends in employment discrimination and litigation will require close attention from managers in the coming years. These trends highlight the fact that the workforce is increasingly diverse and that new managers must be alert to the full impact of antidiscrimination laws.

Discrimination by E-Mail
Recently, more and more complaints about discriminatory company e-mail have surfaced. Racist and sexist jokes passed generally through a company's

e-mail system can create a hostile work environment prohibited under Title VII. Employees at Chevron Corp., Citibank, R.R. Donnelley & Sons Co., and Morgan Stanley & Co. have all sued their employers at least in part because of discriminatory e-mail messages.

Managers must note that legal issues of employee privacy and constitutional free speech do not apply to situations of company e-mail use. Employees should be alerted that computer hard drives store e-mail where plaintiffs in discrimination lawsuits can recover it. Companies should develop formal policies regarding acceptable e-mail use in order to protect themselves. They must also take prompt action against discriminatory e-mail messages and those employees who send them.

Arbitration in Employment Discrimination Disputes

Arbitration is usually cheaper, quicker, and less public than litigation. Accustomed to using arbitration clauses in contracts with customers and suppliers, many employers also have begun placing arbitration clauses in employment contracts and personnel handbooks. These clauses require arbitration in employment discrimination disputes and with other employment controversies.

The Federal Arbitration Act (see Chapter 3) prefers arbitration over litigation, but that act may not apply to certain employment contracts. Although the Supreme Court has upheld arbitration clauses in employment discrimination cases in certain instances, not all of the important issues have been decided. In July 1977 the EEOC issued a policy statement concluding that "agreements that mandate binding arbitration of discrimination claims as a condition of employment are contrary to the fundamental principles" of antidiscrimination laws.

Congress may ultimately decide whether binding arbitration as a condition of working for an employer is an acceptable part of the employment contract. In the meantime, employers who wish to have employment disputes, including discrimination disputes, arbitrated should consider

- paying employees separately from the employment contract to sign arbitration agreements;
- ensuring that arbitration agreements allow for the same range of remedies contained in the antidiscrimination laws;
- allowing limited discovery in arbitration, which traditionally has no discovery process;
- permitting employees to participate in selecting neutral, knowledgeable professional arbitrators instead of using an industry arbitration panel.

These steps should go far toward eliminating many of the objections to the arbitration of employment discrimination disputes.

Proper arbitration agreements should continue to be part of the business response to discrimination in employment disputes. Interestingly, at least one study has found that employees alleging discrimination win more often before arbitration panels than before juries and in only two-thirds of the time.

Insuring against Employment Discrimination Claims

Employers commonly insure against many potential liabilities. However, the general liability policies carried by many businesses, which cover bodily injury and property damage, often do not insure against intentional torts. Intent is a key element in many employment discrimination claims. In addition, general policies may not cover the back pay or damages for mental anguish that many discrimination plaintiffs seek. As a result, employers are beginning to ask for and get employment practices liability insurance, a type of insurance aimed specifically at discrimination claims.

Even with the availability of the new insurance, not all types of employment discrimination can be insured against in every state. States like New York and California do not permit companies to insure against "intentional acts." Disparate treatment discrimination is an example of such an act. Similarly, some states do not permit companies to insure against punitive damages that can arise in intentional violations of Title VII. Managers should also be aware that what the new policies cover and what they exclude vary widely.

Key Terms

Affirmative action   362
Bona fide occupational qualifications (BFOQs)   349
Business necessity defense   351
Comparable worth   360
Disability   369
Disparate impact   351
Disparate treatment   351
Hostile work environment   357
Qualified disabled   370
Reasonable accommodation   355
Reverse discrimination   362
Section 1981   366
Seniority system   365
Sexual harassment   357

Review Questions and Problems

The Civil Rights Act of 1964

1. *General Provisions*
   Martel, a competent male secretary to the president of ICU, was fired because the new president of the company believed it is more appropriate to have a female secretary.
   (a) Has a violation of the law occurred?
   (b) Assume that a violation of the law has occurred and Martel decided to take an extended vacation after he was fired. Upon his return seven months later, Martel filed suit in federal district court against ICU, charging illegal discrimination under the Civil Rights Act of 1964. What remedies will be available to him under the act?

2. *Enforcement Procedures*
   Muscles-Are-You, Inc., a bodybuilding spa targeted primarily toward male body builders, refused to hire a woman for the position of executive director. The spa's management stated that the executive director must have a "macho" image to relate well with the spa's customers. Discuss whether it is likely that the spa has violated Title VII.

3. *Discrimination on the Basis of Race or Color*
   Does Title VII prohibit employment discrimination against members of all races? Explain.

4. *Discrimination on the Basis of National Origin*
   Ace Tennis Co. hires only employees who speak English. Does this policy illegally discriminate against Hispanic job applicants who speak only Spanish? Discuss.

5. *Discrimination on the Basis of Religion*
   Ortega, an employee of ABC, Inc., recently joined a church that forbids working on

Saturdays, Sundays, and Mondays. Ortega requested that his employer change his work schedule from eight-hour days, Monday through Friday, to ten-hour days, Tuesday through Friday. Ortega's request was refused because the employer is in operation only eight hours per day, five days a week. After a month during which Ortega failed to work on Mondays, he was fired. The employer stated that "only a full-time employee would be acceptable" for Ortega's position. What are Ortega's legal rights, if any?

6. *Discrimination on the Basis of Sex*
A male supervisor at Star Company made repeated offensive sexual remarks to female employees. The employees complained to higher management, which ignored the complaints. If the company does not discharge or otherwise penalize the employee, has it violated Title VII? Discuss.

Employment Practices That May Be Challenged

7. *Testing and Educational Requirements*
Jennings Company, which manufactures sophisticated electronic equipment, hires its assembly employees on the basis of applicants' scores on a standardized mathematics aptitude test. It has been shown that those who score higher on the test almost always perform better on the job. However, it has also been demonstrated that the use of the test in hiring employees has the effect of excluding African Americans and other minority groups. Is this practice of the Jennings Company prohibited by the Civil Rights Act of 1964?

8. *Height and Weight Requirements*
(a) An employer hires job applicants to wait tables in the Executive Heights Restaurant only if they are over 6 feet tall. Does this policy likely violate Title VII? Explain.
(b) If a class of job applicants under 6 feet sues the employer, will it likely get compensatory and punitive damages? Explain.

9. *Appearance Requirements*
Silicon Products requires all male employees to wear their hair "off the collar." Does this policy violate Title VII? Discuss.

10. *Affirmative Action Programs and Reverse Discrimination*
Kartel, Inc., found that historically African Americans had been significantly underrepresented in its workforce. It decided to remedy the situation and place African Americans in 50 percent of all new job openings. Discuss the legality of Kartel's action.

11. *Seniority Systems*
Are seniority systems in the workplace legal under Title VII if in fact they discriminate on the basis of gender or race? Explain.

Other Statutes and Discrimination in Employment

12. *Civil Rights Act of 1866*
When is it an advantage for a plaintiff to use Section 1981 as the basis for discrimination litigation as contrasted with using Title VII?

13. *Discrimination on the Basis of Age*
Cantrell, the controller of Xylec's, Inc., was forced to retire at age fifty-eight due to a general company policy. Although Cantrell has a company pension of $50,000 per year, she believes that her lifestyle will soon be hampered due to inflation, since the pension provides for no cost-of-living increases. What are Cantrell's rights, if any?

14. *Discrimination on the Basis of Disabilities*
Ralph is a systems analyst for the Silicon Corporation, a major defense contractor. When Ralph's co-workers learn that he has AIDS, six of them quit work immediately. Fearing that additional resignations will delay production, the company discharges Ralph. Discuss whether or not the company acted legally.

15. *Discrimination in Getting and Keeping Health Insurance*
Why does Title VII not apply to preventing discrimination in the getting and keeping of health insurance?

16. *Other Federal Legislation*
Do employers have an obligation to negotiate with groups of employees over issues of discrimination? Explain.

17. *State Antidiscrimination Laws*
Explain how state antidiscrimination laws protect workers in situations where federal laws do not.

18. *Trends in Employment Discrimination and Litigation*
Can arbitration agreements be used to keep employees from litigating discrimination issues? Discuss.

Terminology Review

For each term in the left-hand column, match the most appropriate description in the right-hand column:

1. Affirmative action

2. Seniority system

3. Reverse discrimination

4. Disparate impact

5. BFOQs
6. Section 1981

a. Selection of employees for hire or promotion in a pattern significantly different from that of racial minorities or women available in the pool of job applicants

b. Job-related employment characteristics based on sex or religion

c. Taking active steps to seek out and employ groups traditionally underrepresented in the work force

d. A system to give priority to those employees who have worked longer for a particular employer

e. Prohibits contractual discrimination based on race

f. Employment discrimination against white males

14

ENVIRONMENTAL LAWS AND POLLUTION CONTROL

Business Decision

The New Project

You are a project manager for the Katerly Paper Company. Recently, you have been given responsibility for construction of a new plant in Robbinsdale, North Carolina, on the edge of the Nantacauga National Forest. You must also secure a lease from the Department of Interior to harvest timber on federal land. Although many residents welcome the new jobs your company will create, others have moved into the area for its natural beauty and are mounting a campaign to keep out your company.

What environmental laws may apply to the new plant construction?

What environmental laws may apply to the national forest lease?

What steps should you take to maintain good community relations?

Environmental regulation remains the single most expensive area of government's regulation of the business community. Over the next decade, industry will spend several hundred billion dollars on pollution control. The primary reason for environmental regulation is concern over the effects of human population growth and the impacts of human technology. Almost daily we hear of threats to the environment arising from human behavior. Destruction of the rain forests, extinction of animal and plant species, depletion of the ozone layer, and the greenhouse effect are only some of the current environmental concerns.

Environmental and pollution-control laws govern regulation on three levels:

- Government's regulation of itself
- Government's regulation of business
- Suits by private individuals

Table 14–1 illustrates this breakdown.

**TABLE 14–1   Categories of Environmental and Pollution-
Control Laws**

Government's Regulation of Itself
National Environmental Policy Act
State environmental policy acts

Government's Regulation of Business
Clean Air Act
Clean Water Act
Pesticide Control Acts
Solid Waste Disposal Act
Toxic Substances Control Act
Resource Conservation and Recovery Act
Other federal, state, and local statutes

Suits by Private Individuals
Citizen enforcement provisions of various statutes
Public and private nuisance
Trespass
Negligence
Strict liability for ultrahazardous activity

This chapter examines environmental and pollution-control laws by looking first at federal environmental policy and then at specific laws aimed at reducing specific kinds of pollution. The emphasis is on the compliance these laws force on business and industry. For a summary of federal environmental and pollution-control laws, see Table 14–2. The final section of the chapter looks at the rights and liabilities of private individuals under environmental law.

Administering environmental laws at the federal level is the Environmental Protection Agency (EPA). Since many of the laws provide for joint federal-state enforcement, the states also have strong environmental agencies. Policies are set at the federal level, and the states devise plans to implement them. States, and even local governments, also enforce their own laws that affect the environment and control pollution.

As the project manager for "The New Project," you must be aware of how both federal and state environmental laws affect your business. At the federal level, the National Environmental Policy Act, the Clean Air Act, and the Clean Water Act will likely apply to the national forest lease and to the new plant construction. Various state laws will also apply. You will have to get numerous permits and follow complicated regulations.

Maintaining good community relations will add even more difficulty to your job. Showing early that your company intends to be a good corporate citizen and emphasizing the jobs and tax revenues that it will bring to the community are a beginning.

Government's Regulation of Itself

The modern environmental movement began in the 1960s. As it gained momentum, it generated political pressure that forced government to reassess its role in environmental issues.

TABLE 14–2 Major Federal Laws Relating to Environmental Protection and Pollution Control

Year	Statute	Summary of Major Provisions
1969	National Environmental Policy Act	1. Establishes broad policy goals 2. Imposes specific duties on all federal agencies 3. Sets up Council on Environmental Quality
Air		
1970	Clean Air Act	1. Directs the EPA to establish air quality standards and timetables 2. Directs states to establish implementation plans 3. Permits required record keeping and inspection 4. Establishes civil and criminal penalties and fines
1990	Clean Air Act amendments	1. Require certain cities to reduce emissions through tougher standards 2. Require certain industries to use *best available technology* to reduce emissions 3. Require cuts in utility power plant emissions 4. Permit utilities to engage in emissions reduction banking and trading
Water		
1972	Clean Water Act	1. Sets goals and timetables to eliminate water pollution 2. Establishes means of enforcement through permits and criminal penalties
1972	Marine Protection, Research, and Sanctuaries Act	1. Requires permit for discharge or dumping various materials into the seas
1974	Safe Water Drinking Act	1. Directs the EPA to set maximum drinking water contaminant levels for chemicals, pesticides, and microbiological pollutants
Pesticides		
1972	Federal Environmental Pesticide Control Act	1. Requires registration and labeling of agricultural pesticides 2. Regulates application of pesticides
1973	Federal Insecticide, Fungicide, and Rodenticide Act	1. Requires registration and labeling of agricultural pesticides
Waste Disposal/Cleanup		
1965	Solid Waste Disposal Act	1. Promotes research
1976		2. Provides technical and financial assistance to the states
	Resource Conservation and Recovery Act	1. Requires a generator to determine whether its wastes are hazardous 2. Requires such wastes to be properly transported to an EPA-licensed disposal facility 3. Prescribes record keeping requirements
1976		4. Assesses penalties for noncompliance
	Toxic Substances Control Act	1. Requires advance notice of manufacture and analysis of new chemical substances that present a *substantial risk* of injury to health or the environment
1980	Comprehensive Environmental Response and Liability Act	1. Establishes Superfund for environmental cleanup of dangerous hazardous wastes 2. Requires notification of unauthorized release of hazardous substances 3. Permits assessment of punitive damages for noncompliance

1. The National Environmental Policy Act

The way the government considers the environmental impact of its decision making greatly interests the business community. For instance, the federal government pays private enterprise almost $100 billion annually to conduct

FIGURE 14.1

Components of the environmental impact statement.

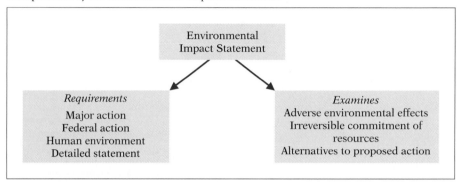

studies, prepare reports, and carry out projects. In addition, the federal government is by far the nation's largest landholder, controlling one-third of the entire area of the United States. Private enterprise must rely on governmental agencies to issue permits and licenses to explore and mine for minerals, graze cattle, cut timber, or conduct other business activities on government property. Thus, any congressional legislation that influences the decision making concerning federal funding or license granting also affects business. Such legislation is the **National Environmental Policy Act (NEPA).**

The NEPA became effective in 1970. It imposes specific "action-forcing" requirements on federal agencies. The most important requirement demands that all federal agencies prepare an **environmental impact statement (EIS)** prior to taking certain actions. An EIS must be included "in every recommendation or report on proposals for legislation and other major federal actions significantly affecting the quality of the human environment." This EIS is a "detailed statement" that estimates the environmental impact of the proposed action. Any discussion of such action and its impact must contain information on adverse environmental effects that cannot be avoided, any irreversible use of resources necessary, and available alternatives to the action (see Figure 14–1).

There have been hundreds of cases that interpret the EIS requirements. In the following case, the Supreme Court decides whether psychological fear caused by the risk of accident at a nuclear power plant is an "environmental effect."

METROPOLITAN EDISON COMPANY V. PEOPLE AGAINST NUCLEAR ENERGY
103 S.Ct. 1556 (1983)

Metropolitan Edison Company decided to reopen its TMI-1 plant at Three Mile Island, Pennsylvania, after it had been shut down when a serious accident damaged the reactor. People Against Nuclear Energy (PANE), an association of Three Mile Island–area residents, sued, claiming that the Nuclear Regulatory Commission failed to consider the psychological harm that reopening the plant and exposing the community to the risk of a nuclear accident might cause.

REHNQUIST, J.: Section 102(C) of NEPA directs all federal agencies to "include in every recommendation or report on proposals for legislation and other major Federal actions significantly affecting the quality of the human environment, a detailed statement by the responsible official on—(i) the environmental impact of the proposed action, [and] (ii) any adverse environmental effects which cannot be avoided should the proposal be implemented. . . ."

To paraphrase the statutory language in light of the facts of this case, where an agency action significantly affects the quality of the human environment, the agency must evaluate the "environmental impact" and any unavoidable adverse environmental effects of its proposal. The theme of section 102 is sounded by the adjective "environmental": NEPA does not require the agency to assess the impact or effect of its proposed action, but only the impact or effect on the environment. If we were to seize the word "environmental" out of its context and give it the broadest possible definition, the words "adverse environmental effects" might embrace virtually any consequence of a governmental action that someone thought "adverse." But we think the context of the statute shows that Congress was talking about the physical environment—the world around us, so to speak. NEPA was designed to promote human welfare by alerting governmental actors to the effect of their proposed actions on the physical environment. . . .

Our understanding of the congressional concerns that led to the enactment of NEPA suggests that the terms "environmental effect" and "environmental impact" in section 102 be read to include a requirement of a reasonably close causal relationship between a change in the physical environment and the effect at issue. The issue before us, then, is how to give content to this requirement. This is a question of first impression in this Court.

The federal action that affects the environment in this case is permitting renewed operation of TMI-1. The direct effects on the environment of this action include release of low-level radiation, increased fog in the Harrisburg area (caused by operation of the plant's cooling towers), and the release of warm water into the Susquehanna River. The NCR has considered each of these effects in its EIS, and again in the EIA. Another effect of renewed operation is a risk of a nuclear accident. The NRC has also considered this effect.

PANE argues that the psychological health damage it alleges "will flow directly from the risk of [a nuclear] accident." But a risk of an accident is not an effect on the physical environment. A risk is, by definition, un-

realized in the physical world. In a causal chain from renewed operation of TMI-1 to psychological health damage, the element of risk and its perception by PANE's members are necessary middle links. We believe that the element of risk lengthens the casual chain beyond the reach of NEPA.

Risk is a pervasive element of modern life; to say more would belabor the obvious. Many of the risks we face are generated by modern technology, which brings both the possibility of major accidents and opportunities for tremendous achievements. Medical experts apparently agree that risk can generate stress in human beings, which in turn may rise to the level of serious health damage. For this reason among many others, the question whether the gains from any technological advance are worth its attendant risks may be an important public policy issue. Nonetheless, it is quite different from the question whether the same gains are worth a given level of alteration of our physical environment or depletion of our natural resources. The latter question rather than the former is the central concern of NEPA.

Time and resources are simply too limited for us to believe that Congress intended to extend NEPA as far as the Court of Appeals has taken it. The scope of the agency's inquiries must remain manageable if NEPA's goal of "ensur[ing] a fully informed and well considered decision," is to be accomplished.

If contentions of psychological health damage caused by risk were cognizable under NEPA, agencies would, at the very least, be obliged to expend considerable resources developing psychiatric expertise that is not otherwise relevant to their congressionally assigned functions. The available resources may be spread so thin that agencies are unable adequately to pursue protection of the physical environment and natural resources. As we said in another context "[w]e cannot attribute to Congress the intention to . . . open the door to such obvious incongruities and undesirable possibilities." . . . [*Reversed*].

Case Questions

1. Why did PANE members want the Nuclear Regulatory Commission to consider "psychological harm" in the EIS?

2. What did the Supreme Court define the statutory language "adverse environmental effects" to mean?

3. Did the Supreme Court think that the risk of nuclear accident was itself an "adverse environmental effect"? Explain.

Several regulatory guidelines have made the EIS more useful. One guideline directs federal agencies to engage in **scoping.** Scoping requires that even before preparing an EIS, agencies must designate which environmental issues of a contemplated action are most significant. It encourages impact statements to focus on more substantial environmental concerns and reduce the attention devoted to trivial issues. It also allows other agencies and interested parties to participate in the scoping process. Scoping helps ensure that formal impact statements will address matters regarded as most important.

Another guideline directs that EISs be "clear, to the point, and written in plain English." This requirement deters the use of technical jargon and helps those reading impact statements to understand them. The Council on Environmental Quality (CEQ) has also limited the length of impact statements, which once ran to more than 1,000 pages, to 150 pages, except in unusual circumstances.

2. Evaluation of Environmental Impact Statements

Importantly, NEPA does not require that federal agencies follow the conclusions of an EIS. However, as a practical political matter, agencies are not likely to proceed with a project when an EIS concludes that the environmental costs outweigh the benefits. EISs have been responsible for the abandonment or delay of many federal projects.

Some critics point out that the present process fails to consider the economic injury caused by abandoning or delaying projects. They also contend that those preparing EISs are forced to consider far too many alternatives to proposed federal action without regard to their economic reasonableness. Other critics maintain that most impact statements are too descriptive and not sufficiently analytical. They fear that the EIS is "a document of compliance rather than a decision-making tool." A final general criticism of the EIS process notes the limits of its usefulness. As follow-ups on some EISs have shown, environmental factors are often so complex that projections concerning environmental effects amount to little more than guesswork.

Although the NEPA applies only to federal actions, many states have enacted similar legislation to assist their decision making. Many interpretive problems found on the national level are also encountered at the state level. In addition, as the states frequently lack the resources and expertise of the federal government, state EISs are often even less helpful in evaluating complex environmental factors than are those prepared by federal agencies.

Government's Regulation of Business

In the past 25 years, the federal government has enacted a series of laws regulating the impact of private enterprise on the environment. More and more companies are hiring environmental managers to deal with environmental compliance issues. This trend reflects the continuing importance of government regulation in this area. Congress may fine-tune environmental acts, but the national commitment to a cleaner environment is here to stay. As the CEO of a large chemical company observed about environmental concern, "Sometimes you find that the public has spoken, and you get on with it."

TABLE 14–3   Responsibilities of the EPA

Conducts research on the harmful impact of pollution
Gathers information about present pollution problems
Assists states and local governments in controlling pollution through grants, technical
  advice, and other means
Advises the CEQ about new policies needed for protection of the environment
Administers federal pollution laws

---

3. The Environmental Protection Agency

One of the first steps taken at the federal level in response to concerns about the environment was the establishment of the **Environmental Protection Agency (EPA)** in 1970. At the federal level, the EPA coordinates public control of private action as it affects the environment.

Today, the EPA is a large agency with a number of major responsibilities (see Table 14–3). Most importantly, it administers federal laws that concern pollution of the air and water, solid waste and toxic substance disposal, pesticide regulation, and radiation. The following sections examine these laws.

4. Air Pollution

In 1257, Queen Eleanor of England was driven from Nottingham Castle because of harsh smoke from the numerous coal fires in London. Coal had come into widespread use in England during this time, following the cutting of forests for fuel and agricultural purposes. By 1307, a royal order prohibited coal burning in London's kilns under punishment of "grievous ransoms." This early attempt at controlling air pollution does not appear, however, to have been very effective. As recently as the London smog of 1952, four thousand people died of air pollution–related causes, including coal smoke.

In the United States the key federal legislation for controlling air pollution is the Clean Air Act.

Clean Air Act and Amendments

The **Clean Air Act** directs the EPA administrator to establish air quality standards and to see that these standards are achieved according to a definite timetable. The administrator has set primary and secondary air quality standards for particulates, carbon monoxide, sulfur dioxide, nitrogen dioxide, hydrocarbons, and lead. **Primary air quality standards** are those necessary to protect public health. **Secondary air quality standards** guard the public from other adverse air pollution effects such as injury to property, vegetation, and climate and damage to aesthetic values. In most instances, primary and secondary air quality standards are identical.

Governmental regulation of private action under the Clean Air Act is a joint federal and state effort. The EPA sets standards, and the states devise implementation plans, which the EPA must approve, to carry them out. The states thus bear principal responsibility for enforcing the Clean Air Act, with the EPA providing standard-setting, coordinating, and supervisory functions. However, the EPA may also participate in enforcement. The administrator can require the operator of any air pollution source to keep such records and perform such monitoring or sampling as the EPA thinks appropriate. In addition, the EPA has the right to inspect these records and data. Various criminal and civil penalties and fines back up the Clean Air Act. In addition, industries that do not obey cleanup orders face payment to the EPA; payment amounts to the economic savings they realize from their failure to install and operate proper antipollution equipment.

In 1990 Congress passed significant amendments to the Clean Air Act. These amendments will add billions of dollars annually to the current cost of complying with environmental regulation.

Since many cities currently do not meet existing Clean Air Act standards, the amendments force businesses in these areas to install new pollution-control equipment to cut emissions. Tailpipe emissions for cars and trucks must be reduced by 30 to 60 percent by 1998, and companies must phase in alternative fuel vehicles for their fleets of vehicles. By 1999 a pilot program for California will introduce up to 300,000 alternative fuel cars. The amendments also required sale of cleaner gasoline blends by 1995 in nine cities with the worst pollution problems. The goal of all these requirements is to cut pollution by 3 percent per year until air quality standards are met. The states have prepared blueprints for meeting these goals.

Expressing concern about airborne toxic chemicals, the 1990 amendments require industry over the next decade to use the "best available technology" on plants to reduce emissions of 189 toxics by 90 percent. Significantly, the plants covered include bakeries and dry cleaning businesses as well as chemical companies. The EPA must also study how to reduce toxic emissions from vehicles and fuels.

To control the sulfur dioxide that contributes to acid rain, the Clean Air Act amendments require cuts in utility power plant emissions. By the year 2000 nationwide sulfur dioxide emissions must be reduced by 10 million tons. After 2000 the new law imposes a nationwide cap on emissions. Reducing these emissions will mean that utilities will burn less soft coal. Miners put out of work because of this may qualify for extra weeks of unemployment pay.

Air Pollution Sources

For control purposes, the Clean Air Act amendments divide air pollution sources into two categories: *stationary source* and *mobile source* (transportation). Under the state implementation plans, major stationary polluters, such as steel mills and utilities, must reduce their emissions to a level sufficient to bring down air pollution to meet primary and secondary standards. Polluters must follow timetables and schedules in complying with these requirements. To achieve designated standards, they must install a variety of control devices, including wet collectors (scrubbers), filter collectors, tall stacks, electrostatic precipitators, and afterburners. New stationary pollution sources, or modified ones, must install the best system of emission reduction that has been adequately demonstrated. Under the act's provision, citizens are granted standing to enforce compliance with these standards.

The act requires both stationary and mobile sources to meet a timetable of air pollution standards for which control technology may not exist at the time. This *technology-forcing* aspect of the act is unique to the history of governmental regulation of business, yet it has been upheld by the Supreme Court.

Technology forcing does not always succeed. It is neither always possible nor always feasible to force new technological developments. In recognizing this fact, developers of the Clean Air Act have allowed the EPA in many instances to grant *compliance waivers* and *variances* from its standards.

5. Clean Air Act Trends

As originally implemented, the Clean Air Act did not try to promote efficient pollution. For instance, if an area's air could tolerate a million tons of pollution per year, the authorities made no attempt to identify those who could make the best productive use of air pollution. Likewise, when a business was permitted to pollute a certain annual amount, the act specified the allowable pollution from each smokestack or other polluting source within the business instead of letting the business arrange its total allowable pollution in the most efficient way.

In the past few years, the EPA has moved to make its regulatory practices more economically efficient. All new pollution control rules are now subjected to cost-benefit analysis. The EPA has also developed specific policies to achieve air pollution control in an economically efficient manner.

Traditionally, the EPA has regulated each individual pollution emission **point source** (such as a smokestack) within an industrial plant or complex. Increasingly, however, the EPA is encouraging the states, through their implementation plans, to adopt an approach called the **bubble concept.** Under the bubble concept, each plant complex is treated as if it were encased in a bubble. Instead of each pollution point source being licensed for a limited amount of pollution emission, the pollution of the plant complex as a whole is the focus of regulation. Businesses may suggest their own plans for cleaning up multiple sources of pollution within the entire complex as long as the total pollution emitted does not exceed certain limits. This approach permits flexibility in curtailing pollution and provides businesses with economic incentives to discover new methods of control. The following case shows that the Supreme Court has upheld the EPA's authority to approve the bubble concept even in states where pollution exceeds air quality standards.

CHEVRON, U.S.A., INC. V. NATURAL RESOURCES DEFENSE COUNCIL
107 S.Ct. 2778 (1984)

The Clean Air Act Amendments of 1977 impose certain requirements on states that have standards established by the EPA, including the requirement that such nonattainment states establish a permit program regulating "new or modified major stationary sources" of air pollution. A permit may be issued only after stringent conditions are met. In 1981, the EPA ruled that the term "stationary source" included treating an entire plant as a single stationary source. Thus, an existing plant could modify the equipment on only one of several pollution-emitting devices in a single plant without meeting the permit conditions as long as the total emissions within the bubble did not increase. The National Resources Defense Council filed a petition for a review of the EPA bubble policy. The Court of Appeals determined that while the Clean Air Act did not explicitly define stationary sources, *the plantwide or* bubble *definition was* inappropriate *as applied to the nonattainment program.*

STEVENS, J.: When a court reviews an agency's construction of the statute which it administers, it is confronted with two questions. First, always, is the question whether Congress has directly spoken to the precise question at issue. If the intent of Congress is clear, that is the end of the matter, for the court, as well as the agency, must give effect to the unambiguously expressed intent of Congress. If, however, the court determines Congress has not directly addressed the precise question at issue, the court does not simply impose its own construction on the statute, as would be necessary in the absence of an administrative interpretation. Rather, if the statute is silent or ambiguous with respect to the specific issue, the question for the court is whether the agency's answer is based on a permissible construction of the statute.

"The power of an administrative agency to administer a congressionally created . . . program necessarily requires the formulation of policy and the making of rules to fill any gap left, implicitly or explicitly, by Congress." If Congress has explicitly left a gap for the agency to fill, there is an express delegation of authority to the agency to elucidate a specific provision of the statute by regulation. Such legislative regulations are given controlling weight unless they are arbitrary, capricious, or manifestly contrary to the statute. Sometimes the legislative delegation to an agency on a particular question is implicit rather than explicit. In such a case, a court may not substitute its own construction of a statutory provision for a reasonable interpretation made by the administrator of an agency. . . .

In light of these well-settled principles it is clear that the Court of Appeals misconceived the nature of its role in reviewing the regulations at issue. Once it determined, after its own examination of the legislation, that Congress did not actually have an intent regarding the applicability of the bubble concept to the permit program, the question before it was not whether in its view the concept is "inappropriate" in the general context of a program designed to improve air quality, but whether the Administrator's view that it is appropriate in the context of this particular program is a reasonable one. Based on the examination of the legislation and its history, we agree with the Court of Appeals that Congress did not have a specific intention on the applicability of the bubble concept in these cases, and conclude that the EPA's use of that concept here is a reasonable policy choice for the agency to make. . . .

Our review of the EPA's varying interpretations of the word "source"—both before and after the 1977 Amendments—convinces us that the agency primarily responsible for administering this important legislation has consistently interpreted it flexibly—not in a sterile textual vacuum, but in the context of implementing policy decisions in a technical and complex arena. The fact that the agency has from time to time changed its interpretation of the term source does not, as respondents argue, lead us to conclude that no deference should be accorded the agency's interpretation of the statute. An initial agency interpretation is not instantly carved in stone. On the contrary, the agency, to engage in informed rulemaking, must consider varying interpretations and wisdom of its policy on a continuing basis. Moreover, the fact that the agency has adopted different definitions in different contexts adds force to the argument that the definition itself is flexible, particularly since Congress has never indicated any disapproval of a flexible reading of the statute. . . .

Judges are not experts in the field, and are not part of either political branch of the Government. Courts must, in some cases, reconcile competing political interests, but not on the basis of the judges' personal policy preferences. . . .

When a challenge to an agency construction of a statutory provision, fairly conceptualized, really centers on the wisdom of the agency's policy, rather than whether it is a reasonable choice within a gap left open by Congress, the challenge must fail. In such a case, federal judges—who have no constituency—have a duty to respect legitimate policy choices made by those who do. The responsibilities for assessing the wisdom of such policy choices and resolving the struggle between competing views of the public interest are not judicial ones: "Our Constitution vests such responsibilities in the political branches."

We hold that the EPA's definition of the term "source" is a permissible construction of the statute which seeks to accommodate progress in reducing air pollution with economic growth. . . . The judgment of the Court of Appeals is [*reversed*].

Case Questions

1. What two questions must courts confront in reviewing an agency's construction of the statute it administers?

2. How did the Supreme Court say that the Court of Appeals had misconceived its role in reviewing the EPA's bubble policy regulations?

3. Why does the EPA's bubble policy depend on the meaning of the term "source"? Explain.

A number of states have developed EPA-approved plans for **emissions reduction banking.** Under such plans, businesses can cut pollution beyond what the law requires and "bank" these reductions for their own future use or to sell to other companies as emission offsets. Eventually, we may be headed for a *marketable rights* approach to pollution control, under which the right to discharge a certain pollutant would be auctioned off to the highest bidder. This approach would promote efficiency by offering to those who have the greatest need for pollution rights the opportunity to obtain them by bidding highest for them. Under the 1990 Clean Air Act amendments, Congress specifically allows utility companies to engage in emissions reduction banking and trading. Since 1992 the Chicago Board of Trade has run an auction in pollution credits given by the EPA to the nation's 110 most polluting utility plants.

Another important policy of the Clean Air Act is the **prevention of significant deterioration.** Under this policy, pollution emission is controlled, even in areas where the air is cleaner than prevailing primary and secondary air quality standards require. In some of these areas, the EPA permits construction of new pollution emission sources according to a strictly limited scheme. In other areas, it allows no new pollution emission at all. Critics of this policy argue that it prevents industry from moving into southern and western states, where air quality is cleaner than standards require.

One of the most controversial issues involving the Clean Air Act concerns the delay and red tape caused by the *permitting process.* Before a business can construct new pollution emission sources, it must obtain the necessary environmental permits from the appropriate state agency. Today, the estimated time needed to acquire the necessary permits to build a coal-fired electric-generating plant is 5 to 10 years. This is nearly twice the length of time it took in the early 1970s. The formalities of the permitting process, the lack of flexibility in state implementation plans, the requirement that even minor variations in state implementation plans be approved by the EPA—all these factors contribute to delay. Both the EPA and Congress are considering ways to streamline the permitting process.

The EPA has also grown increasingly concerned about indoor air pollution. Paints, cleaning products, furniture polishes, gas furnaces, and stoves all emit pollutants that can be harmful to human health. Radioactive radon seeping into homes and buildings from the ground has now been recognized as a major health hazard. Some studies have found that indoor levels of certain pollutants far exceed outdoor levels, whether at work or at home. Although the Clean Air Act does not currently apply to indoor pollution, its application may be extended in the future. (See Tobacco Industry Box.)

In spite of the controversy generated by the Clean Air Act, evidence indicates that the overall air quality in the United States is steadily improving. The 16,000 quarts of air we each breathe daily are cleaner and healthier in most places than they were a decade ago. Yet an estimated 80 million persons in the United States still breathe air that violates one or more primary air quality standards. Note, also, that air pollution is an international problem and that not all countries of the world have, or can afford, our air quality standards. Air pollution is especially severe in developing nations of the world, which are striving to reach our standard of living.

Tobacco Industry Box

Indoor Pollution

The Environmental Protection Agency ranks indoor air pollution as one of the five top pollution problems. Although tobacco smoke is only one type of indoor air pollutant, it may be the most significant. Since 1993, the EPA has classified tobacco smoke as a "Group A" carcinogen and estimates that secondhand smoke kills 3,000 people annually from lung cancer alone. The California EPA concludes that secondhand smoke is responsible for as many as 62,000 deaths from heart disease, 2,700 deaths from Sudden Infant Death Syndrome, and 2,600 new asthma cases annually. Tobacco companies have challenged the research on which these conclusions are based.

Significantly, the EPA does not regulate indoor air pollution under the Clean Air Act, but the Administration does have the authority to regulate indoor workplace pollution. In 1994 OSHA proposed a ban on all workplace tobacco smoking except in specially ventilated smoking rooms. Although the proposed ban has not yet taken final form, numerous major businesses already limit or ban workplace smoking. Many local governments have also strictly regulated indoor smoking in public buildings.

6. Water Pollution

Business enterprise is a major source of water pollution in the United States. Almost one-half of all water used in this country is for cooling and condensing purposes in connection with industrial activities. The resulting discharge into our rivers and lakes sometimes takes the form of heated water, called thermal effluents. In addition to thermal effluents, industry also discharges chemical and other effluents into the nation's waterways.

The principal federal law regulating water pollution is the **Clean Water Act,** passed by Congress in 1972. As with the Clean Air Act, the Clean Water Act is administered primarily by the states in accordance with EPA standards. If the states do not fulfill their responsibilities, however, the federal government, through the EPA, can step in and enforce the law. The Clean Water Act applies to all navigable waterways, intrastate as well as interstate.

The Clean Water Act sets goals to eliminate water pollution. Principally, these goals are to make the nation's waterways safe for swimming and other recreational use and clean enough for the protection of fish, shellfish, and wildlife. The law sets strict deadlines and strong enforcement provisions, which must be followed by industry, municipalities, and other water polluters. Enforcement of the Clean Water Act revolves around its permit discharge system. Without being subject to criminal penalties, no polluter can discharge pollutants from any *point source* (such as a pipe) without a permit, and municipal as well as industrial dischargers must obtain permits. The EPA has issued guidelines for state permit programs and has approved those programs that meet the guidelines.

Since the Clean Water Act applies to "navigable waterways," the criminal penalties of the act cover only the unpermitted point-source pollution of navigable waterways. However, as the following case illustrates, the courts have interpreted the term *navigable* quite broadly to include almost any stream or channel of water that empties into a larger waterway. You should take a lesson from the substantial prison sentences received by the defendants in the case.

UNITED STATES V. HARTSELL

127 F.3d 343 (4th Cir. 1997)

The defendants Gene Hartsell and Keith Eidson owned and operated Cherokee Resources, Inc., (Cherokee) a wastewater treatment and oil reclamation business in Charlotte, North Carolina. Cherokee accepted oil and industrial wastewater from its customers and periodically released water into the public sewer system, which led to a sewage plant that emptied into a creek that ran into a river. After an investigation by the FBI, the defendants were arrested and prosecuted for intentionally dumping untreated water into the sewer in violation of the Clean Water Act (CWA) permits they held. At trial, company employees testified how the defendants bypassed permit-required monitoring devices to dump improperly treated water into the sewer. A jury convicted the defendants, who were each sentenced to 51 months' imprisonment and ordered to pay fines. On appeal, the defendants argued that the trial court lacked jurisdiction because the public sewer was not a navigable waterway as required under the CWA.

ERVIN, Circuit Judge: . . . [W]e must turn our attention to the appellants' assertion that the district court lacked subject matter jurisdiction in the instant case. Although the argument on this matter is not clearly articulated, it appears that Hartsell, Eidson and Cherokee argue that the CWA extends only to "navigable waters." The appellants argue that their discharges into the public sewer system were not into a navigable waterway and, therefore, the federal government lacks the power to punish such pollution and the federal courts lack the power to hear a case involving such pollution. The appellants also seem to argue that, even if Congress did intend for the CWA to extend to waterways such as the sewer system in the instant case, Congress lacked the constitutional power to regulate such waterways.

We find this argument to be without merit for several reasons. First, the CWA clearly provides for regulation of discharge into public sewer systems such as the Irwin Creek system in the instant case. The plain language of the CWA prohibits discharge of pollutants into "navigable waters," except in accordance with a permit issued pursuant to the Act. The Act defines navigable waters as "waters of the United States," and this broad definition "makes it clear that the term 'navigable' as used in the Act is of limited import."

Several courts, including the Supreme Court and this court, have held that Congress clearly intended to regulate pollutant discharge into sewer systems and other non-navigable waters through the CWA, and

that Congress has the constitutional authority to do so. In *Riverside Bayview Home*, the Court stated that Congress intended to allow "broad federal authority to control pollution, for 'water moves in hydrological cycles and it is essential that discharge of pollutants be controlled at its source.'" The Court further held that "Congress clearly intended to exercise its power under the Commerce Clause to regulate at least some waters that would not be deemed 'navigable' under the classical understanding of that term."

We hold that Congress not only intended to legislate against unchecked discharge of pollutants into public sewers which would eventually flow into streams and rivers, but that Congress acted squarely within its power in so doing. Cherokee, Hartsell and Eidson are unable to persuade us that either Congress, in passing the CWA, or the district court, in hearing the criminal case against the appellants, acted beyond its powers. [*Affirmed*].

Case Questions

1. Why does the FBI have jurisdiction to investigate this case?

2. What did the defendants do that violated the Clean Water Act?

3. Why did the defendants argue that the trial court lacked jurisdiction over them?

4. Why does Congress prohibit only the pollution of "navigable" waters instead of just prohibiting all water pollution?

Under the Clean Water Act, industries adopt a two-step sequence for cleanup of industrial wastes discharged into rivers and streams. The first step requires polluters to install *best practicable technology (BPT)*. The second demands installation of *best available technology (BAT)*. Various timetables apply in achieving these steps, according to the type of pollutant being discharged. In 1984, the EPA announced application of the bubble concept to water pollution in the steel industry.

In addition to the Clean Water Act, the EPA administers two other acts related to water pollution control. One, the Marine Protection, Research, and Sanctuaries Act of 1972, requires a permit system for the discharge or dumping of various material into the seas. The other is the Safe Water Drinking Act of 1974, which has forced the EPA to set maximum drinking water contaminant levels for certain organic and inorganic chemicals, pesticides, and microbiological pollutants.

The Clean Water Act and other current statutes do not reach one important type of water pollution: *non–point source pollution*, which comes from runoffs into streams and rivers. These runoffs often contain agricultural fertilizers and pesticides as well as oil and lead compounds from streets and highways. Congress has authorized $400 million for the National Non–Point Source Pollution Program to study the problem.

7. Endangered Species Act

Every day entire species of animals and plants die off. As with the dinosaurs, sometimes great catastrophes like comet impacts cause species to become extinct. Gradual climate changes and competition from other species also can kill off animals and plants. However, in modern times, human activity has caused the vast majority of species extinctions. Air and water pollution, the clearing of land for agriculture, the development of water resources, hunting and fishing, and a growing human population all potentially threaten other species.

In 1973 Congress passed the Endangered Species Act (ESA), the world's toughest law protecting animals and plants and, perhaps, the country's most controversial environmental standard. Under the act the Secretary of the Interior can list any species as "endangered," that is, "in danger of extinction throughout all or a significant portion of its range," except for certain insect pests. ("Threatened" species are also protected.) In determining the factors of endangerment, the secretary must consider the destruction of habitat, disease or predation, commercial and recreational activity, and "other natural or manmade factors." Within a year of listing an endangered species, the secretary is required to define the "critical habitat" of the species which is the area with the biological or physical features necessary to species survival. The Fish and Wildlife Services and the National Marine Fisheries Services administer the ESA for the Department of Interior.

Although no federal agency can authorize, fund, or carry out any action that is likely to jeopardize an endangered species, the ESA's application to private business activity has caused the greater debate in recent years. Section 9 of the act prohibits any person from transporting or trading in any endangered species of fish or wildlife (a separate section applies to plants) or from "taking any such species within the United States" or "upon the high seas."

Taking a species is defined as "harass, harm, pursue, hunt, shoot, wound, kill, trap, capture, or collect, or attempt to engage in any such conduct."

The Secretary of the Interior has further defined the "harm" of taking to mean any act that actually kills or injures wildlife, including harming habitat or essential behavior patterns. Thus, neither private businesses nor individuals can harm the habitats of endangered species. As the following case illustrates, defining the word *harm* to include adverse changes in wildlife habitat has been the subject of much litigation.

BABBIT V. SWEET HOME CHAPTER OF COMMUNITIES FOR A GREATER OREGON
515 U.S. 687 (1995)

Small landowners, logging companies, and families dependent on the forest products industry in the Pacific Northwest and in the Southeast sued the Secretary of the Interior. They challenged the validity of the Secretary's regulation defining the word harm in the Endangered Species Act (ESA) to include habitat modification and degradation. They alleged that application of the "harm" regulation to the red-cockaded woodpecker and the northern spotted owl had injured them economically. When the Court of Appeals ruled that the Secretary's regulation was invalid, the Secretary petitioned the Supreme Court to hear the case.

STEVENS, J.: . . . The Endangered Species Act of 1973 (ESA or Act) contains a variety of protections designed to save from extinction species that the Secretary of the Interior designates as endangered or threatened. Section 9 of the Act makes it unlawful for any person to "take" any endangered or threatened species. The Secretary has promulgated a regulation that defines the statute's prohibition on takings to include "significant habitat modification or degradation where it actually kills or injures wildlife." This case presents the question whether the Secretary exceeded his authority under the Act by promulgating that regulation.

The text of the Act provides three reasons for concluding that the Secretary's interpretation is reasonable. First, an ordinary understanding of the word "harm" supports it. The dictionary definition of the verb form of "harm" is "to cause hurt or damage to: injure." In the context of the ESA, that definition naturally encompasses habitat modification that results in actual injury or death to members of an endangered or threatened species.

Respondents [landowners, companies, and employees] argue that the Secretary should have limited the purview of "harm" to direct applications of force against protected species, but the dictionary definition does not include the word "directly" or suggest in any way that only direct or willful action that leads to injury constitutes "harm." Moreover, unless the statutory term "harm" encompasses indirect as well as direct injuries, the word has no meaning that does not duplicate the meaning of other words that § 3 uses to

define "take." A reluctance to treat statutory terms as surplusage supports the reasonableness of the Secretary's interpretation.

Second, the broad purpose of the ESA supports the Secretary's decision to extend protection against activities that cause the precise harms Congress enacted the statute to avoid. In *TVA v. Hill*, we described the Act as "the most comprehensive legislation for the preservation of endangered species ever enacted by any nation." Whereas predecessor statutes enacted in 1966 and 1969 had not contained any sweeping prohibition against the taking of endangered species except on federal lands, the 1973 Act applied to all land in the United States and to the Nation's territorial seas. As stated in § 2 of the Act, among its central purposes is "to provide a means whereby the ecosystems upon which endangered species and threatened species depend may be conserved. . . ."

Respondents advance strong arguments that activities that cause minimal or unforeseeable harm will not violate the Act as construed in the "harm" regulation. But they ask us to invalidate the Secretary's understanding of "harm" in every circumstance, even when an actor knows that an activity, such as draining a pond, would actually result in the extinction of a listed species by destroying its habitat. Given Congress's clear expression of the ESA's broad purpose to protect endangered and threatened wildlife, the Secretary's definition of "harm" is reasonable.

Third, the fact that Congress in 1982 authorized the Secretary to issue permits for takings that § 9 would otherwise prohibit, "if such taking is incidental to, and not the purpose of, the carrying out of an otherwise lawful activity," strongly suggests that Congress understood § 9 to prohibit indirect as well as deliberate takings. The permit process requires the applicant to prepare a "conservation plan" that specifies how he intends to "minimize and mitigate" the "impact" of his activity on endangered and threatened species, making clear that Congress had in mind foreseeable rather than merely accidental effects on listed species. No one could seriously request an "incidental" taking permit to avert § 9 liability for direct, deliberate action against a member of an endangered or threatened species, but respondents would read "harm" so narrowly that the permit procedure would have little more than that absurd purpose. "When Congress acts to amend a statute, we presume it intends its amendment to have real and substantial effect." Congress's addition to the § 10 permit provision supports the Secretary's conclusion that activities not intended to harm an endangered species, such as habitat modifications, may constitute unlawful takings under the ESA unless the Secretary permits them.

The Court of Appeals made three errors in asserting that "harm" must refer to a direct application of force because the words around it do. First, the court's premise was flawed. Several of the words that accompany "harm" in the § 3 definition of "take," especially "harass," "pursue," "wound," and "kill," refer to actions or effects that do not require direct applications of force. Second, to the extent the court read a requirement of intent or purpose into the words used to define "take," it ignored § 9's express provision that a "knowing" action is enough to violate the Act. Third, the statutory context of "harm" suggests that Congress meant that term to serve a particular function in the ESA, consistent with but distinct from

the functions of the other verbs used to define "take." The Secretary's interpretation of "harm" to include indirectly injuring endangered animals through habitat modification permissibly interprets "harm" to have "a character of its own not to be submerged by its association."

When it enacted the ESA, Congress delegated broad administrative and interpretive power to the Secretary. The task of defining and listing endangered and threatened species requires an expertise and attention to detail that exceeds the normal province of Congress. Fashioning appropriate standards for issuing permits under § 10 for takings that would otherwise violate § 9 necessarily requires the exercise of broad discretion. The proper interpretation of a term such as "harm" involves a complex policy choice. When Congress has entrusted the Secretary with broad discretion, we are especially reluctant to substitute our views of wise policy for his. In this case, that reluctance accords with our conclusion, based on the text, structure, and legislative history of the ESA, that the Secretary reasonably construed the intent of Congress when he defined "harm" to include "significant" habitat modification or degradation that actually kills or injures wildlife." The judgment of the Court of Appeals is [*reversed*].

Case Questions

1. How did the Secretary's regulation economically affect the landowners, companies, and families of employees?

2. What is the issue that the Supreme Court is deciding in this case?

3. What argument do the respondents make that the Secretary exceeded his authority?

4. What arguments does the Supreme Court use in deciding that the Secretary's regulation is valid?

Note that the ESA does not permit courts or regulators to take economic factors into consideration in applying its provisions. There has been much criticism of the act, and amendments to it have been proposed to Congress. Congress has established a review board that can grant exemptions to the ESA for certain important federal projects. However, the exemptions do not apply to private activities.

8. Pesticide Control

Pests, especially insects and mice, destroy over 10 percent of all crops grown in the United States, causing several billion dollars of damage annually. In many underdeveloped countries, however, a much greater percentage of total crop production is lost to pests, as high as 40 to 50 percent in countries such as India. Perhaps the principal reason for our lower rate of crop loss is that the United States uses more pesticides per acre than any other country.

The widespread, continual application of pesticides creates environmental problems, however. Not only is it dangerous to wildlife, particularly birds and fish, but it is also harmful to humans and may eventually threaten our agricultural capacity itself. Rapidly breeding pests gradually become immune to the application of pesticides, and researchers may not always be able to invent new poisons to kill them.

Nationwide, nearly half of the farmers responding to one poll expressed increasing concern about their own safety when using pesticides. In 1992 a National Cancer Institute report concluded that farm families suffer from elevated rates of seven types of cancer, including leukemia, with pesticides suspected as a leading cause.

Federal regulation of pesticides is accomplished primarily through two statutes: the **Federal Insecticide, Fungicide, and Rodenticide Act of 1947,** as amended, and the **Federal Environmental Pesticide Control Act of 1972 (FEPCA).** Both statutes require the registration and labeling of agricultural pesticides, although FEPCA coverage extends to the application of pesticides as well.

Under the acts, the administrator of the EPA is directed to register those pesticides that are properly labeled, meet the claims made as to their effectiveness, and will not have *unreasonable adverse effects on the environment,* which is defined as "any unreasonable risk to man or the environment, taking into account the economic, social, and environmental costs and benefits of the use of any pesticide." In addition to its authority to request registration of pesticides, the EPA classifies pesticides for either general use or restricted use. In the latter category, the EPA may impose further restrictions that require application only by a trained applicator or with the approval of a trained consultant. Today, the EPA requires that employers train agricultural workers in pesticide safety, post safety information, and place warning signs to keep workers out of freshly sprayed fields.

The EPA has a variety of enforcement powers to ensure that pesticide goals are met, including the power to deny or suspend registration. In the 1980s, the EPA used this power and banned several pesticides suspected of causing cancer.

Pesticide control has been attacked by both affected businesses and the environmental movement itself. Pesticide manufacturers complain that the lengthy, expensive testing procedures required by the FEPCA registration process delay useful pesticides from reaching the market and inhibit new research. On the other hand, many in the environmental movement contend that our country's pesticide control policy is hypocritical in that the FEPCA does not apply to pesticides U.S. manufacturers ship to foreign countries. Companies can sell overseas what they cannot sell in this country.

9. Solid Waste

Pollution problems cannot always be neatly categorized. For instance, solid waste disposal processes often create pollution in several environmentally related forms. When solid waste is burned, it can cause air pollution and violate the Clean Air Act. When dumped into rivers, streams, and lakes, solid

FIGURE 14.2

Composition of a typical landfill by volume.

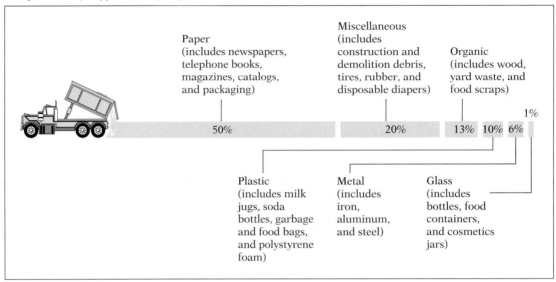

waste can pollute the water beyond amounts permitted under the Clean Water Act. Machinery used in solid waste disposal can also be subject to the regulation of the Noise Control Act.

By all accounts, solid waste pollution problems during the last twenty-five years have grown as pollution has risen and the country has become more affluent and productive. Currently, total solid wastes produced yearly in the United States exceed 5 billion tons, or almost 25 tons for every individual. Half this amount is agricultural waste, another third is mineral waste, and the remainder is industrial, institutional, and residential waste. Some wastes are toxic and hazardous, while others stink or attract pests. All present disposal problems of significant proportion.

Landfills represent the primary disposal sites for most household and much business solid wastes. Figure 14–2 illustrates the composition of solid wastes in the typical landfill. According to Bill Rathje, professor of anthropology at the University of Arizona, paper is the biggest solid waste category in landfills. And paper, which in 1970 constituted 35 percent of landfill volume, today constitutes 50 percent. By contrast, disposable diapers take up less than 1 percent of landfill volume. Polystyrene foam, such as thermal cups, also takes up less than 1 percent of landfill volume.

The **Solid Waste Disposal Act** passed in 1965 represents the primary federal effort in solid waste control. Congress recognized in this act that the main responsibility for nontoxic waste management rests with regional, state, and local management and limited the federal role in this area. Under this act, the federal role in nontoxic waste management is limited mainly to promoting research and providing technical and financial assistance to the states.

In responding to solid waste disposal problems, state and local governments have taken a variety of approaches. These include developing sanitary landfills, requiring that solid waste be separated into categories that facilitate disposal and recycling, and granting tax breaks for industries using recycled materials. A report by the Council of State Governments noted that there are thousands of community recycling centers and that more than one hundred cities and countries burn solid wastes to produce energy.

Eight states and the District of Columbia have recycling laws, usually taking the form of household trash-separation requirements. Nine states, with 25 percent of the nation's population, have beverage container deposit laws, the so-called *bottle bills*. Still, U.S. per capita waste yield, the world's highest, has doubled since 1960.

10. Toxic and Hazardous Substances

According to the opinion research organization Yankelovich, Skelly and White, the control of toxic and hazardous chemicals "ranks first" on the public's list of where the government's regulation of industry is needed. In the last several years, regulation of such chemicals has been expanding rapidly. We can divide public control of private action in this area into three categories:

· Regulation of the use of toxic chemicals
· Regulation of toxic and hazardous waste disposal
· Regulation of toxic and hazardous waste cleanup

Toxic Substances Control Act

Even as the Clean Air and Clean Water Acts are slowly beginning to diminish many types of air and water pollution, attention is being drawn to another environmental problem that is potentially the most serious of all: toxic substances. Hardly a day passes without the news media reporting some new instance of alleged threat to human health and well-being from one or another of the chemical substances so important to manufacturing, farming, mining, and other aspects of modern life.

Threats to human welfare from toxic substances are not new to history. Some scholars have suggested that poisoning from lead water pipes and drinking vessels may have depleted the ranks of the ruling class of ancient Rome and thus contributed to the downfall of the Roman Empire. More recently, some think that the "mad hatters" of the nineteenth-century fur and felt trades likely suffered brain disorders from inhaling the vapors of mercury used in their crafts. Today, however, the problem of toxic substances in the environment is more widespread. More than 70,000 industrial and agricultural chemical compounds are in commercial use, and new chemicals, a significant percentage of which are toxic, are being introduced into the marketplace at the rate of more than 1,000 substances annually.

To meet the special environmental problems posed by the use of toxic chemicals, Congress in 1976 enacted the **Toxic Substances Control Act (TSCA).** Prior to passage of the TSCA, there was no coordinated effort to evaluate effects of these chemical compounds. Some of these compounds are beneficial to society and present no threat to the environment. Some, however, are both toxic and nondegradable, a fact that in the past has been uncovered only after these compounds were introduced into wide use and became important to manufacturing and farming. The primary purpose of the TSCA is to force an early evaluation of suspect chemicals before they become economically important.

The EPA collects information under TCSA sections that require manufacturers and distributors to report to the EPA any information they possess that indicates a chemical substance presents a *substantial risk* of injury to health or to the environment. The TSCA further demands that the EPA be given advance notice before the manufacture of new chemical substances or the processing of any substance for a significant new use. Based on the results of its review, the EPA can take action to stop or limit introduction of new chemicals if they threaten human health or the environment with unreasonable risks.

The law also authorizes the EPA to require manufacturers to test their chemicals for possible harmful effects. Since not all the 70,000 chemicals in commerce can be tested all at once, the EPA has developed a priority scheme for selecting substances for testing based on whether or not the chemicals cause cancer, birth defects, or gene mutations. Today, only a small fraction of the total chemicals in production use have been safety tested.

In view of the beneficial role that many chemical substances play in all aspects of production and consumption, Congress directed the EPA through the TSCA to consider the economic and social impact, as well as the environmental one, of its decisions. In this respect the TSCA is unlike the Clean Air Act, which requires that certain pollution standards be met without regard for economic factors.

Resource Conservation and Recovery Act

The congressional Office of Technology Assessment reports that more than a ton of hazardous waste per citizen is dumped annually into the nation's environment. A major environmental problem has been how to ensure that the generators of toxic wastes dispose of them safely. In the past, there have been instances where even some otherwise responsible companies have placed highly toxic wastes in the hands of less-than-reputable disposal contractors.

To help ensure proper handling and disposal of hazardous and toxic wastes, Congress in 1976 amended the Solid Waste Disposal Act by the **Resource Conservation and Recovery Act (RCRA).** Under the RCRA, a generator of wastes has two primary obligations:

- To determine whether its wastes qualify as hazardous under RCRA
- To see that such wastes are properly transported to a disposal facility that has an EPA permit or license

The EPA lists a number of hazardous wastes, and a generator can determine if a nonlisted waste is hazardous in terms of several chemical characteristics specified by the EPA. The RCRA accomplishes proper disposal of hazardous wastes through the **manifest system.** This system requires a generator to prepare a manifest document that designates a licensed facility for disposal purposes. The generator then gives copies of the manifest to the transporter of the waste. After receiving hazardous wastes, the disposal facility must return a copy of the manifest to the generator. In this fashion, the generator knows the waste has received proper disposal.

Failure to receive this manifest copy from the disposal facility within certain time limits requires the generator to notify the EPA. Under RCRA, the EPA has various investigatory powers. The act also prescribes various record-keeping requirements and assesses penalties for failure to comply with its provisions. The penalties include criminal fines and imprisonment. Between 1983 and 1990 the Department of Justice (at the request of the EPA) brought criminal charges against 253 individuals and corporations under the RCRA.

As amended in 1986, the RCRA is moving the handling of toxic wastes away from burial on land to treatments that destroy or permanently detoxify wastes. By 1990, RCRA requirements cost business an estimated $20 billion annually.

The Superfund

After passage of the TSCA and RCRA in 1976, regulation of toxic and hazardous substances was still incomplete. These acts did not deal with problems of the cleanup costs of unsafe hazardous waste dumps or spills, which are often substantial. Many abandoned dump sites date back as far as the nineteenth century. Even current owners of unsafe dump sites are frequently financially incapable of cleaning up hazardous wastes. Nor are transporters and others who cause spills or unauthorized discharges of hazardous wastes.

In 1980, Congress created the **Comprehensive Environmental Response, Compensation, and Liability Act (CERCLA)** to address these problems. Known as the **Superfund,** this act has allotted billions of dollars for environmental cleanup of dangerous hazardous wastes. Taxes on the petroleum and chemical industries finance most of the fund.

The act requires anyone who releases unauthorized amounts of hazardous substances into the environment to notify the government. Whether it is notified or not, the government has the power to order those responsible to clean up such releases. Refusal to obey can lead to a suit for reimbursement for any cleanup monies spent from the Superfund plus punitive damages of up to triple the cleanup costs. The government can also recover damages for injury done to natural resources. To date, the biggest Superfund case involved Shell Oil and the U.S. Army. These parties agreed to clean up a site outside Denver. Total costs may exceed $1 billion.

The Superfund imposes strict liability on those responsible for unauthorized discharges of hazardous wastes. No negligence need be proved. Responsible parties can include those who currently or formerly operate or own waste disposal sites, those who arrange for disposal of wastes, and those who transport wastes. Responsible parties have liability when there is a release or threatened release of a hazardous substance that causes response costs.

Superfund law has caused land purchasers to be very careful in buying land that may contain hazardous wastes. The law makes current as well as former landowners liable for hazardous wastes. The purchaser may escape liability by proving that it is innocent of knowledge of the wastes and has used *due diligence* in checking the land for toxic hazards. But exercising due diligence can be both costly and difficult to prove.

Fortunately, the Superfund permits a land purchaser to sue a land seller if the purchaser incurs response costs due to hazardous wastes left by the seller. In the following case a purchaser sues the seller in this situation.

Amoco Oil Co. v. Borden, Inc.

889 F.2d 664 (5th Cir. 1989)

Amoco Oil Co. bought a 114-acre tract of land in Texas City, Texas. The seller, Borden, Inc., had for many years operated a phosphate fertilizer plant there. Approximately 35 acres of the land were covered by a pile of mildly radioactive phosphogypsum, a by-product of fertilizer manufacture. Sometime after the purchase the Texas Department of Water Resources told Amoco that parts of the phosphogypsum contained concentrations many times the background level of radiation. Claiming that it had been unaware of the problem previously, Amoco secured the phosphogypsum with fences and guards. It then sued Borden under the Superfund (CERCLA) for its response costs.

REAVLEY, J.: . . . To establish a prima facie case of liability in a CERCLA cost recovery action, a plaintiff must prove: (1) that the site in question is a "facility" as defined in 9601(9); (2) that the defendant is a responsible person under 9607(a); (3) that a release or a threatened release of a hazardous substance has occurred; and (4) that the release or threatened release has caused the plaintiff to incur response costs. If the plaintiff establishes each of these elements and the defendant is unable to establish the applicability of one of the defenses listed in 9607(b), the plaintiff is entitled to summary judgment on the liability issue.

It is undisputed that Amoco's property falls within the statutory definition of a "facility;" that Borden is a responsible party within the meaning of CERCLA; and that the statutory defenses to liability are inapplicable. The question of liability centers around the determination of whether a release of a hazardous substance has occurred.

The plain statutory language fails to impose any quantitative requirement on the term hazardous substance and we decline to imply that any is necessary. Radionuclides meet the listing requirements and therefore the radioactive materials on Amoco's property are hazardous substances within the meaning of CERCLA.

The term "release" is defined to mean: Any spilling, leaking, pumping, pouring, emitting, emptying, discharging, injecting, escaping, leaching, dumping, or disposing into the environment (including the abandonment or discarding of barrels, containers, and other closed receptacles containing any hazardous substance or pollutant or contaminant). . . . As with "hazardous substance," the plain statutory language fails to impose any quantitative requirement on the term "release." We believe that the definition of "release" should be construed broadly.

Borden's actions met the release requirement in two ways. First, it did so by disposing of the phosphogypsum and highly radioactive wastes on the property. Second, the gas emitting from the radionu-

clides constitutes a release within the meaning of the statute.

Borden claims that the radiation generated by the phosphogypsum pile poses a minimal health risk to the surrounding population. According to Borden's calculations, the pile's radiation presents the possibility that one additional cancer death may occur every 400 years. . . .

Borden has pointed out that all matter is radioactive to some degree. While harmless at low concentrations, at some point on a continuum it poses an unacceptable risk to human life and the environment. Given CERCLA's broad liability provisions and the pervasive nature of radionuclides, Borden argues that without a quantitative limit CERCLA liability could attach to the release of any substance and theoretically could reach "everything in the United States." The district court was apparently persuaded by Borden's argument. In finding a standard essential, it noted that "[most] of the radionuclides in the atmosphere come from natural sources [and that] radionuclides are used or produced in thousands of locations throughout the United States."

Yet, concerns about the most extreme reach of liability—extending to naturally occurring hazardous substances—are misplaced. Remedial actions taken in response to hazardous substances as they occur naturally are specifically excluded from [the Superfund] and are therefore not recoverable. While not the exclusive means of justifying response costs, we hold that a plaintiff who has incurred response costs meets the liability requirement as a matter of law if it is shown that any release violates, or any threatened release is likely to violate, any applicable state or federal standard, including the most stringent.

Amoco has clearly met this requirement by showing that the radioactive emissions exceeded the limits set in Subpart B of the Inactive Tailings Standards. . . . Amoco was justified in incurring response costs as a matter of law. Moreover, the excessive radiation in the hot spots, which exceeds any possible standard protective of public health, justified response actions regardless of any overall measure of the sites's radiation.

Amoco's security measures and site investigation are acceptable response costs within the meaning of CERCLA. As there has been a release of a hazardous substance that justified the incurrence of the response costs and the other elements of a prima facie case have been met, Amoco is entitled to summary judgment on the liability issue. [*Reversed and remanded*].

Case Questions

1. What must a plaintiff prove to recover costs under the Superfund law?

2. How did Borden's actions meet the release requirement?

3. Under what circumstances does the court hold that a Superfund plaintiff meets the liability requirement as a matter of law?

Banks and other lenders who take out a security interest (such as a mortgage) in land that turns out to be contaminated and subject to the Superfund are not liable responsible parties. However, if a lender exerts control over a borrower's contaminated land, or assumes ownership of it, the lender will become a responsible party. Many lenders have become very wary about loaning money to borrowers who wish to put up as security land that may be contaminated.

As responsible parties engage in Superfund-required cleanup, they try to pass on the costs to others, often their insurers. In the future insurers may specifically refuse to cover pollution risks in their policies. Some courts, however, have interpreted existing policies to cover waste-cleanup costs as insured-against *damages* arising from an *occurrence*, which includes an *accidental* discharge of pollutants.

The business community has proposed various reforms to the Superfund law. Possible reforms include:

· Prorating liability for companies in Superfund litigation that agree to pay their share of cleanup costs

· Exempting companies from liability when they have contributed very small amounts of waste at a dump site

· Permitting dump site cleanups that meet health and safety standards, rather than requiring that the land be returned to a pristine state

Finally, take note that both the Clean Air Act and the Clean Water Act also contain provisions related to government suits to recover costs for the cleanup of toxic chemicals. Suits under the Superfund and other acts are growing rapidly (see Table 14–4) and will be a major area of environmental litigation in coming years. The U.S. Office of Technology Assessment estimates that it will require as much as $500 billion during the next fifty years to clean up the nation's hazardous waste sites.

Radiation

In 1979, the nuclear power plant accident at the Three Mile Island installation in Pennsylvania and subsequent evacuation of thousands of nearby residents focused the nation's attention on the potential hazards of radiation pollution. Although no single piece of legislation comprehensively controls radiation pollution and no one agency is responsible for administering legislation in this technologically complex area, overall responsibility for such control rests with the Nuclear Regulatory Commission. The EPA, however,

TABLE 14–4   Recent Hazardous Waste Settlements

Company	Amount	Location
Amoco Oil Co.	$40–60 million	South Bend, Ind.
Diamond Shamrock	$12 million	Newark, N.J.
Occidental	$30 million	Niagara Falls, N.Y.
Sharon Steel Corp.	$22 million	Salt Lake City, Utah
Shell Oil (and U.S. Army)	Up to $1 billion	Denver, Colo.
Ten companies	$50 billion	Baton Rouge, La.
Waste Management	$10.5 million	Vickery, Ohio
Westinghouse	$90 million	Bloomington, Ind.

does have general authority to conduct testing and provide technical assistance in the area of radiation pollution control. In addition, the Clean Air Act and the Clean Water Act also contain sections applicable to radiation discharges into the air and water.

Concept Summary: an Environmental Alphabet

Environmental and pollution control legislation seems especially given to acronyms. Here's a key.

BAT: best available technology

BPT: best practicable technology

CEQ: Council on Environmental Quality

CERCLA: Comprehensive Environmental Response, Compensation, and Liability Act

EIS: environmental impact statement

EPA: Environmental Protection Agency

FEPCA: Federal Environmental Pesticide Control Act

NEPA: National Environmental Policy Act

RCRA: Resource Conservation and Recovery Act

TSCA: Toxic Substances Control Act

Suits by Private Individuals

Achieving environmental goals requires coordinated strategy and implementation. As private citizens, individuals and groups of individuals lack both the power and foresight necessary to control pollution on a broad scale. There is a role, however, for the private control of private action in two principal areas:

· Citizen enforcement provisions
· Tort law

The following sections examine suits by private individuals that relate to environmental concerns.

11. Citizen Enforcement

Most of the environmental laws, such as the Clean Air and Water Acts, contain *citizen enforcement* provisions, which grant private individuals and groups the standing to sue to challenge failures to comply with the environmental laws. In many instances, private citizens can sue polluters directly to force them to cease violating the law. Private citizens also have standing to sue public agencies (for example, the EPA) to require them to adopt regulations or implement enforcement against private polluters that the environmental laws require.

12. Tort Theories

A second area of private control of private action lies in tort law and its state codifications. When pollution directly injures private citizens, they may sue offending polluters under various theories of tort law. Thus, the traditional deterrence of tort law contributes to private control of private action. This section further develops tort law's role in pollution control.

Examination of tort law and pollution control reveals little understanding of the interdependence between ourselves and our environment. Instead, tort theories, as they have been applied to environmental problems, focus on the action of one person (or business) as it injures the health or interferes with the property rights of another. In other words, tort law attacks the pollution problem by using the established theories of nuisance, trespass, negligence, and strict liability.

Nuisance

The principal tort theory used in pollution control has been that of **nuisance.** The law relating to nuisance is somewhat vague, but in most jurisdictions the common law has been put into statutory form. Several common elements exist in the law of nuisance in most states. To begin with, there are two types of nuisances: public and private.

A *public nuisance* arises from an act that causes inconvenience or damage to the public in the exercise of rights common to everyone. In the environmental area, air, water, and noise pollution can all constitute a public nuisance if they affect common rights. More specifically, industrial waste discharge that kills the fish in a stream may be held a public nuisance, since fishing rights are commonly possessed by the public. Public nuisance actions may be brought only by a public official, not private individuals, unless the latter have suffered some special damage to their persons or property as a result of the public nuisance.

Any unreasonable use of one's property that causes substantial interference with the enjoyment or use of another's land establishes a common law *private nuisance.* The unreasonableness of the interference is measured by a balancing process in which the character, extent, and duration of harm to the plaintiff are weighed against the social utility of the defendant's activity and its appropriateness to its location. Since society needs industrial activity as well as natural tranquillity, people must put up with a certain amount of smoke, dust, noise, and polluted water if they live in concentrated areas of industry. But what may be an appropriate industrial use of land in a congested urban area may be a private nuisance if it occurs in a rural or residential location.

Note that the proving of nuisance does not demand that a property owner be found negligent. An unreasonable *use* of one's land does not mean that one's *conduct* is unreasonable.

Other Tort Doctrines

Private plaintiffs in pollution cases frequently allege the applicability of tort doctrines other than that of nuisance. These doctrines, however, do overlap that of nuisance, which is really a field of tort liability rather than a type of conduct.

One such doctrine is that of *trespass*. A defendant is liable for trespass if, without right, she or he intentionally enters land in possession of another or causes something to do so. The entrance is considered intentional if the defendant knew that it was substantially certain to result from her or his conduct. Thus, airborne particles that fall on a plaintiff's property can constitute a trespass. In recent years, many courts have merged the theories of nuisance and trespass to such an extent that before plaintiffs can recover for a particle trespass, they must prove that the harm done to them exceeds the social utility of the defendant's enterprise.

Negligence doctrine is sometimes used by private plaintiffs in environmental pollution cases. The basis for the negligence tort lies in the defendant's breach of his or her duty to use ordinary and reasonable care toward the plaintiff, which *proximately* (foreseeably) causes the plaintiff injury. A factory's failure to use available pollution-control equipment may be evidence of its failure to employ *reasonable care.*

Finally, some courts recognize the applicability in pollution cases of *strict liability* tort doctrine. This tort liability arises when the defendant injures the plaintiff's person or property by voluntarily engaging in ultrahazardous activity that necessarily involves a risk of serious harm that cannot be eliminated through the exercise of the utmost care. No finding of *fault,* or *failure of reasonable care,* on the defendant's part is necessary. This doctrine has been employed in situations involving the use of poisons, such as in crop dusting and certain industrial work, the storage and use of explosives, and the storage of water in large quantities in a dangerous place.

Increasing numbers of private plaintiffs are suing companies for pollution-related harm. In one recent case, residents in northeast Denver, Colorado, sued Asarco, Inc., for environmental property damage caused by its smelter. Asarco settled the suit for $35 million.

Trends in Environmental Regulation

A *Wall Street Journal*/NBC News survey suggests strong nationwide support for environment cleanup. A 61 percent majority favored more government regulation of the environment. Only 6 percent thought there should be less environmental regulation.

Public and business awareness of environmental issues has significantly increased. In 1990 at the World Economic Forum, 650 business and government leaders ranked the environment as the greatest challenge facing business. Yet in a recent poll only 36 percent of Americans responded that business is doing an adequate job of keeping the environment clean. After the relaxation of environmental law enforcement under the Reagan administration in the 1980s, the future promises new laws and much stricter enforcement. Civil penalties, criminal fines, and imprisonments are all up dramatically.

13. Emerging Areas of Concern

Meanwhile, researchers almost daily report new instances of how industry and technology affect life on our planet. For every allegation of pollution-caused environmental harm, however, countertheories maintain that the harm is not as significant as alleged or argue that the harm arises from causes unrelated to industrial pollution. Lack of unanimous scientific opinion on many environmental issues underscores their great complexity. It also reveals a key controversy at the heart of environmental regulation: *How much certainty of harm is required to justify regulatory intervention?*

Loss of Natural Ecosystems

In 1992 a report signed by 1,575 scientists, including 100 Nobel Prize winners, warned of the effects of worldwide destruction to natural ecosystems, the cutting of rain forests being the most widely publicized destruction. The report concluded: "If not checked, many of our current practices put at serious risk the future that we wish for human society and the plant and animal kingdoms, and may so alter the living world that it will be unable to sustain life in the manner that we know." At risk in the next thirty years are up to 20 percent of the planet's species of animals and plants.

Ozone

In 1990, 59 countries agreed to stop producing certain chemicals that destroy the earth's protective *ozone layer.* The agreement requires participating countries to stop production of chlorofluorocarbons and halons by the year 2000. Destruction of the ozone layer could lead to hundreds of thousands of cases of cataracts and skin cancer in humans plus unknown serious damage to animals and plants.

Research has recently identified other chemicals that may be at work in destroying the ozone layer, including methane and bromine compounds.

Greenhouse Effect

Overshadowing even ozone destruction as a future pollution concern are increasing atmospheric concentrations of carbon dioxide. The National Academy of Sciences notes that global carbon dioxide levels have increased 6 percent since 1960. The increase is due largely to the burning of fossil fuels such as oil and coal.

Higher carbon dioxide levels will likely lead to warmer global temperatures, the so-called *greenhouse effect.* The last decade has had many of the warmest years on record, and atmospheric scientists believe the rise in global carbon dioxide levels was the cause. Changing climatic patterns and rising sea levels are possible results. In 1997 delegates from 150 nations reached a treaty to reduce emission of various greenhouse gases such as carbon dioxide. Under the Kyoto Protocol the industrialized nations, including the United States, will lower greenhouse gas emission to 7 or 8 percent below 1990 levels. The reductions will be achieved between 2008 and 2012.

However, the United States Senate may not ratify the treaty, a step necessary for it to become law in this country. The reduction in the burning of fossil fuels—coal and oil—necessary to lower greenhouse gas levels might seriously impact the economy. Business production might also relocate in developing countries, which the treaty does not require to reduce greenhouse gas emission.

The United States represents only 5 percent of the world's population, yet it consumes more than 20 percent of the world's energy production, much of it in fossil fuels. Can we reduce our disproportionate production of greenhouse gases without dramatically lowering our standard of living? Is it fair or necessary for us to hold back our standard of living while developing countries use cheap fossil fuels as their own economies grow? These questions are hotly debated. Only one conclusion is clearcut. We possess immense technological power today to change the environment for better and for worse, both intentionally and inadvertently.

Population Growth

The world's population continues to grow. According to a Johns Hopkins University study, if human fertility rates do not drop to roughly two children per woman—merely replacing people who die—the world's population will rise to eight billion by 2025 from its current level of five and a half billion. Concerns about pollution, climate change, and even food production are magnified by population growth, yet birth control raises controversial cultural and religious issues. As a business student, you must be aware of and appreciate the significance of population growth because during your career the social and environmental problems associated with such growth will have to be addressed.

14. The Dilemma of Environmental Ethics

No responsible member of the business community believes that the natural environment is a proper dump site for unlimited amounts of manufacturing, mining, agricultural, and consumer pollutants. The dilemma of environmental ethics is much more complex. It also concerns the level of proof required before a business should take steps to reduce the environmental impact of a certain practice.

Merely waiting for regulation to prohibit a business practice is not always environmentally ethical. This is especially true since both lobbying and time-consuming litigation can delay regulation, even when a practice may cause considerable environmental harm. At the same time, scientific knowledge about environmental effects is seldom certain. A business owes it to its owners, its employees, and the community generally not to stop production every time some group alleges environmental harm.

What, then, is the answer to the dilemma of environmental ethics? It does not lie in legal proofs. Rather, it comes from business commitment to practices that minimize environmental harm. As part of this commitment, a business must ensure that it pays careful attention to potential environmental issues even when the law does not so require. The business must also share information about both environmental and economic impacts with regulators and the public. Only through open, frank dialogue inside the company and with the outside community will a business know ethically when to reduce the environmental impact of a certain practice.

Key Terms

Bubble concept   385
Clean Air Act   383
Clean Water Act   388
Comprehensive Environmental Response,
    Compensation, and Liability Act (CERCLA)   387
Emissions reduction banking   387
Environmental impact statement (EIS)   380
Environmental Protection Agency (EPA)   383
Federal Insecticide, Fungicide, and Rodenticide Act
    of 1947   393
Federal Environmental Pesticide Control Act of 1972
    393
Manifest system   396

National Environmental Policy Act (NEPA)   380
Nuisance   401
Point source   385
Prevention of significant deterioration   387
Primary air quality standards   383
Resource Conservation and Recovery Act (RCRA)
    396
Scoping   382
Secondary air quality standards   383
Solid Waste Disposal Act   394
Superfund   397
Toxic Substances Control Act (TSCA)   395

Review Questions and Problems

Government's Regulations of Itself

1. *The National Environmental Policy Act*
    (a) Your firm has been hired to build a large government facility near a residential neighborhood. A committee of residents has been formed to oppose the building. You have been asked to assist in writing the EIS. What factors must your EIS take into consideration?
    (b) The Avila Timber Company has asked for and been granted permission by the Department of Interior to cut 40 acres of timber from the 10,000-acre Oconee National Forest. Prior to the actual logging, a local environmental group files suit in federal district court, contending that the Department of Interior has not filed an EIS. Can the group challenge the Department's action? Analyze whether an EIS should be filed in light of the facts given.

2. *Evaluation of Environmental Impact Statements*
    Outline criticisms of the EIS process. Why are state EISs often less helpful in evaluating complex environmental factors than are those prepared by federal agencies?

Government's Regulation of Business

3. *The Environmental Protection Agency*
    Explain the function of the EPA.

4. *Air Pollution*
    The Akins Corporation wishes to build a new smelting facility in Owens County, an area where air pollution exceeds primary air quality standards.

    (a) What legal difficulties may Akins face?
    (b) What solutions might you suggest for these difficulties?

5. *Clean Air Act Trends*
    (a) What is the difference between an individual point source approach and a bubble-policy approach to dealing with factory pollution?
    (b) For the factory owner, what are the advantages of employing the bubble concept?

6. *Water Pollution*
    Explain the concept of "navigable waterway" and how it is related to the Clean Water Act.

7. *Endangered Species Act*
    How does the ESA apply to private businesses? Explain.

8. *Pesticide Control*
    Before beginning the manufacture of a new pesticide, what process must a company follow under the pesticide-control acts?

9. *Solid Waste*
    (a) Who has the primary responsibility for nontoxic solid waste disposal?
    (b) Describe the role of the Solid Waste Disposal Act in waste disposal.

10. *Toxic and Hazardous Substances*
    (a) As a manufacturer of paints, you need to dispose of certain production by-products that are highly toxic. Discuss the process the law requires you to follow in disposing of these products.
    (b) An abandoned radioactive waste site is discovered by local authorities. The waste came from a company that manufactured radium

watch faces and is now out of business. Who will pay to clean up these radioactive wastes? Discuss.

Suits by Private Individuals

11. *Citizen Enforcement*
    Explain the standing to sue doctrine as it applies to the citizen enforcement of federal pollution laws.

12. *Tort Theories*
    Several years ago, the Spul Chemical Corporation built a new plant near your neighborhood. About once a month clouds of odorous mist have passed across your property, your children have complained of skin rashes, and you have heard that the water table has been contaminated with toxic chemicals. You and your neighbors are fearful of health hazard from the plant, and the neighborhood property values have dropped significantly. Explain possible tort causes of action you may have against the chemical company.

Trends in Environmental Regulation

13. *Emerging Areas of Concern*
    Give examples of why a key controversy at the heart of environmental regulation concerns how much certainty of harm is required to justify regulatory intervention.

Terminology Review

For each term in the left-hand column match the most appropriate description in the right-hand column.

1. EIS

2. Point source

3. Prevention of significant deterioration

4. Superfund

5. Nuisance

6. Bubble concept

7. Manifest system

8. Primary air quality standards

a. An unreasonable use of one's land that interferes with the use or enjoyment of another's land

b. Treating several point sources at a plant as one source

c. A process that must be followed by federal agencies before undertaking major actions that significantly affect the environment

d. A smokestack, pipe, or other opening that discharges pollution

e. The Comprehensive Environmental Response, Compensation, and Liability Act

f. The tracking process for toxic waste disposal

g. Air pollution levels necessary to protect human health

h. The policy of preventing additional pollution in certain areas that have air cleaner than required by primary standards

INTERNATIONAL LAW AND BUSINESS

Business Decision

Corrupt Business Practices

Now that relations with Vietnam have been normalized, you have been sent overseas by your employer, Global Communications, to obtain a contract with its government to upgrade the communication network between the capital and several outlying villages. After arriving in Vietnam, you are approached by a member of the Parliament, who offers to serve as a consultant and use her influence to help you land the desired contract with the Vietnamese government. She demands a nonrefundable retainer of $100,000 and an additional commission of $1 million should your firm succeed in obtaining the contract. Since this contract is worth nearly $100 million and could result in a hefty profit for your firm, you are considering her offer very seriously. You really need an "inside" link to the government, and she seems to be your best bet.

Do you call your home office to ask for advice?

Do you just agree to her terms and avoid the risk that the boss may say no?

If the boss says to pay the money, should you do it?

What legal problems, if any, are presented by the payment?

As American business is faced with an increasingly competitive global market, some understanding of the legal issues raised by international business transactions is essential. Law supplies the rules for governing the intense competition for business in the global market. Nations enter into treaties and other agreements with other countries that govern competition and the way goods and technology are sold from one country to the next. Every country is interested in developing rules that make its products and services more competitive in the global market.

Who engages in international business? The players are diverse and the results affect virtually every person in the United States. National economies

FIGURE 15.1

Major exporting economies of the world (1996) (billions of dollars)

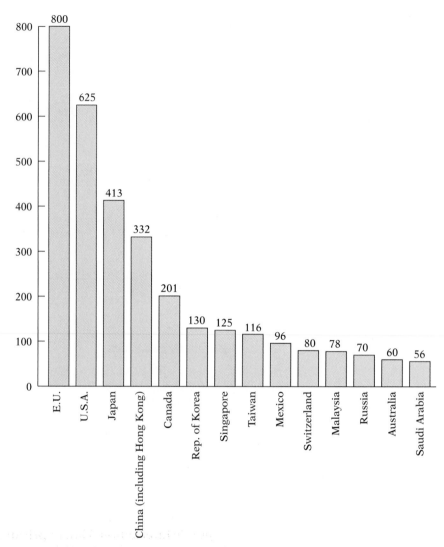

Source: World Trade Organization

rely upon their ability to export products and services abroad to create jobs and economic growth at home (Figure 15–1). The United States continues to run a huge trade deficit as it buys more than it sells abroad (Table 15–1). This chapter focuses on issues important to management decision making by examining the methods and risks of transacting international business. This chapter also considers the role and impact of international organizations and agreements on business and the effect of foreign competition on American business at home.

International Law and Organizations

As you explore international legal transactions as a business manager please remember that, unfortunately, international law does not consist of a cohesive body of uniform principles. Nonetheless, international law can be found

TABLE 15–1   1996 U.S. Trade Deficit

U.S. Exports	U.S. Imports
$625 billion	$ 818 billion

Top Ten Countries with which the U.S. has a Trade Deficit:

Japan	$31.1 billion
China	25.9 billion
Germany	10.6 billion
Canada	10.1 billion
Mexico	9.2 billion
Taiwan	6.8 billion
Italy	5.9 billion
Malaysia	3.6 billion
Thailand	2.7 billion
France	2.4 billion

Source: U.S. Department of Commerce.

in a variety of sources from U.S. domestic law to the law of other countries to international agreements and treaties and even in customary international principles found in the general practice of civilized nations.

In the famous case of *The Paquette Habana* (175 U.S. 677 [1900]), the Supreme Court held that "[i]nternational law is part of our law, and must be ascertained and administered by the courts of justice of appropriate jurisdiction as often as questions of right depending upon it are duly presented for their determination."

1. Sources of International Law

How does one go about finding the principles or rules of international law that apply to a particular contract or dispute? Generally, international law is classified as either **public international law** or **private international law.** Public international law examines relationships between nations and uses rules that are binding on all countries in the international community. Private international law, which is of principal concern to the business manager, examines relationships created by commercial transactions and utilizes international agreements and the individual laws of nations to resolve business disputes.

Public International Law

Article 38 of the Statute of the **International Court of Justice (ICJ)** is the traditional place for ascertaining what is public international law. However, in contrast to what you learned in Chapter 1 regarding U.S. cases, the decisions made by the ICJ, the World Court, do not create binding rules of law or precedent in future cases.

The ICJ is the judicial branch of the United Nations and sits at The Hague in the Netherlands. It consists of 15 judges representing all of the world's major legal systems. The judges are elected by the U.N. General Assembly and the Security Council after having been nominated by national groups, not governments. No more than one judge may be a national of any country.

The ICJ has not been a major force in settling disputes since it began functioning in 1946. The ICJ renders, on average, only one contested decision per year and one advisory opinion every two years. There has been widespread reluctance to resort to the ICJ as a forum for resolving international disputes for several reasons. First, only countries have access to the Court. Private parties or corporations may not directly present claims before the Court. No device exists under U.S. law by which a firm or individual can compel the U.S. government to press a claim on its behalf before the ICJ. Furthermore, only countries that have submitted to the Court's jurisdiction may be parties, since there is no compulsory process for forcing a country to come before the Court. A country may choose to accept the Court's jurisdiction only when the use of the Court may suit its own interests. Moreover, the ICJ has no enforcement authority and must rely on diplomacy or economic sanctions against countries that breach international law. For these reasons, infractions of international law often are settled through diplomacy or arbitration, rather than by the presentation of formal charges to the ICJ.

Of course, deciding whether international law has been violated is often a very difficult question. Article 38 sets forth the following order of importance for determining what is international law in a given case:

> The Court, whose function is to decide in accordance with international law such disputes as are submitted to it, shall apply:
>
> a. *International Conventions,* whether general or particular, establishing rules expressly recognized by the contesting states;
> b. *International Custom,* as evidence of a general practice accepted as law;
> c. *The General Principles of Law* recognized by civilized nations;
> d. *Judicial Decisions and the Teachings of the Most Highly Qualified Publicists* of various nations, as subsidiary means for the determination of rules of law.

Private International Law

Private international law is represented by the laws of individual nations and the multilateral agreements developed between nations to provide mutual understanding and some degree of continuity to international business transactions. Even in purely domestic business deals, the law is rarely predictable or certain. When different national laws, languages, practices, and cultures are added to the transaction, the situation can become very unstable for international business.

International commerce is seldom uncomplicated, and a single business transaction often involves several firms with operations in different nations. For example, in a contract dispute among a German manufacturer, an American wholesaler, and a Canadian retailer, which nation's law controls the transaction may be crucial for determining the outcome of the case. Moreover, determining the proper forum for the case (which nation's court may hear the case) can be difficult.

2. International Organizations and Agreements Affecting Trade

Several international organizations and agreements play important roles in the development of political, economic, and legal rules for the conduct of international business. They include the United Nations, the World Trade Organization, and the Convention on the International Sale of Goods.

United Nations

The **United Nations** was established after World War II and has grown in size from 51 founding nations at that time to almost every nation in the world today. The Charter of the United Nations sets forth as its primary goal "to save succeeding generations from the scourge of war" and to that end authorizes "collective measures for the prevention and removal of threats to the peace, and for the suppression of acts of aggression or other breaches of the peace." Using this authority in 1991, the United States successfully led a concerted effort of nations to remove Iraq as a "threat to peace" in Kuwait.

The General Assembly is composed of every nation represented in the United Nations and permits each country to cast one vote. The real power in the United Nations rests in the Security Council, which is composed of fifteen member states. The council has the power to authorize military action and to sever diplomatic relations with other nations. The five permanent members of the Council (United States, Russia, China, France, and United Kingdom) have veto power over any action proposed in the Council.

A number of organizations affiliated with the United Nations have authority over activities that directly affect international business. The United Nations Commission on International Trade Law (UNCITRAL) was created in 1966 in an effort to develop standardized commercial practices and agreements. One of the documents drafted by the UNCITRAL is the Convention on the International Sale of Goods. The United Nations Conference on Trade and Development (UNCTAD) was created in 1964 to deal with international trade reform and the redistribution of income through trading with developing countries. The UNCTAD has drafted both the Transfer of Technology Code and the Restrictive Business Practices Code, which have gone largely ignored by most nations.

At the Bretton Woods Conference of 1944, two important agencies were also created under the auspices of the United Nations. The International Monetary Fund (IMF) encourages international trade by maintaining stable foreign exchange rates and works closely with commercial banks to promote orderly exchange policies with members. The World Bank promotes economic development in poor countries by making loans to finance necessary development projects and programs.

World Trade Organization

Every nation has the right to establish its own trading policies and has its own national interests at stake when dealing with other nations. Ultimately, after years of economic conflict, many countries concluded that their own interests could be served best by liberalizing trade through reduced tariffs and free markets. The **General Agreement on Tariffs and Trade (GATT)** was originally signed by 23 countries after World War II and represented the determination of a war-weary world to open trade and end the protection of domestic industries. Since GATT was created in 1948, it has undergone eight major revisions, including the 1994 Uruguay Round, which culminated in the creation of the **World Trade Organization (WTO)** as an umbrella organization to regulate world trade. The 1994 agreement was signed by 125 countries.

The WTO expects nations to avoid unilateral trade wars and rely on GATT dispute settlement procedures to avert conflict. At the heart of the 1994 Uruguay Round are several enduring GATT principles: (1) nondiscrimination (treating all member countries equally with respect to trade); (2) national treatment (countries not favoring their domestic products over imported products); and (3) elimination of trade barriers (reducing tariffs and other restrictions in foreign products).

Under the Uruguay Agreement, existing tariffs will be reduced by an average of 38 percent over the next 10 years. The agreement also extends GATT rules to new areas such as agricultural products and service industries and further restricts tariffs on textiles, apparel, and forest products. The lower tariffs are expected to make U.S. goods more competitive in many foreign markets that now impose significant duties on U.S. goods. The agreement also requires countries to upgrade their intellectual property laws to protect patents and copyrights and guard against the piracy of items such as computer software and videotapes.

Since 1995, the WTO has been having some success in resolving trade disputes. Roughly 70 trading disputes were resolved in the first two years, representing an annual rate eight times higher than before 1995. Moreover, the largest and most powerful trading nations have been complying with the WTO rulings. The WTO also can sanction nations that ignore its rulings.

However, early warning signs that the WTO may be in trouble are beginning to emerge. The United States, for example, has begun criticizing the lack of appreciation for competition and antitrust enforcement in WTO rulings. Part of the U.S. frustration arises out of a highly publicized 1997 case against Japan in which the WTO rejected the U.S. claim that Japanese business practices favored Fuji over Kodak film products. Several U.S. trade experts also have criticized the WTO for its inability to gather and collect evidence and for weakening U.S. sovereignty and control over its own trading practices. Many European countries, along with the United States, also are worried that new WTO rules will undermine their ability to compete in many emerging markets such as Asia.

The WTO troubles many environmental groups that believe the WTO's new ability to sanction a violating country may undercut U.S. environmental policies that impact free trade. For example, an earlier 1994 GATT panel found that U.S. embargoes on imports of tuna caught by nations that use purse seine nets were inconsistent with the free-trade provisions in GATT. While the United States imposed these embargoes because these types of nets often kill and maim dolphins, the panel held that the United States may not distinguish between "environmentally friendly" products and those produced in ecologically damaging ways.

Convention on the International Sale of Goods

The **Convention on the International Sale of Goods (CISG)** outlines standard international practices for the sale of goods. It took several years to develop, and it represents many compromises among nations that follow a variety of practices in the area of contracts. It became effective in 1988 and has been adopted by the United States and most of the other countries that engage in large quantities of international trade.

The CISG applies to contracts for the commercial sale of goods (consumer sales for personal, family, or household use are excluded) between parties whose businesses are located in different nations, provided that those nations have adopted the convention. If a commercial seller or buyer in the United States, for example, contracts for the sale of goods with a company located in another country that also has adopted the CISG, the convention and not the U.S. Uniform Commercial Code (UCC) applies to the transaction.

Under the CISG, a significant degree of freedom is provided for the individual parties in an international contract. The parties may negotiate contract terms as they deem fit for their business practices and may, if desired, even opt out of the CISG entirely. One of the most interesting provisions in the CISG includes a rule that contracts for the sale of goods need not be in writing. The CISG also provides that in contract negotiations an acceptance that contains new provisions that do not materially alter the terms of the offer becomes part of the contract, unless the offeror promptly objects to the change. The CISG also sets forth the fundamental elements that will materially alter a contract such as price, payment, quality, and quantity of the goods, place and time of delivery of goods, provisions related to one party's liability to the other, and methods for settling disputes. Since international transactions typically involve sophisticated parties, the CISG also makes it easier to disclaim warranties on goods than under traditional U.S. law.

3. The European Union

Probably the single most significant development affecting international business was the original action by six European countries in 1957 to achieve economic unity by signing the Treaty of Rome, which created the European Community. Now known as the **European Union (EU),** it has grown to include 15 member countries: Austria, Belgium, Denmark, Finland, France, Germany, Greece, Ireland, Italy, Luxembourg, the Netherlands, Portugal, Spain, Sweden, and the United Kingdom. As Figure 15–2 demonstrates, the combined GNP of the top five European countries is very significant when compared to that of either Japan and the United States. Six Eastern European countries, Poland, Hungary, the Czech Republic, Slovenia, Estonia, and Cyprus, have been invited to join the EU and began membership negotiations in late 1997. Several others, including Romania, Latvia, Bulgaria, Lithuania, and Slovakia, have been offered a slower track to EU membership.

The past 10 years have provided remarkable development for the modern Europe. In 1987, the member states passed the Single European Act, which required each country by 1992 to complete many reforms necessary to reach the goal of a unified internal market. The 1987 act mandated the removal of many physical, technical, and tax barriers to the free movement of persons, goods, services, and capital. In 1992, the leaders of the EU member nations signed a far-reaching agreement, known as the Maastricht Treaty, designed to create a more federal system of government and further political and economic union within the EU. The Maastricht Treaty, which took effect in late 1993, created common foreign and defense policies, established

FIGURE 15.2

*Comparative GNP's,
1996 (in billions)*

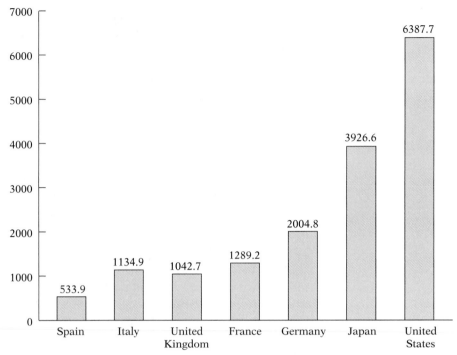

Source: U.S. Department of Commerce

a joint central bank, required member countries to reduce government deficits, and to initiate a single currency by 1999. Moreover, under the treaty, trade barriers between member states essentially are being eliminated under a system similar to the trading policy between states in the United States.

The major institutions of the EU are the Council of Ministers, the Commission, the Parliament, and the Court of Justice. The Council is composed of one representative from each member state. Its purpose is to coordinate the policies of the member states in a variety of areas from economics to foreign affairs. The Commission consists of individuals who represent the will of the entire Union rather than specific national concerns. Much of the executive functions of the EU are carried out by the Commission as it seeks to forge a single identity. The Parliament is comprised of elected representatives from each member state and is divided into political factions that often create coalitions across national borders. Finally, the Court of Justice serves the role of deciding the nature and parameters of EU law. Justices are appointed by the Council and each member nation has justice seated on the Court.

4. The North American Free Trade Agreement

With passage in 1993 of the **North American Free Trade Agreement (NAFTA),** the United States, Mexico, and Canada set in motion increased trade and foreign investment, and unlimited opportunities for economic growth in one of the fastest-growing regions of the world. At the core of NAFTA is free trade with the reduction and eventual elimination of tariffs and other barriers to business between the three countries. NAFTA also provides for a dispute settlement mechanism that will make it easier to resolve trade disputes between the three countries. Based upon concerns that cheap labor and poor environmental controls might cause U.S. firms to relocate to Mexico, side agreements also were reached to improve labor rights and environmental protection in Mexico.

Despite dire predictions that NAFTA would harm the United States, the agreement has proved beneficial to everyone. For example, prior to NAFTA, Mexico was not a member of GATT and its tariffs averaged 10 percent on imports. Since U.S. tariffs averaged only two percent, the United States had to adjust its trade policy only marginally to gain tremendous access to the Mexican marketplace. From 1993 to 1996, bilateral trade between Mexico and the United States rose by $17 billion per year. Mexico is set to overtake Japan in the future as the United States' number two trading partner behind only Canada, the third NAFTA partner.

Methods of Transacting International Business

A U.S. business that wants to engage in international trade is presented with an almost limitless array of possibilities. Choosing a method of doing business in foreign countries not only requires understanding the factors normally involved in selecting an organization and operating a business domestically but also demands an appreciation of the international trade perspective. Depending upon the country, type of export, and amount of export involved in a particular transaction, international trade may involve direct foreign sales, licensing agreements, franchise agreements, or direct foreign investment.

5. Foreign Sales

The simplest, least risky approach for a manufacturer to use when trying to penetrate foreign markets is to sell goods directly to buyers located in other countries. However, with foreign sales, increased uncertainty over the ability to enforce the buyer's promise to pay for goods often requires that more complex arrangements for payment be made than with the usual domestic sale. Commonly, an **irrevocable letter of credit** is used to ensure payment. Transactions using such a letter involve, in addition to a seller and buyer, an *issuing bank* in the buyer's country. The buyer obtains a commitment from the bank to advance (pay) a specified amount (i.e., the price of the goods) upon receipt, from the carrier, of a **bill of lading,** stating that the goods have been shipped. The issuing bank's commitment to pay is given, not to the seller directly, but to a *confirming bank* located in the United States from which the seller obtains payment. The confirming bank forwards the bill of lading to the issuing bank in order to obtain reimbursement of the funds that have been paid to the seller. The issuing bank releases the bill of lading to the buyer after it has been paid, and with the bill of lading the buyer is able to obtain the goods from the carrier. Use of a letter of credit in the transaction thus reduces the uncertainties involved. The buyer need not pay the seller for goods prior to shipment, and the seller can obtain payment for the goods immediately upon shipment.

There is no room in documentary transactions for substantial performance. All of the duties and responsibilities of parties must be evaluated based upon the documents tendered, and these documents must comply strictly with the letter of credit. The tradition and purpose of the letter of credit in international transactions is demonstrated by the following case.

MOOG WORLD TRADE CORPORATION V. BANCOMER, S.A.

90 F.3d 1382 (8th Cir. 1996)

Moog World Trade Corporation, the beneficiary of an irrevocable letter of credit, brought suit in Missouri against Bancomer, S.A., a Mexican issuing bank, for wrongful dishonor of its draw. Bancomer issued the letter of credit at the request of its customer, CRG. The letter of credit promised that Moog as beneficiary would be paid $383,636 at Boatmen's offices in St. Louis upon Moog's timely presentation of a 60-day time draft accompanied by specified documents confirming that Moog had shipped the auto parts to CRG. Bancomer issued the letter of credit by telex to Boatmen's. Boatmen's then sent the letter of credit to Moog.

Two weeks before the letter of credit expired, Moog presented a draft and supporting documents to Boatmen's, which dishonored the draw, noting discrepancies between the shipping documents and the letter of credit's specifications. Moog had time to cure these discrepancies by submitting amended documents to Boatmen's to present the dishonored documents to Bancomer in Mexico. When Bancomer refused to honor the draw, citing six alleged documentary discrepancies, a Moog representative and its attorney visited Bancomer's office in Guadalajara, Mexico, requesting an explanation of the dishonor. Bancomer responded that Moog should contact Boatmen's.

With the letter of credit now expired, Moog brought this diversity action, claiming wrongful dishonor and untimely notice of dishonor by both banks. The district court dismissed Bancomer for lack of personal jurisdiction and dismissed the untimely-notice-of-dishonor claim against Boatmen's on the merits. Moog dismissed its wrongful dishonor claim against Boatmen's with prejudice and appealed the district court's rulings. Moog later dismissed its appeal against Boatmen's, leaving for us only the question whether the district court has personal jurisdiction over Bancomer.

LOKEN, J.: The federal court in a diversity case must determine whether defendant is subject to the court's jurisdiction under the state long arm statute, and if so, whether exercise of that jurisdiction comports with due process. As pertinent here, the Missouri long arm statute confers jurisdiction over "any cause of action arising from . . . (1) [t]he transaction of any business within this state [or] (2) [t]he making of any contract within this state." Missouri courts have construed this statute to extend the jurisdiction of the courts of this state over nonresident defendants to the extent permissible under the Due Process Clause. To put the issues of fair play, reasonable anticipation, and purposeful availing in proper perspective, we must examine the purposes and functioning of an international commercial letter of credit.

Letters of credit have been used for nearly 3000 years. Though they stretch common law contract principles such as consideration, letters of credit were eventually accepted and enforced by Anglo-American common law courts. The commercial letter of credit is widely used to assist sales transactions, including in-

ternational export/import transactions. The parties to such a transaction have conflicting needs and concerns. The exporter-seller does not wish to part with its goods without knowing it will be paid, even if the buyer later changes its mind, becomes insolvent, or claims upon inspection that the goods are nonconforming. The seller also wants prompt payment in its own currency, even if the buyer needs credit financing. The importer-buyer, on the other hand, may need credit financing and in any event does not wish to pay for the goods without firm evidence that they have been shipped. Each party typically fears litigation in the other party's "home court."

The commercial letter of credit bridges these differences. The buyer's bank issues the letter of credit naming the seller as beneficiary. The letter of credit is the issuer's irrevocable obligation to pay a stated amount of money to the seller-beneficiary, at a stated time and place and in a specified currency. To obtain payment, the seller must present specified documents, typically, the seller's invoice and shipping documents, thereby confirming to the buyer that (i) the right goods (ii) are in the hands of a common carrier (iii) with the agreed-upon costs prepaid. The letter of credit usually requires the issuing bank to honor or dishonor the seller's presentation (draw) while the goods are in transit. If the bank dishonors, it must return the shipping documents to the seller, who then has the exclusive right to claim the goods from the carrier. If the draw is honored, the seller is promptly paid, or in a credit sale is promised payment at a specified time by the creditworthy issuing bank, a promise the seller can convert to immediate cash by discounting.

This commercial letter of credit transaction creates three distinct contractual relationships—the underlying transaction between the buyer and seller; the buyer's agreement to reimburse the issuing bank for payments under the letter of credit; and the letter of credit itself. The simplest commercial letter of credit contains the issuer's irrevocable promise to pay drafts drawn by the beneficiary at the issuer's counter (place of business). But in an international transaction, the seller typically wants to present the draw locally and to be paid in its own currency; the seller may also want a local bank to decide whether a draw complies with the letter of credit's documentary requirements. The seller can meet these concerns by persuading the buyer to have its bank issue a letter of credit payable at a bank near the seller's place of business. That bank may be an advising bank—simply a conduit for the issuing bank's decisions—or it may be a confirming bank that decides whether the draw complies and thereby adds its own liability to that of the issuing bank. Here, Moog persuaded CRG to have Bancomer issue the letter of credit with Boatmen's as the confirming bank. With these fundamental commercial concepts in mind, we return to the jurisdiction issue.

When Bancomer issued its letter of credit, it did not make a contract with Moog, it performed a contract with its Mexican customer, CRG. The identity and location of CRG's beneficiary was of little if any concern to Bancomer, because it looked to CRG for both its letter of credit fee and reimbursement of any payment Bancomer might make under the credit. True, the letter of credit created a separate, conditional obligation running from Bancomer to Moog as beneficiary. But that bare letter of credit obligation, while contractual in nature, was not the making of a contract with Moog.

Moreover, relying upon traditional due process principles, other federal courts have been virtually unanimous in holding that a bank issuing a commercial letter of credit at the request of its customer, payable at the bank's offices, does not without more subject itself to personal jurisdiction in a distant forum, such as a court where the letter of credit beneficiary resides.

We conclude that this reasoning is even more compelling when the issuer is a foreign bank that has financed an import transaction with a commercial letter of credit payable at the foreign bank's counter. The U.S. seller-beneficiary could have better protected its interests by delaying shipment until the letter of credit was honored, or by reclaiming the goods from the carrier after dishonor, or by making the letter of credit payable at the counter of a U.S. confirming bank. When the seller has failed to protect itself in this manner, it is not fair play—and it risks the future availability of this inexpensive international banking device—to subject the foreign bank to the burdens of wrongful dishonor litigation in the United States. . . .

In these circumstances, we agree with the district court's resolution of the personal jurisdiction issue. Moog protected its interests under the letter of credit when it obtained confirmation by Boatmen's, which then became subject to suit in Missouri for wrongful dishonor. Bancomer as foreign issuer took no action beyond securing a local confirming bank that would subject it to the jurisdiction of the Missouri courts. It is more consistent with fair play and the need for efficient international markets to limit Moog in this lawsuit to its wrongful dishonor claim against Boatmen's, which it has abandoned. The fact that Bancomer had previously issued numerous commercial letters of credit naming various Missouri beneficiaries to assist other export/import transactions does not, in our view, alter the analysis. The judgment of the district court is [*affirmed*].

Case Questions

1. What three contractual relationships are created by the commercial letter of credit?

2. What is the primary purpose of a letter of credit from the standpoint of the seller? The buyer?

3. Why did the court find no personal jurisdiction with respect to the bank issuing the letter of credit?

6. Licenses or Franchises

In appropriate circumstances, a domestic firm may choose to grant a foreign firm the means to produce and sell its product. The typical method for controlling these transfers of information is the **license** or **franchise** contract. In this manner, intangible property rights, such as patents, copyrights, trademarks, or manufacturing processes, are transferred in exchange for royalties in the foreign country. A licensing arrangement allows the international business to enter a foreign market without any direct foreign investment. Licensing often is used as a transitional technique for firms expanding international operations since the risks are greater than with foreign sales but considerably less than with direct foreign investment.

Licensing technology or the sale of a product to a foreign firm is a way to expand the company's market without the need for substantial capital. The foreign firm may agree to this arrangement because it lacks sufficient research and development capability or the management skills or marketing strategies to promote the product alone. Of course, as with all international trade agreements, there is some level of risk. The licensor must take care to restrict the use of the product or technology to agreed-upon geographic areas and must take adequate steps to protect the confidential information that is licensed to the foreign firm so that third parties cannot exploit it.

7. Direct Foreign Investment

As a business increases its level of international trade, it may find that creation of a **foreign subsidiary** is necessary. Most countries will permit a foreign firm to conduct business only if a national (individual or firm) of the host country is designated as its legal representative. Since this designation may create difficulties in control and result in unnecessary expense, the usual practice for multinational corporations is to create a foreign subsidiary in the host country. The form of subsidiary most closely resembling a U.S. corporation is known as a *société anonyme (S.A.)* or, in German-speaking countries, an *Aktiengesellschaft (AG)*. Other forms of subsidiaries may also exist that have characteristics of limited liability of the owners and fewer formalities in their creation and operation.

Creation of a foreign subsidiary may pose considerable risk to the domestic parent firm by subjecting it to foreign laws and the jurisdiction of foreign courts. The 1983 industrial accident in Bhopal, India, where hundreds of people were killed and thousands injured as a result of toxic gas leaks from a chemical plant, resulted in lawsuits against both the Indian subsidiary corporation and Union Carbide, the parent firm in the United States. In 1989, Union Carbide agreed to pay more than $450 million to settle outstanding claims and compensate the victims of the disaster.

In many instances, however, the only legal or political means a firm has to invest directly in a foreign country is to engage in a **joint venture** with an entity from that host country. A host country's participant may be a private enterprise or, especially in developing countries, a government agency or government-owned corporation. Many foreign countries favor joint ventures because they allow local individuals and firms to participate in the benefits of economic growth and decrease the risk of foreign domination of local industry. Many of the developing countries require that the local partner have majority equity control of the venture and also insist on joint ventures with government participation.

Risks Involved in International Trade

Because international trade means dealing with different legal systems, cultures, and ways of doing business, there are a number of risks involved. Among them are expropriation and nationalization, export controls, pressures for bribes, and ill will resulting from U.S. antitrust laws.

8. Expropriation and Nationalization

If a domestic firm is involved in a foreign country to the extent of locating assets there (whether through branches, subsidiaries, joint ventures, or otherwise), it may be subject to the ultimate legal and political risk of international business activity—expropriation. **Expropriation,** as used in the context of international law, is the seizure of foreign-owned property by a government. When the owners are not fairly compensated, the expropriation is also considered to be a *confiscation* of property. Usually, the expropriating government also assumes ownership of the property, so the process includes **nationalization** as well. In the United States, the counterpart of expropriation is called the *power of eminent domain.*

This power of a government to take private property is regarded as inherent; yet it is subject to restraints upon its exercise. The U.S. Constitution (as well as the constitutions and laws of most nations) prohibits the government from seizing private property except for "public purposes" and upon the payment of "just compensation."

However, the extent of such protection varies widely. Treaties (or other agreements) between the United States and other countries provide additional protection against uncompensated takings of property. It is customary for international law to recognize the right of governments to expropriate the property of foreigners only when accompanied by "prompt, adequate and effective compensation." This so-called "modern traditional theory" is accepted by most nations as the international standard and requires full compensation to the investor including fair market value as a going concern.

9. Export Controls

Another risk involved in doing business abroad is **export controls** placed on the sale of U.S. strategic products and technology abroad. Controlling the export of such items has been the cornerstone of Western policy since the conclusion of World War II. Most of the attention was focused on preventing the acquisition of technology by the former Soviet Union and its allies. However, since the end of the Cold War the policy rationale behind export controls has been drawn into question, with many Western countries contending they should be eliminated to increase trading opportunities with Russia, China, Eastern Europe, and the Middle East. Indeed, the Coordinating Committee for Multilateral Export Controls (COCOM), an organization created by the major Western nations (including the United States, Europe, and Japan) to control exports, came to an end in 1994. Since that time, a new organization of 33 countries, known as the Wassenaar Group, has come into existence to help control the spread of both military and dual-use technology to unstable areas of the world.

The U.S. export control system currently is regulated by the Department of State and the Department of Commerce under authority provided by the

Export Administration Act and the Arms Export Control Act. The Department of Defense also plays a key role in determining the technology to be controlled as does the U.S. Customs Service in the enforcement of the controls. Significant criminal and administrative sanctions may be imposed upon corporations and individuals convicted of violating the law.

Because the Export Administration Act was not renewed by Congress in 1994, President Clinton has used his authority granted under the International Emergency Economics Powers Act to continue the U.S. export control regime currently in place until Congress acts and passes new legislation.

The future of the U.S. system remains in doubt with many proposals pending in Congress to reform and limit the current export control system. Over the past several years, these controls have become an extremely controversial topic in the international business community. Export controls make successful business deals more difficult because foreign buyers may be reluctant to trade with a U.S. firm due to the red tape involved in obtaining governmental approval as compared with Europe or Japan.

The following case illustrates the complexity and international intrigue that often accompany export controls.

United States of America v. Covarrubias

94 F.3d 172 (5th Cir. 1996)

Covarrubias was pulled over by Robstown, Texas, police officer Albert Stout ("Stout") on March 19, 1995 for failing to display a front license plate and for a malfunctioning taillight on his late model Chevrolet pickup truck. Covarrubias was stopped on Highway 77, which comes within approximately one-half mile of the American border with Mexico. As Stout approached the vehicle, he noticed a gas filler hose protruding from near the left double-rear tires of the truck and also detected the odor of fresh paint in this area.

Officer Stout began to inquire about Covarrubias's truck and his destination; the two conversed primarily in Spanish. Stout immediately noticed that Covarrubias was very nervous, gripping the steering wheel tightly with both hands, avoiding eye contact, and speaking in a low, stammering voice. Furthermore, Covarrubias responded inconsistently to Stout's inquiries regarding his destination.

Covarrubias also assured Stout during their conversation that his truck had been painted over a year ago, that it had working dual fuel tanks, and that the hose protruding from the truck was merely a homemade valve designed to fix the truck's broken fuel switch. When asked to demonstrate the use of this homemade valve, Covarrubias suggested that the makeshift fuel switch was not yet operational.

Confronted with a myriad of inconsistent and suspicious information, Stout requested that Covarrubias step outside his pickup as Stout prepared a citation for the vehicle violations. After giving Covarrubias the citation, Stout informed Covarrubias that he was free to leave, but also sought consent to search the pickup truck, expressing misgivings about what Covarrubias might be carrying. Covarrubias provided both oral and written consent to the search.

Officer Stout's search of the vehicle revealed that the gas tank hose was not connected to the left tank and that this tank sounded solid when hit. After securing the assistance of a wrecker service, Stout and another officer, Danny Flores ("Flores"), supervised the mechanic's removal of the left fuel tank from the truck. When the tank was opened, the officers discovered a camouflage flak jacket, ammunition, several firearms, and various weaponry paraphernalia. During trial, the parties stipulated that the firearms found in the gas tank are listed on the United States Munitions List, which requires an individual to obtain a permit before exporting such weapons. The officers read Covarrubias his constitutional rights and placed him under arrest. While in transit to the police station, Covarrubias offered the explanation that he was traveling to Mexico in order to give the firearms to relatives because his girlfriend would no longer tolerate the guns in their house.

Later that afternoon, Covarrubias waived his rights and agreed to an interview with Customs Special Agent Monte Price ("Price"). Stout was present during the interview and testified that Price asked Covarrubias if he knew that it was illegal to move the firearms to Mexico, and Covarrubias answered that "he knew that it was illegal to cross them with-

out notifying the proper authorities," both in the United States and Mexico. Stout further testified that Covarrubias explained that he had no intention of reporting the firearms to any border authorities whatsoever, and that he had hidden the weapons in the fuel tank in order to conceal them "from the Mexican and American police." Covarrubias also expressed relief that he was arrested in the United States, since he feared retribution from Mexican law enforcement.

PER CURIAM: Covarrubias contends that the evidence was insufficient to sustain his conviction for willfully attempting to export without a license firearms on the United States Munitions List because the government did not demonstrate that he had knowledge of the duty to obtain such authorization. As this court has frequently explained, when considering the sufficiency of the evidence underlying a conviction, it is not necessary that the evidence exclude every reasonable hypothesis of innocence or be wholly inconsistent with every conclusion except that of guilt, provided a reasonable trier of fact could find that the evidence establishes guilt beyond a reasonable doubt. A jury is free to choose among reasonable constructions of the evidence. The evidence and reasonable inferences drawn from the evidence are viewed in the light most favorable to the government.

To sustain a conviction, the government must prove beyond a reasonable doubt that the defendant willfully exported or attempted to export defense articles that are on the United States Munitions List without a license. Hence, the statute requires the government to prove that the defendant acted with specific intent to violate a known legal duty.

Covarrubias contends that the government has not sufficiently proved that he acted with specific intent because the government's evidence demonstrates only a general awareness of the illegality of his conduct and falls short of establishing that he was aware of the United States Munitions List or of the duty to obtain a license in order to export the items listed on it.

[T]he jury in the instant case had ample evidence from which it could have reasonably concluded that Covarrubias knowingly attempted to export weapons on the Munitions List without obtaining either the required license or authorization. For instance, the government presented extensive and uncontroverted evidence detailing Covarrubias's efforts to conceal the weapons in a gas tank of his truck. Furthermore, Covarrubias made several inconsistent and incriminating statements before, during, and after his arrest that demonstrate his knowledge that export of the concealed weapons was unlawful. Covarrubias also admitted that he had no intention of declaring the weapons concealed in the gas tank of his truck to authorities on either side of the border because he knew that it was illegal to transport the weapons into Mexico. Finally, despite his insistence to the contrary, Covarrubias owned a vehicle that had crossed the border at regulated ports of entry on at least five occasions since 1993. The government proved at trial that the United States Customs Service displays large signs at these ports of entry that detail the requirement that a license or other form of express authorization is needed before articles on the United States Munitions List can be exported to Mexico.

Viewing this evidence and the other evidence adduced at trial as well as the reasonable inferences in the light most favorable to the government, the evidence was sufficient to support the jury's conclusion that Covarrubias knew that either a license or other form of authorization was required before he could transport the weapons. . . .

For the foregoing reasons, the evidence is sufficient to support the jury's verdict and Covarrubias's conviction is [*affirmed*].

Case Questions

1. What steps must an American exporter follow in order to send goods abroad? Should these controls on business exist? Why or why not?

2. Why is the U.S. system so fragmented among various government agencies—State Department, Commerce Department, Defense Department, and Customs Service? Would it make sense to centralize the responsibility for export controls in one government agency?

3. Can the United States effectively control exports of goods and technology to foreign countries given the many methods available to circumvent the law?

A country's ability to control the entry and exit of products and technology is essential not only for national security purposes, but also for public health and the collection of tax revenues through tariffs and other import duties. The following "Tobacco Box" demonstrates that point most conclusively.

Tobacco Industry Box

In light of the number of lawsuits filed against cigarette manufacturers in the United States, along with increased regulatory scrutiny by many federal agencies, a significant decrease in cigarette sales is expected in the United States in the future. Foreign markets have become increasingly important to the survival of the cigarette industry and there has been a general surge in cigarette sales abroad, particularly for American brands.

Interestingly, large tobacco companies have been accused of selling billions of dollars of cigarettes each year to traders and dealers who funnel them into black markets. The volume of cigarette smuggling around the world has nearly tripled in the last 10 years, according to some researchers. While the cigarette industry claims that they neither encourage nor condone smuggling, company managers have pled guilty to aiding smugglers. Moreover, by selling large quantities of cigarettes to traders and dealers, the pipeline for the smugglers is created. For example, two organized crime groups in Europe are believed to take in hundreds of millions a year from cigarettes they buy from dealers selling products made by U.S. cigarette manufacturers.

Cigarette smuggling costs foreign governments an estimated $16 billion a year in lost revenues from import taxes and custom duties. Moreover, health experts claim that mass smuggling is undermining efforts to discourage smoking by teenagers. The experts claim that young people smoke more when cigarettes are cheaper, and smuggled brands sell for less since they avoid the taxes imposed on legitimate sales.

---

10. Pressures for Bribes

Following widespread disclosure of scandalous payments by domestic firms to officials of foreign governments, Congress enacted the **Foreign Corrupt Practices Act (FCPA)** in 1977. The law is designed to stop bribery of foreign officials and to prohibit U.S. citizens and companies from making payments to foreign officials whose duties are not "essentially ministerial or clerical" for the purpose of obtaining business.

This statute has two principal requirements:

1. Financial records and accounts must be kept "which, in reasonable detail, accurately and fairly reflect the transactions and dispositions of assets" of the business.

2. The business must "devise and maintain a system of internal accounting controls sufficient to provide reasonable assurances" that transactions are being carried out in accordance with management's authorization.

These provisions are intended to correct the previously widespread practice of accounting for bribes as commission payments, payments for services, or other normal business expenses and then illegally deducting the payments on income tax returns.

Many legal observers criticized the FCPA for creating a significantly chilling effect on U.S. companies seeking business in many developing coun-

---

TABLE 15–2 **The Foreign Corrupt Practices Act**

Legal or Permissible Payments
1. Any payments permitted under the written laws of a foreign country
2. Travel expenses of a foreign official for purpose of seeing demonstration of product
3. "Grease" payments to foreign customs officials to speed goods through customs
4. Other small payments for "routine" government action such as obtaining visas, work permits, or police protection

---

tries where under-the-table payments to government officials are an accepted practice. Indeed, many civil servants in other nations are expected to supplement their salaries in this manner. The U.S. prohibition of such payments is perceived as an attempt to impose U.S. standards of morality in other parts of the world, and it has caused resentment and discrimination against U.S. businesses. Moreover, the FCPA puts U.S. firms at a competitive disadvantage with businesses in other countries that are not operating under similar constraints. According to a 1997 study, U.S. exporters are least likely to pay bribes, while companies from Belgium, France and Italy are the most likely. The existence of the FCPA probably accounts for the difference.

As a result of intensive lobbying by the U.S. business community, Congress amended the FCPA in 1988 in an effort to eliminate ambiguity and uncertainty over what constitutes improper conduct. While the law still prohibits bribery and corruption, the amendments establish clearer standards for firms to follow in overseas operations. The amendments limit criminal liability for violations of accounting standards to those who "knowingly" circumvent accounting controls or falsify records of corporate payments and transactions. The amendments also clarify the level of detail required in such record keeping and should improve compliance by businesses and enforcement by the government. Moreover, under the new law otherwise prohibited payments to foreign officials may be defended if they were legal under the written laws of the host country or if they cover "reasonable and bona fide" expenses associated with the promotion of the product and the completion of the contract. Table 15–2 illustrates the types of payments that are legal under the FCPA.

Under the 1988 amendments, criminal penalties for companies violating the FCPA have been increased to a maximum of $2 million and individuals may be fined up to $100,000 and/or five years in prison.

11. Conflicts with U.S. Antitrust Laws

The U.S. antitrust laws, discussed in detail in Chapter 11, represent our nation's legal commitment to free markets and international competition. Perhaps no other aspect of our legal system has generated as much recent controversy and ill will abroad as the extraterritorial application of our antitrust laws to conduct occurring beyond the borders of the United States. To protect the welfare of the U.S. consumer, however, the government's enforcement efforts must sometimes reach foreign defendants as a means of ensuring open and free markets.

The Department of Justice and the Federal Trade Commission have issued guidelines delineating the U.S. government's policy on enforcement of federal antitrust law in the international arena. The guidelines provide that anticompetitive conduct, regardless of where such conduct occurs in the world or the nationality of the parties involved, may be prosecuted if it affects U.S. domestic or foreign commerce. The guidelines also provide that imports intended for sale in the United States by definition affect the U.S. market directly and will, therefore, invariably be subject to control. For example, suppose two foreign firms organize a cartel, produce a product abroad, and agree to fix the price of the finished product sold to the United States. Under the guidelines, this type of conduct is subject to prosecution because the transaction will affect U.S. commerce. Anticompetitive conduct by a foreign firm intended to affect the exports of a U.S. business may be sanctioned as well.

The following case represents the most recent judicial examination of extraterritorialty in a case involving the U.S. prosecution of a foreign corporation for price-fixing which took place entirely in Japan.

UNITED STATES V. NIPPON PAPER INDUSTRIES CO., LTD.

109 F.3d 1 (1st Cir. 1997)

In 1995 a federal grand jury handed down an indictment naming as a defendant Nippon Paper Industries Co., Ltd. (NPI), a Japanese manufacturer of facsimile paper. The indictment alleged that in 1990 NPI and certain unnamed co-conspirators held a number of meetings in Japan which culminated in an agreement to fix the price of thermal fax paper throughout North America. NPI and other manufacturers who were privy to the scheme purportedly accomplished their objective by selling the paper in Japan to unaffiliated trading houses on condition that the latter charge specified (inflated) prices for the paper when they resold it in North America. The trading houses then shipped and sold the paper to their subsidiaries in the United States who in turn sold it to American consumers at swollen prices. The indictment further related that, in 1990 alone, NPI sold thermal fax paper worth approximately $6,100,000 for eventual import into the United States; and that in order to ensure the success of the venture, NPI monitored the paper trail and confirmed that the prices charged to end users were those that it had arranged. These activities, the indictment claims, had a substantial adverse effect on commerce in the United States and unreasonably restrained trade in violation of Section One of the Sherman Act.

NPI moved to dismiss, claiming that if the conduct attributed to NPI occurred at all, it took place entirely in Japan, and, thus, the indictment failed to limit an offense under Section One of the Sherman Act. The government opposed this initiative on two grounds. First, it claimed that the law deserved a less grudging reading and that, properly read, Section One of the Sherman Act applied criminally to wholly foreign conduct as long as that conduct produced substantial and intended effects within the United States. Second, it claimed that the indictment, too, deserved a less grudging reading and that, properly read, the bill alleged a vertical conspiracy in restraint of trade that involved overt acts by certain coconspirators within the United States. Accepting a restrictive reading of both the statute and the indictment, the district court dismissed the case.

POPOFSKY, J.: This case raises an important, hitherto unanswered question. In it, the United States attempts to convict a foreign corporation under the Sherman Act, a federal antitrust statute, alleging that price-fixing activities which took place entirely in Japan are prosecutable because they were intended to have, and did in fact have, substantial effects in this country. The district court, declaring that a criminal antitrust prosecution could not be based on wholly extraterritorial conduct, dismissed the indictment.

Our law has long presumed that legislation of Congress, unless a contrary intent appears, is meant to apply only within the territorial jurisdiction of the United States. In this context, the Supreme Court has charged inquiring courts with determining whether Congress has clearly expressed an affirmative desire to apply particular laws to conduct that occurs beyond the borders of the United States. . . .

The case law now conclusively establishes that civil antitrust actions predicated on wholly foreign conduct which has an intended and substantial effect in the United States come within Section One's jurisdictional reach. Were this a civil case, our journey would be complete. But here the United States essays a criminal prosecution for solely extraterritorial conduct rather than a civil action. This is largely uncharted terrain; we are aware of no authority directly on point, and the parties have cited none.

Be that as it may, one [point] sticks out like a sore thumb: in both criminal and civil cases, the claim that Section One applies extraterritorially is based on the same language in the same section of the same statute: "Every contract, combination in the form of trust or otherwise, or conspiracy, in restraint of trade or commerce among the several states, or with foreign nations, is declared to be illegal." Words may sometimes be chameleons, possessing different shades of meaning in different contexts, but common sense suggests that courts should interpret the same language in the same section of the same statute uniformly, regardless of whether the impetus for interpretation is criminal or civil. . . .

NPI and the Government of Japan urge that special reasons exist for measuring Section One's reach differently in a criminal context. We have reviewed their exhortations and found them hollow.

NPI makes much of the fact that this appears to be the first criminal case in which the United States endeavors to extend Section One to wholly foreign conduct. We are not impressed. There is a first time for everything, and the absence of earlier criminal actions is probably more a demonstration of the increasingly global nature of our economy than proof that Section One cannot cover wholly foreign conduct in the criminal milieu.

There is simply no comparable tradition or rationale for drawing a criminal/civil distinction with regard to extraterritoriality, and neither NPI nor [the Japanese Government] have alluded to any case which does so. NPI and the district court both sing the praises of the Restatement (Third) of Foreign Relations Law (1987), claiming that it supports a distinction between civil and criminal cases on the issue of extraterritoriality. The passage to which they pin their hopes states:

> In the case of regulatory statutes that may give rise to both civil and criminal liability, such as the United States antitrust and securities laws, the presence of substantial foreign elements will ordinarily weigh against application of criminal law. In such cases, legislative intent to subject conduct outside the state's territory to its criminal law should be found only on the basis of express statement or clear implication.

We believe that this statement merely reaffirms the classic presumption against extraterritoriality—no more, no less.

The next arrow which NPI yanks from its quiver is the rule of lenity. The rule itself is venerable; it provides that, in the course of interpreting statutes in criminal cases, a reviewing court should resolve ambiguities affecting a statue's scope in the defendant's favor. Put bluntly, the rule of lenity cannot be used to create ambiguity when the meaning of a law, even if not readily apparent, is, upon inquiry, reasonably clear.

[Finally] international comity is a doctrine that counsels voluntary forbearance when a sovereign which has a legitimate claim to jurisdiction concludes that a second sovereign also has a legitimate claim to jurisdiction under principles of international law.

In this case the defendant's comity-based argument is even more attenuated. The conduct with which NPI is charged is illegal under both Japanese and American laws, thereby alleviating any founded concern about NPI being whipsawed between separate sovereigns. And, moreover, to the extent that comity is informed by general principles of reasonableness, the indictment lodged against NPI is well within the pale. In it, the government charges that the defendant orchestrated a conspiracy with the object of rigging prices in the United States. If the government can prove these charges, we see no tenable reason why principles of comity should shield NPI from prosecution. We live in an age of international commerce, where decisions reached in one corner of the world can reverberate around the globe in less time than it takes to tell the tale. Thus, a ruling in NPI's favor would create perverse incentives for those who would use nefarious means to influence markets in the United States, rewarding them for erecting as many territorial firewalls as possible between cause and effect.

The combined force of these commitments requires that we accept the government's cardinal argument, reverse the order of the district court, reinstate the indictment, and remand for further proceedings. [*Reversed and remanded*].

Case Questions

1. Why did NPI and the Japanese Government claim that a U.S. criminal case could not be initiated under these facts?

2. What reasons did the Court of Appeals offer for permitting prosecution here even though the criminal conduct occurred outside the United States?

3. Given this action by the United States, what additional risks are now posed to U.S. businesses and their employees when engaged in foreign trade?

Resolving International Disputes

12. Suing Foreign Governments in the United States

The doctrine of **sovereign immunity** provides that a foreign sovereign is immune from suit in the United States. Under the doctrine of sovereign immunity, the foreign sovereign claims to be immune from suit entirely based on its status as a state.

Until approximately 1952, this notion was absolute. From 1952 until 1976, U.S. courts adhered to a *restrictive theory* under which immunity existed with regard to sovereign or public acts but not with regard to private or commercial acts. In 1976, Congress enacted the **Foreign Sovereign Immunities Act (FSIA),** which codifies this restrictive theory and rejects immunity for *commercial acts* carried on in the United States or having direct effects in this country.

The Supreme Court has held that the doctrine should not be extended to foreign governments acting in a commercial capacity and "should not be extended to include the repudiation of a purely commercial obligation owed by a foreign sovereign or by one of its commercial instrumentalities." This interpretation recognizes that governments also may act in a private or commercial capacity and, when doing so, will be subjected to the same rules of law as are applicable to private individuals. Of course, a nationalization of assets probably will be considered an act in the "public interest" and immune from suit under the FSIA. The case that follows illustrates the application of a foreign sovereign's immunity from suit in this country.

Phaneuf v. Republic of Indonesia

106 F.3d 302 (9th Cir. 1997)

Plaintiff Curtis A. Phaneuf held several promissory notes allegedly issued by the National Defense Security Council of the Republic of Indonesia ("NDSC"). These notes were part of approximately 505 promissory notes created by several then-members of the NDSC and valued at over three billion U.S. dollars ("NDSC notes"). The notes bore the signatures of two NDSC members and the NDSC crest. The principal maker of the notes, Ibnu Hartomo, traded the "NDSC notes" for promissory notes issued by Hassan Zubaidi, a Syrian financier. Defendant Mawardi, then Indonesia's ambassador to Syria, participated in a signing ceremony in Damascus. At the ceremony Mawardi purportedly confirmed that Hartomo represented the Indonesian government and that the "NDSC notes" were "Official/Governmental." Zubaidi's notes were later discovered to be worthless.

The Republic of Indonesia claims that it did not know about the "NDSC notes" until later, at which time it promptly determined that these notes were unauthorized and invalid under Indonesian law. The NDSC's Secretary General informed Bank Indonesia that neither the NDSC nor any of its officials had authority to issue promissory notes and that the "NDSC notes" were invalid. Bank Indonesia then sent communications to financial institutions advising that Indonesia had detected unauthorized promissory notes allegedly issued by the NDSC. The NDSC issued a press release which disavowed NDSC responsibility for the notes, stating that responsibility lay with the persons who signed the notes. Bank Indonesia has continuously refused to honor the notes.

Phaneuf brought this action to enforce payment on the notes in his possession. The defendants moved to dismiss based on lack of subject matter jurisdiction under the Foreign Sovereign Immunities Act ("FSIA"). The district court denied the defendants' motion to dismiss, stating that defendants had not established a prima facie case of immunity under the FSIA.

BEEZER, J.: The Republic of Indonesia, the National Defense Security Council of the Republic of Indonesia and H.A. Chalid Mawardi (collectively "defendants") appeal the district court's order denying the defendants' motion to dismiss on the basis of sovereign immunity.

The FSIA is the sole basis of subject matter jurisdiction over suits involving foreign states and their agencies and instrumentalities. Under the FSIA, foreign states are immune from suit unless one of the enumerated exceptions to the Act applies.

The district court held that it currently had subject matter jurisdiction, but stated that it might revisit the issue later in the trial based on further discovery. Subject matter jurisdiction under the FSIA, however, must be decided before the suit can proceed. Immunity under the FSIA is not only immunity from liability, but immunity from suit. The district court improvidently postponed its final determination of subject matter jurisdiction under the FSIA.

The district court denied the defendants' motion to dismiss holding that the defendants had not established a prima facie case of immunity. In its order, the district court stated that defendants failed to show that the "acts complained of arise out of a public act." Defendants had argued to the district court that the commercial activity exception to the FSIA did not apply because they had not participated in the issuance of the promissory notes. The district court concluded that the defendants could not consistently argue that they are entitled to immunity (as a foreign sovereign for their sovereign acts) [under] the FSIA and, at the same time, argue that the acts alleged were not sovereign so as to defeat its exceptions.

We, however, have never required a defendant to establish that a plaintiff's claim arose from a public act.

Requiring a foreign state to prove a public act conflicts with the plain language of the statute: A foreign state is immune from suit unless one of the enumerated exceptions applies.

Moreover, requiring a prima facie showing of a public act would prevent the defendants here from asserting a valid argument against the application of the commercial activity exception. The language of the commercial activity exception requires not only that there be "commercial activity," but also that there be commercial activity "of the foreign state." Defendants should be permitted to argue against the application of the exception on the grounds that they did not act: That there was no "commercial activity of the foreign state."

We conclude that the FSIA does not require the defendants to prove a public act to establish a prima facie case of immunity. Instead, they are entitled to a presumption of immunity if they are foreign states within the meaning of the Act. As conceded by Phaneuf, both Indonesia and the NDSC quality as foreign states under the FSIA. The district court erred in determining that the Republic of Indonesia and the NDSC had not established a prima facie case of sovereign immunity.

Because the defendants have established a prima facie case of immunity, the burden of production shifts to the plaintiff to offer evidence that an exception applies. Phaneuf submitted affidavits and other evidence to support the theory that the NDSC members had either actual or apparent authority to issue the promissory notes. Phaneuf asserts that defendants' actions fall within the commercial activity exception.

Because Phaneuf offered evidence that the commercial activity exception applies, the defendants bear the burden of proving by a preponderance of the evidence that the exception does not apply. The issuance of sovereign debt is a commercial act which falls within the exception claimed by Phaneuf. Defendants maintain, however, that the commercial activity exception does not apply because they are not responsible for the issuance of the notes. They contend there was no "commercial activity of the foreign state." Defendants argue they are not bound by the actions of the former NDSC members or Ambassador Mawardi because these government officers exceeded the scope of their authority in issuing and certifying the validity of the notes. The question is whether an agent of a foreign state must have acted with actual authority to invoke the commercial activity exception against a foreign state, or whether apparent authority suffices.

When an agent acts beyond the scope of his authority, however, that agent is not doing business which the sovereign has empowered him to do. If the foreign state has not empowered its agent to act, the agent's unauthorized act cannot be attributed to the foreign state; there is no "activity of the foreign state."

We hold that an agent must have acted with actual authority in order to invoke the commercial activity exception against a foreign state. We express no opinion as to whether the issuers of the "NDSC notes" or Ambassador Mawardi acted with actual authority. We remand to the district court to determine whether the commercial activity exception applies to the defendants. [*So ordered*].

Case Questions

1. In order to sue a foreign government under the FSIA, what must a plaintiff show?

2. What is the rationale for the "commercial activity" exception to the FSIA?

3. Why is the issue of the authority of the agents critical to resolving this case?

13. Suing Foreign Firms in the United States

As foreign products and technology are imported into the United States, disputes may arise over either the terms of contract or the performance of the goods. In order to sue a foreign firm in the United States, the Supreme Court recently has held that the plaintiff must establish "minimum contacts" between the foreign defendant and the forum court. The plaintiff must demonstrate that exercise of personal jurisdiction over the defendant "does not offend traditional notions of fair play and substantial justice."

Once the plaintiff decides to sue in the United States, he or she also must comply with the terms of the Hague Service Convention when serving the foreign defendant notice of the lawsuit. The Hague Service Convention is a treaty that was formulated "to provide a simpler way to serve process abroad, to assure that defendants sued in foreign jurisdictions would receive actual and timely notice of suit, and to facilitate proof of service abroad." Many countries, including the United States, have approved the convention. The primary requirement of the agreement is to require each nation to establish a central authority to process requests for service of documents from other countries. After the central authority receives the request in proper form, it must serve the documents by a method prescribed by the internal law of the receiving state or by a method designated by the requester and compatible with the law.

14. International Arbitration

International businesses now are focusing on the need for new methods of resolving international commercial disputes and, as a result, are frequently resorting to the use of arbitration. The advantages of arbitration in domestic transactions, previously discussed in Chapter 3, are more pronounced in international transactions where differences in languages and legal systems make litigation costs still more costly.

The United Nations Convention on the Recognition and Enforcement of Foreign Arbitral Awards of 1958 (New York Convention), which has been adopted in more than fifty countries, encourages the use of arbitration in commercial agreements made by companies in the signatory countries. Under the New York Convention it is easier to compel arbitration, where previously agreed upon by the parties, and to enforce the arbitrator's award once a decision has been reached.

Once the parties to an international transaction have agreed to arbitrate disputes between them, the U.S. courts are reluctant to disturb that agreement. In the case of *Mitsubishi Motors v. Soler Chrysler-Plymouth* (473 U.S. 614 [1985]) the Supreme Court upheld an international agreement even where it required the parties to arbitrate all disputes, including federal antitrust claims. The Court decided that the international character of the undertaking required enforcement of the arbitration clause even as to the antitrust claims normally heard in a U.S. court.

In the following case, the Court reaffirmed its willingness to enforce foreign arbitration clauses.

Vimar Seguros y Reaseguros, S.A. v. M/V Sky Reefer

115 S.Ct. 2322 (1995)

After a New York fruit distributor's produce was damaged in transit from Morocco to Massachusetts aboard respondent vessel, petitioner insurer paid the distributor's claim, and they both sued respondents under the standard form bill of lading tendered to the distributor by its Moroccan supplier. Respondents moved to stay the action and compel arbitration in Tokyo under the bill of lading's foreign arbitration clause and the Federal Arbitration Act (FAA). The District Court granted the motion, rejecting the argument of petitioner and the distributor that the arbitration clause was unenforceable under the FAA because of the Carriage of Goods by Sea Act (COGSA) in that the inconvenience and costs of proceeding in Japan would "lessen . . . liability" in the sense that COGSA prohibits. In affirming the order to arbitrate, the First Circuit expressed grave doubt whether a foreign arbitration clause lessened liability, but assumed the clause was invalid under COGSA and resolved the conflict between the statutes in the FAA's favor.

KENNEDY, J.: This case requires us to interpret the Carriage of Goods by Sea Act (COGSA), as it relates to a contract requiring arbitration in a foreign country. The question is whether a foreign arbitration clause in a bill of lading is invalid under COGSA because it lessens liability in the sense that COGSA prohibits.

The contract at issue in this case is a standard form bill of lading to evidence the purchase of a shipload of Moroccan oranges and lemons. The purchaser was Bacchus Associates (Bacchus), a New York partnership that distributes fruit at wholesale throughout the Northeastern United States. Bacchus dealt with Galaxie, a Moroccan fruit supplier. Bacchus contracted with Galaxie to purchase the shipload of fruit and chartered a ship to transport it from Morocco to Massachusetts. The ship was the M/V Sky Reefer, a refrigerated cargo ship owned by M.H. Maritima, S.A., a Panamanian company, and time-chartered to Nichiro Gyogyo Kaisha, Ltd., a Japanese company. Stevedores hired by Galaxie loaded and stowed the cargo. As is customary in these types of transactions, when it received the cargo from Galaxie, Nichiro as carrier issued a form bill of lading to Galaxie as shipper and consignee. Once the ship set sail from Morocco, Galaxie tendered the bill of lading to Bacchus according to the terms of a letter of credit posted in Galaxie's favor.

Among the rights and responsibilities set out in the bill of lading were arbitration and choice-of-law clauses. Clause 3, entitled "Governing Law and Arbitration," provided:

"(1) The contract evidenced by or contained in this Bill of Lading shall be governed by the Japanese law."

"(2) Any dispute arising from this Bill of Lading shall be referred to arbitration in Tokyo by the Tokyo Maritime Arbitration Commission (TOMAC) of The Japan Shipping Exchange, Inc., in accordance with the rules of TOMAC and any amendment thereto, and

the award given by the arbitrators shall be final and binding on both parties."

When the vessel's hatches were opened for discharge in Massachusetts, Bacchus discovered that thousands of boxes of oranges had shifted in the cargo holds, resulting in over $1 million damage. Bacchus received $733,442.90 compensation from petitioner Vimar Seguros, Bacchus' marine cargo insurer, that became subrogated to Bacchus' rights. . . .

As the Court observed in *The Bremen v. Zapata Off-Shore Co.*, 92 S. Ct. 1907, when it enforced a foreign forum selection clause, the historical judicial resistance to foreign forum selection clauses "has little place in an era when . . . businesses once essentially local now operate in world markets. The expansion of American business and industry will hardly be encouraged," we explained, "if, notwithstanding solemn contracts, we insist on a parochial concept that all disputes must be resolved under our laws and in our courts."

That the forum here is arbitration only heightens the irony of petitioner's argument, for the FAA is also based in part on an international convention, the United Nations Convention on the Recognition and Enforcement of Foreign Arbitral Awards, intended "to encourage the recognition and enforcement of commercial arbitration agreements in international contracts and to unify the standards by which agreements to arbitrate are observed and arbitral awards are enforced in the signatory countries." The FAA requires enforcement of arbitration agreements in contracts that involve interstate commerce. . . .

If the United States is to be able to gain the benefits of international accords and have a role as a trusted partner in multilateral endeavors, its courts should be most cautious before interpreting its domestic legislation in such manner as to violate international agreements. That concern counsels against construing

COGSA to nullify foreign arbitration clauses because of inconvenience to the plaintiff or insular distrust of the ability of foreign arbitrators to apply the law.

Petitioner [also argues] against enforcement of the Japanese arbitration clause [because] there is no guarantee foreign arbitrators will apply COGSA. This objection raises a concern of substance. The central guarantee of COGSA is that the terms of a bill of lading may not relieve the carrier of the obligations or diminish the legal duties specified by the Act. The relevant question, therefore, is whether the substantive law to be applied will reduce the carrier's obligations to the cargo owner below what COGSA guarantees.

Petitioner argues that the arbitrators will follow the Japanese Hague Rules, which, petitioner contends, lessen respondents' liability in at least one significant respect. The Japanese version of the Hague Rules, it is said, provides the carrier with a defense based on the acts or omissions of the stevedores hired by the shipper.

Whatever the merits of petitioner's comparative reading of COGSA and its Japanese counterpart, its claim is premature. At this stage it is not established what law the arbitrators will apply to petitioner's claims or that petitioner will receive diminished protection as a result. The arbitrators may conclude that COGSA applies of its own force or that Japanese law does not apply so that, under another clause of the bill of lading, COGSA controls. Respondents seek only to enforce the arbitration agreement. The district court has retained jurisdiction over the case and will have the opportunity at the award-enforcement stage to en-sure that the legitimate interest in the enforcement of the . . . laws has been addressed.

Were there no subsequent opportunity for review and were we persuaded that the choice-of-forum and choice-of-law clauses operated in tandem as a prospective waiver of a party's right to pursue statutory remedies . . ., we would have little hesitation in condemning the agreement as against public policy. Under the circumstances of this case, however, the First Circuit was correct to reserve judgment on the choice-of-law question, as it must be decided in the first instance by the arbitrator. As the District Court has retained jurisdiction, mere speculation that the foreign arbitrators might apply Japanese law which, depending on the proper construction of COGSA, might reduce respondents' legal obligations, does not in and of itself lessen liability under COGSA.

Because we hold that foreign arbitration clauses in bills of lading are not invalid under COGSA in all circumstances, both the FAA and COGSA may be given full effect. The judgment of the Court of Appeals is [*affirmed*], and the case is remanded for further proceedings consistent with this opinion. It is so ordered.

Case Questions

1. Why does the Court favor arbitration clauses in international disputes?

2. Why is the petitioner concerned about the application of Japanese law?

3. Why is the petitioner's claim that there is a conflict between COGSA and Japanese law premature?

The advantages of arbitrating international disputes are many. The arbitration process likely will be more streamlined and easier for the parties to understand than litigating the dispute in a foreign court. Moreover, the parties can avoid the unwanted publicity that often results in open court proceedings. Finally, the parties can agree, before the dispute even arises, on a neutral and objective third party to act as the arbitrator. Several organizations, such as the International Chamber of Commerce in Paris and the Court of International Arbitration in London, provide arbitration services for international disputes.

Key Terms

Bill of lading   415
Convention on the International Sale of Goods (CISG)   412
European Union (EU)   413
Export controls   419

Expropriation   419
Foreign Corrupt Practices Act (FCPA)   422
Foreign Sovereign Immunities Act   426
Foreign subsidiary   418
Franchise   418

Review Questions and Problems

International Law and Organizations

1. *Sources of International Law*
   (a) What are the essential differences between the International Court of Justice and the U.S. Supreme Court?
   (b) How does the ICJ determine international law?

2. *International Organizations and Agreements Affecting Trade*
   (a) What are the three major principles of the World Trade Organization?
   (b) How would adherence to those principles improve international trade?

3. *European Union*
   (a) Describe the organization of the European Union?
   (b) How is it similar to the structure of the government of the United States?

4. *The North American Free Trade Agreement*
   What are some of the key benefits that the North American Free Trade Agreement has produced for member countries?

Methods of Transacting International Business

5. *Foreign Sales*
   BMW, a German buyer, opens an irrevocable letter of credit in favor of Goodyear, an American seller, for the purchase of tires on BMW model automobiles. BMW confirms the letter of credit with Goodyear's bank in New York, Bankers Trust. Under what circumstances will the seller obtain payment?

6. *Licenses or Franchises*
   (a) How should a licensor protect its investment in a foreign country?
   (b) Why is licensing less risky for the seller than direct foreign investment?

7. *Direct Foreign Investment*
   What are the advantages and disadvantages of a joint venture with a foreign firm?

Risks Involved in International Trade

8. *Expropriation and Nationalization*
   Explain the "modern traditional theory" of compensation regarding the taking of private property by a foreign government?

9. *Export Controls*
   (a) Why is the future of export controls in doubt?
   (b) What are some of the dangers associated with having an inadequate export control regime?

10. *Pressures for Bribes*
    XYZ Company, a U.S. firm, is seeking to obtain business in Indonesia. XYZ learns that one of its major competitors, a German firm, is offering a key Indonesian governmental official a trip around the world for choosing their firm in the transaction. Can XYZ report this bribe to the Department of Justice and have the German firm prosecuted under the Foreign Corrupt Practices Act?

11. *Conflicts With U.S. Antitrust Laws*
    What are some of the practical and political dangers associated with the United States attempting to apply its laws to business activity in foreign nations?

Resolving International Disputes

12. *Suing Foreign Governments in the United States*
    Belgium arrests an American citizen, while he is visiting Brussels, on suspicion that he is an international drug smuggler. After a thorough investigation, Belgium realizes that it has arrested the wrong person. Can the American citizen successfully sue Belgium in the United States for false arrest?

13. *Suing Foreign Firms in the United States*
    What is the primary requirement of the Hague Service Convention and how does it help a plaintiff when filing a lawsuit?

14. *International Arbitration*
    Why are arbitration clauses in international agreements favored by the courts and likely to be enforced when conflicts arise between the contracting parties?

Terminology Review

For each term in the left-hand column, match the most appropriate description in the right-hand column.

1. International Court of Justice

2. World Trade Organization

3. CISG

4. Letter of credit

5. License

6. Expropriation

7. Export Controls

8. FCPA

9. Sovereign Immunity

10. Arbitration Agreements

a. seizure of foreign-owned private property by a government

b. the traditional place for ascertaining what is public international law

c. ensures payment and delivery of goods in international transactions

d. the umbrella organization for regulating international trade

e. governmental restrictions placed on the sale of products and technology abroad

f. typical method for controlling the transfer of information regarding a product or service

g. document followed by many nations that outlines standard international contract rules for the sale of goods

h. an increasingly common method of resolving international disputes

i. law designed to stop bribery of foreign officials by U.S. firms

j. provides immunity for foreign governments from lawsuits in the United States

APPENDIX

THE CONSTITUTION OF THE UNITED STATES OF AMERICA

We, the People of the United States, in Order to form a more perfect Union, establish Justice, insure domestic Tranquility, provide for the common defense, promote the general Welfare, and secure the Blessings of Liberty to ourselves and our Posterity, do ordain and establish this Constitution for the United States of America.

Article I

Section 1. All legislative Powers herein granted shall be vested in a Congress of the United States, which shall consist of a Senate and House of Representatives.

Section 2. The House of Representatives shall be composed of Members chosen every second Year by the People of the several States, and the Electors in each State shall have the Qualifications requisite for Electors of the most numerous Branch of the State Legislature.

No Person shall be a Representative who shall not have attained the Age of twenty five years, and been seven Years a Citizen of the United States, and who shall not, when elected, be an Inhabitant of that State in which he shall be chosen.

Representatives and direct Taxes shall be apportioned among the several States which may be included within this Union, according to their respective Numbers, which shall be determined by adding the whole Number of free Persons, including those bound to Service for a Term of Years, and excluding Indians not taxed, three-fifths of all other Persons. The actual Enumeration shall be made within three Years after the first Meeting of the Congress of the United States, and within every subsequent Term of ten Years, in such Manner as they shall by Law direct. The Number of Representatives shall not exceed one for every thirty Thousand, but each State shall have at Least one Representative; and until such enumeration shall be made, the State of New Hampshire shall be entitled to chuse three, Massachusetts eight, Rhode Island and Providence Plantations one, Connecticut five, New-York six, New Jersey four, Pennsylvania eight, Delaware one, Maryland six, Virginia ten, North Carolina five, South Carolina five, and Georgia three.

When vacancies happen in the Representation from any State, the Executive Authority thereof shall issue Writs of Election to fill such Vacancies.

The House of Representatives shall chuse their Speaker and other Officers; and shall have the sole Power of Impeachment.

Section 3. The Senate of the United States shall be composed of two Senators from each State, chosen by the Legislature thereof, for six Years; and each Senator shall have one Vote.

Immediately after they shall be assembled in Consequence of the Election, they shall be divided as equally as may be into three Classes. The Seats of the Senators of the first Class shall be vacated at the Expiration of the second Year, of the second Class at the Expiration of the fourth Year, and of the third Class at the Expiration of the sixth Year, so that one third may be chosen every second Year; and if Vacancies happen by Resignation, or otherwise, during the Recess of the Legislature of any State, the Executive thereof may make temporary Appointments until the next Meeting of the Legislature, which shall then fill such Vacancies.

No Person shall be a Senator who shall not have attained to the Age of thirty Years, and been nine Years a Citizen of the United States, and who shall not, when elected, be an Inhabitant of that State for which he shall be chosen.

The Vice President of the United States shall be President of the Senate, but shall have no Vote, unless they be equally divided.

The Senate shall chuse their other Officers, and also a President pro tempore, in the Absence of the Vice President, or when he shall exercise the Office of the President of the United States.

The Senate shall have the sole Power to try all Impeachments. When sitting for that Purpose, they shall be on Oath or Affirmation. When the President of the United States is tried, the Chief Justice shall preside: and no Person shall be convicted without the Concurrence of two-thirds of the Members present.

Judgment in Cases of Impeachment shall not extend further than to removal from Office, and disqualification to hold and enjoy any Office of honor, Trust or Profit under the United States: but the Party convicted shall nevertheless be liable and subject to Indictment, Trial, Judgment and Punishment, according to Law.

Section 4.   The Times, Places and Manner of holding Elections for Senators and Representatives, shall be prescribed in each State by the Legislature thereof: but the Congress may at any time by Law make or alter such Regulations, except as to the Places of chusing Senators.

The Congress shall assemble at least once in every Year, and such Meeting shall be on the first Monday in December, unless they shall by Law appoint a different Day.

Section 5.   Each House shall be the Judge of the Elections, Returns and Qualifications of its own Members, and a Majority of each shall constitute a Quorum to do Business; but a smaller Number may adjourn from day to day, and may be authorized to compel the Attendance of absent Members, in such Manner, and under such Penalties as each House may provide.

Each House may determine the Rules of its Proceedings, punish its Members for disorderly Behaviour, and, with the concurrence of two thirds, expel a Member.

Each House shall keep a Journal of its Proceedings, and from time to time publish the same, excepting such Parts as may in their Judgment require Secrecy; and the Yeas and Nays of the Members of either House on any question shall, at the Desire of one-fifth of those Present, be entered on the Journal.

Neither House, during the Session of Congress, shall, without the Consent of the other, adjourn for more than three days, nor to any other Place than that in which the two Houses shall be sitting.

Section 6.   The Senators and Representatives shall receive a Compensation for their Services, to be ascertained by Law, and paid out of the Treasury of the United States. They shall in all Cases, except Treason, Felony and Breach of the Peace, be privileged from Arrest during their Attendance at the Session of their respective Houses, and in going to and returning from the same; and for any Speech or Debate in either House, they shall not be questioned in any other Place.

No Senator or Representative shall, during the Time for which he was elected, be appointed to any civil Office under the Authority of the United States, which shall have been created, or the Emoluments whereof shall have been encreased during such time; and no Person holding any Office under the United States, shall be a Member of either House during his Continuance in Office.

Section 7.   All Bills for raising Revenue shall originate in the House of Representatives; but the Senate may propose or concur with Amendments as on other Bills.

Every Bill which shall have passed the House of Representatives and the Senate, shall, before it become a Law, be presented to the President of the United States; If he approve, he shall sign it, but if not he shall return it, with his Objections to that house in which it shall have originated, who shall enter the Objections at large on their Journal, and proceed to reconsider it. If after such Reconsideration two thirds of that House shall agree to pass the Bill, it shall be sent, together with the Objections, to the other House, by which it shall likewise be reconsidered, and if approved by two thirds of that House, it shall become a Law. But in all such Cases the Votes of both Houses shall be determined by Yeas and Nays, and the Names of the Persons voting for and against the Bill shall be entered on the Journal of each House respectively. If any Bill shall not be returned by the President within ten Days (Sundays excepted) after it shall have been presented to him, the Same shall be a Law, in like Manner as if he had signed it, unless the Congress by their Adjournment prevent its Return, in which Case it shall not be a Law.

Every Order, Resolution, or Vote to which the Concurrence of the Senate and House of Representatives may be necessary (except on a question of Adjournment) shall be presented to the President of the United States; and before the Same shall take Effect, shall be approved by him, or being disapproved by him, shall be repassed by two thirds of the Senate and House of Representatives, according to the Rules and Limitations prescribed in the Case of a Bill.

Section 8. The Congress shall have the Power to lay and collect Taxes, Duties, Imposts and Excises, to pay the Debts and provide for the common Defence and general Welfare of the United States; but all Duties, Imposts and Excises shall be uniform throughout the United States;

To borrow Money on the credit of the United States;

To regulate Commerce with foreign Nations, and among the several States, and with the Indian Tribes;

To establish an uniform Rule of Naturalization, and uniform Laws on the subject of Bankruptcies throughout the United States;

To coin Money, regulate the Value thereof, and of foreign Coin, and fix the Standard of Weights and Measures;

To provide for the Punishment of counterfeiting the Securities and current Coin of the United States;

To establish Post Offices and post Roads;

To promote the Progress of Science and useful Arts, by securing for limited Times to Authors and Inventors the exclusive Right to their respective Writings and Discoveries;

To constitute Tribunals inferior to the supreme Court;

To define and punish Piracies and Felonies committed on the high Seas, and Offenses against the Law of Nations;

To declare War, grant Letters of Marque and Reprisal, and make Rules concerning Captures on Land and Water;

To raise and support Armies, but no Appropriation of Money to that Use shall be for a longer Term than two Years;

To provide and maintain a Navy;

To make Rules for the Government and Regulation of the land and naval Forces;

To provide for calling forth the Militia to execute the Laws of the Union, suppress Insurrections and repel Invasions;

To provide for organizing, arming and disciplining, the Militia, and for governing such Part of them as may be employed in the Service of the United States, reserving to the States respectively, the Appointment of the Officers, and the Authority of training the Militia according to the discipline prescribed by Congress;

To exercise exclusive Legislation in all Cases whatsoever, over such District (not exceeding ten Miles square) as may, by Cession of particular States, and the Acceptance of Congress, become the Seat of the Government of the United States, and to exercise like Authority over all Places purchased by the Consent of the Legislature of the State in which

the Same shall be, for the Erection of Forts, Magazines, Arsenals, dock-Yards, and other needful buildings;— And

To make all Laws which shall be necessary and proper for carrying into Execution the foregoing Powers, and all other Powers vested by the Constitution in the Government of the United States, or in any Department or Officer thereof.

Section 9. The Migration or Importation of such Persons as any of the States now existing shall think proper to admit, shall not be prohibited by the Congress prior to the Year one thousand eight hundred and eight, but a Tax or Duty may be imposed on such Importation, not exceeding ten dollars for each Person.

The Privilege of the Writ of Habeas Corpus shall not be suspended, unless when in Cases of Rebellion or Invasion the public Safety may require it.

No Bill of Attainder or ex post facto Law shall be passed.

No Capitation, or other direct, Tax shall be laid, unless in Proportion to the Census or Enumeration herein before directed to be taken.

No Tax or Duty shall be laid on Articles exported from any State.

No Preference shall be given by any Regulation of Commerce or Revenue to the Ports of one State over those of another: nor shall Vessels bound to, or from, one State, be obliged to enter, clear, or pay Duties in another.

No Money shall be drawn from the Treasury, but in Consequence of Appropriations made by Law; and a regular Statement and Account of the Receipts and Expenditures of all public Money shall be published from time to time.

No Title of Nobility shall be granted by the United States: And no Person holding any Office or Profit or Trust under them, shall, without the Consent of the Congress, accept of any present, Emolument, Office, or Title, of any kind whatever, from any King, Prince, or foreign State.

Section 10. No State shall enter into any Treaty, Alliance, or Confederation; grant Letters of Marque and Reprisal; coin Money; emit Bills of Credit; make any Thing but gold and silver Coin a Tender in Payment of Debts; pass any Bill of Attainder, ex post facto Law, or Law impairing the Obligation of Contracts, or grant any Title of Nobility.

No State shall, without the Consent of the Congress, lay any Imposts or Duties on Imports or Exports, except what may be absolutely necessary for executing its inspection Laws: and the net Produce of all Duties and Imposts, laid by any State on Imports or Exports, shall be for the Use of the Treasury of the United States; and all such Laws shall be subject to the Revision and Control of the Congress.

No State shall, without the Consent of Congress, lay any Duty of Tonnage, keep Troops, or Ships of War in time of Peace, enter into any Agreement or Compact with another State, or with a foreign Power, or engage in War, unless actually invaded, or in such imminent Danger as will not admit of delay.

Article II

Section 1. The executive Power shall be vested in a President of the United States of America. He shall hold Office during the Term of four Years, and, together with the Vice President, chosen for the same Term, be elected as follows:

Each State shall appoint, in such Manner as the Legislature thereof may direct, a Number of Electors, equal to the whole Number of Senators and Representatives to which the State may be entitled in the Congress: but no Senator or Representative, or Person holding an Office or Trust or Profit under the United States, shall be appointed an Elector.

The Electors shall meet in their respective States, and vote by Ballot for two Persons, of whom one at least shall not be an Inhabitant of the same State with Themselves. And they shall make a List of all the Persons voted for, and of the Number of Votes for each; which List they shall sign and certify, and transmit sealed to the Seat of the Government of the United States, directed to the President of the Senate. The President of the Senate shall, in the Presence of the Senate and House of Representatives, open all the Certificates, and the Votes shall then be counted. The Person having the greatest Number of Votes shall be the President, if such Number be a Majority of the whole Number of Electors appointed; and if there be more than one who have such Majority, and have an equal Number of Votes, then the House of Representatives shall immediately chuse by Ballot one of them for President; and if no Person have a Majority, then from the five highest on the List the said House shall in like Manner chuse the President. But in chusing the President, the Votes shall be taken by States, the Representation from each State having one Vote; a quorum for this Purpose shall consist of a Member or Members from two thirds of the States, and a Majority of all the States shall be necessary to a Choice. In every Case, after the Choice of the President, the Person having the greatest Number of Votes of the Electors shall be the Vice President. But if there should remain two or more who have equal Votes, the Senate shall chuse from them by Ballot the Vice President.

The Congress may determine the Time of chusing the Electors, and the Day on which they shall give their Votes; which Day shall be the same throughout the United States.

No Person except a natural born Citizen, or a Citizen of the United States, at the time of the Adoption of this Constitution, shall be eligible to the Office of President; neither shall any Person be eligible to that Office who shall not have attained to the Age of thirty five Years, and been fourteen Years a Resident within the United States.

In Case of the Removal of the President from Office, or of his Death, Resignation, or Inability to discharge the Powers and Duties of the said Office, the Same shall devolve on the Vice President, and the Congress may by Law provide for the Case of Removal, Death, Resignation, or Inability, both of the President and Vice President, declaring what Officer shall then act as President, and such Officer shall act accordingly, until the Disability be removed, or a President shall be elected.

The President shall, at stated Times, receive for his Services, a Compensation, which shall neither be increased nor diminished during the Period for which he shall have been elected, and he shall not receive within that Period any other Emolument from the United States, or any of them.

Before he enter on the Execution of his Office, he shall take the following Oath or Affirmation:—"I do solemnly swear (or affirm) that I will faithfully execute the Office of President of the United States, and will to the best of my Ability, preserve, protect and defend the Constitution of the United States."

Section 2. The President shall be Commander in Chief of the Army and Navy of the United States, and of the Militia of the several States, when called into the actual Service of the United States; he may require the Opinion, in writing, of the principal Officer in each of the executive Departments, upon any Subject relating to the Duties of their respective Offices, and he shall have Power to grant Reprieves and Pardons for Offenses against the United States, except in Cases of Impeachment.

He shall have Power, by and with the Advice and Consent of the Senate, to make Treaties, providing two thirds of the Senators present concur; and he shall nominate, and by and with the Advice and Consent of the Senate, shall appoint Ambassadors, other public Ministers and Consuls, Judges of the supreme Court, and all other Officers of the United States, whose Appointments are not herein otherwise provided for, and which shall be established by Law: but the Congress may by Law vest the Appointment of such inferior Officers, as they think proper, in the

President alone, in the Courts of Law, or in the Heads of Departments.

The President shall have the Power to fill up all Vacancies that may happen during the Recess of the Senate, by granting Commissions which shall expire at the End of their next Session.

Section 3. He shall from time to time give to the Congress Information of the State of the Union, and recommend to their Consideration such Measures as he shall judge necessary and expedient; he may, on extraordinary Occasions, convene both Houses, or either of them, and in Case of Disagreement between them, with Respect to the Time of Adjournment, he may adjourn them to such Time as he shall think proper; he shall receive Ambassadors and other public Ministers; he shall take Care that the Laws be faithfully executed, and shall Commission all the Officers of the United States.

Section 4. The President, Vice President, and all civil Officers of the United States, shall be removed from Office on Impeachment for, and Conviction of, Treason, Bribery, or other high Crimes and Misdemeanors.

Article III

Section 1. The judicial Power of the United States, shall be vested in one supreme Court, and in such inferior Courts as the Congress may from time to time ordain and establish. The Judges, both of the supreme and inferior Courts, shall hold their Offices during good Behaviour, and shall, at stated Times, receive for their Services, a Compensation, which shall not be diminished during their Continuance in Office.

Section 2. The judicial Power shall extend to all Cases, in Law and Equity, arising under this Constitution, the Laws of the United States, and Treaties made, or which shall be made, under their Authority;—to all Cases affecting Ambassadors, other public Ministers and Consuls;—to all Cases of admiralty and maritime Jurisdiction;—to Controversies to which the United States shall be a Party;—to Controversies between two or more States;—between a State and Citizens of another State;—between Citizens of different States;—between Citizens of the same State claiming Lands under Grants of different States, and between a State, or the Citizens thereof, and foreign States, Citizens or Subjects.

In all Cases affecting Ambassadors, other public Ministers and Consuls, and those in which a State shall be Party, the supreme Court shall have original Jurisdiction. In all the other Cases before mentioned, the supreme Court shall have appellate Jurisdiction, both as to Law and Fact, with such Exceptions, and under such Regulations as the Congress shall make.

The Trial of all Crimes, except in Cases of Impeachment, shall be by Jury; and such Trial shall be held in the State where the said Crimes shall have been committed; but when not committed within any State, the Trial shall be at such Place or Places as the Congress may by Law have directed.

Section 3. Treason against the United States, shall consist only in levying War against them, or in adhering to their Enemies, giving them Aid and Comfort. No Person shall be convicted of Treason unless on the Testimony of two Witnesses to the same overt Act, or on Confession in open Court.

The Congress shall have Power to declare the Punishment of Treason, but no Attainder of Treason shall work Corruption of Blood, or Forfeiture except during the Life of the Person attainted.

Article IV

Section 1. Full Faith and Credit shall be given in each State to the public Acts, Records, and judicial Proceedings of every other State. And the Congress may by general Laws prescribe the Manner in which such Acts, Records and Proceedings shall be proved, and the Effect thereof.

Section 2. The Citizens of each State shall be entitled to all Privileges and Immunities of Citizens in the several States.

A person charged in any State with Treason, Felony, or other Crime, who shall flee Justice, and be found in another State, shall on Demand of the executive Authority of the State from which he fled, be delivered up, to be removed to the State having Jurisdiction of the Crime.

No Person held to Service or Labour in one State, under the Laws thereof, escaping into another, shall, in Consequence of any Law or Regulation therein, be discharged from such Service or Labour, but shall be delivered up on Claim of the Party to whom such Service or Labour may be due.

Section 3. New States may be admitted by the Congress into this Union; but no new State shall be formed or erected within the Jurisdiction of any other State, nor any State be formed by the Junction of two or more States, or Parts of States, without the Consent of the Legislatures of the States concerned, as well as of the Congress.

The Congress shall have Power to dispose of and make all needful Rules and Regulations respecting the Territory or other Property belonging to the United States; and nothing in this Constitution shall be so construed as to Prejudice any Claims of the United States, or of any particular State.

Section 4. The United States shall guarantee to every State in this Union a Republican Form of Government, and shall protect each of them against Invasion; and on Application of the Legislature, or of the Executive (when the Legislature cannot be convened) against domestic Violence.

Article V

The Congress, whenever two thirds of both Houses shall deem it necessary, shall propose Amendments to this Constitution, or, on the Application of the Legislatures of two thirds of the several States, shall call a Convention for proposing Amendments, which, in either Case, shall be valid to all Intents and Purposes, as Part of this Constitution, when ratified by the Legislatures of three fourths of the several States, or by Conventions in three fourths thereof, as the one or the other Mode of Ratification may be proposed by the Congress; Provided that no Amendment which may be made prior to the Year One thousand eight hundred and eight shall in any Manner affect the first and fourth Clauses in the Ninth Section of the first Article; and that no State, without its Consent, shall be deprived of its equal Suffrage in the Senate.

Article VI

All Debts contracted and Engagements entered into, before the Adoption of this Constitution, shall be as valid against the United States under this Constitution, as under the Confederation.

This Constitution, and the Laws of the United States which shall be made in Pursuance thereof; and all Treaties made, or which shall be made, under the Authority of the United States, shall be the supreme Law of the Land; and the Judges in every State shall be bound thereby, any Thing in the Constitution or Laws of any State to the Contrary notwithstanding.

The Senators and Representatives before mentioned, and the Members of the several State Legislatures, and all executive and judicial Officers, both of the United States and of the several States, shall be bound by Oath or Affirmation, to support this Constitution; but no religious Test shall ever be required as a Qualification to any Office or public Trust under the United States.

Article VII

The Ratification of the Conventions of nine States, shall be sufficient for the Establishment of this Constitution between the States so ratifying the Same.

Amendment I [1791]

Congress shall make no law respecting an establishment of religion, or prohibiting the free exercise thereof; or abridging the freedom of speech, or of the press; or the right of the people peaceably to assemble, and to petition the Government for a redress of grievances.

Amendment II [1791]

A well regulated Militia, being necessary to the security for a free State, the right of the people to keep and bear Arms, shall not be infringed.

Amendment III [1791]

No Soldier shall, in time of peace be quartered in any house, without the consent of the Owner, nor in time of war, but in a manner to be prescribed by law.

Amendment IV [1791]

The right of the people to be secure in their persons, houses, papers, and effects, against unreasonable searches and seizures, shall not be violated, and no Warrants shall issue, but upon probable cause, supported by Oath or affirmation, and particularly describing the place to be searched, and the persons or things to be seized.

Amendment V [1791]

No person shall be held to answer for a capital, or otherwise infamous crime, unless on a presentment or indictment of a Grand Jury, except in cases arising in the land or naval forces, or in the Militia, when in actual service in time of War or public danger; nor shall any person be subject for the same offense to be twice put in jeopardy of life or limb; nor shall be compelled in any criminal case to be a witness against himself, nor be deprived of life, liberty, or property, without due process of law; nor shall private property be taken for public use without just compensation.

Amendment VI [1791]

In all criminal prosecutions, the accused shall enjoy the right to a speedy and public trial, by an impartial jury of the State and district wherein the crime shall have been committed, which district shall have been previously ascertained by law, and to be informed of the nature and cause of the accusation; to be confronted with the Witnesses against him; to have compulsory process for obtaining witnesses in his favor, and to have the Assistance of counsel for his defense.

Amendment VII [1791]

In Suits at common law, where the value in controversy shall exceed twenty dollars, the right of trial by jury shall be preserved, and no fact tried by a jury, shall be otherwise re-examined in any Court of the United States, than according to the rules of the common law.

Amendment VIII [1791]

Excessive bail shall not be required, nor excessive fines imposed, nor cruel and unusual punishments inflicted.

Amendment IX [1791]

The enumeration in the Constitution, of certain rights, shall not be construed to deny or disparage others retained by the people.

Amendment X [1791]

The powers not delegated to the United States by the Constitution, nor prohibited by it to the States, are reserved to the States respectively, or to the people.

Amendment XI [1798]

The Judicial power of the United States shall not be construed to extend to any suit in law or equity, commenced or prosecuted against one of the United States by Citizens of another State, or by Citizens or Subjects of any Foreign State.

Amendment XII [1804]

The Electors shall meet in their respective states and vote by ballot for President and Vice-President, one of whom, at least, shall not be an inhabitant of the same state with themselves; they shall name in their ballots the person voted for as President, and in distinct ballots the person voted for as Vice-President, and they shall make distinct lists of all persons voted for as President, and of all persons voted for as Vice-President, and of the number of votes for each, which lists they shall sign and certify, and transmit sealed to the seat of the government of the United States, directed to the President of the Senate;—The President of the Senate shall, in the presence of the Senate and House of Representatives, open all the certificates and the votes shall then be counted;—The person having the greatest number of votes for President, shall be the President, if such number be a majority of the whole number of Electors appointed; and if no person have such majority, then from the persons having the highest numbers not exceeding three on the list of those voted for as President, the House of Representatives shall choose immediately, by ballot, the President. But in choosing the President, the votes shall be taken by states, the representation from each state having one vote; a quorum for this purpose shall consist of a member or members from two-thirds of the states, and a majority of all the states shall be necessary to a choice. And if the House of Representatives shall not choose a President whenever the right of choice shall devolve upon them, before the fourth day of March next following, then the Vice-President shall act as President. The person having the greatest number of votes as Vice-President, shall be the Vice-President, if such number be a majority of the whole number of Electors appointed, and if no person have a majority, then from the two highest numbers on the list, the Senate shall choose the Vice-President; a quorum for the purpose shall consist of two-thirds of the whole number of Senators, and a majority of the whole number shall be necessary to a choice. But no person constitutionally ineligible to the office of President shall be eligible to that of the Vice-President of the United States.

Amendment XIII [1865]

Section 1. Neither slavery nor involuntary servitude, except as a punishment for crime whereof the party shall have been duly convicted, shall exist within the United States, or any place subject to their jurisdiction.

Section 2. Congress shall have power to enforce this article by appropriate legislation.

Amendment XIV [1868]

Section 1. All persons born or naturalized in the United States, and subject to the jurisdiction thereof, are citizens of the United States and of the State wherein they reside. No State shall make or enforce any law which shall abridge the privileges or immunities of citizens of the United States; nor shall any State deprive any person of life, liberty, or property, without due process of law; nor deny to any person within its jurisdiction the equal protection of the laws.

Section 2. Representatives shall be appointed among the several States according to their respective numbers, counting the whole number of persons in each State, excluding Indians not taxed. But when the right to vote at any election for the choice of electors for President and Vice President of the United States, Representatives in Congress, the Executive and Judicial officers of a State, or the members of the Legislature thereof, is denied to any of the male inhabitants of such State, being twenty-one years of age, and citizens of the United States, or in any way abridged, except for participation in rebellion, or other crime, the basis of representation therein shall be reduced in the proportion which the number of such male citizens shall bear to the whole number of male citizens twenty-one years of age in such State.

Section 3. No person shall be a Senator or Representative in Congress, or elector of President and Vice President, or hold any office, civil or military, under the United States, or under any State, who, having previously taken an oath, as a member of Congress, or as an officer of the United States, or as a member of any State legislature, or as an executive or judicial officer of any State, to support the Constitution of the United States, shall have engaged in insurrection or rebellion against the same, or given aid or comfort to the enemies thereof. But Congress may by a vote of two-thirds of each House, remove such disability.

Section 4. The validity of the public debt of the United States, authorized by law, including debts incurred for payment of pensions and bounties for services in suppressing insurrection or rebellion, shall not be questioned. But neither the United States nor any State shall assume or pay any debt or obligation incurred in aid of insurrection or rebellion against the United States, or any claim for the loss or emancipation of any slave; but all such debts, obligations and claims shall be held illegal and void.

Section 5. The Congress shall have the power to enforce, by appropriate legislation, the provisions of this article.

Amendment XV [1870]

Section 1. The right of citizens of the United States to vote shall not be denied or abridged by the United States or by any State on account of race, color, or previous condition of servitude.

Section 2. The Congress shall have power to enforce this article by appropriate legislation.

Amendment XVI [1913]

The Congress shall have power to lay and collect taxes on incomes, from whatever sources derived, without apportionment among the several States, and without regard to any census or enumeration.

Amendment XVII [1913]

The Senate of the United States shall be composed of two Senators from each State, elected by the people thereof, for six years; and each Senator shall have one vote. The electors in each State shall have the qualifications requisite for electors of the most numerous branch of the State legislatures.

When vacancies happen in the representation of any State in the Senate, the executive authority of such State shall issue writs of election to fill such vacancies: *Provided,* That the legislature of any State may empower the executive thereof to make temporary appointments until the people fill the vacancies by election as the legislature may direct.

This amendment shall not be so construed as to affect the election or term of any Senator chosen before it becomes valid as part of the Constitution.

Amendment XVIII [1919]

Section 1. After one year from the ratification of this article the manufacture, sale, or transportation of intoxicating liquors within, the importation thereof into, or the exportation thereof from the United States and all territory subject to the jurisdiction thereof for beverage purposes is hereby prohibited.

Section 2. The Congress and the several States shall have concurrent power to enforce this article by appropriate legislation.

Section 3. This article shall be inoperative unless it shall have been ratified as an amendment to the Constitution by the legislatures of the several States, as provided in the Constitution, within seven years from the date of the submission hereof to the States by the Congress.

Amendment XIX [1920]

The right of citizens of the United States to vote shall not be denied or abridged by the United States or by any State on account of sex.

Congress shall have power to enforce this article by appropriate legislation.

Amendment XX [1933]

Section 1. The terms of the President and the Vice President shall end at noon on the 20th day of January, and the terms of Senators and Representatives at noon on the 3d day of January, of the years in which such terms would have ended if this article had not been ratified; and the terms of their successors shall then begin.

Section 2. The Congress shall assemble at least once in every year, and such meeting shall begin at noon on the 3d day of January, unless they shall by law appoint a different day.

Section 3. If, at the time fixed for the beginning of the term of the President, the President elect shall have died, the Vice President elect shall become President. If a President shall not have been chosen before the time fixed for the beginning of his term, or if the President elect shall have failed to qualify, then the Vice President elect shall act as President until a President shall have qualified; and the Congress may by law provide for the case wherein neither a President elect nor a Vice President shall have qualified, declaring who shall then act as President, or the manner in which one who is to act shall be selected, and such person shall act accordingly until a President or Vice President shall have qualified.

Section 4. The Congress may by law provide for the case of the death of any of the persons from whom the House of Representatives may choose a President whenever the right of choice shall have devolved upon them, and for the case of the death of any of the persons from whom the Senate may choose a Vice President whenever the right of choice shall have devolved upon them.

Section 5. Sections 1 and 2 shall take effect on the 15th day of October following the ratification of this article.

Section 6. This article shall be inoperative unless it shall have been ratified as an amendment to the Constitution by the legislatures of three-fourths of the several States within seven years from the date of its submission.

Amendment XXI [1933]

Section 1. The eighteenth article of amendment to the Constitution of the United States is hereby repealed.

Section 2. The transportation or importation into any State, Territory, or possession of the United States for delivery or use therein of intoxicating liquors, in violation of the laws thereof, is hereby prohibited.

Section 3. This article shall be inoperative unless it shall have been ratified as an amendment to the Constitution by conventions in the several States, as provided in the Constitution, within seven years from the date of the submission hereof to the States by the Congress.

Amendment XXII [1951]

Section 1. No person shall be elected to the office of the President more than twice, and no person who has held the office of President, or acted as President, for more than two years of a term to which some other person was elected President shall be elected to the office of President more than once. But this Article shall not apply to any person holding the office of President when this Article was proposed by the Congress, and shall not prevent any person who may be holding the office of President, or acting as President, during the term within which this Article becomes operative from holding the office of President or acting as President during the remainder of such term.

Section 2. This article shall be inoperative unless it shall have been ratified as an amendment to the Constitution by the legislatures of three-fourths of the several States within seven years from the date of its submission to the States by the Congress.

Amendment XXIII [1961]

Section 1. The District constituting the seat of Government of the United States shall appoint in such manner as the Congress may direct:

A number of electors of President and Vice President equal to the whole number of Senators and Representatives in Congress to which the District would be entitled if it were a State, but in no event more than the least populous State; they shall be in addition to those appointed by the States, but they shall be considered, for the purposes of the election of President and Vice President, to be electors appointed by a State; and they shall meet in the

District and perform such duties as provided by the twelfth article of amendment.

Section 2.   The Congress shall have power to enforce this article by appropriate legislation.

Amendment XXIV [1964]

Section 1.   The right of citizens of the United States to vote in any primary or other election for President or Vice President, for electors for President or Vice President, or for Senator or Representative in Congress, shall not be denied or abridged by the United States or any State by reason of failure to pay poll tax or any other tax.

Section 2.   The Congress shall have power to enforce this article by appropriate legislation.

Amendment XXV [1967]

Section 1.   In case of the removal of the President from office or of his death or resignation, the Vice President shall become President.

Section 2.   Whenever there is a vacancy in the office of the Vice President, the President shall nominate a Vice President who shall take the office upon confirmation by a majority vote of both Houses of Congress.

Section 3.   Whenever the President transmits to the President pro tempore of the Senate and the Speaker of the House of Representatives his written declaration that he is unable to discharge the powers and duties of his office, and until he transmits to them a written declaration to the contrary, such powers and duties shall be discharged by the Vice President as Acting President.

Section 4.   Whenever the Vice President and a majority of either the principal officers of the executive departments or of such other body as Congress may by Law provide, transmit to the President pro tempore of the Senate and the Speaker of the House of Representatives their written declaration that the President is unable to discharge the powers and duties of his office, the Vice President shall immediately assume the powers and duties of the office as Acting President.

Thereafter, when the President transmits to the President pro tempore of the Senate and the Speaker of the House of Representatives his written declaration that no inability exists, he shall resume the powers and duties of his office unless the Vice President and a majority of either the principal officers of the executive departments or of such other body as Congress may by law provide, transmit within four days to the President pro tempore of the Senate and the Speaker of the House of Representatives their written declaration that the President is unable to discharge the powers and duties of his office. Thereupon Congress shall decide the issue, assembling within forty-eight hours for that purpose if not in session. If the Congress, within twenty-one days after receipt of the latter written declaration, or, if Congress is not in session, within twenty-one days after Congress is required to assemble, determines by two-thirds vote of both Houses that the President is unable to discharge the powers and duties of his office, the Vice President shall continue to discharge the same as Acting President; otherwise, the President shall resume the powers and duties of his office.

Amendment XXVI [1971]

Section 1.   The right of citizens of the United States, who are eighteen years of age or older, to vote shall not be denied or abridged by the United States or any State on account of age.

Section 2.   The Congress shall have power to enforce this article by appropriate legislation.

Amendment XXVII [1992]

No law, varying the compensation for the services of the Senators and Representatives shall take effect, until an election of Representatives shall have intervened.

GLOSSARY

Abatement   Decrease, reduction, or dimunition.

Acceptance   The contractual communication of agreeing to another's offer. The acceptance of an offer creates a *contract*.

Accessory   A term used at the state level that is similar to "aiding and abetting." Accessory to a crime generally is either before the criminal act or after it.

Accord and satisfaction   Payment of money, or other thing of value, usually less than the amount demanded, in exchange for cancellation of a debt that is uncertain in amount.

Actual authority   The authority a principal expressly or implicitly gives to an agent in an agency relationship. This authority may be written, spoken, or derived from the circumstances of the relationship.

Ad infinitum   Without limit; endlessly.

Adjudication   The judicial determination of a legal proceeding.

Adjustment   Under the Bankruptcy Act the procedure followed when a debtor's debts are partly reduced and partly rearranged for repayment.

Administrative agency   An organization, usually a part of the executive branch of government, that is created to serve a specific purpose as authorized by the legislative branch. An agency's function usually is characterized as quasi-legislative or quasi-judicial.

Administrative law   The branch of public law dealing with the operation of the various agency boards and commissions of government.

Administrative law judge   The individual employed by an administrative agency who is in charge of hearing the initial presentations in a quasi-judicial case.

ADRs   An abbreviation for alternative dispute resolution systems that may be used in lieu of litigation.

Ad substantiation program   A program of the Federal Trade Commission under which the FTC demands that an advertiser substantiate any claims made in advertising. Even if the claims are not provably untrue, they are considered deceptive if they cannot be substantiated.

Ad valorem   According to value.

Advisory opinion   A formal opinion by a judge, court, regulatory agency, or law officer upon a question of law.

Affidavit   A sworn written statement made before an officer authorized by law to administer oaths.

Affirmative action   Positive steps taken in order to alleviate conditions resulting from past discrimination or from violations of a law.

Affirmative action program   A program designed to promote actively the position of minority workers with regard to hiring and advancement.

Affirmative defenses   Defenses that must be raised and proved by the defendant.

A fortiori   Even more clearly; said of a conclusion that follows with even greater logical necessity from another that is already included in the argument.

Agent   The person who on behalf of a principal deals with a third party.

Aiding and abetting   A criminal action that arises from association with and from assistance rendered to a person guilty of another criminal act.

Alter-ego theory   One method used by courts to pierce the corporate veil when a shareholder fails to treat the corporate organization as a separate legal entity.

Amicus curiae   A friend of the court who participates in litigation though not a party to the lawsuit.

Annual percentage rate A rate of interest that commercial lenders charge persons who borrow money. This rate is calculated in a standardized fashion required by the Truth-in-Lending Act.

Annuity A contract by which the insured pays a lump sum to the insurer and later receives fixed annual payments.

Answer The responsive pleading filed by a defendant.

Apparent authority The authority that a third party in an agency relationship perceives to exist between the principal and the agent. In fact, no actual authority does exist. Sometimes also called *ostensible authority.*

Appeal The right of the litigation parties to have the legal decisions of the trial judge reviewed by an appellate court.

Appellant The party seeking review of a lower court decision.

Appellee The party responding to an appeal; the winner in the trial court.

Apportionment The concept used by states to divide a company's taxable income so that no one state burdens a company with an unfair tax bill.

Arbitration Submission of a dispute to an extrajudicial authority for decision.

Arbitrator The individual or panel members authorized by disputing parties to resolve a dispute through the arbitration process.

Arguendo For the sake of argument.

Articles of incorporation The legal document that forms the application for a state charter of incorporation.

Articles of organization The document used to create a limited liability company. Its purpose corresponds to the purpose of the articles of partnership and the articles of incorporation.

Articles of partnership Another name for a formally drafted partnership agreement.

Artisan's lien The lien that arises in favor of one who has expended labor upon, or added value to, another person's personal property. The lien allows the person to possess the property as security until reimbursed for the value of labor or materials. If the person is not reimbursed, the property may be sold to satisfy the claim.

Assault The intentional creation of immediate apprehension of injury or lack of physical safety.

Assignee One who receives a transfer of contractual rights from an assignor.

Assignor One who sells or transfers contractual rights to an assignee.

Assumed-name statute A state law that requires partners to make a public filing of their identities if their partnership operates under a name that does not reveal the partners' identities.

Assumption of risk Negligence doctrine that bars the recovery of damages by an injured party on the ground that such a party acted with actual or constructive knowledge of the hazard causing the injury.

Attachment The term "attachment" has three meanings. First, attachment is a method of acquiring in rem jurisdiction of a nonresident defendant who is not subject to the service of process to commence a lawsuit. By "attaching" property of the nonresident defendant, the court acquires jurisdiction over the defendant to the extent of the value of the property attached. Second, attachment is a procedure used to collect a judgment. A plaintiff may have the property of a defendant seized, pending the outcome of a lawsuit, if the plaintiff has reason to fear that the defendant will dispose of the property before the court renders its decision. Third, attachment is the event that creates an enforceable security interest under the Uniform Commercial Code (UCC). In order that a security interest attach, there must be a signed, written security agreement, or possession of the collateral by the secured party; the secured party must give value to the debtor; and the debtor must maintain rights in the collateral.

Award The decision announced by an arbitrator.

Bait-and-switch promotion An illegal promotional practice in which a seller attracts consumer interest by promoting one product, the "bait," then once interest has been attracted switches it to a second, higher-priced product by making the "bait" unavailable or unattractive.

Balance of trade The difference between the amount of exports and imports of goods by a nation. A favorable balance would indicate more exports than imports. The United States has run an unfavorable balance of trade for several years.

Bank Merger Acts Federal laws passed in 1960 and 1966 that require approval of the appropriate administrative agency prior to the merger of banks.

Bankruptcy crime An action involving the falsification of documents filed in a bankruptcy case.

Bargained for A term used in conjunction with the requirement of contractual consideration to represent the exchange of benefits and burdens between the contracting parties.

Beneficiary A person entitled to the possession, use, income, or enjoyment of an interest or right to which legal title is held by another; a person to whom an insurance policy is payable.

Best evidence rule   A principle requiring that the original of a document be submitted to the court as proof of the document's contents.

Beyond a reasonable doubt   The burden of proof required in a criminal case. The prosecution in a criminal case has the burden of proving the defendant is guilty, and the jury must have no reasonable doubt about the defendant's guilt. See also *Burden of proof.*

Bilateral contract   An agreement that contains mutual promises, with each party being both a promisor and a promisee.

Bill of lading   A document issued by a carrier indicating that goods to be shipped have been received by the carrier.

Bill of particulars   In legal practice, a written statement furnished by one party to a lawsuit to another, describing in detail the elements upon which the claim of the first party is based.

Battery   An intentional, unpermitted, offensive contact or touching.

Biodegradable   Capable of being decomposed by organic action.

Bona fide   In good faith; innocently; without fraud or deceit.

Bona fide occupational qualification (BFOC)   A qualification that permits discriminatory practices in employment if a person's religion, sex, or national origin is reasonably related to the normal operation of a particular business.

Breach of contract   A party's failure to perform some contracted-for or agreed-upon act, or failure to comply with a duty imposed by law.

Brief   A written document produced by a party for a reviewing court that contains the facts, propositions of law, and argument of a party. It is in this document that the party argues the desired application of the law and any contentions as to the rulings of the lower court.

"Bubble" concept   A procedure by which the Environmental Protection Agency (EPA) allows a business to treat its entire plant complex as though encased in a bubble. The business suggests its own methods of cleanup, provided the total pollution does not exceed certain limits.

Bulk transfer   A transfer made outside the ordinary course of the transferor's business involving a major part of the business' inventory. Bulk transfers are subject to Article 6 of the Uniform Commercial Code (UCC).

Burden of proof   The term "burden of proof" has two meanings. It may describe the party at a trial with

the burden of coming forward with evidence to establish a fact. The term also describes the party with the burden of persuasion. This party must convince the judge or jury of the disputed facts in issue or else lose that issue. There are various degrees of proof. See also *Beyond a reasonable doubt, Preponderance of evidence,* and *Clear and convincing proof.*

Business judgment rule   A legal principle used by the courts to uphold the decisions of corporate directors and officers who have exercised good faith and due care in their business practices.

Business necessity defense   An affirmative defense under Title VII of the Civil Rights Act. It is raised to disparate impact claims and asserts that a facially neutral but discriminatory policy is job related.

Buy and sell agreement   A contract, usually among partners, but perhaps among shareholders, wherein one party agrees to buy the ownership interest held by another party or the first party agrees to sell such an interest to the other party. These contractual provisions help provide for a transition of owners without harming the business of the organization.

Capacity   Mental ability to make a rational decision that includes the ability to perceive and appreciate all relevant facts. A required element of a contract.

Case law   The legal principles that are developed by appellate judges through their written opinions. See *Common law.*

Categorical imperative   A concept by the philosopher Kant that a person should never act in a certain way unless he or she is willing to have everyone else act in the same way.

Caucus   The name used for a private meeting between a mediator and one of the parties involved in a mediation.

Cause in fact   The actual cause of an event; the instrument that is the responsible force for the occurrence of a certain event. A required element of a tort.

Cause of action   This phrase has several meanings, but it is commonly used to describe the existence of facts giving rise to a judicially enforceable claim.

Caveat emptor   Let the buyer beware; rule imposing on a purchaser the duty to inform him- or herself as to defects in the property being sold.

Caveat venditor   Let the seller beware; it is the seller's duty to do what the ordinary person would do in a similar situation.

Cease and desist order   The sanction that may be issued by an administrative agency to prevent a party from violating the law.

Celler-Kefauver Amendment   Passed in 1950 to amend the Clayton Act by broadening the scope of Section 7 on mergers and acquisitions.

Certification mark   A mark used by someone other than its owner to certify the quality, point of origin, or other characteristic of goods or services. The Good Housekeeping "Seal of Approval" is an example.

Certiorari   A Latin word that means "to be informed of." This is the name of a writ that a higher court grants permitting the review of a lower court's ruling.

Chancery   Originally in England, this word was associated with the king's chancellor rendering decisions that did not involve monetary relief. Today, chancery is another name for courts of equity.

Changing conditions defense   A defense to a price discrimination (Section 2 of the Clayton Act) case wherein the defendant seeks to justify charging different customers different prices due to a change in the conditions of the product or marketplace.

Charter   The legal document issued by a state when creating a new corporation.

Circuit court   This term frequently is used to describe two distinct courts. First, the appellate courts in the federal court system often are called circuit courts of appeals. Second, the trial court of general subject matter jurisdiction in some state court systems also are referred to as circuit courts.

Civil law   The area of law governing the rights and duties between private parties as compared with the criminal law. This term also describes the system of codifying law in many countries as compared with the judicial orientation of the common law system.

Civil rights   The area of law designed to protect an individual's right to freedom from discrimination. In employment, this area of law prohibits unequal treatment based on race, color, national origin, religion, and sex.

Class-action suit   A method of litigation that allows one or more plaintiffs to file a lawsuit on behalf of a much larger group of persons, all of whom have a common interest in the claims being litigated.

Clayton Act   Legislation passed in 1914 that exempts labor unions from the Sherman Act. This law expanded the national antitrust policy to cover price discrimination, exclusive dealings, tying contracts, mergers, and interlocking directors.

Clean-hands doctrine   An equitable principle that requires a party seeking an equitable remedy to be free from wrongdoing.

Clear and convincing proof   A burden of proof that requires the party with the burden to establish clearly the existence of the alleged facts. This burden requires more proof than merely having a preponderance of evidence on one's side.

Closed shop   A contractual agreement between an employer and a union that all applicants for a job with the employer will have to join the union. This type of agreement was outlawed by the Taft-Hartley Act.

Closely held   An organization that is owned by only a few people.

Code   A compilation of legislation enacted by a federal, state, or local government.

Colgate doctrine   The legal principle that allows a form of vertical price fixing in that manufacturers may maintain the resale price of their products by announcing their pricing policy and refusing to deal with customers who fail to comply with the policy.

Collective bargaining   The process used by an employer and a union representing employees to discuss and resolve differences so that the parties can agree to a binding contract.

Collective mark   A mark representing membership in a certain organization or association. The "union label" is an example.

Commerce clause   A provision in Article I, Section 8, of the U.S. Constitution that grants the federal government the power to regulate business transactions.

Commercial impracticability   A Uniform Commercial Code (UCC) defense to contractual nonperformance based on happenings that greatly increase the difficulty of performance and that violate the parties' reasonable commercial expectations.

Commercial speech   Speech that has a business-oriented purpose. This speech is protected under the First Amendment, but this protection is not as great as that afforded to noncommercial speech.

Common law   That body of law deriving from judicial decisions as opposed to legislatively enacted statutes and administrative regulations.

Comparable worth   Jobs that, although different, produce substantially equal value for the employer.

Comparative negligence   A doctrine that compares the plaintiff's contributory fault with the defendant's fault and allows the jury to reduce the plaintiff's verdict by the percentage of the plaintiff's fault.

Comparative responsibility   A doctrine that compares the plaintiff's contributory fault with the defendant's fault and allows the jury to reduce the plaintiff's verdict by the percentage of the plaintiff's fault. Also called *comparative negligence*.

Compensatory damages   Usually awarded in breach-of-contract cases to pay for a party's losses that are a direct and foreseeable result of the other party's breach. The award of these damages is designed to place the nonbreaching party in the same position as if the contract had been performed.

Complaint   In legal practice, the first written statement of the plaintiff's contentions, which initiates the lawsuit.

Complete performance   Degree of performance recognizing that each contracting party has performed every duty required by the contract.

Compulsory bargaining issue   Mandatory bargaining issue regarding wages, hours, or other terms or conditions of employment. Refusal to engage in good-faith bargaining with regard to these issues is an unfair labor practice.

Concealment   An intentional misrepresentation of a material fact occurring through the silence of a party.

Concerted activities   Those activities involving an agreement, contract, or conspiracy to restrain trade that may be illegal under the Sherman Antitrust Act.

Concurrent conditions   Mutual conditions under which each party's contractual performance is triggered by the other party's tendering (offering) performance.

Condition precedent   An event in the law of contracts that must occur before a duty of immediate performance of the promise arises. Contracts often provide that one party must perform before there is a right to performance by the other party. For example, completion of a job is often a condition precedent to payment for that job. One contracting party's failure to perform a condition precedent permits the other party to refuse to perform, cancel the contract, and sue for damages.

Condition subsequent   A fact that will extinguish a duty to make compensation for breach of contract after the breach has occurred.

Conduct   Under the Uniform Commercial Code (UCC) the conduct of contracting parties (i.e., their actions) is important in determining the meaning of a sales contract.

Confiscation   The seizure of property without adequate compensation.

Conflict of law   Rules of law the courts use to determine that substantive law applies when there is an inconsistency between laws of different states or countries.

Conglomerate merger   The merger resulting when merging companies have neither the relationship of competitors nor that of supplier and customer.

Consent order   Any court or regulatory order to which the opposing party agrees; a contract of the

parties entered upon the record with the approval and sanction of a court.

Consequential damages   The amount of money awarded in a breach-of-contract case to the non-breaching party to pay for the special damages that exceed the normal compensatory damages. Lost opportunities may create consequential damages if the breaching party was aware of the special nature of the contract.

Consequentialism   An ethical system that concerns itself with the moral consequences of actions. Also called *teleology*.

Consideration   An essential element in the creation of a contract obligation that creates a detriment to the promisee or a benefit to the promisor.

Consolidation   The process by which two or more corporations are joined to create a new corporation.

Conspiracy   A combination or agreement between two or more persons for the commission of a criminal act.

Constitutional law   The legal issues that arise from interpreting the U.S. Constitution or a state constitution.

Constructive discharge   The event of an employee resigning because the employer has made working conditions too uncomfortable for continued employment.

Consumer   An individual who buys goods and services for personal use rather than for business use.

Consumer investigative report   A report on a consumer's character, general reputation, mode of living, etc., obtained by personal interviews in the community where the consumer works or lives.

Contempt of court   An order by a judge to punish wrongdoing with respect to the court's authority.

Contingency fee   An arrangement whereby an attorney is compensated for services in a lawsuit according to an agreed percentage of the amount of money recovered.

Contract   A legally enforceable promise.

Contract clause   The constitutional provision that prohibits states from enacting laws that interfere with existing contracts. The Supreme Court has refused to interpret this clause in an absolute manner.

Contribution   The right of one who has discharged a common liability to recover from another also liable the proportionate share of the common liability.

Contributory negligence   A failure to use reasonable care by the plaintiff in a negligence suit.

Controlling person   The person who has the control of, or is controlled by, the issuer of securities in securities laws.

Convention on the International Sale of Goods (CISG) A treaty adopted by most major trading countries that outlines standard commercial rules for international contracts involving the sale of goods.

Conversion An unlawful exercise of dominion and control over another's property that substantially interferes with property rights.

Cooling-off period A time provided by the Taft-Hartley Act during which labor and management must suspend the work stoppage (strike or lockout) and continue their working relationship while negotiating a resolution of the dispute. This period is for eighty days.

Copyright The protection of the work of artists and authors that gives them the exclusive right to publish their works or determine who may publish them.

Corporation An artificial, but legal, person created by state law. As a business organization, the corporation's separation of owners and managers gives it a high level of flexibility.

Corrective advertising A Federal Trade Commission (FTC) remedy that requires companies that have advertised deceptively to run ads that admit the prior errors and correct the erroneous information.

Cost justification defense A defense to a price discrimination (Section 2 of the Clayton Act) case wherein the defendant seeks to justify charging different customers different prices due to that defendant's costs varying because of the differing quantities purchased by the customers.

Counterclaim Any claim filed by the defendant in a lawsuit against the plaintiff in the same suit.

Counterdefendant The party involved in litigation against whom a counterclaim is filed. This party is the original plaintiff.

Counteroffer An offer made in response to another's offer. Usually made in place of an acceptance. A counteroffer usually terminates an offer.

Counterplaintiff The party involved in litigation who files a counterclaim. This party is the original defendant who is making a claim against the original plaintiff.

Course of dealing The way parties to a contract have done business in the past. Important in helping to determine the meaning of a contract for the sale of goods.

Covenant An agreement or promise in writing by which a party pledges that something has been done or is being done. The term is often used in connection with real estate to describe the promises of the grantor of the property.

Covenant not to compete An agreement in which one party agrees not to compete directly with the business of the other party; may be limited by geography or length of time.

Criminal law That area of law dealing with wrongs against the state as representative of the community at large, to be distinguished from civil law, which hears cases of wrongs against persons.

Cross-examination The process of questioning a witness by the lawyer who did not call the witness to testify on behalf of that lawyer's client.

Cruel and unusual punishment Protection against such punishment is provided by the Eighth Amendment of the U.S. Constitution. To be cruel and unusual, the punishment must be disproportionately harsh when compared to the offense committed.

Damages Monetary compensation recoverable in a court of law.

D.B.A. Doing business as.

Decree The decision of a court of equity.

Defamation The publication of anything injurious to the good name or reputation of another.

Default The failure of a defendant to answer a plaintiff's complaint within the time period allowed by the court. Upon the defendant's default, a judgment is entered in the plaintiff's favor.

Defect Something that makes a product not reasonably safe for a use that can be reasonably anticipated.

Defendant The party involved in a lawsuit that is sued; the party required to respond to the plaintiff's complaint.

Defined benefit plan A money-purchase plan that guarantees a certain retirement income based on the employee's service and salary under the Employee Retirement Income Security Act. The benefits are fixed, and the contributions vary.

Defined contribution plan A money-purchase plan that allows employers to budget pension costs in advance under the Employee Retirement Income Security Act. The contribution is fixed, and the benefits vary.

Delivery The physical transfer of something. In sale-of-goods transactions, delivery is the transfer of goods from the seller to the buyer.

Demurrer A formal statement by the defendant that the facts alleged by the plaintiff are insufficient to support a claim for legal relief in common law pleading.

De novo judicial review A proceeding wherein the judge or hearing officer hears the case as if it had not been heard before.

Deontology An ethical system that affirms an absolute morality. Also called *formalism*.

Deposited acceptance rule The contractual doctrine that a binding acceptance of an offer occurs when a mailed acceptance is irrevocably placed with the postal service.

Deposition A discovery process outside the court's supervision that involves the sworn questioning of a potential witness. This oral questioning is reduced to a written form so that a record is established.

Derivative action A lawsuit filed by a shareholder of a corporation on behalf of the corporation. This action is filed to protect the corporation from the mismanagement of its officers and directors.

Derivative suit A lawsuit filed by one or more shareholders of a corporation against that organization's management. This suit is brought to benefit the corporation directly and its shareholders indirectly.

Design defect A defect arising when a product does not meet society's expectation for a safely designed product.

Dicta Statements made in a judicial opinion that are not essential to the decision of the case.

Directed verdict A motion for a directed verdict requests that the judge direct the jury to bring in a particular verdict if reasonable minds could not differ on the correct outcome of the lawsuit. In deciding the motion, the judge will view in the light most favorable to the nonmoving party, and if different inferences may be drawn by reasonable people, then the court cannot direct a verdict. In essence, a directed verdict removes the jury's discretion.

Direct examination The process of questioning a witness conducted by the lawyer who called the witness to testify on behalf of that lawyer's client.

Directors Those individuals who are elected by the shareholders to decide the goals and objectives for the corporate organization.

Disability Any physical or mental impairment that substantially limits a major life activity.

Disaffirm To void. Used to describe a minor's power to get out of a contract because of age.

Discharge In bankruptcy the forgiving of an honest debtor's debts. In contract law an act that forgives further performance of a contractual obligation.

Discovery Procedures by which one party to a lawsuit may obtain information relevant to the case from the other party or from third persons.

Discretionary function exception An exception to the waiver of the doctrine of sovereign immunity. Officials of administrative agencies are exempt from

personal liability if their performance or lack thereof is based on a discretionary function.

Discrimination in effect The discriminatory result of policies that appear to be neutral.

Disparate impact A term of employment litigation that refers to the disproportionate impact of a policy neutral on its face on some protected class (e.g., race or sex).

Disparate treatment A term of employment litigation that refers to the illegal discriminatory treatment of an individual in some protected class (e.g., race or sex).

Dissolution The cancellation of an agreement, thereby rescinding its binding force. A partnership is dissolved anytime there is a change in partners. A corporation's dissolution occurs when that business entity ceases to exist.

Diversity of citizenship The plaintiffs filing a lawsuit must be from states different from those of the defendants. This requirement, along with over $50,000 at stake, is one method a federal distict court gains jurisdiction over the subject matter of a lawsuit.

Divestiture The antitrust remedy that forces a company to get rid of assets acquired through illegal mergers or monopolistic practices.

Docket A book containing a brief summary of all acts done in court in the conduct of each case.

Doctrine of abstention A principle used by federal courts to refuse to hear a case. When used by the federal courts, the lawsuit involved is sent to the state court system.

Domestic corporation A business organization created by the issuance of a state charter that operates in the state that issued the charter.

Domicile That place that a person intends as his or her fixed and permanent legal residence; place of permanent abode, as contrasted with a residence, which may be temporary; a person can have a number of residences but only one domicile; the state of incorporation of a corporation.

Dominant commerce clause concept The impact of the commerce clause as a means of limiting state and local governments' powers to regulate business activities.

Donee beneficiary A noncontracting third party who receives as a gift the benefits of a contract made between two other parties. This third party is empowered to enforce the contract to ensure the receipt of the contract's benefits.

Double jeopardy A constitutional doctrine that prohibits an individual from being prosecuted twice by the same governing body based on the same factual situation.

Double tax   A disadvantage of a corporate form of organization in that the corporation must pay a tax on the money earned and the shareholder pays a second tax on the dividends distributed.

Dram shop acts   Statutes adopted in many states that impose strict liability upon tavern owners for injuries to third parties caused by their intoxicated patrons.

Due diligence defense   A defense that experts may assert in a 1933 Securities Act case involving the failure to register securities or the failure to provide accurate documents. The expert utilizing this defense attempts to prove his or her reasonable investigation into all available information.

Due process   Fundamental fairness. As applied to judicial proceedings, adequate notice of a hearing and an opportunity to appear and defend in an orderly tribunal.

Due process clause   A provision found in the Fifth and Fourteenth Amendments of the U.S. Constitution. This clause assures all citizens of fundamental fairness in their relationship with the government.

Dumping   The practice of selling foreign goods in one country at less than the comparable price in the country where the goods originated.

Duress   Action by a person that compels another to do what he or she would not otherwise do. It is a recognized defense to any act that must be voluntary in order to create liability in the actor.

Duty   A legal obligation imposed by the law.

Duty of performance   In contract law the legal obligation of a party to a contract.

Duty of reasonable care   The legal duty owed under negligence doctrine.

Easement   The right of one other than the owner of land to some use of that land.

Economic boycott   Used in three basic forms (primary, secondary, and tertiary), a practice aimed at cutting off trade opportunities for enemy countries.

Eighty-day cooling-off period   A provision in the Taft-Hartley Act that allows the president to require that laborers continue working and that the laborers' representatives and management continue bargaining for at least eighty days during which it is intended that federal mediation will resolve the dispute. This provision can be utilized by the president only when there is a determination that the work stoppage is adversely affecting the national health and safety.

Ejusdem generis   Of the same kind or class; a doctrine of legislative interpretation.

Embezzlement   The fraudulent appropriation by one person, acting in a fiduciary capacity, of the money or property of another.

Eminent domain   Authority of the state to take private property for public use.

Emissions reduction banking   The policy stating that businesses that lower pollution beyond the requirements of the law may use the additional reductions in the future.

Employment at will   A hiring for an indefinite period of time.

En banc   Proceedings by or before the court as a whole rather than any single judge.

Endangerment of workers   A criminal act that involves placing employees at risk with respect to their health and safety in the work environment.

Enjoin   To require performance of or abstention from some act through issuance of an injunction.

Environmental impact statement   A filing of documents required by the National Environmental Policy Act that forces governmental agencies to consider the environmental consequences of their actions.

Equal protection clause   A provision in the Fourteenth Amendment of the U.S. Constitution that requires all citizens to be treated in a similar manner by the government unless there is a sufficient justifiation for the unequal treatment.

Equity   A body of law that seeks to adjust conflicting rights on the basis of fairness and good conscience. Courts of equity or chancery may require or prohibit specific acts where monetary damages will not afford complete relief.

Escrow   A deed, bond, or deposit that one party delivers for safekeeping by a second party who is obligated to deliver it to a third party upon the fulfillment of some condition.

Establishment clause   A provision in the First Amendment of the U.S. Constitution that prohibits the federal government from establishing any government-supported religion or church.

Estoppel   The legal principle that one may not assert facts inconsistent with one's own prior actions.

Ethics   A systematic statement of right and wrong together with a philosophical system that both justifies and necessitates rules of conduct.

European Union (EU)   Created by the Treaty of Rome, an organization that seeks to facilitate the free movement of goods, services, labor, professions, transportation, and capital among European countries.

Exclusive dealing   A buyer agrees to purchase a certain product exclusively from the seller or the seller agrees to sell all of his or her product production to the buyer.

Exculpatory clause   A provision in a contract whereby one of the parties attempts to relieve itself of liability for breach of a legal duty.

Exculpatory contract   A contract that excuses one from accepting responsibility or blame. For example, a contract that excuses one from having to accept liability for one's negligence or another's injury or loss.

Executed contract   A contract that is fully accomplished or performed, leaving nothing unfulfilled.

Execution   To carry out some action to completion. With respect to enforcing a court's judgment, an execution involves the seizure of the debtor's property, a sale of the property, and the payment of proceeds to the creditor.

Executory contract   An agreement that is not completed. Until the performance required in a contract is completed, it is executory.

Exemplary damages   Punitive damages. Monetary compensation in excess of direct losses suffered by the plaintiff that may be awarded in intentional tort cases where the defendant's conduct deserves punishment.

Exhaustion of remedies   A concept used in administrative law that requires any party to an administrative proceeding to give the administrative agency every opportunity to resolve the dispute before appealing to the court system.

Experience rating system   A system of sliding taxation under which employers are charged less unemployment compensation tax as they lay off fewer workers due to economic conditions.

Export controls   Action taken on a national and multilateral basis to prevent the exportation of controlled goods and technology to certain destinations.

Express authority   Actual authority that arises from specific statements made by the principal to the agent.

Express contract   A contract in which parties show their agreement in words.

Express warranty   Any statement of fact or promise about the performance of a product made by a seller

Expropriation   A foreign government's seizure of privately owned property.

Extortionate picketing   Picketing by employees in an attempt to force an employer to pay money to union officials or other individuals when these payments provide personal benefit to the officials or individuals instead of benefiting the union membership generally.

Extradition   The process that one state uses to have another state transfer to the jurisdiction of the first state a person accused of criminal activities.

Failing-company doctrine   A merger bewteen a failing company and a competitor may be allowed, although such a merger wuld be illegal if both companies were viable competitors.

False advertising   Untrue and fraudulent statements and representations made by way of advertising a product or a service.

False imprisonment   The tort of an intentional, unjustified confinement of a nonconsenting person who knows of the confinement.

Family resemblance test   A legal principle used to determine whether or not promissory notes or other similar investment opportunities are securities.

Featherbedding   A term used in the labor laws to describe workers who are paid although they do not perform any work. Under the Taft-Hartley Act, featherbedding is an unfair labor practice by unions.

Federal Employer's Liability Act   The federal act covering transportation workers that establishes an employer's liability to employees for negligence.

Federalism   A term used to describe the vertical aspect of the separation of powers. The coexistence of a federal government and the various state governments, with each having responsibilities and authorities that are distinct but overlap, is called federalism.

Federal question   Litigation involving the application or interpretation of the federal Constitution, federal statutes, federal treaties, or federal administrative agencies. The federal court system has subject matter jurisdiction over these issues.

Federal Rules of Civil Procedure   A law passed by Congress that provides the procedural steps to be followed by the federal courts when handling civil litigation.

Federal Trade Commission Act   Passed in 1914, this legislation created the Federal Trade Commission (FTC) and authorized it to protect society against unfair methods of competition. The law was amended in 1938 (by the Wheeler-Lea amendment) to provide the FTC with authority to regulate unfair or deceptive trade practices.

Fee schedule   A plan, usually adopted by an association, that establishes minimum or maximum charges for a service or product.

Fellow-servant doctrine   The doctrine that precludes an injured employee from recovering damages from his employer when the injury resulted from the negligent act of another employee.

Felony   A criminal offense of a serious nature, generally punishable by death or imprisonment in a penitentiary; to be distinguished from a misdemeanor.

Fiduciary   One having a duty to act for another's benefit in the highest good faith.

Finance charge   Any charge for an extension of credit, which specifically includes interest, service charges, and other charges.

Financing statement   An established form that a secured party files with a public officer, such as a state official or local court clerk, to perfect a security interest under the Uniform Commercial Code (UCC). It is a simple form that contains basic information such as a description of the collateral, names, and addresses. It is designed to give notice that the debtor and the secured party have entered into a security agreement.

Firm offer   An offer in signed writing by a merchant to buy or sell goods; it gives assurances that the offer will be held open for acceptance under the Uniform Commercial Code (UCC).

Foreclosure   If a mortgagor fails to perform his or her obligations as agreed, the mortgagee may declare the whole debt due and payable, and she or he may foreclose on the mortgaged property to pay the debt secured by the mortgage. The usual method of foreclosure authorizes the sale of the mortgaged property at a public auction. The proceeds of the sale are applied to the debt.

Foreign corporation   A business organization, created by the issuance of a state charter, that operates in states other than the one issuing the charter.

Foreign Corrupt Practices Act   A U.S. law that seeks to ban the payment of bribes to foreign officials in order to obtain business.

Foreign Sovereign Immunities Act   A federal law passed in 1976 that codifies the restrictive theory of *sovereign immunity* and rejects immunity for commercial acts carried on in the United States or having direct affects in this country.

Foreign subsidiary   A practice common in a multinational corporation that conducts part of its business operations in a foreign country.

Formalism   An ethical system that affirms an absolute morality. Also called *deontology*.

Forum non conveniens   The doctrine under which a court may dismiss a lawsuit in which it appears that for the convenience of the parties and in the interest of justice the action should have been brought in another court.

Franchise   A marketing technique whereby one party (the franchisor) grants a second party (the franchisee) the right to manufacture, distribute, or sell a product using the name or trademark of the franchisor.

Fraud   A false representation of fact made with the intent to deceive another that is justifiably relied upon to the injury of that person.

Free exercise clause   A provision in the First Amendment of the U.S. Constitution that allows all citizens the freedom to follow or believe any religious teaching.

Frolic and detour   The activity of an agent or an employee who has departed from the scope of the agency and is not, therefore, a representative of his or her employer.

Full faith and credit clause   A provision in the U.S. Constitution that requires a state to recognize the laws and judicial decisions of all other states.

Full-line forcing   An arrangement in which a manufacturer refuses to supply any portion of the product line unless the retailer agrees to accept the entire line.

Functional discount   A reduction in price as the result of the buyer performing some service that usually is provided by the seller.

Garnishment   A legal proceeding whereby a creditor may collect directly from a third party who is obligated to the debtor.

General Agreement on Tariffs and Trade (GATT)   An international treaty that requires member countries to abide by the principles of open and free trade.

General counsel   An individual who is responsible for coordinating all law-related issues, such as the quasi-judicial hearings in administrative agencies. This term is also used to describe the principal lawyer of a company.

General partner   The owner of a limited partnership that enjoys the control of the partnership's operation. This type of partner is personally liable for the debts of the limited partnership.

General partnership   A business organization wherein all owners (partners) share profits and losses and all are jointly and severally liable for the organization's debts.

Geographic extension merger   A combining of companies involved with the same product or service that do not compete in the same geographical regions or markets.

Geographic market   The relevant section of the country affected by a merger.

Going bare   A professional practicing (in her or his field of expertise) without liability insurance.

Good, the   In philosophy the moral goals and objectives that people choose to pursue.

Good faith   Honesty in dealing; innocence; without fraud or deceit.

Good-faith meeting of competition   A bona fide business practice that is a defense to a charge of violation of the Robinson-Patman Act. The Robinson-

Patman Act is an amendment to the Clayton Act, which outlaws price discrimination that might substantially lessen competition or tends to create a monopoly. This exception allows a seller in good faith to meet the equally low price, service, or facility of a competitor. The good-faith exception cannot be established if the purpose of the price discrimination has been to eliminate competition.

Goods   Tangible (touchable), movable personal property.

Greenmail   Forcing a corporation to buy back some of its own stock at an inflated price to avoid a takeover.

Guardian   One charged with the duty of care and maintenance of another person such as a minor or incompetent under the law.

Guardian ad litem   A guardian appointed to prosecute or defend a lawsuit on behalf of an incompetent or a minor.

Guidelines   A result of an administrative agency's quasi-legislative function that assists parties being regulated to understand the agency's functions and intentions. Guidelines do not have the force of the law, but they can be helpful in anticipating the application of an agency's regulations.

Habeas corpus   The name of a writ that orders one holding custody of another to produce that individual before the court for the purpose of determining whether such custody is proper.

Hearsay evidence   Evidence of statements made or actions performed out of court that is offered to prove the truth thereof.

Hearsay rule   The exclusion, with certain exceptions, of hearsay evidence because of the lack of opportunity to cross-examine the original source of the evidence.

Holder in due course   One who has acquired possession of a negotiable instrument through proper negotiation for value, in good faith, and without notice of any defenses to it. Such a holder is not subject to personal defenses that would otherwise defeat the obligation embodied in the instrument.

Horizontal merger   Merger of corporations that were competitors prior to the merger.

Horizontal price fixing   A per se illegal agreement among competitors as to the price all of them will charge for their similar products.

Horizontal territorial agreement   An arrangement between competitors with respect to geographical areas in which each will conduct its business to the exclusion of the others. This type of agreement is illegal per se under the Sherman Act.

Hostile working environment   Under Title VII an environment where co-workers make offensive sex-ual comments or propositions, engage in suggestive touching, show nude pictures, or draw sexual graffiti.

Hot-cargo contract   An agreement whereby an employer agrees to refrain from handling, using, selling, transporting, or otherwise dealing in the products of another employer or to cease doing business with any other person.

Illegal search and seizure   The area covered by the Fourth Amendment that protects individuals and organizations from unreasonable intrusion without a court-issued warrant.

Immunity   Status of exemption from lawsuits or other legal obligations.

Implied authority   Actual authority that is incidental to express authority.

Implied conditions   Conditions to a contract that are implied by law rather than by contractual agreement.

Implied contract   A legally enforceable agreement inferred from the circumstances and conduct of the parties. Also called an *implied-in-fact contract*.

Implied-in-fact contract   A legally enforceable agreement inferred from the circumstances and conduct of the parties.

Implied warranty   A warranty implied by law rather than by express agreement of the parties to a contract

Implied warranty of fitness for a particular purpose   An implied Uniform Commercial Code (UCC) warranty that arises when a buyer specifies a purpose for a product, then relies on the seller's skill and judgment to select the product.

Implied warranty of habitability   A warranty implied by law in a number of states that guarantees the quality of new home construction.

Implied warranty of merchantability   A warranty (implied) that the goods are reasonably fit for general purpose for which they are sold.

Impossibility of performance   A defense to contractual nonperformance based on special circumstances that render the performance illegal, physically impossible, or so difficult as to violate every reasonable expectation the parties have regarding performance.

Incidental beneficiary   A person who may incidentally benefit from the creation of a contract. Such a person cannot enforce any right to incidental benefit.

Incorporators   Those individuals who are responsible for bringing a corporation into being.

Indefiniteness   When the terms of an agreement are not sufficiently specific, the agreement does not rise to the level of a contract because of the doctrine of indefiniteness.

Indictment   A document issued by a grand jury formally charging a person with a felony.

Individual retirement account   A retirement account for persons who can make either tax deductible contributions, which are taxed on withdrawal, or contributions that are taxed, which produce tax-free withdrawals. This latter type of account is known as a Roth IRA.

Industry guide   An issue of the Federal Trade Commission (FTC) defining the agency's view of the legality of an industry's trade practice.

Infliction of mental distress   An intentional tort of the emotions that causes both mental distress and physical symptoms as a result of the defendant's outrageous behavior.

Infringement   Unauthorized use of copyrighted or patented material.

Injunction   A court order directing a party to do or to refrain from doing some act.

Injurious falsehood   A statement of untruth that causes injury or damage to the party against whom it is made.

In pari materia   Concerning the same subject matter. A rule of statutory construction that two such statutes will be construed together.

In personam   The jurisdiction of a court to affect the rights and duties of a specific individual.

In rem   The jurisdiction of a court to affect property rights with respect to a specific thing.

Insider   A person who owns 10 percent or more of a company or who is a director or officer of the company; a term used in securities law. This term is also used to describe a person possessing nonpublic information.

Intangible property   Something that represents value but has no physical attributes, such as a copyright, patent, or franchise right.

Intent   A legal doctrine indicating that parties meant to do what they did.

Intentional tort   Noncontractual legal wrong caused by one who desires to cause the wrong or where the wrong is substantially likely to occur from the behavior.

Intent to defraud   Applies to an individual who knowingly and willfully makes a misrepresentation of a material fact that is relied on and thereby causes injury or harm.

Interference with contractual relations   A business tort in which persons are induced to breach binding agreements.

International Court of Justice   The judicial branch of the United Nations, which sits at The Hague in the Netherlands and consists of fifteen judges representing the world's major legal systems.

Interpleader   A legal procedure by which one holding a single fund subject to conflicting claims of two or more persons may require the conflicting claimants to come into court and litigate the matter between themselves.

Interrogatory   A written question propounded by one party to a lawsuit to another; a type of discovery procedure.

Inter se   Between themselves.

Intestate   A person who dies without a will.

Invasion of privacy   A tort based on misappropriation of name or likeness, intrusion upon physical solitude, or public disclosure of objectionable, private information.

Involuntary petition   The document filed by a creditor to initiate bankruptcy proceedings against a debtor.

Irrevocable letter of credit   Reduces the risk to parties in cases where business is extended across national borders between strangers by providing guarantees of payment and delivery of goods.

Issuer   The term in securities law for an individual or busines organization offering a security for sale to the public.

Jointly and severally liable   The legal principle that makes two or more people, usually partners, liable for an entire debt as individuals or in any proportional combination.

Joint tenancy   A form of ownership in which each of two or more owners has an undivided right to possession of the property. Upon the death of an owner his or her interest passes to the surviving owners because of the survivorship.

Joint venture   Two or more persons or business organizations agreeing to do business for a specific and limited purpose.

Judgment   Official adjudication of a court of law.

Judgment notwithstanding the verdict   The decision of a court that sets aside the verdict of a jury and reaches the opposite result.

Judgment on the pleadings   A principle of litigation, in the form of a motion, whereby one party tests the validity of the allegations contained in the complaint and answer. Upon this motion a judge might determine that the pleadings contain no issues of fact or law and thus grant a judgment prior to a trial.

Judicial activism An activist judge tends to abide by the following judicial philosophies: (1) The political process cannot adequately handle society's difficult issues; (2) the courts can correct society's ills through the decision-making process; (3) following precedent is not crucial; and (4) "judge-made law" is often necessary to carry out the legislative intent of the law. See also *Judicial restraint.*

Judicial restraint A judge who abides by the judicial restraint philosophy (1) believes that the political process, and not the courts, should correct society's ills; (2) decides an issue on a narrow basis, if possible; (3) follows precedent whenever possible; and (4) does not engage in "judge-made law" but interprets the letter of the law. See also *Judicial activism.*

Judicial review The power of courts to declare laws enacted by legislative bodies and actions by the executive branch to be unconstitutional.

Jurisdiction The power and authority of a court or other governmental agency to adjudicate controversies and otherwise deal with matters brought before it.

Jurisdictional strike A stoppage of work that arises from a dispute between two or more unions as to what work should be assigned to the employees belonging to the disputing unions. This work stoppage is an unfair labor practice. This dispute between the unions should be resolved by the NLRB.

Jurisprudence The science of the law; the practical science of giving a wise interpretation of the law.

Jury instruction A statement made by the judge to the jury informing them of the law applicable to the case the jury is bound to accept and apply.

Laches Defense to an equitable action based on the plaintiff's unreasonable delay in bringing the action.

Landrum-Griffin Act The federal law passed in 1959 that provides union members with a "Bill of Rights" and requires union officers to file reports with the Department of Labor. This law, which is known as the Labor-Management Reporting and Disclosure Act, also added unfair labor practices by unions.

Lanham Act A federal law regulating unfair methods of competition regarding trademarks.

Law of agency That body of law concerning one's dealing with another on behalf of a principal.

Leading question A question that indicates the appropriate answer because of the way or manner in which it is asked. Typically, such questions are allowed during the cross-examination of a witness but not during the direct examination.

Legacy A gift of money under a will. It is a type of bequest, which is a gift of personal property. The word "devise" is used in connection with real property distributed by will.

Legal capacity The ability of a business organization to sue and be sued in its own name rather than having to sue or be sued in the name of its owners.

Legal clinic A term referring to a law firm that specializes in low-cost, generally routine legal procedures.

Legislation Laws passed by an elected body such as Congress, a state legislation, or local council/commission. Those laws enacted at the federal and state levels are called statutes. At the local level, such laws are often referred to as ordinances.

Legislative history A technique used by courts in interpreting statutes. Courts often examine the record of the legislators' debate in an attempt to determine what was intended by the legislation.

Letter of credit A document commonly used in international transactions to ensure payment and delivery of goods.

Libel A defamatory written statement communicated to a third party.

License A common method of controlling product or technology transfers across national borders.

Lien A claim to an interest in property in satisfaction of a debt or claim.

Limited liability This term is used to describe the exposure of business owners to pay the debts of their businesses when such exposure does not exceed the owner's investment in the business.

Limited liability company (LLC) A type of business organization that has characteristics of both a partnership and a corporation. The owners of an LLC are called members, and their personal liability is limited to their capital contributions. The LLC, as an organization, is not a taxable entity.

Limited partners Those owners of a limited partnership who forego control of the organization's operation in return for their liability being limited to the amount of their investment.

Limited partnership A partnership in which one or more individuals are general partners and one or more individuals are limited partners. The limited partners contribute assets to the partnership without taking part in the conduct of the business. Such individuals are liable for the debts of the partnership only to the extent of their contributions.

Limited personal liability See *Limited liability.*

Liquidated damages clause A contractual provision that specifies a predetermined amount of damages or a formula for such a determination to be utilized if a breach of contract occurs.

Liquidation The process of winding up the affairs of a business for the purpose of paying debts and disposing of assets. May be voluntary or under court order.

Litigation The process of utilizing the court system to resolve a legal dispute.

Long-arm statute A state statute that gives extraterritorial effect to process (summons) in specified cases. It allows state courts to obtain jurisdiction in civil actions over defendants who are beyond the border of the state provided the defendants have minimum contact with the state sufficient to satisfy due process.

Mail box rule The rule that an acceptance is effective once it is sent. See *Deposited acceptance rule.*

Malfeasance Doing of some wrongful act.

Malice The state of mind that accompanies the intentional doing of a wrongful act without justification or excuse.

Malicious prosecution An action for recovery of damages that have resulted to person, property, or reputation from previous unsuccessful civil or criminal proceedings that were prosecuted without probable cause and with malice.

Mandamus A court order directing the holder of an office to perform his or her legal duty.

Mandatory arbitration A form of resolving a dispute, as an alternative to litigation, that is required by a statute.

Manifest system A documentary system required by the Resource Conservation and Recovery Act. Used in the disposal of toxic chemicals.

Market extension merger An acquisition in which the acquiring company increases its market through product extension or geographical extension.

Master The term used in an agency relationship to describe the principal (employer) of a servant (employee) who is involved in a tort.

Material breach A level of performance below what is reasonably acceptable. A substantial failure, without excuse, to perform a promise that constitutes the whole or part of a contract. A party who has materially breached cannot sue the other party for performance and is liable for damages.

Mayhem Unlawfully depriving a human being of a member of his or her body.

Mechanic's lien A lien on real estate that is created by statute to assist suppliers and laborers in collecting their accounts and wages. Its purpose is to subject the owner's land to a lien for material and labor expended in the construction of buildings and other improvements.

Med-arb An abbreviation for an alternative dispute resolution system that involves parties going through mediation and agreeing to resolve as many issues as possible. These parties agree that any matters not resolved in the mediation process will then be arbitrated.

Mediation An alternative to litigation whereby a third party attempts to assist the disputing parties in reaching a settlement. The third-party mediator lacks authority to impose on the parties a binding solution to the dispute.

Mediator An individual who assists disputing parties in their efforts to resolve their differences. Mediators must rely on their persuasive abilities since they have no authority to settle the dispute.

Members The individuals or business entities that belong to a limited liability company.

Merchant A person who deals in goods of the kind or otherwise by his or her occupation presents himself or herself as having knowledge or skill peculiar to the practice or goods involved.

Merger The extinguishment of a corporate entity by the transfer of its assets and liabilities to another corporation that continues in existence.

Minimum rationality A legal test used by courts to test the validity of governmental action, such as legislation, under the equal protection clause of the U.S. Constitution. To satisfy this test, the government needs to demonstrate that there is a good reason for the government's action.

Minimum wage Minimum hourly wages, established by Congress under the Fair Labor Standards Act, to maintain the health, efficiency, and general well-being of workers.

Ministerial duty An example of a definite duty regarding that nothing be left to discretion or judgment.

Minitrial An alternative dispute resolution system that involves lawyers presenting both sides of a business dispute to the executives of the organizations involved.

Mirror image rule The common law rule that the terms of an acceptance offer must mirror exactly the terms of the offer. Any variation of terms would make the attempted acceptance a counteroffer.

Misappropriation theory The legal doctrine supported by the Securities and Exchange Commission (SEC) and the courts that any person who shares nonpublic information with another party or who trades on the information violates the securities laws if that information was intended to be kept confidential.

Misdemeanor A criminal offense of less serious nature than a felony, generally punishable by fine or jail sentence other than in a penitentiary.

Misfeasance   A misdeed or trespass.

Misrepresentation   An untrue manifestation of fact by word or conduct; it may be unintentional.

Mitigate   To lessen the consequences of. Usually used to refer to the contractual duty to lessen damages following breach of contract.

Mock trial   An alternative dispute resolution system that involves lawyers presenting their clients' cases to a group of citizens who render their opinion about the relative merits of the parties' positions.

Monopoly   Exclusive control of a market by a business entity.

Morality   The values of right and wrong.

Mortgage   A transfer of an interest in property for the purpose of creating a security for a debt.

Motion   The process by which the parties make written or oral requests that the judge issue an order or ruling.

Mutual assent   A contractual doctrine requiring that the minds of the contracting parties must meet before there exists a binding contract.

Mutual mistake   A situation in which parties to a contract reach a bargain on the basis of an incorrect assumption common to both parties.

Nationalization   A claim made by a foreign government that it owns expropriated property.

National Labor Relations Board   The federal administrative agency created in 1935 to conduct certification/decertification elections of unions and to conduct quasi-judicial hearings arising from the labor-management relationship.

Necessaries of life   Food, clothing, shelter, medical care, and, in some states, education. A minor is legally responsible to pay a reasonable value for purchased necessaries of life.

Negligence   A person's failure to exercise reasonable care that foreseeably causes another injury.

Negotiable instrument or document   A special type of written promise to pay money (instrument) or deliver goods (document). Personal defenses do not apply against the holder in due course of a negotiable instrument or document.

Negotiated settlement   A voluntary but binding agreement that settles a legal dispute, such as one involving a contractual breach or a tort lawsuit.

Nexus   A logical connection.

NLRB   National Labor Relations Board

Noerr-Pennington doctrine   This doctrine exempts from the antitrust laws concerted efforts to lobby government officials regardless of the anticompetitive purposes. It is based on the First Amendment freedom of speech.

No-fault laws   Laws barring tort actions by injured persons against third-party tortfeasors and requiring such persons to obtain recovery from their own insurers.

Nolo contendere   A plea entered by the defendant in a criminal case that neither admits nor denies the crime allegedly committed but, if accepted by the court, permits the judge to treat the defendant as guilty.

Norris-LaGuardia Act   The federal legislation adopted in 1932 that attempted to increase union membership by prohibiting the use of injunctions issued by federal courts against certain union activities and by outlawing yellow-dog contracts.

North American Free Trade Agreement (NAFTA)   An agreement reached in 1993 among the United States, Mexico, and Canada to increase economic growth through mutual trade.

Noscitur a sociis   The principle that the scope of general words is defined by specific accompanying words; a doctrine of legislative interpretation.

Notary public   A public officer authorized to administer oaths and certify certain documents.

Notice   Communication sufficient to charge a reasonable person with knowledge of some fact.

Nuisance   A physical condition constituting an unreasonable and substantial interference with the rights of individuals or the public at large.

Obligee   One who is entitled to receive a payment or performance under a contract.

Obligor   One who is obligated to pay or perform under a contract.

Offer   A contractual communication that contains a specific promise and a specific demand. The offer initiates the process of making a contract.

Officers   Those individuals appointed by directors of a corporation to conduct the daily operations of the corporate organization.

Oligopoly   Control of the supply and price of a commodity or service in a given market by a small number of companies or suppliers.

Opinion   The decision of a judge, usually issued in a written form.

Option   A contractual arrangement under which one party has for a specified time the right to buy certain property from or sell certain property to the other party. It is essentially a contract to not revoke an offer.

Oral argument   Attorneys appear in person before the appellate court to explain orally to the court their position in the case and answer the court's questions about the case.

Ordinance   The legislative enactment of a city, county, or other municipal corporation.

Organizers   The parties responsible for bringing a limited liability company into existence. These parties correspond to the functions of incorporators with respect to corporations.

Overbreadth doctrine   A principle used by courts to invalidate legislation that is broader in scope than is necessary to regulate an activity. This doctrine may be utilized to protect constitutional rights, such as freedom of speech, against a wide sweep of some governmental action.

Overt act   An essential element of a crime. Without this action by a party, the intent to engage in criminal activity is not wrongful.

Ownership   The bundle of rights to possess and use property because of title to the property.

Paper fortress   A term referring to the documentation an employer should keep about an employee's performance.

Parker v. Brown doctrine   The name given to the state action exemption to the Sherman Act. See also *State action exemption.*

Parol evidence   Legal proof based on oral statements; with regard to a document, any evidence extrinsic to the document itself.

Parol evidence rule   Parol evidence is extrinsic evidence. In contracts, the parol evidence rule excludes the introduction of evidence of prior written or oral agreements that may vary, contradict, alter, or supplement the present written agreement. There are several exceptions to this rule. For example, when the parties to an agreement do not intend for that agreement to be final and complete, then parol evidence is admissible.

Partnership   A business organization involving two or more persons agreeing to conduct a commercial venture while sharing its profits and losses.

Part performance   The contractual doctrine that says when a buyer of land has made valuable improvements in it or has paid part or all of the purchase price, the statute of frauds does not apply to prevent an oral land sales contract from being enforceable.

Patent   To be patentable, inventions must be nonobvious, novel, and useful. A patent creates a seventeen-year protection period during which there is a presumption of validity if the patent is properly registered with the Patent Office.

Per capita   By or for each individual.

Per curiam   By the court; said of an opinion expressing the view of the court as a whole as opposed to an opinion authored by any single member of the court.

Peremptory challenge   The power granted each party to reject a limited number of potential jurors during voir dire examination. No reason for the rejection need be given.

Perfection   The status ascribed to security interests after certain events have occurred or certain prescribed steps have been taken, e.g., the filing of a financing statement.

Perjury   The giving of false testimony under oath.

Per se   In itself.

Per se illegality   Under the Sherman Act, agreements and practices are illegal only if they are unreasonable. The practices that are conclusively presumed to be unreasonable are per se illegal. If an activity is per se illegal, only proof of the activity is required, and it is not necessary to prove an anticompetitive effect. For example, price fixing is per se illegal. See also *Rule of reason.*

Personal jurisdiction   The power of a court over the parties involved in the litigation process.

Personal property   Physical or intangible property other than real estate.

Petitioner   The party filing either a case in equity or a petition for a writ of certiorari before a supreme court.

Petit jury   The fact-finding body during a trial. Also called a trial or traverse jury.

Petty offenses   Criminal acts that are viewed as minor and thus are typically punished by a fine only.

Piercing the corporate veil   The legal doctrine used by courts to disregard the existence of a corporation thereby holding the shareholders personally liable for the organization's debts.

Plaintiff   The person who initiates a lawsuit.

Plan termination insurance   The insurance required by federal law on regulated pension plans. It protects against plan termination that leaves pension benefits underfunded.

Pleadings   The process by which the parties to a lawsuit present formal written statements of their contentions to create the issues of the lawsuit.

Plenary   Entire; complete in all respects.

Point source   Any source of air pollution that must be licensed under the Clean Air Act.

Police power   The authority a state or local government has to protect the public's health, safety, morals, and general welfare.

Possession   Dominion and control over property; the holding or detention of property in one's own power or command.

Precedent   A prior judicial decision relied upon as an example of a rule of law.

Predatory conduct   An anticompetitive action that is intended to drive competitors out of business. A common example occurs when a business lowers its prices in the hope of gaining such a large market share that it can then raise prices without the fear of competition.

Predatory pricing   A policy of lowering the price charged to customers for the purpose of driving competitors out of business. Typically, this policy involves prices that are below the seller's costs of the products sold with resulting losses to the seller.

Preemption   A condition when a federal statute or administrative rule governs an issue to the extent that a state or local government is prohibited from regulating that area of law.

Preemptive right   A corporation's shareholder's right to maintain the same percentage ownership of the organizaton whenever newly authorized stock is sold.

Preferred stock   A type of stock issued by a corporation that entitles the owner to receive a dividend before owners of common stock.

Prejudicial error   An error in judicial proceedings that may have affected the result in the case.

Preponderance of evidence   In the judgment of the jurors, evidence that has greater weight and overcomes the opposing evidence and presumptions.

Presumption of innocence   The basis of requiring the government to prove a criminal defendant's guilt beyond a reasonable doubt.

Prevention of significant deterioration   A rule implemented under the Clean Air Act that prohibits the degradation of air quality in regions where air quality is better than required by primary air quality standards.

Price discrimination   A seller charging different purchasers different prices for the same goods at the same time.

Price fixing   An agreement or combination by which the conspirators set the market price, whether high or low, of a product or service whether being sold or purchased.

Prima facie   On the face of it; thus, presumed to be true unless proved otherwise.

Primary air quality standards   The standards necessary to protect human health. Secondary air quality standards are stricter standards necessary to protect various environmental amenities.

Primary jurisdiction   A doctrine used by reviewing courts to determine whether a case is properly before the courts or whether it should be heard by an administrative agency first since such an agency might have expertise superior to the courts'.

Principal   The person who gives an agent authority.

Prior consideration   Service or gift from the past that presently induces one to make a promise. Prior consideration does not enable that promise to bind one. It is not legal consideration.

Prior restraint   A principle applicable under the freedom of press and speech clauses of the First Amendment of the U.S. Constitution. The courts have announced decisions that encourage governments to allow the publication or expression of thoughts rather than to restrain such thoughts in advance of their publication or expression.

Private international law   A body of rules that utilizes treaties, agreements, and individual laws of nations to resolve international business disputes between private firms.

Private law   A classification of legal subject matters that deals most directly with relationships between legal entities. The law of contracts and the law of property are two examples of this classification.

Private nuisance   A use of one's property that constitutes an unreasonable and substantial interference with the use of another's property. See also *Nuisance.*

Privilege   A special advantage accorded by law to some individual or group; an exemption from a duty or obligation generally imposed by law.

Privileged communication   A rule of evidence that protects conversations that society deems to be confidential. For example, a witness cannot be required to disclose communications between an attorney and a client.

Privileges and immunities clause   A provision found in Article IV and the Fourteenth Amendment of the U.S. Constitution that prevents a state government from discriminating in favor of its citizens and against citizens from another state. This clause, while not interpreted to be absolute, has emphasized national rather than state citizenship.

Privity   Interest derived from successive relationship with another party; a contractual connection.

Probable cause   The reasonable basis on which law enforcement officials convince a judge that criminal activity has occurred. This is the basis that must be satisfied before a judge will issue a criminal search warrant.

Procedural due process The process or procedure ensuring fundamental fairness that all citizens are entitled to under the U.S. Constitution.

Procedural law The body of rules governing the manner in which legal claims are enforced.

Product extension merger A merger that extends the products of the acquiring company into a similar or related product but one that is not directly in competition with existing products.

Production defect A defect arising when a product does not meet its manufacturer's own standards.

Product liability The liability that sellers have for the goods they sell.

Promissory estoppel Court enforcement of an otherwise unbinding promise if injustice can be avoided only by enforcement of the promise. A substitute for consideration.

Property A legal subject matter that governs the rights and duties of persons to all things. Real property relates to the earth's surface (land) and things attached thereto as well as the area physically above and below the surface. Personal property describes all things that are not real property.

Proportionality review The process that appellate courts use to determine the appropriateness of a criminal sentence.

Prospectus The legal document required by the 1933 Securities Act to be made available to potential purchasers of securities.

Pro tanto So far as it goes.

Protestant ethic A set of beliefs urging that human desire and indulgence be bent to God's will through hard work, self-denial, and rational planning.

Proxy The legal document whereby a shareholder appoints an agent to vote the stock at a corporation's shareholders' meeting.

Proximate causation The doctrine that limits an actor's liability to consequences that could reasonably be foreseen to have resulted from the act.

Public international law A body of rules that examines relationships among nations and seeks to bind them to common principles in the international community.

Public law A classification of legal subject matters that regulates the relationship of individuals and organizations to society.

Publicly held A business organization that has hundreds, if not thousands, of owners who can exchange their ownership interests on public exchanges.

Public nuisance A use of one's property that constitutes an unreasonable and substantial interference with the use of property by the public at large. See also *Nuisance.*

Public policy Accepted standards of behavior. For instance, a contract is illegal if it violates public policy.

Punitive damages Monetary damages in excess of a compensatory award, usually granted only in intentional tort cases where defendant's conduct involved some element deserving punishment. Also called *exemplary damages.*

Purchase-money security interest A security interest given to the party that loans the debtor the money that enables the debtor to buy the collateral.

Qualified pension plan A private retirement plan that gains favorable income tax treatment from the Internal Revenue Service (IRS). A qualified pension plan allows for the deduction of contributions made to fund the plan. Also, earnings from fund investments are not taxable, and employees defer personal income tax liability until payments are received after retirement. To qualify, the plan must cover a high percentage of workers (usually 70 percent) or cover classifications of employees that do not discriminate in favor of management or shareholders.

Quantity discount The practice of giving a lower per unit price to businesses that buy a product in volume than to their competitors that do not.

Quasi-contract A quasi-contract, often referred to as an implied-in-law contract, is not a true contract. It is a legal fiction that the courts use to prevent unjust enrichment and wrongdoing. Courts permit the person who conferred a benefit to recover the reasonable value of that benefit. Nonetheless, the elements of a true contract are not present.

Quasi-judicial Administrative actions involving factual determinations and the discretionary application of rules and regulations.

Quasi-legislative This term describes the rule-making functions of administrative agencies.

Quasi-strict scrutiny A legal test used by courts to test the validity of governmental action, such as legislation, under the equal protection clause of the U.S. Constitution. To satisfy this test, the government needs to demonstrate that the purpose of the action is substantially related to an important governmental objective.

Quid pro quo The exchange of one thing of value for another.

Quitclaim deed The transfer by deed of all the grantor's rights, title, and interest in property.

Quo warranto   An action brought about by the government to test the validity of some franchise, such as the privilege of doing business as a corporation.

Racketeering   A crime under RICO involving a pattern of actions that are indictable under state or federal laws.

Railway Labor Act   The federal law passed in 1926 to encourage collective bargaining in the railroad industry. The law also created the National Mediation Board.

Ratio decidendi   Logical basis of judicial decision.

Real property   Land and fixtures to land.

Reasonable accommodation   The actions that an employer must take under Title VII of the Civil Rights Act and under the Americans with Disabilities Act to adapt employment conditions to an employee's religious belief or disability.

Reciprocal dealing   A contract in which two parties agree to mutual actions so that each party can act as both a buyer and a seller. The agreement violates the Clayton Act if it results in a substantial lessening of competition.

Redlining   An act or refusal to act that results in a discriminatory practice. For example, refusing to make loans in low-income areas can discriminate against minorities in granting credit.

Reformation   A contractual remedy exercised by a court to correct a mistake of drafting or some other nonessential mistake. After reformation the parties remain bound to the contract.

Registration statement   The legal document required to be filed with the Securities and Exchange Commission (SEC) prior to securities being offered for sale to the public.

Reimbursement   Restoration; to pay back or repay that expended; the act of making one whole.

Rejection   The refusal of an offer. A rejection terminates an offer.

Release   The relinquishment of a right or claim against another party.

Remand   The return of a case by an appellate court for further action by the lower court.

Remedial statute   Legislation designed to provide a benefit or relief to a victim of a violation of law.

Remedy   The action or procedure that is followed in order to enforce a right or to obtain damages for injury to a right; the means by which a right is enforced or the violation of a right is prevented, redressed, or compensated.

Reorganization   The legal process of forming a new corporation after bankruptcy or foreclosure.

Replevin   An action for the recovery of goods wrongfully taken or kept.

Representational standing   The requirements that must be satisfied for an organization to have the right to file a lawsuit on behalf of its members.

Request for an admission   A method of discovery used to narrow the issues to be litigated by having a party request that the other party admit the facts are not in dispute.

Request for production of documents   A method of discovery whereby one party asks the other to provide documents for the requesting party's review.

Res   A thing, object, or status.

Res ipsa loquitur   The thing speaks for itself. A rule of evidence whereby negligence of the alleged wrongdoer may be inferred from the mere fact that the injury occured.

Res judicata   The doctrine that deems a former adjudication conclusive and prevents a retrial of matters decided in the earlier lawsuit.

Resale price maintenance   Manufacturer control of a brand- or trade-name product's minimum resale price.

Rescind   To cancel or annul a contract and return the parties to their original positions.

Rescission   The cancellation of a contract and return of the parties to the positions they would have occupied if the contract had not been made.

Respondeat superior   The doctrine imposing liability on one for torts committed by another person who is in his or her employ and subject to his or her control.

Respondent   The party answering a petition in equity or petition for a writ of certiorari.

Restraint of trade   Monopolies, combinations, and contracts that impede free competition.

Retaliatory trade practices   Actions by aggrieved nations responding to tariffs and other unfair trade restrictions imposed by foreign governments.

Reverse   Overturn or vacate the judgment of a court.

Reverse discrimination   The advancement and recruitment of minority workers ahead of similarly qualified nonminority workers.

Revocation   The contractual communication of withdrawing an offer.

RICO   The Racketeer Influenced and Corrupt Organizations Act.

Right of redemption   The right to buy back. A debtor may buy back or redeem his or her mortgaged property when he or she pays the debt.

Right-to-work law   A state statute that outlaws a union-shop contract—one by which an employer agrees to require membership in the union sometime after an employee has been hired as a condition of continued employment.

Robinson-Patman Act   The amendment to Section 2 of the Clayton Act covering price discrimination. As originally adopted, the Robinson-Patman Act outlawed price discrimination in interstate commerce that might substantially lessen competition or tends to create a monopoly.

Rule of reason   Under the Sherman Act, contracts or conspiracies are illegal only if they constitute an unreasonable restraint of trade or attempt to monopolize. An activity is unreasonable if it adversely affects competition. An act is reasonable if it promotes competition. The rule of reason requires that an anticompetitive effect be shown. See also *Per se illegality*.

Rules of evidence   The laws governing the admission of evidence, such as testimony and documents, during the trial of a case.

Sale of business doctrine   The legal principle in securities law that might be used to remove the sale of corporate stock from the securities laws' protection if the purchaser of such stock is to operate the business instead of relying on others to do so.

Sanctions   Penalties imposed for violation of a law.

Scienter   With knowledge; particularly, guilty knowledge.

Scoping   A regulatory step required of a federal agency by the Council on Environmental Quality. Before preparing an environmental impact statement, an agency must designate which environmental issues of a proposed action are most significant.

Search warrant   A court order required by the Fourth Amendment of the U.S. Constitution to be obtained from governmental officials prior to private property being searched or seized.

Secondary air quality standards   Clean Air Act standards designed to protect environmental quality other than human health.

Secondary boycott   Conspiracy or combination to cause the customers or suppliers of an employer to cease doing business with that employer.

Section 402A   That section of the Second Restatement of Torts that imposes strict liability on product sellers who sell a product in a "defective condition unreasonably dangerous to the user or consumer or his property."

Section 1981   That provision of the Civil Rights Act of 1866 that forbids racial discrimination in the making of contracts.

Secured transactions   Any credit transaction creating a security interest; an interest in personal property that secures the payment of an obligation.

Securities Act of 1933   The federal law that regulates (through disclosure requirements) the initial sale of securities to the public.

Securities and Exchange Commission (SEC)   The federal administrative agency that regulates the securities industry.

Securities Exchange Act of 1934   The federal law that regulates sales (other than the initial sale) of securities. This law governs the resale of securities whether by individuals or through brokers and exchanges.

Security   Under the securities law, an investment in which the investor does not participate in management.

Seller   In commercial law, a person who sells or contracts to sell goods.

Seniority system   A plan giving priority to employees based on the length of time an employee has worked for an employer. An employer may apply different standards pursuant to a good-faith seniority system if the differences are not the result of an intention to discriminate.

Sentencing guidelines   Adopted by the U.S. Sentencing Commission as a means of standardizing the sentences given to similar criminals committing similar crimes.

Separation of powers   The doctrine that holds that the legislative, executive, and judicial branches of government function independently of one another and that each branch serves as a check on the others.

Servant   The person hired to act on behalf of a principal in an agency relationship.

Service mark   Any mark, word, picture, or design that attaches to a service and indicates its source.

Set-off   A counterclaim by a defendant against a plaintiff that grows from an independent cause of action and diminishes the plaintiff's potential recovery.

Sexual harassment   Under Title VII, for an employer or workplace supervisor to promise benefits or threaten loss if an employee does not give sexual favors.

Shareholders   The owners of corporations. Typically these owners vote on major decisions impacting their corporations, most commonly the election of a board of directors.

Shark repellent Corporate action to make a threatened acquisition unattractive to the acquiring company.

Shelf registration The process in securities law under Securities and Exchange Commission (SEC) Rule 415 that allows an issuer to satisfy the registration statement requirements, thereby allowing the issuer immediately to offer securities for sale.

Sherman Act An 1890 congressional enactment designed to regulate anticompetitive behavior in interstate commerce.

Short-swing profits The proceeds gained by an insider buying and selling, or vice versa, securities within a six-month time period. Such profits are considered to be illegal.

Simplified employee pension A type of pension permitted by the Revenue Act of 1978. Under this pension type employers contribute up to a specified amount to employee individual retirement accounts.

Slander An oral defamatory statement communicated to a third person.

Small-claims court A court of limited jurisdiction, usually able to adjudicate claims up to a certain amount, such as $3,000, depending on the state.

Social contract theory A theory by John Rawls that proposes a way for constructing a just society.

Sole proprietorship The simplest form of business organization, created and controlled by one owner.

Sovereign immunity A doctrine of state and international law that permits a foreign government to claim immunity from suit in the courts of other nations.

Specific performance Equitable remedy that requires defendants in certain circumstances to do what they have contracted to do.

Standing The doctrine that requires the plaintiff in a lawsuit to have a sufficient legal interest in the subject matter of the case.

Standing to sue The requirement that a plaintiff must satisfy by demonstrating a personal interest in the outcome of litigation or an administrative hearing.

Stare decisis The doctrine that traditionally indicates that a court should follow prior decisions in all cases based on substantially similar facts.

State action exemption The Sherman Act exemption of the sovereign action of a state that replaces competition with regulation if the state actively supervises the anticompetitive conduct.

State-of-the-art defense A defense that the defendant's product or practice was compatible with the current state of technology available at the time of the event in question.

States' relations article Article IV of the U.S. Constitution. Among its purposes, this article prevents a state from favoring its citizens over the citizens of another state, thereby making the United States one nation as opposed to fifty subgroups.

Status quo The conditions or state of affairs at a given time.

Statute A legislative enactment.

Statute of frauds Legislation that states that certain contracts will not be enforced unless there is a signed writing evidencing the agreement.

Statute of limitations A statute that sets a date after which a lawsuit may not be brought. The statute begins running after the happening of a certain event, such as the occurrence of an injury or the breach of a contract.

Statute of repose A statute that applies to product liability cases. It prohibits initiation of litigation involving products more than a certain number of years (e.g., twenty-five) following their manufacture.

Strict liability The doctrine under which a party may be required to respond in tort damages without regard to such party's use of due care.

Strict scrutiny A legal test used by courts to test the validity of governmental action, such as legislation, under the equal protection clause of the U.S. Constitution. To satisfy this test, the government needs to demonstrate that there is a compelling state interest justifying the government's action.

Structured settlement A periodic payment of damages, usually taking the form of a guaranteed annuity.

S corporation A business organization that is formed as a corporation but, by a shareholders' election, is treated as a partnership for taxation purposes.

Subject matter jurisdiction The authority of a court to hear cases involving specific issues of law.

Submission The act or process of referring an issue to arbitration.

Subpoena A court order directing a witness to appear or to produce documents in his or her possession.

Substantial performance Degree of performance recognizing that a contracting party has honestly attempted to perform but has fallen short. One who has substantially performed is entitled to the price promised by the other less that party's damages.

Substantive due process The use of the due process provision of the U.S. Constitution to make certain that the application of a law does not unfairly deprive persons of property rights.

Substantive law A body of rules defining the nature and extent of legal rights.

Summary judgment   A judicial determination that no genuine factual dispute exists and that one party to the lawsuit is entitled to judgment as a matter of law.

Summons   An official notice to a person that a lawsuit has been commenced against him or her that he or she must appear in court to answer the charges.

Superfund   The Comprehensive Environmental Response, Compensation, and Liability Act of 1980.

Supremacy clause   Article VI of the U.S. Constitution, which states that the Constitution, laws, and treaties of the United States shall be the "supreme law of the land" and shall take precedence over conflicting state laws.

Surety   One who incurs a liability for the benefit of another. One who undertakes to pay money in the event that his or her principal is unable to pay.

Taft-Hartley Act   The federal law enacted in 1947 to increase the bargaining power of management by creating unfair labor practices by unions, by outlawing the closed shop, by creating an eighty-day cooling-off period, by permitting states to adopt right-to-work laws, and by creating the Federal Mediation and Conciliation Service.

Tangible property   Physical property.

Teleology   An ethical system that concerns itself with the moral consequences of actions. Also called *consequentialism.*

Tender offer   An invited public offer by a company or organization to buy shares from existing shareholders of another public corporation under specified terms.

Testator   One who has made a will.

Third party   One who enters into a relationship with a principal by way of interacting with the principal's agent.

Third-party beneficiaries   Persons who are recognized as having enforceable rights created for them by a contract to which they are not parties and for which they have given no consideration.

Third-party defendant   A party who is not a party (plaintiff or defendant) to the original litigation. Typically, a defendant might file a claim against a third party stating that if the defendant is liable to the plaintiff, then this third party will be liable to the defendant.

Title   Legal evidence of ownership.

Tippee   A person who learns of nonpublic information about a security from an insider.

Tort   A civil wrong other than a breach of contract.

Trade disparagement   The publication of untrue statements that disparage the plaintiff's ownership of property or its quality.

Trademark   Any word, name, symbol, or device used by a manufacturer or merchant to identify his or her goods.

Trade practice regulation   A term generally referring to laws that regulate competitive practices.

Trade secret   Any formula, pattern, machine, or process of manufacturing used in one's business that may give the user an opportunity to obtain an advantage over its competitors. Trade secrets are legally protectable.

Trade usage   Refers to the particular use of a word in business that may differ from its common use.

Treason   Breach of allegiance to one's government, specifically by levying war against such government or by giving aid and comfort to the enemy.

Treaty of Rome   A historic agreement reached by six European countries in 1957 to achieve economic unity in the European Community. The latter is now known as the European Union, and its membership has grown to fifteen nations.

Treble damages   See *Triple damages.*

Trespass   An act done in an unlawful manner so as to cause injury to another; an unauthorized entry upon another's land.

Trial court   The level of any court system that initially resolves the dispute of litigants. Frequently, but not always, a jury serves as a fact-finding body while the judge issues rulings on the applicable law.

Triple damages (or treble damages)   An award of damages allowable under some statutes equal to three times the amount found by the jury to be a single recovery.

Trust   A fiduciary relationship whereby one party (trustee) holds legal title for the benefit of another (beneficiary).

Trustee   One who holds legal title to property for the benefit of another.

Truth in lending   A federal law that requires the disclosure of total finance charges and the annual percentage rate for credit in order that borrowers may be able to shop for credit.

Tying contract   A contract that ties the sale of one piece of property (real or personal) to the sale or lease of another item of property.

Ultra vires   Beyond the scope of corporate powers granted in the charter.

Unconscionable   In the law of contracts, provisions that are oppresive, overreaching, or shocking to the conscience.

Underwriter   The party that, in securities law, guarantees the issuer that the securitites offered for sale will be sold.

Undue burden   Under the Civil Rights Act of 1964 and the Americans with Disabilities Act an employer need not take action that is excessively costly or creates excessive inefficiency in order to accommodate an employee's religious beliefs or disability. This is the concept of undue burden.

Undue influence   Influence of another destroying the requisite free will of a testator or donor, which creates a ground for nullifying a will or invalidating a gift. A contract will not be binding if one party unduly influences the other since the parties have not dealt on equal terms.

Unfair competition   A group of statutory torts that include misappropriation of trademarks, patent violations, and copyright breaches. One aspect of the Federal Trade Commission's authority. Section 5 of the FTC Act makes unfair methods of competition illegal.

Unfair labor practices   Activities by management or labor unions that have been declared to be inappropriate by the Wagner Act and Taft-Hartley Act, respectively.

Uniform Commercial Code (UCC)   The most successful attempt to have states adopt a uniform law. This code's purpose is to simplify, clarify, and modernize the laws governing commercial transactions.

Unilateral contract   A contract in which the promisor does not receive a promise as consideration; an agreement whereby one makes a promise to do, or refrain from doing, something in return for a performance, not a promise.

Unilateral mistake   Arises when only one of the parties to a contract is wrong about a material fact. It is not usually a basis for rescinding a contract.

Union shop   This term applies, in labor law, to an agreement by management and labor that all employees of a business will be or become union members. Union shops are not allowed in states with right-to-work laws.

Unreasonable search and seizure   A violation of the Fourth Amendment of the U.S. Constitution that occurs when a valid search warrant is not obtained or when the scope of a valid warrant is exceeded.

Usury   A loan of money at interest above the legal rate.

Utilitarianism   A form of consequentialist ethics.

Valid contract   A contract that contains all of the proper elements of a contract.

Venue   The geographical area over which a court presides. Venue designates the court in which the case should be tried. Change of venue means moving to another court.

Verdict   Findings of fact by the jury.

Vertical merger   A merger of corporations where one corporation is the supplier of the other.

Vertical price fixing   An agreement between a seller and a buyer (for example, between a manufacturer and a retailer) to fix the resale price at which the buyer will sell goods.

Vertical territorial agreement   Arrangement between a supplier and its customers with respect to the geographical area in which each customer will be allowed to sell that supplier's products. This type of agreement is analyzed under the rule of reason to determine whether it violates the Sherman Act. Limitations on intrabrand competition may be permitted if there is a corresponding increase in interbrand competition.

Vested rights   Rights that have become so fixed that they are not subject to being taken away without the consent of the owner.

Voidable contract   Capable of being declared a nullity, though otherwise valid.

Void contract   A contract that is empty, having no legal force; ineffectual, unenforceable.

Voir dire   The preliminary examination of prospective jurors for the purpose of ascertaining bias or interest in the lawsuit.

Voluntary arbitration   A method of resolving a dispute, as an alternative to litigation, that the parties agree to utilize. This agreement may be made before or after a dispute arises.

Voluntary bargaining issue   Either party may refuse to bargain in good faith regarding matters other than wages, hours, and other terms and conditions of employment. This refusal does not constitute an unfair labor practice. An issue over which parties may bargain if they choose to do so.

Voluntary petition   The document filed by a debtor to initiate bankruptcy proceedings.

Wagner Act   The federal law passed in 1935 that recognizes employees' rights to organize. This law also created the National Labor Relations Board and defined unfair labor practices by management. It is formally known as the National Labor Relations Act.

Waiver　An express or implied relinquishment of a right.

Warrant　A judicial authorization for the performance of some act.

Warranty of authority　An agent's implied guarantee that he or she has the authority to enter into a contract. The agent is liable for breaching the warranty if he or she lacks proper authority.

Warranty of merchantability　A promise implied in a sale of goods by merchants that the goods are reasonably fit for the general purpose for which they are sold.

Wheeler-Lea amendment　Legislation passed in 1938 that expanded the Federal Trade Commission's authority to protect society against unfair or deceptive practices.

White-collar crime　Violations of the law by business organizations or by individuals in a business-related capacity.

White knight　A slang term that describes the inducement of a voluntary acquisition when an involuntary acquisition is threatened. The voluntary acquisition group is a white knight since it saves the corporation from an unfriendly takeover.

Willful and wanton negligence　Extremely unreasonable behavior that causes injury.

Willfully　With intent to defraud or deceive.

Workers' compensation　A plan for the compensation for occupational diseases, accidental injuries, and deaths of employees that arise out of employment. Compensation includes medical expenses and burial costs and lost earnings based on the size of the family and the wage rate of the employee.

Work rules　A company's regulations governing the workplace, the application of which often becomes an issue in the ability of employees to organize for their mutual benefit and protection.

World Trade Organization (WTO)　Mechanism for enforcing the General Agreement on Tariffs and Trade that allows GATT member countries to bring complaints and seek redress.

Wright-Line doctrine　Establishes procedures for determining the burden of proof in cases involving mixed motivation for discharge.

Writ of certiorari　A discretionary proceeding by which an appellate court may review the ruling of an inferior tribunal.

Writ of habeas corpus　A court order to one holding custody of another to produce that individual before the court for the purpose of determining whether such custody is proper.

Yellow-dog contract　An agreement in which a worker agrees not to join a union and that discharge will result from a breach of the contract.

INDEX